HELP!
WordPerfect
6.0

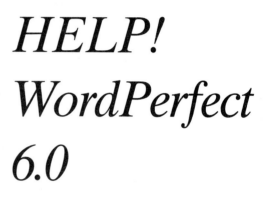

HELP!
WordPerfect
6.0

Stephen G. Dyson

Ziff-Davis Press
Emeryville, California

Development Editor	Valerie Haynes Perry
Copy Editor	Kate Hoffman
Technical Writer	Deborah Craig
Technical Reviewers	Deborah Craig, Edward Mendelson, and Nathaniel Meyers
Project Coordinator	Sheila McGill
Proofreaders	Vanessa Miller and Barbara Dahl
Cover Design	Carrie English
Book Design	Laura Lamar/MAX, San Francisco
Screen Graphics Editor	Dan Brodnitz
Technical Illustration	Cherie Plumlee Computer Graphics & Illustration
Word Processing	Howard Blechman, Cat Haglund, and Allison Levin
Page Layout	Anna L. Marks, Tony Jonick, and Bruce Lundquist
Indexer	Valerie Haynes Perry

Ziff-Davis Press books are produced on a Macintosh computer system with the following applications: FrameMaker®, Microsoft® Word, QuarkXPress®, Adobe Illustrator®, Adobe Photoshop®, Adobe Streamline™, MacLink®Plus, Aldus® FreeHand™, Collage Plus™.

Ziff-Davis Press
5903 Christie Avenue
Emeryville, CA 94608

ISBN 1-56276-014-9

Manufactured in the United States of America
10 9 8 7 6 5 4 3 2 1

CONTENTS AT A GLANCE

TABLE OF CONTENTS

Part 2   Editing the Document Text and Format

Part 3   Professional Documents

Part 4 Form Letters and Mass Mailing

Part 6   Macros and Keyboards

ACKNOWLEDGMENTS

MANY PEOPLE CONTRIBUTED TO THE FINISHED PRODUCT THAT YOU now hold in your hands. Cindy Hudson deserves a round of applause for launching the project. Many thanks to Valerie Haynes Perry, Kate Hoffman, and Deborah Craig for polishing the manuscript. Kudos to Dan Brodnitz who handled the screen illustrations with perfection. I also thank Edward Mendelson, Deborah Craig, and Nathaniel Meyers for their thorough technical review and helpful comments. This book would not exist without the efforts of these fine people.

For the gang at WordPerfect Corporation, thanks go to Jeff Acerson, Don LaVange, Susan Jarvis, Robert Hartley, and a cast of thousands. Randy Nelson had absolutely nothing to do with this book, but he approached me with a cashier's check and asked for his name in print.

Many thanks to Jan, Tyler, and Jake for their support, their love and tolerance. They didn't really help with the book, but they did keep the author sane and awake. Personally, I think that's rather important.

INTRODUCTION

A FEW YEARS AGO, A WORD PROCESSOR WAS CONSIDERED GOOD WHEN the text you typed actually came out of the printer you owned. A truly great word processor could also check your spelling, hyphenate your text, and show rudimentary formatting on your screen. The latest version of WordPerfect shows how our expectations have progressed beyond the boundaries of general word processing.

WordPerfect performs the basics with finesse, adds a graphical editing screen, and includes powerhouse features for advanced formatting, printing, file management, tables, outlines, graphics, hypertext documents, and much more. If the feature you want isn't found in WordPerfect (although that's unlikely), you can use macros, keyboard layouts, merge commands, and styles to create what you need. This book will help you get started and will introduce you to the amazing things you can accomplish with WordPerfect 6.0.

Who Should Read This Book

Are you the person who likes to learn software without a parachute, who has time to burn and nothing to do but explore every nook and cranny of a new software program? If so, you can close this book now. It's not for you.

If, however, you need a solid overview of WordPerfect 6.0 and want to get working as soon as possible, this book will provide the help you need. As with any new software, you may feel some anxiety about learning the new features and getting your work done. In this book, to help you quickly overcome some of that anxiety, the features are presented according to common tasks that you need to perform.

Instead of reading about every feature, *A* to *Z*, you'll learn how to use related features to create something useful. You'll find comprehensive chapters on document editing, tables and spreadsheets, printing, and form letters. The information is presented with step-by-step instructions and clear illustrations.

You won't need to memorize all the formatting commands to create a business memo. You won't need to learn everything about the Sort feature just to alphabetize a list of names. Each exercise is designed to create a finished document or teach you how to complete a specific task. When you're done, you'll have documents that you can modify for your own needs. You'll also develop a good working knowledge of the WordPerfect software, which you can apply to other documents and applications.

How This Book Is Organized

The chapters for *HELP! WordPerfect 6.0* are arranged in six parts. Each part combines related chapters to address a specific application or topic, as described in the following information.

Part 1: WordPerfect Fundamentals

These chapters explain the basics of WordPerfect. Chapter 1 shows you how to start WordPerfect and then create and print a simple document. Chapter 2 explains how to create a document layout and arrange text on the pages. In Chapter 3, you'll learn how to work with different fonts and text attributes. Chapter 4 explains WordPerfect's printing features and fax capabilities. Chapter 5 discusses the file management features, including WordPerfect's new QuickFinder file indexer.

Part 2: Editing the Document Text and Format

These chapters explain editing tasks and procedures. In Chapter 6, you'll find information about changing the layout of text and other elements in your document. Chapter 7 explains special editing tools, such as WordPerfect's button bar, that help you perform editing tasks. In Chapter 8, you'll learn how to use WordPerfect's writing tools, which include the Speller, Thesaurus, and new grammar checker, Grammatik. Chapter 9 covers alphabetizing and sorting operation.

Part 3: Professional Documents

These chapters discuss the WordPerfect features that create manuscripts, legal documents, reports, and other documents for professional publishing and educational applications. Chapter 10 explains how to create and edit footnotes and endnotes. Chapter 11 shows you how to create numbered paragraphs and document outlines. In Chapter 12, you'll see how to create WordPerfect tables and import spreadsheet files from other software programs. Chapter 13 explains applications for legal documents, and Chapter 14 shows you how to create tables of contents and indexes. In Chapter 15, you'll learn about the WordPerfect features that help you create and manage large documents, such as book manuscripts and reports.

Part 4: Form Letters and Mass Mailing

These chapters show how to create labels, envelopes, form letters, and other items for mass mailing. In Chapter 16, you'll see how to create mailing labels and envelopes. Chapter 17 explains how to create form letters and other documents that are created by merging a standard letter with an address list. Chapter 18 discusses some of the advanced Merge features that let you create conditional merge documents and assemble documents based on variable information.

Part 5: Desktop Publishing, Graphics, and Sound

These chapters explain the graphics and layout features for creating newsletters and other desktop publishing applications; this section also includes a chapter on WordPerfect's Sound Clip features. In Chapter 19, you'll learn about the features that let you insert graphic images into your documents. Chapter 20 shows you how to create WordPerfect equations for technical and scientific documents. Chapter 21 explains how to create document columns for newsletters, charts, and other documents where the text should be distributed across two or more columns.

In Chapter 22, you'll learn about WordPerfect's Styles feature, which lets you combine and store formatting commands to create complex document layouts; styles also ensure that certain layout elements remain consistent for each document where you need them. Chapter 23 shows you how to include recorded sound clips and music in your document file; once a sound clip is retrieved into your document, you can play it back to hear dictation notes, distribution instructions, or other sounds.

Part 6: Macros and Keyboards

These chapters explain how to simplify your work with user-defined macros and keyboard definitions. Chapter 24 shows you how to create and edit simple macros, which store a series of commands that you define. Chapter 25 explains how to change the keystroke assignments that invoke WordPerfect commands and features; in this chapter, you'll also learn about the alternative keyboard layouts included with WordPerfect.

At the end of this book, you'll find three appendices that explain how to install and start the WordPerfect software, how to work with WordPerfect's formatting codes, and how to use the utility programs included with WordPerfect.

How to Use This Book

WordPerfect supports two methods of accessing its features: You can press function keys to display the various menus and options, or you can use the menu bar to choose from a list of feature categories. Although most experienced WordPerfect users know the basic function-key assignments, new users will prefer to use the menu bar. If you are using a mouse, you'll probably use the menu bar, as well.

If you are already familiar with at least one version of WordPerfect, you've probably invested some time memorizing function-key assignments. In this book, keystrokes appear in parentheses after the name of the feature they access. When two keys must be pressed at the same time, they are listed with a plus (+) sign between them. If two or more keys must be pressed in succession, they are separated by commas. Here are a few examples:

When You See...	Do This
Save (F10)	Press and release the F10 function key.
Print (Shift+F7)	Hold down the Shift key and press the F7 function key. Then, release both keys.
Ctrl+W	Hold down the Ctrl key and press the letter *w* on the keyboard. Then, release both keys.
Home, Home, ↑	Press and release the Home key twice. Then press the ↑ (up-arrow) cursor key.

Because the function-key assignments are widely accepted as the Word-Perfect standard, this is the primary method described in this book. However, if you prefer to use the menu bar, this book also lists the appropriate menu selection—if one exists for the keystroke—in the margin next to each step.

The menu bar selections appear in the margins and are notated with a mouse icon. These are alternatives to the keystrokes listed in the chapter text. Here are a few examples of how the menu bar selections appear in this book:

When You See...	Do This
Choose File ▶ Save As.	Use the mouse pointer to choose the File option from the menu bar, and then choose Save As.
Choose File ▶ Print ▶ Page.	Choose the File option from the menu bar. Choose the Print option from the File menu. Then, choose Page.
Choose OK until you return to the document screen.	Click on the OK button, displayed on the screen, until all menus or dialog boxes are removed from the screen.

When the menu bar is displayed, you'll notice each menu option has a mnemonic letter, which is underlined. If you do not have a mouse, you can press Alt+Enter to activate the menu bar, and then type the mnemonic letters to choose the menu options.

What's New in WordPerfect 6.0?

The latest version of WordPerfect includes a graphical editing screen, new menus and dialog boxes, advanced formatting, and improved printing capabilities. WordPerfect now allows you to send documents to virtually every printer and fax machine, and it lets you communicate with embedded voice messages. Communicating with other word processors is easy, too; simply retrieve a document from any word processor and WordPerfect automatically converts it to the WordPerfect file format.

This section highlights some of the new features and explains where to find more information throughout this book. Much of the following information is written for WordPerfect 5.1 users who may need to know how their favorite word processor has changed.

Menus and Dialog Boxes

The most obvious changes to WordPerfect are the new menus and dialog boxes. In most cases, the function keystrokes you've memorized will bring up the features you expect, but the menus will look different. The developers at WordPerfect Corporation were careful to make the menus intuitive and easy to use, although, for a while, you may feel a little overwhelmed.

Chapter 1 guides you through the basics of selecting features with function keys or with the menu bar, which is now always displayed at the top of the screen.

If you don't want to see the menu bar, you can remove it by pressing Screen (Ctrl+F3), and then pressing Setup (Shift+F1) to display the screen setup options. Under the group of Screen Options, select Pull-Down Menus, so that an *X* does not appear in the box next to this option. Then press Exit (F7) twice to return to the document screen. This tells WordPerfect to display the document screen without the menu bar, and gives you the "clean screen" you know from WordPerfect 5.1.

Graphical Editing Screens

WordPerfect now includes alternative WYSIWYG (what you see is what you get) editing screens. These editing screens, called the *graphics display mode* and the *page display mode,* let you create and edit documents on a graphical screen that shows all formatting, graphics, and fonts as they will appear on the printed document. When you are using one of the graphical displays, you can use the mouse pointer to size and move graphic boxes. You can also use WordPerfect's Zoom features to get a closer look at detailed areas of your document.

The graphics display mode shows your document with the fonts and graphics that you've placed in your document. The page display mode takes this a step further by also showing page margins, headers, footers, and other items that don't appear in the text display mode and the graphics display mode.

Throughout this book, the text display mode is used for most word processing tasks because it's faster and more efficient. However, some applications, like desktop publishing, are easier to do with the graphics display mode or page display mode. Where appropriate, you will be instructed to switch to one of the graphic displays to edit your document in the WYSIWYG mode. See Chapter 1 for information about using the graphics display mode and page display mode. Chapter 7 also explains the editing tools that are available while using one of the graphical display modes.

Intelligent Code Placement

WordPerfect 6.0 intelligently inserts formatting codes where they belong. You don't need to worry about putting the cursor at the precise location where a formatting code should be. Paragraph formatting codes are automatically placed at the beginning of the paragraph, page codes are inserted at the top of the current page, and document codes are placed at the beginning of the document. If, however, you don't want automatic code placement, you can turn it off from the Setup Environment menu. Also, WordPerfect automatically deletes some kinds of duplicate codes.

These new features make it easier for you to create and manage a document layout and will let you spend less time in the Reveal Codes window. Throughout this book, you'll find references to the Auto-Code Placement feature; see Chapters 1 and 2 for general information about Auto-Code Placement. Appendix B also includes useful information about working with WordPerfect formatting codes.

Drag and Drop Text

If you have a mouse attached to your computer, you'll see the mouse pointer on your screen when you move the mouse across your desk. When a section of text in your document is selected as a block, you can use the mouse pointer to drag the selected text to another location in your document. This is how it works:

1. First, block the section of text that you want to move. You can block a section of text by holding down the mouse button while moving—or dragging—the mouse pointer across the text you want to move.

2. After you've blocked a section of text, use the mouse to move the mouse pointer over the selected text. Then, hold down the mouse button.

3. While holding down the mouse button, move the mouse pointer to the place where you want to move the text.

4. Release the mouse button and the blocked text is moved to the new location.

This is a quick and easy way to move sections of text. If you hold down the Ctrl key while dragging the mouse pointer, the blocked text is copied, rather than moved, to the new location. For more information about other editing tasks, see Chapter 1 and Chapter 6.

Button Bar and Ribbon

Similar to the Windows version of WordPerfect, WordPerfect 6.0 includes a button bar feature to allow quick access to common features. When the button bar is displayed on the screen, you can use the mouse pointer to click on the on-screen buttons to select the features that the buttons represent. WordPerfect includes several predefined button bar layouts that you can use, or you can create custom button bar layouts for the features you use most.

WordPerfect's ribbon provides quick access to common formatting features, such as fonts, line spacing, justification, and styles. See Chapter 7 for information about the button bar and ribbon features.

Fax Communications

In addition to sending your documents to a printer, you can send them to any fax machine if you have a fax board installed in your computer. Chapter 4 explains how to send a document to a fax machine, and the chapter explains other WordPerfect printing features.

Scalable Fonts

WordPerfect 6.0 includes several graphic fonts which are licensed from Bitstream Inc. and Adobe Systems Inc. These fonts may be scaled to any point size and printed from any printer that can produce graphics. You can install additional Bitstream and Adobe fonts for use with WordPerfect. Chapter 3 explains the basics of working with fonts and text attributes. In Appendix C, you'll learn about the utility program that lets you install additional fonts.

Collapsible Outlines

WordPerfect's new Outline feature lets you create collapsible outlines, which hide or display outline text according to paragraphs, subheadings, or main outline entries. You can choose which portions of the outline to show or hide, and you can focus on the displayed entries. The new Outline bar makes it easier to create and manage outline documents with on-screen buttons and controls. You can instantly change the numbering style and sequence of all outline entries. For more information on the Outline feature and the new Outline bar, see Chapter 11.

Table and Spreadsheet Editor

WordPerfect's Table Editor is enhanced to allow spreadsheet editing. You can easily create formulas, insert spreadsheet functions, and create links to other tables, spreadsheet files, or even to special items called floating table cells within your document text. See Chapter 12 for information about WordPerfect tables and the spreadsheet features.

Easy Envelopes

WordPerfect's new Envelope feature lets you create, format, and print envelopes with ease. You can store a permanent return address that is automatically inserted each time you create an envelope. If you use the Block feature to highlight the recipient's address from a business letter, this is also inserted automatically when you create the envelope. When you send bulk mailings, you can include POSTNET bar codes to speed up delivery and reduce your postal rates. For more information on the new Envelope features, see Chapter 16.

File Manager

The File Manager replaces the List Files screen from WordPerfect 5.1. With the new File Manager features, you can display a directory tree, choose different file list layouts, and do advanced file sorting and searching. Chapter 5 explains the new features and also discusses practical file management techniques.

QuickFinder File Indexer

The QuickFinder lets you create an index that catalogs every word or phrase in some or all of the files on your hard disk. Once you've created an index, you can use the QuickFinder to instantly locate all files that contain specific words, phrases, or names. This feature is much faster and more accurate than the Word Search feature from WordPerfect 5.1's List Files screen and will help you manage a large number of documents. Chapter 5 explains how to use the new QuickFinder file indexer.

Expanded Setup Options

In earlier versions of WordPerfect, you pressed Setup (Shift+F1) to display the Setup menu, where you defined the default program and feature settings. These options let you customize the WordPerfect program to suit your preferences. In WordPerfect 6.0, there are several more setup options that you can define.

To accommodate the new features, all setup options are located on the feature menus that they affect. For example, when you display the Print menu or dialog box, you can press Setup (Shift+F1) to define the default print settings. From the Screen dialog box (press Ctrl+F3 to display it), you can press Setup (Shift+F1) to define the default screen display options. Not all features have associated setup options, but you will see "Setup (Shift+F1)" displayed on the menus that do.

References to setup options are found throughout this book; see Appendix A for specifics on the setup options that affect the entire WordPerfect program.

Balanced Columns

WordPerfect now provides an option that lets you create balanced newspaper columns. This is useful when you have a section of columns that does not fill the entire page; instead of having one column longer than the others, the Balanced Column option can automatically distribute column text so that all columns have an even bottom edge.

Also, WordPerfect now allows footnotes, endnotes, comments and other document items within columns. For example, earlier versions of WordPerfect did not allow footnotes within newspaper columns; now, you can place footnotes in columns and all footnote text is formatted within the column layout. For more information on creating and editing text columns, see Chapter 21.

Sound Capabilities

WordPerfect can format text, it can insert graphics, and now it can talk, too! You can insert music or voice sound clips into your document text, and then you can play them while viewing your document on the screen. You can use the Sound Clip feature to add dictation notes, add distribution instructions, or create multimedia documents. Chapter 23 explains how to use the new features and how to record your own sound clips for your WordPerfect documents.

Hypertext Documents

WordPerfect's Cross-reference feature lets you display references to other items in your document, and it lets you "jump" to related items and documents. With WordPerfect's new Bookmarks and Hypertext features, you can mark text and create a link to another section in the current document or to another related document. Then, when you view the document on the screen, you can select the hypertext marker and immediately display the related item or document.

These features let you create on-line documentation, hypertext reference publications, and other large documents that will be viewed from the WordPerfect document screen. When used without the Hypertext feature, the Bookmark feature lets you mark one or more places in your document and move quickly to these places while creating or revising your document. See Chapter 15 for detailed information about the new Hypertext and Bookmark features.

Improved Graphics

WordPerfect 6.0 introduces several enhancements of the graphics features. You can now wrap text around any side of a graphics box, or you can wrap the text around the contour of the image inside the box. You can create custom border styles, fill styles, square or rounded corners, and create a graphics box with a gradually-shaded background. You can create watermarks that appear as a faint image or shaded text on the background of every document page. You can also place graphic borders around any page, paragraph, or column. Chapter 19 explains how to add graphics to your documents and also how to use the new graphics features.

Token-Based Macros

WordPerfect 6.0 includes a token-based macro language that records the end result of a command or task. Keystrokes are no longer recorded—only the effects of the keystrokes are. Each recorded macro creates a script of commands that you can edit like any other WordPerfect document. The only limit to the size of your macros is the amount of disk space available to store the files.

This new macro system does have one disadvantage: Many of your existing macros will not work with WordPerfect 6.0. In Appendix C, you'll learn about the Macro Conversion utility that can help you convert or salvage your existing macros. Chapter 24 explains the basics of recording and editing a macro and how to use the macro programming commands to create complex macros.

Improved On-line Help

It's now easier to learn how to use WordPerfect. An on-line help and tutorial system is available at all times. Simply press the Help (F1) key and you'll get help on the feature you are currently using or information about something you want to do but can't find on the menus. WordPerfect's new menus and dialog boxes put all features where you want to see them—on the screen. If you can't figure out what to do next, WordPerfect is ready to walk you through the procedures with its new Coaches feature. See Chapter 1 for information about the new Help features.

Starting WordPerfect and Creating a Document

Creating the Document Layout

Fonts, Text Attributes, and Special Characters

Using Your Printer with WordPerfect

File Management

P A R T

1

WordPerfect Fundamentals

CHAPTER

1

Starting WordPerfect and Creating a Document

THIS CHAPTER IS YOUR INTRODUCTION TO WORDPERFECT. FIRST YOU'LL learn how to start and use the WordPerfect software; then you will create a simple document, save the document to a file, and print it. You'll also learn how to use the on-line help system to find more information about the features of WordPerfect.

This chapter also provides an overview of several WordPerfect features that are detailed in other chapters; where appropriate, references to these chapters are given.

Starting WordPerfect

Before you can start WordPerfect, you must install the program files as described in Appendix A. The following steps explain how to start WordPerfect.

First, turn on your computer. Then, from the DOS prompt on your screen, follow these steps:

1. At the DOS prompt, type **cd\wp60** and press Enter.

2. Type **wp** and press Enter.

The main editing screen appears, and you're ready to create a new document.

NOTE. *These steps assume that you installed WordPerfect to the C:\WP60 directory. If you installed WordPerfect to a different directory, substitute the correct path name in step 1.*

WordPerfect Screen Basics

When you first start the WordPerfect program, your screen will look like Figure 1.1. Think of this screen as a clean sheet of paper that you've just rolled into a typewriter.

The Cursor and the Mouse Pointer

The blinking dash in the upper-left corner of your screen is the *cursor*; this is where the next character you type will appear. For example, press the spacebar a few times to place some blank spaces on the screen. Then type your name. Notice that as you type each character, it is inserted at the cursor position and the cursor moves one space to the right.

If you are using a mouse pointing device with your computer, you may also see the *mouse pointer*, which appears as a small rectangle on the screen. (If you don't see the pointer on your screen, move the mouse and it will appear.) You can use the mouse pointer to choose menu options, select text for editing, and move the cursor to another location in the document. To move the mouse pointer, simply move the mouse across your table or desk. Notice that the movement of the mouse controls the position of the mouse pointer on the screen.

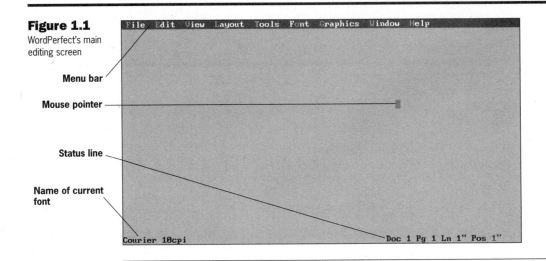

Figure 1.1
WordPerfect's main editing screen

Menu bar

Mouse pointer

Status line

Name of current font

When the mouse pointer is located within the text of your document, you can use it to reposition the cursor. Just move the mouse pointer to the place where you want to move the cursor, and quickly press and release the left mouse button. This "press-and-release" action is called a *click*. When you click on a specific place in your document, the cursor is moved to that position or to the closest available text character. (Note that you can't use this technique to move to an area of the screen that does not already contain text or characters of some sort.)

The Status Line

The *status line*, which appears at the bottom of the screen, tracks where the cursor is located in your document. Four labels appear in the lower-right corner of the status line—*Doc*, *Pg*, *Ln*, and *Pos*:

- *Doc* indicates the number of the current document screen; WordPerfect has nine document screens that you can use for creating and editing documents.

- *Pg* tells you the number of the page displayed on the screen.

- *Ln* shows the distance between the cursor and the top of the current page in your document.

■ *Pos* shows the distance between the cursor and the left edge of the current page in your document.

For example, when you first start the WordPerfect program, the status line looks like this:

```
Doc 1 Pg 1 Ln 1" Pos 1"
```

This tells you that document screen one is displayed, and that the cursor is located on page one, one inch from the top edge of the paper, and one inch from the left edge of the paper. As you type your document, the status line changes to reflect the current cursor position.

TIP. *The WordPerfect Setup feature provides a way to select a different unit of measurement for the status line. For more information about this and other display options, refer to Appendix A under "Defining Program Options."*

As you use WordPerfect, the status line occasionally displays messages that indicate what is happening in the program, and it prompts you, when necessary, to perform an action. For example, if you have not yet saved your document, the lower-left corner of the screen shows the name of the font that is active at the cursor location.

The Menu Bar

The *menu bar*, shown with an open menu in Figure 1.2, makes WordPerfect easier to use, because it lets you choose features from logical menus.

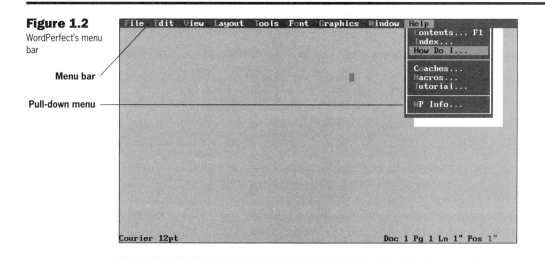

Figure 1.2
WordPerfect's menu bar

Menu bar

Pull-down menu

Follow these steps for a brief exercise in the use of the menu bar:

1. While holding down the Alt key, press the equal (=) key. Throughout this book, this keystroke command appears as Alt+=. It activates the menu bar at the top of the screen.

2. Press → four times to highlight the word *Tools* on the bar. Then press Enter to display the Tools pull-down menu.

3. Press ↓ five times to highlight the word *Date,* and press Enter to display the menu of Date options, shown here:

4. Notice that the first date option, Text, is now highlighted. Press Enter to choose this option, and WordPerfect types the date into your document. After you choose an option, WordPerfect deactivates the menu bar.

TIP.   *If you don't want to see the menu bar in WordPerfect, press Screen (Ctrl+F3), press Setup (Shift+F1), and choose Screen Options. Then choose Pull-Down Menus to turn off this feature, and press Exit (F7) until you return to the document screen. You can also choose Pull-Down Menus from the View menu to accomplish the same thing.*

Making Selections

When the menu bar is active, you can press → or ← to highlight adjacent menus. Notice that each feature name has a boldfaced or underlined letter, called a *mnemonic*, or simply *shortcut*. (In this book, the mnemonic selections appear as underlined characters.) You can type the letter to choose a feature, rather than pressing the arrow keys. Press Cancel (Esc) to close pull-down menus and to deactivate the menu bar.

If you are using a mouse with WordPerfect, you can display the menu bar by clicking the right mouse button. Then move the mouse pointer over a menu item, and click the left mouse button to choose it. To remove a menu without making a selection *and* deactivate the menu bar at the same time, click the right mouse button.

The exercises in this book include margin notes that tell mouse users how to make the menu selections. Here is one example of these notes:

Choose Tools ▸ Date ▸ Text.

This example tells you how to choose the Date Text feature from the menu bar. First, use the mouse pointer to click on the Tools option on the menu bar; this opens the Tools pull-down menu. From the Tools pull-down menu, choose Date to display the Date menu. Then, from the Date menu, choose Text. These mouse margin notes are also helpful for keyboard users who prefer to make selections through the pull-down menus.

Menu-bar Elements and Icons

Symbols and text on the pull-down menus provide more details about the features. If a menu item is dimmed or gray, this means you cannot choose it under the current circumstances. Menu items followed by a solid triangle (▸) will open another pull-down menu when you choose them. Menu items followed by an ellipsis (…) open a larger menu called a *dialog box*. (Dialog boxes are covered later in this chapter.) If you prefer to use the function keys, keystroke equivalents are listed beside most of the menu items.

When a label on the menu bar is highlighted, the menu bar is active and you cannot type text. To resume working on your document, press Cancel (Esc), or click both mouse buttons, until all pull-down menus are closed and none of the labels on the menu bar are highlighted.

Using WordPerfect's Graphics Display

WordPerfect now supports two types of display modes to help you work more effectively. The first type is called the *text display mode*, in which only text characters are visible on the screen. The second type is called the *graphics display mode*, in which your document is shown on the screen as it will appear on the printed pages, complete with proportional text spacing, fonts, and graphics. The graphics display mode is also referred to as the WYSIWYG mode (What You See Is What You Get). The process of creating and editing documents is the same in both display modes, although you may have a display preference for certain applications.

In Figure 1.3, the upper screen shows the text display mode; the lower screen shows the same document in the graphics display mode. Notice the differences between the cursor and the mouse pointer in the two display modes. In graphics mode, the cursor appears as a thin vertical line (sometimes called the *insertion point*), and the mouse pointer becomes an arrow.

When you first start WordPerfect, the text display mode is automatically enabled, but you can follow these steps to change to the graphics display mode:

Choose View ▸ Graphics Mode.

1. Press Screen (Ctrl+F3) to display the Screen dialog box. Then, from the group of Display mode options, choose Graphics.

Figure 1.3

A document shown in both text (a) and graphics display (b) modes

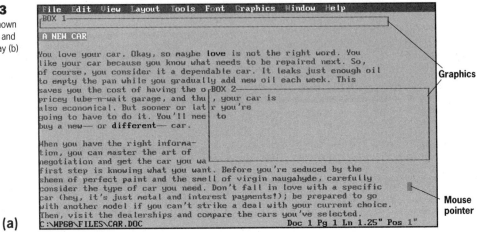

(a)

(b)

2. When you are finished working in the graphics display mode, press Screen (Ctrl+F3). Then choose Text Mode.

Choose View ▶ Text Mode.

You can easily switch between the two display modes at any time. Menu selections and cursor movement work identically in each display mode. A third display mode option, P<u>a</u>ge Mode, is a variation of the graphics display mode. When the Page Mode option is enabled, you'll see the document with page margin spacing, headers, footers, and footnotes—exactly as they'll appear on the printed pages.

When you want speedy word processing, use the text display mode, which is faster than the graphics modes and better suited to general word processing. Switch to one of the graphics display modes when you are using various text fonts, creating a complex page layout, or when you are working with WordPerfect's graphics and desktop publishing features.

Working with Dialog Boxes

Dialog boxes are menus that appear within a box on the screen and usually contain a list of related features. Some dialog boxes also display messages that prompt you to do something or to make a selection. Figure 1.4 shows the types of menu items that may appear in a dialog box.

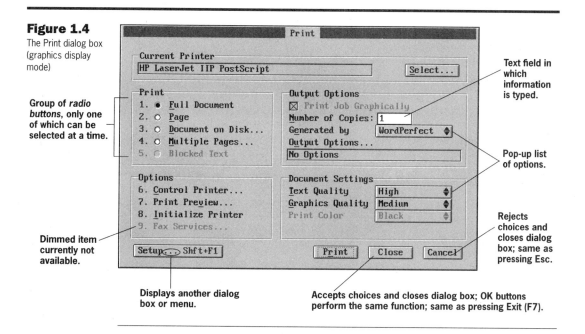

Figure 1.4

The Print dialog box (graphics display mode)

Group of *radio buttons*, only one of which can be selected at a time.

Dimmed item currently not available.

Text field in which information is typed.

Pop-up list of options.

Rejects choices and closes dialog box; same as pressing Esc.

Displays another dialog box or menu.

Accepts choices and closes dialog box; OK buttons perform the same function; same as pressing Exit (F7).

In this example, the dialog box is shown as it appears in WordPerfect's graphics display mode, which makes the options slightly easier to use. Figure 1.5 shows how the same dialog box appears when the text display mode is active. Notice that the items in the dialog box are arranged in groups within *group boxes*. In this example, there are five group boxes: Current Printer, Print, Output Options, Options, and Document Settings.

Figure 1.5

The Print dialog box (text display mode)

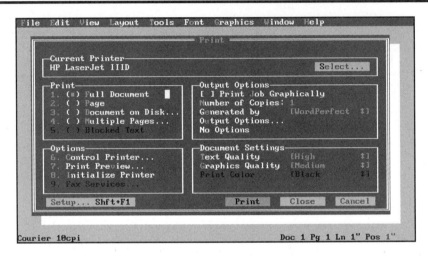

Although the dialog box items may look a little different, they work the same in both text and graphics display modes. When a dialog box is displayed, you can type a highlighted number or mnemonic letter to choose a feature. Or you can press Tab and Shift+Tab to highlight each of the items in a dialog box in turn (Shift+Tab selects the items in reverse order); when the item you want is highlighted, press Enter to choose it. Single items that appear in a rectangle are called *buttons*. Items followed by an ellipsis (…) open another menu or dialog box with additional options.

The following steps provide a quick lesson on using the keyboard to choose dialog box options:

Choose File ▸ Print.

1. Press Print (Shift+F7) to display the Print dialog box, shown earlier.

2. Notice that the Print button at the bottom of the dialog box is highlighted. Press Tab to highlight each of the items in the dialog box in turn.

3. Press Tab and Shift+Tab until the Text Quality item is highlighted, and then press Enter to open a pop-up list of choices.

4. Press ↑ to highlight the Draft text quality option, and press Enter to select it.

5. Choose Text Quality and then choose High to reset printing for high text quality.

Choose Close to
accept and close
the dialog box. Or
choose Cancel to
close it without
accepting the
selections.

6. To accept what you've done in the dialog box, press Exit (F7). Or press Cancel (Esc) to close the dialog box without accepting what you've done.

After you've pressed Exit (F7) or Cancel (Esc), you are returned to the document screen.

If you are using a mouse with WordPerfect, you can choose dialog box items with the mouse pointer. Simply move the pointer over the item you want to choose and click the mouse button. When you are finished making selections, click on the Close or OK button in the lower-right corner of the dialog box. This accepts the choices you made and returns you to the document screen. Or click on the Cancel button or the right mouse button to return to your document without accepting the dialog box choices.

When a dialog box item is gray or dimmed, this means you cannot select this item under the current circumstances. Some dialog boxes contain a group of items preceded by parentheses or round buttons. These buttons mean that only one item from the group may be selected at once. For example, in the Print dialog box, you'll see five items in the Print group box: Full Document, Page, Document on Disk, Multiple Pages, and Blocked Text. These items let you choose an option for printing, but you cannot choose all of them at the same time. For this reason, only one of the items is marked with a small box in parentheses or a filled button. Also note that the Blocked Text option is dimmed because no text is currently blocked in the document.

Your Keyboard and WordPerfect

Figure 1.6 shows the location of important keys on your keyboard. Don't worry if there are a few differences between your keyboard and the one shown in the illustration; the basic functions are the same. The following sections explain techniques for using your keyboard with WordPerfect, emphasizing the most frequently used keystrokes.

NOTE. *Some keystroke assignments in WordPerfect 6.0 differ from those in earlier versions of WordPerfect. See Chapter 25 for more information about selecting a keyboard layout that mimics the keyboard layout from WordPerfect 5.1.*

Using the Function Keys

Your keyboard has at least ten *function keys*, labeled F1 through F10, which access different WordPerfect features. Most keyboards also have two additional function keys, F11 and F12. To see how the function keys work, press F1 now to access WordPerfect's Help feature and then choose the Template option to display an on-screen function key template. Then press Exit (F7) or Cancel (Esc) to return to the document screen.

Figure 1.6

Important keys in
WordPerfect

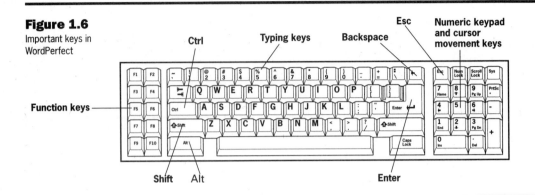

The Ctrl, Shift, and Alt keys are often used in combination with the function keys, which means each function key can have up to four feature assignments. One example of this is the Retrieve (Shift+F10) feature, which is accessed by holding down the Shift key, and then pressing and releasing the F10 function key.

The plastic keyboard template, included in your WordPerfect package, fits over the function keys on your keyboard. Feature names are printed in four different colors to identify the four roles that each key plays:

- *Black*   Press the function key alone to access this feature.

- *Blue*   Hold down the Alt key and press the function key to select this feature.

- *Green*   Hold down the Shift key and press the function key to select this feature.

- *Red*   Hold down the Ctrl key and press the function key to access this feature.

The features assigned to the function keys are also accessible from the pull-down menus, which list the keystroke assignments next to the menu items. You can invoke WordPerfect features and actions by pressing the appropriate function keys or by choosing the features from the pull-down menus, whichever you prefer.

Cancel (Esc) and Help (F1)

The Esc key cancels a program command or a menu selection. For example, if a menu or dialog box is displayed, pressing Esc removes it from the screen. When no menus or messages are displayed, Esc activates the Undelete feature, which allows you to restore things you have deleted from your document. (You'll learn more about the Undelete feature later in this chapter.) The F1 key accesses WordPerfect's help system, which is also explained later in this chapter.

If you are familiar with earlier versions of WordPerfect, note that Esc and F1 do not behave as you might expect. In WordPerfect 5.1, the F1 key performs the Cancel function; in WordPerfect 6.0, this function is performed by the Esc key, and F1 accesses the Help feature. If you're in the habit of pressing F1 to cancel a menu, you'll get the main Help screen instead; when this happens, simply press Esc to return to the document screen.

NOTE. *See Chapter 25 for information about selecting a WordPerfect 5.1 keyboard layout or defining your own keystroke assignments.*

Backspace and Delete

The Backspace and Delete keys remove single characters from your text. Backspace deletes the character to the *left* of the cursor; Delete removes the character *at* the cursor. When you press and hold down either of these keys, you delete several characters; Backspace deletes to the *left* of the cursor, Delete erases to the *right*.

If you've followed the previous exercises, you now have text on your screen. Press ← until the cursor is at the middle of the text line on the screen. Then remove some text using Backspace and Delete, as follows:

1. Press Delete once to remove the character at the cursor. Notice that the next character on the line moves left to fill the space of the deleted character.

2. Hold down Delete until you delete several characters to the right of the cursor.

3. Press Backspace once to remove a character to the left of the cursor.

4. Hold down Backspace to delete several characters to the left of the cursor.

5. Use Backspace and Delete to remove any remaining text from your screen.

These keys can also remove formatting codes that WordPerfect places in your document to format the text. You'll learn more about formatting codes in later chapters.

NOTE. *The Backspace and Delete keys can also remove a block of text from your document. For more information, see Chapter 2.*

Caps Lock and Num Lock

The Caps Lock key helps you type uppercase text. Press Caps Lock and the Pos label on the status line appears as POS. Now type some text, and it appears in uppercase letters. When you hold down the Shift key and type a character while the Caps Lock is on, you'll get a lowercase letter. Caps Lock affects only the letter keys (A through Z). When you're finished typing uppercase text, press Caps Lock again to toggle back to the normal typing mode.

Pressing the Num Lock key activates the *numeric keypad*, located at the right edge of your keyboard, which allows you to type numbers without using the number keys along the top of your keyboard. When Num Lock is enabled, the Pos label on the status line is highlighted to remind you that the numeric keypad is active; it remains highlighted until you press another key. To turn off the numeric keypad, press Num Lock again.

Using the Enter Key

The Enter key performs two different functions in WordPerfect:

- When you are typing text, pressing Enter indicates that you want to end the current line or paragraph and move the cursor to the next line.

- When a menu or prompt is displayed on the screen, you can press Enter to accept something you've typed, such as a measurement or file name.

You'll use the Enter key many times as you work through the exercises in this book. Sometimes you'll press Enter to end a text line or add a blank line, and sometimes you'll press Enter to accept something you've typed, in response to a menu item or prompt.

Typing Text for a New Document

Now that you've learned a little about the WordPerfect program, you're ready to type your first document. WordPerfect has predefined margins, tab settings, and line spacing, so you can begin typing immediately. In Chapter 2, you'll learn how to change these and other layout settings.

Figure 1.7 shows a simple letter that you will create. You'll begin by typing the lines of text for the date, address, and salutation. Then you'll type the paragraphs that make up the body of the letter. Later, you'll save and print the document.

Figure 1.7
A basic letter

September 12, 1994

Roger Filbert
32 North Shore Road
Port Charlotte, FL 33952

Dear Mr. Filbert:

We recently received a shipment of 24 domestic parakeets from your farm, and they're quite lovely. Do you breed parakeets with colors other than yellow, blue, and white? We've had several requests for mauve, salmon, and taupe. Are birds available in these hues?

We've tried spray-painting the little guys, but they don't really like that. My assistant and I now wear a lovely mix of taupe and salmon coloring; unfortunately, the birds are no more colorful than before. Can you help us find an effective—and humane—alternative?

Sincerely,

Mavis Brimley
Pat's Pets Incorporated

Typing Text Lines

Follow these steps to insert the date, recipient's name and address, and the salutation for your letter. (If you make a mistake while typing, press Backspace to delete any unwanted characters.)

1. Type today's date and press Enter.

2. Press Enter again to insert a blank line.

3. Type **Roger Filbert** and then press Enter.

4. Type **32 North Shore Road** and press Enter.

5. Type **Port Charlotte, FL 33952** and press Enter.

6. Press Enter twice to add two blank lines.

7. Type **Dear Mr. Filbert:** as the salutation.

8. Press Enter twice.

At this point, your screen should resemble Figure 1.8 (the date and status line may differ). In this exercise, you typed single lines of text, and you pressed Enter to end each line and to add blank lines for spacing. In the next section, you'll type the paragraphs for the body of the letter.

Figure 1.8

The opening lines of the letter

```
File  Edit  View  Layout  Tools  Font  Graphics  Window  Help
September 12, 1994

Roger Filbert
32 North Shore Road
Port Charlotte, FL 33952

Dear Mr. Filbert:




Courier 12pt                              Doc 1 Pg 1 Ln 2.89" Pos 1"
```

Typing Paragraphs with Word-Wrap

WordPerfect includes a feature called *word-wrap*, which breaks lines automatically to fit the current margin settings. When your typed text enters the area reserved for the right margin, WordPerfect automatically "wraps" the text to the next line on the page. You press Enter only when you're ready to end the paragraph. This allows you to concentrate on writing without worrying about whether there's room to fit your text on the current line.

To see how this works, type the following text as the first paragraph for your letter. Notice how WordPerfect automatically breaks the lines for you:

```
We recently received a shipment of 24 domestic parakeets
from your farm, and they're quite lovely. Do you breed
parakeets with colors other than yellow, blue, and white?
We've had several requests for mauve, salmon, and taupe.
Are birds available in these hues?
```

When you're finished typing this text, press Enter twice to end the paragraph. Your screen should look like Figure 1.9. Notice that when text extends beyond the right margin, WordPerfect wraps it to the next line, so that it fits within the margins of the paragraph.

Figure 1.9

The first paragraph of the letter

```
 File  Edit  View  Layout  Tools  Font  Graphics  Window  Help
September 12, 1994

Roger Filbert
32 North Shore Road
Port Charlotte, FL 33952

Dear Mr. Filbert:

We recently received a shipment of 24 domestic parakeets from your
farm, and they're quite lovely. Do you breed parakeets with colors
other than yellow, blue, and white? We've had several requests for
mauve, salmon, and taupe. Are birds available in these hues?




Courier 12pt                                  Doc 1 Pg 1 Ln 3.83" Pos 1"
```

Now finish typing the text of the letter, as shown in Figure 1.7. Later in this chapter, you'll edit, save, and print the letter. To save the letter now before continuing, press Save (F10), type **letter.doc**, and then press Enter.

Word-wrap makes editing easier, because, as you'll see later in this chapter, it automatically reformats the paragraphs when you add or delete text. This wouldn't be possible if you were to press Enter at the end of each line in a paragraph, because WordPerfect would then assume that each line is separate from the other lines, rather than a paragraph unit. So remember to press Enter *only* when you want to end a text line or paragraph, or insert a blank line into the text.

Moving the Cursor

Now that you have your letter on the screen, you can use the arrow keys to move the cursor through your document and make any necessary changes. Later in this chapter, you'll get plenty of practice moving the cursor when you edit your letter.

Moving the Cursor with the Arrow Keys

Use the arrow keys on your keyboard to move the cursor through your text:

- Press ↑ to move the cursor to the line above.

- Press ↓ to move the cursor down to the next line.

- Press ← to move the cursor to the previous text character.

- Press → to move the cursor to the next character.

Extended Cursor Movement

Fortunately, WordPerfect provides other keystroke combinations that enhance and magnify the limited power of the arrow keys. Other keys allow you to move quickly between the pages of your document. Table 1.1 shows a complete list of WordPerfect's cursor movement keystrokes.

Table 1.1	**WordPerfect's Cursor Movement Keystrokes**
Keystroke	**Moves Cursor**
←	Left to next character
→	Right to next character
↑	Up one line

Table 1.1   **WordPerfect's Cursor Movement Keystrokes (Continued)**

Keystroke	Moves Cursor
↓	Down one line
Ctrl+←	Left to previous word
Ctrl+→	Right to next word
Home ←	Left end of current line
Home →	Right end of current line
End	Right end of current line
Home ↑	Top of displayed text
Home ↓	Bottom of displayed text
Home, Home ↑	Beginning of document, *before* text but *after* formatting codes
Home, Home, Home, ↑	Beginning of document, *before* text and formatting codes
Home, Home ↓	End of document
PgUp	Previous page
PgDn	Next page
– (minus on keypad)	One screen up
+ (plus on keypad)	One screen down
Ctrl+Home, *n,* Enter	Page *n* in document

Moving the Cursor with the Mouse

As mentioned earlier in this chapter, you can use the mouse pointer to move the text cursor within your text. You can also use the mouse pointer to scroll through your document. Here's how to accomplish these maneuvers:

- To move the cursor to another place in the displayed text, move the mouse pointer to the new location, and click the left mouse button.

- To scroll up or down through your document, hold down the right mouse button, and move the mouse pointer to the top or bottom of the screen. Release the mouse button to stop scrolling.

■ To scroll right or left across the screen, hold down the right mouse button, and move the mouse pointer to the right or left edge of the screen. Release the mouse button to stop scrolling.

The last scrolling option is useful when you are working with small or proportional fonts that cause your text to extend beyond the width of your screen. For smoother scrolling, you can use WordPerfect's *scroll bars* to move through document text. To display the scroll bars:

Choose <u>V</u>iew ▸ <u>V</u>ertical Scroll Bar, or choose <u>V</u>iew ▸ <u>H</u>orizontal Scroll Bar.

1. Press Screen (Ctrl+F3), and then press Setup (Shift+F1) to display the Screen Setup dialog box.

2. Choose <u>W</u>indow Options, and then select <u>V</u>ertical Scroll bar or <u>H</u>orizontal Scroll Bar.

3. Press Exit (F7) until you return to the document screen.

When you return to your document, you'll see a long bar at one edge with an arrow icon at each end. The length of the bar represents the length of your document. The small box inside of the bar—called a *scroll box*—shows you the relative position of the cursor in your document. If you click the mouse pointer over a scroll bar arrow, WordPerfect scrolls your document in that direction. You can also move the mouse pointer over the scroll box, hold down the mouse button, and drag the box along the length of the scroll bar. When you release the mouse button, WordPerfect quickly jumps to the position indicated by the scroll box. Note that you are free to display both scroll bars at once if you like. You can turn off the scroll bars by selecting the scroll bar options again.

TIP.   *WordPerfect configures the mouse buttons for right-handed users. If you are left-handed, you can switch the button assignments from the Setup Mouse dialog box. See Appendix A for details.*

Editing the Text

Once you begin typing the text for your document, you'll probably want to make changes. You can add new text, delete characters and words, and move sentences and paragraphs around. The following sections explain some of these basic editing tasks.

Inserting New Text

You can easily add new text to a document that is displayed on the screen. Simply move the cursor to the place where the new text should be inserted, and type it. WordPerfect will automatically reformat the paragraph with the additional text.

Follow these steps to insert a new word into the letter you began earlier in the chapter:

1. At the end of the first paragraph, move the cursor just before the letter *A*, in the sentence that begins "Are birds available...."

2. Press the spacebar once, and type the following to add a new sentence to the paragraph:

   ```
   We also trust that plum and shepherd's blue will be
   popular again next season.
   ```

As you type new text, WordPerfect reformats the existing text within the current page margins.

Typing Over Existing Text

WordPerfect supports two methods of typing text in your document. The first method is called *Insert mode*, in which any text you type is *added* to the text that is already in the document. This is the standard typing mode in Word-Perfect. The second method is called the *Typeover mode*; when Typeover mode is active, any text you type *replaces* the text in the document.

Follow these steps to try both typing modes in the letter displayed on your screen:

1. Move the cursor to the beginning of the line that reads "Port Charlotte, FL 33952."

2. Press Insert to activate the Typeover mode. You will see a "Typeover" message in the lower-left corner of the screen.

3. Type the following to replace the current line of text: **Grand Junction, CO 81501**.

4. Press Delete twice to delete the last two numbers from the previous line of text.

5. Press Insert again to turn off the Typeover mode. Notice that the "Type-over" indicator is removed from the status line.

6. Move the cursor between the words "yellow" and "blue" in the second sentence of the first paragraph.

7. Type **green,** to insert a new word into the sentence.

Watch the new text push the existing text to the right; you're in Insert mode now.

When Typeover mode is on, any text you type replaces the existing text with a few exceptions. The Typeover mode will not replace layout codes, such as margin settings and center alignment codes. Instead, WordPerfect temporarily switches to the Insert mode when the cursor encounters a code in the text. You can force the cursor to move beyond the hidden code by pressing →. Also, pressing the Tab key when Typeover mode is active causes the cursor to jump to the next tab stop, but it does not insert tabular spacing in the text.

Deleting Words, Sentences, and Paragraphs

You've seen how the Backspace and Delete keys can remove single characters from your text. The following methods explain other techniques for removing text from your document:

- Press Ctrl+Backspace to delete the word where the cursor is located. This deletes the word, as well as the space that follows it.

- Press Ctrl+End to delete all the text between the cursor position and the right margin. This is called *Delete to End of Line*. This does *not* delete a complete sentence, just the text between the cursor and the right margin.

- Press Move (Ctrl+F4), choose Sentence, and then choose Delete to remove the sentence where the cursor is located.

This last technique also provides options for deleting a full paragraph or page of text. Instead of the Sentence option, choose Paragraph or Page from the dialog box that appears. This will delete the paragraph or complete page where the cursor is located.

Restoring Deleted Text

You can use the Undelete feature to restore text that you have deleted or removed with any of the previous techniques, or removed using the Typeover feature. Follow these steps to restore removed text:

Choose Edit ▶ Undelete.

- Press Cancel (Esc) from the normal document screen. WordPerfect displays the Undelete dialog box.

- At the cursor position, WordPerfect displays the last thing you deleted or the text that you typed over.

- Choose Restore to restore the highlighted text at the current cursor position.

- Choose Previous Deletion to view the second most recent deletion.

■ Choose <u>P</u>revious Deletion again to view the third deletion (WordPerfect can remember the last three things you deleted from the document).

When you see the text you want to undelete, choose <u>R</u>estore, and the deleted text is restored to your document.

Note that the Undelete feature restores the text at the current cursor position, and this may *not* be the original position of the deleted text. For this reason, make sure the cursor is positioned properly before you restore text.

TIP. *You can use the Undelete feature to quickly move text to another place in your document. Simply delete a section of text, and put the cursor at the place where the text should be moved. Then use the Undelete feature to restore the text at the new location.*

Using the Undo Feature

WordPerfect's Undo feature lets you cancel or reverse the effect of the last thing you did in the software. For example, suppose you've just made an editing change to a paragraph, but decide you like the original paragraph better. The Undo feature can cancel the change you made.

Follow these steps to see how the Undo feature works:

1. Move the cursor to the middle of a paragraph in the current document.

2. Type the following to introduce a new sentence to the paragraph:

    This intrusive little sentence does not belong here.

Choose <u>E</u>dit ▸ <u>U</u>ndo.

3. Press Undo (Ctrl+Z) to remove the sentence and restore the original paragraph.

4. Move the cursor to one of the words in your paragraph. Press Delete Word (Ctrl+Backspace) to remove it.

5. Press Home, Home, ↑ to move the cursor to the top of the document.

Choose <u>E</u>dit ▸ <u>U</u>ndo.

6. Press Undo (Ctrl+Z), and the deleted word is restored to its original location.

Unlike the Undelete feature, Undo restores text to its original state—which means restoring deleted text to its original position or removing the last text you typed.

Undo also cancels the effect of formatting changes and other document layout features. If, for example, you don't like the appearance of a font you've just selected, you can choose Undo to cancel the font change. Suppose you've just changed your document margins and find that they cause your tables to wrap in the wrong place; choose Undo to remove the new margin settings and restore the original document layout.

Saving the Document

When you type and edit a document in WordPerfect, it is stored in your computer's memory. When you turn off your computer, this memory is cleared. If you turn off your computer without saving your document, you will lose your letter and will not be able to revise or print it. So it's important to *save* your document to a file on disk; then it can be retrieved at a later time.

Follow these steps to save the letter you created earlier in this chapter:

Choose File ▶ Save As from the menu bar.

1. Press Save (F10) and WordPerfect prompts you with Filename.

2. Type **letter.doc** as the name of your document, and press Enter.

WordPerfect saves the current document under the file name LETTER-.DOC and stores it in the default directory (the directory in which WordPerfect is currently working). After you save the file, its name is displayed in the status line in the lower-left corner of the screen.

If you want to save the file in a specific directory, type the directory name immediately before the file name. For example, if you want to save your letter in a directory called C:\FILES, you would type **c:\files\letter.doc** when prompted to enter the file name.

It is important to save your document often as you create and edit the text. This ensures that your document is stored in a file with the most recent changes.

NOTE.　*For complete information about the Save and Retrieve features, see Chapter 5.*

Previewing and Printing Your Document

WordPerfect lets you preview your document to help you discover and fix any problems before you send your document to the printer. The following sections explain how to first preview and then print the document displayed on your screen.

Previewing the Printed Pages

WordPerfect's text display mode cannot show different fonts, graphics, or precise formatting. For this reason, WordPerfect includes a Print Preview screen that shows your document as it will appear when printed. Figure 1.10 shows a preview of your letter in the Print Preview screen.

Figure 1.10

Previewing your document

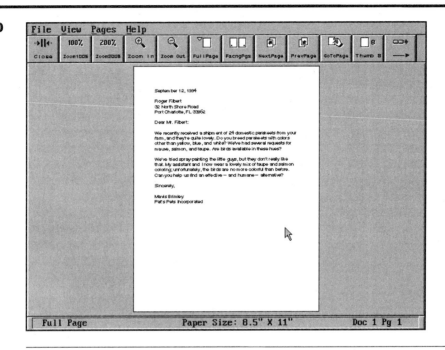

The Print Preview screen is also useful when you are working in the graphics display mode, which *does* show fonts and graphics but cannot show more than one page at once. The Print Preview screen lets you preview two or more document pages simultaneously. You can also choose to view small pages, called *thumbnails;* up to 255 thumbnails may be viewed at once on the Print Preview screen.

Follow these steps to preview the on-screen document:

1. Press Print (Shift+F7) to display the Print dialog box.

Choose File ▶ Print Preview.

2. Choose Print Preview, and a graphic screen appears that shows how your document will look when printed.

3. If your document has more than one page, you can press PgDn and PgUp to view each of the pages.

Choose File ▶ Close to return to the document editing screen.

4. When you are finished viewing your document, press Exit (F7) to return to the document editing screen.

The menu bar at the top of the Print Preview screen provides options for viewing your document. Use the File menu to choose options for the Print Preview feature and to return to the document screen. The View menu includes options for viewing your documents, and the Pages menu lets you move be-tween the document pages. For more information about the Print Preview screen, see Chapter 4.

Printing Your Document

The following steps explain how to print the displayed document using the Print dialog box, shown earlier in this chapter. Before you attempt to print your document, make sure that the printer is turned on and ready to print. If you have not yet installed and selected a printer, refer to Chapter 4.

Choose File ▸ Print.

1. Press Print (Shift+F7) and the Print dialog box appears.

2. Choose Full Document to indicate that you want to print the entire docu-ment displayed on your screen.

3. Choose Print (highlight the Print button and press Enter) to send your document to the printer.

WordPerfect sends a copy of your document to the printer. While Word-Perfect is printing, you can continue to edit the current document or clear the screen and begin a new document.

This is the basic procedure for printing a document; for detailed informa-tion about printing and print options, read Chapter 4.

Clearing the Screen

When you are finished working with a document, you should clear the screen before you create a new document or retrieve a different document file. Fol-low these steps to clear the document displayed on your screen:

Choose File ▸ Exit.

1. Press Exit (F7), and WordPerfect prompts you about saving your document.

2. Choose Yes if you need to save changes before clearing the screen. Other-wise, choose No.

3. WordPerfect prompts you with Exit WordPerfect?. Choose No to remain in WordPerfect and clear the current document screen.

WordPerfect clears your document. Now you can create or retrieve a new document. Before you complete the clearing process, remember to save im-portant documents. Once a document is cleared, the only way to get it back is to retrieve it from a file on disk.

Opening and Retrieving Documents

As you work with WordPerfect, you'll want to retrieve files to edit and print existing documents. When you retrieve a document, you have two options: You can open a file into an unused or new document screen, or you can retrieve a file and insert it into a document that is currently displayed on your screen. The following sections explain each of these options.

Opening a File into a New Document Screen

When you open a document file, WordPerfect places it into the next available document screen. Up to nine document screens can be opened at once. The following steps outline the procedure for opening the LETTER.DOC file that you created earlier in this chapter:

Choose File ▸ Open.

1. Press Open (Shift+F10), and the Open Document dialog box appears.

2. In the Filename text field, type **letter.doc** and press Enter. Or press ↓ to display a list of the last four documents that you created or retrieved in WordPerfect; highlight the file you want and press Enter.

A copy of your document is opened in the next available document screen; note the current document number shown after the Doc label on the status line. The document you see is only a copy of the information in the LETTER.DOC file. Changes you make to the displayed document are not updated to the file until you save the document again under the same file name. For complete information about the Save and Retrieve features, see Chapter 5.

Retrieving a File into the Displayed Document

Suppose you have created several reports for different managers in your office; you may want to combine them all into one report, which you will edit as one document. When you use the Open option, WordPerfect places each document you retrieve into its own document window. The following steps explain how to retrieve and insert a file into a document displayed on your screen:

Choose File ▸ Retrieve.

1. Choose Retrieve from the File menu and the Retrieve Document dialog box appears.

2. In the Filename text field, type the name of the file you want to retrieve, and then press Enter. Or press ↓ to choose from a list of the last four documents that you created or retrieved in WordPerfect.

A copy of your document is inserted into the document displayed on your screen. (Note that the document number at the bottom of the screen does not change.) When you are finished editing the text, save the document.

This combines the text from both documents into one file. The original file that you retrieved remains unchanged.

Getting Help

WordPerfect includes a friendly Help feature that provides information about the program; this help system displays *context-sensitive* help for any menu or dialog box that is currently displayed. An on-line tutorial also helps you learn some of the basic word processing tasks. The following sections explain the basics of using the help system.

If you need information that is not available in the help system or in the WordPerfect manual, you can contact WordPerfect's Customer Support group for further assistance.

Using the Main Help Index

WordPerfect's Help feature is built around an on-line index, shown in Figure 1.11, that lets you look up information according to feature names. For example, suppose you want to know more about the graphics features. You can look up *graphics* in the index to display specific help information. The following steps show you how to accomplish this:

Figure 1.11
WordPerfect's Help
Index

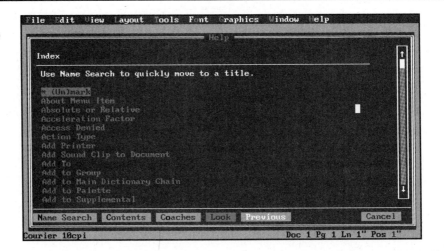

1. Press Help (F1) to display the Help Contents screen. Make sure Index is highlighted and press Enter to display the Help Index.

Choose <u>H</u>elp ▸
Index.

2. Choose <u>N</u>ame Search, type **graphics**, and press Enter to highlight the Graphics index entry.

3. Press Enter again to display the help information for the Graphics feature.

4. If you wish, choose <u>P</u>revious to go back to the previously viewed screen, and look up other graphics entries.

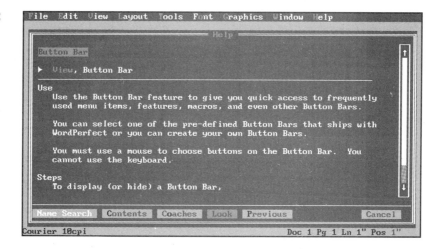

Click on Cancel to exit the help system.

5. When you are finished with the help system, press Cancel (Esc) or Exit (F7) to return to the document screen.

Jumping to Related Help Information

When you are reading help information, you may notice that some of the words are bold or underlined, as shown in Figure 1.12.

Figure 1.12

Jump terms and glossary terms in the help text

Bold words in the help text are called *jump terms*; if you press one of the arrow keys to highlight a jump term and then select Look to choose it, you'll display a related screen of help information. Mouse users can simply double-click on a jump term to choose it. When you're finished reading the related information, choose the <u>P</u>revious button at the bottom of the help window to jump back to the help screen where you started.

Underlined words in the help text are *glossary terms*. Pressing one of the arrow keys to highlight a glossary term and then selecting Look displays a definition for the highlighted word. Again, mouse users can choose a glossary term by double-clicking on it. When you are finished reading the definition, you can press Exit (F7) or choose OK to return to the help system.

If you're using a color monitor, jump terms and glossary terms may instead be displayed in different colors or in reverse video.

Displaying Help for Menus and Dialog Boxes

When a menu item is highlighted or a dialog box is displayed, you can press Help (F1) to view context-sensitive help information about the active feature. You must press the Help (F1) keystroke to get context-sensitive help; there is no equivalent method for mouse users. When you are finished reading the help text, press Exit (F7) to return to the displayed menu or dialog box.

Getting Help with Common Tasks

The help system provides three options on the Help menu that aid you with common word processing tasks: How Do I, Coaches, and Tutorial. The How Do I option lets you view information about common tasks that you'll need to perform in WordPerfect; choose How Do I when you know what you want to do but don't know which features to choose. WordPerfect's on-line tutorial also provides guided instruction on basic word processing features.

To use the How Do I option, choose Help from WordPerfect's menu bar. Then choose How Do I. WordPerfect displays a list, similar to a table of contents, with various task categories. Choose the task that you want to learn about, and WordPerfect displays the procedure for performing the task. When you are finished, press Exit (F7) to return to the document screen.

To run WordPerfect's on-line tutorial, choose Help from the menu bar, and then choose Tutorial. Follow the instructions displayed on the screen to choose and view information about the basic word processing tasks. When you are finished using the tutorial, press Exit (F7) until you return to the document screen.

Getting Interactive Help

The WordPerfect Coaches feature can help you perform specific tasks in your documents. Coaches is appropriate when you are first learning WordPerfect, or when you need to review a feature that you don't use very often. Instead of just telling you how to use a feature, Coaches can walk you through each step to perform a finished task. This is how it works:

Choose Help ▸ Coaches from the menu bar.

- Press Help (F1) and then choose Coaches. WordPerfect displays the Coaches dialog box with a list of word processing tasks.

- Scroll through the list and highlight the task you want to perform. Then, press Enter or choose Select.

■ WordPerfect then displays a series of prompts and instructions that help you perform each step of the selected task.

At some point, WordPerfect may divide the screen into different windows so you can read instructions while performing one of the steps in your document. When you're done, the Coaches feature will congratulate you on the completed task.

The following exercise will give you some practice with the Coaches feature. Suppose you want to know how to create italic text in your document. The Coaches feature can show you how:

Choose <u>H</u>elp ▸
C<u>o</u>aches from the
menu bar.

1. Press Help (F1) and then choose C<u>o</u>aches. WordPerfect displays the Coaches dialog box with a list of word processing tasks.

2. From the list of tasks, highlight the task called "Bold, Italicize, Underline, etc." Then, press Enter or choose <u>S</u>elect, and then press Enter again.

3. WordPerfect asks whether you want to change the same text you've previously typed. Choose <u>N</u>o to simply add italic text.

4. You are prompted with "Position the cursor where you want to begin typing." Position the cursor and choose Continue (or press F7) and WordPerfect tells you to choose an attribute from the <u>F</u>ont menu..

5. Press Enter or choose Show Me, and the Coaches feature will show you the menu where you can choose different font attributes.

6. From the F<u>o</u>nt menu, choose <u>I</u>talics, and type **This is Italic Text**. As you type the text, it appears in the Italics attribute.

7. Choose Continue (F7) and WordPerfect asks if you'd like to be coached in next step: turning off the Italics attribute. Press <u>Y</u>es and then press Enter or choose Show Me, and Coaches displays the appropriate menu.

8. Choose <u>N</u>ormal to turn off the Italics attribute and the Coaches feature reports that the task is completed.

Don't worry about making mistakes while performing a task. The Coaches feature monitors everything you do, tells you when something is incorrect, and gives you the chance to fix a problem before you complete the task.

As mentioned earlier, you won't want to use the Coaches feature for every WordPerfect task. This help option is designed to help new WordPerfect users learn the software. Coaches is also useful when you need to learn a new feature or to review a task—like creating a table of contents—that you don't perform very often.

Finding the Right Keystroke

Sometimes, you'll want to know which keystroke to press to access a specific feature. When you display a pull-down menu, keystrokes are listed next to the menu items they access. If you want a complete list of all keystroke assignments, press F1, choose Keystrokes, and then select Look.

Press ↓ or use the mouse to click on the down arrow at the right edge of the screen. This lets you scroll the text and view the entire list. When you are finished, press Exit (F7) to close the help system and return to the document screen.

For a complete list of the function key assignments, press F1, and then choose Template. This displays an on-screen diagram of the keyboard template, shown in Figure 1.13.

Figure 1.13

Viewing the function key template

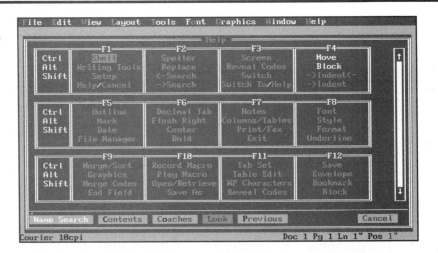

Additional Help from WordPerfect Corporation

WordPerfect Customer Support operators can help you when you have problems with the software or need additional information. This support won't cost you anything if you are a registered user of WordPerfect—a good reason to send in your registration card. To reach WordPerfect Customer Support, call the telephone number listed in your WordPerfect manual. If possible, call from a touch-tone phone so you can take advantage of their automated tech support system.

Before you call, try to solve the problem on your own. Answers for most problems are found in your WordPerfect manual or in the text of the help system. If you still need assistance, start the WordPerfect software and call WordPerfect Customer Support.

If the operator asks for information about your computer system, choose Help from the menu bar, and then choose WP Info. This displays information about your computer system and the version of WordPerfect that you are running. This information will help the support operator diagnose the problem.

Exiting WordPerfect

You've seen how WordPerfect's Exit feature can both save the displayed document and clear the screen. Now, you'll use Exit to leave WordPerfect and return to DOS:

Choose File ▸ Exit.

1. Press Exit (F7). WordPerfect asks whether you want to save the current document.

2. Choose No to exit without saving the document. WordPerfect now prompts you with "Exit WordPerfect?"

3. Choose Yes to exit the program.

If you select No instead of Yes at the Exit WordPerfect? prompt, WordPerfect clears the screen and resets the program options to the standard settings.

CHAPTER

**Creating the
Document Layout**

A DOCUMENT LAYOUT DETERMINES THE GENERAL PLACEMENT AND appearance of the text on your pages and includes *formatting commands* for margin and tab settings, line spacing and alignment, and paragraph indenting. You can apply these formatting commands either to specific sections of text in your document or to the entire document. You can, for example, change tab settings at different places within your document text, or you can define standard tab settings that affect the entire document.

This chapter explains how to use the formatting commands to create a document layout. Throughout this chapter, you'll create various sample documents, like the document shown in Figure 2.1.

About WordPerfect Formatting

WordPerfect gives you substantial control over the text formatting process. Creating a document layout isn't difficult, but it does require some understanding of a few basic formatting principles. The following sections explain some of the "rules" that WordPerfect uses to format text and manage document information.

Formatting Codes

WordPerfect is a *document-oriented* word processor. This means that as you type text and insert formatting commands, WordPerfect automatically reformats the entire document to reflect the changes you've made. You won't have to guess where a text line will wrap or where a page will end, because Word-Perfect shows the format of the document on the screen.

As you create a document, you select commands that determine the format of the text. If you want to change your margins, for example, you select a formatting command that lets you enter new measurements for the margins. After you do so, a code is inserted into your text that tells WordPerfect where to start the new margins. You won't see the code on the document editing screen—WordPerfect hides all codes so you can read your text—but you can view the codes by displaying the *Reveal Codes window*; this is explained later in this chapter.

Figure 2.2 shows where the formatting commands were applied in the document shown earlier. In this example, the cursor was moved to each place in the text where the format changes were to begin, and then the desired formatting command was selected. Every formatting command you choose, including line spacing, indents, and tabs, inserts a code into your text that produces the desired effect.

Figure 2.1

A sample document

TEAM MEETING

Manufacturing   2nd Quarter

First quarter sales increased 35% from last year's figures. This is a direct result

of improved communication with our suppliers, the installment of a computer

network in our West Valley warehouse, and, of course, the excellent

accomplishments of our manufacturing team.

A recent issue of Hang Gliders' Quarterly features an article about the P8500

Glider; here is an excerpt from that article:

> "Although there are relatively few competitors in the
> hang glider industry, the Dalworth Company produces
> quality equipment, and continually raises the standard
> for excellence and safety. Their dedication to the sport
> is evident in the y P8500, which is the first new model to
> appear since 1992."

Dalworth continues to enjoy enormous success, despite the recessed market.

We feel confident our success will continue throughout the next quarter as we

introduce a new line of sporting equipment. In addition to the new hang glider

models, we will begin manufacturing two new products: the Sail•Chute®, and

the Dalworth wind surf board. Next year, we will also offer a complete line of

sportswear for hang gliding, boating, and parachuting.

Figure 2.2

The effects of applying formatting commands

Double line spacing —

Paragraph indent —

Single line spacing —

Double line spacing —

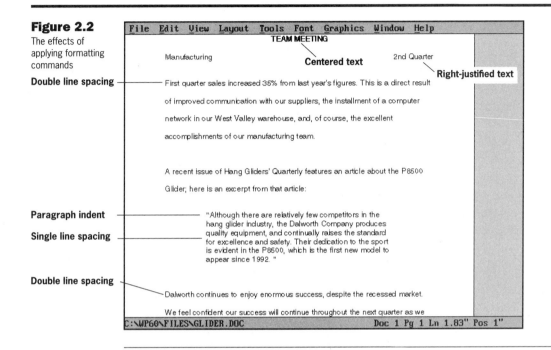

Open and Paired Codes

WordPerfect formatting codes come in two varieties: open and paired. An *open code* affects all the document text that follows it. Margin changes, line spacing, and text justification use open codes to create a formatting command. An open code remains in effect until the end of the document or until another code is later inserted to change the format.

As shown in Figure 2.3, *paired codes* affect only the specific section of text they surround. The first code in the pair turns on the format feature, and the second code turns off the feature. Text *attributes*, such as bold, underline, and italic, all use paired codes to indicate where the attribute will begin and end. (Attributes are discussed in the next chapter.) Other WordPerfect features, such as Outline, Tables, and Columns, use paired codes to create a specific format for a section of your document.

Viewing the Codes in Your Document

You usually won't see the formatting codes as you create your documents. You can view the codes by using Reveal Codes (press Alt+F3 or F11) or by choosing View, Reveal Codes from the menu bar. This divides the screen into two *windows*, as shown in Figure 2.4.

Figure 2.3

Paired codes surrounding a section of text

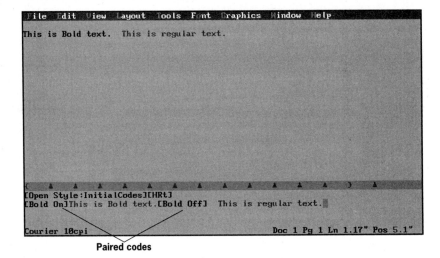

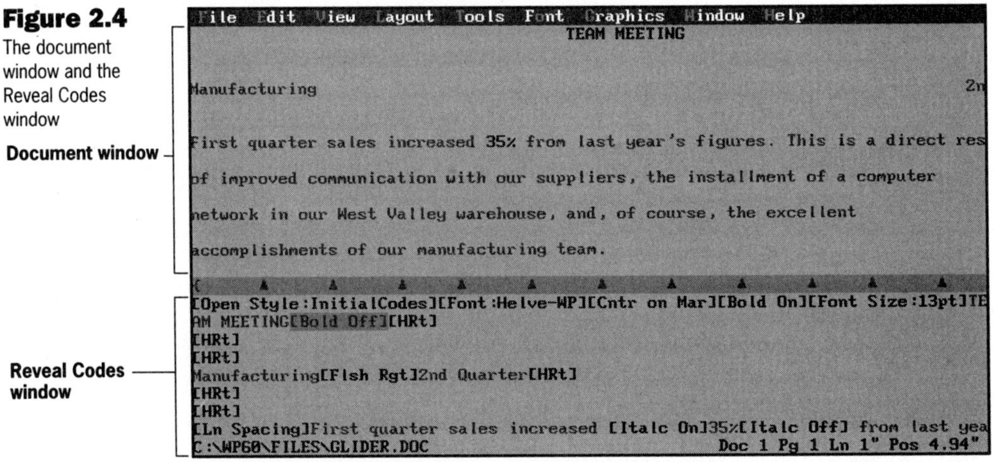

Paired codes

Figure 2.4

The document window and the Reveal Codes window

Document window

Reveal Codes window

The document window shows your text as it normally appears on the screen, and the Reveal Codes window shows the same text with the embedded formatting codes, which appear in square brackets (for example, [Bold On]). The Reveal Codes window makes the codes visible so you can more easily delete or change the formatting codes you've placed in your document. See Appendix B for a complete list of WordPerfect's formatting codes.

Code Placement

In earlier versions of WordPerfect, codes were inserted at the position of the cursor in the text. WordPerfect 6.0 includes an Auto Code Placement option that automatically places each code where it belongs without requiring you to move the cursor to the beginning of the text line or to the top of the page.

For example, when you choose a paragraph formatting command—such as Margins or Indent—the code is automatically inserted at the beginning of the paragraph in which the cursor is located; if you choose a page formatting command, such as Page Numbering or Page Header, the code is inserted at the top of the page in which the cursor is located. Formatting commands that affect only a specific section of text, such as font changes, are inserted at the precise location of the cursor.

When you first start WordPerfect 6.0, the Auto Code Placement option is turned on. If you do not want to use this option, use Setup (press Shift+F1) or choose File, and then choose Setup from the menu bar. Choose Environment, and you'll see an *X* next to the check box for Auto Code Placement; choose this option to uncheck the box and turn off the option. Then press Exit (F7) until you return to the document screen. The Auto Code Placement setting (on or off) remains in effect until you change it again from the Setup Environment dialog box.

Document Pagination

Pagination is the process of arranging text across the pages of a document. WordPerfect automatically displays *page break* indicators as part of the pagination process to show where one page ends and another page begins. It can also number pages automatically. When you add or delete text, WordPerfect repaginates your document to reflect your changes. This makes editing easier for you and ensures that the document will print correctly. For more information on page breaks, see "Starting a New Page" later in this chapter, and see Chapter 14 for detailed information about page numbering.

Working with Page Margins

Margins are the space between the edges of the paper and the text on the page, as shown in Figure 2.5. Think of the margins as a frame around your text; you can edit your text, add footnotes, or insert graphics, and the entire document is formatted within the boundaries of the margins you've set.

WordPerfect's standard margin is 1 inch at each side of the printed page (top, bottom, left, and right). You can easily change the amount of space by entering a new measurement for any of the four margins. If you're working with WordPerfect's text or graphics display mode, the screen doesn't show the margin space. Only the page display mode shows margin space on the screen as you create and edit your documents.

Figure 2.5
Margins frame your text.

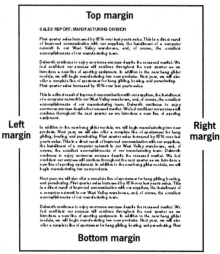

In the figure:

Top margin

SALES REPORT : MANUFACTURING DIVISION

Left margin ... **Right margin**

Bottom margin

Defining Page Margins

WordPerfect provides several options for defining the margins in your document. You can change the space for one or more sides of the page (left, right, top, or bottom), or you can change all margins at once. The following steps explain how to change the left, right, top, and bottom margins for the current page, using the Margin Format dialog box shown in Figure 2.6.

- Move the cursor to the place in your document where the new margins should begin. (If you're starting a new document from a clear screen, you don't need to worry about moving the cursor.)

Choose Layout ▶
Margins.

- Press Format (Shift+F8) and choose Margins.

- Choose Left Margin, type a measurement for the new left margin, and press Enter.

- Choose Right Margin, type a measurement for the new right margin, and press Enter.

- Choose Top Margin, type a measurement for the new top margin, and press Enter.

Figure 2.6

The Margin Format
dialog box

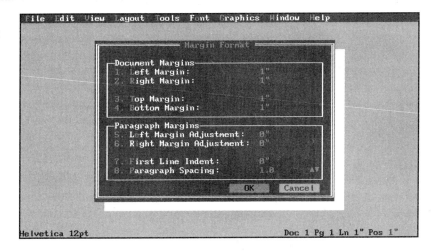

Choose OK to
accept the margin
settings.

■ Choose <u>B</u>ottom Margin, type a measurement for the new bottom margin, and press Enter.

■ Press Exit (F7) until you return to the document screen.

TIP. *Instead of pressing Enter after typing each measurement, you can press ↓ or ↑ to move the cursor to the next or previous margin option.*

These steps insert four hidden codes to define each margin setting for the page: [LftMar], [RgtMar], [Top Mar], and [Bot Mar]. The new margins affect the text that follows the codes, but not the preceding text. You don't need to set all four margins at once; you can make a single margin change, and it will affect the text that follows it.

NOTE. *When the Auto Code Placement option is active, the [LftMar] and [RgtMar] codes are inserted at the beginning of the line where the cursor is located, and the [Top Mar] and [Bot Mar] codes are inserted at the top of the current page.*

The following exercise shows you how to define new margins for a document. This is the first step in creating the document shown at the beginning of this chapter. Before you begin, press Exit (F7) and type **n** twice to clear the document screen.

Choose <u>L</u>ayout ▶
<u>M</u>argins.

1. Press Format (Shift+F8) and then choose <u>M</u>argins.

2. Choose <u>L</u>eft Margin. Type **.75** as the measurement for the left margin. Then press ↓ to move to the next margin setting.

Click on Right Margin to move to the next margin setting.

3. At the Right Margin setting, type **.75**, and then press ↓ to move to the next margin setting.

4. At the Top Margin setting, type **.75**, and then press ↓ to move to the next margin setting.

5. At the Bottom Margin setting, type **.75**, and then press Enter to accept your changes.

Choose OK to return to the document screen.

6. Press Exit (F7) twice to return to the document screen.

When you return to the document screen, you'll notice that the status line shows the cursor location according to the new margin settings. Use Reveal Codes (press Alt+F3 or F11), or choose View from the menu bar and then choose Reveal Codes, to see the margin codes embedded in the text. Press ← to move the cursor over the [Bot Mar] code. When the code is highlighted by the cursor, it expands to show its setting: [Bot Mar:0.75"]. If you move the cursor over each of the margin codes, you'll see the measurement assigned to each margin. When you are finished with Reveal Codes, press Alt+F3 or F11 again to restore the document screen.

TIP. *If you don't like the margin settings you've defined, choose Edit, and then choose Undo; this cancels the last task you completed in WordPerfect.*

Editing the Defined Margins

You can change the margins you've defined by moving the cursor to the same place where the previous margins were set and then defining new margin settings. WordPerfect replaces the old margins with the new margins you define. Try the following steps to change all the current margin settings:

1. Move the cursor to the text line where you set the previous margin codes. If you don't remember where you set the codes, use Reveal Codes (press Alt+F3 or F11) and scroll through the text to locate them.

2. Press Format (Shift+F8) and choose Margins.

Choose Layout ▶ Margins.

3. Choose each of the margin settings (Left Margin, Right Margin, Top Margin, Bottom Margin), and type **.5** for each margin.

4. Press Exit (F7) twice to return to the document screen.

Choose OK to return to the document screen.

The new margin settings replace the older codes, provided that the cursor is located on the same page and paragraph as before. To see the change, view the new settings from the Reveal Codes window. Keep the margin codes in the current document screen; you'll build on them to create a document later in this chapter.

When you want to cancel all margin changes and return to the default settings of 1 inch on each side, you can open the Margin Format dialog box and set all four margins to **1"**. Or you can display the Reveal Codes window (press Alt+F3 or F11), highlight each margin code, and press Delete to remove them. When you're done, choose the Reveal Codes option again to remove the Reveal Codes window.

Setting Margins for a Laser Printer

Most laser printers allow a small border of space, called the *unprintable region*, where the printer cannot print information. Usually, this space is about ¼ inch wide. If you specify margins that are smaller than the unprintable region for your printer, WordPerfect increases the margins to that minimum.

For example, if you are using an HP LaserJet Series III printer, and you enter 0" for both left and right margins, WordPerfect increases the margins to about 0.3" for each side. These are the minimum margins allowed for the HP LaserJet Series III printer. Your printer may also have a minimum margin allowance; check your printer documentation to see whether your printer has an unprintable region that affects the margins you may set.

Entering Measurements in Centimeters, Points, and Fractions

WordPerfect is preset to measure margins, tabs, and other format settings in inches. There are, however, other measurement types that you can specify at any layout or format option by typing one of these four letters at the end of the measurement numbers you enter:

c for centimeters

m for millimeters

p for typesetting points

w for 1200ths of an inch (the *w* stands for WordPerfect units)

u for WordPerfect 4.2 units

The last option (WordPerfect 4.2 units) displays measurements in terms of nonproportional units, that is, units that display the line numbers and fixed character numbers across the page, rather than precise measurement numbers. This is the measurement method for WordPerfect 4.2, which assumes that you're working with nonproportional fonts.

Just type one of these letters at the end of the number you enter, and WordPerfect converts to the equivalent inch measurement. For example, suppose you usually work with inch measurements, but a client gives you document specifications in centimeters. You must enter ten centimeters for the top margin. Select the Top Margin feature, type **10c**, and press Enter to accept the measurement. The letter *c* tells WordPerfect that you want the inch equivalent of 10 centimeters. WordPerfect converts the centimeter measurement into inches and displays the result as the margin.

TIP.   *You can change the default measurement type for all WordPerfect menus with the Units of Measurement feature. For instructions, refer to "Defining Program Options" in Appendix A.*

In addition, you can enter fractional amounts by using the forward-slash (/) character. If you're typing a whole number and a fraction, make sure to type a space between them. For example, you would type **1 ³/₄** to specify a margin of one and three-quarter inches. Other possibilities include **2 ⁷/₈, ¹/₂,** and **3 ¹⁵/₁₆.** After you enter the fraction, WordPerfect converts it to the decimal equivalent (for example, 1 ³/₄ becomes 1.75).

Creating Centered and Right-Aligned Text

WordPerfect's text *alignment* features let you center and align text according to the left and right margins. The Center feature can center a headline, title, or any line of text precisely between the page margins. The Flush Right feature aligns text against the right margin; this is useful for inserting dates, page numbers, and text for a return address on a letter. If you change your margins, you won't have to worry about making adjustments; WordPerfect keeps your text alignment true to the new margins.

Typing a Centered Text Line

This is the procedure for centering a line of text:

- Move the cursor to a new line in your document.

- Press Center (Shift+F6).

Choose Layout ▸
Alignment ▸ Center.

- Type the text to be centered.

- Press Enter to end the centered line, and move the cursor to a new line.

When you choose the Center command, you insert a [Cntr on Mar] code at the beginning of the line. WordPerfect then centers everything that lies between the [Cntr on Mar] code and the end of the line.

TIP. *Usually, you'll center only single lines of text. However, it is possible to center the lines of an entire paragraph or page. See "Selecting Justification for Text Alignment" later in this chapter.*

Follow these steps to type a centered title for the document on your screen:

1. Press Home, Home, ↓ to move the cursor past the margin codes you've inserted.

2. Press Center (Shift+F6).

Choose Layout ▸ Alignment ▸ Center.

3. Type **TEAM MEETING** and press Enter to end the line.

When you are finished, your document screen will look like Figure 2.7. WordPerfect inserted a [Cntr on Mar] code where your cursor was located. As you typed, the text was centered between the left and right margins; pressing Enter ended the centered line and moved the cursor to the beginning of the next line.

Figure 2.7
Centering a
document title

Centered text

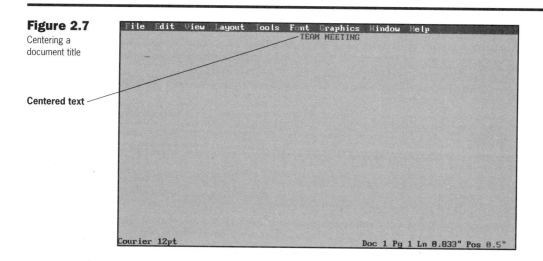

Centering an Existing Line of Text

Sometimes you'll want to center an existing line of text. To center an existing line of text:

■ Move the cursor to the beginning of the line you want to center.

Choose Layout ▸
Alignment ▸ Center.

- Press Center (Shift+F6).

WordPerfect centers the text line between the left and right margins.

If part of the title or text line wraps to the next line after you center it, this means there isn't enough room to center the whole title. You can fix this by dividing the title into two lines and then centering each line. First, move the cursor to the place where you want to divide the title into two lines, and press Enter to break the line. Move the cursor to the beginning of the first line, and press Center (Shift+F6). Then repeat the Center command with the cursor at the beginning of the second line.

Aligning Text at the Right Margin

The Flush Right feature lets you align dates and other text at the right margin of the page. This is the procedure:

Choose Layout ▸
Alignment ▸ Flush
Right.

- Press Flush Right (Alt+F6).

- Type the text that should be right-aligned.

- Press Enter to end the line and move the cursor to a new line.

When you choose the Flush Right command, you insert a [Flsh Rgt] code at the cursor. At the right margin, WordPerfect aligns everything you type between the [Flsh Rgt] code and the end of the line.

TIP. *Usually, you'll align only single lines of text at the right margin. However, it is possible to align an entire paragraph or page. See "Selecting Justification for Text Alignment" later in this chapter.*

Try this exercise to add a subheading to the document on your screen. You'll use Flush Right to align some of the text:

1. Press Home, Home, ↓ to move the cursor to the end of the document.

2. Type **Manufacturing** to begin the subheading text, but don't press Enter at the end of the line.

Choose Layout ▸
Alignment ▸ Flush
Right.

3. Press Flush Right (Alt+F6).

4. Type **2nd Quarter** and press Enter twice to end the line and add a blank line below the subheading.

As you typed "2nd Quarter," the text was aligned at the right margin. Now the document on your screen has a centered title and a subheading with right-aligned text.

Aligning Existing Text

To align an existing line of text, simply move the cursor to the first character of the text you want to align, and then press Flush Right (Alt+F6). You don't need to move the cursor to the beginning of a line before you choose Flush Right. However, the cursor should be located on the first character of the text that should be aligned at the right margin.

Canceling Centered and Right-Aligned Text

To cancel the effect of the Center or Flush Right command, you can delete the code that creates the format. You accomplish this by following these two steps:

- Move the cursor to the first character of the text that is centered or right-aligned.

- Press Backspace to delete the centering or right-alignment.

Creating Dot Leaders for Aligned or Centered Text

Figure 2.8 shows examples of *dot leaders* in a document. A dot leader is a line of dots that leads the eye across the page to a label or page number. Dot leaders are commonly used to help display the page numbers after the entries in a table of contents.

Figure 2.8
Dot leaders with right-aligned text

Dot leaders

Table of Contents

Introduction 1
Shopping for Tools 3
Wood and Materials 8
Basic Carpentry Skills 12
Framing 22
Solving Special Problems 48
Door and Windows 52
Finish Carpentry 60

You can use WordPerfect's Tab Set feature (explained later in this chapter) to create special tab settings with dot leaders. Or you can use the Center and Flush Right features to create the same effect:

Choose Layout ▸ Alignment ▸ Flush Right.

- Press Flush Right (Alt+F6) once to align the cursor at the right margin.

- Press Flush Right (Alt+F6) again to create the dot leader.

- Type the text to be right-aligned after the dot leader.

You can also press Center (Shift+F6) twice to create a dot leader for centered text. In each case, WordPerfect inserts a line of dots between the right-aligned or centered text and the previous text on the line. If you add or delete text on the line, the dot leader is automatically adjusted to span the gap between the text. Flush Right and Center codes with dot leaders appear as [Flsh Rgt (Dot)] and [Cntr on Mar (Dot)] in the Reveal Codes window.

If you want to cancel the dot leader but retain the centered or flush-right alignment, move the cursor to the aligned text, and press Flush Right (Alt+F6) or Center (Shift+F6) a third time. This removes the dot leader from the text.

Changing the Line Spacing

Line spacing determines the amount of space between the lines of text in your document. Figure 2.9 shows an example of double line spacing in a document. To double-space on a typewriter, you need to add the extra line spaces manually, but WordPerfect's Line Spacing feature handles line spacing for you automatically.

In addition to the double-spaced lines shown in Figure 2.9, you can enter other numbers for the line spacing—even fractional numbers. It's also easy to change or delete the line spacing format.

Selecting a New Spacing for Lines

The standard line spacing in WordPerfect is single-spacing. The following steps explain the procedure for changing the line spacing in your document:

- Move the cursor to the beginning of the line where the new line spacing should begin.

Choose Layout ▸ Line.

- Press Format (Shift+F8) and choose Line to display the Line Format dialog box.

- Choose the Line Spacing option.

Click on ▲ or ▼ to change the line spacing setting.

- Type a number and press Enter. For example, enter **2** for double-spacing, **1.5** or **1 ½** for one-and-one-half spacing, or **1** for single-spacing.

Figure 2.9

A double-spaced document

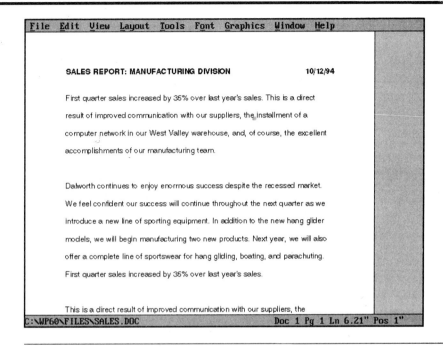

```
 File  Edit  View  Layout  Tools  Font  Graphics  Window  Help


        SALES REPORT: MANUFACTURING DIVISION              10/12/94

        First quarter sales increased by 35% over last year's sales. This is a direct

        result of improved communication with our suppliers, the installment of a

        computer network in our West Valley warehouse, and, of course, the excellent

        accomplishments of our manufacturing team.


        Dalworth continues to enjoy enormous success despite the recessed market.

        We feel confident our success will continue throughout the next quarter as we

        introduce a new line of sporting equipment. In addition to the new hang glider

        models, we will begin manufacturing two new products. Next year, we will also

        offer a complete line of sportswear for hang gliding, boating, and parachuting.

        First quarter sales increased by 35% over last year's sales.


        This is a direct result of improved communication with our suppliers, the

 C:\WP60\FILES\SALES.DOC                    Doc 1 Pg 1 Ln 6.21" Pos 1"
```

Choose OK to return to the document screen.

■ Press Exit (F7) twice to return to the document screen.

A [Ln Spacing] code is inserted into the text. This is an open code, which means that all text following the code will have the new line spacing.

Line spacing is not measured in inches or any other unit of measure. The number you enter for line spacing is multiplied by the height of the text line and applied to each line of text that follows the [Ln Spacing] code. If, for example, you type **2** as the line spacing and your text line is 0.16 inches high, the space allowed for one text line would be 0.32 inches (2×0.16). Since the text is only 0.16 inch high, double-spacing creates an extra 0.16 inch of space between the current line and the next line.

In the following exercise, you will type a few paragraphs of text and change the line spacing for the document you're creating on the screen:

1. Press Home, Home, ↓ to move the cursor to the end of the document. Then type this paragraph:

```
First quarter sales increased 35% from last year's
figures. This is a direct result of improved communication
with our suppliers, the installment of a computer network
in our West Valley warehouse, and, of course, the
```

excellent accomplishments of our manufacturing team.

2. Press Enter twice to end the first paragraph. Then type the second paragraph:

A recent issue of Hang Gliders' Quarterly features an article about the P8500 Glider; here is an excerpt from that article:

Choose Layout ▸ Line.

3. Press Home, Home, ↑ to move the cursor to the top of the document.

4. Press Format (Shift+F8) and choose Line.

Choose Line Spacing and click on ▴ until the line spacing number changes to 2.00.

5. From the Line Format dialog box, choose Line Spacing, and enter **2** to create double-spacing.

6. Press Exit (F7) twice to return to the document screen.

Choose OK to return to the document screen.

7. Now you'll change back to single-spacing after the second paragraph you typed. Press Home, Home, ↓ to move the cursor to the end of the document.

8. Press Format (Shift+F8), choose Line, and then choose Line Spacing.

Choose Layout ▸ Line ▸ Spacing.

9. Type **1** and press Enter to choose single-spacing. Press Exit (F7) twice to return to the document screen.

10. Type this quote as the second paragraph:

Click on ▾ until the line spacing number changes to 1.00. Then choose OK.

"Although there are relatively few competitors in the hang glider industry, the Dalworth Company produces quality equipment, and continually raises the standard for excellence and safety. Their dedication to the sport is evident in the P8500, which is the first new model to appear since 1992."

11. Press Enter three times to end the quote. Now you'll resume double-spacing for the rest of the text.

12. Repeat steps 4, 5, and 6 of this procedure to resume double-spacing.

13. Finish the rest of the document by typing this paragraph:

Dalworth continues to enjoy enormous success, despite the recessed market. We feel confident our success will continue throughout the next quarter as we introduce a new line of sporting equipment.

14. Press Enter twice to end the paragraph.

Choose File ▶
Save As.

15. Press Save (F10) to display the Save Document dialog box.

16. Type **team.doc** as the document name, and then press Enter to save it to a file on disk.

You've just inserted [Ln Spacing] codes into your text to change the line spacing at three points in your document. Display the Reveal Codes window (press Alt+F3 or F11), and scroll through the text to view the codes. The first code was inserted at the beginning of the document to specify double-spacing. The second code was inserted before the quote to change the quote text to single-spacing. The last code was inserted to resume double-spacing after the quote. Figure 2.10 shows the document you've completed.

Figure 2.10

The effects of line spacing changes

Double-spacing ————

Single-spacing ————

Double-spacing ————

```
 File   Edit   View   Layout   Tools   Font   Graphics   Window   Help
   Manufacturing                                      2nd Quarter

   First quarter sales increased 35% from last year's figures. This is a direct result

   of improved communication with our suppliers, the installment of a computer

   network in our West Valley warehouse, and, of course, the excellent

   accomplishments of our manufacturing team.


   A recent issue of Hang Gliders' Quarterly features an article about the P8500

   Glider; here is an excerpt from that article:

                   "Although there are relatively few competitors in the
                   hang glider industry, the Dalworth Company produces
                   quality equipment, and continually raises the standard
                   for excellence and safety. Their dedication to the sport
                   is evident in the P8500, which is the first new model to
                   appear since 1992. "


   Dalworth continues to enjoy enormous success, despite the recessed market.

   We feel confident our success will continue throughout the next quarter as we

   introduce a new line of sporting equipment. In addition to the new hang glider

 C:\WP60\FILES\GLIDER.DOC                        Doc 1 Pg 1 Ln 1.63" Pos 1"
```

Remember, the [Ln Spacing] code affects only the text that follows it and remains in effect until the end of the document or until a different [Ln Spacing] code is placed in the text. If you want a line spacing change to affect only one or two paragraphs in your text, you can use the Block feature (press Alt+F4 or F12) to highlight a section of text, and then choose the line spacing you desire. When you block the text first, WordPerfect inserts a [+Ln spacing] code at the beginning of the block and a [–Ln spacing] code at the end of the block. The + code turns on the specified line spacing; the − code reverts back to the line spacing that was active before the blocked text.

Canceling the Line Spacing Setting

You can easily cancel any line spacing you've defined by deleting the code that creates it. The following steps show you how to accomplish this:

Choose <u>V</u>iew ▸
Reveal <u>C</u>odes.

- Press Reveal Codes (Alt+F3 or F11) to display the Reveal Codes window.

- Use the arrow keys to move the cursor, and highlight the code that you want to cancel.

- Press the Del (Delete) key to remove the code.

- Press Reveal Codes (Alt+F3 or F11) again to restore the document screen.

You can also press Undo (Ctrl+Z), or choose <u>E</u>dit and then choose <u>U</u>ndo to cancel a line spacing command immediately after you've selected it. Undo is useful when you don't like the effect of the line spacing and want to reverse the effect of the command.

Adding Extra Space after Each Paragraph

WordPerfect's Paragraph Spacing option adds extra space after the paragraphs in your document. This will save you the effort of pressing Enter twice to add a blank line at the end of each paragraph.

To set paragraph spacing:

- Move the cursor to the place where the extra paragraph spacing should begin.

Choose <u>L</u>ayout ▸
<u>M</u>argins.

- Press Format (Shift+F8) and then choose <u>M</u>argins.

- Choose <u>P</u>aragraph Spacing and enter a number for the number of blank lines that should appear *after* each paragraph.

Choose OK to return
to the document
screen.

- Press Exit (F7) to return to the document screen.

This inserts a [Para Spacing] code, which indicates the amount of spacing after each paragraph.

To determine the paragraph spacing, WordPerfect multiplies the current line spacing number by the number you enter for the paragraph spacing. For example, if your text is single-spaced, and you want a blank line between paragraphs, you can enter 2 as the number for paragraph spacing. The result is a single-spaced document with double-spacing *between* paragraphs. If the line spacing number is 2 and the paragraph spacing number is also 2, your document will be double-spaced with four blank lines between paragraphs.

Selecting Justification for Text Alignment

Earlier in this chapter, you learned how to center and right-align a single line of text. WordPerfect also provides *justification* features that let you choose the text alignment for a whole paragraph, page, or the entire document.

Justification determines how text is aligned and distributed between the margins on the page. Figure 2.11 shows examples of justification. You can align the text at the left margin, which is the default format for WordPerfect, or you can align the text at the right margin, center all lines between the margins, or extend each text line to meet both margins.

Figure 2.11

Left, center, right, and full justification

Left Justification
The text in this paragraph is left-justified, where each text line is aligned with the left margin. This is the standard setting for WordPerfect.

Center Justification
The text in this paragraph is center-justified, where each text line is centered between the left and right margins.

Right Justification
The text in this paragraph is right-justified. When Right Justification is turned on, WordPerfect aligns each text line against the right margin.

Full Justification
The text in this paragraph is full-justified. The text lines extend to create a clean edge at both margins. Use this justification option to create straight margins at each side of the page.

Full Justification All Lines
All text in this paragraph is full-justified. Each text line fills the space between left and right margins. If a text line does not meet the right margin, WordPerfect stretches the   text   to   do   so .

To justify text in any way:

- Move the cursor to the first text line to be justified.

- Press Format (Shift+F8) and choose <u>L</u>ine. Then choose <u>J</u>ustification.

Choose Layout ► <u>J</u>ustification.

- Choose the justification option you want to use: <u>L</u>eft, <u>C</u>enter, <u>R</u>ight, <u>F</u>ull, or Full, <u>A</u>ll Lines.

- Press Exit (F7) twice to return to the document screen.

Choose OK ► Close to return to the document screen.

After you select the justification option, WordPerfect inserts a [Just] code into your text to start the justification type you specified. If you choose <u>L</u>eft, all text is aligned with the left margin. Choose <u>R</u>ight to align all text at the right margin. If you choose <u>C</u>enter, all text lines—even paragraph text—are centered between left and right margins.

The <u>F</u>ull option aligns text at both the left and right margins; if you press Enter at the end of a text line to end it, the line is aligned with the left margin and does not meet the right margin. The Full, <u>A</u>ll Lines option forces *all* lines to extend the full width of the page to meet the right margin, even text lines in which you've pressed the Enter key to end the line.

If you want justification to affect only one section of the text, you can use the Block feature (press Alt+F4 or F12) to highlight a section of text, and then choose the justification you want to apply to the text. WordPerfect inserts a [+Just] code at the beginning of the block, and a [–Just] code at the end of the block. The + code turns on the specified setting, and the – code restores the justification that was active before the blocked text.

To cancel or remove the justification setting, turn on Reveal Codes (press Alt+F3 or F11). Highlight the [Just] code and press Delete. WordPerfect deletes the code and restores justification to the previous setting.

Indenting Paragraphs

The Tab and Indent features let you indent the text in your document. Using the standard indent features, you can indent only the first line of a paragraph, indent the paragraph margins, or create a hanging indent. You can also create a "permanent" indent that applies to two or more paragraphs in your document. (Permanent indents are covered later in this chapter.) Figure 2.12 shows examples of the different indents you can create.

Figure 2.12

Four examples of indented text

This paragraph is not indented, and the text is aligned with the left margin.

> **First Line Indent:** Only the first line of this paragraph is indented. You can press Tab to indent the first line of a single paragraph. Or you can choose the First Line Indent feature to indent the first line of all paragraphs in your document.

> **Left Margin Indent:** The left side of this paragraph is indented. The tab stop on the left determines the amount of space for the indent.

> **Left/Right Margin Indent:** This paragraph is indented by the same amount on both sides. The tab stop of the left determines the amount of space for the indent on each side.

Hanging Indent: This paragraph begins with a hanging indent, where all paragraph lines—except the first line—are indented from the left margin. Again, the amount of space for the indent is determined by the defined tab stops.

Indenting the First Line of the Paragraph

You can press Tab to indent the first line of a single paragraph. If you need to indent the first line of all paragraphs in your document, use WordPerfect's First Line Indent feature, as described below:

- Move the cursor to the place where you want the first-line indent to begin.

- Press Format (Shift+F8) and then choose <u>M</u>argins.

Choose <u>L</u>ayout ▸ <u>M</u>argins.

- Choose <u>F</u>irst Line Indent. Type the measurement you want for the indent, and then press Enter.

Choose OK to return to the document screen.

- Press Exit (F7) twice to return to the document screen.

   This inserts a [First Ln Ind] code into your document. All paragraphs that follow the code will have a first-line indent of the measurement that you entered. You can cancel the first-line indent by deleting the [First Ln Ind] code or by choosing the First Line Indent feature again and entering a measurement of **0**.

Indenting the Paragraph Margins

WordPerfect's Indent feature lets you temporarily change the left and right margins of a single paragraph. You can choose to indent only the left margin of a paragraph or both the left and right margins. The latter option is useful for offsetting a quote from the rest of your text.

Here is the general procedure:

Choose Layout ▸ Alignment ▸ Indent →.

- Move the cursor to the beginning of the text you want to indent.

- To indent the left margin of the paragraph, press Indent (F4).

Choose Layout ▸ Alignment ▸ Indent →←.

- To indent both margins of the paragraph, press Left/Right Indent (Shift+F4).

WordPerfect inserts a [Lft Indent] or [Lft/Rgt Indent] code at the cursor position, which indents the text of the paragraph to the next tab stop. If you change your mind and want to cancel the indent, move the cursor to the first character of the paragraph, and press Backspace.

Now that you know how to use the Indent feature, retrieve the TEAM–.DOC file you created earlier, and try the following steps to indent a paragraph:

Choose Layout ▸ Alignment ▸ Indent →←.

1. Move the cursor to the beginning of the quotation that begins, "Although there are relatively few...."

2. Press Left/Right Indent (Shift+F4) to indent the quote by one-half inch on each side. Press Shift+F4 again to indent each side by a full inch.

3. Press Exit (F7) and choose Yes when prompted about saving your document. WordPerfect updates your changes to the TEAM.DOC file.

Choose File ▸ Exit ▸ Yes.

4. WordPerfect prompts you about exiting WordPerfect. Choose No and the document screen is cleared, but you remain in WordPerfect.

In these steps, you used the Indent feature to indent a quote in your document. You also saved your document and cleared the screen.

This exercise shows how you can indent an existing paragraph in your document, but you can also indent a new paragraph as you type it. Simply use either Indent key (press F4 or Shift+F4) before you begin to type. The text you type will be indented until you press Enter, which inserts an [HRt] (hard-return) code and ends the paragraph.

Remember, the indent applies to only one paragraph of text. When Word-Perfect encounters an [HRt] code, the indent is turned off and a new line begins at the left margin in the document.

TIP.   *The Indent features use the current tab stops to indent your text. You can change the amount of space for an indent by defining new tab stops as described later in this chapter.*

Creating a Left-Margin Heading

Figure 2.13 shows a document with a heading in a "column" at the left margin. You can use the Indent feature to create headings like these in your own documents.

Figure 2.13

Using indents to create a left-margin heading

INTERVIEWS	Employee interviews should be conducted every 6 months. The purpose of the interview is to evaluate each employee's progress and to discuss concerns about job activities. Remember that communication is important between the supervisor and the employee; this is the employee's opportunity to discuss problems that affect the department goals. Appendix VI includes sample questions and interview scenarios.

Try the following steps to create a left-margin heading:

Choose F<u>o</u>nt ▸ <u>B</u>old.

1. At the beginning of a new line, press Bold (F6) to turn on the Bold text attribute.

2. Type the text for the left-margin heading. Or type a number, an asterisk, or any other character to offset the paragraph.

Choose F<u>o</u>nt ▸ <u>B</u>old.

3. Press Bold (F6) again to turn off the Bold attribute.

4. Press Indent (F4) to insert a left margin indent code.

Choose <u>L</u>ayout ▸
<u>A</u>lignment ▸ <u>I</u>ndent →.

5. Type the paragraph that will appear next to the heading or character you typed in step 2.

As you type the paragraph, the text remains indented from the heading or character at the left margin. When you press Enter to end the paragraph, WordPerfect turns off the Indent feature, allowing you to start a new paragraph or line.

The amount of space between the heading and the paragraph is determined by the current tab settings. Later in this chapter, you'll learn how to change the tab settings for your document.

NOTE. *Bold is one of several attributes covered in Chapter 3.*

Creating a Hanging Indent

In Figure 2.12, you saw an example of a *hanging indent*. For some professional documents, a hanging indent is required to offset a paragraph in the text. Hanging indents are also used to create bibliography entries, like this:

Schoen, Wally. *Uncle Wally's Home Repair Guide and Cajun Cookbook.* Louisiana: Red Bayou Press, 1992. pp. 116-121.

This is the procedure for creating text with a hanging indent:

Choose Layout ▸ Alignment ▸ Hanging Indent.

- Move to the beginning of the text where the hanging indent should occur.

- Press Indent (F4) to indent the paragraph, and then press Margin Release (Shift+Tab) to release the first line from the indentation.

As with the other Indent features, you can also insert a hanging indent before typing a new paragraph.

If you want to cancel the indent, turn on Reveal Codes (press Alt+F3 or F11) to display the Reveal Codes window. You will see two codes, [Lft Indent] and [Back Tab], at the beginning of the paragraph. You can then highlight each code and press the Delete key to remove them from the text.

TIP. *When you need to edit the text of a hanging indent, do so with the Reveal Codes window displayed. Sometimes it is difficult to know where the cursor is located when a hanging indent is active; the Reveal Codes window will show you the precise placement of codes and text.*

Creating a Permanent Indent

The Margin Adjustment feature lets you create a permanent indent from the current margin settings. Use this feature when you want to indent a list of paragraphs or items with a single command. Unlike the indents described earlier, the Margin Adjustment feature indents the text *from* the left or right margin, and not according to the tab stops. The indent remains in effect until you turn off the margin adjustment. If you later change your margins, the margin adjustment keeps your text indented by the same amount you specified without requiring you to redefine the measurements that create the indent.

This is the procedure for creating a margin adjustment:

Choose Layout ▸ Margins.

- Move the cursor to the place where the margin adjustment should begin.

- Press Format (Shift+F8) and choose Margins.

- To indent the left margin, choose Left Margin Adjustment, and enter a measurement for the indent.

■ To indent the right margin, choose R̲ight Margin Adjustment, and enter a measurement for the indent.

■ Press Exit (F7) twice to return to the document screen.

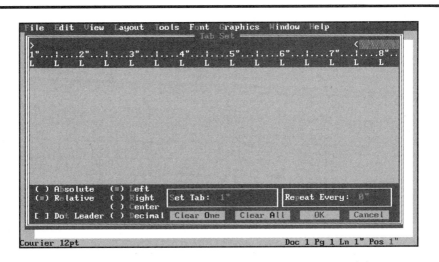

Choose OK to return to the document screen.

These steps insert the [Lft Mar Adj] and [Rgt Mar Adj] codes into the text. The measurements you entered are the amount of space that WordPerfect indents the text from the current left and right margins.

Incidentally, you could create a permanent hanging indent by combining a Left Margin Adjustment setting with a *negative* First Line Indent setting.

Defining the Tab Settings

Tab stops, or *tabs*, are measurements that allow you to indent and align the text in your document. WordPerfect automatically sets tabs at every half-inch across the page, but you can easily redefine the number and position of the tab stops anywhere in your document, and you can do so as often as you like.

Tab stops are defined in the Tab Set dialog box, shown in Figure 2.14, in which you can add, delete, and move tab stops for your document. The changes you make at the Tab Set dialog box determine how text will be indented when you press the Tab key or choose the Indent features at the document screen.

Figure 2.14

The Tab Set dialog box

On the Tab Set dialog box, you'll see a ruler that measures the space across that page and notes where each tab stop is currently set. Each *L* on the ruler represents one tab stop. The *L* stands for *left-aligned* tab, which means that the left edge of the text will be aligned at the tab stop.

Defining New Tabs

This section explains how to define new tab settings. The new tab settings take effect from the cursor position forward in your document.

To define new tab settings:

Choose Layout ▸ Tab Set.

Double-click on a ruler measurement to set a tab.

Choose OK until you return to the document screen.

- Move the cursor to the place in your document where the new tab settings should begin.

- Press Format (Shift+F8), choose Line, and then choose Tab Set.

- Choose Clear All. This clears the ruler of the current tab stops.

- To set new tab stops, press ← or → to move the cursor along the ruler and type **L** to set each tab. Or type a measurement and press Enter to insert a new tab at that distance from the left margin.

- When you're finished setting tabs, press Exit (F7) until you return to the document editing screen.

When you enter tab stop measurements, you can also enter decimal numbers, such as **2.5** and **1.75**. Or, if you prefer, you can type fractions instead of decimal numbers—for example, type **1 1/2** instead of **1.5**, or **3/4** instead of **0.75**.

CAUTION. *When you type a measurement that is a decimal number less than 1, make sure you type a zero before the decimal amount, as in* **0.5**, **0.2**, *or* **0.75**. *If you type a decimal point first before typing a number, WordPerfect creates a dot leader for the tab at the cursor location on the ruler.*

When the Tab Set dialog box is displayed, the tab ruler measurements begin with the measurement of your left margin. So, for example, if your left margin is set at 1 inch, this will be the first measurement you see on the tab ruler. You can't see the entire tab ruler on the screen at once, because it begins at the zero inch mark and extends to a length of 54.5 inches. You can, however, press → or ← to scroll the length of the tab ruler. This lets you set tabs beyond the width of the displayed page.

After you exit the Tab Set dialog box, WordPerfect inserts a [Tab Set] code into your document. Now you can press the Tab key to move to the first tab stop you defined and type the text that should be located at that tab stop. Press Tab to move to each of the tab stops, and type the desired text.

Special Tabs for Text Alignment

The Tab Set dialog box lets you select different types of tabs that align text on the tab stops. Figure 2.15 shows examples of each type. A left tab aligns text at the left edge, a right tab aligns at the right edge, a center tab centers the text over the tab stop, and a decimal tab aligns numbers at the decimal points.

Figure 2.15

Left, right, center, decimal, and dot leader tab stops

Dot leader option applied to this tab stop

Left Tab	Right Tab	Center Tab	Decimal Tab
One 1		George	10.16
Two 2		Amy	72.002
Three 3		Scott	106.5
Four 4		Laura	0.3326

Here is the procedure for setting different tab types:

Choose Layout ▸ Tab Set.

Double-click on a ruler measurement to set a tab.

Choose OK to return to the document screen.

- Press Format (Shift+F8), choose Line, and then choose Tab Set.

- Enter a measurement for the tab you want to set.

- Choose Left, Right, Center, or Decimal to indicate the type of tab you want to set.

- Repeat the procedure until you've set all the tabs you want.

- Press Exit (F7) until you return to the document screen.

Here is another method for setting the different tab types: With the cursor on the tab ruler, press → or ← to move the cursor to the place where you want to set a tab stop; then type **R** for Right, **C** for Center, **D** for Decimal, or **L** for Left to change the desired tab stop. When you're finished, exit the Tab Set dialog box to accept the new tab settings.

You can also select an option that creates dot leaders between the tab stops. Simply type a period (.) while the cursor is located over a tab stop, or choose the Dot Leader option at the bottom of the Tab Set dialog box when you set a tab. This instructs WordPerfect to insert a dot leader between the current and previous tab stops. When the dot leader option is applied to a tab stop, the tab letter appears in reverse video. You can remove the dot leader by either typing a period or choosing the Dot Leader option again while the cursor is located over the tab stop, or you can simply replace the tab with a new tab stop.

Setting Tabs for the Entire Line

WordPerfect offers a shortcut for setting tabs of the same type at specific increments along the entire line. Assume you want to set multiple tabs at every inch mark across the page, and you want to begin 2.5 inches from the left edge of the page. These steps describe how to create these multiple tabs:

- From the Tab Set dialog box, choose Clear All to clear the current tab settings.

- Type **2.5** and press Enter to set a tab at the 2.5-inch mark.

- Choose Left, Right, Center, or Decimal to indicate the type of multiple tabs you want to set.

- Choose Repeat Every, type **1**, and press Enter. WordPerfect creates evenly spaced tabs at every 1-inch interval.

- Press Exit (F7) until you return to the document screen.

Choose OK to return to the document screen.

The first number you type is a measurement for the place where the tabs should start. The Repeat Every number specifies how WordPerfect should space the tabs; in this example, it's 1 inch apart.

If a centered, right-aligned, or decimal tab is located at the measurement you specify as the beginning number for multiple tabs, WordPerfect uses that tab type to create the other tabs on the line.

Relative Tabs and Absolute Tabs

When you define tabs, an option on the Tab Set menu lets you select *Relative* or *Absolute* tabs. Relative is the standard method for measuring tabs in WordPerfect. The Relative tab method sets tabs in relation to the left margin of your document. This ensures that tabs will be spaced correctly if you later change your margins. For example, if your left margin is set at 1 inch and you create a tab stop at the 1.5-inch mark, the tab stop is set at one-half inch from the left margin. If you later change your left margin to 2 inches, the relative tab stop moves to the 2.5-inch mark to keep the half-inch distance from the margin. This ensures that the tab spacing remains consistent if you change the left and right margins in your document.

Absolute tabs, on the other hand, are set to fixed measurements. With the Absolute method, all tabs you set are assigned to absolute measurements from the left edge of the printed page. If you later change your margins, these tabs remain at their original defined positions.

To change the method in which tabs are set, simply choose Absolute or Relative from the Tab Set dialog box before you set your tabs. Remember, Relative tabs are the standard method for WordPerfect; if you use Absolute tabs, your text may not format correctly when you change the margins in your document.

Changing the Decimal-Align Character

The *decimal-align* character is the character that WordPerfect uses to align text and numbers over a decimal tab stop. The standard decimal-align character is the period (.), but in some countries commas rather than periods are used to note the decimal places in numbers. WordPerfect lets you change the character used for decimal alignment. When you do so, you'll also have the opportunity to change the character used as the *thousands separator*; the standard character is the comma, but you can choose any character as the thousands separator.

This is the procedure for changing the character assignments:

- Move the cursor to the place where you want the new decimal-align character to take effect.

Choose Layout ▸ Character.

- Press Format (Shift+F8) and choose Character.

- Choose Decimal/Align Character, and type the character you want to use as the decimal point.

- Choose Thousands Separator, and type the character you want to use for the thousands separator.

- Press Exit (F7) until you return to the document screen.

Choose OK to return to the document screen.

WordPerfect inserts [Dec/Align Char] and [Thousands Char] codes into the text. These are both open codes, so any decimal tabs located to the right of the code or below it will be aligned on the new decimal-align character and formatted with the new thousands separator. For example, if you change the decimal-align character to a comma and the thousands separator to a period, you can set a decimal tab to align a column of numbers, like this:

DM 105.120,20
20.500,50
132.307,00

The DM in this example stands for deutsche marks, one of the European currencies that uses periods for thousands placement and commas for decimal placement.

You can also change the decimal-align character to solve special alignment problems in your document. For example, suppose you're creating a table like the one shown here:

Item No.	Description
QRFT/163	Snow Gaiters, Lt.
CEA/1456	Climbing Harness
QRFT/81	Ice Piton, Driving (10)
CEF/2116	Climbing Boots
RFT/100	Nylon Climbing Rope (100 ft.)

In this example, the item numbers are aligned on the forward-slash character. To create such a list, first you change the decimal align character to the forward slash. Next, create new tab settings with a decimal tab stop defined for the first column. Then type your text. All decimal tabs that follow the [Dec/Algn Char] code are then aligned on the new character that you specified.

Using Tabs to Create a Chart

The following exercise will give you some practice with the Tab features. In this exercise, you'll create and adjust a set of tab stops for a text chart.

Creating a Chart

In the following steps, you'll define new tab settings and then type the text for the chart. Figure 2.16 shows how the completed chart will look on the screen.

Before you proceed with this exercise, you may need to clear the current document. Press Exit (F7), and choose Yes to save the current document, or choose No to continue without saving. Then choose No to indicate that you do not want to exit WordPerfect. Now you're ready to create the chart:

1. Type **SUPPLY CATALOG** and press Enter twice to create the title for the chart.

2. Press Format (Shift+F8), choose Line, and then choose Tab Set.

Choose Layout ▸ Tab Set.

3. Choose Clear All to remove the current tab stops from the ruler.

4. To set the first tab, type **1.5** and press Enter.

5. Type **2.5** and press Enter to set the next tab at 2.5 inches from the left margin.

6. Type **4.5** and press Enter. Type **R** to change this tab to a right-aligned tab.

Figure 2.16
A chart formatted with custom tab settings

```
 ile  dit  View  Layout  Tools  Font  Graphics  Window  Help
SUPPLY CATALOG
    269    Copy Toner. . . . . . . . . 2      89.90
    321    Diskettes . . . . . . . . 10       6.75
    128    Paper . . . . . . . . . 13         5.50
    003    Labels. . . . . . . . . . 8        8.85
    415    Note Pads . . . . . . . . 11       1.25




Courier 10cpi                        Doc 1 Pg 1 Ln 1.33" Pos 1"
```

7. Type **5.75** and press Enter to create the last tab. Type **D** to change this to a decimal-aligned tab.

8. Press Exit (F7) three times to accept the tab settings and return to the document screen.

Choose OK to return to the document screen.

9. Press Tab and type **269** as a number for the first column.

10. Press Tab to move the cursor to the next tab stop, and type **Copy Toner**.

11. Press Tab to move to the third tab stop, and type **2** as the page number for the entry.

12. Press Tab once more and type the decimal number **89.90**.

13. Press Enter to end the line and start a new line.

14. Using Figure 2.16 as a guide, type the last four lines to complete the table.

As you type the text at each tab stop, notice how WordPerfect aligns the text.

For now, keep this chart on the screen. In the next section, you'll edit the tab settings and adjust the position of the tab stops.

Editing the Tab Settings

WordPerfect makes it easy to adjust the position of the tab stops you've defined. Simply display the Tab Set dialog box, make the desired changes, and WordPerfect updates the previous [Tab Set] code in your document. When you edit tabs, it's important to put the cursor on the same line as the [Tab Set] code you want to change; if the cursor is on a different line, you'll create a second [Tab Set] code, rather than editing or updating the existing code.

When the Tab Set dialog box is displayed and the cursor is on the ruler, you can press ↑ or ↓ to move the cursor to each of the defined tab stops. With the cursor on a tab stop, you can do one of the following:

- Press Delete or Backspace to remove the tab from the line.

- Hold down the Ctrl key and press → or ← to adjust the position of the tab stop.

- Type **C** (Center), **D** (Decimal), **R** (Right), or **L** (Left) to change the type of tab, as explained earlier.

- Type a period to create a dot leader between the current and previous tab stops on the line. Type the period again to remove a dot leader that is already set.

Now you can try these tab editing techniques. Follow these steps to adjust the tab settings for the chart on your screen:

1. Move the cursor to the line where you defined the tab settings (the "Copy Toner" line in the chart).

Choose Layout ▸ Tab Set.

2. Press Format (Shift+F8), choose Line, and then choose Tab Set. Your screen will look similar to Figure 2.17.

Figure 2.17

Editing the tab settings

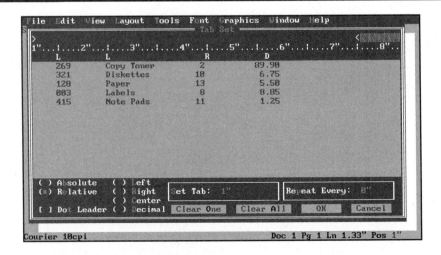

3. Press ↑ until the cursor moves to the second tab stop at the 2.5-inch mark. Hold down the Ctrl key, and press ← a few times to move the tab stop to the 2-inch mark.

4. Press ↑ again to move the cursor to the right-aligned tab stop. Hold down the Ctrl key and press → a few times to move the tab stop to the 5-inch mark.

5. While the cursor is still located on this tab stop, type a period (**.**) to add a dot leader to this tab.

6. Press ↓ twice to move back to the first tab stop. Type **C** to change it to a centered tab stop.

Choose OK to return to the document screen.

7. Press Exit (F7) three times to accept the edited tab settings and return to the document screen.

As you edit each tab stop, the effect is shown in the middle area of the Tab Set dialog box; this shows you how each change will affect the text and allows you to cancel the change or make further adjustments before you return to your document.

When you are finished, your screen will look similar to Figure 2.16, as shown earlier. WordPerfect updated the previous [Tab Set] code with the edited tab stops.

Aligning Text without Setting Tabs

You don't have to change your tab settings to create centered, right-aligned, or decimal-aligned text over an existing tab stop. Another way to create these text alignments is by pressing special keystrokes, known as *hard tabs*, at the document editing screen.

Hard tabs use the current tab settings to determine where text should be placed. However, they carry their own type of text alignment and require no special tab settings. Try the following procedures at the main editing screen:

■ Press Home, Tab to insert a hard left-aligned tab. A [LFT TAB] code is inserted into the text, which creates a left-aligned tab over the current tab stop—regardless of the alignment defined by the current tab settings.

■ Press Home, Shift+F6 to insert a hard centered tab. The [CNTR TAB] code appears in the Reveal Codes window, overriding the existing tab and centering text over the tab stop.

■ Press Home, Alt+F6 to insert a hard right-aligned tab. This inserts a [RGT TAB] code into the text and creates a right-aligned tab over the existing tab stop.

■ Press Tab Align (Ctrl+F6) to insert a hard decimal-aligned tab, [DEC TAB], where the text is aligned on a specific character, usually a decimal point. If the text you type after inserting this hard tab does not include a decimal point, then WordPerfect aligns the right edge of the text against the tab stop.

Centering Text on the Page

Suppose you have a brief document, such as a business letter, that fills only a portion of the page. WordPerfect's Center Page feature lets you center the text vertically on the page to create a more appealing layout. This is also useful for title pages, on which the text should be centered between the top and bottom margins of the page. The Center Page feature works for a single page or for several consecutive pages in your document.

This is the procedure to vertically center one or more pages of text:

■ Move to the page where the text should be vertically centered.

Choose Layout ▸ Page.

■ Press Format (Shift+F8) and choose Page to display the Page Format dialog box.

■ To center a single page, choose Center Current Page (an *X* should appear in the check box next to this option).

■ To center the current page and all pages that follow, choose Center Pages (an *X* should appear in the check box next to this option).

Choose OK to return to the document screen.

■ Press Exit (F7) until you return to the document screen.

Depending on which option you selected, you inserted a [Cntr Cur Pg] or a [Cntr Pgs] code at the beginning of the current page. If you chose Center Current Page, the text of the current page is centered between the top and bottom margins; this option affects only the current page. If you chose Center Pages, all pages are vertically centered, starting with the current page; this option is useful when you have several single-page business letters compiled in the same document.

If you decide you don't want to center the page(s) after you've selected the command, move the cursor to the page that is vertically centered. Then display the Page Format dialog box (press Shift+F8 and choose Page), and choose either Center Current Page or Center Pages again, so that no *X* appears in the option you selected earlier.

Although the Center Current Page command places your text precisely between the top and bottom margins on the printed page, it often appears that the text is lower than it should be. This is an optical illusion that you can fix by adding blank lines at the end of the text; this creates some "empty" space at the bottom of the page that is included in the centered text, which helps to balance the look of the text on the page. To add the lines, press Ctrl+Home, ↓ to move the cursor to the end of the current page. Then press Enter about four times to add extra blank lines. Since WordPerfect includes blank lines in the centering, this moves the text slightly higher on the printed page to create a more balanced look. Experiment with the number of blank lines you enter, and make adjustments to suit your own preferences.

Applying a Formatting Command to a Section of Text

In earlier versions of WordPerfect, you need to manually insert two different codes to change the margins, for example, for a single paragraph or text passage. First you would move the cursor to the beginning of a paragraph and change the margins. Then you would move the cursor to the end of the paragraph and choose the Margins feature again to restore the margin settings that were active before the current paragraph. Although this method still works in WordPerfect 6.0, it's a clumsy way to change margins and other layout settings for a single section of text.

WordPerfect 6.0 simplifies this process by allowing you to apply margins, line spacing, and other "open" document formatting commands to only a blocked section of text. Also, if you change the format of your document, the blocked section won't alter the format of the text that follows it. This is the general procedure:

- First, use the Block feature (press Alt+F4 or F12) or drag the mouse pointer to select the section of text that you want to affect.

- Next, choose the formatting command—left/right margins, line spacing, justification, hyphenation, fonts, or other formatting commands—that you want to apply to only the blocked text.

After you select a formatting command, WordPerfect inserts two codes: one code to turn on the command at the beginning of the block and another code at the end of the block to turn off the command (or, in other words, to return to the formatting command that was active before the blocked text).

Try the following exercise, which demonstrates a practical example of this concept. Suppose you want to change one paragraph to double line spacing within a document that is now set to single line spacing. These are the steps you would perform:

1. Move the cursor to the beginning of the paragraph that should be affected by the line spacing change.

Hold down the mouse button, and drag the mouse pointer to the end of the paragraph.

2. Press Block (Alt+F4 or F12) and then press Enter to move the cursor to the end of the paragraph (when Block is turned on, the cursor will move to the next [HRt] code when you press Enter).

3. Press Format (Shift+F8), choose Line, and then choose Line Spacing.

4. Type **2** to indicate that you want to create double line spacing for the paragraph. Then press Enter to accept the number.

5. Press Exit (F7) twice to return to the document screen. The new spacing is applied to the paragraph, and the Block feature is turned off.

To observe how WordPerfect 6.0 works differently from previous versions, press Reveal Codes (Alt+F3 or F11) to display the Reveal Codes window. In your document, you'll find that two codes were inserted to create the line spacing change: [+Ln Spacing] and [-Ln Spacing]. The first code turns on the line spacing you specified, and the second code reverts to the line spacing that was active before the first code; if you later change the line spacing for the entire document, the [-Ln Spacing] code will change to reflect the new line spacing.

These plus and minus codes appear only when you block a section of text before applying a formatting command. If you choose Line Spacing, for example, when Block is *not* turned on, you'll insert only one code—[Ln Spacing]—at the cursor position.

In the previous example, the Line Spacing command was selected, but the plus and minus codes also appear whenever you choose Justification, Margins, Tab Set, Hyphenation, Font, and other formatting commands with the Block feature turned on.

Inserting the Date into Your Document

WordPerfect's Date features read the date stored in your computer and insert it anywhere you wish in your document. You can also insert a [Date] code that will update your document with the current date whenever your document is retrieved. When you use these date features, you can define the format for the dates that you insert—including dates in a different language format.

Inserting the Date as Text

Follow this procedure to insert today's date as text in your document:

■ Move the cursor to the place in the text where the date should be inserted.

■ Press Date (Shift+F5) and then choose Insert Date Text.

Choose Tools ▸
Date ▸ Text.

WordPerfect reads the current date stored in your computer and inserts it as text in your document. It's that simple. To remove the date, delete it the same way you delete other text.

Inserting an Automatic Date Code

For documents that should display the current date whenever they are displayed on your screen or printed, you'll want to insert a [Date] code instead of text. The [Date] code ensures that whenever your document is retrieved, viewed, or printed, the current date will always be displayed as part of the text. This is useful for contracts, memos, and other professional documents that are frequently revised and reused.

To have a current date inserted automatically:

■ Move the cursor to the location in your document where the date should appear.

■ Press Date (Shift+F5) and then choose Insert Date Code.

Choose Tools ▸
Date ▸ Code.

The date that WordPerfect inserts in your document will appear as regular text. When you view the date text in the Reveal Codes window, however, you'll see a [Date] code in the document. This code guarantees that today's date will always be placed in the text (assuming, of course, that your computer keeps track of the correct date). To remove the [Date] code, just highlight it in the Reveal Codes window and press Delete.

Changing the Date Format

The Date Formats dialog box, shown in Figure 2.18 lets you change the format or layout of the date that WordPerfect inserts.

To change the date format:

■ Move the cursor to the location in your document where the date format should take effect.

■ Press Date (Shift+F5) and then choose Date Format.

■ Choose one of the predefined date formats from the list of options.

■ Press Exit (F7) until you return to the document screen.

Choose Tools ▸
Date ▸ Format.

Choose OK to return
to the document
screen.

If you want to create a custom format, you can choose Edit from the Date Formats dialog box. This displays the Edit Date Format dialog box shown in Figure 2.19.

Figure 2.18

Choosing a date format

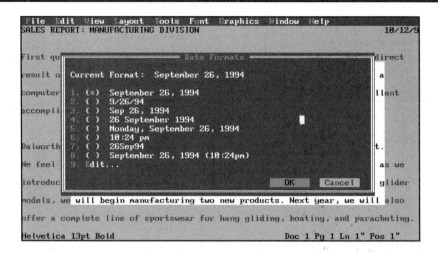

Figure 2.19

Creating a custom date format

Date codes

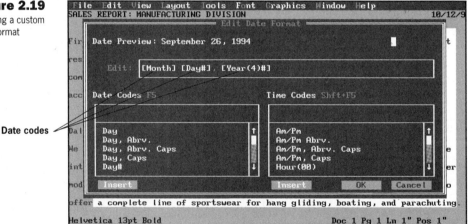

In the Edit box, you'll see that codes and characters are combined to create a date format. When this dialog box is displayed, you can do one or more of the following to create a custom date format:

- Press Ctrl+End to delete the current format. Press Delete or Backspace to delete a single date code or character.

- Press Date Codes (F5) and choose a date code.

- Use Time Codes (press Shift+F5) and choose a time code.

■ Type a character to add punctuation to the date format.

Suppose you want to change the standard date format to display the day of the week, the month, and finally the date, as in "Wednesday, May 9." With the cursor inside the Edit box:

1. Press Ctrl+End to delete the current date format.

2. Press Date Codes (F5), highlight the word *Day*, and press Enter.

3. Type a comma and a space. Then press Date Codes (F5). Scroll down to the word *Month*, or type **month** to highlight the Month date code. Press Enter to insert it.

4. Type a space. Press Date Codes (F5) and type **day#** to highlight the Day# entry. Press Enter to insert it.

5. Press Exit (F7) until you return to the document screen.

Choose OK to return to the document screen.

After you choose or create a new date format, WordPerfect inserts a [Date Fmt] code into your document that determines the format for all dates inserted after this point in the text. (Note that this code does not affect dates already inserted with the Date Text option; it will change the format of dates inserted with Date Code.) The date format is saved with your document and will remain in effect until you change it again.

When you create a new date format, you can also combine regular text with date codes to create a custom format. For example, to display the date as:

```
Synodyne Corporation / November 30, 1994
```

you would start the date format by typing **Synodyne Corporation /** in the Edit box. Then you would choose and insert the date codes and type punctuation to create the rest of the date format:

```
[Month] [Day#], [Year(4)#]
```

When you are finished, you would press Exit (F7) until you return to the document screen. Then, when you insert the date, the entire *Synodyne* text string is inserted with the date.

The month and day names used by the date features are stored in a file called WP{WPC}.LCN. This is a WordPerfect file that controls how certain text and program options are displayed for specific languages. WordPerfect Corporation provides optional language modules that let you display dates in different languages; if you have installed one of these language modules, you can choose a different language (press Shift+F8, choose Other, and then choose Language) to display dates with the names and abbreviations of the selected language.

Starting a New Page

WordPerfect calculates how much text can fit on each page and is constantly making adjustments so that the text is formatted and printed correctly. Word-Perfect uses a *page break* code to separate the pages in your document. The following sections show the difference between WordPerfect's two types of page breaks and explain how to start a new page.

Soft Page Breaks

When the text you are typing fills the current document page, WordPerfect displays a thin line across the screen to show where one page ends and the next page begins; Figure 2.20 shows how this will appear. This is called a *soft page break* [SPg]. "Soft" means that WordPerfect automatically inserts this command as needed. You don't have to do anything; your text will automatically flow to the next page. As you insert or delete text from your document, WordPerfect adjusts the placement of the soft page break as needed to correctly format your pages.

Figure 2.20
Soft page breaks on the document screen

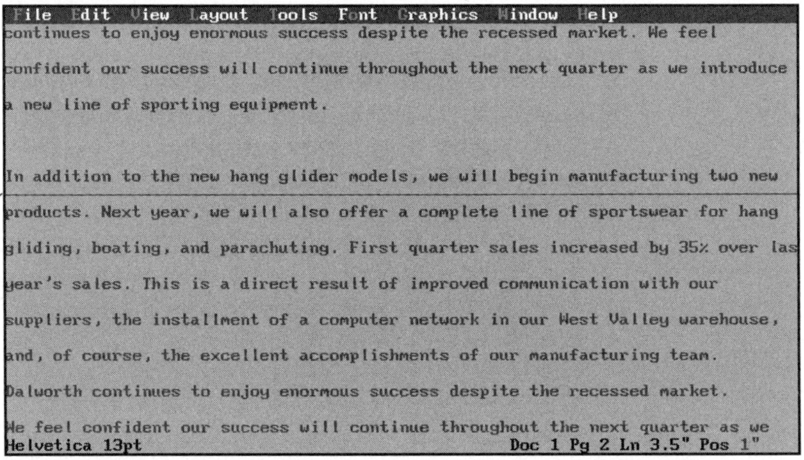

Soft page break

```
 File  Edit  View  Layout  Tools  Font  Graphics  Window  Help
continues to enjoy enormous success despite the recessed market. We feel
confident our success will continue throughout the next quarter as we introduce
a new line of sporting equipment.

In addition to the new hang glider models, we will begin manufacturing two new
products. Next year, we will also offer a complete line of sportswear for hang
gliding, boating, and parachuting. First quarter sales increased by 35% over las
year's sales. This is a direct result of improved communication with our
suppliers, the installment of a computer network in our West Valley warehouse,
and, of course, the excellent accomplishments of our manufacturing team.
Dalworth continues to enjoy enormous success despite the recessed market.
We feel confident our success will continue throughout the next quarter as we
Helvetica 13pt                                    Doc 1 Pg 2 Ln 3.5" Pos 1"
```

Hard Page Breaks

Sometimes you'll want to begin a new page even before the current page is filled. This is important when you want to isolate specific pages, such as a title page, table of contents, or index, from the rest of your document. You can insert a *hard page break* by pressing Ctrl+Enter. WordPerfect inserts an [HPg] code into your text, which appears as a solid double line, as shown in

Figure 2.21. This code ends the current page and starts the next one, ensuring that the current page remains separate from the pages that follow.

Figure 2.21

Hard page break on
the document screen

Hard page break

```
File  Edit  View  Layout  Tools  Font  Graphics  Window  Help
continues to enjoy enormous success despite the recessed market. We feel
confident our success will continue throughout the next quarter as we introduce
a new line of sporting equipment.


In addition to the new hang glider models, we will begin manufacturing two new
products. Next year, we will also offer a complete line of sportswear for hang
gliding, boating, and parachuting. First quarter sales increased by 35% over las
year's sales. This is a direct result of improved communication with our
suppliers, the installment of a computer network in our West Valley warehouse,
and, of course, the excellent accomplishments of our manufacturing team.
Dalworth continues to enjoy enormous success despite the recessed market.
Helvetica 13pt                                      Doc 1 Pg 1 Ln 7.88" Pos 1"
```

A hard page break is inserted by the person who creates the document. Unlike the soft page break, the hard page break remains in its original position when your document text is reformatted. To remove a hard page break, highlight and delete the [HPg] code from the Reveal Codes window.

Formatting a Document with Document Initial Codes

Generally, you insert formatting codes into your document where the format changes should occur. When you want margins, line spacing, and other layout settings to apply to the entire document, you can use the Document Initial Codes feature. One advantage of Document Initial Codes is that you can create a global layout from anywhere within your document; you don't need to worry about moving the cursor to the beginning of the text before changing the formatting codes. For some formatting codes, this makes editing easier, because you can edit the document layout from a single Document Initial Codes window. This also saves you the trouble of searching through the Reveal Codes window to find the right codes.

Creating and Editing Document Initial Codes

At the Document Initial Codes dialog box, shown in Figure 2.22, you can define the codes that create the initial layout for your document. These codes, such as margin settings, line spacing, tab settings, and justification, would normally be placed at the beginning of your document.

Figure 2.22

The Document Initial Codes dialog box

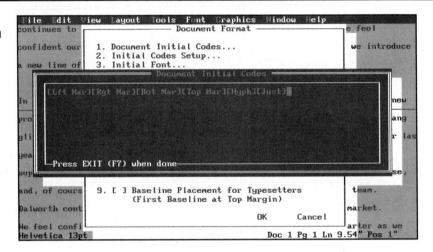

Follow these steps to create an initial document layout from the Document Initial Codes dialog box:

Choose Layout ▸ Document ▸ Document Initial Codes.

1. Press Format (Shift+F8), choose Document, and then choose Document Initial Codes.

2. Insert formatting codes by choosing features from the format menus, just as you would in the editing screen.

3. Press Exit (F7) until you return to the document editing screen.

The formatting codes you select are inserted into the [Open Style:Initial-Codes] code that automatically appears at the beginning of each document you create; this code stores the initial document codes. If you want to edit the Document Initial Codes, simply display the Document Initial Codes dialog box again, and delete or revise existing codes or add new ones. When you return to the document screen, the revised layout is applied to your document.

TIP. *You can display (but not edit) the initial document codes without calling up the Document Initial Codes screen. Just display the Reveal Codes window and move the cursor over the [Open Style:Document] code. When this code is* *highlighted in the Reveal Codes window, it expands to show all the initial document codes.*

Creating a Default Document Layout

The Document Initial Codes option lets you create and edit the intial codes for the current document, but these changes do not affect other documents you will create. The Initial Codes Setup feature, however, does let you create a default document layout that will apply to every document you will create in WordPerfect. Use this feature to change WordPerfect's default margins, tab settings, and other layout options that are already defined when you start the WordPerfect program.

These are the steps for creating a default document layout with the Initial Codes Setup feature:

Choose Layout ▶ Document.

- Press Format (Shift+F8) and choose Document.

- Choose Initial Codes Setup to display a dialog box that is similar to the one shown in Figure 2.22.

- Choose features from the format menu to insert the codes that you want to apply to all documents.

- Press Exit (F7) twice to accept the layout and return to the document screen.

After you close the Initial Codes Setup dialog box, WordPerfect updates the [Open Style:InitialCodes] code at the beginning of the current document. Also, whenever you create a new document, the codes you inserted at the Initial Codes Setup dialog box become the default layout settings for the document.

You cannot delete the [Open Style:InitialCodes] code, but you can use the Document Initial Codes option, described earlier, to edit or remove the codes that the style inserts. When you edit the default layout with the Document Initial Codes option, this changes the initial codes for the current document but it does not change the default layout you defined at the Initial Codes Setup dialog box. The layout stored in Initial Codes Setup will remain in effect for each new document until you change the codes stored in this dialog box.

3

Fonts, Text Attributes, and Special Characters

N RECENT YEARS, BUSINESS COMMUNICATIONS HAVE BECOME MUCH MORE sophisticated. Open any magazine or corporate report, and you'll see many different text styles, called *typefaces* or *fonts*. Most people use the words *typeface* and *font* interchangeably; you may also hear the term *typefont*, which is a combination of the two words. In the world of computers, these terms refer to the same thing: the style of your text. *Text attributes* such as bold, underline, and italic are used to change or emphasize the appearance of each typeface. You'll also notice a variety of text sizes for superscript text, labels, and headlines. These typefaces and text attributes can help you create attractive documents that are livelier, more expressive, and also more professional.

WordPerfect includes all the features you need for selecting text fonts, attributes, and sizes. You can change fonts to create headlines, captions, and tables. The various text attributes and sizes provide enhancements that help you communicate your message more effectively. Need a large headline? No problem. In addition to the fonts provided by your printer, WordPerfect includes several graphic fonts that can be scaled to any size and printed on any printer. Figure 3.1 shows some of the fonts that are included with the Word-Perfect software.

Figure 3.1
WordPerfect fonts

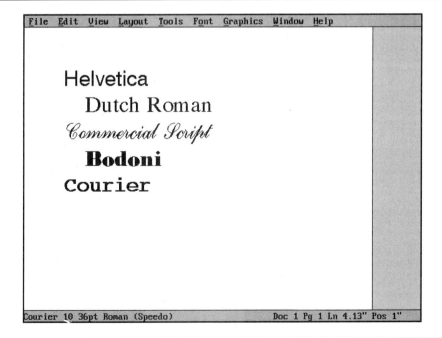

WordPerfect also provides over 1,200 *extended characters*. These include typographic symbols, accented characters, mathematic symbols, and the alphabets of many languages—including Russian, Japanese, Hebrew, and Greek. You can insert any of these characters into your text, and print them as part of your document.

Enhancing Text with Appearance Attributes

WordPerfect supports a wide variety of appearance attributes that you can apply to your text. These include Bold, Underline, and Italic, plus a few less common attributes like Double Underline, Shadow, and Outline. They all help you to create professional-looking documents. The effects of some of the attributes—Bold and Underline, for example—can be seen when you're working with WordPerfect's text display mode; others are only visible when you are working with the graphics display mode or when you print your document.

Each time you select an appearance attribute, you insert a pair of codes into your text: The first code turns on the attribute, the second one turns it off. Figure 3.2 shows an example of this code sequence.

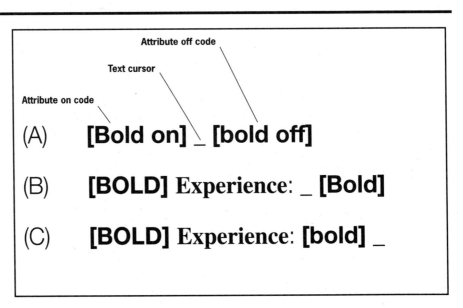

Figure 3.2
Typing a word with the Bold appearance attribute

In this example, Bold (F6) is pressed, and the [Bold On] and [Bold Off] codes are inserted at the cursor position (as shown as part A of the figure. The cursor is located between the codes, so that you can type the text that will appear with the attribute. After the text is typed (part B), Bold (F6) is pressed again to move the cursor to the other side of the Bold Off code (part C). When the Reveal Codes window is displayed, you can also press the → key to move the cursor past the second code; this has the same effect as selecting the attribute again. After turning on any attribute, you can select the attribute again to turn it off; however, it's usually easier to move the cursor outside of the paired attribute codes.

TIP. *The following exercises show you how to select the appearance attributes. Use these attributes sparingly in your documents, however. If you include too many attribute changes, your document will look cluttered and unprofessional.*

Creating Bold Text

Bold text is useful for creating headlines, titles, and other labels that should stand out from the rest of the text in your document.

Follow these steps at your computer to select the Bold appearance attribute while typing a line of text:

1. If there is text on the document screen, clear the screen by pressing Exit (F7), and then choosing <u>N</u>o twice.

2. Begin a line by typing

   Welcome to

Choose F<u>o</u>nt ▸ <u>B</u>old.

3. Without moving the cursor, press Bold (F6).

4. Type

   Barney & Wally's

Choose F<u>o</u>nt ▸ <u>B</u>old again.

5. Press Bold (F6) again to turn off the Bold attribute. Finish the line of text by typing

   Olde-Time Circus!

The text on the screen will now look like this:

   Welcome to **Barney & Wally's** Olde-Time Circus!

When you select the Bold feature, WordPerfect inserts two codes into your text, [Bold On] and [Bold Off]. Press Reveal Codes (Alt+F3 or F11), and you'll see the codes shown in Figure 3.3. The first code turns on the Bold attribute, the second turns it off. Any text that is typed or inserted between these paired codes is displayed and printed as bold text. Should you change your mind and want to remove the Bold attribute, just display the Reveal

Codes window and delete either of the Bold codes. Since these are paired codes, they are both removed when either of the pair is deleted.

Figure 3.3

[Bold On] and [Bold Off] codes in the Reveal Codes window

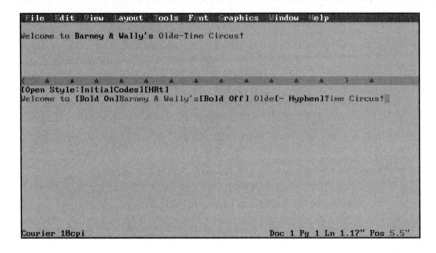

TIP.   *See "Applying Attributes to a Block of Text" later in this chapter for information about applying the Bold attribute to text that is already typed.*

Underlining Text

Underlining can help you emphasize a document title, a publication reference, or any word or phrase. (Ideally, italic is used for this kind of emphasis; however, if a selected font cannot produce the Italic attribute, underlining is the acceptable substitute.) For forms or memos, the Underline feature can also create an empty line for a "fill-in-the-blank" effect.

These steps demonstrate how to underline text as you are typing it:

1. If you already have text on your screen, press Home, Home, ↓ and press Enter twice to add a blank line at the bottom of your document.

2. On a new line, type

    ```
    For related information, see
    ```

3. Without moving the cursor, press Underline (F8).

4. Type

    ```
    The Pacific Machine,
    ```

Choose F<u>o</u>nt ▶
<u>U</u>nderline.

Choose F<u>o</u>nt ▶
<u>U</u>nderline again.

5. Press Underline (F8) again to turn off the Underline attribute.

6. Finish the line of text by typing

```
Wallace York, Clason & Sons Publishing, Chicago, 1993, p.
237.
```

7. When you are finished, press Enter twice to end the paragraph.

Your screen will display

```
For related information, see The Pacific Machine, Wallace
York, Clason & Sons Publishing, Chicago, 1993, p. 237.
```

When you select the Underline attribute, WordPerfect inserts two codes into your text, [Und On] and [Und Off]. The first code turns on the Underline attribute, and the second turns it off. Any text that is typed or inserted between the codes is displayed and printed as underlined text. Should you change your mind and want to remove the underlining, simply display the Reveal Codes window and delete one of the Underline attribute codes. Remember, when you delete one code in the pair, the other code is automatically removed.

There is also a Double Underline attribute available to you. It places a double underscore beneath each character of text that occurs between the [Dbl Und On] and [Dbl Und Off] codes. To select this attribute, press Font (Ctrl+F8), choose <u>A</u>ppearance, and choose <u>D</u>bl Undline. Then Press Exit (F7). Like Bold and Underline, Double Underline inserts a pair of codes to turn the attribute on and off. When you are finished typing the text, choose Double Underline again to turn off the attribute.

Italicizing Text

You can use the Italic feature to italicize text as you type it. The following steps show you how to do this. See "Applying Attributes to a Block of Text" later in this chapter, to learn how to italicize text you've already typed.

NOTE. *Your printer can print italic text only if the selected font supports the Italic attribute. If the Italic attribute is not available, the printer will substitute underlined text.*

1. On a new line, type

```
For related information, see
```

Choose F<u>o</u>nt ▶
<u>I</u>talics.

2. Press Font (Ctrl+F8), choose <u>A</u>ppearance, and choose <u>I</u>talics. Then press Exit (F7) to return to the document screen.

3. Type

```
Wilma's Guide for Lovelorn Doggies
```

4. Press Font (Ctrl+F8), choose <u>A</u>ppearance, and choose <u>I</u>talics. Then press Exit (F7).

Choose F<u>o</u>nt ▶
<u>I</u>talics again.

5. Finish the line of text by typing

```
Turtle Rock Publishing, San Diego, 1990, p. 206.
```

6. Press Enter twice to end the paragraph.

When you are finished, your screen will display

```
For related information, see Wilma's Guide for Lovelorn
Doggies, Turtle Rock Publishing, San Diego, 1990, p. 206.
```

Like the other attribute features, the Italic option inserts two codes, [Italc On] and [Italc Off], in your document. The first code turns the attribute on, and the second one turns it off. To remove the Italic attribute, just display the Reveal Codes window and delete one of the Italic codes.

Outline, Shadow, and Small Caps

In addition to Bold, Underline, and Italic, WordPerfect provides five other font attributes: Outline, Shadow, Small Caps, Redline, and Strikeout. (Redline and Strikeout are explained in the next section.) You can choose a combination of all possible attributes from the Font dialog box. Note that some of these attributes may not be supported by the font you've selected.

To select the Outline attribute, press Font (Ctrl+F8), or choose F<u>o</u>nt and then choose F<u>o</u>nt again. From the Font dialog box, choose <u>A</u>ppearance, and then <u>O</u>utline, and press Exit (F7). Then type the text to appear with this attribute. As shown here, Outline text is printed as an outline of the regular typeface:

Regular Text

Outlined Text

Choosing <u>O</u>utline inserts a pair of [Outln On] and [Outln Off] codes. To remove the attribute, simply delete one of the codes. Remember, you can select this attribute freely, but in order to print it, the font you're using must support the Outline attribute.

Shadow text is similar to bold, except there is a slight shadow next to the text. To select the Shadow attribute, press Font (Ctrl+F8), or choose F̲ont, and then F̲ont from the menu bar. From the Font dialog box, choose A̲ppearance and then choose Sh̲adow. Press Exit (F7). Finally, type the text that you want to have the Shadow attribute.

When the document is printed, the Shadow text will appear similar to this:

Shadow Text

WordPerfect inserts a pair of codes, [Shadw On] and [Shadw Off], into your text; to cancel this attribute, simply delete one of the paired codes.

If the selected font does not support the shadow attribute, WordPerfect creates a shadow effect by printing the text twice. The second printing of the text is shifted slightly up and to the left, thus creating the appearance of a shadow. Some printers won't allow WordPerfect to do this, and you may need to enhance your text with the Bold attribute instead.

When the Small Caps (small capitals) attribute is applied to text, all capital letters appear as they normally do, but lowercase letters appear as capitals that are one size smaller than the normal text. To select Small Caps, press Font (Ctrl+F8), or choose F̲ont and then F̲ont from the menu bar. Choose A̲ppearance and then choose Small C̲aps. Press Exit (F7) to close the Font dialog box.

When you select this attribute, WordPerfect inserts two codes: [Sm Cap On] and [Sm Cap Off]. Text that is typed or inserted between these paired codes prints is illustrated below. (Lines of regular text and capitalized text are also shown to better demonstrate the Small Caps effect.)

WordPerfect Text Regular text

WORDPERFECT TEXT Small capitals

WORDPERFECT TEXT Capitalized text

As you can see, the Small Caps attribute can subtly enhance names, abbreviations, or acronyms—without the impact of fully capitalized text. To cancel the Small Caps attribute, display the Reveal Codes window and delete one of the paired Small Caps codes.

Redline and Strikeout Text

The Redline and Strikeout attributes are often selected for editing purposes. Redline is commonly used to indicate text that has been added; Strikeout generally indicates text that will be deleted from the document.

To select the Redline or Strikeout attribute, press Font (Ctrl+F8), or choose Font, and then Font again. Next, choose Appearance and then Redline or Strikeout. Redlined and Strikeout text may look like this on your screen:

Redlined Text

~~Strikeout Text~~

The actual appearance of redlined text will vary based on your printer.

When you choose Redline, WordPerfect inserts the [Redln On] and [Redln Off] codes into your document; when you select Strikeout, the paired codes [StkOut On] and [StkOut Off] are inserted. You can remove these attributes by deleting one of the paired codes. (See Chapter 13 for examples of document editing with the Redline and Strikeout attributes.)

Combining Text Attributes

Sometimes, you'll want a text headline to be bold *and* underlined. Or perhaps you need to create italic text that is also redlined. WordPerfect makes these and other combinations possible by allowing you to select two or more attributes from the Font dialog box to create a unique style of text.

The process is simple. Suppose you want to create text that is bold, underlined, and italic: Display the Font dialog box, choose all the attributes you want to use, and return to the document screen. Then type your text. You can also select new attributes while other attributes are still turned on, thus creating new combinations. As you turn on each attribute, the appropriate pair of On/Off codes is inserted into the text. Of course, the appearance of the printed text is determined by your printer's capabilities and the font you've selected. If, for example, you create text that is bold and underlined, you'll need a font that supports both of these attributes.

Try the following exercise to combine different attributes on the same line. When you're finished, you'll see this sentence on your screen:

`This sentence contains `**`Bold`**`, `**`Underlined`**`, `*`Italic`*` text.`

Choose <u>V</u>iew ▸
<u>R</u>eveal Codes.

Choose F<u>o</u>nt ▸ <u>B</u>old.

Choose F<u>o</u>nt ▸
<u>U</u>nderline.

Choose F<u>o</u>nt ▸
<u>I</u>talics.

1. Press Reveal Codes (Alt+F3 or F11). This will let you see how the attribute codes are placed and combined in the text.

2. Begin by typing

   `This sentence contains`

3. Press Bold (F6). Notice the paired codes that are inserted into the document.

4. Continue the sentence by typing

   `Bold,`

5. Without moving the cursor, press Underline (F8). Notice that the [Und On] [Und Off] codes are embedded within the [Bold On] [Bold Off] codes.

6. Continue the sentence by typing

   `Underlined,`

   When the word "Underlined" is printed, it will be bold *and* underlined, because the text is located within the paired codes for both of these attributes.

7. Press Font (Ctrl+F8) and choose <u>A</u>ppearance. Then choose <u>I</u>talics and press Exit (F7). (Alternately, you may press Ctrl+I.)

8. Type **Italic** as the next word in the sentence.

9. Press Font (Ctrl+F8). Choose each of the selected <u>A</u>ppearance options— <u>B</u>old, <u>U</u>nderline, and <u>I</u>talics—so that the check boxes next to these options appear without an *X*. Then press Exit (F7).

10. Finish the sentence by typing

    `text.`

Your screen should now look similar to Figure 3.4. (This figure is shown in WordPerfect's graphics display mode so you can see the effect of the codes; your screen may look different from the figure.)

   In our example, you combined the Bold, Underline, and Italic attributes, but you aren't limited to these three. You can select any attribute while another attribute is still working. Create any combination you like by selecting the desired attributes from the Font dialog box, but remember that the results you get depend on the fonts you've selected. If you don't have the right fonts to create the attribute combination you've chosen, WordPerfect will print plain text.

Figure 3.4
Using several text
attributes

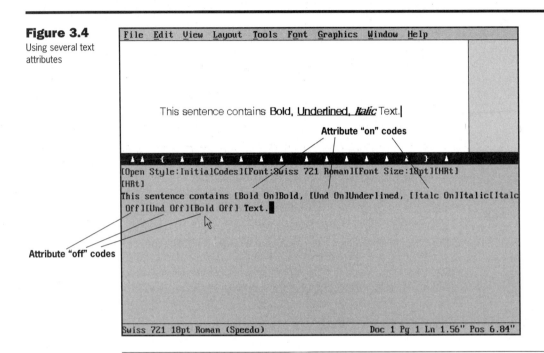

Attribute "on" codes

Attribute "off" codes

Canceling one or more attributes in a combination is no different than what you've already learned. Display the Reveal Codes window and delete one of the paired codes of the attribute you want to remove. This cancels the attribute without removing the other attributes in the combination.

Applying Attributes to a Block of Text

Now that you know how to select different text attributes as you're typing, you're probably wondering how to apply the attributes to text that is already entered. This is easy to do with WordPerfect's Block feature. First you define a section of text, called a *block,* that you want to have appear in the new attribute. Then you select the attribute to change the appearance of the blocked text. It's that simple. WordPerfect inserts the On code for the attribute at the beginning of the block, and the Off code at the end of the block.

To see how this works, let's try changing the attribute for a block of text. Before you begin, you may want to clear your screen; to do so, press Exit (F7) and type **N** twice.

1. Begin by typing this paragraph on the document screen:

   Our sales reps will be arriving in Seattle on the morning of January 6. Please make reservations at the Westshore Hotel for that evening through January 12. We will need ten single rooms, preferably on the same floor, and one executive suite for Mr. Beckstrand.

2. Move the cursor to the beginning of the phrase "Westshore Hotel." If you're using a mouse, move the pointer to the first character of the hotel name.

While holding down the mouse button, move the mouse pointer over the "Westshore Hotel" text to block it.

3. Press Block (Alt+F4 or F12). As you move the cursor, you'll notice the "Block On" message at the bottom of the screen, which lets you know that the Block feature is now turned on.

   TIP. *From the keyboard, press Ctrl+→ twice to quickly move past two words.*

4. Move the cursor or mouse pointer to the space that follows "Westshore Hotel." As you move the cursor, the text is displayed with a reverse-video highlight bar, shown in Figure 3.5. This highlight indicates the text that is included in the block.

Figure 3.5

Blocking text to assign an attribute code

Blocked text ⟶

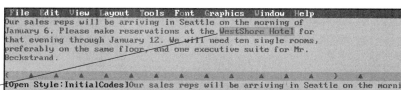

5. Press Font (Ctrl+F8), choose <u>A</u>ppearance, and choose <u>I</u>talics. Then press Exit (F7). (Alternately, you may press Ctrl+I.)

Choose F<u>o</u>nt ▸ <u>I</u>talics.

   After you select the Italic attribute, WordPerfect inserts an [Italc On] code at the beginning of the block, and an [Italc Off] code at the end of the block. Of course, you can select any of the text attributes to change the blocked text. Just block the text you want to change, and select the desired attributes.

If attribute codes are already present in a defined block of text, these codes will remain in effect and work together with the attributes you add—as long as they can all be printed in the font you are using. For example, if your block of text contains a word in italic, it remains italic if you also apply the Bold attribute to the block. This assumes, however, that you have a font that includes both the Italic *and* Bold attributes for printed text. If you do not have a such a font, the italic text may not print as you would expect. WordPerfect does its best to print the text as you've specified, but, because of font limitations, your printer may not be able to produce certain combinations of attributes.

Underlining Spaces and Tabs

When you turn on the Underline attribute, WordPerfect's standard operation is to underline characters typed from the keyboard and spaces inserted with the spacebar, but *not* the spaces inserted by pressing the Tab key. If you wish, you can tell WordPerfect whether to underline spaces, tabs, or both.

When WordPerfect is set to underline spaces, it's easy to create a form like the one shown in Figure 3.6. The blank spaces to be filled in are simply underlined character spaces. In the figure, tabs are also underlined to create the horizontal lines.

The following steps show you how to change the setting for underlining spaces and tabs. This setting only affects the spaces and tabs that are placed between the paired Underline On/Off attribute codes; it does not affect spaces and tabs located within regular text. In this exercise, you will also create a simple form with the new Underline settings (clear the screen before you begin):

Choose Font ▸
Font ▸ Underline .

1. Press Font (Ctrl+F8) and choose Underline.

2. Choose Tabs, so that an *X* appears next to this option. The Underline Spaces option should already be turned on. When you select this Underline feature, WordPerfect inserts an [Undrln Tab] code at the cursor position. Since underlined spaces are the default WordPerfect setting, you won't see a code for the Underline spaces option. From this point on, any tabs or spaces you type within Underline On/Off codes will be underlined in the printed document.

Choose OK to return
to the document
screen.

3. Press Exit (F7) to return to the document screen. Then press Tab once.

Choose Font ▸
Underline.

4. Press Underline (F8) to turn on the Underline attribute.

5. Type **Name:** as the first label for your form.

Figure 3.6
A form with
underlined spaces
and tabs

DEPARTMENT SURVEY

Name: _____ Date: _____

Hire Date: _____ Dept.:_____

Please note the scheduled conference/trade show dates below.
Circle those that you plan to attend, and indicate the number
of people from your department who are registered for the shows.

Date	City	No. Attending
04/12/95	New York	4
05/02/95	Chicago	6
06/21/95	Dallas/Ft. Worth	3
07/06/95	Los Angeles	5

Comments:

_____

_____

_____

_____

6. Press Tab four times to start the second column in the table. Notice that the Underline attribute continues through the tab columns.

7. Type **Phone Number** as the label for the second column. Then press Tab twice to extend the underline a little farther to the right.

8. Press → to move the cursor past the [Und Off] code. Then press Enter twice to move to the next line.

9. Press Tab, and then type your name as the first entry in the table.

10. Press Tab until the cursor is beneath "Phone Number." Type your phone number, and then press Enter to move to the next line.

When you are finished, your screen will look similar to Figure 3.7. You created the underlined areas by pressing the spacebar and the Tab key while the Underline attribute was turned on. As you can see, you can get the same effect with either method; you don't need to use both tabs and spaces. Generally, however, you'll want to use underlined spaces for normal text, and underlined tabs for charts created with tabs.

Figure 3.7

Using underlined spaces and tabs

File   Edit   View   Layout   Tools   Font   Graphics   Window   Help
Name: Phone Number
Dana Heath   607-555-7214
I
Swiss 721 14pt Roman (Speedo)   Doc 1 Pg 1 Ln 1.89" Pos 1"

Changing the Font in Your Document

So far in this chapter, you've learned how to select and change the different appearance attributes for text. These are merely variations on the typeface (font) for your document. Now let's look at how to change the font to print the text in a different typeface. There are two ways to do this: You can change the font at a given point within the text, or you can select a font for the entire document.

The fonts you can choose depend on the fonts available for use with your printer. Most printers have some built-in fonts that you can select. If you have purchased separate *font cartridges* or *soft fonts* (fonts on disk), these must be installed for use with your printer before you can select them for your document text. For more information about setting up the fonts for your printer, see Chapter 4.

WordPerfect includes several graphic fonts that you can choose for your text; these fonts are scalable to different sizes and can be printed on any printer.

Changing the Font for a Section of Text

When you select a new font for your text, WordPerfect displays a list of the fonts that are available for use with your printer. After you choose a new font, WordPerfect inserts a [Font] code at the cursor position. This is an open code, meaning that any text coming after the font code is formatted and printed in the new typeface. The active font remains in effect until the end of the document or until another [Font] code is inserted.

Figure 3.8 shows the effect of a font change inserted into the text. (In the next section, you'll see how to change the base font for the entire document.)

The steps that follow show you how to insert a font change code into the text of your document.

1. Move the cursor to the place in the text where you want the font change to begin.

Choose Font ▸ Font ▸ Font.

2. Press Font (Ctrl+F8) and choose Font. The screen shown in Figure 3.9 appears. The list shows the fonts available for use with your printer, plus the fonts that WordPerfect provides. On the Font list, an asterisk appears next to the name of the current font in the document.

3. Press ↓ or ↑ to highlight the name of the font you want to select. If you're using a mouse, simply move the pointer to the font name, and click the left mouse button.

Double-click on the Font name and choose OK.

4. Press Enter to select the highlighted font, and then press Exit (F7).

Figure 3.8
Font changes in a document

SCHEDULE

04/30: **Monday**
Arrive in Seattle to discuss new expansion plans. Meet with sales reps regarding improvements to distribution channels.

05/01: **Tuesday**
Meeting with Dr. Crutchfield regarding research grants. Visit with Anna. Dinner at the Harbor Café.

05/02: **Wednesday**
Meet with faculty to discuss Warner's involvement with research. Execute contractual agreement.

05/03: **Thursday**
Take the shuttle to Vancouver. Visit with Terry's parents. Fly back to Chicago.

Figure 3.9
A list of available fonts in graphics display mode

If the font you've selected can be scaled to different sizes, you can also choose the Size option to specify a size. After you select the font, WordPerfect inserts a [Font] code into your text. You can display the Reveal Codes window to view the font change code. The characteristics of the font are generally not visible on the standard text display screen; however, WordPerfect's graphics display will show the font as it should appear when printed. You can also use the Print Preview feature (press Shift+F7 and then choose Print Preview) to see the effect of the font change on your text.

Although WordPerfect sets no limits on the number of font changes you can insert on a page (or in one document), the actual number may depend on the type of printer you have and the amount of memory available for printing. To find out whether your printer has such limits, perform the following steps:

Choose File ▸ Print.

1. Press Print (Shift+F7).

2. Choose Select from the Print dialog box.

3. Highlight the name of your printer, and choose Information.

A dialog box appears with information specific to your printer. If there is a limit to the number of fonts you can select for each page or document, it will be noted on this screen. When you are finished reading the printer help information, press Exit (F7) three times to return to the document.

Changing the Font for the Entire Document

One way to select a font for the entire document is by moving the cursor to the beginning of the document and inserting a font change code, as you just learned. This works well for most cases, but there are a few exceptions. For example, font changes placed in your text don't always affect the *invisible text* you'll be adding to your documents later on—that is, page numbering, headers and footers, footnotes, endnotes, and any other text that is printed with the document but may not appear on the document screen. Generally, font change codes you insert from the document screen affect only the main body of text.

Because of this, WordPerfect offers an important feature, Document Initial Font, that lets you select a font for all text in the document. When you use this option, you can still insert specific font changes within your text. The Document Initial Font option simply guarantees that all document text will be printed with the same font, except when you insert font codes to change specific passages of text within the document.

Choose Layout ▸ Document.

1. Press Format (Shift+F8) and choose Document.

2. From the Document Format dialog box, choose Initial Font. The Initial Font dialog box appears.

3. Choose <u>F</u>ont; a list of available fonts appears.

4. Highlight the name of the font you want to select, and press Enter. If necessary, choose <u>S</u>ize and specify a size for the font.

Double-click on a font name to select it.

5. Choose <u>C</u>urrent Document Only if you want to apply this font only to the document you have on your screen. Or, choose All <u>N</u>ew Documents to select this font as the default font for all new documents.

Choose OK twice.

6. Press Exit (F7) twice to return to the document screen.

The Initial Font option does not insert a code into your text, but rather applies a font change to the entire document. All text in your document will appear in this new font, except when you insert font changes directly into the text. When you want to change or remove the initial font assignment for the document, repeat the steps you just took, and choose a different font.

Changing the Font for a Block of Text

You can change the font for only one section of text by first blocking the text and then choosing the font you want. Try these steps to see how this works:

Move the mouse pointer to the letter *S* in *Spain*. Hold down the mouse button and move the pointer to the space after *Spain*. Then release the mouse button.

1. Clear the document screen and type the following line of text:

   `The rain in Spain is mostly wet.`

2. Move the cursor to the *S* in *Spain*. Press Block (Alt+F4 or F12) and move the cursor to the space after the word *Spain*.

3. Press Font (Ctrl+F8), and choose <u>F</u>ont from the dialog box.

4. Press ↓ or ↑ to scroll through the list of fonts until you highlight the font named "Bodoni WP-Bold (Type 1)." Press Enter to select the font.

Choose F<u>o</u>nt ▸ F<u>o</u>nt ▸ <u>F</u>ont.

5. Choose <u>S</u>ize, type 24, and then press Enter to change the font size.

6. Press Exit (F7) to return to the document screen.

Click on the ↑ or ↓ in the font list, to scroll through it.

The font selections are applied to the blocked text, and the Block feature is turned off. Press Reveal Codes (Alt+F3 or F11), and you'll see four codes, shown in Figure 3.10, surrounding the word *Spain*: [+Font: Bodoni-WP Bold] [+Font Size: 24pt] and [-Font Size: 12pt] [-Font: Courier].

Choose OK to return to the document screen.

The codes that begin with a plus sign (+) are the codes that are inserted at the beginning of the block to turn on the font and font size; the codes that begin with a minus sign (–) are inserted at the end of the block to "turn off"—or more accurately, reset—the font and font size that were active before you made the font change. These + and – codes let you apply fonts to blocked text, without disturbing the font selections that are already applied to the document text.

Figure 3.10
Applying fonts to
blocked text

Font and size
change code

Code reset
original font and
size

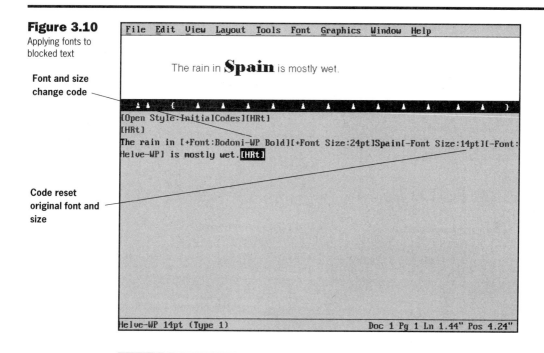

Removing Text Attributes and Fonts

When you want to remove font or attribute changes from your text, you need to use the Reveal Codes window to delete the codes that create the changes.

This is different from earlier versions of WordPerfect, in which you could delete bold and underlining codes without displaying the Reveal Codes window. WordPerfect 6.0 does not let you delete font and formatting codes unless the Reveal Codes window is displayed. (Without Reveal Codes displayed, you can only delete codes by actually deleting the text affected by the codes.)

Choose View▶ Reveal Codes.

- Press Reveal Codes (Alt+F3 or F11).

- Move the cursor to highlight the attribute code or the font code that you want to delete.

- Press Delete to remove the font code.

If you delete an attribute or font code by mistake, choose Edit and then choose Undo; this restores the deleted codes—even paired attribute codes—to your text. For example, if you accidentally delete a [Bold Off] code, both bold codes are removed from your text. When this happens, choose Edit and then Undo to restore the bold attribute to the text where it was applied.

Changing the Relative Size of Your Text

When you choose a font, you can select a Size to specify the text size you want. WordPerfect also provides relative size options for generic sizes. Figure 3.11 shows the relative sizes you can choose in WordPerfect. Note that relative sizes are measured as percentages of the current font. The results you get depend entirely upon the font and font size selections that are available for your printer.

Figure 3.11
WordPerfect's text size options

Fine (60%)

Small (80%)

Large (120%)

Very Large (150%)

Extra Large (200%)

For some printers, sizes are already assigned to the fonts in the printer. If, for example, the current font is Times Roman 12 point, and you select Large text, WordPerfect searches for a Times Roman font that is larger than 12 points. If it can't find a larger Times Roman font, it looks for another typeface that matches the requested size. When a suitable font cannot be found, WordPerfect uses one of its graphic fonts to produce the text size you've indicated.

If you have a PostScript printer or a printer with *scalable* fonts, WordPerfect can always create the text size you select.

Selecting a Size while Typing

The following procedure selects different text sizes while you are typing the text in your document. (To change the size of existing text, refer to "Changing the Size of Existing Text" later in this chapter.)

Choose F̲ont ►
Size/Position.

1. Press Font (Ctrl+F8) and choose R̲elative Size.

2. Select a text size from the following options:

<u>F</u>ine, <u>S</u>mall, <u>L</u>arge, <u>V</u>ery Large, or <u>E</u>xtra Large

3. Press Exit (F7).

4. Type the text that will appear in the new size.

5. When you are finished typing the text, turn off the text size change by selecting it again from the Font dialog box.

6. Press Exit (F7) to return to the document editing screen.

Size attributes are similar to the appearance attributes. You can use WordPerfect's graphics display mode or the Print Preview feature to see the effect of the size changes. Whenever you select a new size, you insert two codes. The first code turns on the size you select, and the second code turns it off. If you change your mind and want to cancel the size change, simply delete either code from the Reveal Codes window.

Superscripts and Subscripts

Included in the Font dialog box are options for creating superscript and subscript text. These help you create mathematical expressions, chemistry symbols, and other special text like this: 5^2, CO_2, $\log_b 45$, and "…now only \$19.95*." Superscript reduces the size of the text (assuming you've got a smaller font available) and raises it up one-half line. Subscript reduces the size of the text and lowers it one-half line.

NOTE. *The Superscript and Subscript options are useful for creating simple figures and basic equations. If you need to create complex equations, see Chapter 20 for information about WordPerfect's Equation feature.*

Follow these steps at your computer to create a few examples of superscript and subscript text. Before you begin, press Home, Home, ↓ to move the cursor to the end of the current document, and press Enter twice to start a new paragraph. Or press Exit (F7) and type **N** twice to clear the screen.

1. Type this text:

25 = x

2. Now add an exponent of *2* to the equation. Press Font (Ctrl+F8), choose <u>P</u>osition, and then choose <u>S</u>uperscript. Press Exit (F7).

3. Type **2**. Then press Font (Ctrl+F8), choose <u>P</u>osition, and then choose <u>N</u>ormal to turn off the effect of Superscript. Press Exit (F7).

Choose F<u>o</u>nt ▸
Size/Position ▸
Su<u>p</u>erscript.

4. Press Enter twice and type

```
CO
```

5. Now create a subscript *2*. Press Font (Ctrl+F8), choose Position, and then choose Subscript.

Choose Font ▸
Size/Position ▸
Subscript.

6. Type **2**. Press Font (Ctrl+F8), choose Position, and choose Normal. Then press Enter twice.

7. Press Font (Ctrl+F8), choose Position, and then choose Superscript.

8. Type an asterisk (*), turn off the Superscript attribute, and type

```
Batteries not included
```

9. Press Print (Shift+F7) and choose Print Preview to view the text as it will be printed. Your text now looks like this:

```
25=x²
CO²
*Batteries not included
```

10. When you are finished viewing the text, press Exit (F7) to return to the editing screen.

WordPerfect inserts the paired codes [Suprscpt On][Suprscpt Off] and [Subscpt On][Subscpt Off] into your document. Any text typed between the codes is superscript or subscript. You aren't limited to just one character when you use these attributes; a string of superscript or subscript text can be as long as you like. If you're using WordPerfect's text display mode, you won't see the Superscript or Subscript attribute on the editing screen; to see these attributes while editing, use WordPerfect's graphics display mode.

To create super- and subscript text, WordPerfect looks for the next smallest font. If a smaller font that matches the current font is not available, WordPerfect looks for a smaller font in a different typeface. If an appropriate font cannot be found, WordPerfect substitutes one of its graphic fonts to create the super- and subscript text.

Removing superscript and subscript is easier than selecting and inserting them. Simply display the Reveal Codes window (Alt+F3 or F11) and delete one of the paired attribute codes. Like other text attributes, the attribute is removed from the text when you delete one of the paired codes.

TIP. *Press → to move the cursor past the super- and subscript off codes. This is easier than displaying the Font dialog box to turn off the attributes.*

Changing the Size of Existing Text

To change the size of existing text in a document, you can use the Block feature. Here's how to do it.

While holding down the mouse button, drag the mouse pointer over the text to block it. Then release the mouse button.

1. Move the cursor to the beginning of the text you wish to change.

2. Press Block (Alt+F4) or hold down the left mouse button to begin defining a block of text.

3. Move the cursor to the end of the block.

4. Press Font (Ctrl+F8) and choose <u>R</u>elative Size.

Choose Fo<u>n</u>t ▸ Size/Position.

5. Choose one of the sizes from the list of size options.

When you select the size, a "Size On" code is inserted at the beginning of the block, and a "Size Off" code is inserted at the end of the block. If you change your mind about the size, you can delete one of the paired size codes. This restores your text to the normal size.

If size codes already exist in the block of text you define with an additional size code, the effect of the existing codes will change, depending on the text size you select for the entire block. For example, suppose the Small text size is applied to a single word in a paragraph. Then you block the entire paragraph and assign the Large text size. When the paragraph is printed, the "small" word will be produced in the original font size, because the change to Large text made everything in the paragraph one size larger.

Special Characters and Symbols

Your computer and printer use a standard set of characters to display and print documents. Called the *ASCII* (American Standard Code for Information Interchange) *character set*, it includes all the characters and symbols that you can type from your keyboard. It also includes a few accented characters and symbols. These are fully supported by WordPerfect. If you need to type something in French, *pas de problème!* WordPerfect makes it easy to insert the special characters you need.

Sometimes, however, you'll need characters that the ASCII character set doesn't provide. For example, have you ever wanted to include the trademark symbol (™) or the copyright symbol (©) in your text? Or, if you work with other languages, you may need to produce a phrase in Greek or Hebrew— not as a phonetic equivalent, but in the actual symbols of the language.

For these and other situations, WordPerfect supports 12 additional *extended character sets* with multinational characters, typographic symbols, mathematical and scientific characters, and the alphabets for Greek, Hebrew,

Cyrillic (Russian), and Hirigana and Katakana (Japanese). When possible, WordPerfect uses your own printer fonts to produce these extended characters. However, if your fonts do not support these characters, WordPerfect uses its graphic fonts to generate the characters for the printer. One way or the other, you'll be able to put these characters on paper with most printers.

There are a few different techniques for inserting these characters into your text. For special ASCII characters, you can use the Alt key with the numeric keypad to insert the characters you want. For accented characters and some symbols, the WordPerfect Characters feature lets you create the characters from the keyboard; this feature also lets you insert characters from the other 12 WordPerfect character sets.

Inserting Characters with the Alt key

Each character in the ASCII character set is assigned a unique number. Table 3.1 shows the numbers of several familiar characters found in the ASCII character set.

NOTE. *See your DOS manual for a complete list of ASCII characters and their assigned numbers.*

Table 3.1   **ASCII Characters and Their Numbers**

ASCII Character	ASCII Number
ü	129
é	130
â	131
å	134
ç	135
ö	148
á	160
ó	162
ú	163
ñ	164
£	156

Table 3.1   **ASCII Characters and Their Numbers (Continued)**

ASCII Character	ASCII Number
¥	157
û	158
ƒ	159
¶	20
☺	1
♪	14
♥	3
⌂	127
Σ	228

You can't type these characters directly from a standard U.S. keyboard, but you can insert them into your document by holding down the Alt key and typing the ASCII number assigned to the character you want. The ASCII number *must* be typed from the numeric keypad—the cluster of number keys at the right side of your keyboard. If you use the number keys at the top of the keyboard, nothing happens.

Follow these steps to practice inserting ASCII characters:

1. At a blank editing screen, hold down the Alt key and, using the keys on the numeric keypad, type **164**. This is the ASCII number assigned to the ñ character. When you release the Alt key, the ñ character is inserted at the cursor position.

2. Hold down the Alt key and type **130** on the numeric keypad. Release the Alt key to insert the é character into your document.

3. Choose one of the characters listed in Table 3.1. Hold down the Alt key and type the number (on the numeric keypad) assigned to the character you chose. Release the Alt key, and the character is inserted into your document.

This is a quick way to insert special characters, but it does have limitations. For example, you have to know the ASCII numbers of the characters you want to insert. You can memorize the numbers of the extended characters you use often, but you may not want to do this for a lot of other characters. Also, the ASCII character set does not include all characters supported by WordPerfect—for example, the ù character. For these cases, you can use the WordPerfect Characters feature explained in the following sections.

Composing Characters with Diacritical Marks

The WordPerfect Characters feature lets you quickly create characters or symbols that have accents and other diacritical marks. It's simple: Just press Ctrl+2 and type two characters from the keyboard; the first character represents the letter you need, and the second character represents the diacritical mark. For example, *e* and ´ create *é*; and *a* and ^ create *â*. Table 3.2 shows the accents and diacritics that WordPerfect supports.

Table 3.2   **Characters with Accents and Diacritics**

Accent/Diacritic	Keyboard Character	Example
Acute	'	**e'** = é
Caron	v	**Nv** = Ñ
Cedilla	,	**C,** = Ç
Centered Dot	:	**L:** = Ŀ
Circumflex	^	**o^** = ô
Crossbar	-	**D-** = Đ
Dot above	.	**e.** = ė
Grave	`	**y`** = ỳ
Macron	_	**u_** = ū
Ogonek	;	**i;** = į
Ring Above	@	**a@** *or* **ao** = å
Slash	/	**o/** = ø
Stroke	\	**L** = Ł
Tilde	~	**n~** = ñ
Umlaut	"	**u"** = ü

NOTE. *The Characters feature also lets you insert other more elaborate characters from the WordPerfect character sets. See "Using the WordPerfect Character Sets" later in this chapter.*

This is the general procedure for inserting a character with an accent or diacritical mark:

- At the WordPerfect document screen, press Ctrl+2.

- Type the two characters for the accented character you want to create. The accented character is inserted at the cursor automatically.

In the following exercise you'll use the Compose feature to insert a few characters with diacritics:

1. To insert the *é* character, press Ctrl+2. Then type **e** followed by ' (apostrophe or single quote mark).

2. Let's try the *ñ* character. Press Ctrl+2. Then type **n** followed by a tilde (~).

3. To insert the *ỳ* character, press Ctrl+2. Then type **y`** (that is, **y** followed by the accent mark on the tilde key).

4. Press Ctrl+2 and type **u"** to inset the *ü* character.

This method of creating special letters is easier than using the Alt key, because you don't need to memorize any ASCII numbers. You only need to remember the keys that produce the accent marks you want. Using Table 3.2 as a guide, experiment with this feature to create different letters and accent marks from the keyboard.

Bullets and Other Symbols

A bullet is any character used to offset an item in a list. For example, in the past you may have used asterisks (*) or hyphens (-) to emphasize each item in a list of objectives. WordPerfect lets you insert true bullet characters, including •, ●, °, and ◆.

In addition, there are other common symbols that you can compose and insert into your text. These include the trademark symbol (™), the copyright symbol (©), mathematical symbols (≥, ±, ≈, ½), and currency symbols (¢, £, ƒ, ¥).

Bullets and symbols are created in the same way as characters with diacritical marks. Instead of typing Alt with a keyboard character, you type two characters that WordPerfect interprets as the desired symbol. Table 3.3 shows the bullets and symbols, with the characters you would type after pressing Ctrl+2.

Table 3.3 **Bullets and Other Symbols**

To Create This	Press Ctrl+2 and Type This
Bullets	
.	*.
•	**
∘	*o
o	*O
Typographic Symbols	
™	tm
℠	sm
©	co
®	ro
R	rx
« *or* »	<< *or* >>
ª	a=
º	o=
¶	Pl
¿	??
¡	!!
ß	ss
–	n–
—	m– *or* –
Mathematical Symbols	
±	+–
≤	<=
≥	>=
≅	==
≈	~~

Table 3.3 **Bullets and Other Symbols (Continued)**

To Create This	Press Ctrl+2 and Type This
≠	=/
½	/2
¼	/4
Currency Symbols	
ƒ	f–
£	L–
¥	Y=
₨	Pt
¢	c/

Let's try creating a few of these symbols.:

1. From the editing screen, press Ctrl+2. Then type ** to insert the • bullet.

2. Press Ctrl+2 and type *O to insert the ° bullet.

3. To insert the copyright symbol, press Ctrl+2 and type **co**.

4. Press Ctrl+2 and type **tm** to insert the trademark symbol.

5. To insert the cents symbol, press Ctrl+2 and type **c/**.

6. Press Ctrl+2 and type **/2** to insert the ½ fraction.

7. To insert the not equal to symbol (≠), press Ctrl+2 and type **=/**.

Each symbol you insert is considered one character in your text. When you are working with the text display mode, some of the characters or symbols appear as small boxes (■) on your screen; this is because of the limitations of the text display mode. To view these characters as they will appear when printed, use WordPerfect's graphics display mode or use the Print Preview feature.

Using the WordPerfect Character Sets

In addition to the characters and symbols just described, WordPerfect supports more than 1,500 additional characters and symbols. These include characters for different alphabets, large mathematical symbols, and special icons.

To insert these characters into your document, you'll use the WordPerfect Characters feature. However, instead of typing a two-character combination as described earlier, you'll choose from a palette of different characters. If you're working with WordPerfect's text display mode, you won't see all the characters as they will print on the pages. For this reason, you may want to switch to WordPerfect's graphics mode or page mode before you use the WP Characters feature (press Ctrl+F3 and choose Graphics or Page).

Here is the procedure for inserting a character from one of WordPerfect's extended character sets:

Choose Font ▸ WP Characters

1. Press WP Characters (Ctrl+W) to display the WordPerfect Characters dialog box.

2. Press Tab to deactivate the Number option. Then choose Set to display a list of possible character sets, shown in Figure 3.12.

Choose Set to display the character set list.

3. Highlight the desired character set, and then press Enter. WordPerfect updates the Characters palette to show the characters of the selected set.

4. Choose Characters and use the arrow keys to highlight the character you want to insert. Then press Enter to insert it into your document text.

Figure 3.12

Choosing one of WordPerfect's character sets

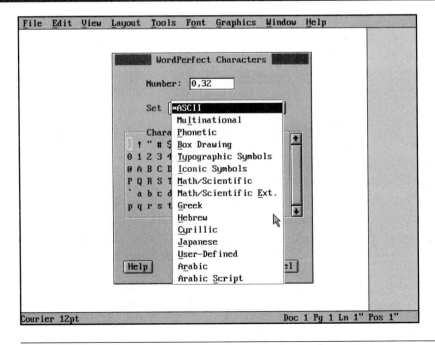

That's all you do. This technique works well when you need to insert a few characters at a time. However, if you need to type complete documents with an alphabet from one of the character sets, you should create a new keyboard layout that includes the characters you need. See Chapter 25 for instructions on assigning WP Characters to a new keyboard layout.

Note that you can use the Characters feature to insert some of the characters you inserted earlier with the Compose (Ctrl+2) feature. For example, the Multinational character set provides numerous accented letters, and the Typographic Symbols character set provides a variety of bullet characters. Use the method that you find the easiest.

Adjusting Automatic Font Changes

When WordPerfect encounters an attribute code such as [Bold On], it uses the code to make an automatic font change that matches the active font in your document. For example, if the active font is Times Roman, WordPerfect interprets a [Bold On] code as a change to the Times Roman Bold font, and a [Bold Off] code as a change back to the regular Times Roman font. WordPerfect does this to ensure that your text is consistent when attribute changes are applied to the text.

If WordPerfect does not switch to the right fonts when you apply attributes, you can adjust the automatic font changes from the Font dialog box. This is how you do it:

Choose Font ▸ Font.

- Press Fonts (Ctrl+F8) to display the Font dialog box.

- Press Setup (Shift+F1) to display the Font Setup dialog box.

Choose Setup.

- If you are having problems with WordPerfect's graphic fonts, choose Edit Automatic Font Changes for Graphic Fonts. Or, choose Edit Automatic Font Changes for Printer Fonts to adjust the automatic font changes for your printer's fonts.

- Scroll through the list of fonts and highlight that name of the font that is active when problems occur with attributes. Then, choose Edit. WordPerfect displays the Edit Font Attribute dialog box, as shown in Figure 3.13.

Choose OK until you return to the Font Setup dialog box.

- This dialog box shows which fonts WordPerfect will switch to when you choose different attributes. Scroll through the list and make sure that each attribute is correctly assigned the appropriate font.

- If you need to adjust one of the automatic font changes, highlight the attribute and choose Edit. Then, highlight the new font that you want to use for the attribute and choose Select. WordPerfect changes the font assignment for that attribute.

Figure 3.13
Edit Font Attribute
dialog box

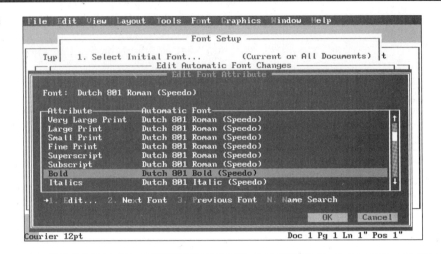

- When you are finished editing the automatic font changes, press Exit (F7) until you return to the Font Setup dialog box.

- If you are using scalable fonts or graphic fonts, and you want to adjust the text sizes that appear, choose Size Ratios. Choose Fine, Small, Large, Very Large, Extra Large, or Super/Subscript, and then enter a percentage to indicate the size for the selected size attribute. For example, you could decide to change Fine print to 50 percent of the current point size (by default it's 60 percent).

Choose OK until you return to the document screen.

- If you are editing the automatic font changes for graphic fonts, choose Update Graphic Fonts from the Font Setup dialog box to save your changes for WordPerfect's internal graphic fonts.

- Press Exit (F7) until you return to the document screen.

Now, when you choose different size and attribute options, WordPerfect uses the fonts and sizes you indicated on the Font Setup and Edit Font Attribute dialog boxes. The changes you made at the Font Setup dialog box are updated to the printer driver file (.PRS) that you are now using with WordPerfect. These changes remain in effect until you change them again.

NOTE. *If you're editing the automatic font changes for scalable fonts, you won't see specific font sizes in the Edit Font Attribute dialog box. Font sizes are handled as part of the Size Ratios feature on the Font Setup dialog box, explained earlier in this chapter.*

4

Using Your Printer with WordPerfect

WHEN COMPUTERS WERE FIRST INTRODUCED, IT WAS PREDICTED that the "paperless office" would soon become a reality. Today, that's hardly the case. In fact, we produce more printed documents than ever before, because computers have made the process easier. Software and printers now allow for multiple fonts, graphics, and color printing.

WordPerfect offers the best printing capabilities of any word processor. You can print the document displayed in WordPerfect or print a saved document without retrieving it. You can print all pages of your document or only a select few. If your printer allows, WordPerfect can also print color text and graphics on both sides of the page. You can preview the printed document before you actually print it and can have up to 255 pages displayed at once on your screen. Then, if necessary, you can adjust the layout and arrangement of pages before you send the document to the printer.

With support for over 900 printers, WordPerfect can send your documents to virtually any laser printer, PostScript printer, dot-matrix or daisy-wheel printer, or even a plotter. It's almost certain that the printer you use will work with WordPerfect.

Suppose you work with two or more different printers; you can select the one you want for each document you create. WordPerfect specifically formats the text for the printer you've selected. In fact, WordPerfect automatically adjusts fonts, layout, and text spacing according to the capabilities of the selected printer—even when that printer is not the one you used to create the document. This allows you to share document files with someone else without having to adjust the layout for a different printer.

WordPerfect 6.0 also introduces an important new feature—the ability to send your documents to any fax machine. If you have a fax board installed in your computer, you can send documents, receive documents from other computers or fax machines, and keep a log of fax transmissions.

This chapter shows you how to use your printer with WordPerfect. You'll learn how to preview and print a document, and how to manage the printing process. Additional information describes how to add new printer definitions, set up fonts, and solve potential printing problems. At the end of this chapter, you'll also learn how to send WordPerfect documents to a fax machine.

Getting Ready to Print

There are a few things you should know and do before you begin printing your WordPerfect documents. The following general information will help you get started with printing.

WordPerfect Document Files and Your Printers

Before you begin printing, you should understand how WordPerfect works with your printer. When you installed WordPerfect for your computer, you were asked to identify the printer you're using. The installation program then configured WordPerfect to work with that printer. Press Print (Shift+F7) or choose File and then Print, and you will see the name of your printer inside the Current Printer box. This is the printer definition that WordPerfect is currently using. Choose Full Document from the Print dialog box, and then choose Print to send a copy of the document from the document screen to your printer in the format your printer expects.

When you save a document, WordPerfect records information about the currently selected printer and saves it with the document file. WordPerfect uses the printer information to make formatting decisions for text spacing, margins, and fonts that are dependent on the capabilities of your printer. For example, each font has its own size and width, and these measurements affect the amount of text your printer can fit on a page. WordPerfect even changes the options for certain menus, such as the list of available fonts, to reflect the capabilities of the printer that is currently selected.

When you retrieve a document, information in the file tells WordPerfect which printer was selected when the document was created. If the document was created with the same printer you're now using with WordPerfect, the document is retrieved without alteration. If, however, the document was created for a different printer, WordPerfect changes the fonts and formatting to match the current printer's capabilities. WordPerfect attempts to use fonts that most closely resemble the fonts originally selected for the other printer, but the appearance of the altered document may differ from its original design.

Figure 4.1 shows an example of this adjustment. The original document (Figure 4.1a) was created for a laser printer. The same document printed on a dot-matrix printer is shown in Figure 4.1b. Notice that the dot-matrix printout retains the intended format, with only a few minor differences. The major difference in the appearance of the two documents occurs because the dot-matrix printer does not have the same fonts as the laser printer. However, WordPerfect has reformatted the second version to get the best possible match for the original document layout.

Selecting a Printer

If you work with only one printer, you do not need to select it each time you print a document; WordPerfect remembers the printer selection you make and continues to work with that printer definition until you select a different one. If you work with more than one printer, however, you need to select the appropriate printer definition from within WordPerfect *before* you send a document to the printer.

Figure 4.1a
WordPerfect adjusts the document layout to accommodate the selected printer's capabilities.

CORPORATE SALES REPORT

Manufacturing   2nd Quarter

First quarter sales increased 45% from last year's figures. This is a direct result of improved communication with our suppliers, the installment of a computer network in our West Valley warehouse, and, of course, the excellent accomplishments of our manufacturing team. A recent issue of Hang Gliders' Quarterly featured an article about the P8500 Glider; here is an excerpt from that article:

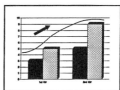

> *"Although there are relatively few competitors in the hang glider industry,* [The Dalworth Company] *produces quality equipment, and continually raises the standard of excellence and safety. Their dedication to the sport is evident in the P8500, which is the first new model to appear since 1989."*

Dalworth continues to enjoy enormous success, despite the recessed market, and we feel confident our success will continue throughout the next quarter as we introduce the new line of sporting equipment. Please note the schedule for the second quarter, as shown in the table below.

I.D.	ITEM	ORDERS	SHIP DATE	NET SALES
3492	P8500 Glider	9000	4/15/92	$960,300.50
1845	DX-9 Sailboard	8000	4/07/92	$840,750.00
2798	Roller Blades	12000	5/15/92	$276,540.50
0026	12' Trampoline	3000	5/30/92	$150,200.00

Figure 4.1b
Continued

CORPORATE SALES REPORT

Manufacturing   2nd Quarter

First quarter sales increased 45% from last year's
figures. This is a direct result of improved
communication with our suppliers, the installment of
a computer network in our West Valley warehouse,
and, of course, the excellent accomplishments of our
manufacturing team. A recent issue of Hang Gliders'
Quarterly featured an article about the P8500
Glider; here is an excerpt from that article:

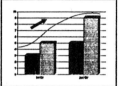

> *"Although there are relatively few competitors in the
> hang glider industry, [The Dalworth Company]
> produces quality equipment, and continually raises
> the standard of excellence and safety. Their
> dedication to the sport is evident in the P8500, which
> is the first new model to appear since 1989."*

Dalworth continues to enjoy enormous success, despite the recessed
market, and we feel confident our success will continue throughout the next
quarter as we introduce the new line of sporting equipment. Please note
the schedule for the second quarter, as shown in the table below.

I.D.	ITEM	ORDERS	SHIP DATE	NET SALES
3492	P8500 Glider	9000	4/15/92	$960,300.50
1845	DX-9 Sailboard	8000	4/07/92	$840,750.00
2798	Roller Blades	12000	5/15/92	$276,540.50
0026	12' Trampoline	3000	5/30/92	$150,200.00

NOTE. *If you did not specify a printer when you installed WordPerfect, refer to "Setting Up a New Printer" later in this chapter before you continue here.*

Follow these steps to select a printer definition from the list of installed printers:

Choose File ▶ Print.

1. To display the Print dialog box, press Print (Shift+F7).

2. Choose Select, and a list of printer definitions like the one in Figure 4.2 is displayed. An asterisk appears next to the printer that is now selected.

Figure 4.2

The Select Printer screen

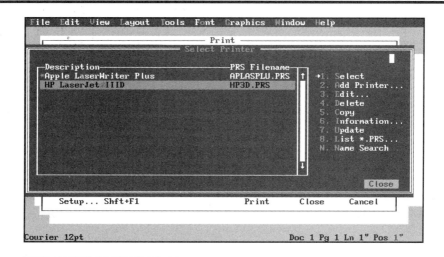

NOTE. *The list of printers on your screen will reflect the printers you specified when you installed the WordPerfect software.*

Use the mouse pointer to click on the name of the printer you want to use.

3. Press ↑ or ↓ to highlight the printer you want to use.

4. From the menu at the right edge of the dialog box, choose Select to choose the highlighted printer definition.

WordPerfect again displays the Print dialog box, with the name of the current printer inside the Current Printer box.

Before you continue, confirm that the printer is turned on and ready to print. Also make sure the printer has enough paper to print your document. Now you can choose to print the current document (choose Print), or you can press Exit (F7) or choose Close to return to the document editing screen.

Previewing a Document

When you're working with WordPerfect's text display mode, you can use the Print Preview feature to see how your document will look on the printed pages. Print Preview lets you view your document with graphics, different fonts and text sizes, page numbers, headers, footnotes, and other elements of your document that don't appear when you're working in text display mode.

This feature is also useful when you're working with graphics display mode and page display mode, because Print Preview is the only way to view two or more document pages at once—up to 255 document pages on the screen at one time.

Using the Print Preview Screen

When you choose the Print Preview feature, you'll see a preview of the current page in your document, like the example shown in Figure 4.3. At the top of the Print Preview screen, you'll see a menu and a row of buttons (called a *button bar*) that provide different viewing options.

Figure 4.3
Previewing a
document

Menu bar

Button bar

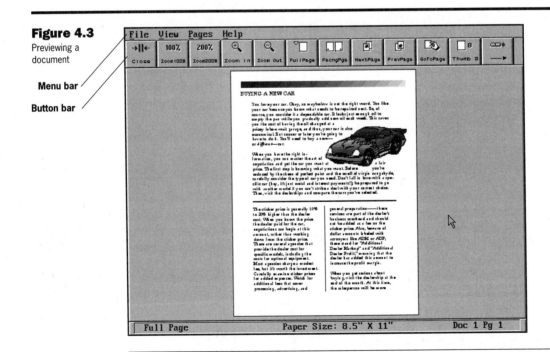

Choose File ▶ Print Preview.

Click on the NextPage or PrevPage buttons on the button bar.

Click on the Facing-Pgs button on the button bar.

The following steps explain how to preview a document and how to use the viewing options on the Print Preview screen. Before you begin the steps, create or retrieve a document in WordPerfect.

1. Press Print (Shift+F7) to open the Print dialog box. Then choose Print Preview.

2. If your document includes two or more pages, press PgDn and PgUp to display each page in your document.

3. To view two pages together, as you would view the pages of a book, choose View from the menu at the top of the screen. Then choose Facing Pages. Figure 4.4 shows how facing pages will look.

Figure 4.4

Previewing facing pages

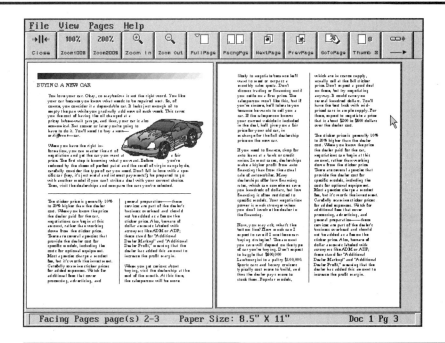

Click on the Zoom 100% button on the button bar.

4. For a closer look, choose View, and then choose 100% View. Your document is now displayed in the approximate size of the printed page.

5. Choose View, and then choose 200% View to see a magnified view of the text.

Click on the horizontal and vertical scroll bars to scroll through the text.

6. Press ↑ or ↓ to scroll through the text in small increments. Press End to move to the right end of the page; press Home, ← to move to the left end of the page.

7. Choose <u>V</u>iew and then <u>F</u>ull Page to return to the standard Print Preview display.

8. When you are finished previewing your document, press Exit (F7) to return to the document screen.

When you return to the document screen, WordPerfect displays the page that you were viewing on the Print Preview screen. This makes it easier to edit a specific page when you find text or layout problems in the preview.

The Print Preview screen will help you verify that your document is formatted correctly—especially when the formatting commands affect several pages of text. Print Preview shows headers, footers, footnotes, endnotes, font changes, and graphics as they will appear when printed. If you find a formatting error on the Print Preview screen, you can return to the document screen and make changes to the document layout. Then print the completed document.

Moving between the Document Pages

In the previous exercise, you pressed PgDn and PgUp to display each of the document pages on the Print Preview screen. You can also "jump" to a specific page by using WordPerfect's Go To feature. First press Go To (Ctrl+Home) or choose <u>P</u>ages, <u>G</u>o To Page from the menu bar in the Print Preview area. Then enter the number of the page you want to display. WordPerfect displays that page on the Print Preview screen. The status line, in the lower-right corner of the Print Preview screen, tells you the document number and the number of the page that is currently displayed.

Previewing Several Pages at Once

The Print Preview screen lets you view two or more pages on the screen. You've already seen how to view a single page (choose <u>V</u>iew, <u>F</u>ull Page) and facing pages (choose <u>V</u>iew, Fa<u>c</u>ing Pages), but the Print Preview screen can display any number of pages, between 1 and 255. Figure 4.5, for example, shows the Print Preview screen with 55 pages displayed.

To view multiple pages, choose <u>V</u>iew from the Print Preview menu bar, and then choose <u>T</u>humbnails. Another menu appears that lets you choose between 1 and 32 pages for viewing. You can also choose <u>V</u>iew, <u>T</u>humbnails, <u>O</u>ther, and then enter a number between 1 and 255. WordPerfect then updates the preview screen to show the number of pages you specified.

Figure 4.5

Previewing 55 pages

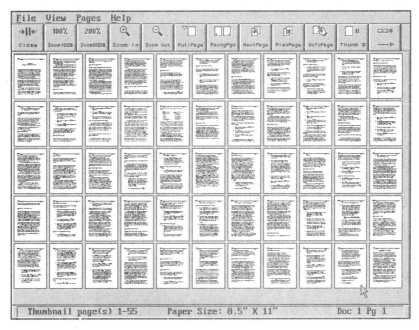

When two or more pages are displayed at once, WordPerfect puts a red border or thicker border around the page to which you will return when you exit the Print Preview screen. Pressing PgDn or PgUp moves the border to the next or previous page in your document and lets you choose the page you want to display when you return to the document screen.

Although your documents may include 200 or more pages, you'll probably want to preview no more than 20 to 30 pages at once. You'll lose text clarity when you increase the number of displayed pages, which makes the text difficult—if not impossible—to read. Remember that the Thumbnails option isn't designed for proofreading; use this feature to check the layout of your entire document.

Close-up Viewing Options

When you are previewing your document, you can choose 100% View or 200% View to get a close-up view of your text. The Print Preview screen provides other *zoom* options that let you choose the section of the page you want to see. These features will help you examine small text and intricate graphics on the Print Preview screen. With the Print Preview screen displayed, you can choose one of these options to switch to a close-up view of your text:

- Choose Ⅴiew and then 200% View to see your document at 200 percent of its actual size.

- To magnify the current view by 100 percent, choose Ⅴiew and then Zoom Ⅰn.

- To reduce the view, choose Ⅴiew and then Zoom Ⅹut. This works until you return to a 100 percent view.

- To magnify the view for a specific area on the page, choose Ⅴiew and then Zoom Ⅹrea. Then, while holding down the mouse button, move the mouse pointer diagonally across the page to define a viewing area. Release the mouse button and WordPerfect magnifies the specified area. Note that the smaller the zoom area you select, the larger it is magnified.

Figure 4.6 shows a zoomed view of a document on the Print Preview screen. When you choose one of the zoom options, WordPerfect places scroll bars at the sides of the screen to let you scroll through the magnified page. (You saw the scroll bars earlier in this chapter when you first learned how to preview a document.) Simply use the mouse pointer to click on the scroll bar arrows and move through the text; you can also use the mouse pointer to drag the slider buttons between the scroll bar arrows and quickly display another section of the document.

When a zoomed view is displayed, you can use the Select Area option to move quickly to another part of the displayed page. First, use the Zoom Ⅹrea or Select Area feature to display a magnified view of your document. Then choose Ⅴiew and then Select Area, and WordPerfect displays a frame with an overview of the current page (see Figure 4.7). Within the frame, you'll see a dotted-lined box that represents the area of the zoomed view.

You view a different part of the page by dragging the dotted-line box with the mouse pointer. Move the mouse pointer over the box, and then, while holding down the mouse button, move the box to the section of the page you want to view. When you release the mouse button, WordPerfect removes the Select Area frame and displays a magnified view of the selected area.

When you are finished with the zoomed views, choose Ⅴiew and then Ⅹull Page to restore the standard Print Preview screen.

Figure 4.6
Zooming in for a closer look

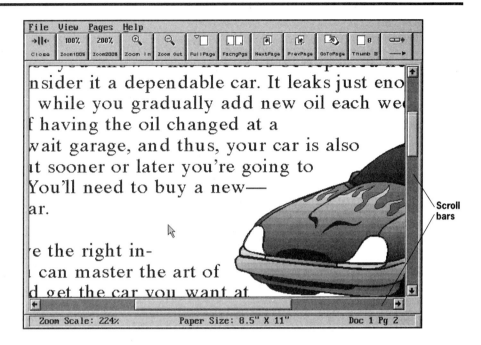

Scroll
bars

Figure 4.7
Using the Select Area feature

Select Area frame

Dotted-line box
represents
zoomed area

Different Ways to Print a Document

This section explores the various ways to print a document from WordPerfect. The print features are selected from the Print dialog box, shown in Figure 4.8. Before you continue, you may want to clear the screen (press F7 or choose File, Close, and then choose No). Next, retrieve a document file that you've already created, or create a new document. For this section, it's best to have a document with three or more pages of text.

Figure 4.8

The Print dialog box

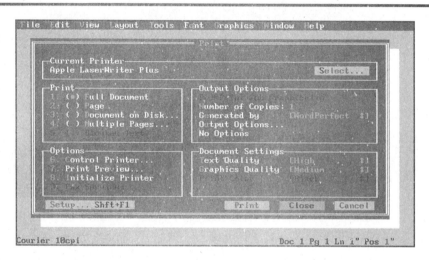

Printing the Entire Document

This exercise shows how to print the entire document displayed on your screen:

Choose File ▸ Print.

1. Press Print (Shift+F7).

2. Make sure the correct printer name is displayed as the current printer on the Print dialog box. If it isn't, choose Select, highlight the correct printer name, and choose Select.

3. Choose Full Document and then Print. Note that the Print option is highlighted by default; after you type *f* to choose Full Document, you can press Enter to select the Print option. WordPerfect sends a copy of your document to the printer.

That's all you need to do. As WordPerfect is printing, you can continue to edit the current document, or clear the screen and retrieve or create a new document. This is possible because WordPerfect handles printing in the *background*, which means that you don't have to wait for the print job to finish before continuing your work.

NOTE. *If your printer isn't working correctly, refer to "Solving Printing Problems" near the end of this chapter.*

WordPerfect offers other ways to print. Let's take a look at how to print a block of text and specific pages from the document.

Printing a Block of Text

To print only a portion of your document, you can choose the Print feature while a block of text is defined. First you use the Block feature (press Alt+F4, or choose <u>E</u>dit and then <u>B</u>lock) to highlight a section of text; display the Print dialog box (press Shift+F7, or choose <u>F</u>ile, and then <u>P</u>rint from the menu bar) and then choose P<u>r</u>int. Only the blocked text will be sent to the printer. See Chapter 7 for detailed information.

Try this exercise to print a block of text from the document on your screen:

Hold down the mouse button, and drag the pointer to the end of the text you want to block.

Choose <u>F</u>ile ▶ <u>P</u>rint.

1. Move the cursor or mouse pointer to the beginning of a sentence in the document on the screen.

2. Press Block (Alt+F4 or F12) and move the cursor to the end of the text you want to include in the block. As you move the cursor, the text for the block is highlighted.

3. Now that you've blocked the text, press Print (Shift+F7) to display the Print dialog box.

4. Notice that the <u>B</u>locked Text option is now selected. Choose P<u>r</u>int to send the block to the printer.

After you select the Print feature, the Block feature is automatically turned off.

Text printed from a block begins on the printed page at the same vertical position where it falls on the displayed document page. For example, if the blocked text is located four inches from the top of the document page, the printed block is also located four inches from the top edge of the paper, and the rest of the page is left blank.

Printing a Single Page

Rather than print the entire document, you'll sometimes want to print only a single page. For example, suppose you've just printed a lengthy report, and as you are proofreading the pages, you discover an error in the text. Instead of printing the entire document again, you can fix the mistake and print only the corrected page.

Follow these steps to print a single page from the document on your screen:

■ Press PgUp or PgDn to display the page you want to print. If a page break (soft or hard) appears on the screen, make sure the cursor is positioned within the page to be printed.

Choose File ▸ Print ▸ Page ▸ Print.

■ Press Print (Shift+F7), choose Page and then Print.

WordPerfect sends a copy of the page to the printer.

Printing a Group of Pages

WordPerfect also includes a feature that lets you print a group of pages at once. The Multiple Pages option lets you select and print a consecutive series of pages or a group of random pages from your document. It works like this:

Choose File ▸ Print ▸ Multiple Pages.

■ Press Print (Shift+F7) and then choose Multiple Pages. The Print Multiple Pages dialog box appears as shown in Figure 4.9.

Figure 4.9

Printing multiple pages

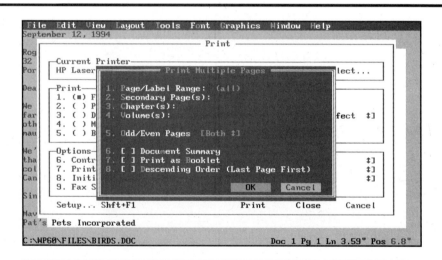

■ Choose Page/Label Range. Then, using the formats shown in Table 4.1, enter the page or page numbers for printing. Choose OK to close the Print Multiple Pages dialog box and then choose Print. The pages you specified are then sent to the printer.

Table 4.1	Typing Page Numbers for the Multiple Pages Option
Type This Format	**To Print These Pages**
x	Page x
x,y,z	Pages x, y, and z
$x\ z$	Pages x and z
x-	Beginning with page x, all the pages until the end of the document
-y	From the beginning of the document up to page y
x-z	Pages x through z
E	Even-numbered pages only
O	Odd-numbered pages only
S	The Document Summary only
S-	The Document Summary, followed by the entire document

When you enter a series of page numbers, they must be typed in numeric order. For example, if you want to print pages 5 and 7, you enter **5,7**. If you enter **7,5** instead, page 7 is printed, but page 5 is ignored because it doesn't occur after page 7 in the document.

Suppose you're working on a long document that is divided into different sections or chapters. If you've used WordPerfect's New Page Number feature to restart page numbering at the beginning of each chapter, you can tell WordPerfect to print pages from specific sections. To do this, select Multiple Pages and choose the Secondary Page(s), Chapter(s), or Volume(s) to indicate the section type. Then enter the page numbers, chapter numbers, or volume numbers you want to print.

NOTE. *See Chapter 15 for detailed information about the page numbering features.*

Options for Printing

Included on WordPerfect's Print dialog box are several other features that help you use your printer more effectively. You can add extra space for binding, print numerous copies, adjust the print quality, print on both sides of the paper, and print sideways on the page. When you choose these print options, the settings are saved with your document file. As you work with your document, the print options you select and change will be saved and used when that document file is again retrieved.

Adding Space for Binding

Large documents, like corporate reports and thesis papers, often need to be bound before they can be presented. For bound documents that are printed on both sides of the page, you can use WordPerfect's Binding Offset feature to shift the text and allow extra space for the binding. Figure 4.10 shows how this works. The binding space occurs alternately on the left edge of odd-numbered pages and on the right edge of even-numbered pages.

Figure 4.10
Using the Binding Offset feature

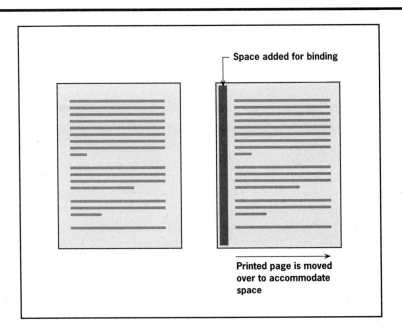

Here is the procedure for adding extra space for binding:

Choose Layout ▸ Other ▸ Printer Functions.

- With the document displayed on the editing screen, press Format (Shift+F8), choose Other and then Printer Functions.

- Choose Binding Offset. Then choose From Edge and select the edge of the page that will be bound.

- Choose Binding Offset again. Then choose Binding Offset (Add to Margin) and enter a measurement for the binding space.

Choose OK until
you return to the
document screen.

■ Press Exit (F7) until you return to the document screen.

■ Display the Print dialog box, and print your document.

When you choose this feature, WordPerfect inserts a [Binding Width] code at the top of your document. The extra binding space doesn't show on the document screen, but you can see it when you preview your document with the Print Preview feature.

Because the binding space is an option on the Format dialog box, the setting is saved as a code in your document file. After you exit the editing screen, the binding offset is restored to its default (usually 0").

If you are printing a single-sided document and you want a wider left margin to allow for binding space, just alter the left and right margins as described in Chapter 2.

Printing Several Copies

Suppose you need to distribute a corporate memo or a flyer to several people in your organization. You intend to print one copy of your document and then produce the copies you need on a copy machine. However, as fate would have it, the copy machine needs servicing (again), and you need to distribute the memo now. WordPerfect comes to the rescue!

It's easy to print duplicate copies by specifying the number of copies you want each time you send a document to your printer. This time-saving feature appears in the Print dialog box. Before you select the option, retrieve the document to be printed. Then follow these steps:

Choose File ▸ Print.

■ Press Print (Shift+F7).

■ Select the Number of Copies option from the Print dialog box.

■ Type the number of copies that you want to print, and press Enter.

■ Choose Full Document (or Page) and then choose Print. WordPerfect will print the number of duplicate copies you chose.

■ When you are finished printing, display the Print dialog box again, and change the Number of Copies back to 1 to restore single-copy printing.

Make sure you perform the last step—it ensures that your next print job doesn't produce multiple copies that you don't want.

Duplicate copies can be generated by WordPerfect, by your printer, or by your network software if you're running WordPerfect from a network server. It's a little faster to have your printer generate the copies if your printer has that capability. From the Print dialog box, choose Generated by, and then select either WordPerfect or Printer. (Note that some printers cannot generate the number of copies. In this case, the Printer option will be grayed.) If you are running WordPerfect from a network, you may also see a third option, Network, which instructs the network software to generate the copies for you. After you've selected the method for the copies to be generated, indicate the number of copies and print your document.

Changing the Print Quality

WordPerfect's Print dialog box includes options for controlling the quality of both printed graphics and text. You can choose three degrees of quality—draft, medium, and high—and each can affect the speed of printing, as well as the appearance of your document. Figure 4.11 shows samples of the three types of print quality.

Documents that include graphics take longer to print than documents with only text. The Graphics Quality option in the Print dialog box lets you speed up the printing process for graphics or choose a slower but better-quality image. The option for Text Quality lets you select the quality of printed text; this option affects the quality of all text—including text printed with one of WordPerfect's graphic fonts. Here are the general instructions to change the print quality for graphics and text:

NOTE.   *In Chapter 19, you'll learn how to put graphics in your documents.*

Choose File ▸ Print.

- Press Print (Shift+F7) to display the Print dialog box.

- Select Text Quality from the Document Settings group. A pop-up list appears with four options:

  ```
  Do Not Print
  Draft
  Medium
  High
  ```

- Choose the desired print quality from the list.

- Select Graphics Quality from the Print dialog box, and choose the desired print quality for text.

- Select Full Document or Page, and then choose Print to print your document.

Draft quality prints the least refined graphics and text; choose this when you're in a hurry and when professional-looking pages aren't important. Medium quality (which is the standard setting for graphics) produces a good image within a reasonable amount of time. High quality, of course, produces the sharpest possible graphics and text, and takes the most time to print. Select high quality when you want to print the final version of your document.

Figure 4.11

Samples of draft-, medium-, and high-quality printing

 This text and graphic image were printed with the Draft print quality. Choose Draft Quality to create a rough printout of your document for editing.

 This text and graphic image were printed with the Medium print quality. Choose Medium Quality to create a quick printout of your document.

This text and graphic image were printed with the High print quality. Choose High Quality to create the final version of the printed document.

As the name implies, the Do Not Print option leaves blank spaces where graphics will normally appear; this option is useful when you want to proof-read only the text in a large document or when graphics may slow printing to an unacceptable level. If chosen for text, Do Not Print turns off the printing of text and produces only the graphics images in a document.

Generally, the Text Quality feature is useful only with dot-matrix or similar printers, because these printers can produce different print qualities. Most laser printers print only high-quality text.

When you save a document with the print quality settings, they are re-corded with your document file and will automatically take effect whenever the document is retrieved. For this reason, make sure you check the quality settings on the Print dialog box *before* you print your document.

Printing Graphical Pages

The Print Job Graphically option lets you send your text as graphic images to your printer. This gives you greater control over the print quality and allows some printers to print effects that their text fonts do not support. When this option is turned on, WordPerfect converts or *rasterizes* each page as a graphic image and sends it to the printer.

To use this option, display the Print dialog box and choose Print Job Graphically before you send your document to the printer. The Graphics Quality option, also on the Print dialog box, determines the quality of the printed page. If the Graphics Quality is set to High, your page will look the same as printing without the Print Job Graphically option turned on.

Network Options

If you are running WordPerfect on Novell NetWare or other network soft-ware, you may see two additional options on the Print dialog box: Banners and Form Number.

NOTE. *Your network must be set up to take advantage of the options de-scribed in this section before they will work correctly. For more information, talk to your network administrator.*

A banner is an extra printed page that displays your network ID and other information about your network. This helps to identify your printed documents when the network printer is receiving files from several different users. To tell the network to print a *banner* at the beginning of each print job, check the box for Banners. To turn off banner printing, choose Banners again from the Print dialog box, so that no *X* appears in the box next to the option.

The Form Number option is similar to selecting a specific paper size/type from WordPerfect's Page Format dialog box (described later in this chapter), except that the network handles the paper selection with its own defined forms. This option is not often used, because WordPerfect does a good job of controlling the paper selection; however, if your office usually selects form numbers from the network for other software programs, you might want to do so within WordPerfect also.

Ask your network administrator about which numbers to enter for the defined forms. Zero (0) is the default form number. To select a different form, choose the F__o__rm Number option and enter the number of the form you want to use. Then, when you print your document, WordPerfect surrenders its own paper size/type selection and uses a form on the network.

Printing Sideways on the Page

Sometimes your document may not fit on an 8 $\frac{1}{2}$-inch-wide sheet of paper. For example, tables, charts, and spreadsheet information often need to be printed sideways on the page to accommodate a large number of items or columns of information.

You can tell WordPerfect that you want to print sideways by selecting a new paper definition or paper size/type. A *paper definition* determines the size and dimensions of the paper on which you are printing, and also indicates the *orientation* of the text on the page. There are two ways to place text on a page, as shown in Figure 4.12. The standard orientation is called *portrait*, in which the text is printed as it would appear in a normal business letter. *Landscape* orientation means the text is printed sideways on the page, but this arrangement can be used only if your printer has fonts that can be printed sideways.

Figure 4.12
Portrait versus
landscape orientation

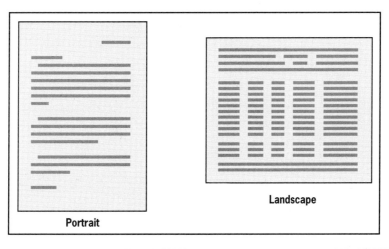

Portrait

Landscape

WordPerfect uses landscape fonts to print sideways, and you'll need to select a new paper type that specifies this orientation. Follow these steps to select a paper type that lets you print sideways on the page:

1. With your document on the screen, use the cursor keys to move the cursor to the top of the page that you want to print sideways.

2. Press Format (Shift+F8) and choose <u>P</u>age.

Choose Layout ▶
<u>P</u>age.

3. Choose Paper <u>S</u>ize/Type to display a dialog box similar to Figure 4.13. This is a list of the paper types and sizes you can select for the current printer. (Your list may differ from the one shown here.)

Figure 4.13
The Paper
Size/Type list

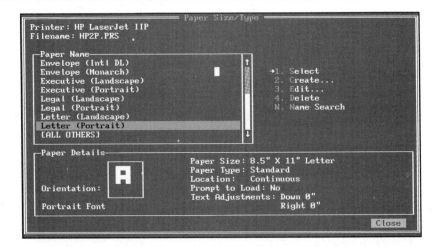

4. Press ↓ to highlight the Letter (Landscape) paper definition, and choose <u>S</u>elect.

Click on Letter
(<u>L</u>andscape).

5. Press Exit (F7) until you return to the document screen.

Choose OK to return
to your document.

WordPerfect inserts a [Paper Sz/Typ] code at the top of the current page, and each page that falls after this code will be printed sideways on the paper. Remember, WordPerfect can print sideways only if your printer has the required landscape fonts or fonts that can be rotated sideways.

TIP.   *To print an entire document sideways, open the Document Initial Codes screen before you choose the new paper size.*

If your printer does not support landscape fonts or cannot rotate fonts, you can still print sideways by feeding the long edge of the paper into your printer. Just feed the 11-inch (long) edge of the paper into the printer, instead of the 8 ½-inch (short) edge. If you're using a tractor paper feeder, you may need to remove your regular paper and insert standard 8 ½-by-11-inch paper to print the document. Then select the Letter (Landscape) paper type from the Paper Size/Type dialog box, and print your document.

To designate only one or two pages for sideways printing, place the cursor at the beginning of the first page to be printed sideways, and choose the landscape paper definition as described earlier. Then move the cursor to the beginning of the next page that should print normally (in portrait), and reset the paper type back to Letter (Portrait). To do this:

Choose Layout ▸ Page.

- Press Format (Shift+F8) and then choose Page.

- Choose Paper Size/Type, and select the Letter (Portrait) paper definition.

Choose OK ▸ Close.

- Press Exit (F7) until you return to the document screen.

- Preview your document to make sure all the pages are correct.

- Print your document.

This inserts a new [Paper Sz/Typ] code into the document; all pages that lie after this code will be printed with portrait orientation on 8 ½-by-11-inch paper.

Double-sided Printing

Some laser printers can print in *duplex mode*, where text is printed on both sides of each page. This saves paper and reduces the cost of reproducing your document. If you have a printer that can perform duplex printing, you can choose a special option from the Page Format dialog box that tells WordPerfect to print on both sides of the paper. To use this option, press Format (Shift+F8) and choose Page, or choose Layout, Page from the menu bar. Then choose Double-sided Printing, and select Long Edge for portrait printing or Short Edge for landscape printing. Then print your document.

If your printer can't print on both sides of the paper at once, you can use the Multiple Pages print option to produce double-sided documents, regardless of your printer type. In the following exercise, you will print a document using both sides of the paper. You will first print the odd pages of the document. Then you will feed the paper back into the printer and print the even pages on the blank sides of the paper. Before you print, consider adding page numbers to your document; this will help you verify that the pages are printed in the correct order.

TIP. *If you plan to fasten a printed document with staples or place it in a three-ring binder, remember to use the Binding Offset feature (described earlier) to allow extra space at the edge of each printed page.*

Choose File ▸ Print ▸ Multiple Pages.

1. With your document displayed on the screen, press Print (Shift+F7) and then <u>M</u>ultiple Pages.

2. Choose <u>O</u>dd/Even Pages and then <u>O</u>dd. This tells WordPerfect to print only the odd pages in the document.

3. Press **D** to select the <u>D</u>escending Order option (an *X* should appear in the check box). The <u>D</u>escending Order option stacks the printed pages so that they'll be in the correct order when you feed them back into the printer to print the even pages.

4. Press Exit (F7) to return to the Print dialog box.

5. From the Print dialog box, choose <u>P</u>rint and WordPerfect prints only the odd pages from your document.

6. Feed the pages back into your printer, placed so that the printer will print on the blank side of the paper. When you place the pages into the printer, don't change the order of the pages. Also, if the last page in your document falls on an odd page number, don't insert this page back into the printer.

Choose File ▸ Print ▸ Multiple Pages.

7. Press Print (Shift+F7), and then choose <u>M</u>ultiple Pages.

8. Choose <u>O</u>dd/Even Pages and select <u>E</u>ven. This tells WordPerfect to print only the even-numbered pages from the document.

9. Choose <u>D</u>escending Order so that an *X* is in the check box next to this option.

Choose OK to return to the Print dialog box.

10. Press Exit (F7) to return to the Print dialog box.

11. Choose <u>P</u>rint to print the even pages on the blank sides of the paper.

If you've fed the paper correctly into your printer, the even pages are now printed on the backs of the odd pages—page two is printed on the back of page one, page four is on the back of page three, and so on.

Printing on Different Paper Sizes

WordPerfect supports dozens of paper types and sizes for document printing. These include the standard 8 ½-by-11-inch paper, various styles of letterhead and stationery, envelopes, labels, and many others. Earlier, you learned how to print sideways on the paper by selecting specific paper definitions. Like the other formatting features, such as margins and line spacing, you can also insert a formatting code that instructs WordPerfect to print the document on a specific type or size of paper. You can select any of the predefined paper sizes or create your own, if necessary.

In the following sections, you'll get more practice choosing a different paper size, and you'll create and edit a new paper definition. You'll also learn how to create a paper definition specifically for business letterhead, which includes predefined margins for the page. Before you continue with the exercises, you'll need to have a document on the editing screen; retrieve one that you've already created, or type a few paragraphs of text.

Choosing a Different Paper Size

Here is the general procedure for choosing a different paper size for the text in your document:

Choose Layout ▶ Page.

- With your document displayed on the screen, move the cursor to the page that will be printed on a different size paper.

- Press Format (Shift+F8) and select Page.

- From the Page Format dialog box, choose Paper Size/Type. You'll see a list of the paper sizes that are defined for the selected printer, much like the dialog box shown earlier in Figure 4.13. Remember, your list may be different.

- Highlight the name of the paper definition you want to use, and choose Select.

Choose OK to return to the document screen.

- Press Exit (F7) twice to return to the document screen.

You have just inserted a [Paper Sz/Typ] code into the document at the cursor position. As you scroll through the document, you may notice that WordPerfect reformats your text to fit the new paper size.

On the Paper Size/Type dialog box, you'll see a list of the common paper sizes that the selected printer can handle. All printers allow the standard paper types: 8.5" x 11" paper, legal-sized paper (8.5" x 14"), and at least one envelope size. For some printers, special paper definitions exist to take advantage of unique printer features. For example, if your printer can handle various paper sizes, you'll see paper definitions for envelopes, legal paper, and labels.

Adjusting Margins for Paper Size

When you choose a new paper size, you don't need to worry about changing the margins; WordPerfect automatically measures these from each edge of the paper, regardless of the paper size. The only case where you need to change your margins to accommodate paper size is when the total space allowed for the margins exceeds the width or height of the defined paper size.

If the combined margin space is equal to or greater than the dimensions of the paper, there won't be room to type any text.

For example, assume your margins are currently set at 3 inches on each side of the page. These margins are acceptable for an 8 ½-by-11-inch sheet of paper and leave an area of 2 ½ by 5 inches on the page for the printed text—not much room, but still valid. Now, suppose you keep your margins at 3 inches all around, but want to select a paper size of 5 ½ by 8 ½ inches. Word-Perfect won't let you do it, because the total space for the right and left margins (3 + 3 = 6) is greater than the width of the paper you want to use, thus leaving no space on the page for typing text. In this case, you'll need to first reduce your margins for the smaller paper size and then select the new paper definition.

Creating a New Paper Definition

The paper definitions on the Paper Size/Type dialog box will be adequate for most of the documents you will produce. It's possible, however, that you'll need to print on a paper size that isn't listed on the Paper Size/Type dialog box. In this case, you can choose the Create option from this dialog box to define a new paper size for the list.

When you create a new paper definition, you will select a paper type, size, and other attributes for the form. Here is the procedure for creating a new paper definition:

Choose Layout ▶ Page.

- At the document screen, press Format (Shift+F8) and choose Page.

- Choose Paper Size/Type and then Create to create a new paper size/type definition. This displays the dialog box, shown in Figure 4.14.

Figure 4.14
Selecting a paper type

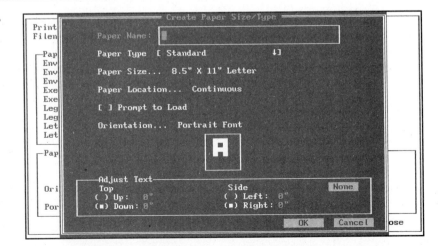

- At the Paper Name option, type a name for the new paper definition. Then press Enter.

- Choose Paper Type and choose one of the predefined paper types as a model for the new paper definition.

- Choose Paper Size, and the Define Paper Size dialog box (shown in Figure 4.15) appears with the standard paper sizes. Highlight one of the sizes from the list, and then choose Select. If you don't see the size you want, choose Other and enter the width and height for the new paper definition.

Figure 4.15

The Define Paper Size dialog box

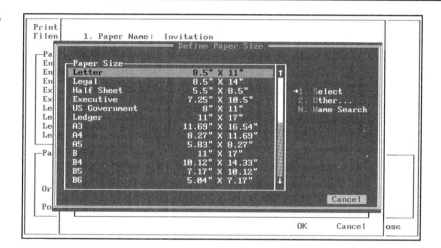

- Choose Paper Location, and you'll see a list with at least two options, Continuous and Manual Feed, plus any additional options that may apply to your printer. Highlight Continuous if the paper you're defining is tractor-fed paper or is always available from a standard printer's paper tray. Highlight Manual for paper types that must be manually inserted into the printer as the document is printed. If the paper is located in a sheet-feeder tray, highlight the tray option. Then choose Select to accept the paper location and return to the Create Paper Size/Type dialog box.

The other options in the dialog box allow for a more refined paper definition:

- Use the Prompt to Load option to designate whether WordPerfect will notify you when a specific paper type should be inserted into the printer. Check the box for this option when the paper location is defined as Manual, and WordPerfect will sound a beep to remind you to insert the correct paper for the current print job.

- Choose <u>O</u>rientation to specify the font orientation for the page (portrait or landscape). If you selected a paper size where the width is greater than the height, WordPerfect assumes that you need a landscape font. Otherwise, portrait orientation is the default.

- The last option, <u>A</u>djust Text, is helpful when the text is printing too low or too high on the page; it can also fix incorrect left/right margin placement. Usually, Adjust Text values are set to 0", and you won't enter these measurements when you first create the paper definition. Don't bother changing the Adjust Text measurements until you've printed a page or two with the new paper definition. Then, if problems occur, you can edit the paper definition and adjust the text. You'll have the chance to do this in the next section, "Editing a Paper Definition."

When you are finished creating a paper definition, press Exit (F7) and the Paper Size/Type dialog box appears with the new paper definition highlighted. If you wish to use it immediately, you can choose <u>S</u>elect to insert the paper definition into your document at the cursor position. Then press Exit (F7) again until you return to the editing screen.

The Paper Size/Type information, which includes the new paper definitions you create, is stored in the printer driver file for the printer you're currently using. When you want to use a paper definition you've created, you must make sure the associated printer is selected; if it's not, you won't see your new paper definition on the Paper Size/Type list.

Editing a Paper Definition

You may need to change the paper definitions that you've defined or the predefined paper types included on the list. This is often necessary when you add a sheet feeder to your printer or change the location of a particular paper type. You've already seen how to create a new paper definition on the Paper Size/Type dialog box. Now, you'll edit one:

Choose <u>L</u>ayout ▶ <u>P</u>age ▶ Paper <u>S</u>ize/ Type.

1. From the WordPerfect document screen, press Format (Shift+F8) and choose <u>P</u>age. Then choose Paper <u>S</u>ize/Type.

2. On the list, highlight the name of the paper definition you want to edit; then choose <u>E</u>dit. This displays the Edit Paper Size/Type dialog box in which the options for this paper type are defined.

3. To change the displayed name for the paper definition, choose Paper <u>N</u>ame and type a new name. Then press Enter.

4. Choose Paper <u>S</u>ize and select a new size. Or choose Paper <u>T</u>ype to select a different paper type.

5. Now let's assume the printer isn't placing the printed pages correctly on the paper. For example, suppose there's only a 1-inch top margin defined, but the printed text begins 1 ½ inches from the top of the paper. The printer is starting the top of the page ½ inch lower than it should. Choose <u>A</u>djust Text.

6. Because the text is printing too low on the page, choose <u>T</u>op and then select <u>U</u>p to shift the text upward. Enter **.5** and press enter to move the text up ½ inch.

Practice selecting and changing the settings for each option on the Edit Paper Size/Type dialog box. When you are finished, press Exit (F7) until you return to the document editing screen.

CAUTION! *When you edit a paper definition, WordPerfect does not automatically adjust the paper definition codes you previously inserted into a document. If you want the edited paper definition to affect the current document on your screen or other documents you've already created, you'll need to delete the existing [Paper Sz/Typ] code and then select the edited paper definition to insert a code reflecting the update.*

Printing on Letterhead

Letterhead is any stationery that has information already printed on the paper—usually at the top edge of the sheet. This information may include a logo, slogan, or other information, as well as the company name and address. When you print on letterhead, you'll need to allow more space at the top margin, so that your text doesn't print over the letterhead information.

Instead of changing the margins for each document, you can define a special letterhead paper definition that includes the extra space at the top edge. Then, when you want to print on letterhead, you can select the applicable paper definition, and the margins will automatically adjust for the letterhead form.

The following exercise explains how to create a new paper definition that lets you print documents on preprinted letterhead. As you go through the steps, you'll select a few options that are normally reserved for printing on sheets of mailing labels, but for this application they will help you create a definition for letterhead. (Complete information about mailing labels appears in Chapter 16.) Clear the editing screen (choose <u>F</u>ile, choose <u>C</u>lose, and then choose <u>N</u>o) before you begin this exercise.

Choose <u>L</u>ayout ▸ <u>P</u>age.

1. At the editing screen, press Format (Shift+F8) and choose <u>P</u>age.

2. Choose <u>L</u>abels to display the Labels dialog box. (If WordPerfect does not know which label file to use, it presents the Label File dialog box. Select the appropriate label file and continue.) Then choose <u>C</u>reate to create a new labels definition. WordPerfect displays the screen shown in Figure 4.16.

Figure 4.16

Figure 4.16
Using the Labels
option to create a
letterhead form

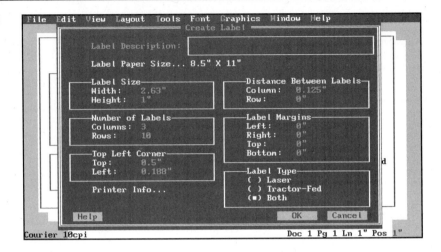

3. At the Label <u>D</u>escription option, type **Letterhead** and press Enter.

4. If your letterhead paper is a size other than 8 ½ by 11 inches, choose Label Paper Size, and select the correct paper size from the list of possible sizes. If the correct size is not listed, choose <u>O</u>ther and enter the measurements for the width and height of your paper.

5. Choose Label <u>S</u>ize, and for the <u>W</u>idth and <u>H</u>eight settings, enter the same width and height measurements that are listed next to the Label <u>P</u>aper Size option. If, for example, your letterhead is the standard size, enter **8.5"** for the width and **11"** as the height.

6. Select <u>N</u>umber of Labels. Type **1** as the number of <u>C</u>olumns and press Enter. Then type **1** as the number of <u>R</u>ows and press Enter. This tells WordPerfect that this paper (label) definition includes only one "label" on the page.

7. Select Top Left <u>C</u>orner, and enter **0"** twice to cancel the offset, which is normally added for labels.

8. Now you'll define the margins for the letterhead page. Choose Label <u>M</u>argins. For both the Left and Right margins, type **1** and press Enter.

9. For the Top margin, measure from the top edge of your letterhead to the place where you want text to begin on the page, and enter this measurement. Usually, when the letterhead information is at the top of the page, you'll need a top margin of about 2 ½ inches. Finally, enter **1** for the Bottom margin.

Choose OK to return to the Labels dialog box.

10. Press Exit (F7) to accept the paper definition and return to the Labels dialog box. The new letterhead definition will be highlighted on the list.

11. Choose <u>S</u>elect to select the new letterhead paper (label) definition, and press Exit (F7) until you return to the document editing screen.

Notice that the *Ln* indicator on the status line shows the measurement that you entered for the top margin. Because you've selected the letterhead definition, this margin setting is in effect, even though you haven't actually changed the margins for the document text.

Now, all you need to do is create the text that should be printed on the letterhead. Go ahead and create or retrieve a business letter for your letterhead. Then press Print (Shift+F7) and select the Print Pre<u>v</u>iew option to see how the text will be printed on the page. Notice that the blank space added at the top margin allows enough room for the preprinted letterhead information. Then press Exit (F7) to return to the document screen, insert the letterhead paper into your printer, and print the document (press Shift+F7 and choose <u>F</u>ull Document).

This technique can be used to create any paper definition with predefined margins. If you do not want margins assigned to the paper definition, just create a new paper definition without using the Labels option from the Page Format dialog box.

TIP. *When your document contains more than one page, only the first of which is to be printed on letterhead, you'll want to eliminate the extra top margin space for page 2 and beyond. You can accomplish this by moving the cursor to the top of page 2 and selecting the Standard paper size/type, using the technique you've learned in this chapter.*

Printing from Files on Disk

In addition to printing a document displayed on your screen, you can print a file directly from disk without retrieving it. This feature is useful when you want to send something to the printer without interrupting the current editing session.

Printing a Disk File

This next exercise shows you how to print a document from a file on disk:

Choose <u>F</u>ile ▸ <u>P</u>rint.

1. From the document screen, press Print (Shift+F7).

2. Choose <u>D</u>ocument on Disk, and WordPerfect prompts you for the document name.

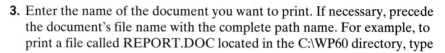

3. Enter the name of the document you want to print. If necessary, precede the document's file name with the complete path name. For example, to print a file called REPORT.DOC located in the C:\WP60 directory, type

```
c:\wp60\report.doc
```

Or, instead of typing a file name, you can press List Files (F5) to select from a list of file names.

4. Click on OK or press Enter. WordPerfect displays the Print Multiple Pages dialog box. Choose P̲age/Label Range and enter the specific pages you want to print (see Table 4.1, earlier in this chapter, for the format). Or press Exit (F7) to indicate that you want to print the entire document.

5. Choose P̲rint from the Print dialog box.

WordPerfect prints the document and redisplays the document screen.

Printing from the File Manager

It is also possible to print your documents from WordPerfect's File Manager:

- First, select File Manager (press F5 or choose F̲ile and then F̲ile Manager), and press Enter to display a directory of the files in the default directory.

- Highlight the name of the file you want to print, and choose P̲rint from the File Manager menu.

- WordPerfect displays the Print Multiple Pages dialog box. You can choose P̲age/Label Range and enter the numbers of the specific pages you want to print, or press Exit (F7) to indicate that you want to print all the pages.

NOTE.   *You'll learn all about the File Manager feature in Chapter 5.*

As with other print options, this technique works only when the file you've highlighted was created for the current printer. If you print a file created for a different printer from the File Manager, the text may not print correctly. Again, the solution is to retrieve the document into the editing screen, which allows WordPerfect to adjust the format for the selected printer. Then you can print from the document screen.

Printing without WordPerfect

If you ever need to print a WordPerfect document on a printer that is attached to a different computer, and that computer does not have a copy of WordPerfect, you can still print your document. This section explains how.

In this case, when you create your WordPerfect document, instruct WordPerfect to format the document for the printer to be used—even if that printer is not attached to your computer—and then save the information to a special file on a floppy disk. Take the floppy to the other computer, and send the document file to the printer from the DOS prompt. The result is a printed document that looks like it was printed from within WordPerfect.

The following exercise lets you try this printing technique. As part of the exercise, you'll copy a printer definition, and then edit it to specify "printing to disk." Before you continue, clear the document screen, and retrieve a document that you've already created.

Choose File ▸ Print ▸ Select.

1. From the editing screen, press Print (Shift+F7). Choose Select and highlight the name of the printer for which the document should be formatted. (You will use this printer as a model for a new printer definition you'll now create.) Then select Edit, Port, Filename.

2. Choose Copy, and WordPerfect prompts you with "New Printer Filename."

3. Type a name for the new printer file. For this exercise, type **diskprnt.prs** and press Enter. After you enter the name, WordPerfect displays the Information dialog box for this printer. Press Exit (F7) to go to the Edit Printer Setup dialog box.

4. Choose Description and enter **Print to Disk** as the name to be displayed on the Select Printer dialog box. Then press Enter.

5. Because you want WordPerfect to print to a file on a floppy disk, place a disk in drive A or B. Choose Port and then choose Filename from the Port dialog box.

6. At the Filename option, type **a:** or **b:** (depending on which drive you're using), followed by the file name you want to use. For this exercise, let's print to a file called PRINTDSK.DOC on the disk in drive A. Type **a:\printdsk.doc** and press Enter.

7. Press Exit (F7) until you to return to the Select Printer dialog box. Then select the new printer definition you just created.

Choose OK until you return to the Select Printer dialog box.

Whenever this printer definition is selected, the print job will be "sent" to the file name that you entered at the Port option, instead of through the computer port where your printer is connected.

CAUTION!   *Because WordPerfect can print to only one file, each print job you "send" will replace the previous PRINTDSK.DOC file. Note also that the print file WordPerfect generates cannot be retrieved into WordPerfect.*

8. From the Print dialog box, choose Full Document and then Print. Word-Perfect generates the document for the selected printer and saves the information in the PRINTDSK.DOC file.

Choose File ▸ Exit ▸
No ▸ Yes.

9. Press Exit (F7). Choose No once and then Yes to exit WordPerfect. Make sure the DOS prompt is displayed before you continue.

10. At the DOS prompt, type this DOS command for sending the file to the printer:

```
copy a:\printdsk.doc /b prn
```

In this DOS command, the */b* specifies that you're sending a *binary file*, which is the format WordPerfect uses to translate your documents for the printer. The *prn* indicates that the file should be sent to the printer connected to the computer. (If you know which port the printer is using, you can type **lpt1:** or **com1:**, instead of **prn**.) After you enter the DOS command, the document is sent to the printer, and it should look exactly as though it were printed from within WordPerfect.

Before you proceed to the next section, display the Print dialog box again and select the printer definition that you normally use. If you continue to print files with the Print to Disk printer definition selected, all your print jobs will be sent to the PRINTDSK.DOC file in your floppy-disk drive, and not to your printer.

Managing Print Jobs with the Control Printer Dialog Box

Each document you send to your printer is considered a *print job*. You can send several print jobs to the printer at once, and you don't need to wait for each one to finish before you send another one. WordPerfect assigns a unique number to each document you send and displays a list of your print jobs—called a *print queue*—at the Control Printer dialog box. This dialog box also includes prompts, messages, and information on the status of each job.

Viewing the Print Queue

This next exercise acquaints you with the Control Printer dialog box (before you begin, you'll need to temporarily stop the printing process):

1. Press the on-line or select button on your printer to turn *off* the printer light and temporarily prevent the printer from accepting any input.

2. Retrieve a document to your screen.

Choose <u>F</u>ile ▸ <u>P</u>rint
▸ <u>P</u>rint.

3. Press Print (Shift+F7) and then choose P<u>r</u>int to send the current document to the printer. Repeat this step two or three times to resend the document.

4. Press Print (Shift+F7) and choose <u>C</u>ontrol Printer to display the screen shown in Figure 4.17.

Figure 4.17
The Control Printer screen

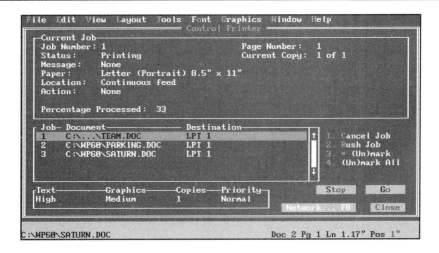

The upper half of the Control Printer dialog box displays messages regarding the status of printing. If WordPerfect sounds a beep while you are printing a document, this usually means something's gone wrong with the printing process. When this happens, display the Control Printer dialog box. You'll see an error message on the screen and may find advice on what you can do to fix the problem. The lower half of the Control Printer dialog box shows a list of the print jobs you've sent to the printer.

5. If more than five print jobs are waiting to be printed (that is, they are queued), you can press ↓ or use the scroll bar to view a display of the entire queue. Try this now; in the queue you'll see an entry for each instance in which you sent your document to the printer in step 3 of this exercise.

Choose Close to return to the document screen.

6. Press Exit (F7) until you return to the document editing screen.

Make sure your printer stays "off line" for now; later, you will cancel the print jobs that you've sent.

Sending a Rush Job

Sometimes you'll want to rush a document to the printer, ahead of any other documents waiting to be printed. This can be done from the Control Printer dialog box. Let's assume the document on your screen is the one you want to rush to the printer. Try this exercise to place a rush job ahead of the other jobs in the print queue:

Choose File ▸ Print.

1. From the document screen, select Print (Shift+F7).

2. Choose Full Document and then Print to send a copy of the on-screen document to the printer. This places the document as the last print job on the Control Printer queue.

3. Again choose Print and then Control Printer. If there are more than five jobs waiting to be printed, press ↓ to scroll to the end of this list. The document you just sent should be the last print job on the list; this entry should be highlighted. Note the number assigned to the print job.

4. Choose Rush Job, and WordPerfect prompts you with "Rush highlighted job?" Choose Yes to continue.

WordPerfect now moves the highlighted print job to the beginning of the list. If a long document is currently printing when you select the Rush Job option, WordPerfect asks you if you want to interrupt the current job to print the rush job. Choose Yes at this prompt, and WordPerfect finishes the current page of the current job, prints the rush job, and then resumes printing the previous document. Choose No at the prompt, and WordPerfect sends the rush job after the current print job is finished.

Before you continue with the next subject, press Exit (F7) to return to the editing screen.

Canceling a Print Job

From the Control Printer dialog box, you can cancel a print job that is currently printing or waiting to be printed.

Follow this exercise to cancel the print jobs that you sent earlier:

Choose File ▸ Print.

1. Press Print (Shift+F7), and choose Control Printer. Because you previously took your printer off line, you should see a "Fix Printer…" message on the screen.

2. Choose Cancel Job from the Control Printer menu, and WordPerfect prompts you with

```
Cancel highlighted print job?
```

3. Choose <u>Y</u>es to cancel the job.

You can also type an asterisk to mark specific jobs in the list and cancel them. For this exercise, type asterisks to mark the remaining jobs. Then choose <u>C</u>an-cel Job to cancel them.

In the Action field of the Control Printer dialog box, you may see additional messages that tell you what to do next to cancel the print jobs. This varies by printer. Follow the instructions displayed on the screen until the print job is removed and the Control Printer screen is clear. Press Exit (F7) to return to the editing screen. Then press the on-line button on your printer so that it will accept information.

Setting Up a New Printer

When you installed the WordPerfect program, special files called *printer drivers* were copied to your WordPerfect directory or disk. As shown in Figure 4.18, a printer driver works like a translator between WordPerfect and your printer. Because each printer speaks a different "language," the printer driver file is necessary to help WordPerfect communicate with your printer.

Figure 4.18
The printer driver helps WordPerfect communicate with your printer.

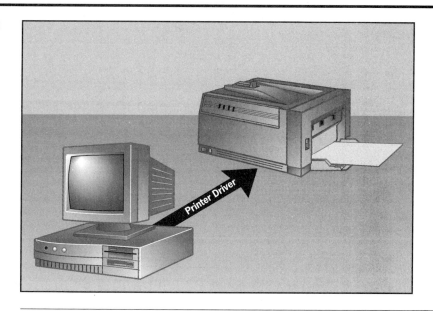

Installing a printer involves two different tasks. First, the necessary printer driver files must be copied to your WordPerfect directory. Then the *printer definition* must be established from within WordPerfect. If you specified a printer when you installed WordPerfect, the Installation program performed both tasks for you, and WordPerfect should be ready to work with your printer. If you work with two or more printers, you can install as many printer drivers as you need. Before printing, you can then select the one you want from the Select Printer dialog box.

If the Installation program could not install a printer or if you want to set up additional printers, this section explains how to install the necessary printer drivers.

A Word about Printer Memory

Like your computer, your printer has its own memory—a place to store information that it receives from WordPerfect and from other software programs. A portion of this memory, called the *print buffer*, is reserved as the area where documents (or sections of long documents) are stored while waiting to be printed. Your printer's memory also stores any font information that is copied (*downloaded*) from disk files.

Just as your computer has a limited amount of memory, so too is your printer memory limited for storing document and font information. WordPerfect works with your printer to send this information as needed, waiting until the print buffer is clear before sending the next batch of data.

The amount of memory in your printer varies based on the printer type. Your printer manual lists the amount of memory in your printer as it was shipped from the factory. For certain printers, you can add additional memory to increase the storage capacity and thus speed up the printing process. If you work with soft fonts, additional memory may be required for storing the font information, but this is not always necessary. To find out more about additional memory for your printer, consult the dealer from whom you purchased your printer.

Setting Up a New Printer Definition

As mentioned earlier, you set up the appropriate printer drivers when you installed the WordPerfect software. If you need to update a printer driver or set up a driver for a new printer, you can do so by running the Installation program again and selecting the new printer drivers. These are the steps:

1. From the set of disks included in your WordPerfect package, insert the Install 1 floppy disk into the A drive of your computer.

2. Exit WordPerfect. Then, from the DOS prompt, type **a:install**. Choose <u>Y</u>es or <u>N</u>o to indicate whether you are using a color monitor. Then, the WordPerfect 6.0 Installation menu appears.

3. Choose Device, and the Installation program prompts you to verify the location of the Install 1 disk ("Install Files From"). Press Enter to continue.

4. The Installation program prompts you to verify the location of your WordPerfect program files. Press Enter to continue, and the Install Device dialog box appears.

5. Choose Printer Files and a list of supported printers appears. Scroll through the list, or use the Name Search option to locate the printer driver you want to install. Then press Enter to select the driver.

6. Choose Yes to verify that you want to install the highlighted printer driver. The Installation program then starts WordPerfect to complete the printer driver installation.

7. You may be prompted to choose the Port number to which your printer is attached. If so, choose the appropriate port, and then press Exit (F7) to continue.

8. The program prompts you to choose an initial font for the printer. Scroll through the list of available fonts and press Enter to select the default font for the printer driver.

During installation, the software creates a *.PRS file for the selected printer driver in your printer file directory; the default printer file directory is C:\WPC60DOS. When the installation of the new printer driver is completed, the program returns you to the DOS prompt. At this point, you can start WordPerfect and the new printer driver appears on the list of printers you can select from the Print dialog box.

The latest installed printer driver becomes the current selected printer when you start WordPerfect. Before you print your documents, make sure the printer that appears at the top of the Print dialog is the printer to which you want to send your documents.

Editing Your Printer Definition

In most cases, your printer driver will work correctly with WordPerfect. However, there may be situations where you need to edit the settings that make up the definition for one or more printer drivers. You can change the printer port, default font, sheet-feeder definition, or the name that appears for a printer driver on the Select Printer list.

If your printer is working without problems in WordPerfect, you don't need to change these settings. However, if your printer is taking paper from the wrong sheet-feeder trays, is using the wrong default font, or doesn't print at all, you may need to edit the printer definition. These steps explain how to do this:

Choose File ▸ Print
from the menu bar.

- Press Print (Shift+F7) to display the Print dialog box.

- Choose Select and WordPerfect displays the list of printer drivers you've installed for WordPerfect.

- Highlight the printer driver you want to edit (the one that isn't working right). Then choose Edit. WordPerfect displays the dialog box shown in Figure 4.19.

Figure 4.19

The Edit Printer
Setup dialog box

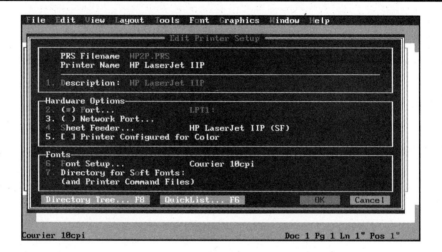

- To change the name that appears on the Select Printer list, choose Description and enter a new name.

- To change the printer port, choose Port and select the correct printer port type and number. If you are running WordPerfect from a network, you can choose Network Port and specify the correct communications port.

- Choose Sheet Feeder to select the correct sheet-feeder definition for your printer. This option is designed for sheet feeders that you must purchase separately and install for your printer.

- If your printer can produce color text and graphics, you can choose Printer Configured for Color to enable (or disable) color printing.

- The Font Setup option lets you adjust the default font selection, graphic font options, relative text size ratios, and automatic font changes for the current printer definition.

Choose OK until
you return to the
document screen.

■ When you are finished with the Edit Printer Setup dialog box, press Exit
(F7) until you return to the document screen.

After you edit a printer definition, WordPerfect updates your changes to
the appropriate *.PRS file for the printer driver. The new settings remain in
effect until you change them again from the Edit Printer Setup dialog box.

Setting Up Cartridge Fonts and Soft Fonts

When you install a new printer driver, WordPerfect automatically recognizes
the built-in fonts that come with your printer. However, you need to tell
WordPerfect whether you've installed additional soft fonts or cartridge fonts.

Soft fonts are software files that WordPerfect can send to your printer to
create fonts for your documents. Cartridge fonts are stored in cartridges that
you can plug into your printer and use. Both font options are common for
laser printers, but some dot-matrix printers allow soft fonts and cartridge
fonts, too. Ask the dealer about additional font options for your printer.

After you've purchased additional soft fonts for your printer, you need to
install them as described in the documentation that came with the font cartridge or font software. After you install the fonts, you can follow these steps
to tell WordPerfect which fonts to add to the font list:

Choose File ▸ Print
from the menu bar.

■ Press Print (Shift+F7) to display the Print dialog box.

■ Choose Select and WordPerfect displays the list of printer drivers you've
installed for WordPerfect.

■ Highlight the printer driver for which you've purchased and installed additional fonts. Then choose Edit. WordPerfect displays the Edit Printer
Setup dialog box.

■ Choose Font Setup, and then choose Select Cartridges/Fonts. WordPerfect displays the dialog box shown in Figure 4.20, with the different font
types: Built-In, Cartridge, and Soft Font.

■ If you are installing additional soft fonts, highlight the Soft Font item in
the list and choose Quantity. This displays the amount of printer memory
that is available for soft fonts. If you've installed additional memory in
your printer, make sure the displayed number reflects the amount of
printer memory you have available for soft fonts.

■ Highlight Cartridges or highlight Soft Font to indicate the type of fonts
you want to add. Then choose Edit.

■ If you highlighted Cartridges, WordPerfect displays a list of cartridges
you can select for your printer. If you highlighted Soft Font, WordPerfect

asks you to choose a font group. Then, the Select Fonts dialog box appears as shown in Figure 4.21.

Figure 4.20

Choosing a category for additional fonts

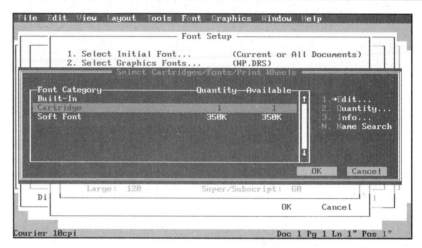

Figure 4.21

The Select Fonts dialog box

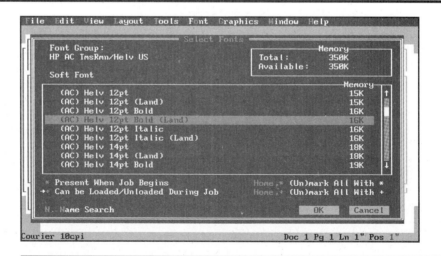

■ From the list, highlight and type an asterisk to mark each font you've installed for use with WordPerfect. Each font you mark with an asterisk is considered available each time you create or print a document.

- If you're marking soft fonts, you can also type a plus sign (+) to mark a font as unloadable. This means that WordPerfect can load or unload the font as needed to free memory for printing tasks.

Choose OK until you return to the Edit Printer Setup dialog box.

- When you are finished marking the fonts you've installed, press Exit (F7) until you return to the Edit Printer Setup dialog box.

- If you marked soft fonts, choose Directory for S<u>o</u>ft Fonts, and enter the full path name where the soft font files are stored. Note that all soft fonts must be stored in the same directory.

Choose OK until you return to the document screen.

- When you are finished marking the fonts you've installed, press Exit (F7) until you return to the document screen.

WordPerfect updates the *.PRS file for the printer driver and includes the fonts you marked. When the printer driver is selected, WordPerfect includes the new fonts on the list of fonts you can apply to your document text.

When marking the fonts you've installed, make sure you highlight the correct fonts. It's possible to mark fonts that you haven't installed; when you do so, WordPerfect will let you choose the fonts when you create your documents, but the text will not print correctly.

Installing Additional Graphic Fonts

As mentioned earlier, WordPerfect includes several scaleable fonts that are licensed from Bitstream Inc. and Adobe Systems Inc. If you have purchased additional graphic fonts or outline fonts from Bitstream, Adobe, or other font manufacturers, you need to use WordPerfect's Font Installer program to install them for use with WordPerfect.

Appendix C explains how to use the Font Installer program from the DOS prompt. You can also choose the <u>I</u>nstall Fonts option from the Font Setup dialog box to start the Font Installer utility. Use this option to set up additional Bitstream Speedo fonts, CG Intellifont software, Adobe Type 1 fonts, TrueType fonts, or bitmapped fonts for use with WordPerfect.

Solving Printing Problems

According to the WordPerfect Corporation, users of WordPerfect have more problems with printing than with any other aspect or feature of the program. There are literally hundreds of printers that may be used with WordPerfect; when you consider the abundance of font options, available computer equipment, and options for customizing WordPerfect's printer definitions, it's clear that there are endless possibilities for printers and thus a greater chance for complications.

If you ever experience a problem with your printer, the information in this section will help you ask the right questions until you find the cause of the trouble. Should you be unable to correct the problem yourself, call the WordPerfect Customer Support group at the number listed in your manual.

The Printer Does Not Work at All

One of the most common difficulties is that the printer simply won't print anything. There are several possible reasons for this. To troubleshoot a printer that doesn't work:

- First, make sure your printer is turned on. Check to see that the printer cables are correctly attached. These may be loose or plugged into the wrong computer ports.

- Is there paper in the printer? Most printers will not let you continue if you run out of paper.

- Check the on-line button on the computer. Most printers have a light next to this button; if the light is off, press the button—the light should go on, indicating that the printer is ready to print.

- Make sure the correct printer is selected from the Print dialog box. For more information, refer to "Getting Ready to Print" earlier in this chapter.

- If the correct printer is selected, make sure WordPerfect is sending print jobs to the correct port. For more information, refer to "Editing a Printer Definition" earlier in this chapter.

- Can you view the document from the View Document screen or with Word-Perfect's graphics display mode? Do the fonts, text, and format look correct? If the document looks okay on the View Document screen or graphics display screen, there may be a problem with your printer equipment.

The Printer Does Not Print Correctly

Once you get the printer working, it may not work as you'd expect. For example, the printer may not place the text correctly on the page, or it might use the wrong fonts. Here are the explanations of these and other dilemmas, and some suggestions for correcting the errors.

Printer Is Printing Garbage

In this case, "garbage" is a series of letters, symbols, and odd characters that are printed on the page. From a distance—a long distance—it may look like a document, but anything more than a glance reveals a mess of computer gibberish. Although there are a few possible causes of this type of error, the most common is that the selected printer definition does not match the printer receiving the information. You can easily correct the situation by choosing Select from the Print dialog box, and then highlighting and selecting the correct printer definition. Your document should then print correctly. For more information on selecting a printer, see "Getting Ready to Print" earlier in this chapter.

If selecting the right printer definition doesn't solve the difficulty, there may be another problem with your printer. In this case, consult the dealer where your printer was purchased, or call WordPerfect Customer Support for assistance.

Margins Aren't Printing Correctly on the Page

Perhaps you've specified 1-inch margins on each side of the page, but instead, you're getting $1/2$ inch at the top and 1 $1/2$ inches at the bottom. Text printed too high or too low on the page is a common error on dot-matrix printers. You may also see incorrect side margin spacing. Obviously, you first should check the margin settings in your document, but it may not be the margins that are at fault. If your printer is not placing the text correctly on the page, it's possible that you'll need to adjust the paper in the printer.

On dot-matrix printers, you can physically reposition the tractor-fed paper so that the top of the next page is higher or lower in the printer and thus will better receive the printed text. You may also need to slide the tractor-feed mechanism to the left or right to accommodate incorrect left or right margins.

On laser printers, you can't alter the way paper is fed into the printer, but you can change the position of the printed text on the page. This involves amending the page offset for the defined paper/size type. See "Editing a Paper Definition" earlier in this chapter.

The Document Is Printing on the Wrong Paper

When you have a printer with multiple paper trays or a sheet feeder with multiple bins, WordPerfect uses the paper size/type definitions (under Page: Format) to determine the location of each paper type you are using. If your documents are printing on the wrong paper, there are a few possible reasons.

First, make sure you have defined a sheet feeder for your printer. Check that you've selected the correct paper size/type definitions for your document layout and that each one is assigned the proper location or bin number. The Information screen available from the Sheet Feeder dialog box should list the numbers assigned to each bin. For more information on selecting and editing the paper size/type definitions, see "Printing on Different Paper Sizes" earlier in this chapter.

Printer Isn't Using the Right Fonts

There are two possible causes for fonts printing incorrectly: The fonts in the printer definition are not correctly defined, or WordPerfect cannot locate the appropriate font information to send to the printer. This often occurs when you are using font software (soft fonts) with your printer. To check for both of these possibilities:

■ First make sure you've installed the correct cartridges or fonts for your printer. Soft font files must all be installed in the same directory on your hard disk.

■ After the soft fonts or cartridges are installed, display the Edit Printer Setup dialog box (press Shift+F7 and choose Select and then Edit). Choose the Cartridges and Fonts option, and make sure you've marked the correct fonts. If you've marked fonts that you don't have, WordPerfect can't use them for printing, despite the fact that it displays them on the Font dialog box.

■ Finally, make sure that Directory for Soft Fonts in the Edit Printer dialog box correctly lists the directory where the soft font files are located. (If you're working only with font cartridges, you don't need to worry about this option.)

Another problem that may occur is that the printer isn't using the correct fonts for the font attribute changes you have inserted. For example, you may have the Helvetica and Helvetica Italic fonts available for your printer, and yet WordPerfect does not recognize the Italic attribute when you choose it within Helvetica text. If this happens in your printed documents, you may need to correct the *Automatic Font Changes*. Automatic Font Changes are the settings that determine which fonts are used to create the different text attributes. Because these depend on whatever font is active in your document, it can be a tricky task for WordPerfect to find the right font for the selected attribute. The Setup (Shift+F1) option in the Font dialog box lets you tell WordPerfect which fonts should be used for each attribute when specific fonts are active.

Using WordPerfect's Fax Capabilities

The Fax Services option on the Print dialog box lets you send your documents to a fax machine through a fax board installed in your computer. If your fax software allows, you can receive faxes and retrieve them into WordPerfect. You can also view and manage a list of the faxes you've sent and received. In this section, you'll learn how to set up your fax software for WordPerfect's Fax Services feature and how to send documents to a fax machine.

The success of the Fax Services feature depends on the type of fax software you are using. WordPerfect tries to account for the differences among various types of fax and communications software, but certain features in your software may be incompatible with WordPerfect's fax features. Also, WordPerfect cannot provide capabilities that are not supported by your existing fax software.

The main advantage of WordPerfect's Fax Services feature is that it allows you to send documents from within WordPerfect. WordPerfect converts your document to reproduce the fonts, text attributes, and graphics that you see on the printed page and sends a copy of this to the fax machine you choose. The result is a fax that closely resembles the documents you get from your printer.

NOTE. *If you have problems setting up your software and sending faxes from WordPerfect, call WordPerfect's Customer Support Group for assistance. The number is listed in your WordPerfect reference manual.*

Setting Up Your Fax Board for WordPerfect

Before you can send documents to fax machines, you must first install a fax board in your computer, and you must install the fax software that allows your computer to send faxes through the board. The documentation that came with the fax board will explain how to do this.

After you've installed the board and the fax software, try sending a few faxes from the fax software to verify that the board is working correctly. Then, you're ready to set up the fax board for WordPerfect documents. You will need to use the WordPerfect Installation program to install and load the fax-board driver files that allow WordPerfect to communicate with the fax software. This is the procedure:

1. From the set of disks included in your WordPerfect package, insert the Install 1 floppy disk into the A drive of your computer.

2. Exit WordPerfect. Then, from the DOS prompt, type **a:install**. Choose Yes or No to indicate whether you are using a color monitor. Then, the WordPerfect 6.0 Installation menu appears.

3. Choose Device, and the Installation Program prompts you to verify the location of the Install 1 disk ("Install Files From"). Press Enter to continue.

4. The Installation program prompts you to verify the location of your WordPerfect program files. Press Enter to continue, and the Install Device dialog box appears.

5. Choose Fax Files, and the Fax Device Options dialog box appears, as shown in Figure 4.22. This dialog box lists the types of fax software that

are supported by WordPerfect, but not necessarily all brands of fax software that will work with WordPerfect.

Figure 4.22
Setting up a fax
board for
WordPerfect

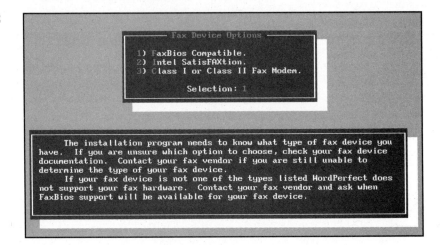

6. Choose the fax option that matches the type of fax software you've installed: FaxBios Compatible, Intel SatisFAXtion, or Class I/Class II Fax Modem. If you choose Intel SatisFAXtion or Class I/Class II, the Installation program will copy the appropriate driver files to your WordPerfect directory.

7. The Installation program then displays instructions that will tell you how to complete fax setup so that WordPerfect can communicate with your fax software. After you read the message (you might want to take notes), press Enter to continue.

8. Press Exit (F7) until you are prompted with Exit Installation? Choose Yes to return to the DOS prompt.

9. From the DOS prompt, change to the directory where your WordPerfect program files are stored. Then, follow the instructions that the Installation Program displayed for completing the fax setup.

For example, if you selected Intel SatisFAXtion from the Fax Device Options dialog box, you would load the INTELFAX.COM driver before starting WordPerfect. Simply change to the WordPerfect directory, type **intelfax**, and then press Enter. This loads the fax driver file that WordPerfect needs to communicate with Intel SatisFAXtion boards. Once the fax setup is completed, you can start WordPerfect and choose Fax Services option from the Print dialog box.

TIP. *You may want to include the fax driver commands in your AUTOEXEC-.BAT file so that the fax setup is performed each time you start your computer. When you do so, include the commands to load the fax driver that WordPerfect needs to communicate with your fax board.*

Creating a Fax Phone Directory

WordPerfect uses the phone directory from your fax software to display a list of fax machines to which you can send documents. A phone directory allows you to select a fax machine before you send a document, saving you the trouble of remembering each fax number you use. Consult the documentation that came with your fax software for instructions on creating the phone directory or phone book.

When you choose the Fax Services option from within WordPerfect, you'll see the phone directory entries that you've already created in your fax software. If the phone directory list is blank, this means you haven't created a phone directory for your fax software or that WordPerfect can't use the fax software's phone directory. If WordPerfect can't use the phone directory you've created from your fax software, the Fax Services dialog box provides an option for manually dialing the fax machine number; this is explained in the next section.

Sending a Document to a Fax Machine

After you've set up the fax software, as described earlier, sending a document to a fax machine is as simple as printing. The following steps explain how to send a fax from within WordPerfect.

NOTE. *If the Fax Services option is disabled when you display the Print dialog box, this means that the correct drivers are not loaded to allow fax communication with WordPerfect. You can fix this by installing the correct software drivers, as explained earlier in this section. If you still have problems with the Fax Services feature, contact WordPerfect's Customer Support Group for assistance.*

Choose File ▸ Print.

1. Retrieve or create the document you want to send to a fax machine. Then, press Print (Shift+F7) to display the Print dialog box.

2. Choose the Fax Services option, and WordPerfect displays the dialog box shown in Figure 4.23. The Phonebook Entries list displays the phone directory entries you've defined from within your fax software.

Figure 4.23

The Fax Services dialog box

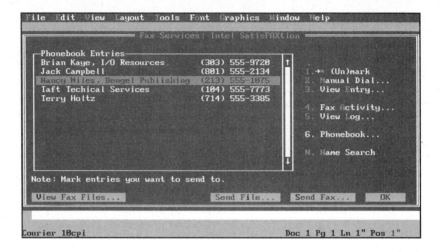

3. Highlight the phone-book entry to which you want to send the current document, press Enter to select it, and then choose §end Fax. Or, choose §anual Dial, enter the recipient's name, and then enter the fax phone number.

4. The Send Fax dialog box appears, as shown in Figure 4.24. Choose §ull Document, §age, or §ultiple Pages to indicate which portion of the displayed document you want to send. Or, choose §ocument on Disk and enter the name of a file stored on disk.

5. Choose §oversheet to select the cover sheet you want to send with the fax. These are usually defined by your fax software.

6. The §end Time option displays the current date and time. If you want to delay the send time, choose this option and enter a new date and time for Deliver §ate and Delivery §ime.

7. Choose §esolution and select Standard or Fine to indicate the print quality for the fax; note that the actual resolution depends on the quality of the receiving fax machine.

8. When you are finished choosing options, choose §end Fax. WordPerfect displays the Fax Job Status message box, which reports on the conversion of the document to the fax format.

The Fax Services dialog box reappears. WordPerfect uses your fax software to dial the phone number and connect to the selected fax machine. Once a connection is established, WordPerfect sends the current document.

Figure 4.24

The Send Fax dialog box

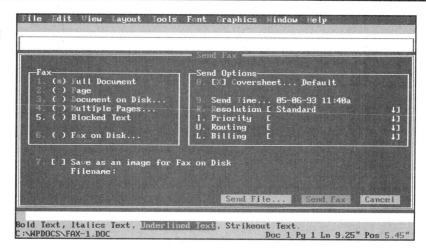

At this point, you can return to the document screen and continue working. Or, choose Fax Activity from the Fax Services dialog to view information about the progress of the fax; after the fax is sent, press Exit (F7) until you return to the document screen.

Viewing the Fax Log

The Fax Log feature, if supported by your fax software, allows WordPerfect to display a list of faxes that you've sent and received. The log is divided into two different lists: Send Log and Receive Log.

From the Fax Services dialog box, choose View Log and WordPerfect prompts you to choose which list you want to see; choose either Send Log or Receive Log. Figure 4.25 shows how the Send Log list displays the faxes you've sent. This information is taken from the fax log created by your fax software. From the Send Log list, you can choose Show Detail to view more information about the highlighted fax entry.

When you display the Receive Log list, you'll see the faxes that your computer has received. From the Receive Log list, you can choose View Fax to view a scanned copy of a fax you've received. Or, choose Print Fax to send a copy of the highlighted fax to your printer.

After you view the list of sent or received faxes, press Exit (F7) or choose OK until you return to the document screen.

Figure 4.25

Viewing a list of
faxes sent

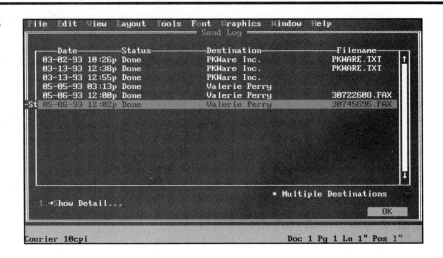

CHAPTER

File Management

FILE MANAGEMENT BECOMES AN IMPORTANT ISSUE ONCE YOU'VE CRE-
ated several WordPerfect documents. Your daily work will probably
include copying and moving files to other directories or disks, changing the names of existing files, and converting documents for use
with other word processors. As time goes by, you'll want to delete some of
your older files and archive others. WordPerfect includes features that perform these and other file management tasks.

In this chapter, you'll learn how to save and retrieve documents, use the File
Manager, add password protection to your documents, and assign descriptive file
names. You'll see how to use WordPerfect's Backup feature as insurance against
power or computer failures. The chapter also explains how to create a document
summary and how to archive files to floppy disks for long-term storage.

Saving Document Files

When you create a document in WordPerfect, the text and formatting information is stored in the memory of your computer—but only temporarily.
Once you exit WordPerfect, the document is cleared from your computer's
memory. Thus, as you've learned in previous chapters, it's important to save
your work to a file on disk.

WordPerfect 6.0 provides two different ways to save the document on
your screen. The Save As feature lets you save the displayed document and
assign a file name. Choosing File and then choosing Save As from the menu
bar is the same as pressing Save (F10). This displays the Save Document dialog box and lets you enter a file name. Use this method to save a new document or to save a copy of the displayed document to a different file name.
The Save feature on the File menu updates editing changes made to a document after you've already saved the document in a file. Remember that the
Save option on the File menu is not the same as pressing Save (F10). Choosing File and then choosing Save automatically saves your document without
prompting you about replacing the previous file. This assumes, of course, that
you've already saved the document to a file on disk; if you haven't yet assigned a file name, WordPerfect will prompt you to do so.

Using the Save and File Save As Features

You've already learned that you can save the displayed document by choosing the Save feature and then entering a file name for the document. Let's go
through this process again in a little more detail. Begin by typing a brief sample
document:

1. Start from a clear screen and type the following paragraph:

Barefoot Elementary is pleased to offer your child a

quality educational experience. We have the finest
facilities and equipment in our county, and take great
pride in our instructional staff. Of course, we cannot
accept full responsibility for your child during the
schooling years. As a parent, you can lend your assistance.
For example, we now have an important question that you
can answer: Which one is your child? Is he the one who
always wears green overalls, or is she the moody one with
the bongo drums? Perhaps you could give us a call and help
us locate him or her.

With the cursor at the end of the text, press Enter twice to end the paragraph.

Choose File ▸ Save As.

2. Press Save (F10) to display the Save Document dialog box, shown in Figure 5.1.

Figure 5.1

The Save Document
dialog box

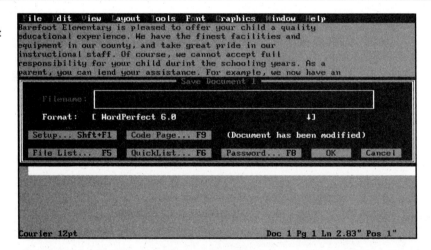

3. At the Filename prompt, type **barefoot.doc** as the file name.

4. Press Enter to accept the file name.

NOTE. *See the section "Choosing File Names" for complete information about the file names you can use for your documents.*

If you make a mistake while typing the file name, you can press Backspace to delete the unwanted characters, or press Cancel (Esc) to end the entire Save procedure and start again. Once you accept the name, WordPerfect saves the document and displays the name in the lower-left corner of the screen. When you divide your screen into different document windows, the document name appears at the top of the window borders. In Chapter 7, you'll learn how to display and switch between document windows.

Saving a Copy of the Displayed Document

After you've saved a file, you can make a copy by saving it again under a different file name. For example, suppose you've created a business letter that you want to use as a model for a new letter. You can retrieve the original letter, make changes to the format and text, and then press Save (F10), or choose File and then Save As from the menu bar. At the Filename prompt, you'll see the current file name displayed. Instead of pressing Enter to accept this name, create a copy of the document by typing a new file name and pressing Enter. The original document remains unchanged and stored under the original file name.

Before you continue to the next section, you should clear the screen. To do so, press Exit (F7) and choose No twice, or choose File, Close from the menu bar.

Choosing File Names

When you save a document, you can type up to eight characters for the file name, plus a period and up to three characters as an extension to the file name. This is according to the pattern required by MS-DOS. WordPerfect 6.0 also includes a feature that allows you to assign descriptive document names of 30 characters or more. (For more information, see the sections on document summaries later in this chapter.) Table 5.1 shows examples of file names that you can enter, along with other names that are unacceptable.

Table 5.1 **Valid and Invalid File Names**

Invalid	Valid	Explanation
DENVER.REPORT	DENVER.RPT	File names must have eight characters or less before the period, and three or fewer characters after the period.
MR.SMITH.LTR	MR_SMITH.LTR	Use only one period in the file name to separate the eight-character name from the three-character extension.
1 2 3.REP BIN NO 12	1-2-3.REP BIN#12	Instead of spaces, use dashes (-) or underscore characters (_) to separate the characters in a file name.

Table 5.1 **Valid and Invalid File Names (Continued)**

Invalid	Valid	Explanation
"LUCKY".DOC	'LUCKY'.DOC	You can include the single quote mark or apostrophe character in a file name, but not the double quote mark.
YES/NO.Q/A	YES-NO.QA	Do not use slashes (forward or backward) in a file name. These are reserved for specifying path names and other DOS functions.
NITE+DAY.MEM	NITE&DAY.MEM	Insert the ampersand (&) symbol, instead of the plus sign (+) in a file name to indicate an abbreviation for the word "and."
REPORT,92.MO	RPRT-92.MO	Do not include commas in a DOS file name.

You can use any alphanumeric characters (A through Z, and 0 through 9) to create a file name, and most of the punctuation characters (! @ # $ % ^ &), including parentheses. You cannot use a space, a comma, double quotes ("), an asterisk (*), a forward slash (/), a backward slash (\), or the plus sign (+). The period character (.) may only be inserted once to separate the eight-character name from the three-character extension. When you type a file name, it doesn't matter whether you type the letters in uppercase or lowercase.

The three-character file name extension is not required, but it can help to identify the type of file you've created. For example, you may want to add an .LTR label to the file name of each business letter you create. An .RPT extension might be added for all reports, a .DOC extension for large document files, or a .MEM extension for memo files.

Certain text strings are reserved for DOS program files and commands, and cannot be used for your documents. These include AUX, CLOCK$, COM, CON, LPT, LST, NUL, and PRN. In addition, the following file name extensions are assigned to identify WordPerfect program files: .ARS, .BIN, .BK!, .BKS, .CHK, .CUX, .DL, .DRS, .EXE, .FIL, .FRS, .HLM, .HLP, .ICR, .INS, .IRS, .LCN, .LRS, .MRS, .ORS, .OVL, .PRS, .QRS, .SET, .SPC, .STY, .TRS, .VRM, .VRS, .WFW, .WPB, .WPK, and .WPM. Avoid using any of these extensions to name your document files; if you confuse your documents with WordPerfect program files, problems may arise when you need to copy, move, and delete these files.

Updating a Document File

After you've saved your document to a file, you can quickly update any editing changes by using the Save option on the File menu. Choose File and then choose <u>S</u>ave from the menu bar; WordPerfect updates the displayed document to its disk file.

Be careful with the Save option on the menu bar. Remember, when you choose <u>F</u>ile and then <u>S</u>ave, WordPerfect automatically updates the changes you've made to the file on disk without asking whether you really want to update the file. You won't have the opportunity to confirm or cancel the replacement of the original document.

Here's an example of how the Save feature may cause a problem. Suppose you want to retrieve a business letter you've already created and use it as a model for a new letter; you still want to keep the original letter, so you plan to save the edited letter under a different file name. In this case, you want to press Save (F10) or choose <u>F</u>ile and then choose Save <u>A</u>s from the menu bar. These commands will prompt you to enter a file name for the edited document. If, instead, you choose <u>F</u>ile and then choose <u>S</u>ave from the menu bar, WordPerfect replaces the original document file with the edited letter on your screen, and your original document is lost.

Saving to Other File Formats

When you need to retrieve your WordPerfect documents into other word processors—such as Microsoft Word and Ami Pro—you can use the Save As feature to convert your documents to one of over 40 different file formats. You can also use this feature if you need to retrieve your WordPerfect 6.0 document files into an earlier version of WordPerfect. For example, before you can retrieve a WordPerfect 6.0 document into WordPerfect 5.1, you must save it as a WordPerfect 5.1 file.

To save the displayed document to a different file format:

Choose <u>F</u>ile ▸ Save <u>A</u>s to display the Save Document dialog box.

1. Press Save (F10) to display the Save Document dialog box.

2. At the Filename prompt, type a file name for the document.

Click on the For<u>m</u>at option.

3. Press Tab and then press Enter to open the For<u>m</u>at list, shown in Figure 5.2.

Scroll through the list and double-click on a format name.

4. When the For<u>m</u>at list is open, scroll through the list to highlight the file format you want to use, or type the format name to highlight it. Then press Enter to select the file format.

5. Press Exit (F7) to save the displayed document to the new format.

Choose OK to save the document.

WordPerfect loads its built-in conversion program and converts the document to the new format. When you save a document to a different file format, consider adding a special extension to the file name to indicate the format you selected. For example, if you've saved a document to the WordStar 4.0 format, you might want to end the file name with .WS4 to help you identify the file type.

Figure 5.2

Choosing a file
format

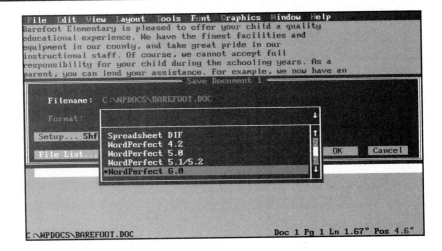

Options on the Save Document Dialog Box

The Save Document dialog box provides different options that will help you
save and protect your files. To view these options, first press Save (F10), or
choose File, Save As from the menu bar. When the Save Document dialog
box is displayed, you can choose one or more of the following options:

- When the cursor is in the Filename box, you can press File List (F5) to
  view a list of files on your hard disk. You can use this option to either select a file name under which you want to save the current document or to
  verify that a file name you've typed isn't already assigned to an existing file.

- The QuickList (F6) option is similar to the File List (F5) option. When
  the cursor is in the Filename box, you can press QuickList (F6) to view a
  file list under a list of directory aliases; see "Using Descriptive Directory
  Names" later in this chapter for information about the QuickList feature.

- Press Code Page (F9) to select a different country specification for the
  document; this option simply converts the internal document commands
  so that your document can be retrieved on a computer designed for a different country.

- Press Password (F8) to assign a password to the current document. See
  "Protecting Your Document with a Password" later in this chapter for
  more information.

- Press Setup (Shift+F1) to display the Save Setup dialog box, which provides two options for saving documents: Fast Save and Default Save Format.

The Setup options determine the default save settings for WordPerfect; these options remain in effect until you change them again. When the Fast Save feature is turned on, WordPerfect won't reformat each document before saving; this reduces the amount of time required for saving a document.

TIP. *If you want to keep the Fast Save option turned on and reformat your documents, simply press Home, Home, ↓ before saving; this performs the reformatting that the Fast Save feature disables.*

The Default Save Format determines which format WordPerfect displays in the Format box each time you use the Save Document dialog box. If, for example, you want all your documents saved in the WordPerfect 5.1 format, display the Save Document dialog box, press Setup (Shift+F1), choose Default Save Format, and then select the WordPerfect 5.1/5.2 format. From then on, whenever you save your documents, this format is automatically listed in the Format box on the Save Document dialog box.

Retrieving Documents

When you're ready to edit or print a previously created document, you can retrieve it and make the desired changes. There are two ways to retrieve a document file. The Open feature lets you retrieve a document file into a new document window, which won't disturb any other documents you may have open. The Retrieve feature inserts a file into the document displayed on your screen. The following sections explain these options, and show you additional ways to open or retrieve a document file.

Using the Open Feature

Let's start by opening the BAREFOOT.DOC file that you created at the beginning of this chapter. Before you continue, make sure the screen is clear (press F7 and choose No twice).

Choose File ▸ Open.

1. Press Open/Retrieve (Shift+F10) to display the Open Document dialog box, shown in Figure 5.3.

2. At the Filename prompt, type **barefoot.doc.**

3. Press Enter to accept the name.

Figure 5.3

The Open Document dialog box

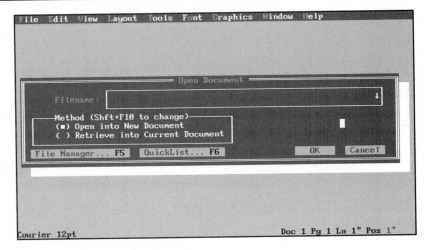

WordPerfect retrieves and displays the BAREFOOT.DOC file in the main editing screen. If you see a "File Not Found" message when you attempt to retrieve a file, this means that WordPerfect could not find the file in the default directory; in this case, you should precede the file name with the directory path where the file is stored. If you don't remember where a file is located, press File Manager (F5) or QuickList (F6) from within the Open Document dialog box to browse through a directory and select the file you want to open.

Once a document is retrieved, you can edit the text or format of the document, view the document, or print it. Then you use the Save feature to update your changes to the document file.

Retrieving from a List of Files

WordPerfect's File Manager feature lets you select and retrieve a file from a displayed directory of files. This is most useful when you can't quite remember the name of a particular file. The following steps explain how to use the File Manager to open or retrieve a file:

Choose File ▸ File Manager.

■ Press File Manager (F5). The name of the current directory is displayed in a dialog box on the screen.

■ Press Enter to accept the current directory, or type the path name of another directory that contains the files you want listed. Then press Enter.

■ The File Manager screen is displayed, as shown in Figure 5.4. (The file names on your screen will differ from those shown in the illustration.)

Use the arrow keys to move the highlighted cursor to the name of the file you want to open or retrieve.

Figure 5.4
WordPerfect's File Manager

Highlighted file ──────

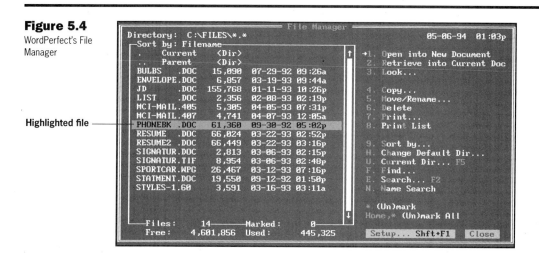

```
═════════════════════ File Manager ═════════════════════
Directory:  C:\FILES\*.*                              05-06-94  01:03p
┌─Sort by: Filename─────────────────────┐
│  .    Current    <Dir>                 │ ↑  →1. Open into New Document
│  ..   Parent     <Dir>                 .    2. Retrieve into Current Doc
│  BULBS    .DOC   15,090   07-29-92 09:26a   3. Look...
│  ENVELOPE.DOC     6,857   03-19-93 09:44a
│  JD      .DOC   155,768   01-11-93 10:26p   4. Copy...
│  LIST    .DOC     2,356   02-08-93 02:19p   5. Move/Rename...
│  MCI-MAIL.405     5,305   04-05-93 07:31p   6. Delete
│  MCI-MAIL.407     4,741   04-07-93 12:05a   7. Print...
│ PHONEBK  .DOC    61,360   09-30-92 05:02p   8. Print List
│  RESUME  .DOC    66,024   03-22-93 02:52p
│  RESUME2 .DOC    66,449   03-22-93 03:16p   9. Sort by...
│  SIGNATUR.DOC     2,813   03-06-93 02:15p   H. Change Default Dir...
│  SIGNATUR.TIF     8,954   03-06-93 02:48p   U. Current Dir... F5
│  SPORTCAR.WPG    26,467   03-12-93 07:16p   F. Find...
│  STATMENT.DOC    19,550   09-12-92 01:50p   E. Search... F2
│  STYLES-1.60      3,591   03-16-93 03:11a   N. Name Search
│                                        │
│                                        │    *  (Un)mark
│                                        │ ↓  Home,* (Un)mark All
└─Files:    14──────Marked:      0───────┘
  Free:  4,601,856  Used:     445,325       ┌─Setup... Shft+F1─┐ ┌Close┐
```

- With the file name highlighted, choose <u>O</u>pen into New Document, or choose <u>R</u>etrieve into Current Doc.

If you are using a mouse with WordPerfect, you can open a file from the File Manager without selecting a menu option. First, move the mouse pointer onto the file name, and then double-click the mouse button (quickly click the mouse button twice). This automatically opens the highlighted file into a new document window.

For complete information about the File Manager, see "Using the File Manager" later in this chapter.

Retrieving a File into an Existing Document

The Retrieve feature lets you combine two or more documents into one document file. Instead of opening a file into a new document window, the Retrieve feature inserts the file into the document displayed on your screen.

Follow the steps of this exercise to combine two files. Before you begin, make sure the document screen is displayed. If the File Manager or a dialog box is displayed, press Cancel (Esc) until you return to the document screen. Then clear the screen by pressing Exit (F7) and choosing <u>N</u>o twice.

1. Type the following paragraph to create a brief document:

```
February 21, 1994

Occupant
52 North Maple Lane
Salem, Virginia  24153

Dear Occupant,

The school board welcomes you to the neighborhood.
```

Keep the cursor positioned at the end of the last sentence.

Choose Eile ▸ Retrieve.

2. Press Open/Retrieve (Shift+F10) to display the Open Document dialog box, and then press Shift+F10 until the Method called "Retrieve into Current Document" is marked.

3. At the Filename prompt, type **barefoot.doc** and press Enter.

WordPerfect now retrieves the BAREFOOT.DOC file into the current document. When a file is retrieved in this manner, it is added to the document already on the screen. This procedure does not change the name of the existing document. If you haven't yet saved the document on your screen, it remains unnamed until you save it.

Remember, when you retrieve a file, only a *copy* of the file contents is inserted on the document screen; the actual file remains unchanged under its original file name until you save it again under the original file name.

CAUTION! *Notice that the file was retrieved at the location of the cursor. It is therefore important to always position your cursor at the right place in the text before you retrieve the file into it.*

You'll need to save this new document for a later exercise, so press Save (F10), or choose Eile and then choose Save As. At the Filename prompt, type **barely.doc**, press Enter, and the document is saved. For now, keep this document on the screen.

Directories and Path Names

Whenever you save a document, it is stored as a file on your hard disk or on a floppy disk. Unless you specifically tell WordPerfect where the file should be located, WordPerfect will save it to the *default directory*. The default directory is the place where your computer is currently set to look for files.

To indicate a specific location in which the file should be stored, you can change the default directory, or you can type a *path name* immediately before the name of the file. Similar to a ZIP code, the path name is an address for a place on your hard disk. Since you also have different disk drives to which you can save files, the path name can also include the drive letter of a specific drive.

For example, press File Manager (F5) or choose Eile, Eile Manger. The path name for the default directory is displayed at the bottom of the screen. Let's assume the path name reads

```
C:\WPDOCS\*.*
```

This means WordPerfect is currently set to work with the \WPDOCS directory on the C drive. When you save or retrieve a file without specifying a path name, WordPerfect assumes the file should be stored in this directory. Press Cancel (Esc) now to remove the path name.

NOTE. *This section discusses directories and path names as they relate to WordPerfect. For complete information about directories and paths, refer to your DOS manual.*

In the following section, you'll see how to enter path names to save or retrieve files that are stored somewhere other than the default directory. You'll also learn how to change the default directory and to create a special directory for WordPerfect document files.

Specifying a Path Name for Saving and Retrieving

Up to this point, whenever you've saved or retrieved documents, you've been instructed to type only a file name. But you can also type a specific path name before the file name to tell WordPerfect exactly where the file is to be stored (or where to find it). For example, when you typed **barely.doc** at the Save File-name prompt, that file was saved in the default directory, whatever that may be. If you had typed **c:\barely.doc** instead, the BARELY.DOC file would be saved to the C:\ directory (the root directory on drive C).

The next exercise shows you how to include a path name when saving and retrieving files. First you will create a brief sample document and use a path name to save it. Then you will clear the screen and retrieve the file.

If you already have a document on the screen, you can add the paragraph to the document. Although you will save this document now, you'll delete it later in this chapter.

1. Press Home, Home, ↓ to move the cursor to the end of the displayed document. Then type the following paragraph on your screen:

   Also, it has come to our attention that you own an all-terrain urban assault vehicle. May we include you in our parent-counselor team for the annual three-day discovery jaunt in the Appalachians? We expect this will be a rewarding experience for our 6th graders. You are, of course, fully insured?

Choose File ▸ Save As.

2. Press Save (F10) to display the Save Document dialog box.

3. Type **c:\school.ltr** and press Enter. Notice that the path name and file name now appear on the document window.

Choose File ▸ Close.

4. Clear the screen by pressing Exit (F7) and choosing No twice.

5. Press Open/Retrieve (Shift+F10).

Choose File ▸ Open.

6. Type **school.ltr** and press Enter. Because the file is not stored in the default directory, a "File not found" message appears. Press Enter or choose OK, and WordPerfect displays the path and file name that you entered and allows you to correct it.

7. Type **c:\school.ltr** and press Enter.

This time, the file is retrieved.

If you get the "File not found" message when you're attempting to retrieve a file, this means that the file name you've entered isn't located in the specified directory. If you know where the file is stored, you can always type a path name before any file name you enter. If you don't know where a file is stored, press File Manager (F5) while the cursor in on the Filename prompt; this lets you browse through a directory list until you find the file you want to retrieve.

Although a specific path name is sometimes necessary with a file name, you shouldn't have to enter the path every time you save or retrieve a document. If you find that you're always entering path names before file names, you may want to change your default directory, as described in the next section.

Changing the Default Directory

You can easily change the default directory, which is the place where WordPerfect looks first when you save or retrieve a document file:

Choose File ▸ File Manager.

- Press File Manager (F5). The current default directory path name appears in a dialog box.

- Type = and the Change Default Directory dialog box appears. Type the path name for the directory that you want as the new default directory.

- Press Enter, and WordPerfect displays the path name you typed as the default directory.

■ Press Cancel (Esc) to close the dialog box.

Now you try it. Follow these steps at your computer to change the default directory for your copy of WordPerfect:

Choose Eile ▸ Eile Manager.

1. Press File Manager (F5) to display the Specify File Manager List dialog box, in which the default directory is displayed.

2. Type **=c:** and press Enter. This indicates that you want to change the default directory to the root directory of the C drive.

3. Press Cancel (Esc) to return to the document screen.

Now, when you save or retrieve files without specifying a path name, WordPerfect will automatically work with the C:\ directory to locate and store your files. It's important to remember that the change you've just made to your default directory, as instructed above, is only a temporary change—the next time you start WordPerfect, the default directory will be the document directory specified on WordPerfect's Location of Files dialog box.

You can use the Location of Files feature to permanently change the default directory for saving, opening, and retrieving documents. These are the general steps:

Choose Eile ▸ Setup ▸ Location of Files.

■ Press Setup (Shift+F1) and choose Location of Files.

■ From the Location of Files dialog box, choose Documents.

■ Type the path name for the directory where you want to store your document files, and then press Enter.

■ Press Exit (F7) until you return to the document screen.

Choose OK to return to the document screen.

The Documents option on the Location of Files dialog box specifies the default directory for the documents that you save, open, and retrieve in Word-Perfect. When you enter a new path name for this option, WordPerfect will look to this directory when you save or retrieve document files—assuming that you don't specify a path name in the Save Document, Open Document, or Retrieve Document dialog boxes. The new path name remains the default directory for document files until you change the path again on the Location of Files dialog box or until you temporarily change the default directory as described earlier. See Appendix A for more information about the Location of Files feature.

Creating a Document Directory

In the following exercise, you will create a document directory and specify it as the directory where all document files should be stored:

NOTE. *This exercise instructs you to create a subdirectory within the Word-Perfect directory called C:\WP60\FILES. If you prefer, you can substitute a different directory and then enter that path name as your new document directory (for example, C:\DOCUMENT or C:\WPFILES).*

Choose File ▸ File Manager.

1. From the editing screen, press File Manager (F5).

2. To create a document directory called FILES as a subdirectory of the main \WP60 directory, type =**c:\WP60\files**, and press Enter.

3. WordPerfect prompts you with

```
Create Directory c:\WP60\files?
```

4. Choose Yes, and the new directory is created. Then press Cancel (Esc) to return to the document screen.

Choose File ▸ Setup ▸ Location of Files.

5. Press Setup (Shift+F1), and then choose Location of Files.

6. From the Setup Location of Files dialog box, choose Documents, type **c:\WP60\files**, and press Enter.

Choose OK to return to the document screen.

7. Press Exit (F7) to return to the document screen.

Now, whenever you save files without typing a path name before the name, WordPerfect will store them in this directory. When you retrieve files without typing a path name, WordPerfect will look here to find them. You've made a permanent change to the program settings of WordPerfect; this change will remain active unless you repeat the steps just listed and enter a new path name for the Document option on the Location of Files dialog box.

Including a Document Summary

When you work with several documents, it can be difficult to remember what each document file contains. A *document summary* lets you keep a record of the document author, typist, and other supplemental information that would not normally be printed with the document text. When you create a document summary, you can also type or retrieve a brief description of the document contents. If a file has a document summary, the summary information appears when you look at the file contents from the File Manager, as explained later in this chapter. Document summaries are also addressed in Chapter 15.

This section tells you how to create a new document summary and retrieve information into it from the text of your document. You'll also see how to print the summary, how to save it as a separate file, and how to remove a summary after you've created it. Other information explains how to set up WordPerfect so that a summary is always created when you first save a document.

Before you continue, you'll need to create the memo shown in Figure 5.5 and save it as MEMO.DOC. It doesn't matter whether the format of your memo is identical to the one shown in the illustration; however, it is important to include the SUBJECT label at the beginning of the memo.

Figure 5.5
A sample memo
document

MEMORANDUM

DATE: September 5, 1994

TO: Kaden Scott

FROM: Shauna Olsen

SUBJECT: Health Spa Membership

According to our records, it's time for you to renew your health spa membership. We have spent a great deal of time and money improving our gym facilities for our customers.

This year the annual membership fee is $250. The fee increase will help cover the cost of the newly added equipment, which includes several new fitness stations and an indoor swimming pool. If you have questions regarding your membership, please contact Karen Ridley at our business office.

Thank you.

Creating a New Summary

All document summaries are created from the Document Summary dialog box, as shown in Figure 5.6.

Figure 5.6

The Document
Summary dialog box

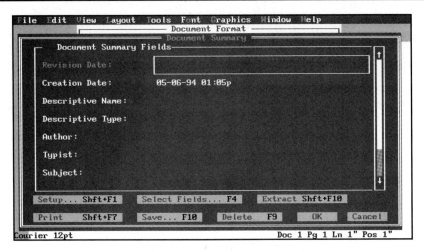

You can display this dialog box by pressing Format (Shift+F8); then choose <u>D</u>ocument and <u>S</u>ummary. At the top of the dialog box, you'll see the Revision Date label. This displays the date when you last saved the current document. If you're creating a new document but haven't yet saved it, this entry will be blank. The Creation Date option automatically displays the date when the document was created, but you can always choose this option and change the date.

The next two options, Descriptive Name and Descriptive Type, let you type a document name and a descriptive phrase about the type of document you've created. The descriptive name can be displayed on the File Manager instead of the standard DOS file name. The document type can also be displayed on the File Manager and will help you organize your documents into categories. For example, you may want to enter words like MEMO, LETTER, REPORT, or ENVELOPE as the document type. Or you can type a description such as First Quarter Prospectus, December Orders, or Birthday Records.

Press ↓ or use the scroll bar to view the complete list of options. The other document summary options include the name of the author and typist for the document, subject information, an account number or title, special document keywords, and an *abstract* or brief summary of the document contents. Many of these options—such as Subject, Account, and Keywords—are provided to accommodate the needs of different business groups. You don't need to enter information for all the document summary items; select only the features that you want to use.

Follow these steps to create a document summary for the memo document on your screen. If you have not yet created the memo, do so before continuing with this exercise.

Choose <u>F</u>ile ▸ S<u>u</u>mmary.

1. With the memo file (MEMO.DOC) displayed on your screen, press Format (Shift+F8), choose <u>D</u>ocument, and then choose <u>S</u>ummary. This displays the Document Summary dialog box (see Figure 5.6 earlier).

2. Press ↓ until the cursor is at the Descriptive Name field. Then type

   ```
   Sample Memo Document from "Help! WordPerfect 6.0."
   ```

   Press Enter.

3. The cursor automatically moves to the Descriptive Type field. Type **MEMO** and press Enter.

4. In the Author field, type your name and press Enter.

5. The cursor automatically moves to the Typist field. In this case, the author and typist are the same, so press Enter to skip this option.

6. Press ↓ until the cursor moves to the Abstract field. Type a summary of the document contents. (You are allowed up to 780 characters, including spaces.)

Choose OK to return to the document screen.

7. When you are finished typing the abstract, press Exit (F7) until you return to the document screen.

If you wish, you can enter additional information for the other summary options. The Subject option lets you enter a subject for the document. The Account option is for an account number or description. Select the Keywords option to enter specific phrases or words to help you find the document from the File Manager (see "Finding Files with Specific Words and Phrases" later in this chapter).

TIP. *You can press F4 at the Document Summary screen to choose the fields that will be included in the summary.*

Inserting Information from the Document

When the Document Summary dialog box is displayed, you can fill in the Subject and Abstract fields with text from the document itself. Here is the general procedure:

- With the Document Summary dialog box displayed, choose Extract (Shift+F10) and WordPerfect prompts you with "Extract Document Summary information?"

- Choose <u>Y</u>es and WordPerfect inserts information from your document to fill the Subject and Abstract fields of the summary. (Note that subject information is inserted automatically only if your document is set up properly, as described in a moment.)

- When you are finished creating the Summary, press Exit (F7) to return to the editing screen.

The first 400 characters of your document are inserted into the Abstract field of the summary, and the subject information is inserted according to the defined *subject search text*. The subject search text is a standard word or phrase that you use to label the subject information in the text of your documents. This is the word WordPerfect looks for to find information that should be inserted into the Subject field of the Summary screen. The abbreviation *RE:* is the standard subject search text, but you can change this to any word you want. If the subject search text is found in your document, the first 35 characters that follow it are inserted into the document summary.

In the memo that you created earlier, the word SUBJECT is used to label the purpose of the memo. By default WordPerfect suggests RE: as the Subject Search Text. You can easily change the Subject Search Text, so that WordPerfect can find and insert the subject of each memo or document into the document summary. The following steps show how to change the subject search text and insert the document information into the Subject and Abstract fields:

Choose <u>F</u>ile ▸ <u>S</u>ummary.

1. From the document screen, press Format (Shift+F8). Choose <u>D</u>ocument and then <u>S</u>ummary.

2. Press Setup (Shift+F1) to display the Document Summary Setup dialog box shown in Figure 5.7.

3. Choose <u>S</u>ubject Search Text. Notice that RE: currently appears in this field.

4. Type **Subject:** as the new subject search text, and press Enter.

5. Press Exit (F7) to return to the Document Summary dialog box.

Choose OK.

6. Choose Extract (Shift+F10), and WordPerfect prompts you with "Extract Document Summary information?"

7. Choose <u>Y</u>es, and WordPerfect looks through your document to find the Subject Search Text. Then in the Subject field, it inserts the text line that follows the subject search text in your document.

Choose OK.

8. When you are finished with the summary, press Exit (F7) to return to the editing screen.

Figure 5.7

Changing the
subject search text

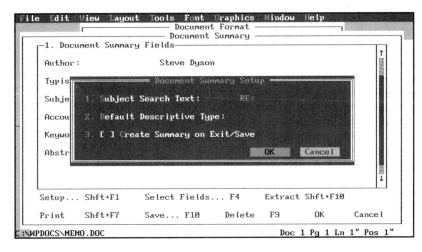

When WordPerfect finds the subject search text, it inserts into the Subject field the line that follows the search text (up to 35 characters). In addition, the first 400 characters of the document text are inserted for the summary abstract.

If you wish, you can now move the cursor to the Subject or Abstract field from the Document Summary dialog box and edit the information that was inserted into these fields. The subject search text that you defined at the Document Summary Setup dialog box remains in effect until you change it again with the steps listed above.

Saving and Printing the Summary

When the Document Summary dialog box is displayed, you can either save the summary information to a separate file or send the information to your printer:

Choose File ▸
Summary.

- From the document screen, press Format (Shift+F8), choose Document, and then choose Summary. This displays the Document Summary dialog box for the current document.

- Press Print (Shift+F7) to send a copy of the screen to the printer, or press Save (F10) and enter a file name to save the summary to a separate file on disk. This file can then be retrieved at the document screen, but you can't retrieve the file back into the Document Summary screen.

Removing a Summary from the Document

If you want to remove a summary from a document, begin by retrieving the document into WordPerfect. Press Format (Shift+F8), choose Document, and then choose Summary. Press Delete (F9), and WordPerfect prompts you with "Delete document summary?" Choose Yes and WordPerfect removes the summary from your document and returns you either to the Document Format dialog box or directly to your document.

Creating a Summary When Saving Documents

If you need to create summaries for all your documents, you can have Word-Perfect prompt you to create a summary each time a new document is saved. This saves you time and ensures that every document will include summary information.

To turn on this feature, you'll need to display the Document Summary Setup dialog box:

1. From the Document Summary dialog box, press Setup (Shift+F1).

2. Choose Create Summary on Exit/Save, so that an X appears in the box next to this option.

3. Press Exit (F7) until you return to the document screen. Now you can try out this feature.

Choose OK until you return to the document screen.

4. Press Exit (F7) and choose No twice to clear the screen.

5. Type a few lines of text, and press Save (F10).

The Document Summary dialog box is automatically displayed for you, in which you can create the summary for the current document. This will happen every time you save a new document.

If you decide not to create a summary for a particular document, just click on Cancel (or press Esc twice) when the Document Summary dialog box is displayed. This cancels the summary and displays the Save Document dialog box, in which you can enter a file name for the document. Before you continue, turn off the "auto-create" feature. From the Document Summary Setup dialog box, choose Create Summary on Exit/Save so that an X does not appear in the check box beside this option.

In this section, you've learned how to create and manage document summaries. You can easily view the summary for a given document by highlighting the document file name at the File Manager and choosing the Look option. This is explained later in "Viewing the Contents of a Document File."

Protecting Your Document with a Password

Some documents, such as payroll records, marketing strategies, and account ledgers, may contain confidential information that should be protected against unauthorized access. WordPerfect's Password feature lets you assign passwords to secure such documents. Once a document is password-protected, no one can view, retrieve, or print the file without first entering the correct password.

Assigning a Password

To assign a password, you first need to retrieve the document that will be protected. Then press Save (F10) and press Password (F8). Type the password you want to assign, which can be up to 23 characters. (As you type, you won't see the password on the screen; this serves as an extra security measure, so that no one will see what you're typing.) WordPerfect then asks you to enter the password again; this is a safeguard against any typing errors. When you finish, press Exit (F7) to save the document with the password.

Try the following steps to assign a password to the SCHOOL.LTR document you created earlier in this chapter:

Choose File ▸ Close.

1. Clear the screen by pressing Exit (F7) and choosing No twice.

2. Press Open/Retrieve (Shift+F10).

Choose File ▸ Open.

3. At the Filename prompt, type **school.ltr** and press Enter.

4. Press Save (F10) and then press Password (F8).

Choose File ▸ Save As ▸ Password.

5. Type **Uncle Fred** as the password, and press Enter. WordPerfect prompts you to reenter the password.

6. Type the same password again, and press Enter to accept it.

7. Press Exit (press F7 twice) to save the document with the password.

Choose OK.

8. When WordPerfect asks if you want to replace the existing file, choose Yes.

Your document is now protected by the password you've assigned.

REMEMBER. *Save the document after you've assigned the password. It is important that the file on disk includes the password change you've made to the document on screen.*

Now you'll clear the screen and retrieve the file again to see how the password works:

Choose File ▸ Close.

1. Press Exit (F7) and choose No twice to clear the screen.

Choose File ▸ Open.

2. Press Retrieve (Shift+F10) and enter **school.ltr** to retrieve the file.

3. WordPerfect prompts you to enter the password for this document. Type the password, **Uncle Fred**, and press Enter. The document is retrieved into the editing screen.

CAUTION! *Be very careful when using the Password feature. Make sure you keep a record of the passwords you've assigned. If you forget the password, there's absolutely no way to recover your document.*

The Password feature secures a file against unauthorized retrieval, printing, or viewing. It also prevents the file from being deleted or copied to another directory or disk, but only from within the WordPerfect software.

Changing the Password

If the password for your document is discovered or if you find it difficult to remember, you may need to change your password. Fortunately, this is easy to do. Just retrieve the file and assign a new password; this automatically replaces the old password. In the following exercise you will change the password that you assigned to the SCHOOL.LTR document. Make sure this file is displayed on the main document screen before you continue.

Choose File ▸
Save As.

1. Press Save (F10) and press Password (F8).

2. Type a new password to replace the old one, and press Enter. WordPerfect prompts you to reenter the new password.

3. Type the same password again, and press Enter to accept it.

4. Press Exit (press F7 twice) to save the file.

Choose OK to save
the file.

5. When WordPerfect asks if you want to replace the existing file, choose Yes.

When you save the file, the new password replaces the old one, and you'll need to enter the new password when you next retrieve the file. If you forget to save the file after changing the password, the old password will still apply to the file on disk.

It's wise to occasionally change passwords to ensure the security of your documents. However, if you change a password too often, you may forget it, in which case there is absolutely no way to recover your document for viewing, retrieval, or printing. So make sure you keep a record of the passwords you use, or use the same password for similar documents.

Removing a Password

Should a specific document no longer need the security that a password provides, the password can be removed as easily as it was assigned. To remove a password, first open the document. Press Save (F10) and press Password (F8). Choose the Remove (F6) option, and the password is removed from your document. Then save the document to replace the file on disk.

If this seems too easy, and you are worried that anyone could take the password from your file, there is no cause for alarm. Remember, you have to enter the password *before* you can open a password-protected file, and the only way to remove a password is by selecting Remove (F6) option while the file is displayed on the screen.

Anytime you want to reassign a password to a document, just follow the usual procedure for assigning a password.

Using the File Manager

If you are familiar with the DOS DIR command, you know that it displays a list of files stored on your disk. Other DOS commands, such as COPY, REN, and DEL, let you copy, rename, and delete files from the list. These features work well, but WordPerfect has a better way to manage your document files—with the File Manager feature.

The File Manager displays a list of all files stored in one directory. From this screen you can retrieve a file, copy it, move, delete, or rename it, and even print it. These features can also be performed on a group of files. You can search for files that contain specific words or phrases, view the contents of files before retrieving them, print copies of the directory list, create new directories, and delete empty ones. There is even an expanded file list available for displaying the descriptive document names from the Document Summary dialog box.

Because the File Manager provides all these powerful options from within WordPerfect, you don't have to exit to DOS to manage your files. You also work more efficiently, because the File Manager lets you quickly locate and retrieve specific documents. You can examine and print files without clearing the current document from your screen, and you can archive document files with accuracy and speed.

Displaying a Directory List

When you want to look at a list of files, press File Manager (F5), or choose File and then File Manager. The path name of the default directory or current directory appears on the Specify File Manager List dialog box. If this is the directory you want to see, press Enter to accept the path name, or type in a different directory path name. After you press Enter, the File Manager is displayed, as shown earlier in Figure 5.4.

Notice that the File Manager is divided into two parts: the list of files and a menu of options at the right side of the dialog box. At the top of the dialog box, you'll see the path name of the displayed directory and today's date. At the bottom of the dialog box, you'll see the amount of free and used space on your disk, and the number of files in the current directory.

The file list presents the files in alphabetical order—something DOS doesn't always do for you. The reverse-video bar in the list is used to highlight and select one of the files. You can use the arrow keys to move the bar, or move the mouse cursor onto the desired file name and click the left mouse button.

At the right edge of the dialog box, a menu displays the File Manager options from which you select the file operations you need to perform.

When you are finished using the directory list, you can return to the document screen by pressing either Exit (F7) or Cancel (Esc), or by choosing OK.

Searching for a File Name

The standard file list displays up to 19 files at once (more if you're using a 43- or 50-line display), but there's virtually no limit to the number of files you can store in a directory. When the number of files in your directory exceeds the amount that can be displayed on the screen at once, you can press ↓ to move the highlight bar cursor through the list. To scroll with a mouse, click on the scroll bar arrows next to the list.

A better way to move to a particular file is with the Name Search option. Name Search can help you quickly find a specific file name on a long list:

- First, choose <u>N</u>ame Search from the File Manager menu. This enables the Name Search box at the bottom of the screen.

- Begin typing the name of the file you want to find. As you type, the characters appear in the Name Search box, and WordPerfect highlights the file name that matches what you're typing.

- If you make a mistake, you can press the Backspace key to cancel the last character you typed.

When enough characters match, WordPerfect highlights the file you want. Then you can press Enter or an arrow key to turn off the Name Search mode. With the file name highlighted, you can now choose one of the file options from the File Manager menu.

Searching for Directory Names

You can also use Name Search to find a specific subdirectory in the list. Choose <u>N</u>ame Search to activate the Name Search box, and type a backslash (\) to indicate that you want to find a directory on the list. Then type the name of the directory, and WordPerfect highlights the directory name that matches the characters you're typing. Again, you can press Enter or an arrow key to turn off Name Search.

Viewing the Contents of a Document File

The Look option on the File Manager menu lets you view a document file without actually retrieving it into the document editing screen. This lets you verify that a file is the one you need before you retrieve it into the editing screen. Follow these steps to view the contents of a file in the list:

Choose File ▸ File Manager ▸ OK.

1. From the document screen, press File Manager (F5). Then press Enter to accept the directory path and open the File Manager.

2. On the File Manager dialog box, move the cursor to highlight a file on the list.

3. Choose Look from the File Manager menu, and the contents of the high-lighted file are displayed in the Look dialog box.

Figure 5.8 shows a document on the Look screen. A header at the top shows the file name of the displayed document, the type of file (such as WP 4.2, 5.0, 5.1, or 6.0), and the date and time that the file was last saved. A menu at the bottom lets you view the next or previous documents in the current directory, open or delete the displayed document, search for a word or phrase, or scroll through the text.

Figure 5.8

A document in the Look screen

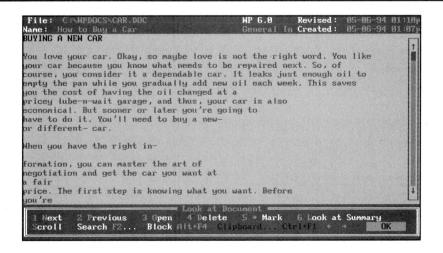

If the document you select from the File Manager has a document summary, the summary is displayed first as shown in Figure 5.9. You can then choose Look at Text to view the contents of the document. You can also choose Next or Previous to view the next document. Select Print Summary to print the document summary or Save to File to save the summary to a separate disk file.

Figure 5.9

A document summary in the Look screen

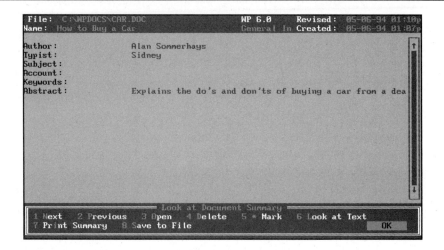

When you are finished viewing the document, press Exit (F7) or choose OK to return to the File Manager screen.

Using Other Options on the Look Screen

When you are viewing the contents of a document in the Look screen, you can either press the ↑ or ↓ keys, or click on the scroll bar arrows to scroll through the text. You can also type plus (+) to scroll down a screen or minus (–) to scroll up a screen. For faster scrolling in long documents, choose Scroll and the text scrolls up continuously until you press a key.

Sometimes, the font in a document causes text to extend beyond the right edge of the screen. (This often happens with proportionally spaced fonts.) You can press End to view the text that extends beyond the right edge, and then press End again to return to the left margin of your document.

If you are running WordPerfect from the Shell program (included with WordPerfect), you can also use the Block (Alt+F4) feature to "clip" document information from the Look screen:

■ Highlight a document in the File Manager list, and choose Look to display the contents of the document.

- Using the arrow keys, move the cursor to the beginning of the text line you want to clip, and press Block (Alt+F4).

- Move the cursor to the end of the text you want to clip, and press Shell (Ctrl+F1).

- A dialog box displays two options: <u>S</u>ave Block to Clipboard and <u>A</u>ppend Block to Clipboard. Choose <u>S</u>ave Block to Clipboard, and the blocked text is saved to WordPerfect's clipboard.

- Press Exit (F7) until you return to the document.

Choose OK until you return to your document.

- Press Shell (Ctrl+F1) and select <u>R</u>etrieve Clipboard from the menu.

The text you blocked at the Look screen is retrieved from the clipboard into your current document.

Moving and Renaming Files

WordPerfect lets you move and/or rename the files in a directory, and both of these features are found under one option on the File Manager menu: <u>M</u>ove/Rename. To try it follow these steps at your computer:

1. Display the File Manager and highlight the barely.doc file that you created earlier.

2. Choose <u>M</u>ove/Rename from the File Manager menu.

3. WordPerfect prompts you with New Name. To rename the document file, type **letter.doc** and press Enter.

WordPerfect changes the name of the highlighted file. You renamed one of the files on the list, but the Move/Rename option can also move the highlighted file to another directory. This is how you do it. First, highlight a file and choose <u>M</u>ove/Rename. If you enter a file name at the New Name prompt, WordPerfect renames the file. If you enter a path name at the prompt, Word-Perfect moves the file to that location. If you enter a path name *and* a new file name, WordPerfect renames the file and moves it to the new location.

Copying and Deleting Files

From the File Manager screen, you can copy files to other directory locations and delete unwanted files.

To copy a file:

- Highlight the file you want to copy.

- Choose <u>C</u>opy from the File Manager menu.

- WordPerfect prompts you with "Copy Highlighted File to." Type the path name where you want the copy to be placed, and press Enter.

WordPerfect makes a copy of the file and stores it in the directory that you specified. If you type a new file name, instead of a path name, you will create a copy of the file in the current directory under the new name.
To delete a file:

- Highlight the file that you want to remove from your directory.

- Choose Delete from the List Files menu.

- WordPerfect asks you to verify that you want to delete the designated file. Choose Yes, and the file is removed from your disk. If you choose No, WordPerfect cancels the operation.

CAUTION! *Be careful when you use the Delete feature; once you delete a file, you cannot restore it unless you have special data recovery software.*

Printing from the File Manager

WordPerfect provides two ways to print information while a directory list is displayed. To print the directory list itself, press Print (Shift+F7), or choose Print List from the File Manager. You'll see a "Please Wait" message and then WordPerfect sends a copy of the displayed file list to the printer. The printed copy includes the screen header, plus all file and directory names in the current directory.
You can also print a document from the File Manager. Just highlight the document you want to print, and choose Print from the File Manager menu. The Print Multiple Pages dialog box appears, in which you can choose the specific page numbers you want to print from the document. Then press Exit (F7) or choose OK. WordPerfect then sends the document to the printer.
For complete information about printing files from disk, see Chapter 4.

Copying, Deleting, or Moving a Group of Files

When you select a File Manager option, it usually affects only the highlighted file. However, there are situations where you'll want to copy, move, or delete a group of files on the list. At the File Manager screen you can *mark* several files and perform a file operation, such as copy or delete.
Here is the procedure for marking and manipulating a group of files:

- To mark a file, highlight the file name and type an asterisk (*). The asterisk appears next to the file name, indicating that it is marked. (To unmark a file name, simply highlight it and type * again.) Highlight and mark the other files that should be included in the group.

- When all files that you want to affect are marked, choose an option from the File Manager menu, such as <u>C</u>opy, <u>D</u>elete, or <u>M</u>ove.

- WordPerfect asks whether you want to perform the selected action on the marked files. Choose <u>Y</u>es and the action is performed.

NOTE. *To quickly mark all files on the File Manager screen, press Home, * (press and release Home, and then press the * key) or Alt+F5. To unmark all files, press Home, * or Alt+F5 again.*

For example, suppose you want to copy all your memo files from the current directory to a floppy disk. First, mark the files you want to copy. Choose <u>C</u>opy from the File Manager menu, and WordPerfect prompts you with "Copy marked files?" Choose <u>Y</u>es and you are prompted with "Copy Marked Files to." Type the path name for the directory where the files should be copied and press Enter. Copies of the marked files are stored in the directory you specified. You can follow this same procedure to delete or move a group of files from the displayed directory.

Finding Files with Specific Words and Phrases

When the File Manager screen is displayed, you can use the find options to locate documents that contain specific words and phrases. This is how you use the Find option: First, display the File Manager, and then choose <u>F</u>ind. WordPerfect displays the Find dialog box, shown in Figure 5.10.

Figure 5.10
The Find Files dialog box

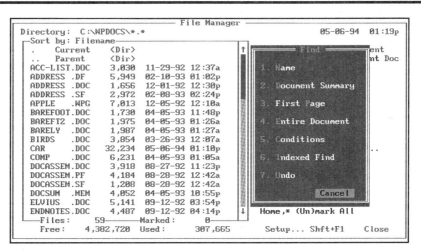

From this dialog box, you can choose one of the following options and locate files that meet a specific search criterion:

- To search for a document name, choose <u>N</u>ame and enter the name of the file you want to find.

- To find files that have specific information in a document summary, choose <u>D</u>ocument Summary and enter the word or phrase.

- Choose First <u>P</u>age, and enter a word or phrase to search only the first page of the documents in the list. This is the quickest way to find documents—such as memos—that contain key words on the first page.

- Choose <u>E</u>ntire Document and enter a word or phrase to search the complete text of all documents for a specific word or phrase.

- Choose <u>C</u>onditions to locate files with multiple search criteria. When you choose this option, you can enter different words or phrases for the first page text, the entire document, and all fields in the document summaries.

- Choose <u>I</u>ndexed Find to start WordPerfect's QuickFinder; the QuickFinder is explained later in the section "Using WordPerfect's QuickFinder."

When you type the word or phrase for a find option, you can create a word pattern by typing a question mark (?) to represent one character or an asterisk (*) to represent two or more characters. If, for example, you want to search for all files that contain the name "Anderson," but you aren't sure whether the name is speller "Ander*son*" or "Ander*sen*;" you can type **anders?n** and WordPerfect will find all documents that contain both "Anderson" and "Andersen." If you want to find all documents with the root word of "inform," you could enter **inform*** as the word pattern.

After you choose one of the find options and enter a word or phrase as the search criterion, WordPerfect searches through the displayed file list to find all files that match the word or phrase you typed. Then the file list is updated to show only those files that match. You can redisplay the complete (or original) file list by choosing <u>F</u>ind and then <u>U</u>ndo.

Sorting a Directory List

The File Manager usually displays all files alphabetically, but you can sort the file list according to the file name extensions, the date/time each file was created, or the byte size of the files. You can also choose to display only the WordPerfect document files.

From the File Manager, choose <u>S</u>ort by and WordPerfect displays the File Manager Setup dialog box. From this dialog box, choose <u>S</u>ort List by and then choose one of the following options: <u>F</u>ilename, <u>E</u>xtension, <u>D</u>ate/Time, or

Size. The N̲o Sort option displays the files in the order in which they appear on your hard disk; this is similar to the list you see when you use the DIR command at the DOS prompt to view your files.

From the File Manager Setup dialog box, choose the W̲P Documents Only option to show only WordPerfect documents on the file list. When you're finished choosing the setup options, press Exit (F7) or choose OK to return to the File Manager. WordPerfect updates the file list according to the sort options you selected.

Viewing Another Directory's Files

When you are finished working with the files in one directory, but need to continue your work in another directory, you can change to a different directory. The following exercise shows you how:

1. Select C̲hange Default Dir from the File Manager menu. You'll see a New Directory prompt at the bottom of the screen, followed by the current directory path name.

2. Type the path name of the directory you wish to view, and press Enter. For example, enter **c:** to view the root directory of drive C. (If you are working with floppy drives, type **a:** and press Enter to view the files on the disk in drive A, or enter **b:** for drive B.)

3. The path name is initially displayed with the pattern for all files (*.*). Press Enter to accept this, and all the files of the new directory are displayed on the File Manager screen.

In this example, the file name pattern *.* is displayed after the path name, which means that all files in the new directory will be displayed. The asterisks in the pattern act as wildcard characters and represent any combination of characters that precede or follow the period that separates the file name from the file extension.

To indicate another file name pattern, press End to move the cursor to the end of the pattern, press Backspace to delete the *.* characters, and type a new pattern.

For example, if you want to view only the files with a .WPG extension, replace the *.* with ***.wpg.** Suppose you want to be more specific and list only these files: REP-23.RPT, REP-27.RPT, REP-50.RPT, and REP-57.RPT. You'd need to enter REP-*.RPT as the pattern. Only the files that match the pattern will be displayed on the List Files screen for the new directory.

TIP. *When you use the Change Default Directory dialog box to view a new list of files, the path name you enter will become the new default directory during the rest of the current editing session. If you don't want this to happen,*

change the default directory by highlighting the directory name and selecting
Look to view the files in that directory.

Shortcuts for Viewing a Directory

Near the top of the File Manager screen, you'll see two labels, Current <Dir>
and Parent <Dir>. The first label, Current <DIR>, represents the directory
that is currently displayed. You can highlight this label and press Enter to
change the directory to be displayed.

This can be useful if you want to view the contents of several floppy disks.
For example, place the first floppy disk in drive A, choose Change Default Dir,
and enter **a:** as the drive. The directory of files on the disk in drive A will be
displayed. Next, replace the disk in drive A with a different disk. This time, instead of selecting Change Default Dir, you can highlight the Current <Dir>
line and press Enter to redisplay the directory for drive A.

When you are viewing a hard disk directory or subdirectory on the File
Manager screen, you can highlight the Parent <Dir> label and press Enter
twice to display the directory one level up from the current list of files (the
parent directory). In the File Manager, the <Dir> label in the file list indicates
a directory or subdirectory in the current list. You can quickly display the files
of any of these directories by highlighting it and pressing Enter.

Redisplaying the Previous Directory List

You can quickly redisplay the File Manager screen from the document editing
screen. Just press F5 twice and WordPerfect shows the last directory list that
was displayed, exactly as it appeared before you exited to the document screen.

Creating a New Directory

There will be times when you need to create a new directory or subdirectory
to accommodate a new group of files. You can do this from the File Manager
screen. Select Change Default Dir from the File Manager menu. "New Directory" appears on the screen, followed by the current directory path name.
Type the path name of your new directory—one that does not yet exist—and
press Enter. WordPerfect recognizes that the path name you entered doesn't
exist and asks if you want to create it. Choose Yes, and WordPerfect creates
the directory for you.

The new directory is not automatically displayed, because it doesn't contain any files. After you've copied or saved files to the new path name, select
Change Default Dir again, and view the contents of the new directory.

Viewing a Directory Tree

WordPerfect provides an option that lets you view your files according to the hard disk directory structure—called a *directory tree*—instead of a list of files. Figure 5.11 shows how a directory tree will look on your screen.

Figure 5.11

The File Manager with a directory tree

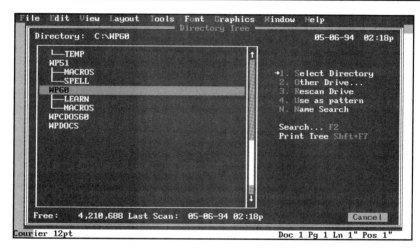

To view a directory tree, press File Manager (F5) or choose File and then File Manager from the menu bar. When the Specify File Manager List dialog box is displayed, choose Directory Tree (F8). WordPerfect then displays the File Manager with a directory tree instead of a file list.

You can press the arrow keys or use the scroll bar to move through the directory structure. When a directory name is highlighted, you can press Enter to display the list of files for that directory. When you are finished with the directory tree, press Exit (F7) or choose Close to return to the document screen.

Using Descriptive Directory Names

WordPerfect's QuickList feature lets you assign descriptive names to the directories where your files are stored. Then you can look up files by selecting them from the descriptive list—called a *quicklist*—instead of browsing through different directories until you find the files you need. Figure 5.12 shows the QuickList dialog box, where the descriptive directory names are listed. Each item in this list represents a directory of files on your hard disk.

Figure 5.12

The QuickList dialog box

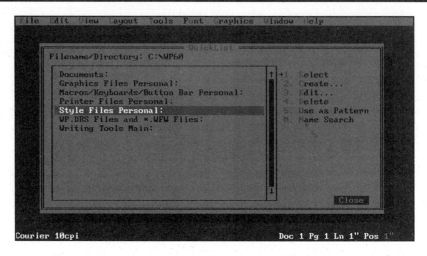

Suppose you want to view all of the graphics files that you use with Word-Perfect. You don't need to look through different directories until you find the right list of files. Simply display the QuickList dialog box and select "Graphic Files Personal." WordPerfect then displays the list of all graphics files assigned to this QuickList item.

The following steps explain how to use the QuickList feature to assign a descriptive name to the C:\FILES directory that you created earlier in this chapter:

1. Press File Manager (F5). Then choose QuickList (F6).

Choose File ▸ File Manager ▸ QuickList.

2. From the QuickList dialog box, choose Create, and WordPerfect displays the dialog box shown in Figure 5.13.

3. Type **WordPerfect Document Files** as the descriptive name for the directory. Then press Enter. The cursor moves to the Filename/Directory field.

4. Type **c:\files** as the directory name that contains the files to which you want to assign the descriptive name. Then press Enter. In this example, you type a directory path name, but you can also enter a file name pattern, such as **c:\files*.doc**, to assign only the files that match a specific pattern.

Choose OK to return to the Quick-List dialog box.

5. Press Exit (F7) to return to the QuickList dialog box. The descriptive name "WordPerfect Document Files" now appears on the list.

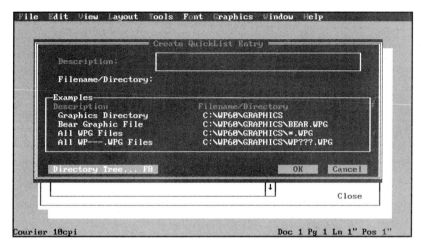

Figure 5.13
Creating a QuickList item

Double-click on the WordPerfect Document Files item.

6. Highlight the WordPerfect Document Files item, and choose Select, or simply press Enter. WordPerfect displays the files stored in the C:\FILES directory.

You can display QuickList from most dialog boxes where you need to specify or select a file name. You can, for example, press Open/Retrieve (Shift+F10) and choose QuickList (F6). Once the QuickList dialog is displayed, you can choose a descriptive name from the QuickList items, and WordPerfect displays the file list assigned to that name.

If you need to change the descriptive name or file list assigned to a quick-list item, first highlight the item you want to change on the QuickList dialog box. Then choose Edit and enter a new Description or Filename/Directory. When you return to the QuickList dialog box, WordPerfect updates the QuickList item to include your changes.

Using WordPerfect's QuickFinder

WordPerfect's QuickFinder provides a fast and easy way to index and locate any text saved in your document files. This feature is ideal for bibliographers, writers, educators, and librarians who keep a large number of documents stored on their computers. Unlike the Find feature on the File Manager, the QuickFinder uses one or more text indexes to instantly locate the text you want to find.

Creating a QuickFinder Index

Before you can use the QuickFinder, you need to create an index of the directories or file groups that you want to search. Each QuickFinder index contains an alphabetical list of all unique words found in your files and records where each of these words are found.

Choose File ▸ File
Manager.

1. Press File Manager (F5) to display the File Manager dialog box.

2. Press Use QuickFinder (F4), and then choose Setup (Shift+F1). WordPerfect displays the dialog box shown in Figure 5.14.

Figure 5.14

Setting up a
QuickFinder Index

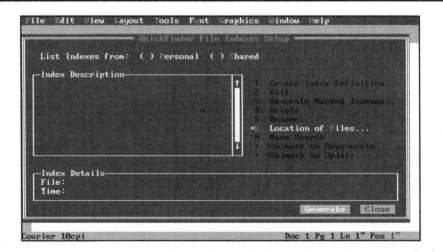

3. Choose Location of Files, choose Personal Path, and enter the name of the directory where you want to save the index files. Most people will want to enter C:\WP60 at this prompt to create the index files in their WordPerfect directories.

Choose OK to
continue.

4. After you enter the personal path or shared path information, press Exit (F7) to continue.

5. Choose Personal to switch to the personal index list. Then choose Create Index Definition.

6. At the Create Index Definition dialog box, type a descriptive name for the current QuickFinder index. Type a description, like "Tax Records, 1994," that indicates the type of files the index will search. Then press Enter.

7. The cursor moves to the Index Filename field and condenses the index description to create an eight-character file name. Press Enter to accept this name, or type a new name and press Enter. Note that an .IDX extension is automatically added to the file name.

8. Choose Add to accept the new index definition. WordPerfect prompts you to enter a file name pattern. This can be a directory name, like C:\FILES, or a full path name with a pattern, like C:\FILES*.DOC, that specifies certain files.

9. After you enter the file name pattern, choose Include Subdirectories if you want to index to also search in the subdirectories within the specified directory/path.

Choose OK to continue.

10. Press Exit (F7) to return to the Create Index Definition dialog box. You can repeat steps 8 and 9 to add other directories and file name patterns to the index.

11. When you are finished defining the index, press Exit (F7) until you re-turn to the QuickFinder dialog box.

12. From the QuickFinder dialog box, choose Generate Marked Indexes. WordPerfect examines each of the files specified by the index definition and catalogs each unique word in an alphabetized list.

NOTE. *The Shared Path option lets you specify a directory that will be shared by different people running WordPerfect from a network server.*

After the indexing process is finished, WordPerfect displays QuickFinder File Indexer dialog box. At this point, you're ready to use the QuickFinder feature.

Using the QuickFinder to Locate Files

After you've created QuickFinder indexes, you can use them to locate any text in your document files. These steps explain how to use the QuickFinder feature:

Choose File ▸ File Manager.

1. Press File Manager (F5) or choose File and then File Manager from the menu bar.

2. Choose Use QuickFinder (F4) to display the QuickFinder File Indexer, shown in Figure 5.15.

3. Type a word, phrase, or pattern that represents the text you want to find. Or choose Operators (F5) to create a logical statement that indicates the text you want to file. Then press Enter.

Figure 5.15
The QuickFinder File
Indexer

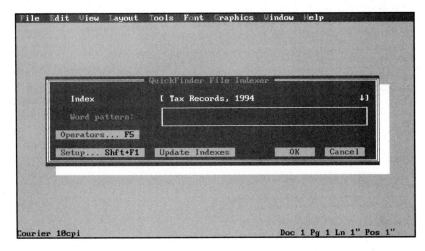

4. Press Exit (F7) to continue.

WordPerfect instantly displays a list of all files that contain the text, specified by the word pattern you entered.

Choose OK to
continue.

Editing the QuickFinder Indexes

If you later want to create additional QuickFinder indexes or edit existing indexes, simply display the QuickFinder File Indexer dialog box again and choose the Setup (Shift+F1) option. Follow the steps listed above to create additional indexes. To edit an existing index, highlight it on the list and choose Edit; then make whatever changes you need to apply to the index. When you're finished creating or editing indexes, press Exit (F7) until you return to the QuickFinder File Indexes Setup dialog box, and choose the Generate Marked Indexes option to regenerate your indexes. This last step is important; otherwise the QuickFinder will not recognize the changes you've made to the indexes.

Updating the QuickFinder Indexes

After you create new document files or edit existing files, you need to update the QuickFinder indexes. This includes any new text as part of the indexes that the QuickFinder uses to search through your files. To update the indexes:

■ Press File Manager (F5) or choose File and then File Manager from the menu bar.

- Choose Use QuickFinder (F4). Press Tab to highlight the Update Indexes option, and then press Enter.

WordPerfect regenerates the indexes you've defined for the QuickFinder and includes any additional text you've added to your document files. If you don't update your indexes, the changes made to your documents and any new documents will not be included in a QuickFinder search.

Automatic Backup Features

WordPerfect includes two backup features that help protect you against file loss from a power failure or computer problem. The first feature, Timed Document Backup, makes regular backup copies of your documents, so that you can restore a file that you were editing when a computer failure occurred. Original Document Backup automatically makes a backup copy of the original file each time you save a revised version of it. This guarantees that you'll always be able to retrieve the previous version of a file after you've edited and saved it.

Backing Up at Regular Intervals

Although computers are powerful tools, they are vulnerable to power failures and static electricity. At some point, you may experience a computer or electrical problem that prevents you from saving your document and exiting WordPerfect properly. With WordPerfect's Timed Document Backup feature, you can concentrate on your documents and not worry about equipment failure. Timed Document Backup makes backup copies of your document at regular timed intervals, ensuring that you can recover the document if a computer failure does occur.

CAUTION! *The Timed Document Backup feature does* not, *however, eliminate the need to regularly save your documents and make floppy disk backup copies as a precaution against disk failure. This is very important!*

When you properly exit the program, WordPerfect deletes its timed backup file, because it assumes you've had the chance to save your document before exiting. If, however, you cannot or do not use the Exit command to properly exit WordPerfect, the timed backup file remains in place. It is this file you can retrieve to recover your document.

This is the procedure for turning on the Timed Document Backup feature. Once you enable this option, it remains active until you turn it off again.

- Press Setup (Shift+F1) and choose Environment.

Choose File ▸ Setup
▸ Environment.

■ Choose Backup Options. The menu shown in Figure 5.16 appears.

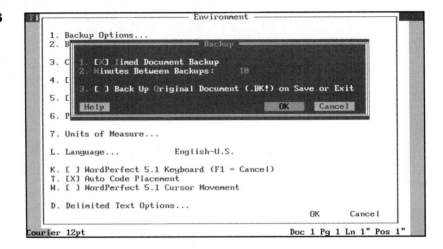

Figure 5.16

Setting
WordPerfect's
backup options

■ Choose the first option, Timed Document Backup, to turn it on. An *X* should now appear in the box next to this option.

Choose OK.

■ Choose the next option, Minutes between Backups. Enter the backup interval in minutes. For example, if you want WordPerfect to backup your files every 20 minutes, type **20** and press Enter. The default time is 10 minutes.

■ Press Exit (F7) to return to the document screen.

With Timed Document Backup enabled each time the backup interval passes, the document on your screen is saved to a temporary backup file. For example, if you entered 20 minutes as the interval between backups, Word-Perfect backs up your document every 20 minutes. When this occurs, you'll see a "Please Wait" message while WordPerfect saves the file. As you work with the file, it is updated at regular intervals, so you can recover a relatively current version of the document if necessary.

If the Timed Document Backup feature becomes a nuisance, and you are constantly waiting while WordPerfect backs up your documents, you may want to change the interval between backups or perhaps turn off the Timed Document Backup feature altogether. To do this, follow the same steps you took to turn on Timed Document Backup. Choosing Timed Document Backup again turns off the feature. Then press Exit (F7) to return to the document screen, and the new backup settings become active.

Retrieving a Backup File

WordPerfect creates a temporary backup file for each document you retrieve. Each file is named WP{WPC}.BKn, where n is the number of the document screen that is open. The WP{WPC}.BKn backup files are all deleted when you properly exit WordPerfect. However, if you experience a computer problem that prevents you from exiting the program, the backup file remains on disk.

NOTE. *Backup files are stored in the WordPerfect directory unless you've specified a backup directory with the Setup, Location of Files option, which is explained in Appendix A.*

When you start WordPerfect again, the "Backup File Exists" message box appears on the screen to let you know that you can recover a backup file. You can choose one of three options before you continue: Rename, Delete, or Open. Choose Rename to save the backup file as a regular document file, choose Delete to remove the backup file, or choose Open to retrieve the file into WordPerfect. If there were two or more files open when you last used WordPerfect, you will be prompted to rename, delete, or open each of the backup files on disk.

Backing Up the Original Document File

The Original Document Backup feature lets you keep a copy of the previous version of an edited file. Suppose you are editing a business report, and you delete a paragraph of text that contains old sales figures from ten years ago. After you finish editing the file, you save it under the same file name and replace the previous version of the file. Then you discover that the paragraph you deleted is your only record of that particular sales data. If you are using the Original Document Backup feature, however, WordPerfect will have saved a copy of the original file under a different file name when you saved the edited version of the report. You can retrieve this original file and thus recover the sales figures.

This is only one example of how Original Document Backup can help you. It is also valuable for documents that need to be edited by a group of users, because it guarantees that you'll always have a copy of the previous version of a document.

To turn on Original Document Backup:

- Press Setup (Shift+F1), and choose Environment.

- Choose Backup Options, and then choose Back Up Original Document (BK!) on Save or Exit.

Choose File ▸ Setup ▸ Environment.

Choose OK.

■ Press Exit (F7) to return to the editing screen.

Now, whenever you save and replace a document file, WordPerfect automatically makes a copy and saves it as *Name*.BK!, where *Name* is the original file name.

Managing Original Backup Files

If you plan to use the Original Document Backup feature, you'll want to avoid creating files with names like REPORT.1, REPORT.2, and REPORT.3. Notice that these file names are identical, except for the extension, which is the only thing that makes each file name unique. This file-naming style can cause you problems, because WordPerfect uses the original file name but replaces the extension with BK! to create the backup file.

For example, when you retrieve a file named REPORT.1, WordPerfect makes a copy under the file name REPORT.BK!. If you later retrieve RE-PORT.2 and REPORT.3, WordPerfect will use the same file name, RE-PORT.BK!, to make backups of these documents, too, thus replacing the backup of REPORT.1. Consider, however, these file names: REPORT-1.DOC, REPORT-2.DOC, and REPORT-3.DOC. For these, WordPerfect would create backup files called REPORT-1.BK!, REPORT-2.BK!, and REPORT-3.BK!, so each file would have its own unique original backup.

Keep in mind that the Original Document Backup option makes backup copies each time a file is retrieved, and, unlike the temporary timed backup files, WordPerfect does not delete original backup files when you exit the program. Therefore, if you use the Original Document Backup feature everyday, you will eventually have duplicate files of every document you've edited since Original Document Backup was turned on. This will consume a great deal of disk space. If you frequently use this feature, it's wise to regularly delete the *.BK! files from your disk drive after you know that you won't need them.

Specifying a Backup Directory

Backup files are usually created in the WordPerfect directory, but you can indicate a specific path name for storing these files. Here's an exercise in which you'll designate a backup directory:

Choose File ▸ Setup ▸ Location of Files.

1. Press Setup (Shift+F1) and choose Location of Files to display the dialog box shown in Figure 5.17.

2. Select Backup Files, type the path name where you want the backup files to be stored, and press Enter. For example, you may want all backup files saved to the C:\FILES directory. If so, type **c:\files** and press Enter.

Choose OK.

3. Press Exit (F7) until you return to the document screen.

Figure 5.17

Designating a directory for backup files

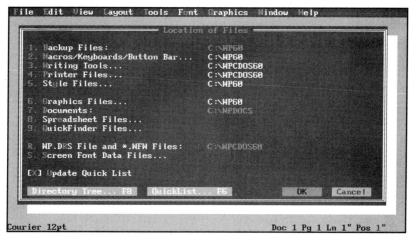

```
File  Edit  View  Layout  Tools  Font  Graphics  Window  Help
┌─────────────────────── Location of Files ───────────────────────┐
│ 1. Backup Files:                         C:\WP60                 │
│ 2. Macros/Keyboards/Button Bar...        C:\WP60                 │
│ 3. Writing Tools...                      C:\WPCDOS60             │
│ 4. Printer Files...                      C:\WPCDOS60             │
│ 5. Style Files...                        C:\WP60                 │
│                                                                  │
│ 6. Graphics Files...                     C:\WP60                 │
│ 7. Documents:                            C:\WPDOCS               │
│ 8. Spreadsheet Files...                                          │
│ 9. QuickFinder Files...                                          │
│                                                                  │
│ R. WP.DRS File and *.WFW Files:          C:\WPCDOS60             │
│ S. Screen Font Data Files...                                     │
│                                                                  │
│ [X] Update Quick List                                            │
│  Directory Tree... F8    QuickList... F6         OK    Cancel    │
└──────────────────────────────────────────────────────────────────┘
Courier 12pt                                   Doc 1 Pg 1 Ln 1" Pos 1"
```

Now all backup files will be stored in the directory path you entered. This setting remains operative until you change it again at the Location of Files dialog box.

Archiving Document Files

Archiving files is different from using WordPerfect's automatic Backup features. When you use the Backup features, WordPerfect creates temporary files that will eventually be deleted. In contrast, archiving is the process of copying inactive files to another location or disk, with the intent of storing them as records or references for future use. The following sections explain how to archive your document files to floppy disks.

Copying Your Files to an Archive Disk

Archiving is important because it clears your hard disk of long-unused files, yet you still have copies—on floppy disks—of files you may need for future reference. Here are the steps to follow when you need to archive your document files:

1. Put a blank formatted disk into drive A of your computer.

Choose File ▶ File Manager.

2. Press File Manager (F5).

3. Press Enter to accept the current directory, or enter the name of the directory that contains the files you want to archive.

4. For each file you want to archive, first highlight the file and then type an asterisk (*) to mark it. (If you are archiving an entire directory, you can mark all files by pressing Home and typing *, or by simply pressing Alt+F5.)

5. Choose Copy from the File Manager menu.

6. At the Copy marked files? prompt, choose Yes.

7. At the "Copy Marked Files to" prompt, type **a:** and press Enter. Each marked file is copied to the disk in drive A.

NOTE.   *If, while you are copying files, you fill up the first disk, WordPerfect will prompt you to replace it with another blank formatted disk.*

After the files are copied, you can use the Delete option on the File Manager screen to remove the archived files from your hard disk. However, before you do so, you should verify that the files were correctly copied to the disk in drive A.

8. Choose Change Default Dir, type **a:** and press Enter. This displays the files you copied to drive A.

9. Verify that the files were correctly copied, making sure the file names and file sizes are correct.

10. Choose Change Default Dir again, and type **c:** (or the drive letter where the original files are still stored). Press Enter.

11. Mark the archived files again, and choose Delete on the File Manager menu.

12. WordPerfect prompts you with "Delete marked files?" Choose Yes to confirm the deletion, and the files are removed from the directory.

CAUTION!   *Before you delete any original files, it's important to verify that the files are archived correctly. WordPerfect does a fine job of moving files around, but there are several possibilities for computer error.*

If you delete original files without first checking the archived files carefully, you may lose some valuable data and time, so be cautious. When you suspect a problem, try copying the files again, or use a new floppy disk.

How Many Disks Do I Need?

Here's a tip for estimating how many floppy disks you'll need for archiving your files. When you mark files on the File Manager dialog box, WordPerfect displays the total byte size for all the marked files. (Look for this information after the Used label at the bottom of the screen.) Divide this number by the maximum storage capacity of the disks type you're using, and the result is a close estimate of the number of disks you'll need.

For example, suppose you've marked 20 files, and their total byte size in the Used field is 3,295,043, or about 3.3MB. If each of your floppies can store 720,000 bytes (720K), you'll need about five disks. Remember—this is only an estimate. Because your file sizes will vary, you probably won't be able to fit the same number of files on each disk, so always keep one or two extra disks ready.

Editing Your Documents

High-Powered Editing Tools

Using the Speller, Thesaurus, and Other Writing Tools

Alphabetizing and Other Sort Operations

2

**Editing the Document
Text and Format**

6

Editing Your Documents

WORDPERFECT INCLUDES MANY TOOLS THAT ARE DEDICATED TO editing. Mastering these tools is as important for you as learning how to type text, change margins, and select a new font. After you've created a document layout and typed the text, there are dozens of adjustments you can make to refine and perfect your document. You may need to delete a paragraph, or repeatedly copy and edit a passage of text. Sometimes you'll want to rearrange information. Now that you know how to insert formatting codes, you'll also need to know how to view and edit them.

This chapter will help you become proficient with editing the text and format of your documents. The chapter begins with an overview of important cursor movement commands. Then you'll learn how to delete text from your document—and how to restore text you've deleted. You'll also explore techniques for moving and copying passages of text, and you'll use WordPerfect's Block feature to select a section of text for editing and other tasks.

You will discover how the Reveal Codes window helps you work with the invisible codes that you've used to create your document format. You'll also see how to perform simple tasks with paragraphs, including how to protect certain text from being separated by page breaks.

Before you continue, you'll need to create a document for the editing exercises. First, clear the screen (press F7 and choose <u>N</u>o twice) and type a few paragraphs of text. Figure 6.1 shows a full page of text you can use as a sample document. You can type this entire page now or only a few of the paragraphs. If you prefer, retrieve another document that you have already saved to a file on disk. To do this, press Open (Shift+F10) or choose <u>F</u>ile and then <u>O</u>pen from the menu bar. Type the name of the file you want to open, and press Enter.

Cursor Movement for Text Editing

If you prefer to use the mouse pointer, moving the cursor is a simple task; just move the pointer to the place in your text where you want to reposition the cursor, and click the mouse button to move the cursor to the pointer's location. (If the text you want to move to is not currently visible on the screen, you can use the scroll bars to get there. See "Scrolling with the Mouse" later in this chapter for details.) If you prefer to use the keyboard, the following sections will give you some practice with the cursor movement keystrokes. As you work with the cursor movement keys, you'll learn a few tricks for moving the cursor more efficiently. When you master these simple procedures, you'll be ready to do the other editing tasks in this chapter.

Figure 6.1

Sample text for use with editing exercises

Buying a New Car

You love your car. Okay, so maybe *love* is not the right word. You like your car because you know what needs to be repaired next. So, of course, you consider it a dependable car. It leaks just enough oil to empty the pan while you gradually add new oil each week; this saves you the cost of having the oil changed at a pricey lube-n-wait garage, and thus, your car is also economical. But sooner or later you're going to have to do it. You'll need to buy a new—or *different*—car.

When you have the right information, you can master the art of negotiation and get the car you want at a fair price. The first step is knowing what you want. Before you're seduced by the sheen of perfect paint and the smell of virgin naugahyde, carefully consider the type of car you need. Don't fall in love with a specific car (hey, it's just metal and interest payments!); be prepared to go with another model if you can't strike a deal with your current choice. Then, visit the dealerships and compare the cars you've selected.

The sticker price is generally 10% to 20% higher than the dealer cost. When you know the price the dealer paid for the car, negotiations can begin at this amount, rather than working down from the sticker price. There are several agencies that provide the dealer cost for specific models, including the costs for optional equipment. Most agencies charge a modest fee, but it's worth the investment. Carefully examine sticker prices for added expenses. Watch for additional fees that cover processing, advertising, and general preparation—these services are part of the dealer's business overhead and shouldn't be added as a fee on the sticker price. Also, beware of dollar amounts labeled with acronyms like ADM or ADP; these stand for "Additional Dealer Markup" and "Additional Dealer Profit," meaning that the dealer has added this amount to increase the profit margin.

When you get serious about buying, visit the dealership at the end of the month. At this time, the salesperson will be more likely to negotiate because he'll want to meet or surpass a monthly sales quota. Don't discuss trading or financing until you settle on a firm price. The salesperson won't like this, but if you're sincere, he'll tolerate you because he wants to sell you a car. If the salesperson knows your current vehicle is included in on the deal, he'll give you a fair price for your old car, in exchange for the full dealership price on the new car.

If you need to finance, shop for auto loans at a bank or credit union. In most cases, dealerships make a higher profit from auto financing than from the actual sale of automobiles. Many dealerships offer low financing rates, which can sometimes save you hundreds of dollars, but low financing is often restricted to specific models. Your negotiation power is much stronger when you don't involve the dealer in the financing.

Moving the Cursor Right, Left, Up, and Down

The most basic cursor movement keystrokes are the arrow keys: →, ←, ↑, and ↓. Press → and the cursor moves one character to the right; press ← and the cursor moves one character to the left. As you press → and ← keys, notice that the number after the *Pos* indicator (on the status line) changes to indicate the distance between the cursor and the left edge of the page.

Press ↑ and the cursor moves up to the previous line of the document; press ↓ and the cursor moves to the next line down. As you press these two arrow keys, the number after the status line's *Ln* indicator shows the distance between the cursor and the top of the page.

The Home key lets you magnify the effects of the arrow keys. For example, press Home and then press → to move the cursor to the right edge of the line; pressing the End key does the same thing. Press Home, ← to move the cursor to the left edge of the current line. Pressing Home, ↑ moves the cursor to the top of the displayed screen; pressing Home, ↓ moves the cursor to the bottom of the screen. If the text cursor is already at the top or bottom of the screen, pressing either Home, ↑ or Home, ↓ will display the next screen of text.

Now let's try all these keystrokes. For this exercise, you should have at least one-half page of text on your screen—that is, the current document should have enough text to fill the entire screen.

1. Press → several times to move the cursor to the right. Then hold down the → key, and watch the cursor move forward through the text until you release the → key.

2. Press ← to move the cursor to the left. Hold down the ← key, and the cursor moves backward through the text until you release the ← key.

3. Press ↑ to move up to the previous line of text. To scroll up through the text, hold down the ↑ key.

4. Press ↓ to move down to the next line. Hold down the ↓ key, and the cursor scrolls down through your text until you release the ↓ key.

5. Press and release the Home key, and then press →. This moves the cursor to the right end of the current text line. (You can also press End to perform this same action.)

6. Press Home, ← to move the cursor to the beginning, or left end, of the current line.

7. To move the cursor to the top of the displayed screen of text, press and release the Home key, and then press the ↑ key.

8. Press Home, ↓ to move the cursor to the bottom of the screen.

The Home, → and Home, ← keystrokes position the cursor so that you can add new text to the current line or paragraph. Pressing Home, ←, for example, places the cursor at the beginning of the text line but *after* any formatting codes that begin the line, excluding tabs and indents. Pressing Home, → or the End key places the cursor at the end of the current text line, on the code that ends the line ([SRt] or [HRt]). (If there are multiple formatting codes at the end of the line, pressing Home, → or the End key places the cursor on the first of these codes.) If you then type text, it is placed on the current line, provided that there's room for it.

TIP. *If you want to move the cursor before any formatting codes that begin the line, press Home, Home, Home, ←.*

There will be times when you'll want more control over the distance for cursor movement than is allowed by the arrow and Home+arrow keystrokes. As you'll see next, WordPerfect also lets you move the cursor one word or one paragraph at a time.

Moving to the Next Word or Paragraph

Two of the most useful WordPerfect keystrokes are called Word Right and Word Left. These keystrokes move the cursor right or left to the first character of the next or previous word, and can save you time as you move the cursor through the text. Word Right and Word Left are easy keystrokes to remember: Just hold down the Ctrl key and press → or ←. Ctrl+→ moves the cursor to the next word on the right, and Ctrl+← moves the cursor to the previous word on the left.

You can also move the cursor to the beginning of the next or previous paragraph in your document by pressing the Ctrl key with the ↓ and ↑ keys.

Move the cursor to the middle of the text on your screen, and try this exercise:

1. Hold down the Ctrl key and press →. Notice that the cursor moves to the beginning of the next word at the right of the cursor. (If the cursor is at the end of the line, Ctrl+→ moves it to the first word on the next line.)

2. Press Ctrl+←, and the cursor moves to the beginning of the word located at the left of the cursor. (If the cursor is at the beginning of the line, Ctrl+← moves it to the last word on the previous line.)

3. Hold down the Ctrl key and press ↑. The cursor moves to the beginning of the previous paragraph.

4. Press Ctrl+↓, and the cursor moves to the beginning of the next paragraph in the document.

Moving through the Pages

WordPerfect provides three ways to move through the pages of your documents: You can move to the top of each page, you can scroll through the text in half-page increments, or you can instruct WordPerfect to move directly to a specific page number.

Remember, WordPerfect automatically inserts soft page breaks into the document to indicate where each page ends and begins. A soft page break appears on the editing screen as a single line. A hard page break is something you can insert (press Ctrl+Enter) to end a page at a specific point. To move through your document one page at a time, you can press PgDn to move to the top of the next page or PgUp to move to the top of the previous page. With Num Lock turned off, you can press the plus key (+) on the numeric keypad to display the next screen of text. Press the minus key (–) on the numeric keypad, and the cursor moves to the previous screen of text.

For documents with several pages, you can also tell WordPerfect to go to a specific page. This is conveniently called the Go To feature, and here's how it works:

Choose Edit ▸ Go To.

- Press Go To (Ctrl+Home) to display the Go To dialog box.

- In the Go To dialog box, type the number of the page you want to see, and press Enter. WordPerfect displays the page with your cursor at the top.

- Alternatively, type a character to move the cursor just after the next occurrence of that character. (Note that WordPerfect is case sensitive in this context.)

That's all you need to do. In longer documents, Go To is the quickest way to move to a specific page. If your document is only three or four pages long, the PgUp/PgDn keys are the most efficient way to get to the page you want.

Scrolling with the Mouse

In addition to the PgUp/PgDn keys and the Go To feature, you can use WordPerfect's *scroll bars* to move through the pages of your document. You must have a mouse to use this feature. There are two scroll bars you can display and use: a vertical scroll bar and a horizontal scroll bar. Figure 6.2 shows how the scroll bars look on the screen. You can display the scroll bars with the Screen Setup menu (press Ctrl+F3 and then press Shift+F1), or from the View pull-down menu (choose View and then Vertical Scroll Bar, or View and then Horizontal Scroll Bar).

Figure 6.2

WordPerfect's scroll
bars

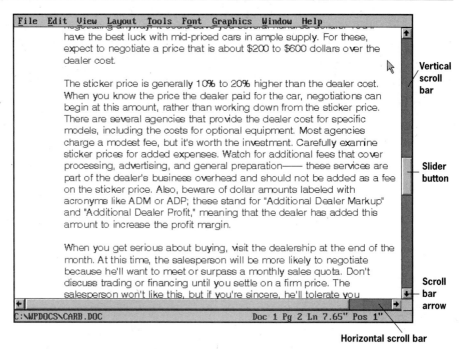

The illustration shows the scroll bars on WordPerfect's graphics screen, but you can display and use them with the text display mode screen, also. When a scroll bar is displayed, you'll see an arrow icon at each end of the bar. The length of the bar represents the entire area in your document through which you can scroll. The box within the scroll bar, called the *slider button*, represents the section of your document that is now shown on your screen. As you scroll through the text, the slider button moves to show you where you are within the document. (Note that the smaller your document, the larger the slider button.)

When a scroll bar is displayed, you can do one of the following to scroll through your text:

- Click on a scroll bar arrow to scroll the text in that direction. For example, to scroll down, move the mouse pointer over the bottom arrow on the vertical scroll bar, and then click the mouse button. WordPerfect moves the cursor one line for each click on a scroll bar arrow.

- Drag the slider button inside of the scroll bar to quickly jump to another place in the document. For example, to move to the middle of the document, move the mouse pointer over the slider button. Then, while holding down the mouse button, drag the slider to the center of the scroll bar. When you release the mouse button, WordPerfect displays the middle page in your document.

■ Click inside of a gray area within the scroll bar to move up (if you click above the slider button) or down (if you click below the slider button) one screen at a time. You can also click and *hold down* the mouse button to quickly scroll to that place in your document.

Use the vertical scroll bar to scroll through your document pages; use the horizontal scroll bar to scroll across and view text that extends past the right edge of the screen.

Try these steps to display and use the vertical scroll bar:

Choose <u>V</u>iew ▸ <u>V</u>ertical Scroll Bar.

1. Press Screen (Ctrl+ F3) and then press Setup (Shift+F1). Choose <u>Win</u>dow Options and then <u>V</u>ertical Scroll Bar. Press Exit (F7) until you return to the document screen.

2. Move the mouse pointer over the arrow at the bottom of the scroll bar. Then click the mouse button several times to scroll through your text.

3. Move the mouse pointer over the slider button between the top and bottom arrows. Then hold down the mouse button and drag the slider to the top of the scroll bar. This moves the cursor to the beginning of the document.

4. Click inside the gray area between the slider button and the bottom scroll bar arrow. WordPerfect scrolls the text down a screenful. If you hold down the mouse button, the slider button moves to the place where you clicked.

Remember that the vertical scroll bar is used to move vertically through your document. The horizontal scroll bar is used to scroll across the page when your text goes beyond the left or right edge of your screen. When you are finished using the scroll bars, choose <u>V</u>ertical Scroll Bar or <u>H</u>orizontal Scroll Bar again to remove them from the screen.

Moving to the End of the Paragraph or Page

To move to the end of the current paragraph, press Go To (Ctrl+Home) and then press Enter. This moves the cursor past the next occurrence of the Hard Return code [HRt], which is inserted when you press Enter to end a paragraph. (Choosing Go To, Enter also stops at Hard Return codes inserted as blank lines; in WordPerfect, a *paragraph* is any amount of text ending with a hard return.) Choosing Go To, Enter is somewhat similar to pressing Ctrl+↓, except Ctrl+↓ moves the cursor to the beginning of the next paragraph, whereas Go To, Enter moves the cursor to the end of the current paragraph.

If you have paragraphs separated by multiple hard returns, Ctrl+↓ is the more efficient way to move between paragraphs.

The Go To feature can also move the cursor to the beginning or end of the page displayed on the screen. To move to the beginning of the displayed page, press Go To (Ctrl+Home) or select Edit and then Go To, and press ↑. This moves the cursor to the top of the current page. Choosing Go To and then ↓ moves the cursor to the end of the current page.

Dividing and Joining Paragraphs

As you edit your documents, you may need to divide one paragraph into two or join two paragraphs together. These operations are performed quickly and easily with the Enter, Backspace, and Delete keys.

To divide one paragraph into two:

■ Begin by moving the cursor to the beginning of the word that will start the new second paragraph.

■ Press Enter to split the paragraph at that point.

■ If you are leaving a blank line between paragraphs, press Enter again to insert the line.

■ If you are indenting the first line of the new paragraph without the leading blank line, press Tab instead.

When you divide one paragraph into two, pressing Enter simply inserts a [HRt] code to separate the text. Later in this chapter, you'll see how to view this and other formatting codes.

To join two paragraphs together:

■ Start with the cursor at the beginning of the second paragraph.

■ Press Backspace (or press Delete with the cursor at the *end* of the first paragraph) until the second paragraph is wrapped into the previous paragraph.

When you join two paragraphs together, you can use either the Backspace or Delete key. Simply delete the [HRt] codes that lie between the paragraphs. You don't need to see the codes to delete them; just move your cursor to the beginning of the second paragraph, and press Backspace until the paragraphs become one. If you prefer to use the Delete key, move the cursor to the end of the first paragraph, and press Delete to join the paragraphs.

Try this exercise to divide one of the paragraphs on your screen, and then combine the two paragraphs into one again:

1. With the cursor positioned anywhere in one of the paragraphs of your document, press Ctrl+→ or Ctrl+← to move the cursor word by word to the beginning of any sentence in the paragraph.

2. Press Enter twice to divide the paragraph and add a blank line. This inserts two [HRt] codes into the text.

3. Now you'll join the two paragraphs. Move the cursor to the beginning of the second paragraph.

4. Press Backspace twice to remove the [HRt] codes.

TIP. *You can follow this same procedure to divide a headline or title into two or more lines.*

Remember that pressing Enter inserts a [HRt] code into your text, which tells WordPerfect to end the current line and begin the next one.

Deleting Text

Perhaps the most important editing task is removing unwanted text from your document, and WordPerfect provides several techniques for doing this. You can delete single characters of text, or you can delete whole sentences, paragraphs, or pages.

NOTE. *For information on deleting formatting codes, see "Viewing and Editing the Formatting Codes" later in this chapter.*

Deleting Single Characters and Words

Chapter 1 of this book lists the keys you can press to delete single characters and words from your text. Here is a quick review of those keystrokes:

- Press the Delete key to delete the character at the cursor position. After the character is removed, the next character to the right moves over to fill the empty space. When you hold down the Delete key, WordPerfect continues to delete characters to the right of the cursor.

- Press Backspace to delete the character to the left of the cursor. Hold down the Backspace key, and WordPerfect continuously deletes characters to the left of the cursor.

- Press Delete Word (Ctrl+Backspace) to delete the entire word where the cursor is located. (The cursor can be at any location within the word.)

■ Press and release the Home key, and then press Delete to delete everything from the cursor to the right end of the word where the cursor is found. For example, to delete only the suffix *-ful* from the word *successful*, move the text cursor to the letter *f,* press Home, and then press Delete. This also deletes any spaces or punctuation located after the deleted characters.

■ Press Home and then press Backspace to delete from the character immediately to the left of the cursor to the left end of the word where the cursor is located. For example, to delete the prefix *pre-* from the word *predefined*, move the text cursor to the letter *d,* press Home, and then press Backspace. This deletes all the characters between the cursor position and the previous character space, but does not delete the space.

■ Press Ctrl+End to delete from the cursor to the end of the line.

■ Press Ctrl+PgDn to delete all text from the cursor to the end of the current page. WordPerfect prompts you with "Delete Remainder of page." Select <u>Y</u>es to go ahead with the deletion.

Deleting Sentences, Paragraphs, and Pages

The Delete keys (Backspace and Delete) are the perfect tools for deleting single characters from your text, but WordPerfect offers other methods for deleting whole passages of text. With the Move feature, for example, you can select a sentence, paragraph, or page, and then delete it, like this:

NOTE.   *To delete more or less than a sentence, paragraph, or page, you'll need to use the Block feature to select and delete the text. Block is discussed later in this chapter.*

■ Move the cursor anywhere within the sentence, paragraph, or page that you want to delete. You don't need to place the cursor at the beginning of a sentence to delete it; just make sure the cursor is within the passage to be removed.

Choose <u>E</u>dit ▸ <u>S</u>elect.

■ Press Move (Ctrl+F4). This displays the Move dialog box. Notice that the Select options are available and the Action options are grayed.

■ To select an item for deletion, choose <u>S</u>entence, Pa<u>r</u>agraph, or P<u>a</u>ge. Based on your cursor location, WordPerfect highlights the text for the item you selected and redisplays the Move dialog box. Notice that the Action options are now available.

Choose <u>E</u>dit ▸ Cu<u>t</u>.

■ From the Move dialog box, choose Delete, and the highlighted text is removed from your document.

In the following exercise, you'll practice actually deleting some text from the document displayed on the screen. Afterward, you'll use WordPerfect's Undelete feature to restore the text you've removed.

1. Pick a sentence to delete from the text on the screen, and move the text cursor to it.

Choose Edit ▸ Select ▸ Sentence.

2. Press Move (Ctrl+F4). Then choose the first option, Sentence, to highlight the sentence where the cursor is located. With the sentence highlighted, your screen will look similar to Figure 6.3. (If you used the menu bar to select the sentence, you will not see the Move dialog box.)

Figure 6.3

Highlighting a
sentence for deletion

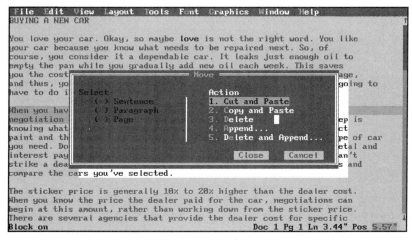

3. From the Move dialog box, choose Delete, and the sentence is removed from your document.

Choose Edit ▸ Cut.

4. Now delete a paragraph. Move the cursor anywhere within one paragraph in the text.

5. Press Move (Ctrl+F4). Then choose Paragraph to highlight the paragraph where your cursor is located.

Choose Edit ▸ Select ▸ Paragraph.

6. From the Move dialog box, choose Delete and the highlighted paragraph is removed from the text.

Choose Edit ▸ Cut.

7. Finally, delete an entire page of text. Place the cursor anywhere on the page you want to delete; if there's only one page of text in your document, place the cursor anywhere within that text.

Choose Edit ▸
Select ▸ Page.

Choose Edit ▸ Cut.

8. Press Move (Ctrl+F4). Then choose Page to highlight the entire page.

9. Choose Delete from the Move dialog box, and the page is removed from the text.

This is a quick way to delete a sentence, paragraph, or page, but the Move (Ctrl+F4) key can do much more than delete text. Later in this chapter, you'll follow a similar procedure to *move and copy* text to another location in your document.

Now that you've deleted some text, don't clear the screen or exit Word-Perfect—in the next section, you're going to restore the deleted text.

Restoring Deleted Text

It's inevitable that you will change your mind about some recently deleted text and wish you could bring it back. Fortunately, as you remember from Chapter 1, WordPerfect includes the Undelete feature, which keeps track of your last three deletions in the current work session and lets you restore any of them to your document. This feature works only at the editing screen, when no menus or prompts are displayed.

Here is how Undelete works:

Choose Edit ▸
Undelete.

■ Move the cursor to the place in your document where you want the deleted text to be restored.

■ Press Cancel (Esc). WordPerfect displays the Undelete dialog box and temporarily inserts the last text you deleted at the cursor position. This appears as highlighted text.

■ Continue to choose Previous Deletion until you've cycled through all three "saved" deletions. (If you've made less that three deletions, Word-Perfect cycles through the deletions on record.)

■ When you see the text you want to restore displayed as highlighted text, choose Restore, and the text is restored to the document. If you decide not to restore any text, press Cancel (Esc) to remove the Undelete dialog box.

Now that you know WordPerfect remembers the last three things you deleted, you may be wondering what is included in one deletion. A single deletion consists of everything you delete at one time, between typing text, moving the cursor, or pressing a function key. For example, pressing Back-space several times to delete an entire word or one character at time is considered one deletion. However, if you delete part of a word, move the cursor, and then delete the remainder of the word, you've created two deletions.

This next exercise will give you some hands-on practice with the Undelete feature. First you'll restore the text that you deleted earlier. Then a few brief steps will illustrate what WordPerfect considers a single deletion. On your screen, make sure you still have the document you used earlier as a sample for the deletion exercise.

Choose Edit ▸ Undelete.

1. In the previous exercise, the last thing you did was to execute the deletion of a page of text. Now, press Cancel (Esc) to display the Undelete dialog box.

2. The page of text you deleted is now highlighted at the cursor position.

3. Choose Restore, and the highlighted text is restored to your document.

Choose Edit ▸ Undelete.

4. Press Cancel (Esc). Notice that the page text is again highlighted at the cursor position. Although you've restored this deletion, it's still one of the last three deletions and remains on the "list" of items you can restore.

5. Choose Previous Deletion from the Undelete dialog box. This inserts the paragraph you deleted previously as highlighted text at the cursor position. Choose Restore to restore the paragraph to your document.

Choose Edit ▸ Undelete.

6. Press Cancel (Esc) to display the last deleted text and the Undelete dialog box. Choose Previous Deletion twice, and this time you'll redisplay the sentence that you deleted earlier.

7. Choose Restore to restore the highlighted sentence. Or choose Previous Deletion, and WordPerfect will complete the cycle and display the most recent deletion again—in this case, the page of text.

   Remember: The Undelete feature restores text *at the cursor position*, which is not necessarily the original location of the text.

8. Now let's delete a few words to see how WordPerfect counts the deletions. Pick a word in the text, and move the cursor to the space at the end of that word.

9. Press Backspace to delete one character at a time until the entire word is gone from the text.

Choose Edit ▸ Undelete.

10. Press Cancel (Esc). Choose Previous Deletion twice to cycle through the list of deletions. Because you have deleted a fourth item (the word), the earliest deletion on the list (the sentence) has been bumped from the list and cannot be restored.

11. Choose Previous Deletion again to display the word you just deleted (the most recent deletion), and choose Restore to restore the word.

12. Pick another word and move the cursor to the space right after it. Press Backspace a few times to delete two or three characters at the end of the word.

13. Stop before you delete the entire word, and press ↑ to move the cursor to the previous line. Then press ↓ to move the cursor back to the word you partially deleted, and use the Backspace key to finish deleting it.

Choose <u>E</u>dit ▸
U<u>n</u>delete.

14. Now press Cancel (Esc) to display the deletion. Notice that the first part of the word is available to be restored but not the entire word. Choose <u>R</u>estore to restore the first half of the word.

15. Press Cancel (Esc), and select <u>P</u>revious Deletion from the Undelete dialog box. This shows you the previous deletion, which includes the first characters that you deleted from the end of the word.

Let's examine what's happening here. Remember that WordPerfect counts everything deleted at one time as a single deletion. For instance, you deleted an entire word by pressing Backspace several times to delete each character. Although you pressed Backspace several times, it was considered one deletion because you deleted the whole word without typing additional text or moving the cursor.

On the other hand, when you deleted the last word, you interrupted the process by moving the cursor—first you deleted a few characters at the end of the word, then you moved the cursor, and finally you completed the deletion. WordPerfect considered this two separate deletions.

Now you know how to remove unwanted text, and, if necessary, to restore text that has been mistakenly deleted. (Note that you can on occasion use the Undo feature to retrieve deleted material. Refer back to Chapter 1 for additional details.)

Moving and Copying Text

NOTE. *This section explains how to use Move and Copy to manipulate a sentence, paragraph, or page, but you can also use the Block feature (described later) to select and move any section of text.*

Deleting may be the most important editing task, but moving and copying are close runners-up. WordPerfect's Move and Copy features give you the freedom to reorganize your documents with ease. You can quickly move or copy a sentence, paragraph, or entire page of text, and place it anywhere in your document. Here's the general procedure for moving or copying text within your document:

■ Move the cursor to any part of the sentence, paragraph, or page that you want to move or copy.

Choose <u>E</u>dit ▸ <u>Se</u>-
lect ▸ <u>S</u>entence,
<u>P</u>aragraph, or P<u>a</u>ge.

Choose <u>E</u>dit ▸ Cu<u>t</u>
and Past<u>e</u> or Cop<u>y</u>
and Paste.

Choose <u>E</u>dit ▸ <u>P</u>aste.

■ Press Move (Ctrl+F4). Then choose <u>S</u>entence, Pa<u>r</u>agraph, or P<u>a</u>ge to select and highlight a segment of text.

■ Choose Cu<u>t</u> and Paste or <u>C</u>opy and Paste to indicate the task you want to
perform. If you choose Cu<u>t</u> and Paste, WordPerfect removes or cuts the
highlighted text from your document. Choose <u>C</u>opy and Paste, and Word-
Perfect keeps the highlighted text at its current position, but stores a
copy in memory.

■ A message at the bottom of the screen prompts you to

```
Move cursor; press Enter to retrieve.
```

Move the cursor to the place in your document where the text should be
moved or copied. Then press Enter to retrieve the text.

You don't have to retrieve the text immediately. You may need to select a
section of text to be moved and then add some text or new formatting codes
before you retrieve it into its new location. To do this, at the "Move cursor;
press Enter to retrieve" prompt, press Cancel (Esc). This cancels the Move or
Copy operation and removes the prompt. However, the highlighted text is
still stored in memory until the next time you store something in memory
with another move or copy operation.

When you've finished editing and are ready to retrieve the text into its
new location, position your cursor there, and press Open (Shift+F10). At the
Open Document dialog box, press Enter without typing a file name, and
WordPerfect retrieves the text stored in memory. Note that you can also use
the Ctrl+V shortcut to accomplish the same thing more efficiently.

After you've retrieved the text, a copy remains stored in memory until
you move or copy something else. So, if you want to repeatedly retrieve copies of a certain passage of text, you don't need to select and copy it over and
over again. Just press Open (Shift+F10), and then Enter without typing a file
name. This always retrieves the text that is currently stored in memory. You
can accomplish the same thing by selecting <u>P</u>aste from the <u>E</u>dit menu or by
using the Ctrl+V shortcut.

Manipulating Blocks of Text

So far in this chapter, you've explored how to move, copy, and delete complete
sentences, paragraphs, and pages in the document. However, suppose you need
to work with a section of text that doesn't fall into one of these neat categories.
For example, you may want to move two or more sentences from a paragraph.
WordPerfect lets you do this. You can also move only a half page of text, instead of an entire page. It's also possible to delete or copy only a small group
of words that don't form a complete sentence. You can accomplish all these

editing tasks with WordPerfect's Block feature. (This feature was introduced briefly in Chapter 3.)

Block allows you to select a precise section of text to be deleted, moved, or copied. You can also use the Block feature to apply formatting commands to a specific section of text. Additionally, when you have blocked a section of text, you can move it with your mouse by using WordPerfect 6.0's new drag and drop feature.

First, here is the general procedure for defining a block of text, using the keyboard:

- Move the cursor to the beginning of the text you want to block.

- Press Block (Alt+F4 or F12). A "Block on" message will appear in the lower-right corner of the screen.

- Use the arrow keys or any other cursor movement keys to move the cursor to the end of the text you want to block. As you move the cursor, the blocked text is highlighted.

- When the block includes all the text to be changed, choose the editing or layout feature you want to use on the block. After you choose a feature, Block is automatically turned off.

If you're using a mouse with WordPerfect, you can use the mouse pointer to block a section of text. Here is the procedure for that method:

NOTE. *See Appendix A for information about setting up WordPerfect for the mouse.*

- Move the mouse pointer to the first character of text to be included in the block.

- Hold down the left mouse button—don't release it—and move the pointer *just past* the last character of the block. The "Block on" message will appear at the bottom of the screen. Moving the mouse with the mouse button held down is called *dragging* with the mouse.

- When the highlighted block includes all the text you want to affect, release the left mouse button and choose the feature you want to apply to the block. Again, after you choose a feature, Block is automatically turned off. You can also drag a highlighted block of text to move it to a new location, as described in a moment under "Moving and Copying Blocks of Text with the Mouse."

Many people prefer using a mouse for block editing, because it's faster than using the keystrokes for relatively small amounts of text. However, if you need to block your entire document, it's probably easier to use cursor keys such as PgDn; Home, Home, ↓; or the Go To feature.

After you select a feature for the blocked text, WordPerfect performs the desired action, and the block is turned off. If you want to apply another feature to the same block, you can press Block (Alt+F4 or F12) and then press Go To (Ctrl+Home) twice. Pressing the Go To key twice causes the cursor to return to its previous position—in this case, the position it was in before the block was defined. Press Block (Alt+F4 or F12) or Cancel (Esc) to turn off Block without selecting a feature.

The foregoing is only a general description of the blocking process, but the following sections provide detailed information about deleting, moving, and copying text, and applying attributes to a block of text. You'll use the Block feature often to select and edit text.

Deleting a Block

Deleting text with the Block feature is easier than using the Move (Ctrl+F4) key described earlier in this chapter. This is because Block lets you specify exactly which text you want to remove from the document. Once a block is defined, you just press one of the delete keys (Backspace or Delete) to remove the blocked text. Follow these steps at your computer to define and delete a block of text from your document:

1. Move the cursor or mouse pointer to the beginning of the text you want to delete.

2. Press Block (Alt+F4 or F12). If you are using a mouse, just press and hold down the left mouse button.

3. Using the cursor movement keys or the mouse, move the cursor to the end of the text that you want to delete. If you're using a mouse, be sure to hold down the left mouse button as you move the cursor. As the cursor moves, the text block is highlighted.

4. Press Backspace or Delete.

Choose Edit ▶ Cut.

Moving or Copying a Block

The Block feature also simplifies the tasks of moving and copying text. Like Block Delete, WordPerfect supports special keystrokes for Block Move and Block Copy. Here is an exercise to practice moving and copying a block of text in your document:

1. Move the cursor or mouse pointer to the beginning of the text you want to move or copy.

2. Press Block (Alt+F4 or F12) and move the cursor to highlight the text you want to move or copy. If you are using a mouse, hold down the left

mouse button as you move the mouse pointer to the end of the block; then release the mouse button.

3. To move the highlighted text, press Block Move (Ctrl+Del). To copy the highlighted text, press Block Copy (Ctrl+Ins).

Choose Edit ▸ Cut and Paste or Edit ▸ Copy and Paste.

NOTE. *You can also press Move (Ctrl+F4) with a block selected, choose Block from the Move Block dialog box, choose Cut and Paste or Copy and Paste, to move or copy the block. But pressing Block Move (Ctrl+Del) or Block Copy (Ctrl+Ins) is easier.*

4. WordPerfect prompts you with "Move cursor; press Enter to retrieve." Position the cursor where you want the text moved or copied. Then press Enter to retrieve it at the new location.

Remember: The Block Move (Ctrl+Del) and Block Copy (Ctrl+Ins) keys work as described here only when the "Block on" message is visible. As mentioned, you can also highlight a block and then press Move (Ctrl+F4) to move, copy, or delete a block of text, but the method described here requires fewer keystrokes.

Moving and Copying Blocks of Text with the Mouse

WordPerfect 6.0 supports a new feature, called "drag and drop," that enables you to easily move or copy blocks of text using just your mouse. The procedure for moving text is pleasantly simple:

1. Use your mouse to highlight the block of text you'd like to move.

2. Position the mouse over the text in question and *hold down* the left mouse button. (You must keep the button held down until you are ready to complete the move operation.) If you're in graphics display or page display mode, you'll see a drag and drop icon below the mouse pointer (it looks like two overlaid boxes). In any of the display modes, you'll see the message "Release mouse button to move block" at the bottom of the screen.

3. With the mouse button held down, drag with your mouse until the cursor is in the desired spot, and then release the mouse button to deposit ("drop") the block of text in its new home. As you drag, make sure to keep your eye on the cursor (the vertical bar in graphics display mode and the blinking horizontal line in text display mode) rather than the mouse pointer itself. It's the cursor that indicates exactly where the text will be inserted.

You can also use drag and drop to copy blocks of text. The procedure is almost the same as moving text with drag and drop. The only difference is that you hold down the Ctrl key while dragging. If you try this, you'll notice that the drag and drop icon changes somewhat in page display mode or graphics display mode: The second box becomes shaded. In addition, in any of the display modes, you'll see the message "Release mouse button to copy block" at the bottom of the screen.

If you work with a mouse, the drag and drop technique is one of the most handy for moving or copying blocks of text. It's intuitive, visual, and enables you to bypass the sometimes cumbersome menu system. However, it may not be the ideal method for moving large blocks of text or for moving text over long distances. in these cases, you may want to revert to using the Block Move or Block Copy feature.

Applying Text Attributes to a Block

In Chapter 3, you learned how to select different text attributes and to use the Block feature to apply the attributes to a block of text. These attributes include text size selections, such as Superscript and Large, and appearance attributes like Bold, Underline, and Italic. Here is a review of the basic procedure for applying attributes with the Block feature:

Use the mouse pointer to block the text.

Choose Font ▸ Font.

- Move the cursor to the beginning of the text that will be printed with the new attribute. Press Block (Alt+F4 or F12). Then move the cursor to highlight the block of text you want to change.

- Press Font (Ctrl+F8) to display the Font dialog box.

- Choose the Appearance and Relative Size options to define the appearance of the blocked text.

- When you are finished with your selections, press Exit (F7) to apply them to the block.

After you apply these attributes to the highlighted text, the Block feature is turned off.

Incidentally, note that the Font dialog box is often more convenient than the Font menu when you're changing multiple text attributes at once.

Changing the Case of Blocked Text

WordPerfect includes a nice helpful feature that lets you change the letter case for an entire block of text. So, when you have a word, phrase, or even a whole paragraph that you want to appear in capital letters, you can quickly change it all to uppercase (or, of course, vice versa).

Here's how it works:

- Use the Block feature (Alt+F4) to define the block of text to be affected by the case change.

Choose <u>E</u>dit ▸ Con<u>v</u>ert Case.

- Press Shift+F3 to display the Convert Case dialog box.

- To change the blocked text to uppercase letters, choose <u>U</u>ppercase. To change the text to all lowercase letters, choose <u>L</u>owercase. To change the text to initial caps (for the first letter of each word to be capitalized), choose <u>I</u>nitial Caps.

After you make your selection, WordPerfect converts the highlighted block to the specified case.

Generally, this operation converts all letters in the block to either upper- or lowercase; however, when you change uppercase to lowercase, there are a few situations in which you won't want the conversion to apply. WordPerfect therefore makes these exceptions when you select <u>L</u>owercase:

- A capital *I* followed by a space or an apostrophe (as in *I'll*) remains uppercase.

- WordPerfect automatically keeps the first letter in a sentence capitalized.

Appending Blocked Text to a File on Disk

WordPerfect's Append feature lets you block a section of text and insert a copy of it at the end of a file you've already created and saved on disk. Follow these steps to append a block of text to a file on disk:

1. At the editing screen, use Block (Alt+F4) to highlight the block of text you want to copy to another file.

Choose <u>E</u>dit ▸ Append ▸ To <u>F</u>ile.

2. If you are using the function keys, press Move (Ctrl+F4) and choose <u>A</u>ppend.

3. In the Append To dialog box, type the file name of the document to which the text should be appended. Then press Enter. Or choose File List (F5) to choose a file from a directory list.

After you enter the file name, WordPerfect appends the highlighted block to the end of the document file you specified, and the Block feature is automatically turned off. If a file with the name you entered does not exist, WordPerfect creates it for you and copies in the text that you've blocked.

TIP.   *You can also append text without using the Block feature. Position the cursor, press Move (Ctrl+F4), and choose <u>S</u>entence, <u>P</u>aragraph, or P<u>a</u>ge to highlight a section of text. Then, from the Move dialog box, choose <u>A</u>ppend.*

WordPerfect prompts you to enter the name of the disk file to which you want the highlighted text added. Type the file name, press Enter, and the text is copied to the end of the file you specified.

Tricks with the Block Feature

While the Block feature is turned on, you can extend the block to a specific character by typing that character at the keyboard. For example, let's say you want to define a block from the cursor position to the end of the sentence. First, press Block (Alt+F4). While the "Block on" message is displayed, type a period (.)—WordPerfect then extends the block to include all the text up to the next period encountered in the document.

TIP. *Whenever you use this technique, remember that when a sentence ends with an exclamation point or question mark, WordPerfect skips these and continues the block until it finds a period. Also, remember that a decimal point in a number (as in $12.75) is considered a period.*

The period is obviously one of the most common characters you'll type when using this technique to define a block—but you certainly aren't limited to this character. To extend a block to the next occurrence of any character, just type that key. To extend the block to the end of the current word, type a space. To extend the block to the end of the current paragraph, or more precisely, to the next occurrence of the [HRt] code, press Enter. In addition, to extend the block to any character that you can see on the screen, just hold down the Shift key and click in the desired location with your mouse.

As described earlier, the Block feature is automatically turned off after you choose an editing feature or a text attribute. Suppose, however, that you want to immediately block the same text again and select another feature. WordPerfect provides a way to return to the previous cursor position and re-block the text—with only two keystrokes. This is especially useful if you want to apply more than one formatting command to the same block of text. Here's how it works.

Say you've just blocked some text and used Bold (F6) to apply the Bold attribute. Now you want to also underline the same block of text. Press Block (Alt+F4) to turn on the Block feature again. Then press Go To (Ctrl+Home) twice. This causes the cursor to jump back to its original position (before the first block was defined). The same text will be highlighted and you can now press Underline (F8) to apply the second text attribute. (Incidentally, if you're applying multiple text attributes, it's often quick to work through the Text dialog box.)

Viewing and Editing the Formatting Codes

In Chapter 2, you were introduced to the concept of creating a document layout with codes. You know that formatting codes tell WordPerfect when to indent a paragraph, create new margin settings, print the text with a different font, and so on. All codes are embedded in the text of your documents, but are invisible at the standard editing screen.

Some word processors don't allow you to view and edit the codes that create the document format, but the designers of WordPerfect decided to include this option. In WordPerfect, the task of editing formatting codes is made easier by a special screen called the Reveal Codes window. You've had some experience already with this screen; in the following sections we will explore it in detail.

Why Do I Need to See the Codes?

To understand the concept of document codes, let's look at how early word processors handled text formatting. When first introduced, word processors required the user to insert commands directly into the text in order to create a document format. For example, in WordStar 1.0, visible commands called *control characters* were inserted into the document to create the desired format, like ^C to begin centering or ^B for bold. Eventually, software designers decided to hide these codes so they wouldn't interrupt the flow of the text. Since the codes were not visible on the printed page, it was assumed that users wouldn't need to see them in the text on the screen. However, knowledge of commands and codes is still necessary to create a formatted document; when codes are invisible, it's difficult to see and edit them. For example, if you turn on the Bold text attribute and later decide to insert new text, how can you be sure where the bold attribute begins or ends? WordPerfect's status line helps by displaying certain text attributes after the *Pos* label, but you also need to see other codes like tab and margin settings, for editing purposes. Reveal Codes lets you view them all.

Displaying the Reveal Codes Window

To display the Reveal Codes window, press Reveal Codes (Alt+F3 or F11). If you prefer to use the menu bar, choose View and then Reveal Codes. This displays the window shown in Figure 6.4.

The bar in the middle of the screen shows the current tab stops and margin settings. The top section of the screen shows your document as it usually appears during editing, and the bottom section of the screen is the Reveal Codes window. When the Reveal Codes window is displayed, you can use the cursor movement keystrokes or the mouse pointer to move the cursor through the text.

Figure 6.4

Displaying the
Reveal Codes
window

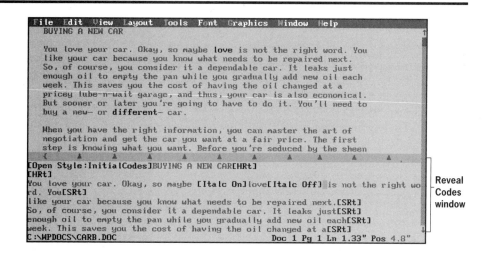

In the Reveal Codes window, the cursor appears as a solid box. You'll also see codes, which appear as words or symbols inside of square brackets. (Appendix B provides a complete list of the codes you may see inside the Reveal Codes window.)

When you are finished viewing the codes, press Reveal Codes (Alt+F3 or F11) or choose Edit and then Reveal Codes again to restore the full document screen.

Editing the Formatting Codes

When the Reveal Codes window is displayed, you can edit the text and codes of your document. As you do so, remember that the cursor appears as a box within the Reveal Codes window, which corresponds to the cursor shown in the document screen. As you move the cursor over each code, the code is highlighted and shows the specific settings that the code creates.

For example, a 1.5-inch left margin code appears like this in the Reveal Codes window: [Lft Mar]. When you move the cursor over the code, it changes to show the specific margin setting, like this: [Lft Mar:1.5"]. This feature keeps the code details hidden so you can view more text. If you prefer to see the code details, a screen setup option lets you display them always; this is explained later in "Displaying Detailed Codes."

To edit the settings that a code creates while the Reveal Codes window is displayed:

■ Remove the code by highlighting it with the cursor and then pressing Delete.

■ Move the cursor to the immediate right of the code, choose the feature that created the code, and then enter the new settings.

When you use the latter method to edit a code, WordPerfect replaces the previous code with the new code settings. For example, suppose you want to change tab settings that are already defined. Display the Reveal Codes window and move the cursor onto the character or code that immediately follows the [Tab Set] code. Then display the Tab Set dialog box and edit the tab settings.

When you return to the document screen, WordPerfect replaces the original [Tab Set] code with a code that stores the new tab settings. The original code is replaced because WordPerfect will not let you put two like codes together; it keeps the latest code and removes the original code. Note that this works only when you put the cursor *after* the code you want to edit. If you highlight or place the cursor *before* the original code, the new code settings will not take effect.

Using the Edit Code Macro

Another way to edit codes is with WordPerfect's Edit Code feature, which is included as a macro on WordPerfect's Macros keyboard. To use this feature, you must first choose the Macros keyboard layout. Press Setup (Shift+F1) or choose File and then Setup from the menu bar. Then choose Keyboard Layout, highlight the "MACROS" name on the keyboard list, and then choose Select.

When the Macros keyboard is selected, you can press Ctrl+E to edit a code. First, display the Reveal Codes window, and then highlight the code you want to edit. Press Ctrl+E and WordPerfect displays the dialog box that created the code. There, you can change the settings that create the code. When you're finished, exit the dialog box and WordPerfect updates the highlighted code with the new settings.

If you want to use the Edit Code feature but don't want to keep the Macros keyboard layout selected, you can create a new keyboard layout and assign a keystroke for the EDITCODE.WPM macro stored in your WordPerfect macros directory. See Chapter 25 for information about creating and editing a keyboard layout.

Displaying Detailed Codes

WordPerfect's standard settings cause the Reveal Codes window to display only generic codes, like [Lft Mar], [Tab Set], and [Ln Spacing]. Most formatting codes have specific measurements or other settings assigned to them, but you won't see these measurements until you move the cursor to highlight each code.

You can change this and display all code settings at once with an option on the Screen Setup dialog box. Press Screen (Ctrl+F3) and press Setup (Shift+F1), or choose View and then Screen Setup from the menu bar.

Choose <u>R</u>eveal Codes and select <u>D</u>isplay Details, so that an *X* appears in the check box next to this option. When you return to the document screen and display the Reveal Codes window, every code you see will be shown in its expanded form with all measurements and settings displayed.

The detailed code option will remain in effect until you turn it off in the Screen Setup dialog box.

Adjusting the Size of the Reveal Codes Window

When you first display the Reveal Codes window, it will take up about 25 percent of the document screen. If you want to view more (or less) of the codes at once, you can change the size of the Reveal Codes window. These steps explain how to do so:

Choose <u>V</u>iew ▸
Scree<u>n</u> Setup.

Click on the upward
pointing triangle to
increase the per-
centage, or the
downward pointing
triangle to de-
crease it.

- First, press Screen (Ctrl+F3) and then press Setup (Shift+F1) to display the Screen Setup dialog box.

- Choose <u>R</u>eveal Codes and then choose <u>W</u>indow Percentage.

- At the Window Percentage option, enter the number that represents the portion of the screen you want to allocate to the Reveal Codes window. For example, enter **50** if you want the Reveal Codes window to take up 50 percent of the screen when the window is displayed.

- Press Exit (F7) until you return to the document screen.

The new Reveal Codes window size takes effect immediately and will remain so until you change the setting again on the Screen Setup dialog box.

CHAPTER

7

High-Powered Editing Tools

WORDPERFECT INCLUDES MANY POWERFUL TOOLS TO HELP YOU EDIT your documents more efficiently. The Search and Replace features work together to let you search for specific words, phrases, and formatting codes, and then replace these with other text or codes if you wish. The Repeat command can save time and effort by repeating keystrokes, including cursor movements, keyboard characters, and some function keys. The Hyphenation feature can automatically hyphenate text to evenly distribute it and create smooth margins. WordPerfect provides multiple editing screens that you can use to open several documents at once. You can even divide the screen to edit multiple documents at once, place a format ruler to show where tabs and margins are set, and use WordPerfect's Button Bar feature to provide quick access to the features you use most often.

In this chapter, you'll learn about special editing tools and practice using them. You'll find and replace text in a sample document, use the Repeat feature, experiment with editing screen options, and use the new Button Bar feature. You may not need all of the tools in this chapter, but you're bound to find several useful tips and techniques.

NOTE. *If you haven't yet read Chapter 6, you should do so before continuing with this chapter.*

Searching for Text and Codes

As you edit your documents, you'll sometimes need to locate a specific word or phrase. This would be a tedious chore if the arrow keys were the only method available for moving through the document; you would have to read each word or scan a lot of pages to find what you were looking for. Fortunately, with WordPerfect, you have better alternatives.

With the Search feature, you can type the text you want to find, and if it's in your document, WordPerfect will take you directly to it. And you aren't limited to text—you can also search for formatting codes.

Searching for Text

WordPerfect's Search options provide quick ways to find things in your document. Think of the Search feature as your personal WordPerfect detective; you tell WordPerfect which text or code you hope to find, and it will show you where it appears in the document. This text or code is called the *search criterion* or *search text.*

Here is the process for finding a word or phrase in your document. Later, you'll have the chance to try it yourself.

- With your document displayed at the WordPerfect editing screen, move the cursor to the place where you want the Search operation to begin.

Choose Edit ▸ Search.

- To search forward from the cursor position, press Search (F2) to display the Search dialog box shown in Figure 7.1.

Figure 7.1

The Search dialog box

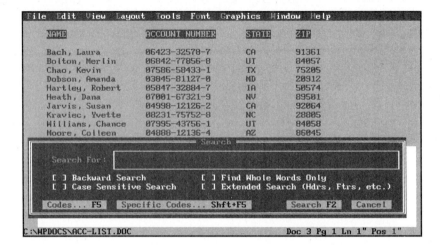

- At the Search For prompt, type the text you want to find, and press Enter to accept it.

- Choose Search (F2) to initiate the search. If the search criterion is found in your document, WordPerfect will move the cursor just past the matching text. After a search, you can move the cursor back to its original position by pressing Ctrl+Home twice.

Whenever you perform a search, it begins at the cursor position and usually continues to the end of the text. The standard Search feature searches forward through all text that lies between the cursor position and the end of the document. If you check the Backward Search option in the Search dialog box, WordPerfect searches backward through all text that lies between the cursor position and the beginning of the document. You can also press Backward Search (Shift+F2) to display the Search dialog box with the Backward Search option selected. (See the next section, which covers the details of using the Search dialog box.)

When the Case Sensitive Search option is selected in the Search dialog box, WordPerfect will look only for text that exactly matches what you typed. When this option *is* selected, WordPerfect finds all instances of the search string, no matter what their case.

After the search is completed, the Search feature turns off. Should you want to look for additional items in the text, you must select Search again.

Now that you know the basics for using Search, let's give it a try:

1. Clear the WordPerfect screen (press F7 and choose <u>N</u>o twice), and type the following text:

   Representatives from the Jamestown Business Park announced a new no-smoking policy for all business offices in the complex, beginning 01/15/95. A small outdoor pavilion is now reserved as a smoking area for employees and guests. This may allow business patrons to breathe cleaner air, but the 39 employees who smoke will be left out in the cold.

2. Press Home, Home, ↑ to move the cursor to the beginning of the document.

Choose <u>E</u>dit ▶
Searc<u>h</u>.

3. Press Search (F2) to display the Search dialog box.

4. At the Search For prompt, type **9**, and press Enter. Then choose Search (F2) again. WordPerfect moves the cursor to the right of the 9 in 01/15/95.

Choose <u>E</u>dit ▶
Searc<u>h</u>.

5. To find the next occurrence of 9, press Search (F2). The Search dialog box reappears, displaying the previous search criterion.

6. Select Search (F2) again to continue with the search. The cursor moves just past the next 9 found in the text.

Choose <u>E</u>dit ▶
Searc<u>h</u>.

7. Press Search (F2) to display the Search dialog box. Then type **01/15/95** as the new search criterion.

8. Choose <u>B</u>ackward Search to indicate that you want to search backward from the cursor position. Then choose Search (F2) to initiate the search operation. The cursor moves to the right of the 01/15/95 date.

9. Press Home, Home, ↑ to move to the beginning of the document. Choose the Search feature again to display the Search dialog box. Note that the <u>B</u>ackward Search option has been turned off automatically.

10. Type **Business** and press Enter to create the new criterion. Check the option for <u>C</u>ase Sensitive Search, and then choose Search (F2) again. WordPerfect locates the word *Business*.

Choose <u>E</u>dit ▶
Searc<u>h</u> ▶ S<u>e</u>arch.

11. Press Search (F2) twice to locate the next occurrence of the word *Business*. Notice the "Not found" message in the middle of the screen, which indicates that *Business* with a capital *B* is not found in the remainder of the text. Press Cancel (Esc) or Enter to remove the message.

NOTE. *When you see the "Not found" message, this means either that there is no matching text in your document or that the last occurrence of your search text has been located and no other text in your document matches the search criterion.*

12. Press Home, Home, ↑ to move to the top of the document. Choose Search again to redisplay the search criterion.

13. Press Enter to accept the criterion, and then choose Case Sensitive Search again, so that no *X* appears in the check box. Then use the Search feature again to find all three occurrences of the word *business*.

14. Press Home, Home, ↑ to move to the beginning of the document. Display the Search dialog box. Type **employees and guests** as the new criterion, and choose Search (F2) again. WordPerfect locates the phrase *employees and guests*.

15. Press Backward Search (Shift+F2).

Choose Edit ▸ Search ▸ Backward Search.

16. Type **Jamestown Business Park** as the new criterion, and choose Search (F2) again. WordPerfect finds *Jamestown Business Park*.

Remember: You don't need to enter new search text each time you use the Search feature. If you want to find the next occurrence of the word or phrase you last searched for, press Search (F2) twice. To go back to the previous occurrence of the search text, press Backward Search (Shift+F2) twice.

To change or edit the search text, press Search (F2) to display the Search dialog box with the current search text. Then type a new criterion or edit the existing one. Choose Search (F2) again to initiate the search, and WordPerfect locates the text that matches the new criterion. If the text is not found, WordPerfect displays the usual "Not found" message, and the cursor remains at the place where the search was attempted.

The Search Dialog Box

Other options on the Search dialog box let you control the results of the search operation. You select each of these from the Search dialog box before you initiate the search. When an *X* appears in the box next to a search option, this means the option will affect the current search operation. Table 7.1 describes each option.

Table 7.1　　**The Search Dialog Box Options**

Option	Result
Backward Search	Searches from the cursor position to the beginning of the document. Choose Backward Search again—so that no *X* appears in the box next to this option—and you'll search from the cursor position to the end of the document.

Table 7.1	The Search Dialog Box Options (Continued)	
Option	**Result**	
Case Sensitive Search	Matches the upper- and lowercase letters exactly as you typed them in the search criteria.	
Find Whole Words Only	Searches for complete words in the document; this option is described later in the chapter.	
Extended Search	Searches through all text in the document. When this option is not selected, WordPerfect searches only through the main body of text and ignores the text stored in headers, footers, footnotes, and endnotes.	
Codes (F5)	Inserts the generic codes into the search criterion. The cursor must be at the Search For prompt before you can choose this option. If, for example, you want to find the next margin codes, you can use this option to insert a generic margin code from a list of possible codes. Then, when you initiate the search, you'll find the next margin code in your document. Note that this option only works when Find Whole Words Only is *not* selected.	
Specific Codes (Shift+F5)	Looks for a code that has specific settings. You may, for example, want to find the next margin code that has a setting of 0.75 inch. You can choose Specific Codes (Shift+F5), choose the margin code from the list, and WordPerfect prompts you for the specific margin setting that you want to find. Enter the measurement and initiate the search to find the margin code that matches the measurement you entered. Note that this option only works when Find Whole Words Only is *not* selected.	

Searching for Single Words

Although the Search feature helps you find specific words, some of the words it finds may not be what you wanted. For example, if you enter **the** as the search criterion, WordPerfect will stop at the words *there* and *theory*, as well as *the*, because all of these words contain the three characters specified in the search criterion. If you want to find each occurrence of the explicit word *the* without stopping at other words that contain these same characters, you need to choose the Find Whole Words Only option on the Search dialog box.

To see how this works, try the following exercise. First you'll search for *the* without choosing the Find Whole Word option. Then you'll search again to find *the* as a single word.

1. Press Home, Home, ↑ to move to the beginning of the text on your screen.

2. Press Search (F2). Type **the** as the new criterion, and then choose Search (F2) again. The cursor moves to the first occurrence of *the*.

Choose Edit ▶ Search.

3. Continue to search for each occurrence of *the* by pressing Search (F2) twice. Notice that the cursor stops at the word *breathe*, because it contains the three characters in the search text.

4. Press Home, Home, ↑ to move back to the top of the document. Then press Search (F2) to display the Search dialog box with current search criterion.

5. Press Enter to accept the criterion. Then choose Find Whole Words Only. This tells WordPerfect to find only the cases where *the* has spaces on each side of the group of characters—in other words, the actual word *the*.

6. Choose Search (F2) again to find the first occurrence of the word *the*.

7. Press Search (F2) twice to continue searching for each occurrence of the word *the* until the "Not found" message is displayed.

Notice that this time WordPerfect did not stop at the word *breathe*, because it was looking only for *the* preceded and followed by spaces.

Using Wildcard Characters

Sometimes you may not know the precise spelling of the text for which you're searching. This is common when you're looking for names for which different spellings are possible (such as *Andersen* or *Anderson*). WordPerfect lets you use special wildcard characters in the search criterion to help you in this kind of search.

Follow these steps at your computer to try out the wildcard characters:

1. Press Home, Home, ↑ to move to the top of the text on your screen. Or 'move the cursor to the place in the text where you want to begin the search.

Choose Edit ▸
Search.

2. Press Search (F2). At the Search For prompt, type **n** to start the search criterion. Now, you'll insert a wildcard character.

3. Choose Codes (F5) to display the Search Codes list shown in Figure 7.2. Highlight *? (One Char)* in the list, and press Enter to insert it into the search criterion.

4. Type **w** to complete the search criterion. When you are finished, press Enter to accept the search text, which now looks like this: n[?]w. This search criterion tells WordPerfect to look for all words that match this pattern, in which [?] represents any single character that falls between the letters *n* and *w*.

Figure 7.2

Choosing a wildcard character for the search criterion

Inserting wildcard into the search criterion

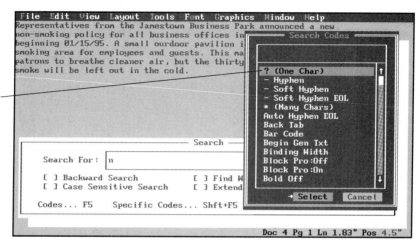

5. Choose Search (F2) to initiate the search. The cursor moves to the word *new*, which matches the pattern because it begins with *n*, ends with *w*, and has a single character between those two letters.

6. Continue to search for words that match the pattern by pressing Search (F2) twice. The next word that matches the pattern is *now*.

The [?] wildcard character is also useful for locating dates and other text that fit a specific pattern. For example, suppose you want to find each occurrence of these dates in your document: 4/2/95, 4/7/95, and 4/9/95. If you create the search text as **4/[?]/95**, this tells WordPerfect to find each date that follows the pattern: 4/[?]/95.

Keep in mind that the [?] represents only a single character. Thus, the wildcard pattern from the previous paragraph might not get correct results for dates like 4/12/92, 4/25/94, and 4/30/95. The search criterion 4/[?]/95 finds dates like 4/2/95, where the day of the month is a single-digit number. Dates like 4/01/95 would not be found because the day of the month consists of two numbers, and the [?] represents only one.

When you want to search for words that may have more than one number or character at the wildcard position, you can use the [*] wildcard character. To insert the [*] wildcard character into the search criterion, choose Codes (F5) as you did to insert the [?] wildcard character. Then highlight * (*Many Chars*) from the displayed list and press Enter.

Where the [?] wildcard character represents only a single character, the [*] character represents any number of characters. If, for example, you insert the [*] wildcard character to create the search criterion 4/[*]/95, you'll locate dates like 4/7/95, 4/21/95, and even 4//95. This happens because the [*] can represent any number of characters—even the absence of characters.

Locating Codes

The Search dialog box can also help you locate formatting codes in the text. This is especially useful for editing, because it can help you find codes without having to display the Reveal Codes window. Here is the basic procedure:

Choose Edit ▸
Sear<u>c</u>h.

■ Press Home, Home, Home, ↑ to move the cursor to the top of your document before any formatting codes.

■ Press Search (F2) to display the Search dialog box. Make sure the Find <u>W</u>hole Words Only option is *not* selected; if it is, this feature will not work.

■ With the cursor inside the Search For box, choose Codes (F5) to display a list of generic formatting codes.

■ Scroll through the list to highlight the code you want to insert into the search criterion, or simply type the code name, and WordPerfect will highlight the code for you. When the code you want to locate is highlighted, press Enter to insert it into the search criterion.

■ Choose Search (F2) from the dialog box to initiate the search.

If the code you specified is found in your document, WordPerfect will move the cursor just to the right of it, which is exactly where the cursor should be for deleting or editing the code. If you turn on Reveal Codes (Alt+F3 or F11), you can press Backspace to delete the code. Or if you want to edit the code, select the feature that you used to insert the original code, and then define your new format settings.

For example, suppose you've searched for and found a [Tab Set] code. With the cursor now located to the right of the code, you can select the Tab Set feature (press Shift+F8, choose <u>L</u>ine, and then choose <u>T</u>ab Set) to edit the tab settings. The Tab Set ruler will reflect the tab stops defined previously, and you can change them as you wish. When you exit the Tab Set menu, WordPerfect replaces the original code with the updated tab settings.

At the Search For prompt, you can also press a function key to specify one of WordPerfect's formatting codes. For example, press Bold (F6) to include a [Bold On] code as part of the search criterion, or press Indent (F4) to search for a [Lft Indent] code. (For a complete list of WordPerfect codes and the keystrokes that insert them, see Appendix B.)

Searching for Specific Code Settings

WordPerfect 6.0 includes enhanced search capabilities that let you locate formatting codes with specific settings. For example, suppose your document has several different font changes; rather than searching for each font change, you want to locate only the font codes that change to a specific font. Another example involves formatting codes for margins and tab settings; instead of locating each margin or font change, you may want to find only those codes with specific layout settings.

From the Search dialog box, you can include specific codes in the search criterion. These are the general steps:

Choose Edit ▶ Search.

- Move the cursor to the place in your document where the search operation should begin.

- Press Search (F2) to display the Search dialog box. If necessary, press Delete to clear the current search criterion. In addition, make sure the Find Whole Words Only option is *not* selected.

- With the cursor in the Search For box, choose Specific Codes (Shift+F5) to display a list of codes.

- Scroll through the list and highlight the code you want to find. Then press Enter to select the code.

- WordPerfect displays a dialog box or list that lets you select the specifics for the code. Enter a measurement or make a selection to indicate the precise code you want to find.

- After you specify a measurement or make a selection, choose Search (F2) from the Search dialog box, and WordPerfect locates the precise code in your document.

When you use the Specific Codes option to select a code for the search criterion, WordPerfect displays a dialog box or a list of different choices that apply to the selected code. For example, if you select a margin code, WordPerfect prompts you to enter the margin measurement you want to find. If you select a font or style code, WordPerfect displays a list that lets you choose which font or style you want to locate in the current document. After you complete the code selection, you'll see the code in the Search For box, precisely as it appears in the Reveal Codes window. Then choose Search (F2) to find the code in your document.

This feature is invaluable for locating document codes during the editing process. Later in this chapter, you'll see how you can use the Specific Codes option to locate and replace formatting codes with different layout settings.

Performing an Extended Search

The Search feature, as described earlier, searches only the text displayed on the editing screen. If you want to search through all the possible document text elements, you'll need to use WordPerfect's Extended Search feature. The Extended Search not only looks through the text you see in the editing screen, but also searches through the "hidden" text found in headers, footers, footnotes, endnotes, text boxes, and graphics box captions. Here's how to use it:

■ Press Home, Home, Home, ↑ to move the cursor to the top of the document before any formatting codes.

Choose Edit ▸ Search.

■ Press Search (F2) and enter the criterion for the text you want to find. You can search for any text element, as well as formatting codes.

■ Choose Extended Search, so that an *X* appears in the check box next to this option.

■ Select Search (F2) again, and WordPerfect searches through all text—including headers, footers, footnotes, endnotes, text boxes, and graphics box captions—for the search criterion.

You can also invoke the Extended Search feature by pressing Forward Extended Search (Home, F2) or Backward Extended Search (Home, Shift+F2). These keystrokes display the Search dialog box with the Extended Search option already selected. Then you can enter the criterion and choose the Search (F2) option to initiate the search.

Although the Extended Search feature looks through the document's hidden text elements, it cannot find text in a document summary or comment. As a general rule, use Extended Search to search through the main body of text; if you are using the text display mode, this tells WordPerfect to search through any text that does *not* appear at the regular document screen, but will be printed with the document.

Other Search Methods

You have seen how the Search feature lets you find specific words or codes located in the document on your screen, and there are other helpful ways to locate text. For example, you can also use the Search feature while you are viewing the contents of a document file from the File Manager screen. It works like this:

Choose File ▸ File Manager.

■ Press File Manager (F5). Press Enter to accept the displayed directory, or enter a different path name.

- Highlight one of the document files on the list. Then choose <u>L</u>ook from the File Manager menu at the right edge of the dialog box to display the contents of the document.

- With the document in view, press Search (F2) to display the File Manager Search dialog box.

- Type a search criterion, and choose Search (F2) or press Enter to initiate the search.

If the word or phrase specified in the search criterion is in the document, WordPerfect displays the page where the item is found and highlights the search text. You can choose Search again to continue the search. In this case, the Search feature helps you locate text in your document without first requiring you to retrieve the file. If you discover this isn't the file you want to retrieve, you can press Exit (F7) to exit the Look screen and highlight a different file. You can't edit the text or search for codes from the Look screen.

Also on the File Manager dialog box is another WordPerfect feature, called Find, that helps you find the document files that contain certain words, names, or phrases. For example, you can find all files in a given directory that contain the name Smith or Brown. Like the Search feature, Find lets you type a search criterion, and then it shows you which files contain the text you've typed. For more information about the Look and Find features, see Chapter 5.

Replacing Text and Codes

The Replace feature, like Search, can locate specific words or phrases—but Replace has an important additional capability: It also lets you replace the text or codes that you find. If, for instance, you have misspelled a client's name throughout a contract, you can use the Replace feature to quickly locate and replace each occurrence of the incorrect spelling. You can use Replace to update numbers and figures, substitute text information, and replace some formatting codes, too.

Replacing Text

As with Search, the Replace feature also prompts you for a search criterion; in this case, the criterion indicates which text you want to replace. Then WordPerfect will ask you for the text that will replace the text you're searching for. You can replace everything that matches the search criterion, or you may want WordPerfect to prompt you for each replacement.

These are the general steps for replacing text:

■ Move the cursor to the place in your document where you want to begin the Search and Replace operation.

■ Press Replace (Alt+F2) to display the Search and Replace dialog box, shown in Figure 7.3.

■ In the Search For box, type the text you want to find, and then press Enter.

Choose Edit ▸ Replace to display the Search and Replace dialog box.

Figure 7.3

The Search and Replace dialog box

```
 File  Edit  View  Layout  Tools  Font  Graphics  Window  Help
Representatives from the Jamestown Business Park announced a new
non-smoking policy for all business offices in the complex,
beginning 01/15/95. A small ourdoor pavilion is now reserved as a
smoking area for employees and guests. This may allow business
patrons to breathe cleaner air, but the thirty-nine employees who
smoke will be left out in the cold.




              ════════════ Search and Replace ════════════

     Search For:  [                                              ]

     Replace With:  <Nothing>

     [ ] Confirm Replacement        [ ] Find Whole Words Only
     [ ] Backward Search            [ ] Extended Search (Hdrs, Ftrs, etc.)
     [ ] Case Sensitive Search      [ ] Limit Number of Matches:

     Codes... F5  │ Specific Codes... Shft+F5 │    Replace F2  │ Cancel

                                        Doc 4 Pg 1 Ln 1" Pos 1"
```

■ In the Replace With box, type the text that will replace what you're searching for, and then press Enter.

■ Choose Replace (F2) from the dialog box, and WordPerfect initiates the replace operation. Every word or phrase in your document that matches the search criterion is replaced with the designated replacement text.

When the Search and Replace dialog box is displayed, you can choose options that affect the Replace operation. When an *X* appears in the box next to an option, this means the option will affect the current Replace operation. The options for Backward Search, Case Sensitive Search, Find Whole Words Only, and Extended Search work the same as the options described earlier for the Search dialog box.

When you choose Confirm Replacement from the Search and Replace dialog box, WordPerfect will prompt you about replacing each occurrence of matching text; choose Yes at the prompt and the text is replaced, or choose

No and WordPerfect continues to look for the next matching text. If you choose Replace All, WordPerfect goes ahead and replaces all instances of the matching text.

Choose Limit Number of Matches and enter a number to control the number of replacements that will occur. You might use this option when you want to replace only the next five font changes, for example, that appear in your document. Make sure to remove the X from this option when you're done using it, so that it does not affect future Replace opeartions.

The following exercise will give you some hands-on practice with the Replace feature. If you already have text on the screen, don't bother clearing it. Press Home, Home, ↓ to move the cursor to the bottom of the document, press Enter a few times to insert blank lines, and type the text shown in Figure 7.4. (*Hint:* Press Indent (F4) to indent the text from the dashes.)

Figure 7.4

Sample text to search and replace

These additional items were also discussed during the city council meeting:

-     Development of median strip along Janss Road will begin on 04/01/95. Direct inquiries to Robert Andersen.

-     Forest Inc. expressed interest in renting mall facilities for cultural events. Contact Sarah Andersen.

-     The water main along Ventura Boulevard will be extended west to accommodate the North Ranch subdevelopment. Robert Andersen will supervise construction.

Choose Edit ▸ Replace.

1. Move the cursor to the beginning of the text you've just typed. Press Replace (Alt+F2) to display the Search and Replace dialog box.

2. First, assume you want to replace the dashes with asterisks. At the Search For prompt, type - as the search criterion, and then press Enter.

3. At the Replace With prompt, type * as the replacement text, and then press Enter.

4. Choose Replace (F2) to begin the Replace operation. Each dash or hyphen in the text is replaced with an asterisk. You'll see a message indicating that the Search and Replace operation is complete and listing the number of occurrences of the search text that were found as well as the number of replacements made. Press Enter or click on OK and the cursor is located after the last replacement.

5. Press Ctrl+Home twice to return to the original cursor position.

Now let's use Replace to correct the spelling of Robert Anderson's name. Notice, however, that there's another Andersen (Sarah) in the text, and her name is spelled correctly, so you'll need to confirm each replacement.

Choose <u>E</u>dit ▸
Re<u>p</u>lace.

1. Press Replace (Alt+F2) to display the Search and Replace dialog box again.

2. At the Search For prompt, type **Andersen** as the search criterion, and then press Enter.

3. At the Replace With prompt, type **Anderson** as the replacement text, and then press Enter.

4. Choose Con<u>f</u>irm Replacement, so that an *X* appears in the check box next to this option. Then choose Replace (F2) to begin the Replace operation.

5. WordPerfect stops at the first occurrence of *Robert Andersen* and asks you to confirm the replacement; choose <u>Y</u>es.

6. WordPerfect stops at *Sarah Andersen* and asks you to confirm replacement; choose <u>N</u>o.

7. Finally, the cursor stops at the last occurrence of *Robert Andersen*. Choose <u>Y</u>es to confirm the replacement and then press Enter to remove the "Search and Replace Complete" message from your screen.

After you've performed this Replace operation, try pressing Ctrl+Home twice to return to the original location of the cursor before the replacements were made. Note that in this case, because you confirmed the replacements, pressing Ctrl+Home twice just moves you to the beginning of the last word that was replaced. To move back to your original location in this case, you'll need to make use of the arrow keys.

CAUTION. *When you expect to replace several occurrences of matching text, you should turn on the Confirm Replacement option before initiating the replace operation. Remember, without Confirm Replacement, all matching text is replaced, and there is no way to undo the replacements without manually editing the text or performing another Search and Replace operation. If you choose to turn off the Confirm Replacement option, make sure you save a backup copy of your document that you can recover if the replacements do not work as expected.*

Replacing Generic Codes

You've seen how to use Replace to change text in your document, and you can also replace certain formatting codes. Here is a simple exercise that shows how to replace the [→Indent] codes in your document with [Tab] codes.

1. Press Home, Home, ↑ to move the cursor to the beginning of the document on your screen.

2. Press Replace (Alt+F2) to display the Search and Replace dialog box.

Choose Edit ▸ Replace.

3. At the Search For prompt, type an asterisk (*) as the first character for the search criterion.

4. Choose Codes (F5) to display a list of codes, type **lft i** to highlight the Indent code, and then press Enter. This inserts the [Lft Indent] code into the Search For box.

5. The search criterion should look like this:

   ```
   *[Lft Indent]
   ```

   Press Enter to accept it.

6. At the Replace With prompt, choose Codes (F5). From the code list, type **lft t** and then press ↓ to highlight the [Lft Tab] code, and then press Enter to insert the code into the search criterion. Press Enter again to accept the replacement text (code).

7. Choose Replace (F2) and WordPerfect replaces each asterisk and Indent code with a Left Tab code.

Note that when you replace codes as described here, you can choose Backward Search, Extended Search, Confirm Replacement, or any other Search and Replace options before you initiate the Replace operation.

In these steps, you used the code list to insert generic codes into the search criterion. You can also press function keys—like Indent (F4) and Decimal Tab (Ctrl+F6)—to insert the codes, but the keystrokes do not work for all codes. Pressing Tab, for example, moves to the next item in the dialog box, rather than inserting a [Lft Tab] code into the search criterion. In most cases, you'll want to use choose Codes (F5) to select from a list of codes.

Note that the previous steps describe how to replace generic codes. Using this method, you can replace codes like [Lft Indent], [Lft Tab], [Bold On], merge codes, and other codes that do not have layout measurements or styles associated with them. If you want to replace codes that include specific layout measurements or styles—margin codes or font codes, for example—you need to use the Specific Codes list from the Search and Replace dialog box, as explained in the next section.

Replacing Specific Codes

The Specific Codes option in the Search and Replace dialog box lets you replace codes that have specific measurements or settings with another specific code. Using the Specific Codes option, you can, for example, replace all margin codes that are set to 1" with another margin code set to 0.75" or some other measurement. You can convert all Helvetica 12-point font changes to Palatino 14-point. You can also replace a style with another style defined for your document. (See Chapter 22 to learn more about styles.)

The following exercise shows how to replace specific codes. The first part of this exercise instructs you to insert margin codes and font changes into the text on your screen. The result of these changes will simulate a document with multiple margin and font codes—the ideal situation in which to use the Specific Codes option. If the WordPerfect screen is empty, type or retrieve a sample document before you begin the steps.

1. Press Home, Home, ↑ to move the cursor to the beginning of the document displayed on the screen.

Drag the mouse pointer over a section of text.

2. Press Block (Alt+F4 or F12) and move the cursor to block a section of text.

3. Press Font (Ctrl+F8) to display the Font dialog box.

Choose Font ▸ Font.

4. Choose Font to display the font list. Highlight the Roman-WP (Type 1) font name, and press Enter to select it. Then press Exit (F7) to close the Font dialog box.

5. Move the cursor to two other places in your document, and repeat steps 2 through 4 to insert additional Roman-WP (Type 1) font changes in your document.

6. Press Home, Home, ↑ to move the cursor to the beginning of your document.

Drag the mouse pointer over a paragraph of text.

7. Press Block (Alt+F4 or F12) and move the cursor to block a paragraph of text.

8. Press Format (Shift+F8), and then choose Margins to display the Margin Format dialog box. Choose Left Margin and enter **.5** as the measurement. Then press F7 until you return to the document screen.

Choose Layout ▸ Margins.

9. Move to two other paragraphs and repeat steps 7 and 8 to insert additional margin changes in your document.

10. Now you're ready to try the Specific Codes option. Press Home, Home, Home, ↑ and then press ← three times to move the cursor to the beginning of your document before any formatting codes.

Choose Edit ▸ Replace.

11. Press Replace (Alt+F2) to display the Search and Replace dialog box.

12. At the Search For prompt, press Specific Codes (Shift+F5) to display the Specific Codes list.

13. Scroll through the list or type **font** to highlight the item for font changes. Then press Enter to select the font item. WordPerfect scans your document for all font changes, and then displays the dialog box shown in Figure 7.5.

Figure 7.5

The Font Search and Replace dialog box

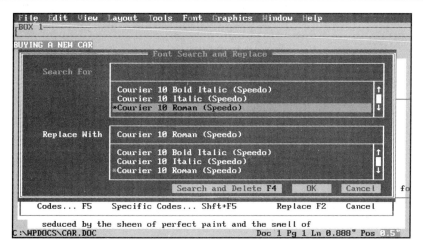

14. At the Search For prompt, you'll see a list of all available fonts. Highlight the font you want to replace and then press Enter. In this case highlight Roman-WP (Type 1).

15. At the Replace With prompt, you'll see a list of all fonts that are defined for the printer that is currently selected. Scroll through the list to highlight the Swiss Roman font name, and press Enter; this is the font that will replace the Roman-WP (Type 1) font.

16. Press Enter or click on OK. WordPerfect redisplays the Search and Replace dialog box, in which you can see both font selections in the Search For and Replace With boxes. Choose Replace (F2) and WordPerfect replaces each case of Roman-WP (Type 1) with Swiss Roman.

17. Press Home, Home, Home, ↑ and then press ← three times to move the cursor to the beginning of the document.

18. Press Replace (Alt+F2) and then choose Specific Codes (Shift+F5).

Choose Edit ▸ Replace ▸ Specific Codes.

19. Scroll through the list or type **l** to highlight the left margin item from the list. Then press Enter to select it. WordPerfect displays the Left Margin Search and Replace dialog box, shown in Figure 7.6.

Figure 7.6
The Left Margin Search and Replace dialog box

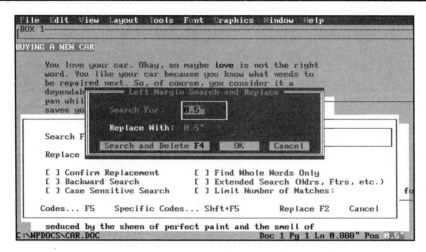

20. At the Search For prompt, type the margin measurement you want to replace, and then press Enter. For this example, enter **.5**.

21. At the Replace With prompt, type the margin measurement that should replace the previous measurement, and then press Enter. For this example, enter **1.5**.

22. Click on OK or press Enter. WordPerfect redisplays the Search and Replace dialog box with the margin settings that you specified. Choose Replace (F2), and WordPerfect replaces the previous margin setting with the new measurement you specified under Replace With.

These are just two examples of how you can replace one specific code with another. Scroll through the Specific Code list, and you'll see all the codes you can replace; when you choose each one, you'll get a dialog box that lets you enter replacement information for that code.

In this exercise, you used the Block feature to create sections of text where the font and margin codes were turned on and off. Note that after the replacements were done, there is only one font change code and one left margin code at the top of the document. This happened because the margin and font codes you inserted specified only one type of change, and WordPerfect does not let you place one identical font or layout code after another.

For example, WordPerfect will not insert a 1.5-inch margin change code when a previous code has already specified that measurement as the current margin setting; if, however, your document contains mixed margin settings of 1.5" and 0.75", and you want to replace the 1.5" settings with 0.5", WordPerfect would replace each of the 1.5" margin settings and leave the 0.75" setting intact.

Using Replace to Delete Text or Codes

You can also use the Replace feature to delete text and codes without disturbing the surrounding text. Consider again the text in our previous example. Let's say you don't want tabs in your document; you can replace them with *nothing*—effectively removing them from the text. This is much faster than scrolling through the text and manually deleting tabs. Try this with the text on your screen:

TIP. *If you're not happy with the results of a Replace operation, you can undo them if you act quickly, selecting undo before you perform any other undoable operation.*

1. Move the cursor to the beginning of the sentence that begins "These additional items...."

Choose Edit ▸ Replace.

2. Press Replace (Alt+F2) to display the Search and Replace dialog box.

3. At the Search For prompt, choose Codes (F5), type **lft t**, and press ↓ to highlight the [Lft Tab] item. Then press Enter to insert the code into the search criterion. Press Enter again to move to the Replace With prompt.

4. At the Replace With prompt, press Enter to indicate that you want to replace [Lft Tab] with nothing.

5. Choose Confirm Replacement so that an *X* appears in the check box for this option.

6. Choose Replace (F2) to begin the Replace operation.

7. At each occurrence of a [LFT TAB] code, WordPerfect prompts you to confirm the replacement. Choose Yes and the [LFT TAB] code is replaced with nothing, and thus is removed from the document. Choose No and WordPerfect skips the current [LFT TAB] code and moves to the next matching code. Choose Replace All and WordPerfect continues the replacement without confirmation.

Repeating Keystrokes

WordPerfect's Repeat feature repeats or multiplies the effect of a keystroke you press. As you'll soon discover, the Repeat feature allows you to move the cursor more quickly and produces character lines with ease. Move the cursor to the middle of the text on your screen. Then follow these steps to experiment with the Repeat feature:

Choose Edit ▸ Repeat.

1. At the editing screen, press Repeat (Ctrl+R). WordPerfect displays the message "Count: 8" in the middle of the screen. This tells you that the next key you press will be repeated eight times.

2. Press ↓ and the cursor moves down eight lines, just as if you'd pressed ↓ eight times.

3. Press Repeat (Ctrl+R) to display the "Count: 8" message, and press Delete Word (Ctrl+Backspace) to delete eight words from the text. Since this is considered one deletion, you can press Undelete (Esc) and choose Restore to bring back the deleted words.

4. Move the cursor to the bottom of the text or to the beginning of a blank line. Press Repeat (Ctrl+R) and type the equal sign (=). WordPerfect repeats the key to create a line of eight characters.

You can easily change the repeat value by typing a different number while the Repeat dialog box is displayed. Try this: Either press Repeat (Ctrl+R) or choose Edit and Repeat to display the "Count: 8" message. Then type a new number (for example, **30**) and press the key you want to repeat. If, for example, you want to create a character line with asterisks, move the cursor to a blank line. Press Repeat (Ctrl+R), type **60** to change the repeat value, and then type an asterisk (*) to create the line.

Use the Repeat feature for cursor movement keystrokes like the arrow keys (↓, ↑, →, and ←), Word Right and Word Left (Ctrl+→ and Ctrl+←), and PgUp/PgDn. You can use this feature to repeat most keys on the keyboard. A few exceptions are Enter, Backspace, Tab, and, of course, the number keys, which are used to change the repeat value.

Working with Document Windows

When you first start the WordPerfect program, you see one document window. Each time you open a document, WordPerfect places it in a new document window; you can open up to nine document windows at once. The following steps explain how to open multiple documents and switch between them. You'll also learn how to display multiple documents at the same time to allow editing of two or more documents at once.

Choose File ▸ Open.

1. Press Open (Shift+F10) to display the Open Document dialog box.

2. If the option for Open into New Document is not selected, press Shift+F10 until it is (a small filled button precedes the option when it is selected).

3. Type the name of the file you want to open, and press Enter. Or press File Manager (F5), press Enter, and select a file from the list. WordPerfect opens a new window and retrieves the document into it.

4. Repeat steps 1 through 3 to open additional documents. Open at least three document windows for this exercise. As you open each new document window, you'll see its number after the *Doc* label on the status line.

Choose <u>W</u>indow ▸ S<u>w</u>itch to.

5. When you have two or more document windows open, you can switch between them. Press F3 or press Home, 0 to display a list of all open documents, like the example shown in Figure 7.7. Then type one of the numbers (1 through 9) to switch to one of the documents.

Figure 7.7
Switching between open documents

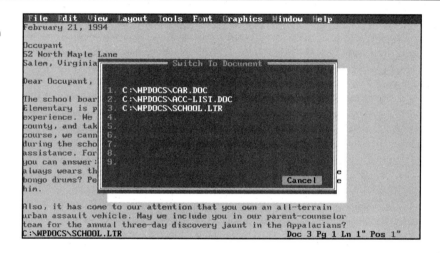

6. Another way to switch between documents is by pressing the Home key, followed by the number of the document you want to see. For example, press Home, 3 to display document window 3. Press Home, 1 to move to document window 1. You can also press Switch (Shift+F3) to switch between the last two documents that you opened.

Choose <u>W</u>indow ▸ S<u>w</u>itch.

7. To view all open documents on the screen, press Screen (Ctrl+F3), choose <u>W</u>indow, and then choose <u>T</u>ile. This arranges the open document windows as shown in Figure 7.8. The window with the double-lined border (or the highlighted title bar, in graphics display mode) is the document you are currently editing.

Choose <u>W</u>indow ▸ <u>T</u>ile.

8. When windows are "tiled," you can move to a different window by pressing Home, followed by the number of the window, or by pressing Home, 0 to select a window from the Switch Document dialog box.

Click the mouse pointer on a window to move to a different document.

Figure 7.8

Tiled document
windows

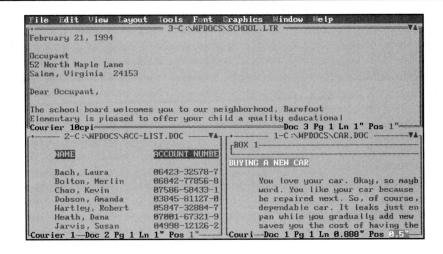

Choose Window ▸
Cascade.

9. To arrange the windows as overlapping documents, press Screen (Ctrl+F3), choose Window, and then choose Cascade. This arranges the windows as shown in Figure 7.9.

Figure 7.9

Cascading
document windows

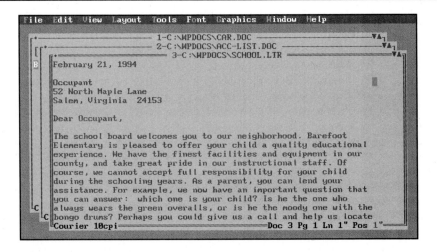

10. When you are finished working in one of the document windows, press Exit (F7). At the Save prompt, choose Yes if you want to save the document. Then choose Yes to close the document window.

When two or more document windows are open, you can also use the mouse pointer to size and move the windows. Figure 7.10 shows the window controls along each window's border. To size a window, position the mouse pointer over a side or corner of the window's border; then drag the border (hold down the mouse button while moving the mouse pointer) to change the window's size and shape. To move a window, move the mouse pointer over the document title at the top side of the window; then drag the mouse pointer to reposition the window.

Figure 7.10

Controls for moving and sizing a window

Click on the bullet (•) to close or exit the window

Drag the title to move the window

Drag a corner or side to change window size

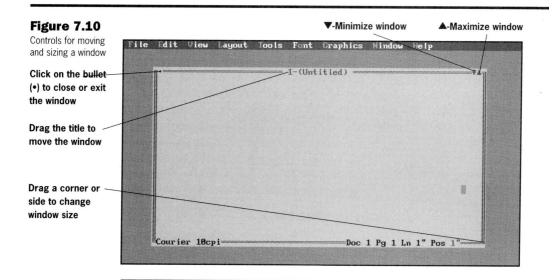

▼-Minimize window   ▲-Maximize window

TIP. *If the document you're viewing fills the entire screen and you don't see a border, choose* <u>Window</u> *and then* <u>Frame</u> *and the border will appear.*

Other controls along the border let you quickly adjust the window's size. Click on the *minimize icon* (▾), and the current document window shrinks to its smallest possible size. Click on the *maximize icon* (▴), and the window expands to its original size. When both the maximize (▴) and minimize (▾) icons appear at the same time, and you click on the maximize icon, the current document window expands to fill the entire screen.

The following steps will give you some practice with sizing and moving a document window:

Choose <u>W</u>indow ▸ <u>F</u>rame.

1. If you can't see the borders for the current document window, press Screen (Ctrl+F3), choose <u>W</u>indow, and then choose <u>F</u>rame.

Drag a corner or side of the border to change the window's size.

2. To size the window, press Screen (Ctrl+F3), choose <u>W</u>indow, and then choose <u>S</u>ize. Use the arrow keys on your keyboard to change the size of

Drag a corner of the border to change the window's size.

Click on the ▾ icon in the upper-right corner of the window.

Click on the ▴ icon in the upper-right corner of the window.

Click on the bullet (•) icon in the upper-left corner of the window.

the window, noting the dashed lines that indicate the new window size. Press Enter to accept the new size.

3. To move the window, press Screen (Ctrl+F3), choose <u>W</u>indow, and then choose <u>M</u>ove. Then use the keyboard arrow keys to move the window, noting the dashed lines that indicate the new window location. Press Enter to accept the new position.

4. To shrink the window, press Screen (Ctrl+F3), choose <u>W</u>indow, and then choose M<u>i</u>nimize.

5. To expand the window, press Screen (Ctrl+F3), choose <u>W</u>indow, and then choose M<u>a</u>ximize.

6. To close the window, press Exit (F7).

When you press Exit (F7) or click on the bullet (∘) icon, WordPerfect asks whether you want to save the document inside the window if you have made any changes to the document. Choose <u>Y</u>es or <u>N</u>o.

Zooming In for a Closer Look

When you are working with WordPerfect's graphics mode display or page mode display, you can use the Zoom feature to magnify or reduce your view of the current document. In Chapter 4, you learned about the Zoom features for the Print Preview screen; the Zoom features described in this section are a little different because they let you edit your document at the magnified or reduced view.

Figure 7.11 shows two examples of how you might use the Zoom feature. The first screen shows a close-up view of the document text, which, in this case, helps you read small footnote text. The second screen shows a reduced or "zoomed-out" view of the document, which gives an overview of the complete page. In each example, it's possible to edit the document text and insert new layout codes—you can do whatever you need to do for the current document.

To use the Zoom features, first switch to the graphics display mode or page display mode (press Ctrl+F3 and choose <u>G</u>raphics or <u>P</u>age). Then you can choose one of the following Zoom options:

Choose <u>V</u>iew ▸ <u>Z</u>oom ▸ <u>F</u>ull Page.

- To display the full height of the current document page, press Screen (Ctrl+F3), choose <u>Z</u>oom, and then choose <u>F</u>ull Page. Press Exit (F7) to return to your document.

Choose <u>V</u>iew ▸ <u>Z</u>oom ▸ Page <u>W</u>idth.

- To display the full width of the current document page, press Screen (Ctrl+F3), choose <u>Z</u>oom, and then choose Page <u>W</u>idth. Press Exit (F7) to return to your document.

Figure 7.11

Zoom lets you choose a different view of your document.

200 % Zoom

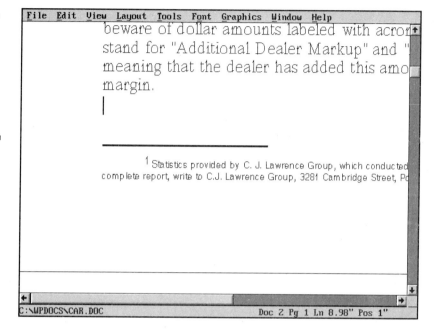

Full page Zoom

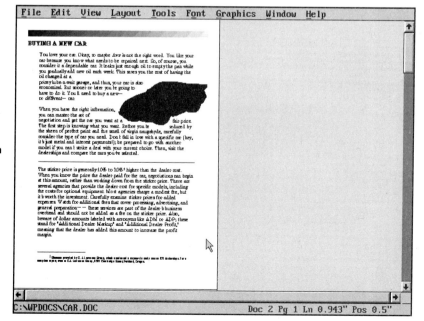

Choose View ▶ Zoom, and then choose one of the following: 50%, 75%, 100%, 125%, 150%, or 200%.

- To zoom in according to a specific percentage, press Screen (Ctrl+F3), choose Zoom, and then choose Percentage. Enter the percentage number, and press Exit (F7). You can enter a number between 40 and 800.

When you are finished with the zoomed view, press Screen (Ctrl+F3) and select Zoom, or choose View and then Zoom from the menu bar. Choose Margin Width to restore the standard screen setting. Remember that when the zoomed view is displayed, you can move the cursor, type or delete text, and perform any other task to create and edit the document. When you are viewing a close-up view of your document, you'll probably want to display both the vertical and horizontal scroll bars to help you move through the document text.

Using WordPerfect's Ribbon Bar

The ribbon bar, shown in Figure 7.12, provides convenient access to some of WordPerfect's important editing tools. When the ribbon bar is displayed, you can select a zoomed view, apply a style to document text, create document columns, choose a justification setting, or select a specific font and point size for your text. (See Chapter 22 to learn more about styles.)

Figure 7.12
WordPerfect's ribbon bar

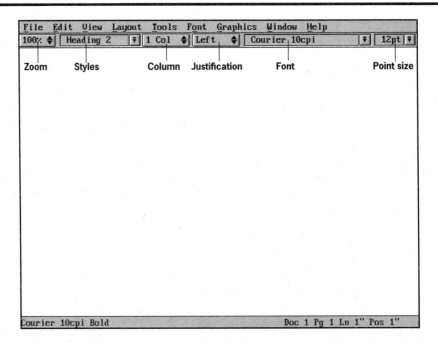

Note the names assigned to each of the buttons on the ribbon bar. Although the graphic screen is shown in the illustration, you can also use the ribbon bar with the text display mode. You must use the mouse pointer to select options from the ribbon bar.

To display and use the ribbon bar:

Choose View ▸ Ribbon.

- Press Screen (Ctrl+F3) and then press Setup (Shift+F1). Choose <u>S</u>creen Options and then <u>R</u>ibbon. Press Exit (F7) until you return to the document screen. The ribbon bar is now displayed.

- To choose a font from the ribbon bar, click on the Font button and double-click to select a font from the list, as shown here:

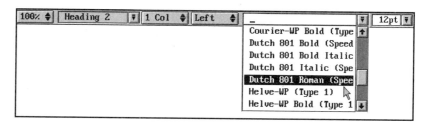

- You can also click on the Point Size button and double-click on one of the listed point sizes to change the size of text when you've selected a scalable font.

- To create document columns, move the cursor to the place where columns should begin. Then click on the Column button, and double-click to select the number of columns you want. Note that choosing "1 Col" is the same as turning off the Column feature.

- To choose one of the styles you've defined for the document, click on the Styles button, and select the desired style.

- Click on the Justification button and choose one of the options to select a justification type for your text.

- When you're working with WordPerfect's graphics display mode or page display mode, you can click on the Zoom button to choose a zoom option.

When you choose an option from the ribbon bar, the effect is the same as if you had selected the feature from a menu or dialog box. Before you click on the Styles, Column, Justification, Font, or Point Size button, you need to position your cursor at the place where you want the change to take effect. The result is a formatting or font code inserted at the cursor position.

When you are finished with the ribbon bar, press Screen (Ctrl+F3) and Setup (Shift+F1). Choose Screen Options and then Ribbon, so that no *X* appears in the check box next to this option. Then press Exit (F7) until you return to the editing screen. Or simply choose View and then Ribbon from the menu bar. The ribbon bar is removed from the screen.

Using WordPerfect's Button Bar

WordPerfect's button bar, shown in Figure 7.13, provides quick access to common features in WordPerfect. Instead of choosing a feature from a menu or dialog box, you can click on one of the button-bar buttons to print or save a document or choose one of the layout features. The best aspect of the button bar is that you can customize it to include the features you use most. You can also record a series of commands in a macro and then include the macro as one of the buttons on a button bar. In this section, you'll see how to display and use the button bar feature.

Figure 7.13
WordPerfect's button bar

WordPerfect's button bar

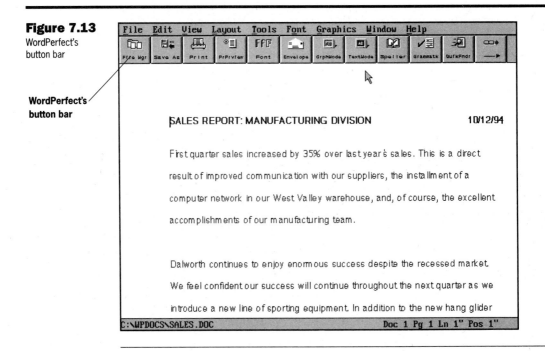

The illustrations in this section appear in WordPerfect's graphics display screen, but you can use the button bar on any of WordPerfect's display types: Text Mode, Graphics Mode, or Page Mode. For each display type, you must use the mouse pointer to access features on the button bar.

Displaying the Button Bar

Try the following steps for a brief exercise in displaying and using the button bar:

Choose View ▸ Button Bar.

- Press Screen (Ctrl+F3) and press Setup (Shift+F1). Choose <u>S</u>creen Options and then choose <u>B</u>utton Bar so that an *X* appears next to this option. Then press Exit (F7) until you return to the document screen. WordPerfect displays the main button bar at the top of the screen.

- On the button bar, move the mouse pointer over the button labeled "File Mgr" and click the mouse button. This starts the File Manager. Press Esc or choose Cancel to close the File Manager.

- Click on the Speller button to start WordPerfect's Speller. When you're finished with the Speller, return to your document.

- At one end of the button bar, you will see a set of "triangle" buttons, like this:

Click on these buttons to scroll to the next set of buttons

These buttons indicate that there are more buttons on the current button bar layout that you can't see. Click on the ▾ button and the button bar scrolls to reveal more buttons that you can choose. Click on the ▴ button and you'll scroll up to the previous set of buttons.

Choose View ▸ Button Bar.

- When you are finished with the button bar, press Screen (Ctrl+F3) and press Setup (Shift+F1). Choose <u>S</u>creen Options, and then choose <u>B</u>utton Bar again. Press Exit (F7) until you return to the document screen. WordPerfect removes the button bar from the screen.

When you choose features from the button bar, they work exactly the same as if you had selected them from the menu bar or with the function keys. If the button bar is displayed when you exit WordPerfect, it will appear again the next time you start WordPerfect.

Choosing a Different Button Bar

When you first display the button bar, you'll see the WordPerfect's standard button-bar layout. WordPerfect also includes other predefined button-bar layouts that are designed to perform specific tasks. To select a different button-bar layout:

Choose <u>V</u>iew ▸
Button Bar <u>S</u>etup ▸
Scree<u>n</u> Setup.

Choose OK until
you return to the
document screen.

- Press Screen (Ctrl+F3) and press Setup (Shift+F1). Choose <u>S</u>creen Options and then choose <u>S</u>elect Button Bar. WordPerfect displays a list of the defined button-bar layouts.

- Highlight the button-bar layout you want to use, and then choose <u>S</u>elect.

- Press Exit (F7) until you return to the document screen. The new button-bar layout is displayed and ready for use.

WordPerfect automatically displays some of its predefined button bars for special editing tasks within the software. Figure 7.14 shows the button bar that automatically appears at the top of the Print Preview screen.

Figure 7.14

The Print Preview
button bar

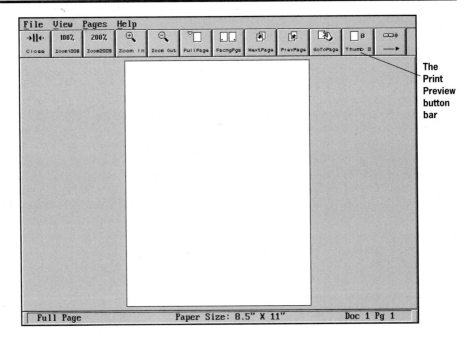

**The
Print
Preview
button
bar**

When each of these screens is displayed, you can choose <u>V</u>iew and then <u>But</u>ton Bar to remove or display the button bar on the screen.

Choosing Button Bar Display Options

WordPerfect also provides other options that affect the display of the button bar. To select button-bar options, choose View, Button Bar Setup, and then Options. Or press Screen (Ctrl+F3), press Setup (Shift+F1), choose Screen Options, and then choose Button Bar Options. This displays the dialog box shown here:

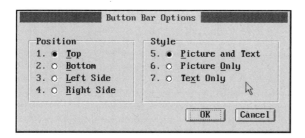

Choose a Position option—Top, Bottom, Left Side, or Right Side—to indicate the edge of the screen where you want the button bar to appear. Choose one of the Style options—Picture and Text, Picture Only, or Text Only—to specify whether you want to see icons and text labels on the buttons, or just icons or text. When you're using WordPerfect's text display mode, the Text Only option is the only one that applies.

When you're finished defining the button-bar options, press Exit (F7) or choose OK until you return to the document screen. The button-bar options you selected remain in effect until you change the options again.

Creating a Custom Button Bar

As mentioned earlier, you can create one or more custom button-bar layouts, and then choose the one you want to use for a specific document or task. The following exercise explains how to do this:

Choose View ▸ Button Bar Setup ▸ Select. Then choose Create.

1. Press Screen (Ctrl+F3) and press Setup (Shift+F1). Choose Screen Options and then Select Button Bar. Choose Create.

2. You are prompted to enter a name for the new button bar. For this exercise, type **helpwp!** and press Enter. WordPerfect displays the Edit Button Bar dialog box, shown in Figure 7.15.

3. Choose Add Menu Item and then choose a feature from the pull-down menus to add a new button to the button bar layout. For this exercise, choose File and then Open; WordPerfect adds the Open button to the button bar.

Figure 7.15

The Edit Button Bar dialog box

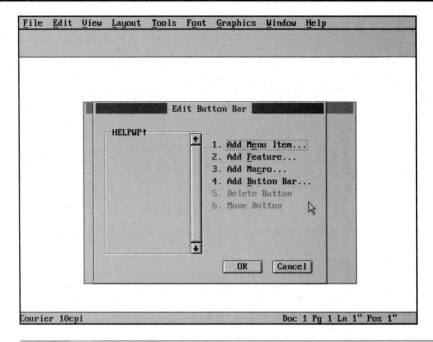

Choose OK to reactivate the Edit Button Bar menu.

4. Continue to select features to add buttons to the button-bar layout. For this exercise, choose the following features: File, Save As; File, Print; Edit, Undo; View, Ribbon; View, Horizontal Scroll Bar; and Font, Font.

5. When you're finished adding buttons to the button-bar layout, press Exit (F7) to reactivate the Edit Button Bar menu.

6. You can also add a button by choosing from a list of WordPerfect features. From the Edit Button Bar dialog box, choose Add Feature and WordPerfect displays a list of features. Highlight the feature you want to assign (you can also type a feature name to move directly to the feature) and then press Enter or click on Select.

7. Suppose you don't want to keep the Ribbon button on the button bar. In the Edit Button Bar dialog box, highlight the Ribbon name on the button-bar list, choose Delete Button, and then choose Yes to remove the Ribbon button.

8. Now move one of the buttons. Highlight the Undo name and choose Move Button. Press Home, ↑ to move to the top of the list, and then choose Paste Button to move the Undo name there.

Choose OK until
you return to the
document screen.

9. When you are finished adding buttons and editing the button bar, your screen will look similar to Figure 7.16. Press Exit (F7) until you return to the Select Button Bar dialog box.

Figure 7.16

A finished button-bar layout

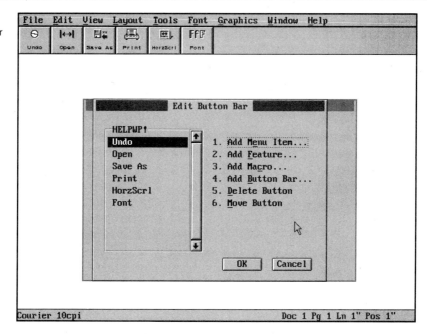

10. If you want to use the new button bar now, highlight the button-bar name and choose Select. Otherwise, press Exit (F7) until you return to the document screen.

The new button-bar layout is saved in the WordPerfect macros directory with a *.WPB extension. For this exercise, your button-bar file is saved in a file called HELPWP!.WPB.

Other options on the Edit Button Bar dialog box let you create a button that displays a different button-bar layout, and create a button that plays back a series of recorded commands, called a *macro*. For more information about creating macros, see Chapter 24. After you've created a macro file, you can choose the Add Macro option from the Edit Button Bar dialog box, and then select your macro and include it as a button on the button bar.

Displaying a Ruler for Editing

WordPerfect's Reveal Codes window also displays the ruler, shown in Figure 7.17, to remind you where the margins and tabs are set.

Figure 7.17
WordPerfect's ruler

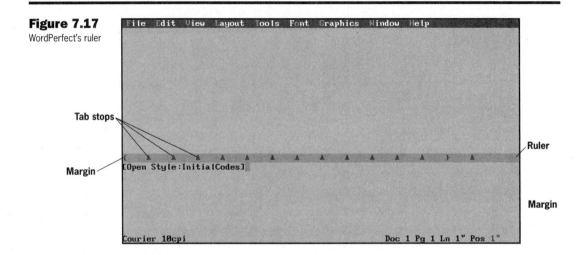

To display the ruler, press Reveal Codes (Alt+F3 or F11). To remove the ruler from the screen, press Reveal Codes (Alt+F3 or F11).

When the ruler is displayed on the screen, it appears inside the document window. The triangles on the ruler show where the current tab stops are set. Square brackets ([]) show where the margins are set. Curly braces ({}) indicate a margin that shares a tab-stop setting. When you close the document, turn off Reveal Codes or exit WordPerfect, the ruler is removed from the screen.

Hyphenating Your Text

Hyphenation is the process of dividing words so that the text wraps more smoothly throughout your document. WordPerfect provides two ways to hyphenate text. You can instruct WordPerfect to automatically hyphenate your text, or you can manually insert special characters and codes to indicate where words should be divided or hyphenated.

Use the following steps to turn on automatic hyphenation for the document on your screen:

1. Move the cursor to the place in your document where you want to begin hyphenation.

Choose Layout ▸
Line ▸ Hyphenation.

Choose OK to return
to the document
screen.

2. Press Format (Shift+F8), choose <u>L</u>ine, and then choose H<u>y</u>phenation (an *X* should be in the check box next to the Hyphenation option).

3. Press Exit (F7) twice until you return to the document screen.

These steps insert a [Hyph] code that you can see in the Reveal Codes window. WordPerfect will now monitor and hyphenate text from the cursor location until the end of the document.

If you want to hyphenate only a section of the text, use Block (Alt+F4) to select the section of text; then turn on automatic hyphenation as instructed above. This inserts a [+Hyph:On] code at the beginning of the block and a [-Hyph] code at the end of the block.

Hyphenation Prompts

When you enable automatic hyphenation, you may be prompted occasionally to help WordPerfect place the hyphens. This happens when WordPerfect needs to hyphenate a word that is not found in the Speller dictionary file. When this occurs, the word is displayed with a prompt on your screen.

For example, suppose WordPerfect needs to hyphenate the word *representative* in your document. If WordPerfect can't figure out how to hyphenate the word, you'll see the Position Hyphen dialog box. You will then need to indicate where the word should be hyphenated, because the program doesn't have enough information to hyphenate it. Use the ← and → keys (or click on the ← and → buttons) to position the hyphen. Then press Enter or choose Insert Hyphen.

If you want to indicate that the word should not be hyphenated, select I<u>g</u>nore Word. WordPerfect will then insert a [Cancel Hyph] code before the word, which will prohibit hyphenation of this single word. If you later want the word to be hyphenated, you'll need to highlight and delete the [Cancel Hyph] code from the Reveal Codes window.

WordPerfect lets you determine when it will prompt you regarding the hyphenation of words. This option is found on WordPerfect's Setup Environment dialog box. To specify the type of hyphenation in a document:

Choose <u>F</u>ile ▸
Se<u>t</u>up ▸
Environment.

- Press Setup (Shift+F1) to display the WordPerfect Setup dialog box.

- Choose <u>E</u>nvironment and then <u>P</u>rompt for Hyphenation.

- A list opens with three options for hyphenation prompts: <u>N</u>ever, <u>W</u>hen Required, and <u>A</u>lways. Choose one of the options.

- Press Exit (F7) until you return to the document screen.

The option you select indicates the conditions under which WordPerfect will prompt for hyphenation:

- Choose <u>N</u>ever if you don't want WordPerfect to prompt you at all regarding hyphenation. In this case, if WordPerfect encounters a word that it doesn't know how to hyphenate, it will simply send the word to the next line.

- Choose <u>W</u>hen Required to instruct WordPerfect to prompt you for the hyphen position only when it needs to hyphenate a word that it doesn't recognize. This is the default setting.

- Choose <u>A</u>lways and WordPerfect will ask you to verify the hyphen position for each word that needs to be hyphenated.

WordPerfect's Hyphenation Zone

The *hyphenation zone* is an invisible area of space that surrounds the right margin on the page. As you move the cursor through your document, Word-Perfect hyphenates the words that cross both ends of the *hyphenation zone*. Figure 7.18 shows a diagram of the hyphenation zone to illustrate the two cases in which WordPerfect will hyphenate or wrap the word:

- When a word spans the hyphenation zone, WordPerfect hyphenates the word.

- When the beginning of a word is already within the hyphenation zone and extends through it, WordPerfect wraps the word.

Figure 7.18
WordPerfect's
hyphenation zone

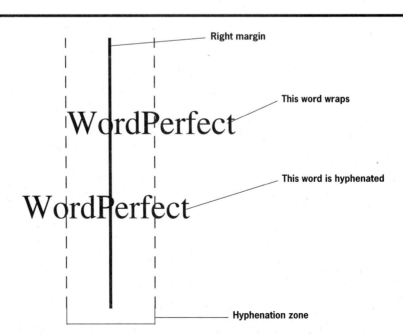

Right margin

This word wraps

This word is hyphenated

Hyphenation zone

You can increase or decrease the amount of space allowed for the hyphenation zone. This is done with the Hyphenation Zone option in the Line Format dialog box. With this option, you will enter two numbers to define the hyphenation zone. The first number determines how much space is allowed before the right margin (this is called the *left* number); the second number determines how much space is allowed after the right margin (this is called the *right* number).

Both hyphenation zone numbers are entered as percentages of the line width on the page. For example, the standard settings are 10 percent before the right margin (the left number) and 4 percent after the margin (the right number). It's easy to calculate the space for the hyphenation zone. Assume that the page width is 8.5 inches, with 1-inch margins set on each side. Subtract 2 inches (1 inch each for the left and right margins), and the line width is reduced to 6.5 inches. Multiply 6.5 times 10 percent and you get a result of 0.65 inch; 6.5 times 4 percent equals 0.26 inch. The result is a hyphenation zone with 0.65 inch of space before the right margin and 0.26 inch after the right margin—almost a full inch of space for the hyphenation zone.

These are the steps for changing the hyphenation zone:

Choose Layout ▸ Line ▸ Hyphenation Zone.

- Move the cursor to the place where the new hyphenation zone will take effect. Usually, this is at the beginning of your document.

- Press Format (Shift+F8) and choose Line. Then choose Hyphenation Zone.

- Type a percentage for the left edge of the hyphenation zone, and press Enter.

- Type a percentage for the right edge of the hyphenation zone, and press Enter.

- Press Exit (F7) or Enter until all dialog boxes are closed, and you return to the document screen.

If you want WordPerfect to hyphenate more often, decrease the numbers to make a smaller hyphenation zone. Enter larger numbers to increase the size of the hyphenation zone, and WordPerfect will hyphenate fewer words.

WordPerfect inserts [Lft HZone] and [Rgt HZone] codes into your document. These codes change the hyphenation zone for all text located after the code. If you don't like the results you get with the new hyphenation zone, you can highlight and delete the codes from the Reveal Codes window.

Preventing Hyphenation of a Single Word

Sometimes there will be words in your document that should never be hyphenated. For these single words, you can insert a code that prevents any hyphenation. Move the cursor to the beginning of the word, press the Home key and then type *I*. This inserts a [Cancel Hyph] code before the word, which tells WordPerfect not to hyphenate it. If the word extends into the hyphenation zone, WordPerfect will simply wrap it to the next line.

Inserting Characters for Hyphenation

WordPerfect does a good job of hyphenating words in your document, but you may want to control how certain words are divided. There are a few characters you can use to manually hyphenate the text in your document. When hyphenation is necessary, WordPerfect will split the words at these characters. Other characters can prevent hyphenation altogether.

The Hyphen Character

A *hyphen character* is a character that should always be displayed as a hyphen in the printed text, regardless of whether the word should be divided. You would insert this character for phrases like: "2-inch," "old-fashioned lemonade," or hyphenated names like "John-Austin." If the word must be split at the end of the line, WordPerfect will do so immediately after the hyphen. To insert this character, simply type a dash (-) from the keyboard. This inserts a [- Hyphen] code into the text.

Soft Hyphens

A *soft hyphen* is a special code that you insert into the text to tell WordPerfect where the word should be hyphenated, if hyphenation is ever necessary. This is useful for technical terms or other unusual words that may not be found in WordPerfect's hyphenation dictionary. To insert this code, hold down the Ctrl key and type a dash (-). This places a hyphen at the cursor position that appears as [- Soft Hyphen] on the Reveal Codes window but is normally invisible in the document text. The soft hyphen remains invisible until the word must be hyphenated. WordPerfect then splits the word after the soft hyphen and displays it as part of the text. If you add or delete text so that the word no longer needs to be hyphenated, the soft hyphen becomes invisible again.

Hard Hyphens

A *hard hyphen* is a character that appears as a hyphen in the text, but it is considered a regular text character. When you insert this character into a word, WordPerfect will not use it as a guide for hyphenation. To insert a hard hyphen, press Home and then type a dash (-). At the Reveal Codes screen, this character appears as a simple dash.

Hyphenation Soft Return

Sometimes you'll want to indicate where WordPerfect should divide a word but you won't want it to insert a hyphen at the division. The best example of this is when you have two words separated by a slash. Phrases like "yes/no," "either/or," and "Smith/Wilson" would look odd if a hyphen were inserted after the slash to separate the word. But there may be situations where the word does need to be separated.

For these cases, you can insert a hyphenation soft return after the slash character. The hyphenation soft return is similar to the soft hyphen, because it remains hidden until the word needs to be separated. Then it tells WordPerfect where the phrase should be broken and wrapped to the next line. To insert this code, move the cursor past the slash character, and press Home and then Enter. This inserts a [Hyph SRt] code into the text. If the word ever needs to be divided, WordPerfect will separate the word at the [Hyph SRt] code without inserting a hyphen. If you add or delete text, so that the word moves out of the hyphenation zone, the hyphenation soft return becomes dormant once again.

8

Using the Speller, Thesaurus, and Other Writing Tools

SUPPOSE YOU'VE DISTRIBUTED AN IMPORTANT BUSINESS REPORT TO your peers, and then a colleague directs your attention to a few errors in that document. As you look through the pages, you discover several embarrassing misspellings—some common typing errors and a few surprising mistakes. Although these types of errors do creep into most documents, the reader can usually decipher what you've written. Still, spelling errors reflect poorly on you, the writer, and may even obscure your message. If you want to impress others with your writing, it's important to correct misspellings and typing mistakes before you print your documents.

Unfortunately, you may not have time to check the dictionary for each word in your document—but WordPerfect can. You have at your fingertips the WordPerfect Speller, a 120,000-word dictionary that you can use to check the spelling of your documents. And the WordPerfect Thesaurus will enrich your documents with exciting word alternatives. WordPerfect also includes Grammatik, an on-line grammar checker to help you fix writing errors and verify that you've used words correctly.

Together, the Speller, Thesaurus, and Grammatik act as your personal editor. They can't guarantee perfect documents or transform a dry business memo into a literary masterpiece, but they will correct your errors with spelling and grammar and will help you find the right words—for truly professional documents.

What Can the Speller Do?

The Speller is a powerful editing tool that helps you correct your documents quickly and efficiently. You can select the Speller feature whenever you type or edit the text in your document. When a misspelled word is found, the Speller highlights it and offers you a list of possible corrections. You can spell-check the entire document, a page, or just a single word. When used with the Block feature, the Speller will check for misspelled words in a defined block of text.

Besides finding misspelled words, the Speller can also make other corrections and perform additional functions in your document:

- The Speller checks for occurrences of *double words*, that is, words that are accidentally typed twice in the text. This often happens with words like *the*, *a*, and *that*. When double words are found, WordPerfect highlights both words and lets you delete the extra one.

- When you've combined numbers with text characters, as in *200W* and *3D*, the Speller asks you to verify that you want the text as it appears. This helps you catch typing errors in which you pressed number or letter keys accidentally.

- The Speller is *case sensitive*, which means that it checks the use of capital letters and allows you to edit any perceived problems with irregular casing.

- An option called <u>L</u>ook Up Word lets you look up the spelling of words before you type them in the text.

Each of these features is explained later in this chapter.

When you consider all it can do, the Speller is one of the most important editing tools you will use. An exercise provided later lets you practice using the Speller to correct misspellings and other errors in the text.

Using the Speller

When you choose the Speller feature, you can indicate whether you want to check the spelling of the open document, the displayed page, or the word at the cursor position. You can also choose to check spelling starting at the location of the cursor. The Speller highlights any misspelled words it finds and may suggest possible replacement words from its dictionary. If you've misspelled the same word in the same way two or more times in the document, you'll need to correct only the first misspelling; WordPerfect corrects all further misspellings for you.

Here is the general procedure to check the spelling for the entire document displayed on the screen:

Choose <u>T</u>ools ▸ <u>W</u>riting Tools ▸ <u>S</u>peller.

- With your document displayed at the editing screen, press Spell (Ctrl+F2). The Speller dialog box appears on the screen, offering options that let you choose what you want to check. (Note that if you have the button bar displayed, you can simply click on the Speller icon.)

- Choose <u>D</u>ocument. Beginning at the top of the document, the Speller compares the words in your text with the words in the Speller's dictionary. When a misspelled word is found in the text, the Speller highlights it and displays possible replacements in the Speller dialog box, as shown in Figure 8.1. Note that each possible replacement is preceded by a letter.

Double-click on the desired replacement word.

- Type a letter to choose a replacement from the list, and the Speller makes the correction. Then it continues examining the words in the document, stopping at each misspelled word and giving you the opportunity to correct it.

Choose OK to continue.

- After the Speller has examined the entire document, a message box indicates the spell-check is finished. You can then press Exit (F7) to return to the normal document editing mode.

Figure 8.1

The Speller dialog box with replacement words

Misspelled word

Suggested replacement words

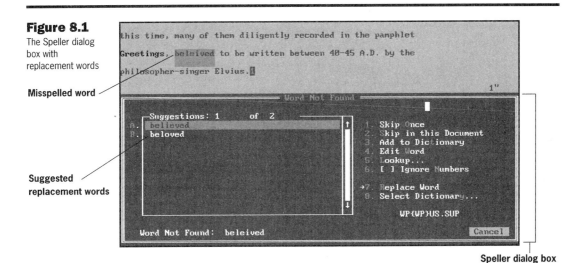

Speller dialog box

Remember that the Speller is using a limited dictionary; there are some words that it will highlight as misspellings, even though the words are spelled correctly. For example, some technical terms or personal names are not recognized as correct spellings, because they are not included as words in the Speller dictionary. You may want the Speller to skip these words. If the Speller constantly highlights a correctly spelled word or other term that you use often, consider adding it to your Speller dictionary.

For these and other cases, you can select options from the menu displayed in the Speller dialog box:

- Choose Skip Once to continue spell-checking without changing the highlighted word; if the same word is found later in the document, the Speller will highlight it again.

- When you want the Speller to completely ignore the highlighted word throughout the document, choose Skip in this Document.

- To add the word to a special dictionary file, choose Add to Dictionary.

- Choose Edit Word to temporarily suspend the Speller, so you can edit the highlighted text if the correct spelling is not included in the replacement words offered.

If you follow the exercise in the next section, you'll have the chance to try each of these options.

Before you perform a spell-check, you may want to save your document. You can undo the effects of a spell-check if you act promptly, selecting <u>U</u>ndo from the <u>E</u>dit menu (Ctrl+Z) before you do anything else in WordPerfect. However, this won't work if, say, you decide to reverse the spell check but you've already performed other actions. If you have saved your document, you can always clear the screen and retrieve the original file.

Correcting Spelling Errors

The following exercise shows you how to use the Speller to correct the text in a simple document. Before you begin, clear the screen (press F7 and choose <u>N</u>o twice), and type the following text. It's important that you type the text exactly as it's shown here, including the grammar and spelling errors—like the embarrassing omission of a *g* in the last sentence.

```
Please inform the independant contractor that the city
counsel will estimated the the building plans for 400W
Street. COnstruction will began after the loan document
are signed, and, as agreed, the construction lone will be
handled by eAST ONE Bank. Make sure the independant trsl
estate agent, T. Olsen, is present for the sining.
```

Now use the WordPerfect Speller to correct the obvious (and not so obvious) errors in the paragraph you've just typed:

Choose <u>F</u>ile ▸ Save <u>A</u>s, and enter **BUILDING.MEM** as the file name.

Choose <u>T</u>ools ▸ Writing Tools ▸ <u>S</u>peller.

1. Before you spell-check the document, save the text you've typed on your screen. Press Save (F10). For this example, enter **BUILDING.MEM** as the file name.

2. Now you're ready to spell-check the document on your screen. Press Spell (Ctrl+F2). Your screen will look like Figure 8.2.

3. To check the entire document, choose <u>D</u>ocument from the dialog box. When the Speller encounters the first misspelled word, *independant*, the Word Not Found dialog box appears, as shown in Figure 8.3.

4. Because *independant* is not in the dictionary, the Speller assumes the word is misspelled and displays a list of possible replacement words (in this case, only one) in the Suggestions list. Notice that the selection letter *A* appears next to the correctly spelled word, *independent*. Type **a**, and the Speller replaces the misspelled word.

5. The Speller continues the spell-check and highlights the double words, *the the*. The Speller asks if you want to skip the double words, delete the duplicate word, edit the text, or disable double-word checking. Since you need only one *the*, choose <u>D</u>elete Duplicate Word, and the second *the* is removed.

Figure 8.2

The Speller dialog box

Spell-check options —

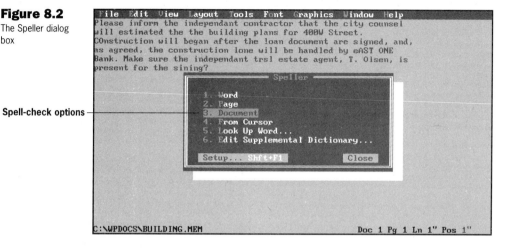

Figure 8.3

The Speller dialog box, suggesting correction for *independant*

Misspelled word —

Suggested replacement —

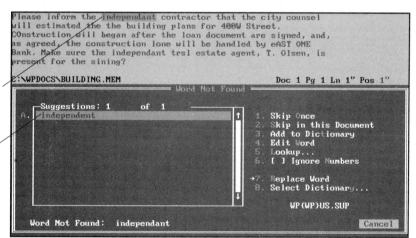

6. The address number *400W* is highlighted next, because it includes numbers and letters mixed together. Choose Skip Once to bypass this. (If you've typed *400W* elsewhere in the document, you may want to choose Skip in this Document, instead, to skip all occurrences of this number.)

TIP. *You can choose Ignore Numbers to tell the Speller to ignore all words that contain both letters and numbers. However, if you do and if a typing error* *exists because you've accidentally pressed a number key, the Speller will not interpret this as an incorrect spelling.*

7. The Speller next highlights the word *COnstruction*. This is an example of an irregular case error. The Irregular Case dialog box appears. Choose the correct case from the list of suggestions and then choose <u>R</u>eplace Word. The Speller replaces the capital *O* with a lowercase *o*.

8. Next the word *eAST* is highlighted as another word with irregular case. Choose the uppercase version of EAST from the list of suggestions and then choose <u>R</u>eplace Word. The Speller changes the lowercase *e* to *E*.

9. The Speller can't find an appropriate replacement for the next highlighted word, *trsl*, so you'll have to edit it yourself. Choose Edit <u>W</u>ord and the cursor appears on the first character of the highlighted word. The Speller dialog box temporarily disappears, and you'll see the message "Editing Misspelled Word. Press F7 or Enter to exit."

TIP. *When replacement words are offered by the Speller, you can also use the Edit <u>W</u>ord option from the Word Not Found dialog box to view the text that surrounds a highlighted word. This lets you analyze the context of the word before you correct it. Then press Exit (F7) to resume the spell-check.*

10. In Spell Edit mode, you can use the → and ← keys to move through the text, type additional text, or press Delete and Backspace to delete characters. So press Delete three times to delete the first three characters of *trsl*. Then replace this with **rea** to create the intended word *real*.

11. Press Exit (F7) to resume the spell-check. The Word Not Found dialog box is restored to the screen, and the next "misspelling," *Olsen*, is highlighted.

12. *Olsen* is actually spelled correctly, but it is highlighted because it doesn't appear in the Speller dictionary. Either choose <u>S</u>kip in this Document to ignore the word, or choose Add to Dic<u>t</u>ionary to add it to the dictionary.

13. The last highlighted word is *sining*, which is obviously a misspelling. A list of possible replacements is displayed in the Suggestions list; type **d** to select and insert the correct spelling, *signing*.

TIP. *You can press Cancel (Esc) to stop a spell-check before it is completed.*

14. The spell-check is now finished. When you're ready to continue, press Exit (F7) to return to the document screen.

Choose OK to
continue.

Choose File ▸ Save
to save the changes.

15. Save the edited text on the screen by pressing Save (F10). At the File-name prompt, press Enter to accept the BUILDING.MEM file name. When asked if you want to replace the existing file, choose Yes.

After you spell-check a document, the cursor is located at the end of the text. You can press Home, Home, ↑ and move to the beginning of the document.

Table 8.1 summarizes the types of errors that the Speller will find and lists the options you can select from the Speller dialog box to correct the errors.

Table 8.1 **Spelling Correction in Various Contexts**

Error	Type Example(s)	Action
Misspelling	*independant, beleive, exercize*	Select a replacement from the Suggestions list.
Proper nouns & words not found in the dictionary	Names, scientific terms, professional jargon	Choose Skip Once, Skip in this Document, or Add to Dictionary.
Double word	*the the, a a, that that*	Choose Skip Duplicate Word, Delete Duplicate Word, Edit Word, or Disable Duplicate Word Checking.
Numbers mixed with text	*200W, 106ne, 3D*	Choose Skip Once, Skip in this Document, Edit Word, or Ignore Numbers.
Irregular case	*COnstruction, eAST BANK*	Select the correct case and choose Replace Word, or choose Skip Word, Edit Word, or Disable Case Checking.
No suggested replacements for misspelled words	Words that should be deleted or edited	Choose Edit Word.

Now let's examine the errors that the Speller corrected in the previous exercise, as well as those it missed. The Speller first stopped at the word *independant*, a true misspelling. This word is used twice in the text, but the Speller stopped only at the first occurrence of the word; when you corrected the first occurrence, the second occurrence was automatically corrected, because the word was misspelled exactly the same way each time. Remember, you only need to correct the first occurrence of a misspelling; WordPerfect will do the rest whenever it finds the same misspelling throughout the text.

The Speller next stopped at the double occurrence of *the*, and you chose the option to delete the duplicate word. The Speller then stopped at *400W* because it contains letters and numbers mixed together. *COnstruction* and *eAST* contained irregular case, and you were prompted to replace each with the correct capitalization. For the word *trsl*, you selected the Edit <u>W</u>ord op-tion and manually edited the word, because the Speller could not find a suit-able replacement. Next, the Speller stopped at the name *Olsen* because it wasn't in the dictionary, and you chose <u>S</u>kip in this Document to bypass it without making a correction. The last misspelling, *sining*, was changed to *sign-ing* when you chose the correct spelling from the list of suggested words.

Now, here's what the Speller missed. The words *counsel* and *lone* are both incorrect in the paragraph. In the context of their sentences, these words are misspelled (*counsel* should be *council*, and *lone* should be *loan*). How-ever, because these are valid entries in the dictionary, the Speller didn't iden-tify these words and other grammatical errors as misspellings. Remember— the Speller simply compares the words in your document with the words in its dictionary. It cannot verify that you've used the words in the correct context. However, WordPerfect's grammar checker, Grammatik, *can* sometimes lo-cate and correct errors like these. Later in this chapter, you'll use Grammatik to correct other errors in the BUILDING.MEM file.

Spell-Checking a Word or Page

After you edit a document that has already been spell-checked, you'll usually want to check the spelling of any additional text that you've inserted, but you won't want to check the entire document again. WordPerfect lets you check the spelling of one page, a single word, or from the cursor position to the end of the document. The process for these shorter spell-checks is similar to checking the entire document.

Choose <u>T</u>ools ▸
<u>W</u>riting Tools ▸
<u>S</u>peller.

- At the editing screen, move the cursor to the word or page you want to check.

- Press Spell (Ctrl+F2). Then choose <u>W</u>ord, <u>P</u>age, or <u>F</u>rom Cursor from the Speller dialog box.

- If a word is misspelled, the Speller highlights it and may display possible replacements in the Speller dialog box. Select a replacement from the list, and the Speller makes the correction. If WordPerfect offers no sug-gestions, choose Edit <u>W</u>ord and change the misspelled word as needed.

- When you check the spelling of a page, the Speller stops at each mis-spelled word on the page and allows you to correct it.

- When you check the document's spelling from the cursor location for-ward, the Speller stops at every misspelled word, as you would expect. The method is particularly handy for checking additions you've made to the end of the document.

- After you've finished the spell-check, the cursor moves to the next word or page, and the main Speller dialog box reappears. This happens only when you spell-check a word or page—if you wish, you can continue to choose <u>W</u>ord to check the next word or <u>P</u>age to check the next page.

- When you are finished, press Exit (F7). The Speller dialog box is removed from the screen, and you are returned to the document screen.

Spell-Checking a Block of Text

Sometimes you'll want to check the spelling of a text passage that is less than the entire document or shorter than a whole page. For this you can use WordPerfect's Block feature to define a specific area of text and check only the words that fall within that block. Once you've defined a block, the Speller can locate and correct the misspelled words within it. The process is similar to correcting words for the whole document or page, as described here:

Drag the mouse pointer to highlight the text you want to check.

Choose <u>T</u>ools ▸ <u>W</u>riting Tools ▸ Speller.

- First define the block for the spell-check. Move the cursor to the beginning of the text for the block. Press Block (Alt+F4 or F12). Move the cursor just past the last word or character in the block.

- Now that the block to be spell-checked is highlighted, press Spell (Ctrl+F2).

- The Speller checks each word included in the defined block. When it finds misspelled words, it stops and highlights them, if possible offering replacement words that you can select.

- When the spell-check is finished, the Block feature turns off, and the cursor moves to the end of the block. Press Exit (F7) to return to the document screen.

Spell-checking a block is similar to spell-checking a document or page; when misspelled words are found in the block, the Word Not Found dialog box appears, and you can choose the same options that are available for correcting the spelling in a page, document, or word.

Editing Text during a Spell-Check

As you know, if, during a spell-check, you need to edit a highlighted word, you can do so by selecting Edit <u>W</u>ord from the Word Not Found dialog box. When you select this option, WordPerfect places the cursor on the first character of the highlighted word and temporarily removes the Word Not Found dialog box from the screen. This allows you to view and edit the text before you continue with the spell-check.

In the Spell Edit mode, however, you can't use all the editing tools that are available at the standard editing screen. The first thing you'll notice is that the ↑ and ↓ keys do not work. In fact, the only keys that move the cursor are the → and ← keys; all other cursor movement keys are inoperative until you continue and finish the spell-check. Hold down the → or ← key until the cursor is on the text that you want to edit.

Backspace and Delete are the only keys you can use to delete text in Spell Edit mode, and the function keys and pull-down menus will not respond until the spell-check is finished. You can, of course, insert new text by simply moving the cursor to the insertion point and typing the text. When you are finished editing, press Exit (F7) to continue the spell-check.

Checking for Upper- and Lowercase Letters

The WordPerfect Speller is case sensitive. As it checks the text in your document, it keeps track of the capitalization you've used. When it replaces misspelled words, it uses the correct case, upper or lower. You may have noticed that the replacement words offered in the Suggestions list are all displayed in lowercase letters. However, if a capitalized word is identified as a misspelling, the Speller suggests uppercase replacements, and if a word with an initial capital letter is identified as a misspelling, the Speller will suggest "initial cap" replacements.

The Speller is also sensitive to irregular case in the document. *Irregular case* is the term for a pattern of upper- and lowercase letters that is inconsistent or does not follow accepted rules of grammar.

In an earlier exercise, the Speller corrected two words with irregular case: *COnstruction* and *eAST*. When the Speller encounters a word with irregular case, it displays the Irregular Case dialog box, shown in Figure 8.4. From the list of suggestions, you can choose the correct case, and then choose Replace Word to fix the word.

Figure 8.4

Correcting irregular case

```
Please inform the independent contractor that the city counsel
will estimated the building plans for 400W Street. COnstruction
will began after the loan document are signed, and, as agreed,
the construction lone will be handled by EAST ONE Bank. Make sure
the independent real estate agent, T. Olsen, is present for the
signing?

C:\WPDOCS\BUILDING.MEM                        Doc 1 Pg 1 Ln 1.17" Pos 6.3"
```

```
                          Irregular Case
  ┌Suggestions:─────────────────────────┐
  │ construction                         │ ↑    1. 2. Skip Word
  │ CONSTRUCTION                         │     →3. Replace Word
  │ Construction                         │      4. Edit Word
  │                                      │ ↓    5. Disable Case Checking
  └──────────────────────────────────────┘

                                              Cancel
```

Other Uses for the Speller

In addition to correcting your misspelled words, the Speller includes features that let you look up words that follow specific patterns, and look up words according to phonetic spelling.

Phonetic Lookup

You might have a valid complaint about the process of looking up words in a dictionary: How can you find the word if you don't know how to spell it? Here is where the Speller really shines. The Speller includes an option that allows you to look up the spelling of words before you type them. To do a lookup with WordPerfect's Speller, you only need to know how the word *sounds*, not how it is spelled. This is called a *phonetic lookup*, and here is how it works:

Choose <u>T</u>ools ▸ <u>W</u>riting Tools ▸ <u>S</u>peller.

- At the editing screen, press Spell (Ctrl+F2).

- From the main Speller menu, choose <u>L</u>ook Up Word. The Look Up Word dialog box appears with this prompt:

  Word or Word Pattern:

- Here you enter the word you want to look up. When you type the word, don't worry about precise spelling; just type the word as it sounds, rather than as you think it's spelled. For example, instead of trying to guess how *souvenir* is spelled, you can enter **sooveneer** or **suevineer** at the prompt and press Enter.

- The Speller compares the phonetic word you've typed with the words in its dictionary and displays the correct spelling of the word.

- The Speller dialog box and its word look-up prompt remain on the screen. You can tab to the "Word or Word Pattern prompt" and enter another word to look up, or press Cancel (Esc) to return to the document screen.

Occasionally, there may be more than one word that fits the phonetic spelling you've typed; in this case, the Speller will display both words and let you decide which one you want.

Try this exercise for some hands-on practice with the Speller's phonetic look-up abilities:

Choose <u>T</u>ools ▸ <u>W</u>riting Tools ▸ <u>S</u>peller.

1. At the document screen, press Spell (Ctrl+F2). (It doesn't matter where the cursor is located when you invoke the feature.)

2. Select <u>L</u>ook Up Word from the list of options. WordPerfect displays the Look Up Word dialog box and the "Word or Word Pattern" prompt.

3. Do you know how to spell *pneumonia*? At the prompt, type the characters that represent how the word sounds to you. For example, type **new-moanya** and press Enter. The Look Up Word dialog box now displays possible choices of words from the dictionary that have a sound similar to your phonetic entry. Among the choices that appear in the Speller dialog box, you'll see *pneumonia*.

Now that you know how to look up specific words without knowing how to spell them, use the preceding exercise to find the correct spellings for *tera-dacktil*, *wate*, *layzer*, and *konseat*. You aren't limited to these phonetic spellings; type in whatever sounds best to you. After you've tried these, experiment with other words. You might even want to practice with words that you already know how to spell, just to see what the Speller finds to match your phonetic entries.

TIP. *If the Speller doesn't immediately find the word that you want, try a different phonetic spelling; some combinations work better than others.*

When you're finished looking up words, press Cancel (Esc) until you return to the document screen.

Using Character Patterns to Find Specific Words

The Lookup feature also lets you look up words according to a specific pattern of characters that occurs in the words you want to find. W*ildcard* characters are used in this operation to represent any combination of characters in words, just as wildcards are used in file name operations (see Chapter 5). For the Look Up Word feature, the wildcard characters are the asterisk (*) and the question mark (?). An asterisk represents any number of characters in the pattern—even no characters. A question mark represents a single character.

For example, to find all words beginning with *th* and ending with *gh*, you can look up this pattern: **th*gh**. The asterisk indicates that any number of characters may appear between the *th* and the *gh*. This pattern will display words like *through*, *though*, *thigh*, and *thorough*. On the other hand, the pattern *th?gh* will only find the word *thigh*, because the question mark specifies only one character between the *th* and the *gh*.

For some hands-on experience with the pattern lookup, try this exercise:

1. At the document screen, press Spell (Ctrl+F2).

Choose Tools ▸
Writing Tools ▸
Speller.

2. Select Look Up Word from the list of options. WordPerfect displays the Look Up Word dialog box and the "Word or Word Pattern" prompt.

3. Look up all words that begin with *th* and end with *gh*. At the "Word or Word Pattern" prompt, type **th*gh** and press Enter.

4. The Speller finds and displays all the words that match the pattern you've entered, as shown in Figure 8.5. Then press Tab to move the cursor back into the "Word or Word Pattern" box, so you can continue to look up other words.

Figure 8.5

Using a pattern to look up words

Words that match the word pattern

```
Courier 10cpi                              Doc 1 Pg 1 Ln 1" Pos 1"
                         ═══ Look Up Word ═══
               Suggestions:  1      of   5
           A.  therethrough                                    ↑
           B.  thigh
           C.  thorough
           D.  though
           E.  through




                                                              ↓

        Word or Word Pattern:  th*gh

                                               Cancel
```

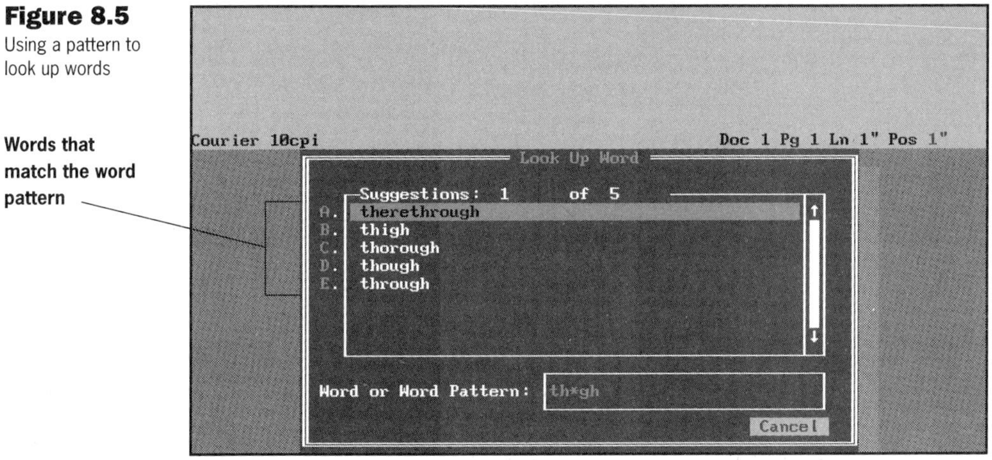

5. This time, type **a?e** as the pattern to find all words that begin with *a*, end with *e*, and have a single character between those two letters. Press Enter to accept the pattern and perform the lookup. This pattern displays words like *abe*, *ace*, *ale*, and *ape*.

6. Now let's try something more complex: a pattern to look up words where the second character is *o*, the sixth and seventh characters are *e* and *r*, and the last character is *t*. For this one, you'll need to use both the question mark and the asterisk wildcards. Press Tab to move the cursor into the word pattern box. Type **?o???er*t** as the pattern, and press Enter. Several words match this pattern, including *WordPerfect* (you can press Home, Home, ↓ to view the "WordPerfect" entry in the list).

7. When you are finished looking up words, press Cancel (Esc) until you return to the document screen.

The Look Up Word feature is especially nice for crossword puzzle fanatics. You can simply type in a pattern that includes what you know about the word you need, and the Speller will show you all possible words that fit the puzzle. For example, suppose you need to find a word that means neutral, where the first letter is *a*, the fifth letter is *o*, and the last letter is *c*. Instead of thinking for days to discover the right word, you can choose <u>L</u>ook Up Word and enter a pattern. But what would the pattern be?

Examine the clues. First, you know the word begins with the letter *a*. If you didn't know that first letter, the pattern would begin with one of the wildcard characters (? or *). You also know that the fifth letter is an *o* and the last letter a *c*. Therefore, you can enter **a*o*c** or **a???o*c** as the pattern. If you want to, try this pattern now on your computer. Among the displayed words in the Look Up Word dialog box, you'll find the answer to the puzzle—the word is *achromatic*. Incidentally, if you try both patterns, you'll notice that the first (a*o*c) finds many more words than the second, making it more difficult to hunt down the word you need. The moral of the story is to be as specific as possible when using wildcards, to avoid generating an unwieldy list of suggested words.

Remember, the asterisk wildcard (*) represents one or more possible characters, and the question mark represents any single character. Use the asterisk when you don't care (or don't know) how many characters fall between the letters you've indicated; use the question mark (or several question marks) to create a pattern for a word with a specific number of characters.

Limitations of the Speller

Bear in mind that the Speller is *not* the grammar checker. If the words you use are found in the Speller's dictionary, the Speller considers them to be correctly spelled—not necessarily correctly used. For example, the Speller would not find any errors in this sentence: "She were at the haws." Of course, there *are* errors in this sentence, but the Speller isn't designed to find them; it checks only individual words, and in this case, each of the words matches a correctly spelled word in the dictionary.

Nor can the Speller display the definitions of the words in its dictionary or guarantee that you're using words correctly. For example, the words *their* and *there* are homonyms; they sound alike but have different definitions. If you type the sentence "Their is there house," the Speller won't fix these obvious errors because the words in the sentence are spelled correctly—even though their use is incorrect. This is a significant concept to remember: Don't assume that your document is correct simply because you've spell-checked it. It's important to proofread your documents carefully, even after using the Speller.

Later in this chapter, you'll see how to use WordPerfect's on-line grammar checker, which can fix the incorrect use of words.

Speller Dictionaries

The WordPerfect Speller uses it own special dictionary file, which includes the correct spellings of over 120,000 words. When you perform a spell-check, the Speller compares the text in your document with the words stored in the dictionary file. The Speller also uses information in the dictionary file when you look up specific words or use the hyphenation features discussed in Chapter 2.

Your copy of WordPerfect probably includes the English-language version of the Speller dictionary (WPUS.LEX), but dictionary files are available for other languages as well. Moreover, you can create your own supplemental dictionary files, which the Speller will use in addition to its own dictionary. A supplemental dictionary file usually contains unique words that are not found in the standard dictionary, including names, technical jargon, acronyms, or professional nomenclature. The following sections explain how to create a supplemental dictionary file, and how to install and use a foreign-language dictionary.

Creating and Using Your Own Speller Dictionary

You've probably noticed that the Speller occasionally stops at words that are actually correctly spelled, but that are not in the Speller dictionary. When the Speller highlights these words, you can always choose Add to Dictionary from the Word Not Found dialog box. This will insert the words into a *supplemental dictionary file* (also called a personal dictionary file), and they will not be highlighted when you spell-check your documents.

The supplemental or personal dictionary file (named WPUS.SUP) is simply a WordPerfect file that contains additional words for the Speller to consider during a spell-check. This file is automatically created the first time you add a word while using the Speller.

In the next exercise, you'll create a new supplemental dictionary file. Follow these steps:

1. Press Spell (Ctrl+F2) and choose Edit Supplemental Dictionary. Word-Perfect displays the Edit Supplemental Dictionary dialog box.

2. Choose Create New Sup, and WordPerfect prompts you to enter a file name. For this exercise, type **newsup** and press Enter. WordPerfect displays the dialog box shown in Figure 8.6.

3. Choose Add and WordPerfect displays the Add to Supplemental dialog box with three options: Word/Phrase to Skip, Word/Phrase with Replacement, and Word/Phrase with Alternates. The Skip option lets you enter a word that the Speller will skip during a spell-check. The Replacement option lets you enter a word and a possible replacement word that will appear in the Suggestions list. The Alternates option lets you add a word and several alternate spellings for the word, which will appear on the Suggestions list.

Figure 8.6

Creating a new supplemental dictionary file

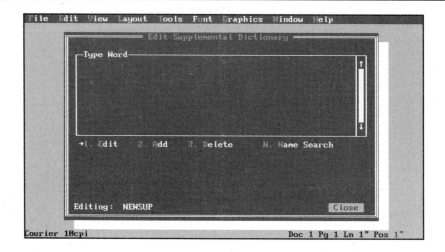

4. Choose Word/Phrase to <u>S</u>kip. WordPerfect prompts you to type the word. For this exercise, type your first name and press Enter.

5. Choose <u>A</u>dd and then Word/Phrase to <u>S</u>kip. Type your last name and press Enter. Repeat this step to add your city's name and other names that you use in your documents.

6. When you are finished adding words for the new dictionary, press Exit (F7) to return to the main Speller dialog box. Then press Exit (F7) to return to your document.

Now, when you spell-check a document, the Speller will recognize your name, city, and the other words you added to the file. You can easily edit or add to the supplemental list at any time by displaying the Edit Supplemental Dictionary dialog box, making your changes, and then replacing the original supplemental dictionary file.

WordPerfect allows you to maintain other supplemental dictionary files. These separately named files can be created to support specific applications. To choose a different supplemental dictionary file before spell-checking a document, simply select the dictionary you need from the Word Not Found dialog box, like this:

Choose <u>T</u>ools ▶ Writing Tools ▶ Speller.

- Press Spell (Ctrl+F2).

- Choose <u>W</u>ord, <u>P</u>age, <u>D</u>ocument, or From Cursor to start the spell-check.

- Choose Select Dictionar<u>y</u>, and highlight the name of the supplemental dictionary you want to use. Then choose Select.

NOTE. *Select Dictionary is only available in the Word Not Found dialog box and there must be at least one misspelled word in the document.*

When you perform the next spell-check, the specified dictionary will be used.

Whenever you create and specify a supplemental dictionary, the Speller uses the words in this file as an additional dictionary source for the spell-check process. If you want the supplemental dictionary words to be included as possible replacement words, you must choose Word/Phrase with Replacement or Word/Phrase with Alternatives when you add words to the supplemental dictionary.

Selecting Dictionaries for Other Languages

Because of WordPerfect's extensive support for international characters, you can use it to create documents in many languages other than English. Obviously, you wouldn't want to use the U.S. English dictionary to check the spelling of a document written in Swedish, German, or even United Kingdom English. And, fortunately, you don't have to.

WordPerfect Corporation provides spelling dictionaries for over 20 different languages—from Japanese to French to Russian and practically every language in between. These spelling dictionaries were originally created for the international versions of WordPerfect, but you can purchase any dictionary from WordPerfect Corporation and use it with your own copy of WordPerfect.

Each Speller dictionary file is named according to the language it supports. You already know that the U.S. English dictionary file is named WPUS.LEX; similarly, the German dictionary is called WPGE.LEX, and WPFR.LEX is the name of the French dictionary file. All dictionary files must be installed in the same directory with your WordPerfect program files (usually named with the .WP*n* extension). Each foreign-language Speller disk contains an installation program (LMINSTAL.EXE) that helps you copy the file.

After an additional dictionary file is copied to your program directory, you need to insert a code into your document that tells WordPerfect which dictionary the Speller should use for this document. This is done with the Layout/Other/Language feature, as described here:

- Press Home, Home, ↑ to move the cursor to the beginning of the document. (If you have a document containing multiple languages, position the cursor at the beginning of the text in the other language.)

- Press Format (Shift+F8). Choose Other from the Format dialog box and then choose Language. WordPerfect displays a list of supported languages.

- Scroll through the list and highlight the dictionary of the language you want to use. Then press Enter to select it.

Choose Layout ▸
Other ▸ Language.

Choose OK to return to the document screen.

- Press Exit (F7) until you return to the editing screen.

WordPerfect inserts a [Lang] code into your text at the cursor position, specifying the dictionary to be used for spell-checking the text that follows the code. As usual, you can view the code with Reveal Codes (Alt+F3 or F11).

This language setting is stored with your document when you save it; the setting is not a permanent change to the WordPerfect program. When you leave the document and clear the screen, WordPerfect returns to its default language setting.

NOTE. *The Language feature also determines which Thesaurus file Word-Perfect looks for when you select the Thesaurus feature with Alt+F1 or from the Tools pull-down menu.*

The Language feature also affects the way dates are inserted into your document with the Date feature options. If, for example, you change the language code to French, the date "July 30, 1994" is inserted as "30 juillet 1994" whenever you use the Date options.

NOTE. *The Language feature cannot be used to change the language in the program's displayed menus and prompts.*

Checking for Grammatical Errors

WordPerfect includes Grammatik as one of its on-line writing tools. You can use Grammatik to check the grammar of your document, make adjustments to the content and style of your writing, and determine whether the text is appropriate for the reading level of your audience. In this section, you'll learn practical uses for the on-line grammar checker.

Checking the Grammar of Your Document

The following steps explain the basic procedure for checking the grammar of a document in WordPerfect. Later in this section, you'll retrieve a document you've already created and check the grammar of the text.

To check the grammar of a document in WordPerfect:

- Open the document that you want to check, or create a new document.

Choose Tools ▶ Writing Tools ▶ Grammatik.

- Press Writing Tools (Alt+F1), and then choose Grammatik. WordPerfect starts the Grammatik program and displays the screen shown in Figure 8.7. The document displayed in WordPerfect is now retrieved into the Grammatik program. (Note that if you have the button bar displayed, you can click on Grammatik in the button bar.)

Figure 8.7

The main Grammatik screen

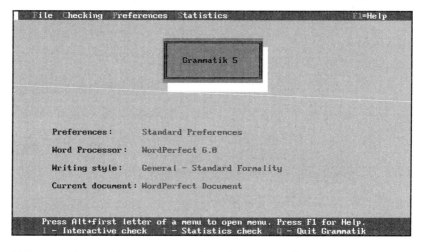

- Choose Interactive Check to check the grammar of your document.

- Grammatik highlights the first grammatical error in your document and displays an explanation of the problem. Figure 8.8 shows how the screen looks when a grammatical error is highlighted.

Figure 8.8

Checking a grammatical error

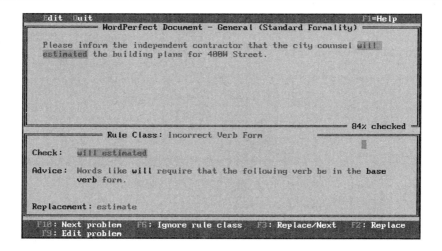

- If the error is a simple one, you may be able to choose Replace (F2) to re-place the error with the correct word or phrase or Replace/Next (F3) to replace the current error and move on to the next. Otherwise, choose Edit Problem (F9) to manually edit the text; the "Advice" message will give you some clues on fixing the problem.

- If necessary, choose Next Problem (F10) to continue the grammar-check and highlight the questionable word or phrase. Choose Replace (F2), Replace/Next (F3), or Edit Problem (F9) to fix each grammatical error. Continue until all errors are reviewed and the main Grammatik screen reappears.

- When you finish the grammar-checking process, choose Quit Grammatik to return to WordPerfect. Your document is updated with the changes you made within Grammatik.

During the grammar-check, the software works with different classes of grammatical rules to give you advice on spelling errors (if they exist) and structure problems, and also tells you when your sentences are too long or too short. In each case, choose Edit Problem (F9) to correct the grammar, and then choose Next Problem (F10) to continue to the next error. When the software encounters spelling errors, you have these additional choices: Replace (F2), Replace/Next (F3), Ignore Word, or Ignore Phrase (F5), and Learn Word (F7).

Press Ignore Rule Class (F6) to turn off a rule class for a specific type of error. For example, if you choose to structure some sentences in the passive voice—"They are being driven here next week," for example—then Grammatik will highlight the "are being driven" text and suggest that you rewrite it in the active voice. If the text is written as intended, you can press Ignore Rule Class (F6) to turn off grammar checking for the passive voice. When you use this option, you will be prompted to save the exclusion of the rule to a custom checking style; the on-screen prompts will explain what you need to do.

After the grammar-check, choose Quit Grammatik and the software updates the changes you made during the grammar-checking process to your document in WordPerfect. At this point, you'll want to save the document file with the new changes. By the way, if you want to halt a grammar check midway, you can simply press Cancel (Esc).

Now that you're familiar with the basics, it's time for some hands-on practice. In the following steps, you'll open the BUILDING.MEM document that you created earlier in "Correcting Spelling Errors." Then you'll use Grammatik to check the document grammar. Start from the WordPerfect document screen.

1. Open the BUILDING.MEM document.

Choose Tools ►
Writing Tools ►
Grammatik.

2. Press Writing Tools (Alt+F1) and then choose Grammatik. WordPerfect transfers your document to the Grammatik program and displays the main Grammatik screen.

3. Choose Interactive Check, and Grammatik displays the grammar-check screen, shown earlier in Figure 8.8. Grammatik highlights the first grammatical error in the text: "will estimated."

4. In this case, the problem is the word "estimated." Next to the Replacement label near the bottom of the screen, you'll see the correct form for this word: "estimate." Press Replace/Next (F3) to substitute the correct term and continue to the next problem.

5. Grammatik highlights the word "counsel" and notes that this may not be the correct use for this word. The Replacement label shows the correct word; press Replace/Next (F3) to replace it with "council" and continue to the next problem. (Note: If "council" is highlighted as an error, press Next Problem (F10) to continue. This may happen because "council" is another word that is often used incorrectly; Grammatik simply highlights the word to make sure that you're using it correctly.)

6. Next, the software highlights "will began." For this error, you could choose one of the Replace options. Instead, press Edit Problem (F9), edit the text, and change "began" to "begin." Then press Next Problem (F10) to continue.

7. The phrase "document are" is highlighted because the word "document" doesn't match the verb "are." In this case, it's not clear which word is wrong, so you press Replace/Next (F3) to display a list of possible corrections for each word. Highlight "documents" as the correct replacement, and press Enter to fix the problem and continue to the next problem.

8. In the next problem, the word "lone" is used incorrectly, and the Replacement label doesn't show the correct replacement word. To fix the problem, press Edit Problem (F9) and change "lone" to "loan." Then press Next Problem (F10) to continue.

9. Now "are signed" is highlighted and Grammatik points out that this phrase is in the passive voice. In this case, press F10 to move on to the next problem.

10. Next "will be handled" is highlighted because it's in the passive tense. Again press F10 to continue.

11. The software completes the grammar check and the main Grammatik screen reappears. Choose Quit Grammatik to return to the WordPerfect document screen.

WordPerfect updates your documents with the changes you made during the grammar-checking process. Press Save (Ctrl+F12) or choose File and then Save from the menu bar to save the changes to your document file.

Remember, you do not need to accept every change the software recommends. In many cases, Grammatik provides guidelines to help you clarify and strengthen the content of your document, but you can decide which changes you want to make.

Marking Grammatical Corrections

The Interactive Check option is the easiest way to fix any grammatical errors in your document, but it isn't the only way. Grammatik also provides a Mark option that marks the grammatical errors without correcting them. This option is useful when you are reviewing documents created by someone else. Rather than change the grammar, the Mark option inserts correction notes into the document that show where changes should be made. This information creates a record of the problems found and can serve as a reference of consistent problems in your writing.

To mark grammatical corrections on a document:

Choose Tools ▸
Writing Tools ▸
Grammatik.

- Open the document that you want to check or create a new document.

- Press Writing Tools (Alt+F1) and then choose Grammatik.

- From the menu bar at the top of the main Grammatik screen, choose Checking and then Mark. Grammatik scans your document and marks the grammatical errors.

- Choose Quit Grammatik to return to the WordPerfect document screen.

When you return to your document, WordPerfect updates your document with the comments you would have seen during the interactive check. These comments appear as regular text in your document, like this: " ¦-- (CONSTRUCTION IS NOT USUALLY FOLLOWED BY 'LONE'.)-- ¦". Each Grammatik comment appears between these characters: ¦--( )-- ¦. At this point, you should save your document under a different file name; you probably won't want the commented file to replace the original document file.

Changing the Writing Style

Students of grammar understand that there are few ironclad rules for acceptable grammar. Grammatik gives advice that follows the guidelines of general grammatical rules, but these rules may not apply to every document you create. For example, a magazine article may have a different style than a business letter or an advertisement.

For this reason, Grammatik lets you choose a different writing style before you start the grammar-checking process. This is how you do it: From the main Grammatik screen, choose Preferences from the menu bar and then choose Writing Style. Grammatik displays a list of different writing style options, including one for business letters, memos, reports, journalism, and fiction. Highlight the style that matches the type of document you're checking, and then choose Enter to continue. When you choose Interactive Check to start the grammar-checking process, Grammatik matches its rules to your style of writing.

Checking the Readability of Your Document

Grammatik's Statistics feature analyses the readability of your document. This feature also shows you the number of paragraphs, sentences, and words—and the average length of these—in the text you've written. This information will help you determine whether your text is appropriate for the audience for which the document is intended. The Statistics feature doesn't change anything in your document; it simply reports on the contents of the text.

To view document statistics, open your document in WordPerfect. Press Writing Tools (Alt+F1) or choose Tools and then Writing Tools from the menu bar. Choose Grammatik. When the main Grammatik screen appears, choose Statistics, Show Statistics, and you'll see the screen shown in Figure 8.9.

Figure 8.9

The Grammatik Statistics screen

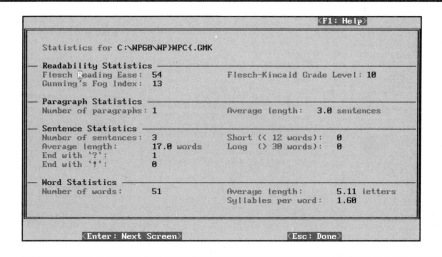

Each heading on this screen displays information about your document. Under Readability Statistics, you'll see the readability scores for your document. You may, for example, want to see whether your text is appropriate for high school reading. For detailed information about the readability of your document, press Enter to switch to the Grammatik Document Summary screen, which explains the reading grade level of your text and the ease of reading score. Then press Enter to return to the Statistics screen.

The headings for Paragraph Statistics, Sentence Statistics, and Word Statistics show the number of paragraphs, sentences, and words in your document, as well as the average length for each of these items. For more information about the Statistics screen, press Help (F1). When you are finished, press Cancel (Esc) until you return to the main Grammatik screen, and then choose Quit Grammatik to return to WordPerfect.

Displaying Document Statistics

Authors and students sometimes need to count the total number of words in a document when a publisher or professor requires a specific document length. The Document Information option shows you the number of characters, words, and sentences in your document, as well as other useful information. Try this exercise:

Choose Tools ▸ Writing Tools ▸ Document Information.

1. With your document displayed on the screen, press Writing Tools (Alt+F1), and choose Document Information. WordPerfect displays the dialog box shown in Figure 8.10.

Figure 8.10

The Document Information dialog box

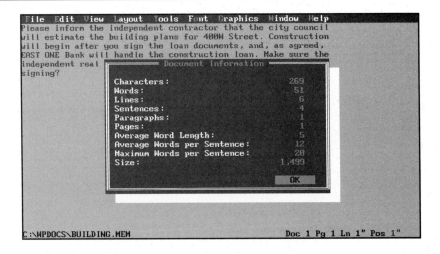

Choose OK to return to your document.

2. When you're finished viewing the document, press Exit (F7) to return to the document screen.

In addition to counting the total words in a document, the Document Information dialog box can show you how many words you've added during a specific editing session. Just retrieve your document, display Document Information, and make a note of the word count before you begin editing. When you're finished editing, display Document Information again. The difference between the first and second word count totals is the number of words you've added to your document.

Using the Thesaurus

WordPerfect's Thesaurus feature can help you enrich your writing vocabulary by offering you alternate words, or *synonyms*, for the text in your document. A sentence like "She traveled through dangerous oceans" can be instantly transformed into "She wandered through perilous billows." You may not want such elaborate text for your own documents, but you will sometimes need appropriate new choices for the words you write. The Thesaurus makes it easy to find refreshing alternatives for common words that you use perhaps too often, or even antonyms when you need them. You can also use the Thesaurus to look up words as you are creating a new document. Here is the general procedure for using the Thesaurus:

- Move the cursor to the word for which you want to find a synonym.

Choose Tools ▸ Writing Tools ▸ Thesaurus.

- Press Writing Tools (Alt+F1) and then choose Thesaurus. WordPerfect highlights the word on your screen and displays the Thesaurus window shown in Figure 8.11.

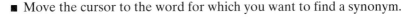

Figure 8.11
The Thesaurus window showing possible alternatives

Replacement words

Word to change

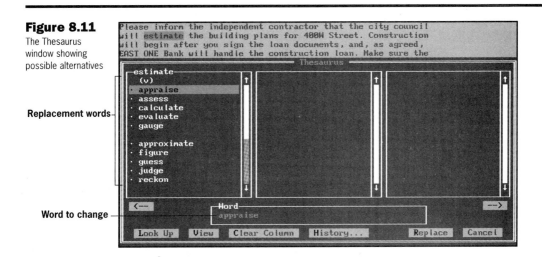

- In the Thesaurus window, you'll see suggested synonyms (and sometimes antonyms) for your word displayed in columns. A small dot (•) appearing next to a word indicates a *headword*—a word that is the heading for another list of synonyms.

- If you don't see the word you want, you can highlight a headword and press Enter, or simply double-click on the desired headword to display its synonyms.

- When you find an appropriate word, highlight it and choose <u>R</u>eplace from the Thesaurus dialog box to replace the highlighted word in your document.

  Other options are available in the Thesaurus dialog box. You can:

- View the document text without leaving the Thesaurus (<u>V</u>iew)

- Look up a specific Thesaurus headword or any word at all (<u>L</u>ook Up)

- Clear a column of words from the Thesaurus window (<u>C</u>lear Column)

- Choose <u>H</u>istory to list the words for which synonyms are currently displayed

When you are finished with the Thesaurus, just press Exit (F7) to remove the Thesaurus and restore the document screen.

TIP.   *The Thesaurus can also help you check the context of most words you've used in your document and can find otherwise elusive alternatives. Use the Thesaurus to display synonyms and antonyms for the word you want to add or replace; these words are the clues you can use to help improve your writing.*

Finding the Right Word

In the following exercise, you'll learn how to use the Thesaurus to replace a word in the document you created earlier. Before you begin, clear the screen and then press Retrieve (Shift+F10). At the prompt, name **BUILDING.MEM** as the file to be retrieved. This is the text you typed earlier in this chapter.

1. Let's say you don't like the use of the word *estimate* in the first sentence. Move the cursor to that word.

Choose <u>T</u>ools ▸
<u>W</u>riting Tools ▸
<u>T</u>hesaurus.

2. Press Writing Tools (Alt+F1) and choose <u>T</u>hesaurus. The Thesaurus window appears on your screen (see Figure 8.11 earlier).

3. Look through the list of words displayed in the first column, and highlight a replacement for *estimate*—perhaps *appraise*, for example.

4. Choose <u>R</u>eplace and the Thesaurus replaces *estimate* with *appraise*.

5. Try another one. The word *independent* is used twice in the paragraph. Find an alternative for the second occurrence of this word. Move the cursor to the word *independent* in the last sentence.

6. Press Writing Tools (Alt+F1) and choose Thesaurus.

Choose Tools ▸ Writing Tools ▸ Thesaurus.

7. Look through the list of displayed synonyms until you see the word *separate*. (Notice, also, that antonyms for *independent* appear at the end of the list.) Choose Replace from the menu to replace *independent* with *separate*.

Choose OK.

It's that simple to find alternate words. When you're looking for common words, the Thesaurus is quite simple to use. However, languages can be complex, and some words share the same or similar meanings. In this example, you easily found alternatives for the two words you needed to replace. Sometimes, however, you may have to look a little deeper to find the right word. The next section shows you how to navigate through the Thesaurus window and call up synonyms for several levels of words.

Moving through the Thesaurus Window

The Thesaurus window uses three columns for its display of synonyms and antonyms. A menu at the bottom of the screen presents the Thesaurus options. Figure 8.12 illustrates the different parts of the display.

Figure 8.12
The Thesaurus window showing antonyms and synonyms

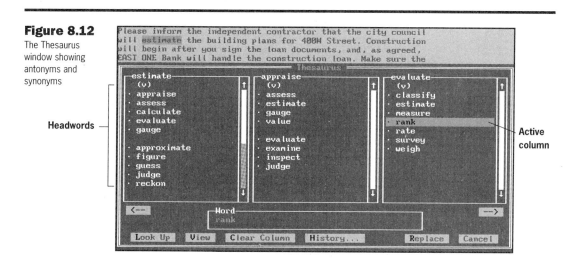

Words with dots before them are called *headwords*. You can view more synonyms by highlighting a headword and then pressing Enter. (Alternatively, you can double-click on a headword.) When you do so, the additional related words are displayed in the adjacent column to the right.

Use the ↑ and ↓ keys to scroll up and down through the list of words within a discrete column. Press ← or →, and you move the list of selection letters into the adjacent column to the left or right. To completely clear the column where the select letters are positioned, choose Clear Column. Look Up lets you display words related to a word that is not on the screen.

Take some time to practice with the Thesaurus screen levels and options. You'll find this feature easy to use and invaluable for finding the precise word you want.

9

Alphabetizing and Other Sort Operations

Alphabetizing Text

Sorting Numbers

Using Keys to Sort Information

Special Cases for Sorting

Sorting a Document without Retrieving It

N SOME DOCUMENTS, SUCH AS LISTS, ADDRESS RECORDS, AND LEDGERS, you'll want to place names, numbers, or words in alphabetical or numeric order. You can easily accomplish this is with WordPerfect's Sort feature.

NOTE. *You can use the Sort feature to arrange records for merge applications. For information about the Merge features, see Chapters 17 and 18.*

Suppose you have an address list stored in a WordPerfect document; using the Sort feature, you can arrange the entries in alphabetical order, or you can sort the list according to city name, state, or ZIP code. In any document, you can alphabetize and sort individual lines of text, paragraphs, or a block of items.

WordPerfect provides options that make the Sort feature a flexible editing tool. You can sort the text displayed on your screen or sort the contents of a file without retrieving it. You can arrange columns of numbers in ascending or descending order, or use the Block feature to alphabetize a section of a list. In addition, you can define guidelines for sorting—called *keys*—that determine how information is arranged.

In this chapter you'll learn how to alphabetize and sort lists of text and numbers. You'll also define keys to fine-tune the sorting process.

Alphabetizing Text

The Sort feature lets you alphabetize a list of text on your screen. Unless you specify otherwise, WordPerfect uses the first word of each text line as the key word for alphabetizing.

Here is the general procedure for alphabetizing a list.

CAUTION. *It's probably best to save your document before you attempt to alphabetize or sort the text. You can undo a sort operation that didn't work as you had hoped, but this only works if you haven't performed any other undo-able operations. However, if you've saved the document before sorting, you can clear the screen, retrieve the original file, and try again.*

- At the editing screen, retrieve or create the list of text that will be alphabetized.

- Press Merge/Sort (Ctrl+F9) and choose <u>S</u>ort.

Choose <u>T</u>ools ▶
Sort ▶.

NOTE. *You'll see how to sort information stored in a file in "Sorting a Document without Retrieving It."*

- In the "From (Source)" box, verify that the option for <u>D</u>ocument on Screen is selected.

Choose OK to
continue.

■ In the "To (Destination)" box, verify that the option for Document on Screen is also selected.

■ Press Enter to continue, and the Sort dialog box appears as shown in Figure 9.1. To alphabetize the list on your screen, choose Perform Action.

Figure 9.1

The Sort dialog box

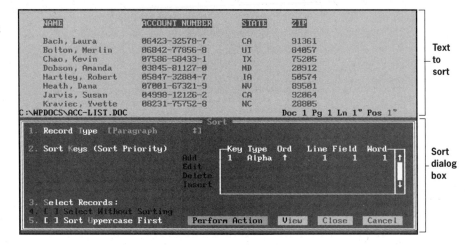

■ When the sort operation is finished, the Sort dialog box is removed from the screen, and the alphabetized list is displayed.

When the Sort dialog box first appears, it may seem a little complicated, but it's actually quite simple. If all you want to do is sort a list of items by the first word of each line, you need only select Perform Action, because the standard settings of the Sort feature are already assigned to alphabetize by the first word of each line. If, however, you want to sort the text in another manner, you must choose options from the dialog box and change the settings before choosing Perform Action. As you work through the exercises in this chapter, you'll learn more about the Sort options.

Alphabetizing a Simple List

Try this exercise to create and alphabetize a list of names on your screen. Before you begin, make sure the screen is clear by choosing Close from the File menu or by pressing Exit (F7) and choosing No twice.

1. Type each name in the following list. At the end of each name, press Enter to move the cursor to a new line.

```
Tracy
Amanda
Sam
Kevin
Colleen
Chance
Geri
```

Choose File ▸ Save As, type **namelist.- doc**, and press Enter.

Choose Tools ▸ Sort ▸ OK.

2. Before you alphabetize the list, you should save the text on your screen. Press Save (F10), type **namelist.doc,** and press Enter.

3. Press Merge/Sort (Ctrl+F9), choose Sort, and press Enter to display the Sort dialog box.

4. Choose Perform Action to alphabetize the list. WordPerfect briefly displays the Sorting Records dialog box to show you the progress of the sort operation.

When the sort is finished, your screen will look like Figure 9.2. Notice that each name in the list now falls in the correct alphabetical order. If you included any blank lines before or within the text, these are placed after the text when the list is alphabetized.

Figure 9.2
An alphabetized list

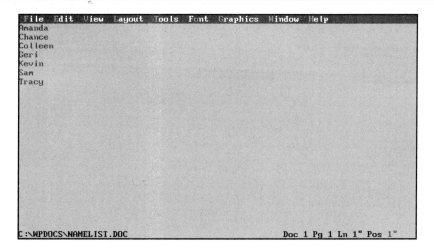

You'll use this list of names for other exercises in this chapter, so save it again now before you continue. Choose File, Save, or press Ctrl+F12. Before you continue, you should also clear the screen. (Choose Close from the File menu.)

Sorting a Block of Text

In the previous exercise, the list you alphabetized was the only text in the document, but such lists are often included as part of a larger document. When you use the Sort feature as outlined earlier, *all* text lines in your document are included in the sort. However, this means that not only will a sort operation alphabetize the text lines in your list, but it will also alphabetize the paragraphs, headlines, and titles—all lines in the document are sorted. This is not only undesirable, it's dangerous. Remember, you can undo a Sort operation, but only if you do so promptly, before performing another undoable operation.

The Block feature lets you indicate exactly which text should be alphabetized or sorted, which protects the rest of your document from being rearranged. This is the basic procedure for defining and sorting a block of text:

■ Move the cursor to the beginning of the first line to be alphabetized.

Drag the mouse pointer over a section of text to highlight and block it.

■ Press Block (Alt+F4 or F12), and then move the cursor to highlight the section of text to be alphabetized.

■ Press Merge/Sort (Ctrl+F9), and the Sort dialog box is displayed.

Choose Tools ▸ Sort ▸ Perform Action.

■ Choose Perform Action from the Sort dialog box. The blocked text is alphabetized or sorted, and the Block feature is turned off.

The Block feature is also useful when you want to sort a list or table with titles above the text, like the table shown in Figure 9.3.

Figure 9.3
Using Block to sort a list with titles

Only the blocked text will be sorted

File Edit View Layout Tools Font Graphics Window Help			
NAME	**ACCOUNT NUMBER**	**STATE**	**ZIP**
Bach, Laura	06423-32578-7	CA	91361
Bolton, Merlin	06842-77856-8	UT	84057
Chao, Kevin	07596-58433-1	TX	75205
Dobson, Amanda	03845-81127-8	MD	20912
Hartley, Robert	05847-32884-7	IA	50574
Heath, Dana	07081-67321-9	NV	89501
Jarvis, Susan	04998-12126-2	CA	92064
Kraviec, Yvette	08231-75752-8	NC	28805
Williams, Chance	07995-43756-1	UT	84050
Moore, Colleen	04888-12136-4	AZ	66045
Olsen, Geri	06978-97843-8	NY	10707
Adamson, Kevin	05537-87593-1	MD	21204
Ragland, Kathy	09873-64125-6	HI	96777
Rosenthal, Sam	07472-19742-3	NJ	07670
Ruttenbur, Joy	06978-47987-8	FL	33400
Shelley, Scott	07954-16897-5	UT	84604
Staheli, Burke	01183-65421-9	VA	24641
Stewart, Tracy	09745-88635-3	NE	68869
Block on		Doc 1 Pg 1 Ln 4.33" Pos 7"	

When you sort this list, you'll want the title line to stay where it is; you won't want it to be alphabetized with the other text. In this case, you can use Block to highlight the table without the titles. Then choose Sort to alphabetize or sort the text. The titles will stay at the top of the list, and the blocked text will be sorted. Later in this chapter, you'll use this technique again to sort a similar table of text.

Sorting Numbers

If you work with numbers, you'll especially appreciate the Sort feature because it can help you quickly arrange columns of numbers in a particular *sort order*. You can choose to sort numbers (and text) in one of two orders. *Ascending* order arranges items from the lowest value to the highest value, as in 1, 2, 3, 4, and so on; this is the standard sort order. *Descending* order, the opposite of ascending, arranges items from the highest to lowest values.

In addition to sort order, there are two sort methods available: *alphanumeric* and *numeric*. Alphanumeric is the standard sort type, because it allows you to sort numbers and text together. The numeric sort type is reserved for sorting numbers only. In the following exercises, you'll use both orders and methods to sort a simple column of numbers.

Sorting a Column of Numbers

Use the following procedure at your computer to sort a simple column of numbers. Make sure the screen is clear before you continue.

1. Type the following list of numbers on the screen. Press Enter after each number to move the cursor to the next line.

   ```
   200
   120
   160
   870
   100
   250
   400
   320
   ```

Choose <u>T</u>ools ▸
Sort ▸ OK.

2. Press Merge/Sort (Ctrl+F9), choose <u>S</u>ort, and then press Enter to display the Sort dialog box.

3. Choose <u>P</u>erform Action, and your list of numbers is sorted from the lowest value to the highest value.

For now, keep this list of numbers on the screen. You won't save these numbers to a file on disk, but you will use the list again in the next section to sort with a different order.

Changing the Sort Order

The standard sort order specifies that numbers and text are sorted in ascending order, from lowest to highest values. Suppose you have these two lists that you want to sort:

List #1	List #2
3	Cari
1	Doug
4	Barbara
2	Allen

If you sort each list with the standard settings, they will look like this after the sort operations are performed:

List #1	List #2
1	Allen
2	Barbara
3	Cari
4	Doug

This sort order is called ascending, because the sorted text is arranged from the lowest value to the highest value.

You can change the sort order to descending, which arranges items from highest to lowest values. If you sorted the two lists with the descending sort order, the result would be:

List #1	List #2
4	Doug
3	Cari
2	Barbara

1   Allen

The descending sort order is useful for ledger sheets or budget lists, in which the highest numbers should be displayed at the top of the list. Use the ascending sort order to arrange the numbers for an itemized list, in which each item should follow a specific sequence. You'll usually use ascending order when alphabetizing a list of text, but you might alphabetize with descending order for some situations.

You can change the sort order from the Sort dialog box before you choose Perform Action to begin the sort:

Choose Tools ▸ Sort ▸ OK.

- From the document screen, press Merge/Sort (Ctrl+F9), choose Sort, and then press Enter.

- In the Sort dialog box, choose Sort Keys, Edit, and then choose Order.

- For ascending sort order, choose Ascending. (Note that this option will be selected by default.) For descending sort order, choose Descending.

Choose OK to return to the Sort dialog box.

- Press Exit (F7) twice to return to the Sort dialog box and highlight Perform Action.

- Choose Perform Action to sort the text with the new sort order.

NOTE.   *The order you select remains in effect for the current editing session until you change it again.*

Here's an exercise that lets you change the order and sort the list of numbers on your screen:

Choose Tools ▸ Sort ▸OK.

1. With the list of numbers displayed on the editing screen, press Merge/-Sort (Ctrl+F9), choose Sort, and then press Enter.

2. From the Sort dialog box, choose Sort Keys, choose Edit, and then choose Order.

3. Choose Descending from the Edit Sort Key dialog box. Then press Exit (F7) twice to return to the Sort dialog box and highlight Perform Action.

4. Choose Perform Action, and your list of numbers is sorted from the highest to the lowest values.

5. Now change the sort order back to ascending. Repeat steps 1 and 2, and then choose Ascending from the Edit Sort Key dialog box. Press Exit (F7) twice to return to the Sort dialog box and highlight Perform Action. Then choose Perform Action to sort the numbers from lowest to highest.

Thus far, you've sorted numbers with the alphanumeric sort type, which allows for the sorting of text *and* numbers. This is the same type used earlier to alphabetize a list of names. In the next section, you'll learn about the differences between the alphanumeric and numeric sort types, and how each affects the sorting of numbers. Make sure you clear the screen before you continue.

Numeric versus Alphanumeric Sorting

As mentioned earlier, there are two sort types: an alphanumeric sort, which arranges both text and numbers (the standard sorting method), and a numeric sort, designed for numbers only. The sorting type is selected with the Type option in the Edit Sort Key dialog box. In the previous exercise, you used the Sort Keys option to change the sort order.

Try the following two exercises to see the effect of the two sort types. First, you'll sort a list of numbers with the alphanumeric type. Then, you'll use the numeric method to improve the results of the sort.

1. From a clear screen, type the following list of numbers. After typing each number, press Enter to move to a new line.

```
5
2
10
3
4
1
20
15
```

Choose <u>F</u>ile ▸ Save <u>A</u>s, type **numbers.-doc**, and press Enter.

2. Before you continue, save this list of numbers to a file. Press Save (F10), type **numbers.doc** as the file name, and press Enter.

3. Press Merge/Sort (Ctrl+F9), choose <u>S</u>ort, and press Enter.

NOTE. *The alphanumeric sort type is the default sort method.*

Choose <u>T</u>ools ▸ Sort ▸ OK.

4. Choose <u>P</u>erform Action, and WordPerfect sorts the list of numbers. The list on your screen should now look like Figure 9.4.

Keep this list of numbers on the screen. Next, you'll use the numeric sort option to sort the list correctly.

Notice that only the first digit of each number is sorted in the correct order (1, 2, 3, and so on); the actual values of the numbers are not in the correct sequence. This is because the alphanumeric sort compares each character (in this case, digit), but it ignores the values that the numbers represent.

Figure 9.4

Sorting numbers
with the
alphanumeric
methods

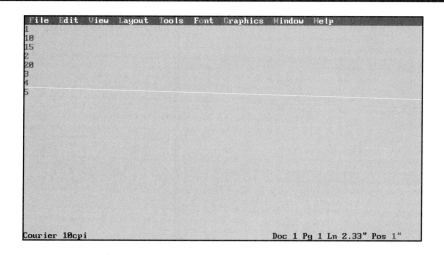

The alphanumeric sort method works well for alphabetizing text because it compares words character by character, but for numbers, the alphanumeric sort works only when each number in the list is the same length (has the same number of digits) as the other numbers in the list. That's why the list of numbers you created earlier in this chapter was sorted correctly; each number in the list had exactly three digits. So when you use the alphanumeric type on numbers, make sure all the numbers to be sorted have the same number of digits—this is the only way the alphanumeric type can produce an accurate sort for a number list.

For most lists of numbers, you'll want to redefine the *sort key* to specify numeric sorting. The numeric sort type correctly arranges any list of numbers, regardless of the number of digits.

Try this exercise to correctly sort the list of numbers on your screen:

1. Press Merge/Sort (Ctrl+F9), choose Sort, and press Enter.

Choose Tools ▸
Sort ▸ OK.

2. Before you continue with the sort, you need to redefine the sort key for numbers. Choose Sort Keys, and the Sort Key list is activated. Choose Edit to edit the first key; this displays the Edit Sort Key dialog box shown in Figure 9.5. Choose Type and then choose Numeric.

3. Press Exit (F7) twice to return to the Sort dialog box and highlight Perform Action.

Choose OK to return to the Sort dialog box.

4. Choose Perform Action, and the number list is sorted again. This time, the list is sorted correctly because you used a numeric sort. In a later section, you'll learn more about keys and how they affect the sorting process.

Figure 9.5

Changing to the
numeric sort type

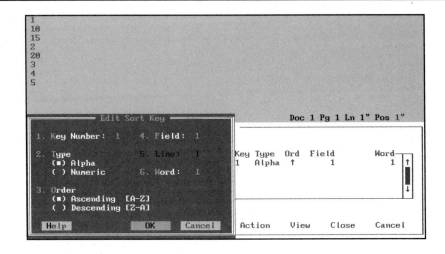

5. You'll need this list later, so choose <u>S</u>ave from the <u>F</u>ile from the menu or press Ctrl+F12.

TIP.   *Although it's generally best to use the numeric sort for any list of numbers, there are several cases in which alphanumeric is okay for numbers, too. For example, you can use the alphanumeric method to correctly sort a column of telephone numbers, account numbers, or five-digit ZIP codes—but only when each number has the same number of digits as the other numbers in the column. On the other hand, sales figures, cash flow listings, and statistics usually do not have a consistent number of digits, and thus, should be sorted with the numeric type.*

Sorting Precedence

The Sort feature assigns precedence to certain characters, depending on the sort method you're using:

■ When you sort text and numbers with the alphanumeric type, lowercase letters are alphabetized before uppercase letters. (Bob will come before BOB.) If you do not want the lowercase letters alphabetized first, check the option for Sort <u>U</u>ppercase First from the Sort dialog box *before* you choose <u>P</u>erform Action. (ZOE will then come before Zoe, although both will still come after Bob.)

■ Text lines that begin with numbers and blank lines are placed before lines that begin with letters.

- When you use the numeric sorting type, letters are sorted before numbers.

- For both alphanumeric and numeric types, lines that begin with punctuation, such as a period (.), question mark (?), or quotation mark ("), will be alphabetized before any numbers or letters.

Using Keys to Sort Information

So far, you have been presented only with limited options for sorting. Each sort you've performed has arranged a list according to the first number or word in each line of text. This method is adequate for simple lists, but you'll often have more elaborate text and tables that require several conditions for sorting.

For example, suppose you add surnames to the list of names you created earlier, and you want to keep the list formatted with the first names at the beginning of each line—as in "Amanda Dobson," and not "Dobson, Amanda." However, when you perform the sort, you want WordPerfect to alphabetize the list according to the *last* names, not the first names.

The Sort Keys option on the Sort dialog box allows you to define keys for sorting—keys that tell WordPerfect to sort the list according to a specific word, phrase, or line. Changes that you make to the sort keys remain active for the current editing session until you change them or exit the WordPerfect program.

Understanding Sort Keys

Sort keys are guidelines that you define which tell WordPerfect how you want the text sorted or alphabetized. In earlier sections, you defined simple keys to change the order and type of sorting. Keys can also help WordPerfect make sorting decisions when certain items have the same values.

Before you can define sort keys, you need to understand how the Sort feature interprets the text or numbers in your list. Each entry in your list is called a *record*. A record contains everything that should remain together during a sort operation. For example, here is a sample record from a list. Each [Tab] code indicates where the Tab key was pressed.

```
Kevin Clark [Tab] Westlake [Tab] CA [Tab] 91360
```

Although there are separate elements in this record, they are kept together when the list is sorted.

Tabs are used to divide records into *fields*; each [Tab] code inserted on the line starts the next field in the record. In the foregoing example, the Tab key was pressed three times, which divided the record into four fields: field 1 is the name (first and last together), field 2 is the city name, field 3 is the state, and field 4 is the ZIP code. Each field may contain one or more *words*; a word can be any text or number that is separated from other words in the field by spaces, forward slashes, or commas. In the foregoing example, there are two words in field 1—*Kevin* and *Clark;* the rest of the fields contain only one word.

When you define keys, you can select the field and the word within that field that you want to use as the guideline for sorting. This lets you format list information any way you like, and still perform a sort according to certain names, numbers, or text.

Alphabetizing First and Last Names

In this exercise, you'll update the list of names that you created earlier, and then define a key to sort by the last names. Before you begin, make sure you clear the screen (choose Close from the File menu).

Choose File ▸ Open, type **namelist.doc,** and press Enter.

1. From a clear screen, open the NAMELIST.DOC that you created earlier. Press Open (Shift+F10). At the Filename prompt, type **namelist.doc** and press Enter.

2. Type surnames for each of the names on the list, as shown here:

   Amanda **Dobson**
   Chance **Williams**
   Colleen **Moore**
   Geri **Olsen**
   Kevin **Clark**
   Sam **Rosenthal**
   Tracy **Stewart**

3. Before you continue, add another name at the top of the list. Press Home, Home, ↑ to move the cursor to the beginning of the list, type **Shauna Williams**, and press Enter to add the name. This will play an important role later in the exercise.

4. Press Merge/Sort (Ctr+F9), choose Sort, and then press Enter.

Choose Tools ▸ Sort ▸ OK.

5. Before you perform the sort, you'll need to redefine the keys that Word-Perfect uses for sorting. Choose Sort Keys and then choose Edit to display the Edit Sort Key dialog box.

6. Choose Type, and then choose Alpha to indicate alphanumeric sorting.

7. Choose Word, type **2**, and press Enter to indicate that you want to sort by the second word on each line, which is the last name.

Choose OK to return to the Sort dialog box.

8. Press Exit (F7) twice to return to the Sort dialog box, which now looks like Figure 9.6.

Figure 9.6
Defining keys to sort
by last name

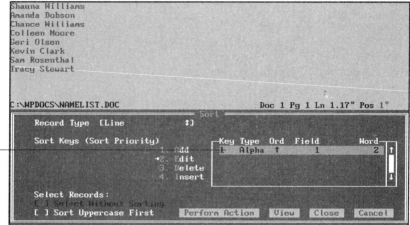

This key sorts
the list by the
last names
(second word)

9. Now you're ready to perform the sort. Choose Perform Action, and WordPerfect sorts the list according to the key definition you've defined.

The names are now alphabetized by the last name of each person on the list, even though the first names remain at the beginning of each line.

Notice that the two records with the same last name, Williams, are sorted correctly by last name, but the first names are not in alphabetical order. Because you defined only one key for the last name, first names were ignored by the sort. To also sort the first names for people with the same last name, you'll need to define a second key that specifies how duplicate records should be sorted. The following steps show you how to define a second key and sort the list again:

Choose Tools ▸
Sort ▸ OK.

1. Press Merge/Sort (Ctrl+F9), choose Sort, and then press Enter.

2. Now you'll create a second key definition that tells WordPerfect to alphabetize the first names. Choose Sort Keys and then choose Add to create a new key.

3. From the Edit Sort Key dialog box, choose Word, type **1**, and press Enter. This designates an alphanumeric sort on the first word in the line. After using the first key definition to sort the last names, WordPerfect will use the second key definition to alphabetize the first names—but only when two or more last names are identical.

Choose OK ▸ Perform Action.

4. Press Exit (F7) twice to accept the key definitions, and choose Perform Action to sort the list of names.

This time, the list is alphabetized according to the last names, but the two people on the list with identical last names—Chance Williams and Shauna Williams—are also alphabetized by the first name. This is only one example of how you can redefine the keys that WordPerfect uses for sorting.

In the next section, you'll add address information to your name list and use the sort features to arrange the text according to city name, state name, and ZIP code.

Sorting an Address List with Keys

In the previous exercise, you defined keys for sorting a list by first and last names. You can use the same procedure to define keys for a list with two or more columns of information. Here, instead of sorting names, you can sort the list according to addresses or other types of information.

In the following exercise, you'll expand the name list displayed on your screen into a list of address information. You'll begin by defining tab settings for the list.

1. Press Home, Home, ↑ to move the cursor to the beginning of the list of names.

Choose Layout ▸ Tab Set.

2. Press Format (Shift+F8), choose Line, and then choose Tab Set.

3. Choose Clear All to clear the current tabs.

4. Type **3** and press Enter to set a tab at 3 inches. Then set additional tabs at **4.5** and **5**. Press Exit (F7) to return to the editing screen.

5. Using the table shown below as a guide, add address information for each name on the list. Remember to press the Tab key before typing each city name, before each state name, and again before each ZIP code. Each Tab across the line creates a new field. Then press ↓ rather than Enter to move the cursor to the next entry in the list.

Kevin Clark	Moab	UT	84532
Amanda Dobson	Fremont	CA	94536
Colleen Moore	Huntsville	AL	35801
Geri Olsen	Verona	PA	15147
Sam Rosenthal	Chelmsford	MA	01824
Tracy Stewart	Southport	NY	14904
Chance Williams	Richmond	CA	94801
Shauna Williams	Bloomfield	NJ	07003

Choose File ▸ Save As.

6. When the table is complete, save it with Save As (F10).

7. At the File Name prompt, type **address.doc** and press Enter.

Choose Tools ▸
Sort ▸ OK.

8. Press Merge/Sort (Ctrl+F9), choose Sort, and then press Enter to display the Sort dialog box.

9. Suppose you want to sort the entire list by the state abbreviations and ZIP codes. You'll need to define two keys: one to sort the entire list by state abbreviations, and one to sort any duplicate state name entries by their ZIP codes. From the Sort menu, choose Sort Keys and then choose Edit to change the first sort key.

10. Choose Type and then choose Alpha for alphanumeric sorting.

11. Because the column that contains the state abbreviations is the third field of each record, choose Field, type **3**, and then press Enter.

12. There is only one word in the third field, so you can leave the Word setting at 1. This completes the first key. Choose Key Number, type **2**, and press Enter, to define the second key.

13. Key 2 will sort the records that have the same state abbreviation. In this case, you'll want WordPerfect to sort the duplicate entries by ZIP code. Because the ZIP code is stored in the fourth field of each record, choose Field, type **4**, and press Enter.

14. Also, choose Type and choose Numeric to specify a numeric sort for this key; this assures correct sorting if some ZIP codes have a 4-digit extension.

Choose OK to
close the Edit Sort
Key dialog box.

15. Again, there's only one word in field 4, so leave Word option set to 1. Press Exit (F7) twice to close the Edit Sort Key dialog box and highlight Perform Action.

16. Now you're ready to sort the table. Choose Perform Action, and the list is sorted first by the state abbreviations. Then, if the same state abbreviation occurs in two or more records, WordPerfect uses Key 2 to sort the duplicate records.

For most tables and lists, you'll usually define one or two keys for sorting. Sometimes, though, you will need to fine-tune the sorting process with multiple key definitions. Each key you define represents one level of sorting, and narrows the sorting procedure for records that match all previous conditions.

The first key (Key 1) you define specifies the main criteria by which the records are sorted. When duplicate records exist, after the first sort, Key 2 defines the sort conditions for these identical records. It's important to understand that Key 2 sorts *only* the duplicate records that match the Key 1 criteria. When you define a third key, it sorts the information that matches both Key 1 *and* Key 2, and so on.

Go ahead and experiment with defining different keys for the sort process. You can sort the table according to city name, for example, or use the sort procedure described earlier to sort by first and last names.

Before you continue, save the document on your screen. Press Save (Ctrl+F12) or choose File and then Save. Later, you'll retrieve this file for other sort operations.

Sorting a Paragraph List

Much of the text you sort will be arranged with one record per line of text. However, some documents may be formatted as paragraphs of information, like the list shown in Figure 9.7. In this context, WordPerfect considers a paragraph to be one or more lines of text, followed by two or more [HRt] codes.

Figure 9.7

A paragraph list

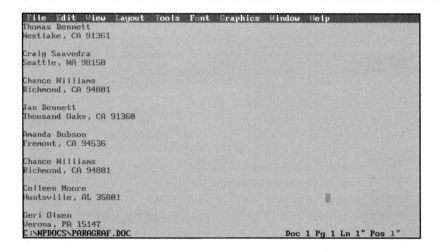

WordPerfect's default sort settings will automatically sort individual lines in your document. So, to sort a paragraph list, you need to tell WordPerfect to sort paragraphs, instead of lines. Here is the procedure:

Choose Tools ▸
Sort ▸ OK.

- With a list of paragraphs on the screen, press Merge/Sort (Ctrl+F9), choose Sort, and then press Enter. This displays the Sort dialog box.

- From the Sort dialog box, choose Record Type, and then choose Paragraph if it's not already selected, to indicate that you want to sort the paragraphs on the screen. In this case, WordPerfect considers a paragraph to be any section of text that ends with at least two Hard Return [HRt] codes.

- If necessary, define keys for sorting the paragraphs. (Notice that when you changed the sort type to Paragraph, the Sort Key list layout changed also. For the Paragraph sort type, you can define keys to sort by Paragraph, Line, Field, or Word.)

- Choose Perform Action, and the paragraphs are sorted according to the first line or by the record fields you designated, in the sorting keys.

Try this example to create and sort a list of paragraphs. As part of the exercise, you'll define three keys to sort the text in this sequence: last name, city name, and ZIP code. Clear the screen before you begin.

1. Type the following address list, remembering to press Enter at the end of each line. Also, press Enter to add a blank line between each paragraph.

```
Thomas Bennett
Westlake, CA 91361

Craig Saavedra
Seattle, WA 98150

Chance Williams
Richmond, CA 94801

Jan Bennett
Westlake, CA 91360
```

Choose Tools ▸ Sort ▸ OK.

2. Save the text to a file called **paragraf.doc**. Press Merge/Sort (Ctrl+F9), choose Sort, and then press Enter.

3. From the Sort dialog box, choose Record Type and then, if necessary, choose Paragraph from the pop-up list.

4. Now you'll define keys to sort the paragraphs first by surname, city name, and ZIP code. Choose Sort Keys. Then use the following table to create the sort keys:

	Type	Line	Field	Word
Key 1:	Alpha	1	1	2
Key 2:	Alpha	2	1	1
Key 3:	Numeric	2	1	3

Choose OK and then
choose Perform Action.

5. Press Exit (F7) to close the Edit Sort Key dialog box and return to the Sort dialog box. Your screen will look like Figure 9.8. Then choose Perform Action.

Figure 9.8

Sorting a paragraph list

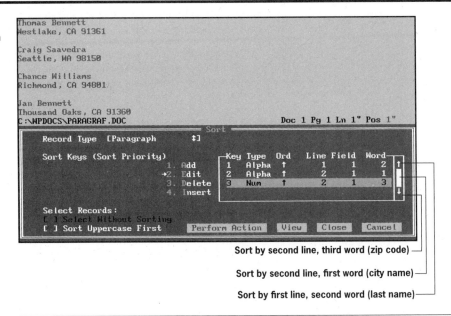

Sort by second line, third word (zip code)

Sort by second line, first word (city name)

Sort by first line, second word (last name)

Key 1 specifies that all records will be sorted by the second word in the first line of each paragraph, which represents the last name for each person in the list. If any last names are the same—for example, Jan and Thomas Bennett—Key 2 specifies that these records should be sorted again by the city name. If the city names are identical, Key 3 sorts the records once again by ZIP code.

This is only one example of how you might sort paragraph information. You can define the keys any way you like or simply sort by the first word of each paragraph without defining keys.

Before you continue, change the sort type back to Line. To do so, press Merge/Sort (Ctrl+F9), choose Sort, and then press Enter to continue. From the Sort dialog box, choose Record Type and then Line. Then press Exit (F7) to save the change and return to the document screen.

The other sort type that appears when you choose the Record Type option, Merge Data File, is used to sort files for merge applications; in Chapter 17 and 18, you'll learn more about the Merge features.

Special Cases for Sorting

There are many formats for names; some people use titles, such as Dr. and Professor, and others add Jr. or Sr. to the end of their names. Some names include a middle initial between the first and last name. Titles and initials add extra words to the sort fields, and since you define keys by counting the precise words from left to right, these extra "words" can cause the sort to be inaccurate.

Fortunately, there are a few tricks you can use to sort these records correctly. In this section, you'll see how to overcome special sorting problems, as well as learn a trick for sorting dates.

Sorting Various Name Formats

Suppose you've created a list of names, in which each record consists of a first name and a last name in a single field. You've specified Word 2—the last name—as the key for sorting the records in the list. Then you add a new name, George T. Hansen, to the list. This name doesn't fit the key definition scheme, because none of the other names in the list include a middle initial. In this record, Word 2 is *not* the last name, but the middle initial.

Remember that WordPerfect doesn't discriminate between a full word and a single initial; it considers everything separated by spaces or commas to be an individual word. Though some names have two words, and others three or more, WordPerfect counts resolutely from left to right to find the word you've specified in the key. Unfortunately, this can produce the wrong arrangement when the sort is performed.

To avoid this kind of inaccuracy, you can tell WordPerfect in the key definition to count *from the right* edge of the field to get the desired word. This technique can be quite useful when the number of words between fields is inconsistent.

Suppose you've added these records to the ADDRESS.DOC file you created earlier:

```
Tracy L. Evans          Arlington    VA    22201
Kevin and Winona Adams   Amarillo    TX    79101
```

Notice that each name is formatted differently from the other names in the existing list. Don't worry—if you define the sort keys correctly, you won't have any problems sorting the names.

In the original ADDRESS.DOC file, the first column (field) contains the first and last names for each record. Word 1 is the first name, and word 2 is the last name. Now consider Tracy L. Evans' name; the second word here is the middle initial, and the last name becomes the *third* word in the field. In the Kevin and Winona Adams entry, the last name becomes the fourth word in the field. Although these names are formatted differently, they have one thing in common: the surname is always the last word in the field.

To accommodate this pattern, you'll need to tell WordPerfect to use the first word from the *right* edge of the field. You do this by entering a negative number under the Word label of the key definition. When you are defining the key, choose the Word option, and type **–1** to indicate that you want to sort by the last word in the field. With this key definition, it doesn't matter how many words are in the field; when you perform the sort, WordPerfect will use the last word in the field as the key. You can also enter –2 or –3 to specify the second or third word from the right edge of the field.

If names in your list are followed by abbreviations such as Jr. or Sr., these can also confuse the sort operation—especially if you've used the foregoing procedure to specify the last word as the sort key. Consider someone with the last name of Hammond, Jr. Here the Sort feature will interpret the Jr. as the last name in this record.

To correct this problem, delete the character space between the two words, Hammond and Jr. Press Home and then Spacebar to insert a Hard Space character code, [HSpace]. On the editing screen and in the printed document, the hard space looks exactly like a regular character space, except that WordPerfect treats it as a text character. With the hard space inserted, the two words are interpreted as one word by Sort and other WordPerfect operations.

Sorting a List of Dates

Use forward slashes or hard hyphens to format dates in WordPerfect documents, such as 07/19/94 or 07-19-94, when you plan to run a sort on those documents. The slash and hyphen characters tell WordPerfect to treat each number as a separate word in the record, with the month number as Word 1, the day number as Word 2, and the year as Word 3. This lets you define different sort keys for each number.

TIP. *A hard hyphen, inserted by pressing Home+Hyphen, is considered a text character in your document, and is not used by WordPerfect's hyphenation feature to divide your text.*

Try this exercise to create and sort a list of dates:

1. Clear the screen, and type the following list:

```
01/30/95
09/12/92
03/19/93
04/02/94
08/26/93
12/20/90
```

11/Ø5/92
12/2Ø/94

Choose Tools ▶
Sort ▶ OK.

2. Press Merge/Sort (Ctrl+F9), choose Sort, and then press Enter.

3. Choose Sort Keys from the Sort dialog box. Make sure the selected sort type is Line.

4. For this exercise, you will sort the information by the year and month. Edit the first key so that Type is set to Numeric, and Word is set to 3.

5. Now edit the second key (if there was only one key in the list, you will have to add a key to edit the second). Choose Word and change the setting to 1. Set Type to Numeric. Then, press Exit (F7) to choose the Edit Sort Key dialog box.

6. If there are three or more keys on the list, highlight the extra keys (below Key 2), and Delete them. Choose Perform Action, and the list of dates is sorted first by the year. For the records with identical years, Key 2 sorts them again by the month number.

Sorting Text in Different Languages

Whenever you perform a sort operation, WordPerfect arranges the text according to established rules of alphabetization. These rules differ, depending on the language you're using to create your documents. For example, if you are using the U.S. English version of WordPerfect, your text is alphabetized according to the conventions of American English.

If, however, you've created your document in another language, such as Spanish or French, certain characters and symbols are not recognized as part of the English language. WordPerfect will not know how to sort these characters, unless you change the language type for the document. To do so, you must insert a language code into the format settings of WordPerfect's Initial Codes screen.

NOTE. *For more information about the Initial Codes screen, see Chapter 2.*

Choose Layout ▶
Document.

■ Display the Document Format by pressing Format (Shift+F8) and choosing Document.

■ Choose Document Initial Codes from the dialog box. This displays the default format settings for your copy of WordPerfect.

Choose Layout ▶
Other ▶ Language.

■ Now, from *within* the Document Initial Codes dialog box, you'll insert a code that tells WordPerfect which language you're using. Press Format (Shift+F8) and choose Other. Select Language to open the Select Language dialog box.

- From the list of languages, choose the language you want to use. Then press Exit (F7) until you return to the Document Initial Codes dialog box where you'll see the [Lang] code that you inserted. If you highlight the code, you can confirm the language that you selected.

- Press Exit (F7) until the document screen is redisplayed.

The [Lang] code that you inserted at the Document Initial Codes dialog box determines the sort rules for all text in the document, according to the language you specified.

Sorting a Document without Retrieving It

Sometimes you'll want to sort the information stored in a file without retrieving the document to the editing screen. For example, suppose you're typing a new list of names and want to add a few of them to the NAMELIST.DOC file that you created earlier. You can block the new names, append them to NAMELIST.DOC, and then tell WordPerfect to alphabetize or sort all information stored in that file, including the names you've just added.

Until now, you've pressed Enter to skip the Source and Destination prompts that appear when you choose the Sort feature. This time, you'll enter file names at these prompts. WordPerfect will then sort the information found in the source file and save it to the destination file. This enables you to sort information from disk without ever retrieving the files. Also, if you're currently working on a document, you won't need to clear the screen before you perform a sort operation with disk files.

Before you continue, make sure you clear the screen. Then follow the general process for sorting files on disk:

Choose Tools ▶ Sort.

- From the document screen, press Merge/Sort (Ctrl+F9) and choose Sort.

- WordPerfect displays the Sort dialog box with the Source and Destination options. From the Source box, choose File and enter the name of the file that contains the information you want to sort.

- From the Destination box, you can choose File and enter the destination file name.

- Press Exit (F7) to accept the source and destination entries.

Choose OK.

- The Sort dialog box appears next. If necessary, define keys to control the sort. Then choose Perform Action, and the information contained in the source file is sorted.

If you entered the same Source and Destination file names, the sorted information replaces the original file. If you entered a file name instead, the sorted information is saved in a file with that name, and the original file remains unaltered.

Try the following exercise to add names to NAMELIST.DOC, and then sort the contents of the disk file without retrieving the file:

1. Move the cursor to a blank line on your screen, and press Enter to start a new line. Then type the following names, remembering to press Enter after each line.

   ```
   Suzanne Kraft
   Terry Brown
   Walt Holland
   ```

2. Now use the Block feature to append these names to the NAMELIST.-DOC file that you created earlier. Move the cursor to the letter *S* in the name Suzanne Kraft.

Drag the mouse pointer over the list to highlight it.

3. Press Block (press Alt+F4 or F12). Move the cursor just beyond the third name, Walt Holland. Make sure all three names are highlighted with the block.

4. Press Move (Ctrl+F4), choose <u>B</u>lock, and select <u>A</u>ppend.

Choose <u>E</u>dit ▸ <u>A</u>ppend ▸ To <u>F</u>ile

5. In the Append To dialog box, type **namelist.doc** and press Enter. WordPerfect appends the highlighted text at the end of NAMELIST.DOC. Now you're ready to realphabetize the information in the file.

6. At the editing screen, press Merge/Sort (Ctrl+F9) and choose <u>S</u>ort.

Choose <u>T</u>ools ▸ So<u>r</u>t.

7. From the Source box, choose File, type **namelist.doc**, and press Enter.

8. From the Destination box, choose Fi<u>l</u>e, type **sorted.doc**, and then press Enter, to indicate that you want the sorted information from NAME-LIST.DOC stored in a file called SORTED.DOC. WordPerfect will create the file when the sort is completed. Press Enter again to go to the Sort dialog box.

9. The Sort dialog box now appears below the contents of the input file name you specified for sorting. If you wish, you can choose <u>V</u>iew from the Sort menu to scroll through the file contents. When you're finished viewing the text, press Exit (F7) to move the cursor back to the Sort dialog box.

10. Choose <u>P</u>erform Action to sort the information in the file. Afterwards, any document you were working on is redisplayed.

Choose <u>F</u>ile ▸ <u>F</u>ile Manager.

11. Now let's look at the contents of the sorted file. Press File Manager (F5). Press Enter to accept the directory path and to see a list of the current directory files.

12. Either use the arrow keys to highlight the file name SORTED.DOC, or choose Name Search and type **sorted.doc** to find the output file. When the file name is highlighted, press Enter to disable Name Search if necessary. Then choose Look to view the contents of the file. You will see the names you added, alphabetized into the list.

13. When you're finished viewing the file contents, press Exit (F7) to return to the editing screen.

During the sort operation, the contents of the input file are displayed for sorting purposes only and do not replace any documents you were working on before you selected the Sort feature. Any documents you were working on are displayed again once the sort operation is completed.

Sorting and Extracting from a List

In addition to the sorting features, the Sort dialog box provides an option that lets you select or *extract* from a list entries that match one or more criterion. This feature is called Select Records. One practical example for this feature would be to sort and locate all of the people in your list that reside in New York. The following steps explain how you would use Select Records to extract entries or records from your list.

- First, open the document that contains the list you want to sort.

- Press Merge/Sort (Ctrl+F9), choose Sort, and then press Enter.

Choose Tools ▶ Sort and then choose OK.

- Use the Sort Keys option to define the keys that you want to use for the sorting process. Make a note of what each key looks for. For example, Key 1 might sort by last name, and key 2 might sort by city name.

  Make sure that at least one key includes the item by which you want to extract items from the list. For example, if you want to extract all the records of people living in New York, at least one key must be defined to sort on the field where the state information is stored.

- Choose Select Records, and the Sort dialog box changes to allow the entry of a search criterion, as shown in Figure 9.9.

- Type **Key***n* where *n* represents the number of the key you want to sort on. Then use the operators listed in the Sort dialog box to create the search criterion. If, for example, Key 2 is defined to sort according to state information, and you want to find all records with New York in the state field, you would type **Key2=New York** and press Enter.

Figure 9.9

Defining a search criterion for the Select Records feature

```
Amanda Dobson       Fremont      CA   94536
Chance Williams     Richmond     CA   94801
Colleen Moore       Huntsville   AL   35801
Geri Olsen          Verona       PA   15147
Kevin Clark         Moab         UT   84532
Sam Rosenthal       Chelmsford   MA   01824
Shauna Williams     Bloomfield   NJ   07003
Tracy Stewart       Southport    NY   14904

C:\WPDOCS\ADDRESS.DOC                       Doc 1 Pg 1 Ln 1" Pos 1"
═══════════════════════════════════ Sort ═══════════════════
    Selection Operators Info
 =  Equal To    >  Greater Than
 <> Not Equal   <  Less Than        ┌Key Type   Ord  Field       Word┐
 &  And         >= Greater or equal │ 1  Alpha    ↑     1          1 │↑
 |  Or          <= Less or equal    │                               │
 Example: Key1=Smith & Key2=Utah    │                               │
   (Select all Smiths from Utah)    └                               ┘↓

    Select Records: ┌─────────────────────────────────────────────┐
  [ ] Select Witho  │                                             │
  [ ] Sort Uppercase First      Perform Action   View   Close   Cancel
```

Enter search criterion here

NOTE. *The <=, >=, >, and < operators also can be applied, for example, so that Key2< New York will list all records where the field is alphabetically before New York.*

■ After you enter the search criterion, choose Perform Action.

WordPerfect first extracts the records that match the search criterion and sorts them according to the keys you've defined. Remember that the Select Records feature deletes the list entries that don't match your search criterion. For this reason, you should save your file before performing the sort procedure.

Working with Footnotes and Endnotes

Paragraph Numbering and Outlines

WordPerfect Tables and Spreadsheets

Preparing Legal Documents

Page Numbering, Tables of Contents, and Indexes

Working with Large Documents

3

Professional Documents

10

Working with Footnotes and Endnotes

N SCHOLARLY AND PROFESSIONAL DOCUMENTS, NOTES ARE OFTEN INSERTED to credit an author or publication, or to acknowledge additional reference materials regarding the content of the text. Such notes provide the reader with related information that would interrupt the flow of the document if placed in the main body of text. For this reason, notes are usually printed separately from the document text.

As shown in Figure 10.1, *footnotes* are printed at the bottom of document pages, and *endnotes* are printed in a list at the end of the document. WordPerfect lets you create both types of notes—you can even combine both types in the same document. (Chapter 25 even explains how to use a special macro to switch footnotes to endnotes and vice versa.)

Figure 10.1

Footnotes and endnotes

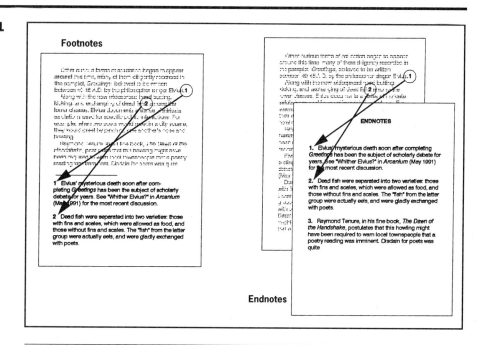

In this chapter, you'll learn how to create footnotes and endnotes in your documents. You'll also see how to edit notes and change the format for the note text. Because most procedures for footnotes and endnotes are identical, many of the instructions in this chapter refer to "notes," which applies to both footnotes and endnotes.

Creating, Inserting, and Viewing Notes

When you use a typewriter to create a term paper or a report with footnotes, you need to calculate how much space to leave at the bottom of each page for the notes you want to insert. On a typewriter, this is a difficult task that requires planning and patience; once footnotes are included in the typed document, it's almost impossible to edit and reorganize the document text.

Fortunately, WordPerfect takes the guesswork out of creating footnotes and endnotes. You need only worry about where the note references should be inserted into the text and what each note should contain—WordPerfect takes care of the numbering and formatting of the notes. Here is the general procedure for inserting notes:

■ Move the cursor to the place in the text where the footnote or endnote reference should be located.

Choose Layout.
Choose Footnote
or Endnote, and
then choose Create.

■ Press Footnote (Ctrl+F7), and choose Footnote or Endnote. Then, choose the first option, Create. An editing screen appears where you can type the text for the note. This screen resembles the document editing screen, except you'll see "Footnote: Press F7 when done" or "Endnote: Press F7 when done" at the bottom of the screen.

NOTE. *If you do not wish to insert the note you've created, press Cancel (Esc) to exit the note editing screen without saving the text and choose Discard Changes and Exit. This will cancel the note.*

■ Notice the number in the upper-left corner of the editing screen; this is the number of the footnote or endnote that you are creating.

■ Press the spacebar or Tab to insert space after the note number. Then, type the text for the note.

■ When you are finished typing the note, press Exit (F7) to save the note text and return to the document editing screen.

A number now appears where your cursor is located in the document. This is the reference number for the note you've just created. Press Reveal Codes (Alt+F3 or F11), or choose View and then Reveal Codes, and you'll see one of these codes:

    [Footnote]

or

    [Endnote]

Move the cursor to highlight the code and the code expands to show the first few words of the contents of the note. Footnote and endnote references are automatically numbered, and if you move, add, or delete a note, Word-Perfect renumbers the notes for you.

You don't need to worry about footnote or endnote placement, either. WordPerfect constantly monitors the note reference; it places each footnote on the page where its reference appears and each endnote in a list at the end of your document. Alternatively, you can create a special endnote page that specifies where endnotes should appear. This procedure is described under "Placing a List of Endnotes" later in this chapter. You'll also create a document with endnotes in that section.

Inserting a Footnote into Your Document

Try this exercise to create a sample document and insert a footnote into the text:

1. Clear the screen by pressing Exit (F7) and typing **N** twice.

Choose File ▶ New to begin at a clear screen.

2. Type the following paragraph to begin a sample document for footnotes:

    Other curious forms of salutation began to appear around this time, many of them diligently recorded in the pamphlet *Greetings*, believed to be written between 40-45 A.D. by the philosopher-singer Elvius.

3. Position the cursor at the end of the paragraph, where you'll insert the reference for the note.

Choose Layout ▶ Footnote ▶ Create.

4. To create a footnote, press Footnote (Ctrl+F7) and choose Footnote. Then choose the first option, Create. The footnote editing screen is displayed, as shown in Figure 10.2.

Figure 10.2
The footnote editing screen

Footnote number in note

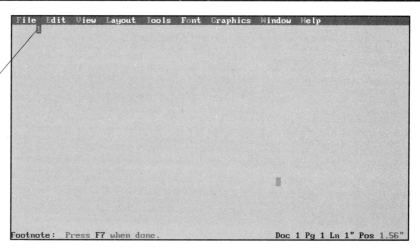

5. The number in the upper-left corner of the editing screen indicates the reference number that will be inserted into the document text. Press the spacebar twice to add space after the note number. Then type this text for the note:

```
Elvius' mysterious death soon after completing Greetings
has been the subject of scholarly debate for years. See
"Whither Elvius?" in Arcanium (May 1993) for the most
recent discussion.
```

NOTE. *When you are typing the text of a footnote or endnote, you can press the Tab or Indent (F4 or Shift+F4) keys to indent text; press Center (Shift+F6) or Flush Right (Alt+F6) to align text; or select font attributes such as Bold (F6), Italic (Ctrl+I), and Underline (F8).*

6. Press Exit (F7) when you're finished typing the note to return to the document editing screen. Figure 10.3 shows the reference number that is inserted into your document for the note.

Figure 10.3

A footnote reference inserted in the document

Footnote reference number in document

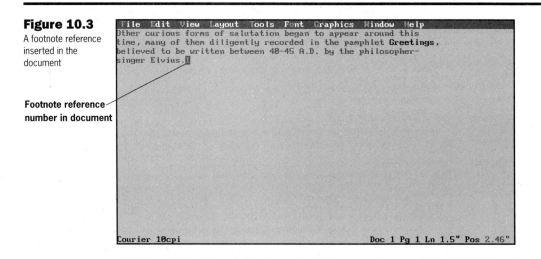

At this point, you may not see the text of the note, even though it will be printed with the rest of your document. If you are working with the text display mode or graphics display mode, WordPerfect keeps the notes hidden until you view or print the document. You can see the notes when you preview or print your document or when you are editing with the page display mode. See "Viewing the Notes," later in this chapter for more information. For now, keep this document on the screen; in the next section you'll add more notes to the text.

When your document is printed, the reference numbers for notes will be printed as superscript numbers, assuming your printer can print this type of text; if not, WordPerfect will attempt to print the reference numbers one-half line higher than the rest of the text on the line.

Inserting Additional Notes

As you edit your documents, you may need to insert additional notes between existing notes. When you insert a new note before existing notes, WordPerfect renumbers all note references to include the new note. Try this exercise to add other notes to your document:

1. Add the following text after the paragraph already on your screen:

   ```
   Along with the now widespread head-butting, kicking, and
   exchanging of dead fish practiced among the lower classes,
   Elvius documents a series of intricate salutations used
   for specific public interactions. For example, when two
   poets would meet in a city square, they would greet by
   pinching one another's nose and howling.
   ```

Choose Layout ▸ Footnote ▸ Create.

2. With the cursor at the end of the additional text, press Footnote (Ctrl+F7) and choose Footnote and then choose Create.

3. On the footnote editing screen, you'll notice that the number 2 appears as the note number in the upper-left corner of the screen. Press the spacebar twice to add space after the note number. Then type this text for the footnote:

   ```
   Raymond Tenure, in his fine book The Dawn of the
   Handshake, postulates that this howling might have been
   required to warn local townspeople that a poetry reading
   was imminent. Disdain for poets was quite high at this
   time.
   ```

4. Press Exit (F7) to return to the document screen. Notice that WordPerfect automatically numbered the second reference.

5. Now you'll insert a footnote between the first and second footnotes. Move the text cursor to the space after the phrase "dead fish."

Choose Layout ▸ Footnote ▸ Create.

6. Press Footnote (Ctrl+F7) and choose Footnote. Then choose Create.

7. At the footnote editing screen, you'll notice that WordPerfect numbers this new note as footnote 2, even though this is the third note you've placed in the text. You're inserting this note after the first note, so the

new note becomes footnote 2. Press the spacebar twice to add space after the note number.

8. Type this text for the footnote:

Dead fish were separated into two varieties: those with fins and scales, which were allowed as food, and those without fins and scales. The "fish" from the latter group were actually eels, and tasted much like fermented footwear. These were gladly exchanged with poets. See *Ancient Fish Folklore*, VI.II, University of California Press, 1962.

9. Press Exit (F7) to save the footnote and return to the document screen. Your screen should now look like Figure 10.4.

Figure 10.4

The finished document with footnotes

Footnote reference numbers

```
File  Edit  View  Layout  Tools  Font  Graphics  Window  Help
Other curious forms of salutation began to appear around this
time, many of them diligently recorded in the pamphlet Greetings,
believed to be written between 40-45 A.D. by the philosopher-
singer Elvius.█

Along with the now widespread head-butting, kicking, and
exchanging of dead fish2 practiced among the lower classes,
Elvius documents a series of intricate salutations used for
specific public interactions. For example, when two poets would
meet in a city square, they would greet by pinching one another's
nose and howling.3




C:\WPDOCS\FOOTNOTE.DOC                           Doc 1 Pg 1 Ln 2" Pos 3.36"
```

Choose File ▸ Save.

10. Before you continue, you'll want to save this document. Press Save (Ctrl+F2), type **footnote.doc**, and press Enter.

Although this example employed footnotes, the procedure works the same for endnotes, as well. Whenever you insert (or delete) footnotes, Word-Perfect will renumber the references according to the correct sequential order. Keep the FOOTNOTE.DOC document on the screen; you'll need it for other exercises in this chapter.

Viewing the Notes

By now, you'll probably want to see how the notes will appear on the printed document. There are two ways to view footnote and endnote text. You can use the Print Preview screen or you can change to WordPerfect's page display mode to include footnotes and endnotes on the document editing screen.

Figure 10.5 shows an example of footnotes on the Print Preview screen. To view your notes on this screen:

Figure 10.5

Footnotes displayed on the Print Preview screen

Document text —————

Footnotes for this page —————

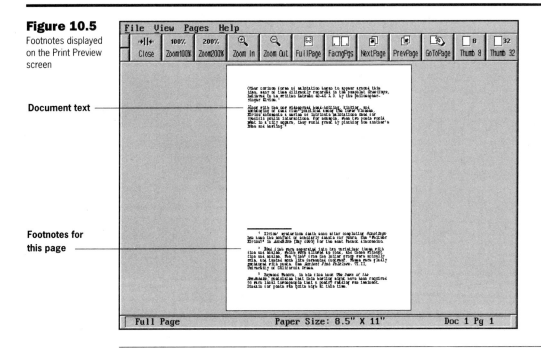

- Choose Print (Shift+F7), and then select Print Preview.

Choose File ▸ Print Preview.

- If necessary, press PgUp or PgDn to view the notes on the document pages. You may also want to zoom in to view the note text more clearly.

- When you are finished viewing the notes, press Exit (F7) to return to the document screen.

When you are using the standard text display mode, or WordPerfect's graphics display mode, the footnote and endnote text remains hidden when you are editing your document. In some cases, you may want to keep the notes hidden because this allows you to scroll and read the main text without being interrupted by footnote text.

You've seen how the Print Preview screen can show a quick view of your document before you print, but sometimes you'll need to view footnote text while you are editing your document. (Note that you can view, but *not* edit, the display mode.) This is possible with WordPerfect's page display mode. To view your notes from the document editing screen, follow these steps:

Choose <u>V</u>iew ▸
P<u>a</u>ge Mode.

■ Press Screen (Ctrl+F3) and then choose the <u>P</u>age option. WordPerfect adjusts the screen display to show the document screen and your text in a graphical mode. Figure 10.6 shows how notes will appear when page display mode is turned on. If the document on your screen doesn't yet fill a complete page, you'll need to press Home, Home, ↓ to move the cursor to the bottom of the text. Then, press Ctrl+Enter to insert a page break and you'll see your footnotes at the end of the first page.

Figure 10.6

Footnotes displayed
with the Page
display mode

```
 File   Edit   View   Layout   Tools   Font   Graphics   Window   Help
      specific public interactions. For example, when two poets would
      meet in a city square, they would greet by pinching one another's
      nose and howling.³



                    ¹ Elvius' mysterious death soon after completing Greetings
             has been the subject of scholarly debate for years. See "Whither
             Elvius?" in Arcanium (May 1993) for the most recent discussion.

                    ² Dead fish were separated into two varieties: those with
             fins and scales, which were allowed as food, and those without
             fins and scales. The "fish" from the latter group were actually
             eels, and tasted much like fermented footwear. These were gladly
             exchanged with poets. See Ancient Fish Folklore, VI.II,
             University of California Press.

                    ³ Raymond Tenure, in his fine book The Dawn of the
             Handshake, postulates that this howling might have been required
             to warn local townspeople that a poetry reading was imminent.
             Disdain for poets was quite high at this time.



 C:\WPDOCS\FOOTNOTE.DOC                              Doc 1 Pg 1 Ln 4" Pos 1"
```

■ Press PgUp or PgDn and use the cursor arrows to scroll through the text of your document. If footnotes exist in the text, they are displayed a the bottom of each document page.

Choose <u>V</u>iew ▸
<u>T</u>ext Mode.

■ You can continue to edit document text in the page display mode, or you can return to the text display mode by pressing Screen (Ctrl+F3) and then choosing <u>T</u>ext.

Creating a Note from Blocked Text

As you are creating and editing your documents, you may decide that certain passages of the text aren't really necessary for the finished document, but may be useful as additional information or resource material. You don't want to delete the text altogether, but you don't want it in the main body of text, either.

Such passages of text are perfect candidates for footnotes or endnotes. WordPerfect's Block feature makes it possible for you to "clip" text from the document and place it in a footnote or endnote. Here is the general procedure:

Drag the mouse pointer to select a section of text.

- Use the Block (Alt+F4 or F12) feature to block the text you want to convert to a footnote or endnote.

- Press Cut (Ctrl+Delete) to cut the blocked text from your document.

- Move the cursor to the place where the note reference number should be inserted.

Choose Edit ▸ Cut and Paste.

- Press Footnote (Ctrl+F7), choose Footnote or Endnote, then choose Create. The note editing screen appears.

- Press the spacebar to add space after the note number.

Choose Layout. Choose Footnote or Endnote. Then, choose Create.

- A prompt at the bottom of the screen reminds you that you have just cut a block of text from your document. Press Enter to retrieve the text into the note screen.

- You can edit the text you've retrieved or add text to the note. When you're finished, press Exit (F7) to accept the text and return to the document. As usual, existing footnotes or endnotes will be renumbered as necessary.

Deleting or Moving a Note

If you delete or move a section of text that contains a reference number for a note, that note is deleted or moved with the text, and the notes are renumbered accordingly.

Sometimes, you may want to delete or move a footnote or endnote without affecting the surrounding text in your document. This can be done quickly and easily with the Delete and Undelete features. Each note you create is stored in a [Footnote] or [Endnote] code; delete the code, and the note is removed from the text. (In fact, you can delete a footnote simply by deleting its reference number within the text.) To move the footnote or endnote to another location in the document, simply delete the code and use the Undelete feature to restore the code at the new location. Alternately, you can use WordPerfect's drag and drop feature to drag a footnote or endnote to a new location in the text. Simply highlight the note number and hold down your left mouse button until you see the drag and drop icon and/or the message "Release mouse button to move block" at the bottom of the screen. Then drag with the mouse until the cursor is in the desired location, and release the mouse button to deposit (drop) the note in its new location.

This is the procedure for deleting a footnote or endnote from the document:

- Move the text cursor onto the note reference number, and press Delete.

- When the reference number is deleted, the note text also is removed from your document.

Now that you know how to remove a footnote or endnote from the text, let's try moving a note reference to another location. The following steps assume the FOOTNOTE.DOC file is displayed on your screen. First you'll delete one of the footnote references on your screen. Then, you'll use the Undelete feature to restore the note to another place in the document.

1. Move the text cursor onto the number of the second footnote reference in the document displayed on your screen.

2. Press the Delete key and the note is removed from the text.

3. Move the cursor to the space after the word "salutation," in the first sentence in your document.

Choose Edit ▸ Undelete.

4. Press Undelete (Esc). The note reference you just deleted is highlighted at the cursor position, and the Undelete dialog box is displayed on the screen. (Notice that the note reference number has changed because of the note's new location in the document.)

5. Choose Restore and the note is restored at the new location in the document.

Choose File ▸ Save.

6. Before you continue, press Save (Ctrl+F12).

After you move the note, it becomes footnote 1, and WordPerfect renumbers the other notes in your document.

Editing Footnotes and Endnotes

When you need to change the information in an existing footnote or endnote, WordPerfect makes it easy for you. Either press Footnote (Ctrl+F7), choose Footnote or Endnote from the Notes dialog box, and then choose Edit; or choose the Edit option from the Footnote or Endnote submenu. Then enter the number of the note you want to edit. It will be displayed again on the footnote/endnote editing screen, where you can edit the text and use all of WordPerfect's editing features, including Delete, Move, and Copy.

Editing a Note

After a footnote or endnote is created, you may need to edit the text contained in the note. To edit a note, you need to return to the editing screen where the footnote or endnote was created. Perform these steps to edit one of the footnotes or endnotes in your document:

- Position the cursor to the left of the reference number for the footnote or endnote you want to edit. For example, if you want to edit footnote 4, move the cursor just before the reference number for that footnote in the document. (This step isn't mandatory, but will save you a step in a moment.)

Choose Layout ▸
Footnote or Endnote ▸
Edit.

- Press Footnote (Ctrl+F7) to display the Notes dialog box. To edit a footnote, choose Footnote; choose Endnote to edit an endnote.

- Choose Edit, and WordPerfect prompts you to enter the number of the footnote or endnote you want to edit. WordPerfect automatically displays the number of the first footnote or endnote located to the right of the cursor.

- If the number displayed in the box is the number of the note you want to edit, press Enter to accept the reference number. If this is not the number of the note you want to edit, type the desired number and press Enter. The note editing screen appears with the text for the selected note.

- Edit the text of the note. When you are finished, press Exit (F7) to save the edited note and return to the document. The reference number remains unchanged, but the note will be displayed and printed with the changes you've made.

Suppose you entered incorrect information in the first footnote of the document you created earlier. Try the following exercise to edit the footnote and change the information:

1. Position the cursor to the left of the reference for footnote 1.

2. Press Footnote (Ctrl+F7) and choose Footnote.

Choose Layout ▸
Footnote ▸ Edit.

3. Choose Edit and WordPerfect displays Footnote Number 1. Press Enter to accept this number, and the footnote editing screen is displayed with the text for the first footnote.

4. Delete the last sentence, "See *Ancient Fish Folklore*, VI.II, University of California Press, 1962." Replace it with:

```
See The Wahlburg Report, 3rd Edition, Banyan Press, 1982,
and Elvius Lives in New Jersey Trailer Park, New England
Herald Gazette, October 5, 1981.
```

5. Press Exit (F7) to save the edited note and return to the document screen.

6. To save the document, press Save (Ctrl+F2).

Choose File ▸ Save.

To edit an endnote, follow the same procedure—except select Endnote instead of Footnote in step 2. As always, it's important to save the edited document to the file on disk.

If you know a word or phrase from the note you want to edit, you can use WordPerfect's Extended Search capabilities to jump directly to the note editing screen. First, move to the top of your document and then press Extended Search (Home, F2). (You can also press F2 and select Extended Search from the Search dialog box.) Type the word or phrase that you know from the note; this must match the note text exactly. Then, press F2 again. WordPerfect locates the note that contains the text you typed and displays it in the editing screen. Make the changes you need, and then press Exit (F7) to return to your document.

Checking the Spelling of a Note

Sometimes you'll want to check the spelling of the text stored in your footnotes or endnote, and there are two ways to do this. You can check the spelling of all notes by running the Speller at the document editing screen; WordPerfect automatically checks footnotes and endnotes when you spell-check the entire document. Or you can use the Speller feature while you are creating or editing a note.

This is how you check the spelling of a note while it is displayed on the footnote/endnote editing screen:

Choose Tools ▸
Writing Tools ▸
Speller. Then choose
From Cursor.

■ While the footnote or endnote text is displayed on the screen, press Spell (Ctrl+F2) and choose Footnote or From Cursor to check the note text.

NOTE. *Usually you can choose any of the first four options to check the spelling of text in the note. If your footnote or endnote is longer than one page, choose Page to check a page at a time.*

■ The Speller dialog box is displayed as it appears for the document screen. Follow the prompts to find and correct any spelling errors in the note text.

- When the Speller is finished checking the text, you'll see the message "Spell Check Completed." Press Enter or click on OK to return to your document.

At this point, you may continue to edit the text of the note, or you can press Exit (F7) again to save the edited note and return to the document editing screen. Because the Speller automatically includes notes when you spell-check your document, the procedure described here is useful only when you want to check the text of a note that is displayed on the note editing screen. If you want to check the note text *and* the document text, run the Speller from the document editing screen.

Searching for Footnote or Endnote Text

When your document has several footnotes or endnotes, you may need some help finding specific notes in your document. If you are using the standard text display or the basic WYSIWYG display, it can be difficult to remember what each note contains and where certain references are located in the document.

WordPerfect's Search feature provides two ways to search for the footnotes and endnotes in your document: You can search for the [Footnote] and [Endnote] codes in the document, or you can search for text which is stored in the footnotes and endnotes. This section explains how to find note codes and locate specific text items which are stored in them. (For more information about the Search and Replace features, see Chapter 7.)

Searching for Footnote/Endnote Codes

The Search feature can help you quickly find a footnote or endnote code in the text, should you need to delete, move, or edit a specific note. Because you are looking for a code instead of text, you need to define a search criterion that contains the appropriate footnote or endnote code. The process is described in the following steps:

- If you want to search the entire document for a footnote or endnote code, begin with the cursor at the top of the document. Press Home, Home, Home, ↑ to move the cursor to the beginning of the document— before any text or hidden formatting codes.

- Press Search (F2) and the Search dialog box appears on the screen.

- To search for a footnote code, press Codes (F5), and scroll through the list that appears until you highlight the word "Endnote" or "Footnote." You can move quickly to either word by typing **footn** or **endn** while the

Choose Edit ▸ Search.

list is displayed. Then, press Enter. This places a note code into the Search For box.

■ Press Search (F2) again to begin the search for the next footnote code in the text. If a code is found, the cursor is moved just past it. You will see the reference number, but you won't see the footnote code unless you display the Reveal Codes window. If a footnote code is not found in the document, WordPerfect displays a "Not found" message box on the screen. Press Enter to clear this message.

■ For each additional note code you want to find, press Search (F2) twice to search for the next code.

This is a quick way to find the note codes in your document. Once you've found a note reference, you can edit, move, or delete it.

Searching for Text in Notes

Searching for text in notes is similar to looking for text in your document, as described in Chapter 7. The difference is that the text in footnotes and endnotes is usually hidden until a document is printed, displayed at the Print Preview screen, or shown in page display mode.

For notes, you'll need to use WordPerfect's Extended Search feature to search through *all* text in the document. While the standard Search (F2) feature searches only the text you can see on the document editing screen, the Extended Search (Home, F2) feature looks through all text—including footnotes and endnotes—that will be printed on the pages. (Remember, you can also press F2 and select Extended Search from the Search dialog box to activate an extended search.)

Here is the general procedure for searching for specific text in footnotes and endnotes:

■ Press Home, Home, Home, ↑ to move the cursor to the beginning of the document—before any text or hidden formatting codes.

■ Press Extended Search (Home, F2). The search prompt appears in the dialog box on the screen.

■ Type a search criterion—a word, phrase, sentence, or name you want to find.

■ Select any other desired options from the Search dialog box, such as Backward Search or Find Whole Words Only.

■ Press Search (F2) again to begin the search for the text you typed. If text is found in a footnote or endnote that matches the search criterion, then the text of that note is displayed on the screen, and the cursor is moved just past the matching text. If the text you typed as the search criterion is not found in the document, WordPerfect displays a "Not found" message on the screen.

■ At this point, you are in the note editing screen where you may make changes to the text in the note. When you are finished, press Exit (F7) to return to the document screen if necessary. You can also continue to hunt for the search string if you do not receive the "Not found" message. Note that if WordPerfect finds an occurence of the search criterion within the main document text, it automatically leaves the note editing screen and returns to the document screen. Continuing to press Extended Search (Home, F2) will eventually turn up all instances of the specified search string, whether thay are in notes or in the main body of the text.

The Extended Search feature will look through *all* text that will be printed on the finished pages, so it's a useful tool for finding a specific phrase or word that may be stored in a footnote or endnote, as well as other hidden text such as document headers or footers.

NOTE. *WordPerfect also supports an Extended Replace feature for replacing one text phrase with another. For more information about the Search and Replace features, see Chapter 7.*

Changing the Format of Notes

WordPerfect uses a standard format for the footnotes and endnotes you'll create; however, several options are available for customizing the appearance of the notes in your document. You can change the spacing of lines and change the style of the reference number displayed in the text. For lengthy footnotes that must be divided across two or more pages, you can tell WordPerfect how much of the note should be kept together; you can even have WordPerfect print a "(continued...)" message when notes must be divided.

Spacing the Note Text

When you create a note, WordPerfect uses single-line spacing for the text and places a blank line—about 0.17 inch of space—between footnotes, at the bottom of the page, and between endnotes displayed in a list. If you want to change the amount of space inserted between notes, you can indicate your preferences as a footnote or endnote option. In these steps, the spacing is changed for footnotes, but you can follow the same procedure to change the spacing for endnotes.

■ Move the cursor to the place in the document where the note spacing change should begin. To change the spacing for all notes in the document, press Home, Home, ↑ to move the cursor to the beginning of the text.

Choose Layout ▶
Footnote ▶ Options.

■ Press Footnote (Ctrl+F7). Then, choose Footnote and Options. Figure 10.7 shows the Footnote Options dialog box that appears.

Figure 10.7
The Footnote
Options dialog box

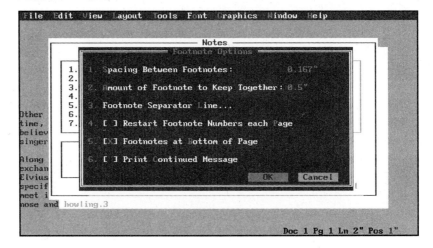

■ Choose the first option, Spacing Between Footnotes, and enter a number to indicate the spacing you want between the footnotes on the page.

■ Press Exit (F7) until you return to the document editing screen.

When you exit the Footnote Options dialog box, a [Footnote Space] code is inserted at the cursor position; all footnotes that are placed after this code will be affected by the spacing change you've made. Notes placed before the [Footnote Space] code are not affected. If you change your mind and don't want the spacing change, simply display the Reveal Codes window (Alt+F3 or F11) and delete the [Footnote Space] code you inserted.

You can also change the spacing *within* a note (rather than between notes). To change the spacing of a single note, you would get into the editing screen for the note in question (press Ctrl+F7, choose Footnote or Endnote, and then choose Edit). Then choose the desired formatting options from either the Layout menu or the Format dialog box (Shift+F8). For example, to double space your note's text, you would press Shift+F8, select Line, choose Line Spacing, type **2** and press Enter, and then press F7 until you return to the document editing screen.

To change the spacing of *all* notes, press Ctrl+F7, choose Footnote or Endnote, select Edit Style in Note, and then insert a spacing code into the Footnote/Endnote Style in Note dialog box by pressing Shift+F8, selecting Line, choosing Line Spacing, and then entering the desired line spacing value.

Keeping Footnotes Together

If one of your footnotes is especially long, WordPerfect may need to divide the note, printing half or part of it on the page where the footnote reference appears. The remainder of the footnote will continue on the next page in the document. WordPerfect automatically takes care of the formatting for you and decides where the longer footnotes should be split. However, you may not always like the way footnotes are divided.

A feature on the Footnote Options dialog box lets you specify how much of the footnote should stay together if WordPerfect decides to divide and print it on two or more pages. You can also indicate whether you want Word-Perfect to print a "(continued...)" message for footnotes that are continued across pages. Here is the procedure:

Choose Layout ▶
Footnote ▶ Options.

- Press Home, Home, ↑ to move the cursor to the beginning of the document.

- Press Footnote (Ctrl+F7), choose Footnote, and then Options.

- From the Footnote Options dialog box, select Amount of Footnote to Keep Together. Type a measurement, and press Enter.

- Choose Print Continued Message to check the box next to this option. This tells WordPerfect to print a "(continued...)" message when footnotes are divided to indicate that the note spans more than one page.

- Press Exit (F7) until you return to the document editing screen.

The measurement you entered indicates the amount of each footnote that WordPerfect will keep on one page, but only when the note needs to be divided. Notice this is a measurement—most likely in inches—and *not* a number of text lines. For example, suppose you want at least 1 inch of each footnote to be kept together on a page whenever a footnote will need to be split between pages. You would select Amount of Note to Keep Together, and enter **1**.

The "(continued...)" message is optional, but it's important because it clarifies the footnote scheme. One possible drawback, however, is that the "(continued...)" message is printed in the same font as your note.

When you exit the Footnote Options menu, two codes are inserted into your document. A [Footnote Min] code is inserted to specify the amount of footnote text to keep together; a [Footnote Cont Msg] code is inserted to print the "(continued...)" message for divided footnotes. All footnotes placed after these codes will be affected by the changes. Notes placed before these codes are not affected.

Changing the Style of the Note Number

The standard format for notes indicates that the reference number is printed as superscript text, but you can easily change the format to suit your needs. In fact, you can specify two different styles for notes: one for the reference number displayed in the text, and one for the number displayed with the footnote or endnote text. Because footnotes and endnotes are numbered independently, you can define a different number style for each note type. This is the procedure for doing so:

- Move the cursor to the place in your document where the number style change should begin. To change the number style for all the notes, move your cursor to the beginning of the document.

Choose Layout ▸ Footnote or Endnote.

- Press Footnote (Ctrl+F7) and choose <u>F</u>ootnote or <u>E</u>ndnote.

- Choose Edit <u>S</u>tyle in Document and the current style definition may appear as:

```
[Suprscpt On][Footnote Num Disp][Suprscpt Off]
```

The [Footnote Num Disp] or [Endnote Num Disp] code represents the footnote or endnote reference number, and the pair of codes, [Suprscpt On] and [Suprscpt Off], indicate that the number will appear as superscript.

- Suppose you want to change the entire note style. Press Ctrl+End to delete the current style definition.

Choose <u>F</u>ont ▸ <u>I</u>talics.

- Press Italics (Ctrl+I) and then press Exit (F7) to return to the previous dialog box. This inserts the code, [Italc On], that turns on italicized text. Now you'll put back the [Footnote Num Disp] or [Endnote Num Disp] code.

- Choose <u>D</u>isplay in Document, and then press Exit (F7) to return to the previous dialog box. Choose <u>F</u>ootnote and then Edit <u>S</u>tyle in Document to return to the Footnote Style in Document dialog box.

Choose <u>F</u>ont ▸ <u>I</u>talics.

- Finally, you'll need to turn off the italic attribute. Press Italics (Ctrl+I) again. This inserts the [Italc Off] code to turn off the font attribute.

- Press Exit (F7) until you return to the document screen.

Choose L<u>a</u>yout ▸
<u>F</u>ootnote, or
choose L<u>a</u>yout ▸
<u>E</u>ndnote.

■ Now you can change the style for the number that appears next to the footnote or endnote text. Press Footnote (Ctrl+F7) and choose <u>F</u>ootnote or <u>E</u>ndnote.

■ From the menu of footnote or endnote options, choose Edit St<u>y</u>le in Note.

■ Change the format for this style, as you did for the <u>S</u>tyle in Document option. After you've defined the number style, press Exit (F7) to return to the Notes dialog box.

■ Press Exit (F7) until you return to the document screen.

When you edit the styles, you can select text attributes, as described here, and you can also insert spaces or include text as part of the numbering style for the notes.

For example, suppose you want each footnote reference number to appear like this: Footnote # 1. To change the style, you would display the Notes dialog box, choose <u>F</u>ootnote, and then choose Edit St<u>y</u>le in Document. Then add "Footnote # " to the current style, so that it appears like this:

```
[Suprscpt On]Footnote # [Footnote Num Disp][Suprscpt Off]
```

This number style specifies that the text "Footnote # " will appear before each footnote reference number in the document. Experiment with different options to see what styles you like best. The number style changes are saved with the internal styles of WordPerfect and are the only footnote/endnote options that do not insert codes into your document. If you don't like the changes, simply edit the styles again to restore the original footnote/endnote numbering styles.

NOTE. *If you want to permanently change the number style, you can do so by editing WordPerfect's internal system styles for Footnote and Endnote numbering. See Chapter 22 for more information on editing styles.*

Separating Footnotes from the Document Text

The standard settings of WordPerfect specify that footnotes will be located at the bottom of the same page where the footnote reference number appears; a 2-inch horizontal line will separate the footnote text from the main body of text. You can select a different length for the separator line and also specify how the footnote text is placed on the page. These features give you more control over the format of footnotes in your document and will help you further customize the appearance of notes.

NOTE. *The two options discussed here apply only to footnotes. Because end-notes are printed in a list at the end of the document, there's no need for a separator line.*

Selecting a Separator Line

WordPerfect allows different settings for the line that separates the footnote text from the main body of your document. You can display any line length you want or choose a line that extends across the full page (margin to margin). Or you can choose to print footnotes without a separator line. WordPerfect also lets you specify the spacing between the line and your text. You can even choose a different line color and style, if you wish. Here's the general procedure for choosing these options:

- Press Home, Home, ↑ to move your cursor to the top of the document. You'll run into problems if you don't perform this step first.

Choose Layout ▸
Footnote ▸ Options.

- Press Footnotes (Ctrl+F7), choose Footnote, and then choose Options.

- Choose Footnote Separator Line. This dialog box is displayed:

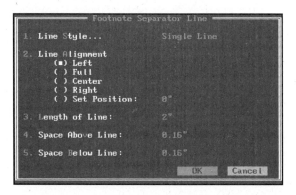

- Choose Line Style to display a list of Line Style options. Highlight the line style that you want to use. To choose a thin solid line for example, highlight "Single Line." Highlight "None" to indicate that you don't want a line printed to separate footnotes from the document text. Then choose Select to accept your choice.

- Choose Line Alignment, and then select the alignment you want. For example, choose Full to specify that you want the line drawn across the entire width of the page to separate the footnote text from the document text.

- When the Line Alignment option is set to anything but Full, you can change the length of the line. Choose <u>L</u>ength of Line, and enter a measurement.

- Choose Space Abo<u>v</u>e Line or Space <u>B</u>elow Line to change the spacing between the line and your text.

Choose OK to return to the document screen.

- Press Exit (F7) until you return to the document screen.

Placing Footnotes on the Page

WordPerfect places all footnotes at the bottom of the same page where the footnote references appear in the text, even when the page has only a line or two of text. Because of this, you may sometimes have a large amount of blank space between the text on the page and the footnote text.

To avoid excessive blank space, you can specify that footnotes be placed after the text, rather than at the bottom of the page. The footnotes will be moved up and inserted immediately after the text on the page. Here are the steps for changing the placement of the footnote text:

- Press Footnote (Ctrl+F7) and choose <u>F</u>ootnote. Then, choose <u>O</u>ptions.

Choose <u>L</u>ayout ▶ <u>F</u>ootnote ▶ <u>O</u>ptions.

- From the Footnote Options dialog box, choose Footnotes at <u>B</u>ottom of Page. This removes the *X* from the box next to the option. If an *X* is in the box, this indicates that footnotes will be printed at the bottom of each page; this is the standard setting. If you want footnotes to immediately follow the last line of text displayed on the page, make sure there is no *X* next to this option.

- Press Exit (F7) until you return to the document screen, and the [Footnote Txt Pos] code is inserted into the text.

When the Footnotes at <u>B</u>ottom of Page option is disabled, WordPerfect prints text—document and footnote—on the page without leaving blank areas between the document text and the footnotes. If you're printing long documents, this may save you some paper.

Changing the Numbers for Footnote References

WordPerfect conveniently numbers the footnotes and endnotes for you, but sometimes you may not want it to do so. For example, when you work with a large document, you may need to divide it between two or more files. This is common for reports and books, where the document is separated into different chapters, sections, or parts. When your document is divided in this manner, you may want the note references to be consecutive throughout the entire text, even though the document is split between several files. Since WordPerfect automatically starts footnote/endnote numbering with *1* at the beginning of each document file, your notes will not be consecutive when all files have been printed and collated.

NOTE. *You'll learn more about managing large documents in Chapter 15.*

On the other hand, for some documents, you may want the footnotes to begin with number 1 on each new page. A few options let you customize the numbering of notes in your document. These include an option for restarting the numbering of footnotes at the top of each page and inserting a special code that assigns a new number for footnote referencing.

Restarting Footnote Numbering with Each Page

For some documents, you may want to reset the footnote numbering at the top of each page. A feature on the Footnote Option dialog box makes this possible, as described in these steps:

- First, press Home, Home, ↑ to move the cursor to the beginning of the document before any text or formatting codes.

Choose Layout ▸ Footnote ▸ Options.

- Press Footnote (Ctrl+F7), and choose Footnote. Then choose Options from the displayed dialog box.

- Choose Restart Footnote Numbers each Page to place an *X* in the box next to this option.

Choose OK.

- Press Exit (F7) to return to the document screen.

The standard setting leaves this option turned off, which means that the footnotes for the entire document are numbered consecutively. When this option is turned on, however, WordPerfect restarts footnote numbering with 1 at the beginning of each document page.

Changing the Numbering for Footnote/Endnote References

If your document is divided between different files, you can insert a code at the beginning of each document that tells WordPerfect to continue footnote or endnote numbering where the previous document file left off.

Here is the procedure for changing or restarting the numbering order for note references:

- Move the text cursor to the place in your document where the numbering for references should change.

Choose Layout ▸
Footnote or Endnote.
Then choose New
Number.

- Press Footnote (Ctrl+F7) and choose Footnote or Endnote.

- Choose Number, and then choose New Number from the Set Footnote Number or Set Endnote Number dialog box.

- Type the number at which the note references should begin, and press Enter. For example, if WordPerfect should begin numbering your footnotes with number *15*, you would type **15** and press Enter.

Choose OK to return
to your document.

- Press Exit (F7) until you return to the document screen.

After you enter the new number, WordPerfect inserts a [Footnote Num Set] or [Endnote Num Set] code at the cursor position in your document. Highlight one of these codes within the Reveal Codes Window and WordPerfect expands the code to show the starting number for footnotes or endnotes. The next note inserted after this code will be referenced with the new number, and all following notes will follow consecutively.

Placing a List of Endnotes

WordPerfect automatically compiles a list of defined endnotes at the end of the last page in your document. However, there are a few situations in which you'll want the list placed elsewhere.

For example, your document may include an index, in which case you'll want the endnotes to appear *before* the index. Another example applies to other long documents, where appendices, bibliographies, or other supplementary materials are added at the end of the document. For some documents, you may want an endnote list placed at the end of each chapter. For these situations, you may want to create a special endnote page to appear before these items.

You can insert an Endnote Placement code that tells WordPerfect where the endnote list should be placed in your document—and this can be anywhere in your document. If you choose to do this, however, WordPerfect can't automatically compile the endnotes as before, and you'll need to use the Generate feature to compile the list yourself. This isn't difficult, but it is an extra step in the endnote process. Here is the general process for creating an endnote list in a specified location in the document:

- Move the text cursor to the place in your document where the list of endnotes should appear.

- Start a new page for endnotes by inserting a Hard Page code (press Ctrl+Enter). Then type a title for the endnote page.

Choose Layout ▸
Endnote ▸
Placement.

■ Insert an Endnote Placement Code by pressing Footnote (Ctrl+F7), and choosing option Endnote Placement.

■ WordPerfect prompts you with "Restart endnote numbering". Choose Yes; WordPerfect inserts an "Endnote Placement" code in the document itself (in Print Preview or page display mode, you'll instead see the actual endnotes). Endnotes inserted after this point in the document will begin numbering with 1, instead of continuing the numbering from the previous list of endnotes. This is useful when you want to generate an endnote list at the end of each chapter in your document. If you choose No instead, any endnotes that follow this list will continue numbering where the previous notes left off.

Choose Tools ▸
Generate ▸ OK.

■ After you've finished adding all endnotes to your document, generate the endnote list by pressing Mark Text (Alt+F5) and choosing Generate. Then, press Enter, or choose OK.

WordPerfect looks for the Endnote Placement code and compiles the list of endnotes there. Once you've generated the list initially, WordPerfect automatically incorporates any changes to your endnotes.

In the following sections, you'll have the chance to create a document with endnotes, and you'll use the Endnote Placement and Generate options to create the endnote list.

Creating a Document with Endnotes

In the following exercise, you'll create a simple document with endnotes. Later, you'll create and generate the endnote list.

Choose File ▸ New

1. Press Exit (F7), and type **N** twice to clear the screen.

2. Type the following paragraph:

```
First quarter sales increased 35% from last year's
figures. This is a direct result of improved communication
with our suppliers, the installment of a computer network
in our West Valley warehouse, and, of course, the
excellent accomplishments of our manufacturing team.
```

Press Enter twice to end the paragraph.

3. Move the text cursor after the phrase "West Valley warehouse."

Choose Layout ▸
Endnote ▸ Create.

4. Press Footnote (Ctrl+F7), select Endnote, and then choose Create.

5. At the endnote editing screen, press the spacebar twice and type the following:

```
The West Valley warehouse opened during the third quarter
last year, but network installations were not implemented
until this year.
```

6. Press Exit (F7) to save the endnote and return to your document. Press Home, Home, ↓ to move the cursor to the end of the text, and type this as the second paragraph for the document:

```
A recent issue of Hang Gliders' Quarterly featured an
article about the P8500 Glider; here is an excerpt from
that article:
```

Choose Layout ▸
Endnote ▸ Create.

7. With the cursor on the colon that follows the word "article," press Footnote (Ctrl+F7), select Endnote, and then choose Create.

8. Press the spacebar twice, and type the following as the second endnote:

```
This article was published in the May 1994 issue of the
Hang Gliders' Quarterly.
```

9. Press Exit (F7) to save the endnote and return to your document. Press End to move the cursor past the colon, and press Enter twice to end the paragraph.

10. Press Left/Right Indent (Shift+F4). Then type the following as the quote from the magazine described in the text:

```
"Although there are relatively few competitors in the hang
glider industry, the Dalworth Company produces quality
equipment and continually raises the standard of
excellence and safety. Their dedication to the sport is
evident in the P8500, which is the first new model to
appear since 1992."
```

Choose Layout ▸
Endnote ▸ Create.

11. With the cursor placed just after the quote, press Footnote (Ctrl+F7), choose Endnote, and then choose Create.

12. At the endnote editing screen, press the spacebar twice and type the following as the third endnote:

```
Reprints of this article are available from our corporate
offices.
```

13. Press Exit (F7) to save the endnote and return to your document. If you want, you can create other endnotes for this document before continuing.

14. Now you'll insert several hard page breaks to simulate a document with several pages. Press Home, Home, ↓ to make sure the cursor is at the end of the text.

15. Press Hard Page (Ctrl+Enter) four or five times to add several page breaks.

16. Before you continue, save the document to a file called ENDNOTES-.DOC.

Your screen will look similar to Figure 10.8. Now that you've finished the document, you're ready to create a special page for endnotes.

Figure 10.8

Creating a document with endnotes

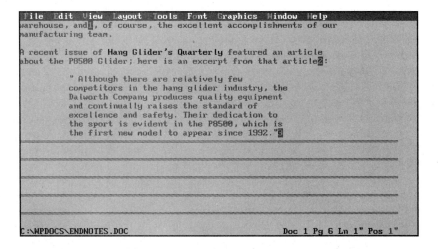

```
 File  Edit  View  Layout  Tools  Font  Graphics  Window  Help
warehouse, and , of course, the excellent accomplishments of our
manufacturing team.

A recent issue of Hang Glider's Quarterly featured an article
about the P8500 Glider; here is an excerpt from that article :

        " Although there are relatively few
        competitors in the hang glider industry, the
        Dalworth Company produces quality equipment
        and continually raises the standard of
        excellence and safety. Their dedication to
        the sport is evident in the P8500, which is
        the first new model to appear since 1992."




C:\WPDOCS\ENDNOTES.DOC                           Doc 1 Pg 6 Ln 1" Pos 1"
```

Creating the Endnotes Page

Using the ENDNOTES.DOC file created in the previous exercise, perform the following steps to create an endnotes page in your document. If you do not create an endnotes page, WordPerfect will automatically place the notes at the end of your document.

1. Move the cursor to one of the blank pages in your document—page 3, for example. When you are creating an endnotes page for a "real" document, you might need to insert a hard page break to start a new page.

2. At the top of a new page, press Bold (F6) to turn on the bold attribute. Type **ENDNOTES** as the title for the page. Then, press Bold (F6) again to turn off the attribute.

Choose Layout ▸
Endnote ▸
Placement.

3. Press Enter twice to add a blank line below the ENDNOTES title.

4. Now you're ready to insert an Endnote Placement code that tells Word-Perfect where to put the list of endnotes. Press Footnote (Ctrl+F7), and choose Endnote Placement.

5. WordPerfect prompts you with "Restart endnote numbering". Choose Yes to indicate that you want to compile a list of all endnotes which are located before this page. The Endnote Placement code is inserted into the document, followed by a hard page break.

As shown in Figure 10.9, the Endnote Placement code appears like a comment in the text. This tells WordPerfect where the endnotes list should be compiled. When you chose Yes at the "Restart endnote numbering" prompt, WordPerfect also inserted an [Endnote Num Set] code after the page break to restart the numbering of any endnotes that follow this page. Next, you'll use the Generate feature to compile the list of endnotes.

Figure 10.9

Inserting the
Endnote Placement
code

```
File  Edit  View  Layout  Tools  Font  Graphics  Window  Help
A recent issue of Hang Glider's Quarterly featured an article
about the P8500 Glider; here is an excerpt from that article▨:

        " Although there are relatively few
        competitors in the hang glider industry, the
        Dalworth Company produces quality equipment
        and continually raises the standard of
        excellence and safety. Their dedication to
        the sport is evident in the P8500, which is
        the first new model to appear since 1992."▨


ENDNOTES


    Endnote Placement


C:\WPDOCS\ENDNOTES.DOC                    Doc 1 Pg 4 Ln 1" Pos 1"
```

Generating the Endnote Text

In previous sections, you created a document with endnotes and designated a special page for the endnotes list. Now, you're ready to generate the endnotes:

Choose Tools ▸
Generate.

1. With your document on the screen, press Mark Text (Alt+F5), and choose Generate. This displays the Generate dialog box shown in Figure 10.10.

Figure 10.10

Generating endnotes

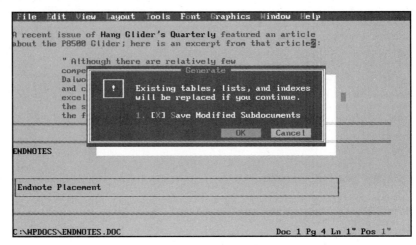

2. WordPerfect reminds you that existing tables, lists, and indexes will be replaced if you continue. Press Enter or choose OK to continue, and Word-Perfect generates the list of endnotes.

3. Move the cursor to the endnotes page. The endnote text will not be visible if you are using WordPerfect's text display mode or graphics display mode but *will* be visible in page display mode or in Print Preview.

Choose File ▸ Print Preview.

4. Press Print (Shift+F7), and choose Print Preview to see the endnotes on the page. When you're finished viewing the document, press Exit (F7) to return to the document editing screen.

5. If you wish, save and print this document. Then, press Exit (F7), and type **N** twice to clear the screen.

You need to create a separate endnotes page as described above only when you want the endnotes to be placed on a page other than the last page in the document. Also, remember that because they are notes, endnotes do not appear with the text on the document editing screen unless you are working with WordPerfect's page display mode. If you are working in text display mode or graphics display mode, you need to use the Print Preview feature to see the notes as they will print.

Using Characters or Letters for Note References

WordPerfect normally assigns numbers to the notes in your document, but there are a few cases in which you will want notes marked with characters or letters instead. For example, you may sometimes need to place a note that is marked with an asterisk (*), a dagger (†), a pound sign (#), or some other character. Figure 10.11 shows three footnotes that are referenced with these symbols.

Figure 10.11

Footnotes numbered with special characters

---

* Elvius' mysterious death soon after completing Greetings has been the subject of scholarly debate for years. See "Whither Elvius?" in *Arcanium* (May 1988) for the most recent discussion.

† Dead fish were separated into two varieties: those with fins and scales, which were allowed as food, and those without fins and scales. The "fish" from the latter group were actually eels, and tasted much like fermented footwear. These were gladly exchanged with poets. See *Greetings,* VI.II, University of California Press, 1962.

Raymond Tenure, in his fine book *The Dawn of the Handshake,* postulates that this howling might have been required to warn local townspeople that a poetry reading was imminent. Disdain for poets was quite high at this time.

Changing the Note Numbering Method

The Numbering Method option, found on the Set Footnote/Endnote Number dialog box, lets you specify characters instead of numbers for marking note references. This is how you would change the note numbering method for characters:

- Move the text cursor to the place in your text where the new note numbering method should go into effect. If you want to change the numbering method for the entire document, move the cursor to the beginning of the document or display the Document Initial Codes screen (press Shift+F8, choose Document, and then choose Document Initial Codes).

Choose Layout ▸ Footnote or Endnote. Then choose New Number.

- Display the Notes dialog box by pressing Footnote (Ctrl+F7). Then choose the type of notes whose numbering method you wish to change, either Footnote or Endnote. Then choose Number.

- From the Set Footnote/Endnote Number dialog box, choose Numbering M̲ethod. A pop-up list appears with these options:

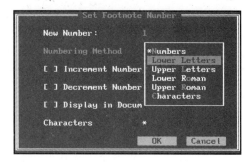

- Choose C̲haracters from the pop-up list. Then choose the Characters option at the bottom of the dialog box, and type up to five characters for note numbering. The procedure is explained in the following section.

- Press Exit (F7) until you return to the document screen.

Choose OK until you return to the document screen.

You can type any characters for the numbering method or use the WP Characters feature (Ctrl+W) to insert extended characters. For example, to use the dagger symbol (†) to mark notes, set the Numbering M̲ethod to "Characters." Then, choose the C̲haracters option, press WP Characters (Ctrl+W), type **4,39**, and press Enter. If you are working in text display mode, this symbol looks like a small box (■) on the screen but will appear as a dagger on the printed page.

Special Conditions for Marking Notes with Characters

If you choose Characters as the numbering method, you can type up to five different (or similar) characters for the numbering cycle; the first note you insert into the document will be marked with the first character, the second with the second character, and so on until each character you specified has been used to number a note. Then, WordPerfect doubles the characters to mark the next set of five notes. Each time WordPerfect cycles through the characters, the number of characters is increased to accommodate the next set of five notes.

For example, suppose you specify that the note numbering method should use these characters: * # ! + @. The note references would be numbered like this in the document:

Note 1	*		Note 11	***
Note 2	#		Note 12	###
Note 3	!		Note 13	!!!
Note 4	+		Note 14	+++
Note 5	@		Note 15	@@@
Note 6	**		Note 16	****
Note 7	##		Note 17	####
Note 8	!!		Note 18	!!!!
Note 9	++		Note 19	++++
Note 10	@@		Note 20	@@@@

You can also choose Lower Letters as the numbering method, and Word-Perfect will use lowercase letters instead of numbers or characters to mark the notes in your document (for example, a, b, c, d, and so on).

No more than 15 characters or letters may be repeated for a single note reference (for example, *************** or aaaaaaaaaaaaaaa). After the note references reach the 15-character limit, WordPerfect restarts the numbering with single characters.

If you want each note to be marked with a single asterisk, type five asterisks (*****) at the Characters option in the Note Numbering Method option. This will mark the next five notes with asterisks; if you will need more than five asterisk notes, you'll need to restart the footnote or endnote numbering at 1, after the fifth note. Just press Footnote (Ctrl+F7), choose Footnote or Endnote, and then choose Number. Then, choose New Number, type * and press Enter. This inserts a [New Ftn Num:1] code into the text to restart the "numbering" with a single asterisk character.

11

Paragraph Numbering and Outlines

WORDPERFECT'S PARAGRAPH NUMBER AND OUTLINE FEATURES CAN help you create outlines, to-do lists, speeches, itineraries, and other documents that require a numbered list of items. If you add or delete items from these lists or move items around, WordPerfect automatically renumbers the items to reflect the new sequence. For outlines and paragraph numbering, you can choose from several pre-defined numbering styles, including roman numerals, alphanumeric characters, legal numbering, and bullets. You can also define custom numbering styles to suit specific applications. For information about numbering the lines in your document, see Chapter 13.

This chapter covers the following topics:

- Paragraph numbering

- Sorting a numbered list

- Creating a bulleted list

- Creating an outline

- Editing outline text

- Moving and copying outline items

- Using WordPerfect's outline bar

- Changing the numbering style for paragraphs and outlines

- Using styles to change the outline format

Paragraph Numbering

Figure 11.1 shows a document with numbered paragraphs. To create a similar document, you can type paragraph numbers, or you can insert them with WordPerfect's Outline feature.

At first glance, you might wonder why you would use the Outline feature. After all, you can easily type numbers before each paragraph. The problem with typing numbers becomes obvious when you change the order or the amount of numbered items: You have to renumber everything in your list.

WordPerfect's Outline feature lets you insert special codes instead of numbers at the beginning of each paragraph in the list. These codes appear exactly like the numbers you would type, but they are always numbered correctly. As you edit your document, WordPerfect automatically updates the paragraph numbers to maintain the correct sequence.

Figure 11.1
A document with
numbered
paragraphs

**Paragraph
numbers** ⎯⎯⎯

RIVER GROVE PROJECT MEETING, Tuesday, 10:00am

1. North Shore statistics indicate a sharp increase in housing demand, due to imported businesses and corporations.

2. National surveys indicate a growing preference for planned communities.

3. Controlled housing tracts and commercial zones allow higher profits for developers.

4. Increased value is passed on to home owners and small businesses.

5. Hearne Corporation will develop 1000 acres of North Shore property.

Creating Numbered Paragraphs

Follow these steps to create the numbered paragraphs shown in Figure 11.1:

1. From a clear document screen, type **RIVER GROVE PROJECT MEETING, Tuesday, 10:00am** and press Enter twice.

2. Press Outline (Ctrl+F5), and then choose Outline Style.

Choose Tools ▸ Outline ▸ Outline Style.

3. Highlight the "Paragraph" style name if it's not already highlighted, and choose Select to activate the Paragraph Numbering style.

4. Press Outline (Ctrl+F5), choose Adjust Levels, and then choose Change to Outline Level. This inserts a paragraph number.

Choose Tools ▸ Outline ▸ Change to Outline Level.

TIP. *Pressing Ctrl+T also inserts a paragraph number. This shortcut toggles text between numbered text and regular body text.*

5. Type the following paragraph:

```
North Shore statistics indicate a sharp increase in
housing demand, due to imported businesses and
corporations.
```

6. Press Enter twice to add a blank line after the paragraph. Notice that WordPerfect automatically inserts the paragraph number for the next paragraph.

7. Type the next paragraph:

```
National surveys indicate a growing preference for planned
communities.
```

8. Press Enter twice to end the paragraph and insert the next paragraph number. Continue entering the text shown in Figure 11.1.

9. When you are done, press Enter twice to end the last paragraph and then press Backspace to delete the extra paragraph number.

You can repeat these steps to create the remaining paragraphs. Notice that WordPerfect numbers each new paragraph sequentially.

What you see in your document looks like a number, but it is actually a code that WordPerfect inserts into the text. Press Reveal Codes (Alt+F3 or F11), and you will see the following code before each paragraph: [Para Style: Level 1;]. The code creates the number you see in your document and the indentation before the paragraph. Choose Reveal Codes again to close the Reveal Codes window.

Choose View ▸ Reveal Codes to see the paragraph number codes.

Moving Numbered Paragraphs

Once you have placed paragraph numbers in your document, you can move paragraphs or items to see how WordPerfect handles the renumbering. Follow these steps to move a numbered paragraph:

Choose Edit ▸ Select ▸ Paragraph to select the current paragraph.

1. Move the cursor to the second paragraph in the document.

2. Press Move (Ctrl+F4), and choose Paragraph.

3. Choose Cut and Paste to cut the selected paragraph from the document.

Choose Edit ▸ Cut and Paste.

4. Move the cursor before the first paragraph in your document, but beneath the RIVER GROVE title.

5. Press Enter to retrieve the paragraph.

During these steps, the paragraph numbers changed twice: once when the second paragraph was cut from the document and again when it was retrieved at the new location. WordPerfect renumbers the paragraphs each time to maintain an accurate sequential list in your document.

NOTE. *When you select a paragraph as described here, remember that a paragraph is defined by the carriage returns (hard returns) that are inserted* *before and after a paragraph. Whenever you press the Enter key, these Hard Return codes [HRt] are inserted into your text. In this context, WordPerfect treats everything placed between two Hard Return codes as one paragraph.*

Note that you can also move numbered paragraphs with WordPerfect's drag and drop feature, which is covered in more detail in Chapter 6.

Working with Numbering Levels

If, after you insert a paragraph number, you press Tab, you'll discover a secret of paragraph numbering: The Tab key changes the paragraph number. Word-Perfect supports eight unique levels of paragraph numbering; when you press Tab on a number, WordPerfect indents to each level in the numbering scheme. (For this technique to work, the cursor must be at the beginning of the line.) To see how this works, move the text cursor to the beginning of a new line and try the following steps:

Choose <u>T</u>ools ▸ <u>O</u>ut-line ▸ <u>C</u>hange to Outline Level.

1. Press Outline (Ctrl+F5), choose <u>A</u>djust Levels, and then choose <u>C</u>hange to Outline Level. Or, go to the end of the last item in your list and press Enter.

2. Press Tab to change the number to the next level of paragraph number-ing. Press Reveal Codes (Alt+F3 or F11) and you'll see that the number-ing code has changed to [Para Style:Level 2;] to indicate that the number style is now set at the second numbering level.

3. Press Tab again to change to the next paragraph numbering level. Con-tinue to press Tab and you'll see the eight levels of numbering, shown in Figure 11.2, that WordPerfect supports. Press Shift+Tab to change the number back to a previous level.

Numbering levels allow WordPerfect's Outline feature to create the dif-ferent groups in an outline structure. WordPerfect uses the same codes to number paragraphs and outlines.

Changing the Numbering Style

WordPerfect includes predefined numbering styles that you can use for num-bering your paragraphs. You can change the numbering style at any time—be-fore or after placing paragraph numbering codes into your text. If you have already selected a paragraph numbering style, you can select a new number-ing style as described here:

Choose <u>T</u>ools ▸ <u>O</u>ut-line ▸ <u>O</u>utline Style.

1. Move the cursor to the beginning of your numbered paragraph list.

2. Press Outline (Ctrl+F5), and then choose <u>O</u>utline Style. This displays the dialog box shown in Figure 11.3.

Figure 11.2

The outline hierarchy created with tabs

1. Level One

    a. Level Two

        i. Level Three

           (1) Level Four

               (a) Level Five

                   (i) Level Six

                       1) Level Seven

                           a) Level Eight

Figure 11.3

The Outline Style List dialog box

Paragraph numbering style

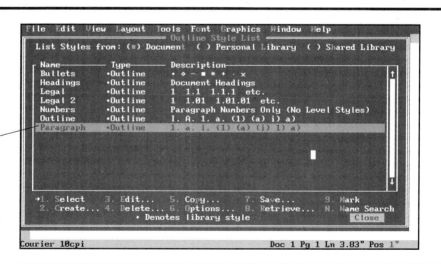

```
File  Edit  View  Layout  Tools  Font  Graphics  Window  Help
                     ─── Outline Style List ───
    List Styles from: (■) Document  ( ) Personal Library  ( ) Shared Library

   ┌Name──────────Type──────Description───────────────────────────┐
   │ Bullets      •Outline  • ◇ - ■ * + · x                        │↑
   │ Headings     •Outline  Document Headings                      │
   │ Legal        •Outline  1  1.1  1.1.1  etc.                    │
   │ Legal 2      •Outline  1  1.01  1.01.01  etc.                 │
   │ Numbers      •Outline  Paragraph Numbers Only (No Level Styles)│
   │ Outline      •Outline  I. A. 1. a. (1) (a) i) a)             │
   │ Paragraph    •Outline  1. a. i. (1) (a) (i) 1) a)           │
   │                                                               │
   │                                                               │
   │                                      ▌                        │
   │                                                               │
   │                                                               │↓
   └───────────────────────────────────────────────────────────────┘
   +1. Select    3. Edit...   5. Copy...     7. Save...    9. Mark
    2. Create... 4. Delete... 6. Options...  8. Retrieve... N. Name Search
                      • Denotes library style              [ Close ]

Courier 10cpi                              Doc 1 Pg 1 Ln 3.83" Pos 1"
```

3. Highlight one of the numbering styles in the list. (The Description column in the dialog box gives you a good idea of what the outline style will look like.) Then choose <u>S</u>elect.

WordPerfect changes the style of the paragraph numbers. When you follow these steps, WordPerfect changes the [Outline] code at the beginning of your document to reflect the numbering style you selected. The new numbering style affects only the paragraph numbers that are placed after the [Outline] code.

NOTE. *Later in this chapter, you'll see how to create a custom numbering style for paragraph numbers and outlines.*

Sorting a Numbered List

You can use WordPerfect's Sort feature to alphabetize a list of numbered paragraphs. When the sort operation is done, your items will be ordered alphabetically and appropriately renumbered.

Consider the list in Figure 11.4. Each item begins with a paragraph number. If your numbered list is structured like this, you would follow these steps to alphabetize the list:

Figure 11.4

An unalphabetized numbered list

Use the block feature to sort only the numbered items.

File   Edit   View   Layout   Tools   Font   Graphics   Window   Help

NAME	ACCOUNT NUMBER	STATE	ZIP
1.	Bach, Laura	06423-32578-7	CA	91361
2.	Bolton, Merlin	06842-77856-8	UT	84057
3.	Chao, Kevin	07586-58433-1	TX	75205
4.	Dobson, Amanda	03845-81127-0	MD	20912
5.	Hartley, Robert	05847-32884-7	IA	50574
6.	Heath, Dana	07001-67321-9	NV	89501
7.	Jarvis, Susan	04998-12126-2	CA	92064
8.	Kraviec, Yvette	08231-75752-8	NC	28005
9.	Williams, Chance	07995-43756-1	UT	84058
10.	Moore, Colleen	04888-12136-4	AZ	86045
11.	Olsen, Geri	06978-97843-8	NY	10787
12.	Adamson, Kevin	05537-87593-1	MD	21204
13.	Ragland, Kathy	09873-64125-6	HI	96777
14.	Rosenthal, Sam	07472-19742-3	NJ	07670
15.	Ruttenbur, Joy	06978-47987-0	FL	33480
16.	Shelley, Scott	07954-16897-5	UT	84604
17.	Staheli, Burke	01183-65421-9	VA	24641
18.	Stewart, Tracy	09745-88635-3	NE	68869

Courier 10cpi	Doc 1 Pg 1 Ln 1.17" Pos 1"

While holding down the mouse button, drag the mouse pointer to block all the text in the list.

1. Move the cursor to the beginning of the first item in the list, and press Home, Home, Home, ← to move to the beginning of the line, before any codes.

2. Press Block (Alt+F4 or F12) to turn on the Block feature, and move the cursor to the end of the last item in the list.

Choose Tools ▸ Sort to display the Sort dialog box.

3. Press Sort (Ctrl+F9) to display the Sort dialog box. Make sure the record type is Line.

4. From the Sort dialog box, choose Sort <u>K</u>eys, and then choose <u>E</u>dit.

5. In the Edit Sort Key dialog box, choose <u>F</u>ield, type 2, and press Enter. Press Exit (F7) twice to return to the Sort dialog box.

6. Choose <u>P</u>erform Action to sort the list. When the sort is completed the list is arranged in alphabetical order.

Note that items are sorted according to the text and not by the numbers. You cannot sort by the number codes, because the numbers will change depending on where they are located in the list.

When your document contains other text, such as a list title or headline, you will not want to include it in the sorted list. This is why you blocked only the list text in steps 1 and 2.

In step 5, you enter the number 2 to specify that you want to sort the second section of text—the text located after the paragraph indentation or tab. The Sort feature recognizes tabs and indents as the separators for sorting a text line. If you have indented your paragraph numbers with one or more tabs, you'll need to enter a different number in step 4. For example, if you pressed Tab after your paragraph numbers, you would enter **3** to specify a sort of the third section of text.

For detailed information about sorting and alphabetizing text, see Chapter 9.

Creating a List with Bullets

Bullets are small dots or symbols that precede each item or paragraph in a list. Figure 11.5 shows a paragraph list with bullets instead of numbers. To create such a list, you'll use a procedure similar to the one used for numbered paragraphs. Instead of a numbered paragraph style, you'll choose a style for bullets.

Follow these steps to create a list with bullets:

1. From a clear screen, type the following as an introductory sentence for the list:

   `The board of directors discussed these items at the last meeting:`

Choose Tools ▸ Outline ▸ Outline Style.

2. Press Enter twice to move the cursor to a new line.

3. Press Outline (Ctrl+F5) and then choose <u>O</u>utline Style to display the Outline Style List dialog box, shown earlier in Figure 11.3.

Figure 11.5

A bulleted list

> The board of directors discussed these items at the last meeting:
>
> • Corporate offices will host a conference on August 15 for the international distributors.
>
> • North Beach Manufacturing will aquire pen computer equipment to allow inventory control and order processing from the warehouse floor.
>
> • On September 27, facilities for the Red Cross Blood Drive will be set up in the west cafeteria. Employees who donate blood will receive four extra vacation hours.

Choose Tools ▸ Outline ▸ Change to Outline Level.

4. Highlight the style for "Bullets," and choose Select.

5. To insert the first bullet character, press Outline (Ctrl+F5), choose Adjust Levels, and then choose Change to Outline Level. (Alternatively, you can simply press Ctrl+T.)

6. Type the following as the first item in the list:

```
Corporate offices will host a conference on August 15 for
the international distributors.
```

7. Press Enter twice to add a blank line after the item. This also inserts the bullet for the next item in the list.

8. Type the following paragraph as the next item:

```
North Beach Manufacturing will acquire pen computer
equipment to allow inventory control and order processing
from the warehouse floor.
```

9. Press Enter twice to end the item and insert the bullet for the last item.

10. Type the following text:

```
On September 27, facilities for the Red Cross Blood Drive
will be set up in the west cafeteria. Employees who donate
blood will receive four extra vacation hours.
```

If you turn on the Reveal Codes window (Alt+F3 or F11) and scroll through the list, you'll see the [Para Style:Level 1;] code where each bullet appears in your document. These are the same codes that are inserted with numbered paragraphs, which are explained earlier in this chapter. In this example, bullets are inserted instead of numbers because you selected the Bullets numbering style in step 4.

You can easily convert a bulleted list to a numbered list by choosing a different numbering style from the Outline Style List dialog box. After you choose a new style, WordPerfect changes the bullets to the new numbering style you selected.

Creating a Simple Outline

Outlines help you organize your thoughts and words. Sometimes, however, the task of creating and managing an outline can stifle your ideas. Standard outlines require numbered entries and text indented according to a hierarchy of groups and subgroups. Fortunately, WordPerfect includes a feature that makes outlines easier to handle. When WordPerfect's Outline style is turned on, outline numbers and formatting are automatically inserted each time you press Enter. And when you rearrange the sequence of your outline entries, WordPerfect renumbers the items for you.

Turning On Outline Style

Figure 11.6 shows an outline you can create in WordPerfect. The first step in creating the outline is selecting the Outline feature. If you want a title for your outline, type it and press Enter before turning on the Outline. This is the general procedure:

■ Type the title for your outline and press Enter twice.

■ Press Outline (Ctrl+F5), and choose Begin New Outline. WordPerfect displays the Outline Style List dialog box.

Choose Tools ▶ Outline ▶ Begin New Outline.

■ Highlight the style for "Outline," and then choose Select. WordPerfect inserts the number for the first outline entry.

At this point, you can type the text for the first item. As long as the Outline style is active, an outline number is inserted each time you press Enter when the cursor is located at the end of outline text. (If you're at the beginning of a text entry, WordPerfect simply inserts a blank line above the current entry.) When you are finished creating the outline, you can turn off the Outline feature by pressing Outline (Ctrl+F5) and choosing End Outline.

Figure 11.6

A standard outline created in WordPerfect

RIVER GROVE PROJECT MEETING, Tuesday, 10:00am

I. OBJECTIVES
    River Grove Project land acquisition, community design and planning, and construction in three phases.

    A. Phase I
        I. Land reclamation
        2. Design and planning
        3. Preliminary construction and development
    B. Phase II
        1. Two-family condominiums
        2. Single-family houses
        3. River Grove Shopping Plaza
        4. Community Center
        5. Sports and Entertainment complex
    C. Phase III
        1. Lakeside development
        2. Exclusive housing community
        3. River Grove Arts Pavilion
        4. River Grove Business Park development

II. MARKETING AND SALES
    River Grove Project marketing, public relations and sales of property. Marketing strategies practiced during all phases of project.

    A. Community alliance
        1. City officials
        2. Local businesses
        3. Special interest groups
    B. Press releases
        1. Emphasize complete community
        2. Explain innovative design
        3. Notice successful precedents
        4. Address criticism from environmentalist groups
    C. Business investment campaign
        1. Profit seminars
        2. Benefit package for corporate participants
        3. Price discounts for employees

Typing Outline Items

Once the Outline feature is turned on, simply type the headings or titles for each entry in your outline. The Enter and Tab keys work differently than in the standard editing mode:

- Pressing Enter from the end of a text entry inserts the number for the next entry in your outline. Pressing Enter twice inserts the next number and inserts a blank line between outline entries.

- If you're at the beginning of a text entry, pressing Tab changes the outline number to the next level in the outline.

- If you're at the beginning of a text entry, pressing Shift+Tab changes the outline number to the previous level in the outline. (Don't use Backspace or you'll turn the entry into an unnumbered entry. If you do this by accident, choose Undo (Ctrl+Z) or press Ctrl+T to change the entry back into a numbered entry.)

Now for some practice with the Outline feature. Follow these steps to create the two-level outline shown in Figure 11.7:

Choose Tools ▸ Outline ▸ Begin New Outline.

1. Press Outline (Ctrl+F5) and choose Begin New Outline.

2. Highlight the "Outline" style, and then choose Select. WordPerfect inserts the number for the first item in your outline.

3. Type **OBJECTIVES** as the first item. Press Enter to insert the next outline number.

Figure 11.7

A brief outline

```
File  Edit  View  Layout  Tools  Font  Graphics  Window  Help
I.   OBJECTIVES
     A.   Phase I
     B.   Phase II
     C.   Phase III

II.  MARKETING AND SALES
     A.   Community alliance
     B.   Press releases
     C.   Business investment campaign




Courier 10cpi                              Doc 1 Pg 1 Ln 2.5" Pos 4.8"
```

4. Press Tab to change the second outline number to the letter *A*, the first item under item I.

5. Type **Phase I**. Press Enter to insert the letter *B* (the second outline number under item I).

6. Type **Phase II**, and press Enter.

7. Type **Phase III**, and press Enter twice to add a blank line before the next item.

8. Press Shift+Tab to change the current number back to the first heading level of the outline.

9. Type **MARKETING AND SALES**, and press Enter to insert the next number.

10. Press Tab to change the current outline number to the letter *A* (the first item under item II).

11. Type **Community alliance**. Press Enter to insert the letter *B* (the second outline number under item II).

12. Type **Press releases** and press Enter.

13. Type **Business investment campaign** as the last entry in your outline.

When you press Enter to create an entry beneath an outline item, Word-Perfect keeps the new items indented at the current level of the outline. For example, if you're at the first level of the outline, at the end of an entry numbered *3.*, pressing Enter creates an entry numbered *4.* To break from the current level, press Tab to move to the next level or press Shift+Tab to move back to a previous outline level.

Inserting a Line without a Number

Most outlines have a continuing list of numbered items, but sometimes you may want to insert a line of text that isn't numbered. This is true for certain notes or paragraphs of explanation that follow an outline heading.

When the Outline feature is active, press Ctrl+T to convert the current line to regular text—or body text—without an outline number. Remember that Ctrl+T is a toggle; you can press it again to convert an entry back to a numbered item.

For example, suppose you want to insert a paragraph after an outline item, as shown in Figure 11.8. Follow these steps to insert body text into the outline that you created in the previous exercise:

1. Move the cursor to the end of the "Objectives" entry in your outline. Then press Enter to insert a new entry.

Figure 11.8

Adding a descriptive
paragraph to an
outline

Body text

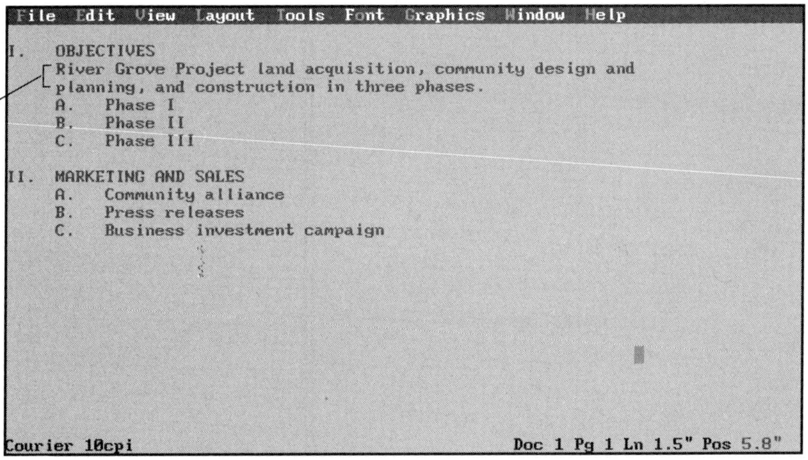

```
 File  Edit  View  Layout  Tools  Font  Graphics  Window  Help
I.   OBJECTIVES
    ┌ River Grove Project land acquisition, community design and
    └ planning, and construction in three phases.
      A.    Phase I
      B.    Phase II
      C.    Phase III

II.  MARKETING AND SALES
      A.    Community alliance
      B.    Press releases
      C.    Business investment campaign
```

```
Courier 10cpi                              Doc 1 Pg 1 Ln 1.5" Pos 5.8"
```

2. Press Ctrl+T to convert the entry to body text.

3. Press Indent (F4) to create the indent for the paragraph. Then type

```
River Grove Project land acquisition, community design and
planning, and construction in three phases.
```

In these steps, you pressed Ctrl+T to convert the outline entry to body text; this is just the shortcut keystroke. You can also press Outline (Ctrl+F5), choose <u>A</u>djust Levels, and then choose <u>C</u>hange to Body Text. If you want to change the body text back to a numbered outline entry, press Ctrl+T again, or press Outline (Ctrl+F5), choose <u>A</u>djust Levels, and then choose <u>C</u>hange to Outline Level.

Turning Off Outline Style

When you are finished creating your outline, you may want to mark the end of it. This turns off the Outline feature and enables you to type regular text after the outline without inserting additional outline numbers. Please note that you do not need to turn off the Outline style unless you plan to type regular text after the outline in your document. To turn off the style and mark the end of your outline:

To turn off the Out-
line mode, choose
<u>T</u>ools ▸ <u>O</u>utline ▸
<u>E</u>nd Outline.

- First, make sure the cursor is located at the end of the outline text.

- Press Outline (Ctrl+F5), and choose <u>E</u>nd Outline.

An [Outline] code is inserted at the cursor position to mark the end of the outlining region. This makes it easier to add and edit outline entries when you return to the document at a later time. Just remember that the Enter key inserts a new outline entry whenever the cursor is located at the end of an outline entry that you've already created.

Editing Outline Text

As with other WordPerfect features, outlines depend on codes to define the beginning and end of the outline. These codes arrange the text and numbers on the page. You can edit outline text as you would regular document text, but be careful not to delete the codes that create the outline numbers and formatting.

Viewing Outline Codes

When you create an outline, [Outline] codes are placed in the text to indicate the beginning and end of the outline. As you've already seen in this chapter, an [Outline] code is inserted to begin the outline. Another [Outline] code marks the end of outline text. As shown in Figure 11.9, [Para Style:] codes are inserted to create the numbers that appear before each item.

Figure 11.9
An outline with codes revealed

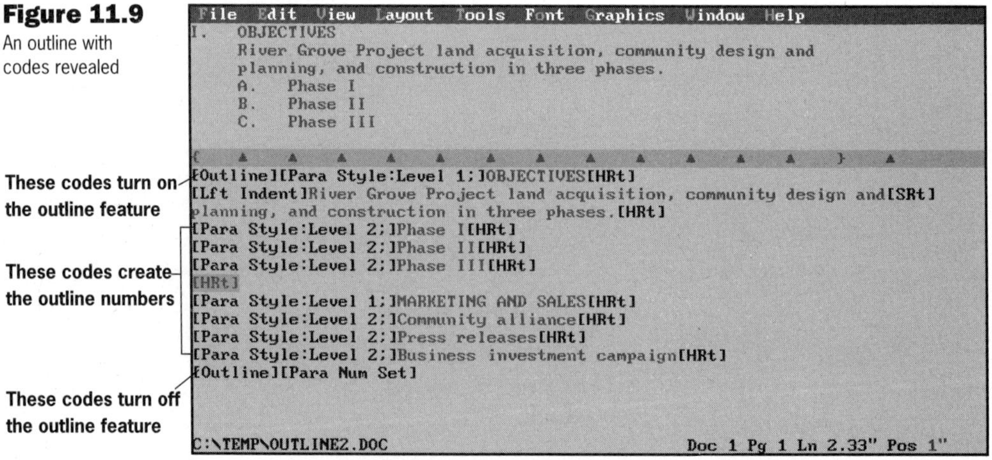

These codes turn on the outline feature

These codes create the outline numbers

These codes turn off the outline feature

```
 File  Edit  View  Layout  Tools  Font  Graphics  Window  Help
I.    OBJECTIVES
      River Grove Project land acquisition, community design and
      planning, and construction in three phases.
      A.    Phase I
      B.    Phase II
      C.    Phase III


{       ▲      ▲      ▲      ▲      ▲      ▲      ▲      ▲      ▲      ▲   }    ▲
[Outline][Para Style:Level 1;]OBJECTIVES[HRt]
[Lft Indent]River Grove Project land acquisition, community design and[SRt]
planning, and construction in three phases.[HRt]
[Para Style:Level 2;]Phase I[HRt]
[Para Style:Level 2;]Phase II[HRt]
[Para Style:Level 2;]Phase III[HRt]
[HRt]
[Para Style:Level 1;]MARKETING AND SALES[HRt]
[Para Style:Level 2;]Community alliance[HRt]
[Para Style:Level 2;]Press releases[HRt]
[Para Style:Level 2;]Business investment campaign[HRt]
[Outline][Para Num Set]
C:\TEMP\OUTLINE2.DOC                        Doc 1 Pg 1 Ln 2.33" Pos 1"
```

To view the codes in your outline, press Reveal Codes (Alt+F3 or F11), or choose View and then Reveal Codes to display the Reveal Codes window.

In the Reveal Codes window, notice that the [Para Style:] code is used for all numbers in the outline. These are the same codes that are inserted as paragraph numbers when you choose a different outline style. The actual numbers that appear in the document depend on the "Level" number that appears within the [Para Style:] code. For example, the [Para Style:Level 1;] codes indicate Level 1 outline numbers (uppercase Roman numerals), the [Para Style:Level 2;] codes specify Level 2 numbering (uppercase letters), and so on.

When you create your outline, you don't need to worry about where these codes are placed, because WordPerfect inserts them for you. When you edit the outline, however, be careful not to delete the [Outline] codes. If you do so, your outline entries will be formatted with the default outline style—the Paragraph style—and not with the style of numbering you selected for the outline.

To convert the text back to an outline, simply move the cursor to the beginning of the text, display the Outline Style List dialog box again, and select the "Outline" style.

Editing the Text

Generally, you edit outline text as you do other text in your document. The Delete and Backspace keys work the same, and pressing Ins turns on the Typeover mode for typing over existing text. You can also use the Block feature to select and manipulate sections of text.

- Use Backspace from the beginning of the text entry line to delete outline numbers. If you make a mistake, press Undo (Ctrl+Z) to undo the last action, or press Ctrl+T to convert the body text back to a numbered outline entry.

- If you use the Block feature or the drag and drop feature to copy or move text, remember that each item in your outline begins with a paragraph numbering code. If you want the number included in the block, press Home, Home, Home, ← to move the cursor to the beginning of the line before turning on the Block feature. You can also turn on Reveal Codes if you want to see the codes as you work.

- Use the Typeover mode to replace existing text in your outline, but make sure the cursor is located to the right of any paragraph numbering codes before you begin typing.

Adding New Items to the Outline

As you already know, the Enter key inserts an outline number for a new entry. This works when you are creating an outline, but also when you are editing an existing outline.

Follow these steps to add a new entry to an existing outline:

■ Move the text cursor to the line where the new entry should be inserted.

■ Press ← until the cursor is located at the end of the previous entry.

■ Press Enter, and then type the new item.

Note that you can also press Enter at the end of an entry to create a new entry after it. After the number is inserted, the outline is renumbered to account for the new entry.

Deleting Outline Items

You can use the Delete and Backspace keys to remove items from your outline, but the Move/Copy feature provides a faster way to delete an entire item.
Follow these steps to delete an item from your outline:

■ Move the cursor to the item you want to delete.

■ Press Move (Ctrl+F4) and select Pa_ragraph.

■ From the menu that appears, choose _Delete.

Choose _Edit_ ▸
Select ▸ _Paragraph_.

This selects and removes the item or paragraph where the cursor is located. If you change your mind about deleting the item, press Undelete (Esc) and choose _Restore to bring it back.

WordPerfect's Outline menu also offers a way to delete a whole section of your outline, including a heading and all items located beneath the heading. To delete a complete section in your outline,

■ Move the cursor to the heading that begins the section you want to delete.

■ Press Outline (Ctrl+F5), choose _Move/Copy, and then choose Cu_t Family.

Choose _Tools_ ▸ _Out-
line_ ▸ Cut _Family_.

This selects and deletes the current outline item and all sublevel headings beneath the item. If you accidentally delete an outline section, press Undo (Ctrl+Z), or choose _Edit and then _Undo to bring it back.

Moving and Copying Outline Items

There are a number of ways to move and copy items in your outline: You can select the items and then move or copy them to another place in the outline, or you can take advantage of special outline features that let you move groups or families of outline items. In addition, you can use WordPerfect 6.0's new drag and drop capabilities to move outline items with just your mouse.

In an outline, a *family* consists of a heading and all the sublevel items listed under the heading. (Remember, you just learned how to delete an outline family.) Consider Figure 11.10; in this example, there are several families. The first heading, OBJECTIVES, begins one family in the outline and includes all items listed under the OBJECTIVES heading. Families are not limited to the first-level headings; a family can start at any heading level and include only the sublevel items that are listed beneath that heading.

Figure 11.10

Outlines organized according to families

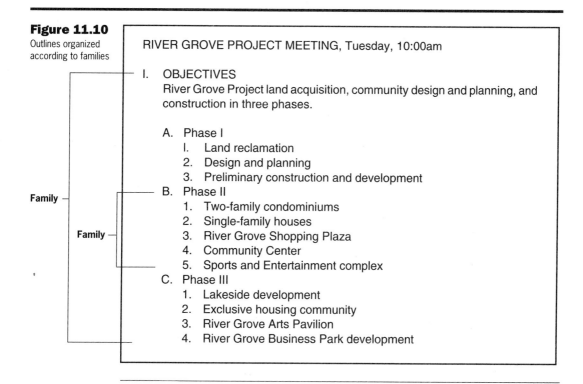

RIVER GROVE PROJECT MEETING, Tuesday, 10:00am

I. OBJECTIVES
    River Grove Project land acquisition, community design and planning, and construction in three phases.

    A. Phase I
        I.   Land reclamation
        2.   Design and planning
        3.   Preliminary construction and development
    B. Phase II
        1.   Two-family condominiums
        2.   Single-family houses
        3.   River Grove Shopping Plaza
        4.   Community Center
        5.   Sports and Entertainment complex
    C. Phase III
        1.   Lakeside development
        2.   Exclusive housing community
        3.   River Grove Arts Pavilion
        4.   River Grove Business Park development

The following sections explain how to arrange outline families with the Move and Copy features on the Outline dialog box or submenu. You'll also learn how to move entries by using the drag and drop feature. Later in this chapter, you'll learn more about WordPerfect's new outline bar and about the outline edit mode, which provides quick and easy methods for editing your outlines.

Moving Outline Entries

Follow these steps to move a section of your outline:

Choose Tools ▸ Outline ▸ Move Family.

- Move the cursor to the item that begins the section you want to move.

- Press Outline (Ctrl+F5), choose Move/Copy, and then choose Move Family.

- Press ↑ or ↓ to move the cursor to another place in the outline.

- Press Enter to accept the new position.

This moves the outline item and all subheadings that appear beneath the item. When you position the cursor at the new location, make sure the cursor is located on the first line where the outline section should be moved. Then, when you press Enter to retrieve the outline section, WordPerfect inserts it beginning with the line where the cursor is located.

Alternatively, you can move outline entries with your mouse alone. To do so, highlight the desired block; then, with your mouse pointer on the block, hold down the left mouse button until you see the drag and drop icon and/or the message "Release mouse button to move block" at the bottom of the screen. Then drag with the mouse until the cursor is in the desired location, and release the mouse button to "drop" the outline entry into its new location in the text.

Copying Outline Entries

Follow these steps to copy a section of your outline:

- Move the cursor to the item that begins the section you want to copy.

Choose Tools ▸ Outline ▸ Copy Family.

- Press Outline (Ctrl+F5), choose Move/Copy, and then choose Copy Family.

- Press ↑ or ↓ to move to the place where you want to insert the copied outline family.

- Press Enter to accept the new location of the copy.

When you select a family for copying, WordPerfect creates the copy and places it at the desired location in the outline.

Incidentally, once you've either moved or copied text with the Move/Copy feature, it remains in memory and can be pasted in repeatedly with the Ctrl+V shortcut. This feature is especially handy if you want to insert repeating text.

Collapsing Outlines

Collapsible outlines let you hide and display sections of a document that is built around an outline. You can, for example, hide the body text that follows the outline headings or hide specific sections of the outline text. This feature can help you create a dynamic document, in which you can not only show an overview of main document headings, but also expand the document to view all text beneath the headings. Figure 11.11 shows an example of a document built around a collapsible outline.

Figure 11.11

The Collapsible
Outline feature lets
you hide outline text

Main headings —

Full document

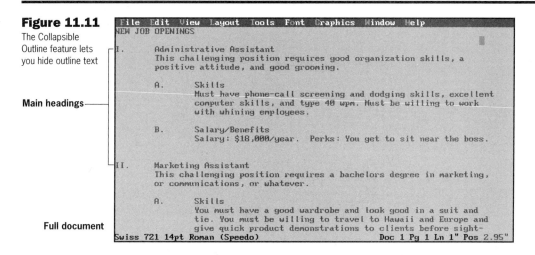

Main headings —

Condensed or
"collapsed"
document

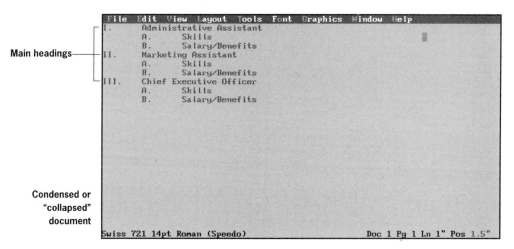

Both screens show the same document. The top screen shows the document with all body text and outline headings displayed; the bottom screen shows the document with only the main outline headings, after the body text is hidden or collapsed.

The collapsible outline feature is ideal for legal briefs, business reports, and other documents that follow a structured outline. In earlier versions of Word-Perfect, you probably created an outline first, and then used it as the model for the finished document. Now, your outline can become your document.

This is how it works. First, you use the Outline feature to create an outline of the main headings and subheadings in your document. Then, beneath each heading, you create the appropriate text as body text within the outline. When you're done, you can choose the Hide <u>B</u>ody Text option from the Outline dialog box to collapse the body text and condense your document to only the outline headings.

If you wish, WordPerfect also lets you selectively collapse one or more outline sections. Then, when you're finished with the outline, you can choose Show Body <u>T</u>ext to expand the document and restore all text beneath the headings.

The best way to visualize this concept is to do it yourself. Try the following exercise to create a document around an outline; Figure 11.12 shows how the document will look. Once the document is finished, you'll learn how to hide or collapse selected sections and then collapse all body text in the document. You'll also see how to expand the document and restore the body text.

1. From a clear screen, type **NEW JOB OPENINGS**, and press Enter twice.

2. Press Outline (Ctrl+F5) and then choose <u>B</u>egin New Outline.

Choose <u>T</u>ools ▸ <u>O</u>utline ▸ <u>B</u>egin New Outline.

3. When the Outline Style List dialog appears, highlight the Outline style name and choose <u>S</u>elect.

4. Now that the Outline feature is turned on, create the outline shown in Figure 11.13.

5. When the outline is finished, you're ready to create the body text. Move the cursor to the end of the Administrative Assistant line.

6. Press Enter to create a new entry beneath Administrative Assistant. Press Ctrl+T to change the next entry to body text. Then, press Indent (F4) and type the following paragraph as the text beneath the heading:

   ```
   This challenging position requires good organization
   skills, a positive attitude, and good grooming.
   ```

7. Move the cursor to the end of the first Skills subheading and press Enter to start a new entry.

8. Press Ctrl+T to change the entry to body text. Press Tab, press Indent (F4), and then type the following paragraph as the text beneath the Skills heading:

   ```
   Must have phone-call screening and dodging skills,
   excellent computer skills, and type 40 wpm. Must be
   willing to work with whining employees.
   ```

Figure 11.12

A sample outline document

NEW JOB OPENINGS

I. Administrative Assistant
    This challenging position requires good organization skills, a positive attitude, and good grooming.

    A. Skills
        Must have phone-call screening and dodging skills, excellent computer skills, and type 40 wpm. Must be willing to work with whining employees.

    B. Salary/Benefits
        Salary: $18,000/year. Perks: You get to sit near the boss.

II. Marketing Assistant
    This challenging position requires a bachelors degree in marketing, or communications, or whatever.

    A. Skills
        You must have a good wardrobe and look good in a suit and tie. You must be willing to travel to Hawaii and Europe and give quick product demonstrations to clients before sightseeing. Must know how to use a gold card.

    B. Salary/Benefits
        Salary: $65,000/year. Perks: Expense account, stock options, free stuff.

III. Chief Executive Officer
    This challenging position requires a masters degree in business management or equivalent experience.

    A. Skills
        No specific skills required. Responsibilities will be determined soon.

    B. Salary/Benefits
        Salary: $2,500,000/year. Perks: Anything you want.

Figure 11.13
Creating the outline

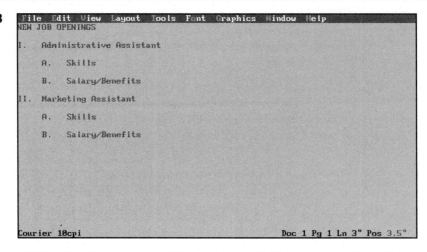

9. Move the cursor to the end of the first Salary/Benefits subheading. Then press Enter to start a new entry.

10. Press Ctrl+T to change the entry to body text. Press Tab, press Indent (F4), and then type the following information:

`Salary: $18,000/year. Perks: You get to sit near the boss.`

11. Using Figure 11.12 as a model, finish the rest of the document, and add body text for each of the numbered outline entries. When you are finished, save the document as JOBS.DOC.

Choose Tools ▸ Outline ▸ Hide Body Text.

12. Now you're ready to see how the Collapsible Outline feature works. To hide all body text, press Outline (Ctrl+F5), choose Hide/Show, and then choose Hide Body Text. Your screen will look similar to Figure 11.14.

Choose Tools ▸ Outline ▸ Show Body Text.

13. Press Outline (Ctrl+F5), choose Hide/Show, and then choose Show Body Text, to restore the full document.

14. You can also collapse specific sections of your outline document. Move the cursor to the Administrative Assistant heading.

Choose Tools ▸ Outline ▸ Hide Family.

15. Press Outline (Ctrl+F5), choose Hide/Show, and then choose Hide Family (-). Your screen will look like Figure 11.15. Notice that the subheadings beneath the Administrative Assistant heading are now hidden.

Choose Tools ▸ Outline ▸ Show Family.

16. Press Outline (Ctrl+F5), choose Hide/Show, and then choose Show Family (+) to restore the hidden subheadings.

Figure 11.14

The collapsed
document

```
File  Edit  View  Layout  Tools  Font  Graphics  Window  Help
I.      Administrative Assistant
        A.      Skills
        B.      Salary/Benefits
II.     Marketing Assistant
        A.      Skills
        B.      Salary/Benefits
III.    Chief Executive Officer
        A.      Skills
        B.      Salary/Benefits




Swiss 721 14pt Roman (Speedo)               Doc 1 Pg 1 Ln 1" Pos 1.5"
```

Figure 11.15

Hiding an outline
family

**Subheadings
for this entry
are hidden.**

```
File  Edit  View  Layout  Tools  Font  Graphics  Window  Help
NEW JOB OPENINGS

I.      Administrative Assistant
        This challenging position requires good organization skills, a
        positive attitude, and good grooming.

II.     Marketing Assistant
        This challenging position requires a bachelors degree in marketing,
        or communications, or whatever.

        A.      Skills
                You must have a good wardrobe and look good in a suit and
                tie. You must be willing to travel to Hawaii and Europe and
                give quick product demonstrations to clients before sight-
                seeing. Must know how to use a gold card.

        B.      Salary/Benefits
                Salary: $65,000/year.  Perks: Expense account, stock options,
                free stuff.

III.    Chief Executive Officer
        This challenging management position requires a masters degree in
Swiss 721 14pt Roman (Speedo)               Doc 1 Pg 1 Ln 1.44" Pos 1.5"
```

The Outline dialog box also includes two other options for hiding and showing outline sections. Press Outline (Ctrl+F5) to display the dialog box, and then choose <u>H</u>ide/Show. You've already seen what the Hide Family (-), Show Family (+), and Hide <u>B</u>ody Text options do.

The <u>S</u>how Levels option lets you choose the number of outline levels that are visible. Suppose your outline includes eight numbering levels, but you only want levels 1 through 4 to appear on the printed page; you can choose <u>S</u>how Levels and select <u>4</u> to indicate that you want to see only the first four levels.

The Hide Outline option hides the entire outline—in other words, everything between the two [Outline] codes that define the outline area. When the entire outline is hidden, you can choose Show Outline from the Outline dialog box to restore it to your document.

When an outline is collapsed, WordPerfect stores the body text inside of embedded [Hidden] codes; display the Reveal Codes window and you'll see these codes. If you save your document while it is collapsed, the body text will remain hidden until you show it again. Remember that hidden text will not display on the screen nor appear on the printed pages of your document.

As you've already seen, you specify collapsible text by creating it as body text beneath outline headings. You can change an outline entry to a numbered outline item or to body text by pressing Ctrl+T; this is the same as choosing Change to Body Text or Change to Outline Level from the Outline menu or dialog box. If the cursor is on an outline entry, pressing Ctrl+T changes it to body text; if the current entry is body text, pressing Ctrl+T changes it to a numbered outline entry.

NOTE. *If you plan to create several collapsible outline documents, make sure you read the next section. The previous exercise shows how to use the menu system to collapse an outline, but the outline bar provides an easier way to do this and other outline editing tasks.*

Using the Outline Bar

Until now, you've used the menu options or options in the Outline dialog box to move, copy, delete, and hide outline entries, but these methods are not the only way to edit your outlines. WordPerfect's outline bar lets you edit your outline by choosing on-screen buttons and controls that are easier and faster to use than the methods you've learned so far.

To display the outline bar, press Outline (Ctrl+F5) and choose Display Outline Bar, or choose Outline Bar from the View pull-down menu. The outline bar appears at the top of your screen, as shown in Figure 11.16; if you're working with WordPerfect's text display mode, the outline bar will look a little different than the screen shown here, but the controls work the same.

When the outline bar is displayed, you can change outline entries to regular text (and vice versa), change the numbering level of any outline entry, collapse and expand outline entries, and change the outline style. The outline bar can also activate a special outline edit mode that lets you quickly rearrange the outline entries. Although the outline bar doesn't offer any features that you haven't already seen, it does simplify the process of creating and editing outlines.

Figure 11.16

The outline bar

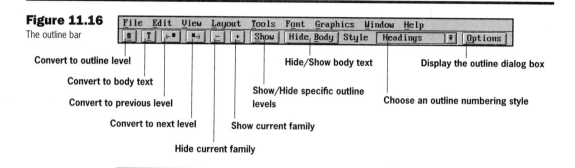

NOTE. *When you are using the standard document editing mode, you must use the mouse pointer to select options from the outline bar. You can, however, press Ctrl+O to switch to the outline edit mode, and then choose outline-bar options by pressing the appropriate underlines mnemonics on the outline bar buttons.*

The following information describes the function of each option on the outline bar. You can use the mouse pointer to choose any of these options while creating or editing an outline in your document.

- Click on the # button to convert a body text entry to a numbered outline entry. This works only when the current line or paragraph does not already begin with a [Para Style:Level *n*;] code.

- Click on the T button to convert a numbered outline entry to body text. This works only when the current line/paragraph begins with a [Para Style:Level *n*;] code.

- Click on the ←■ button to change the current outline number to a previous numbering level. For example, this changes a [Para Style:Level 3;] code to [Para Style:Level 2;]. Each click on this button changes the current entry to the previous level. The keystroke equivalent of this button is Shift+Tab.

- Click on the ■→ button to change the current outline number to the next numbering level. For example, this changes a [Para Style:Level 1;] code to [Para Style:Level 2;]. Each click on this button changes the outline number to the next numbering level. Tab is the keystroke equivalent of this feature.

- Click on the - button to collapse (hide) all subentries and body text beneath the outline entry where the cursor is located. It assumes that subentries exist; if not, this key does nothing.

- Click on the + button to expand (show) all subentries and body text beneath the outline entry where the cursor is located. This feature assumes that subentries exist beneath the outline entry where the cursor is located; if not, it does nothing.

- Click the Show button to display a pop-up list that lets you choose which levels of the outline you want to see. Choosing *1*, for example, displays only the main outline headings (Level 1). Choosing *2* displays the main headings plus the first set of subheadings (Levels 1 and 2), and so on. Choosing All displays the complete outline, up to the maximum of eight levels.

- Click on the Hide Body/Show Body button to toggle the display of all body text within the current outline. Remember that body text is any line or paragraph that is not preceded by a [Para Style:Level *n*;] code.

- Click on the Style button to choose a different outline numbering style from a pop-up list of outline styles. This option changes the style for the entire outline, not just the outline entry where the cursor is located. To select a new outline style, highlight it and press Enter, or just double-click on it using your mouse.

- Click on the Options button to display the Outline dialog box where you can choose the equivalent options for each of the outline-bar controls, and other outline options.

As mentioned, these options and others are also available from the Outline dialog box, and the Outline submenu. When you are finished with the outline bar, press Outline (Ctrl+F5) and choose Display Outline Bar again, or choose View and then Outline Bar from the menu system.

Working in the Outline Edit Mode

When the outline bar is displayed, you can press Ctrl+O to turn on the outline edit mode, which lets you rearrange and edit your outline according to outline families. This is the one of easiest ways to move, copy, and delete outline entries. When outline edit mode is turned on, you can press ↓ or ↑ to select the next or previous family in the outline.

Then, when a family is selected, press Ctrl+↓ or Ctrl+↑ to change its position in the outline. You can also press Cut and Paste (Ctrl+Delete), Copy and Paste (Ctrl+Insert), Cut (Ctrl+X), Copy (Ctrl+C), Paste (Ctrl+V), Undo (Ctrl+Z), Delete, and Backspace to manipulate the selected outline family.

The outline edit mode also lets keyboard users access the outline bar. When outline edit mode is turned off, you need to use the mouse pointer to select options from the outline bar; when outline edit is turned on, you can type any of the underlined mnemonics on the outline bar to choose one of the options.

Remember that the outline edit mode is designed for editing the order of the existing outline families. When outline edit mode is active, you can't edit the outline text. For this reason, you'll need to press Exit (F7) or press Ctrl+O again to switch back to the document editing mode to insert additional outline entries or to type body text. Then, press Ctrl+O to switch back to outline edit mode when you need to rearrange the outline entries.

Using Styles to Create the Outline Format

Outline *styles* define the appearance and layout for paragraph numbering and outlines. You can change the type of numbers that WordPerfect displays by selecting one of the predefined numbering styles. You can also create your own custom styles for specific documents and applications.

Styles ensure that your outline formatting is consistent. They also simplify the task of making changes to your format, because you won't need to edit every case where outline or paragraph numbering is used. Just change the style you used to create the numbering and all numbers in your document are updated with the new format.

Using the Predefined Outline Styles

WordPerfect includes seven predefined outline styles that you can choose for paragraph and outline numbering; you've already experimented with a few of these. Figure 11.17 shows the different formatting and numbering for some of the styles. You can choose a style before you create an outline or replace the style of an existing outline. To choose one of the predefined styles, follow these steps:

Choose Tools ▶ Outline ▶ Outline Style, and then double-click on the desired style.

- Press Outline (Ctrl+F5) and choose Outline Style. The dialog box shown in Figure 11.18 appears.

- Highlight the name of the style you want to use, and then choose Select.

If you choose a different style when the cursor is located in an outline you've already created, the existing outline numbers are updated for the new style.

Defining a Custom Numbering Style

When no predefined style suits your needs, you can create your own style with the desired format and numbering style. If you are already familiar with WordPerfect's Styles feature, you'll feel comfortable with the Outline Styles feature. There are, however, a few notable differences.

NOTE. *See Chapter 22 for complete information about WordPerfect's styles.*

Figure 11.17
Predefined styles for
outline and
paragraph numbering

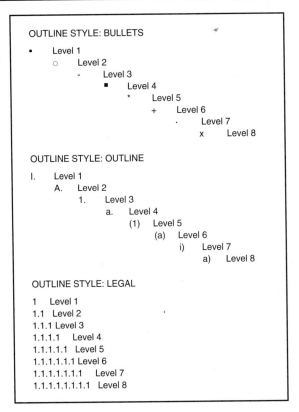

Figure 11.18
The Outline Style
List dialog box

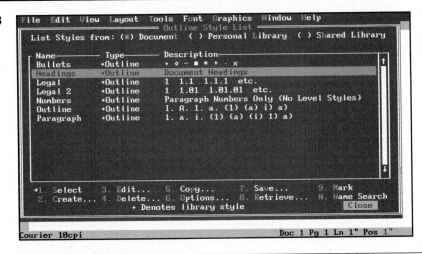

First, an outline style controls the numbering and formatting codes that are inserted when you are working with outlines and paragraph numbering. You cannot select an outline style from the Style List dialog box (Alt+F8). Second, an outline style is actually a compilation of up to eight different styles—one style for each level supported in the outline style. When you define an outline style, you will define the numbering method and layout for each outline numbering level that the outline style will support.

Suppose you want to create a style that lines up the outline numbers on the number punctuation. You would follow these steps to create the outline style:

Choose Tools ▸ Outline ▸ Outline Style.

1. Press Outline (Ctrl+F5), and choose Outline Style.

2. From the Outline Style List dialog box, choose Create to display the Create Outline Style dialog box.

3. Type **RIGHTNUM** and press Enter twice to assign a name to the style. The Edit Outline Style dialog box appears, as shown in Figure 11.19.

Figure 11.19
The Edit Outline Style dialog box

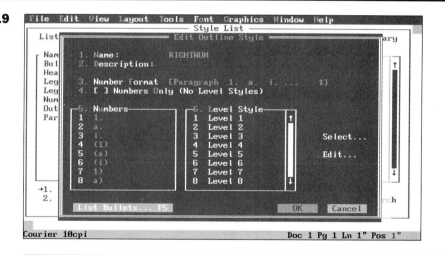

4. Choose Description and enter the following: **Numbers Aligned on the Punctuation.**

5. Choose Number Format and select the numbering style on which the new style will be based.

6. Choose Level Style and Level 1 is highlighted in the style list. This is the style for the first level of outline numbering.

7. Choose Edit to open the Edit Style dialog box.

8. Choose Style Contents and move the cursor onto the [Para Num] code. This code inserts the outline number for the current level.

9. Press Decimal Tab (Ctrl+F6) to insert a code that will align the outline number on the punctuation. Then press Exit (F7) until you return to the Edit Outline Style dialog box.

10. Highlight the each level and repeat steps 9 through 10 to add the decimal tab code before each [Para Num] code in the styles.

11. When you're finished, press Exit (F7) until you return to the Outline Style List dialog box, noting that it now includes the RIGHTNUM style.

Now, when you create a new outline, you can choose the RIGHTNUM style to create outline numbers that are aligned on the punctuation marks.

HINT. *If you accidentally delete the [Para Num] code while you are creating the style, you can restore it by pressing Undelete (Esc) and choosing Restore.*

In this example, formatting codes were placed in the style to create the desired layout. You can choose any layout features to create the format you need, including margin releases, tab settings, indents, and spacing. You can even include regular text or special WordPerfect characters as part of the style for any level. When you are finished creating a style, you can select it for your outline, as described earlier in this chapter. For more information about creating styles, see Chapter 22.

Editing an Outline Style

Once you've created an outline style, you may need to make changes to the numbering style or layout. The following steps explain how to do so. After you edit a style, the outlines you create with the style are automatically updated to reflect your changes.

Choose Tools ▸ Outline ▸ Outline Style.

■ Press Outline (Ctrl+F5), and choose Outline Style.

■ Highlight the name of the style you want to edit.

■ Choose Edit to display the Edit Outline Style dialog box.

■ To change the style name, choose Name and enter a new name.

■ To edit the description of the style, choose Description to enter the new text.

■ To edit the number format being used, choose Number Format and select the desired format from the list that appears.

- Choose Numbers after the types of numbers to be used in the outline style.

- Choose Level Style and highlight the outline level you want to change. Then choose Edit.

- Make the desired changes to the style format. When you are finished, choose OK.

- Highlight and edit the other outline levels you want to change. When you are finished, press Exit (F7) or choose OK until you return to the document screen.

The changes you make to the styles are immediately updated in your document. In addition, if you have used the style in other documents, your changes to the style will be updated to these documents also when they are retrieved into WordPerfect.

12

WordPerfect Tables and Spreadsheets

WORDPERFECT'S TABLES FEATURE LETS YOU CREATE PERFECT TAbles, lists, and forms. Figure 12.1 shows an example of what the Tables feature can do for you. To create a table, you tell WordPerfect how many columns and rows you want, and it creates the table structure. Then, you type the text—it's that simple.

Figure 12.1
A WordPerfect table

Pack-Wrap INDUSTRIES
2634 West Hadley Road • Provo, Utah 84604

INVOICE

BILL TO		SHIP TO		
ADDRESS		ADDRESS		
CITY,STATE	ZIP	CITY,STATE		ZIP
ORDER NO.	SHIPPING CO.	SHIP DATE	TERMS.	

Item No.	Description	Unit Price	Quantity	Total cost
1				
2				
3				
4				
5				
6				
7				
8				
9				
10				
11				
12				
13				
14				
15				
16				
17				
18				
		GRAND TOTAL		

Authorized Signature:	DATE

Unlike tabular columns, which are easily disturbed by editing changes, WordPerfect tables keep your text within column and row boundaries. You won't need to bother with tab settings, because the column dividers are set for you. When you add or delete text, WordPerfect automatically adjusts the table, table rows growing or shrinking to the size required by the current text. If you need to modify the table layout, it's easy to change the column widths, align text, and move information between columns and rows.

You can also apply various formulas to total a column of numbers, estimate percentages, and perform other mathematical calculations. In fact, WordPerfect 6.0 can transform your table into a working spreadsheet, complete with links to data stored in other document or spreadsheet files.

In this chapter, you'll see how to create a basic table and how to use the table editor to define the structure and calculations of table data. You'll also see how to create tables by forming links to your spreadsheet files.

Creating WordPerfect Tables

As shown in Figure 12.2, tables are divided into *columns* and *rows*, which is similar to the structure of standard spreadsheets. A *cell* is a single "box" in the table, which occurs wherever a column and row intersect. Cells in a table can contain any combination of numbers and text. Although most tables contain no more than a page of text, WordPerfect lets you create tables with up to 32 columns across and over 32,000 rows in length—which means you can create a table with over 1 million cells!

Defining the Table Structure

This section explains how to create the structure for a simple table. Later in this chapter, you'll see how to select layout options for changing the column widths, choosing text alignment, changing table lines and shading, and applying attributes to text.

Follow these steps to create the structure for the table shown in Figure 12.3.

Choose Layout ▸ Tables ▸ Create.

1. Press Columns/Tables (Alt+F7) and choose <u>T</u>ables. Then choose <u>C</u>reate.

2. At the "Columns" prompt, enter **3** if necessary to specify three columns for the table.

3. At the "Rows" prompt, enter **6** to specify six rows for the table.

Choose OK.

4. Press Exit (F7) and WordPerfect displays the table structure within the Table Editor, shown in Figure 12.4. (Note the menu of options at the bottom of the screen.) Table columns are assigned letters and rows are numbered.

5. Press Exit (F7) to return to the document screen.

Choose Close.

Figure 12.2

Tables divided into columns and rows

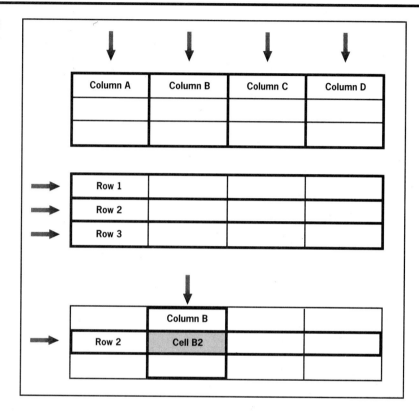

Figure 12.3

Creating a simple table

Part #	Unit Price	Description
A-5000	21.50	Piston/Pin Assembly
A-5001	22.30	Rod Assembly. Requires Part #s A-6000 and A-6002.
A-5004	6.00	Starter Hub
A-5002	00.75	Piston Pin Retaining Ring. Requires Part #s A-5000 and A-5001.
A-5005	35.70	Flywheel

Figure 12.4
WordPerfect's Table Editor

Cursor position

Row numbers

Cell address

Column letters

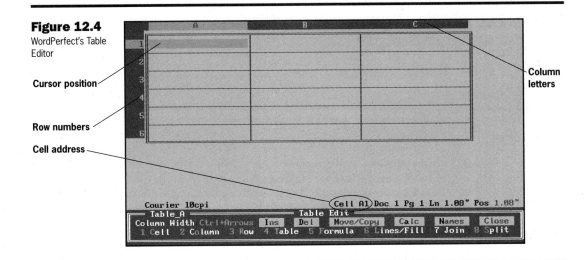

When you return to your document, you won't see the column letters and row numbers, but you'll see the table grid, and the status line will indicate where the cursor is located in the table. Notice that the status line now displays a "Cell" label, followed by "A1." This tells you that the text cursor is now in the first column (column A) and in the first row (row 1). This letter/number combination, known as a *cell address,* is unique for each cell in the table. Move the cursor through the table, and the "Cell" label displays the address for each cell in which the cursor is located.

One of the most important things to understand about tables in WordPerfect is that you can work on them in two different modes. In the Table Editor, which is displayed when you first create a table, you can manipulate the table as a whole, adding and deleting columns and rows, changing column widths, moving and copying columns and rows, applying formatting to cells, columns, and rows, and so forth. You also have to be in the Table Editor to perform table-specific operations such as entering formulas, changing number formats, and changing the line and fill styles used in the table. (You'll learn about all of these topics later in the chapter.) However, you cannot enter and, for the most part, cannot edit text in the Table Editor. To do this, you must return to your document screen (just press F7 or click on Close from within the Table Editor). In the Table Editor, the cursor appears as a highlight bar filling the entire cell it occupies. When you return to your regular document editing screen, the cursor regains its normal appearance, and you are free to enter and edit text as you normally do. At the same time, you'll still see the table grid, and can keep track of your location in the table by noting the cell address listed in the status line.

You can also navigate through the table in slightly different ways, depending on whether you're in the Table Editor or in regular editing mode, as you'll learn in the next section.

Moving the Cursor in a Table

When the text cursor is located within a table, the action of some keystrokes changes to let you easily move the cursor through the table. For example, you press the Tab key to move the cursor to the next available cell to the right; press Shift+Tab to move left to the previous cell. Table 12.1 shows the keystrokes that move the insertion point through the columns and rows of a table when you're in normal editing mode. Table 12.2 lists the keystrokes you use when in the Table Editor. The Alt+*arrow* keystrokes work only on keyboards with a set of dedicated arrow keys. You cannot use Alt in combination with the arrow keys on the numeric keypad.

Table 12.1   **Cursor Movement in Tables**

To Move to	Press
Next cell, right	Tab or Alt+→
Previous cell, left	Shift+Tab or Alt+←
First cell in table	Ctrl+Home, Home, Home, ↑
Last cell in table	Ctrl+Home, Home, Home, ↓
Next cell, down	Alt+↓
Previous cell, up	Alt+↑
Beginning of row	Ctrl+Home, Home, ←
End of row	Ctrl+Home, Home, →
Top of column	Ctrl+Home, Home, ↑
Bottom of column	Ctrl+Home, Home, ↓

Note: Do *not* use the arrow keys on the numeric keypad.

Table 12.2   **Cursor Movement in the Table Editor**

To Move to	Press
Next cell, right	Tab or Right Arrow
Previous cell, left	Shift+Tab or Left Arrow
First cell in Table	Home, Home, ↑
Last cell in table	Home, Home, ↓
Next cell, down	↓
Previous cell, up	↑
Beginning of row	Home, ←
End of row	End, or Home, →
Top of column	Home, ↑
Bottom of column	Home, ↓

In the Table Editor, you can also move the cursor to a specific cell in the table by pressing Go To (Ctrl+Home) and entering the cell address. For example, to move directly to cell C3, press Go To (Ctrl+Home) and enter **C3**. To jump back to the previous cell, press Ctrl+Home twice.

NOTE. *If you are using a mouse with WordPerfect, you can move the cursor by clicking on a table cell.*

Typing Text and Numbers

Once you create a table and have mastered cursor movement, you're ready to enter text information. Simply move the cursor to each cell and type the text you need.

The following steps explain how to enter text into the table created earlier. You'll start by typing the titles for the table columns. Then, you'll enter text for the items inside the table. You will create the table in Figure 12.3, so use the figure as a reference.

1. Move the cursor to cell A1 and type **Part #**.

2. Press Tab to move to cell B1 and type **Unit Price**.

3. Press Tab to move to cell C1 in the row, and type **Description**.

4. Press Tab to move to the first cell in the next row (cell A2), and type **A-5000**.

5. Press Tab to move to the next cell (cell B2) and type **21.50**.

6. Press Tab to move to cell C2 and type **Piston/Pin Assembly**.

7. Press Tab to move to the beginning of the next row, and type **A-5001**.

8. Press Tab to move to the next cell (cell B3) and type **22.30**.

9. Press Tab to move to cell C3 and type **Rod Assembly. Requires Part #s A-6000 and A-6002**.

10. Continue to enter the rest of the text shown in Figure 12.5.

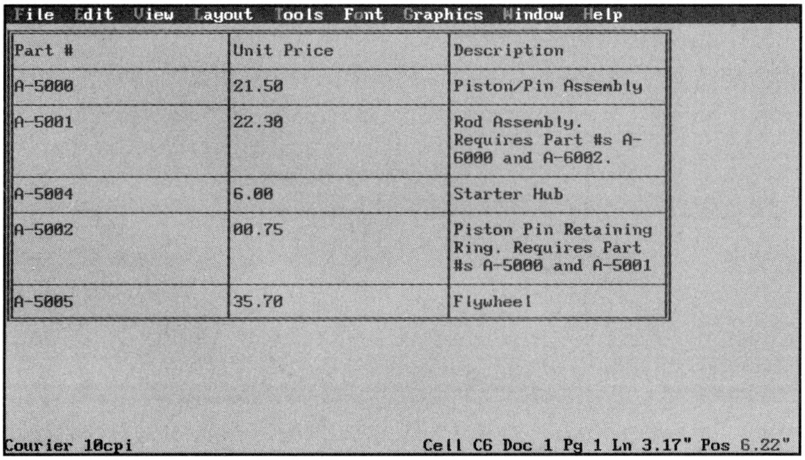

Figure 12.5
The completed table

| File Edit View Layout Tools Font Graphics Window Help |
Part #	Unit Price	Description
A-5000	21.50	Piston/Pin Assembly
A-5001	22.30	Rod Assembly. Requires Part #s A-6000 and A-6002.
A-5004	6.00	Starter Hub
A-5002	00.75	Piston Pin Retaining Ring. Requires Part #s A-5000 and A-5001
A-5005	35.70	Flywheel

Courier 10cpi — Cell C6 Doc 1 Pg 1 Ln 3.17" Pos 6.22"

11. When you are finished creating the table, save your document to a file called PARTS.DOC. You'll use this table for other examples in this chapter.

Notice that when you type more text than the width of the cell can hold, WordPerfect automatically increases the height of the cell and wraps the text on two or more lines. You can type as much text as you need in a cell; WordPerfect will adjust the height of the current row without changing or upsetting the structure of the table. If you edit the text later, WordPerfect will adjust the height of the row again to allow for more or less text.

TIP. *As you type text in a table, you can press Home, Tab to insert a tab into cell text. Remember, Tab by itself takes you to the next cell.*

In this example, you moved across the table rows to enter the text, but you can move the cursor in any sequence. Instead of pressing Tab to move across the row, you can press Alt+↓ to move down the column and type text. (You may want to refer to Table 12.1 earlier in this chapter for a review of cursor movement within tables.)

Converting Tabular Columns into a Table

Another way to create a table is by applying the table structure to a set of tabular columns. Figure 12.6 shows columns of text separated by tabs. If you have text formatted in this manner, you can convert the tabular columns to a table by blocking the text and then choosing the Table Create feature. WordPerfect examines the selected text and replaces the tabs with column separators for the table. The hard returns at the end of each line are replaced with row separators.

Figure 12.6
Converting tabular columns to a table

Tabular columns

	Monday	Tuesday	Wednesday	Thursday	Friday
Week 1	21	10	07	25	16
Week 2	17	11	27	40	37
Week 3	42	39	12	14	09
Week 4	15	03	32	29	18

Tabular columns converted to a table

	Monday	Tuesday	Wednesday	Thursday	Friday
Week 1	21	10	07	25	16
Week 2	17	11	27	40	37
Week 3	42	39	12	14	09
Week 4	15	03	32	29	18

Before you convert tabular text, make sure that only one [Tab] code is present between the items in the tabular columns. If you pressed Tab two or more times between items, the table structure will have incorrect column breaks. This happens because WordPerfect starts a new column at each place where a [Tab] code exists in the original text. Instead of pressing Tab repeatedly to make items line up, you should define new tab stops to eliminate unnecessary tabs between the columns.

Follow these steps to convert tabular text to a WordPerfect table:

Drag with the mouse to select the text that should be converted to a table.

- Move the cursor to the beginning of the first line of tabular text.

- Press Block (Alt+F4 or F12). Then, move the cursor to the end of the last line of tabular text.

- Press Columns/Tables (Alt+F7). Choose Tables, and then choose Create.

- Choose Create from Tabular Text. Then press Enter or choose OK.

Choose Layout ▸ Tables ▸ Create.

- WordPerfect applies the table structure to the text and displays it in the Table Editor. Press Exit (F7) to return to the document screen.

This converts the text into a WordPerfect table; each tab stop begins a new column, and each text line becomes a row in the table.

Changing the table back to tabular text is just as easy. Simply turn on Reveal Codes (Alt+F3 or F11), highlight the [Tbl Def] code that begins the table, and press Delete to remove the table definition code. WordPerfect converts the table to tabular columns, using the current tab stops in your document.

Editing Text and Numbers

To edit table text, use the same editing features you use for regular text. First, move the cursor to the cell that contains the text you want to edit. Press Tab to move to the next cell or press Shift+Tab to move to the previous cell in the current row. When a cell has only one line of text, you can press ↑ or ↓ to move to the previous or next cell in the column; when a cell has two or more lines of text, press Alt+↑ or Alt+↓ to move to the previous or next cell in the column. (You may want to refer to Table 12.1 earlier in this chapter to review cursor movement within tables.)

To edit the text, press Backspace and Delete to remove single characters; Ctrl+Backspace deletes entire words. To add new text, simply type it; WordPerfect will adjust the size of the current cell to accommodate the text. Within the cell, you can use the standard cursor keystrokes to move the cursor. When the current cell contains two or more lines of text, press Ctrl+Home, ↑ to move to the beginning of the cell text. Press Ctrl+Home, ↓ to move to the last line of text within a cell.

Moving and Copying Text in Tables

Use WordPerfect's Move/Copy feature to move or copy text to another cell in the table. The following steps describe how to move or copy cell text:

Drag the mouse to select the text you want to move or copy.

Choose Edit ▸ Cut and Paste, or Edit ▸ Copy and Paste.

- Use Block (Alt+F4 or F12) to highlight the text you want to move or copy.

- Press Cut and Paste (Ctrl+Del) or Copy and Paste (Ctrl+Ins).

- Move the cursor to the cell where the text should be moved or copied.

- Press Enter to retrieve the text.

Note that you can also use WordPerfect 6.0's new drag and drop capabilities to move or copy table text. For details on drag and drop, consult Chapter 6.

If you block text across columns or rows, all highlighted text will be moved or copied into a single cell. This happens because blocked text cannot include column and row separators; column separators are converted to tabs, and row separators become Hard Return codes. To move or copy complete columns or rows of text, see "Moving or Copying Rows and Columns," later in this chapter.

Changing the Table Size and Structure

WordPerfect provides several options for customizing the structure and appearance of your tables. The following sections describe how to adjust the width of table columns, how to move or copy columns and rows, and how to change the table size with new columns and rows. You'll also learn how to join and split cells to create unique tables and forms.

Adjusting Column Widths

Figure 12.7 shows the table from earlier in this chapter. Notice that some of the columns look crowded, while other columns have too much empty space. You can fix this problem by adjusting the width of the columns and more evenly distributing the text across the table.

You can change column widths at any time—it doesn't matter whether you have already typed text in the table. Perform these steps to change the column widths in your table; you may want to try these on the table from the PARTS.DOC document that you created earlier.

Choose Layout ▸ Tables ▸ Edit.

- Move the cursor into the table you want to edit.

Figure 12.7

Adjusting column
widths to evenly
distribute text

Part #	Unit Price	Description
A-5000	21.50	Piston/Pin Assembly
A-5001	22.30	Rod Assembly. Requires Part #s A-6000 and A-6002.
A-5004	6.00	Starter Hub
A-5002	00.75	Piston Pin Retaining Ring. Requires Part #s A-5000 and A-5001.
A-5005	35.70	Flywheel

Too much empty space in these columns.

The text in this column is too crowded.

- Press Columns/Tables (Alt+F7), choose <u>T</u>ables, and then choose <u>E</u>dit. WordPerfect opens the Table Editor. Note that you can also use the Alt+F11 shortcut to open the Table Editor without going through the menu system.

- Move the cursor to the table column you want to change. Notice how, in the Table Editor, the cursor has become a large highlight bar that highlights the entire contents of the active cell.

- Press Ctrl+→ to make the column wider, or press Ctrl+← to make the column narrower.

TIP. *If you want a specific measurement for the column width(s), you can choose C<u>o</u>lumn from the Table Editor menu at the bottom of the screen. Then, enter the desired measurement at the <u>W</u>idth option.*

- To adjust other columns in the table, move to each column and increase or decrease the width, as described above.

- Press Exit (F7) to close the Table Editor and accept the new column widths.

Choose Close to
exit the Table Edi-
tor and return to
your document.

When you change the width of a column, WordPerfect may need to adjust other column widths in the table. If, for example, you make a column narrower, this decreases the width of the entire table. If you make a column wider, any columns located to the right of the current column are moved further to the right.

If you increase a column width until your table extends the full width of the page, WordPerfect proportionately decreases the width of the columns to the right of the column you're widening. It needs to "shrink" these columns to make room for the wider column. You can assign a fixed width to any column to prevent WordPerfect from changing the column width when other columns in the table are widened. To assign a fixed width,

Choose Layout ▸ Tables ▸ Edit.

- Press Columns/Tables (Alt+F7), choose Tables, and then choose Edit; or, press Alt+F11.

- Move the cursor to the column that should have a fixed width.

- Choose Column to display the Column Format dialog box. Then check the box for Fixed Width.

- Choose Width, and enter the measurement that you want for the column. (The current width is displayed by default.) Then press Exit (F7) to return to the Table Editor.

When you change other column widths in the table, WordPerfect will not adjust the column that has a fixed width.

Moving or Copying Rows and Columns

As you create your tables, you'll want to experiment with different table arrangements. Sometimes you'll want the items in cells arranged alphabetically, and sometimes you'll want the entries sorted by part or identification number. WordPerfect makes it easy to move rows and columns in your table, so that you can experiment when you aren't sure how you want the table to look. If your table already contains text, the text moves with the columns and rows when they are moved or copied to another place in the table.

You can also make copies of rows and columns and place them in other sections of your table; this is useful when your table spans two or more pages, and a specific column or row should appear on each page.

To move or copy a row in the table:

Choose Layout ▸ Tables ▸ Edit.

- Press Columns/Tables (Alt+F7), choose Tables, and then choose Edit; or, simply press Alt+F11.

Choose Mo̲ve/Copy.

- Move the cursor to the row you want to move or copy.

- Press Move (Ctrl+F4) or select Move/Copy to display the dialog box shown in Figure 12.8.

Figure 12.8
Moving or copying a row

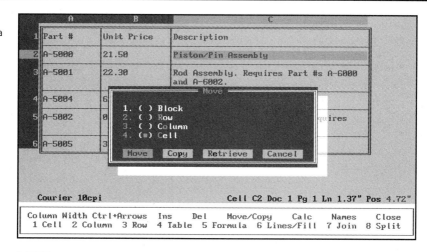

- Choose R̲ow, and then choose M̲ove or C̲opy.

- Move the cursor to the row that should follow the row you are moving or copying. Press Enter to retrieve the row.

- Press Exit (F7) to close the Table Editor and return to your document.

  When you retrieve the table row, remember that it will be inserted just *above* the row where the cursor is located.
  To move or copy a column in the table:

Choose La̲yout ►
Ta̲bles ► E̲dit.

- Press Columns/Tables (Alt+F7), choose T̲ables, and then choose E̲dit; or, press Alt+F11.

- Move the cursor to the column you want to move or copy.

Choose Mo̲ve/Copy.

- Press Move (Ctrl+F4) to display the Move dialog box.

- Choose C̲olumn, and then choose M̲ove or C̲opy.

- Move the cursor to the column that should follow the column you are moving or copying. Press Enter to retrieve the column.

■ Press Exit (F7) to close the Table Editor and return to your document.

When you retrieve the table column, remember that it will be inserted to the *left* of the column where the cursor is located. When you add a new column though copying, WordPerfect adjusts the widths of the other columns in the table to accommodate the copied column.

Adding Rows and Columns

Sometimes you'll need to add a row or column of information to your table. This is accomplished with the Insert option on the Table Editor menu. (The Tables option on the Layout menu also provides a quick way to add or remove table rows.) When you insert a row or column, WordPerfect copies the layout of the current row or column to create the new item.

Retrieve the PARTS.DOC document you created earlier in this chapter, and then try the following exercise to add a row to your table:

Choose Layout ▸ Tables ▸ Edit.

1. Press Columns/Tables (Alt+F7), choose Tables, and then choose Edit; or, press Alt+F11.

2. Move the cursor to the row that contains the "Starter Hub" entry.

3. Choose Ins from the Table Editor menu or press the Insert key to display the dialog box shown in Figure 12.9.

Figure 12.9

Inserting a row into a table

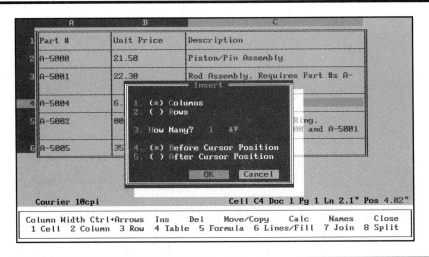

Choose OK.

Choose Close.

4. Choose Rows, choose How Many?, and, if necessary, enter **1** as the number of rows you want to insert.

5. Choose Before Cursor Position if its not already selected to insert the row before the current row. Then press Exit (F7).

6. Press Exit (F7) to close the Table Editor and return to your document.

The inserted row takes its format from the row where you started. Now you can type text in the new row. The pull-down menus also provide a quick way to insert a row without opening the Table Editor. Simply position the cursor within your table and choose Layout, then Tables, and then Insert Row. Alternatively, you can simply press Ctrl+Ins from within a row to insert a new row above it. In addition, you can insert multiple rows in the Table Editor by blocking the desired number of rows, and the pressing Ctrl+Ins.

Inserting new columns is just as easy to do. Try the following steps to add a column to your table:

Choose Layout ▸
Tables ▸ Edit.

1. Press Columns/Tables (Alt+F7), choose Tables, and then choose Edit; or, press Alt+F11.

2. Move the cursor to the "Part #" column in the table you created earlier.

3. Choose Ins or press the Insert key.

4. Choose Columns, choose How Many?, and enter **1** if necessary.

Choose OK.

5. Choose Before Cursor Position to insert the column before the current column. Then press Exit (F7).

6. Press Exit (F7) to close the Table Editor and return to your document.

These steps insert a new column before the "Part #" column. The new column also takes its format from the "Part #" column, which is the column where the cursor was located when you chose Insert. When you return to the document editing screen, you can type text in the new row or column.

Notice when you add a row or column, the table cell addresses are adjusted to account for the new item. For example, suppose you insert a new column between columns A and B. The new column becomes column B and all columns to the right of the new column are changed to column C, column D, column E, and so on. Insert two new rows between rows 4 and 5, and the new rows become rows 5 and 6; the rows that follow the new rows are renumbered, beginning with row 7.

You probably won't notice the change in cell addresses when you add or delete columns and rows, but these address changes are important when you're working with other table features, such as the formulas described later in this chapter.

Deleting Rows and Columns

You will want to remove rows and columns from your table when a row or column of information is no longer needed in the table or when you want to remove duplicate columns and rows.

To delete a row or column from a table, you can position the cursor on the row you want to remove, and then choose Layout, then Tables, and then Delete Row. Or you can remove rows from the Table Editor, as described here:

Choose Layout ▶ Tables ▶ Edit.

- Press Columns/Tables (Alt+F7), choose Tables, and then choose Edit; or, press Alt+F11.

- Move the cursor to the row or column you want to delete.

- Choose Del or press the Delete key to display the dialog box shown in Figure 12.10.

Figure 12.10

Deleting a row or column

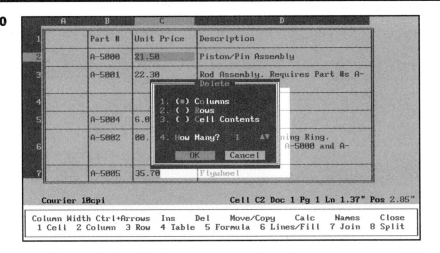

- Choose Rows to delete rows or Columns to delete columns.

Choose OK.

- Choose How Many? and enter the number of rows or columns you want to remove. Then press Exit (F7).

- Press Exit (F7) to close the Table Editor and return to your document.

TIP. *You can press Ctrl+Del to delete the row where the cursor is located. You'll see the prompt "Delete Row?" Respond Yes to delete the row. This technique works whether ot not you are in the Table Editor. In the Table Editor, you can also delete multiple rows by highlighting at least one cell from each row to be deleted and pressing Ctrl+Del.*

Deleting a row or column removes the row or column from the table structure and also deletes any text stored in those cells. After you delete columns or rows, the cell addresses in the table are updated to reflect the new table structure.

TIP. *To delete the text for a whole row or column while in the Table Editor, use Block (Alt+F4 or F12) to select all text in the row or column. Then press Delete to remove the text. This removes just the text, not the rows or columns themselves.*

Restoring Deleted Rows or Columns

If you make a mistake, you can restore a deleted row or column with the Undelete feature. You can restore only the row or column you most recently deleted. Rows will be restored above and columns will be restored to the left of the current cursor position.

To restore the last row or column deleted:

Choose Layout ▸
Ta<u>b</u>les ▸ <u>E</u>dit.

- If the Table Editor is not displayed, press Columns/Tables (Alt+F7), choose <u>T</u>ables, and then choose <u>E</u>dit; or, press Alt+F11.

- Press Undelete (Esc), and type **Y** at the "Undelete Row(s)" or "Undelete Column(s)?" message.

You can also restore deleted rows or columns with the Undo feature. Just press Ctrl+Z immediately after having unintentionally deleted any number of rows or columns. They will be restored to their original location.

Specifying the Table Position

When you first create a table, it will fill the space between the left and right margins on the page. If you have changed the size of the table by reducing the width or number of columns, you can place the table against the left or right margin, center it between margins, or place the table at a specific measurement from the left edge of the page.

To specify a position for your table:

Choose Layout ▸
Ta<u>b</u>les ▸ <u>E</u>dit.

- Move the cursor into the table, press Columns/Tables (Alt+F7), choose <u>T</u>ables, and then choose <u>E</u>dit; or, press Alt+F11.

- Choose <u>T</u>able, select <u>P</u>osition, and then choose one of the position options. If you choose the <u>S</u>et option, you are prompted to enter a measurement that represents the amount of space you want between the left edge of the page and the left edge of the table.

Choose OK ▸ Close.

- Press Exit (F7) twice to return to the document screen.

Figure 12.11 shows how each of the options affect the position of the table on the page. The Left and Right options align the table with the left or right margin, Center aligns the table precisely between left and right margins, and Full stretches the table so that it extends evenly to both left and right margins. As mentioned earlier, the Set option lets you specify how far the table will be placed from the left edge of the printed page.

Figure 12.11

Aligning the table at different positions

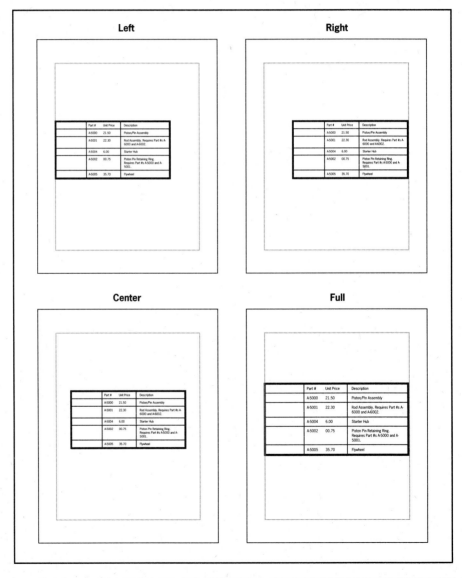

Joining Two or More Cells

For some tables and forms, you may need to combine or *join* cells together to create a larger cell. Figure 12.12 shows an example of cells that have been combined in a table. Joining does more than erase the lines between two or more cells; it actually combines the different cells into one cell in the table.

Figure 12.12

Joining two cells into one

Before joining

Description	Opening/Closing	
	12.50	12.75
	16.20	15.85

After joining

Description	Opening/Closing	
	12.50	12.75
	16.20	15.85

Choose Layout ▸ Tables ▸ Edit.

Drag to highlight the cells you want to join.

Choose Close to return to the document screen.

You can join cells from the Table Editor, as described here:

- Press Columns/Tables (Alt+F7), choose Tables, and then choose Edit; or, simply press Alt+F11.

- Use the Block feature to highlight all the cells you want to join.

- Choose Join and type **Y** at the "Join Cells?" prompt.

- Press Exit (F7) to return to the document screen.

After joining cells, the cell order for cursor movement may change. Consider the example in Figure 12.13; the numbers in the diagram indicate the order in which the cursor moves to each cell when you press Tab to move through the table. Although this may seem odd, there is some logic to the order in which the cursor moves between the cells. When you press Tab to move the cursor, WordPerfect moves the cursor across each row before moving to the next row. In Figure 12.13, the center column has more rows than the other columns; WordPerfect moves the cursor across the top cells first, and continues to the next row in the center column.

Figure 12.13

Joining cells affects the order in which the cursor moves to each cell.

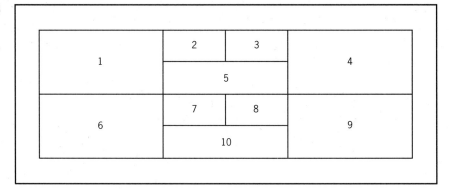

Splitting Cells

Figure 12.14 shows an example of a cell that has been divided into three different rows. You may want to do this in your table when a column of information should provide two or more places to type information for a entry (row) in the table.

Figure 12.14

Dividing a cell into rows

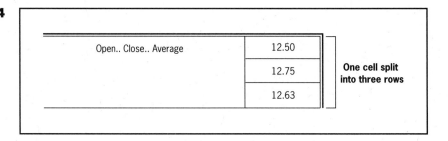

To split one cell into two or more cells from the Table Editor, follow these steps:

■ Press Columns/Tables (Alt+F7), choose <u>T</u>ables, and choose <u>E</u>dit; or, press Alt+F11.

■ Move the cursor to the cell you want to split.

Choose <u>L</u>ayout ▸ Ta<u>b</u>les ▸ <u>E</u>dit.

- Choose <u>S</u>plit and the dialog box shown in Figure 12.15 appears.

- Choose <u>C</u>olumns to divide the cell vertically, or choose <u>R</u>ows to divide the cell horizontally.

- If necessary, choose <u>H</u>ow Many?, and type the number of cells you want to create with the split.

Choose OK ▸ Close.

- Press Enter to accept the settings, and then press Exit (F7) to return from the Table Editor.

Figure 12.15
The Split Cell dialog box

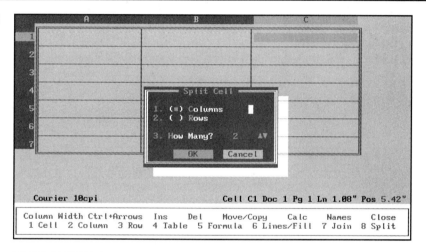

When cells are split, WordPerfect tries to match the dividing lines with existing lines in the table. Figure 12.16 shows a cell before and after splitting. The cell in this example is adjacent to three rows. After splitting, WordPerfect divides the cell to match the lines of the rows in the next column.

Table Lines and Shading

The lines that divide the rows and columns instantly show how the table information is organized and make it easier for you to work with the table data. The standard settings for lines place a double-lined border around the outer edge of the table, and single lines show where the rows and columns are separated. You can change the lines in your table by selecting columns, rows, cells, or other table sections, and choosing different line styles for each. You can also create and choose different shading or fill styles to emphasize certain cells, columns, and rows.

Figure 12.16

When dividing cells, WordPerfect tries to match the existing table's lines

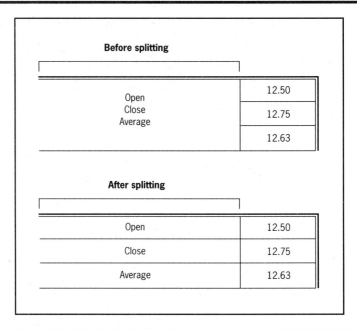

The Table Lines dialog box provides different ways to change table lines and shading. From the Table Editor, choose Lines/Fill to display the Table Lines dialog box. The options listed under Entire Table affect the default table lines and the border and fill settings for the entire table; use these options when you want to define uniform line and border settings for all table cells. The options listed under "Current Cell or Block" let you choose line and fill settings for the current cell or group of blocked cells; use these options when you want to mix different line and fill settings within the same table.

Understanding Table Lines

Table lines are set according to the boundaries of each cell in your table. You can change the lines for a single cell, a row, a column, or a block of cells. When you define table lines, think of each cell as a distinct plot of land with a fence encompassing it; there may be adjoining cells that also have a complete "fence" or border. Figure 12.17 shows an example of this. When the cells are next to each other, their combined borders affect the general appearance of the lines in the table.

Figure 12.17

Each table cell has a border for each side of the cell

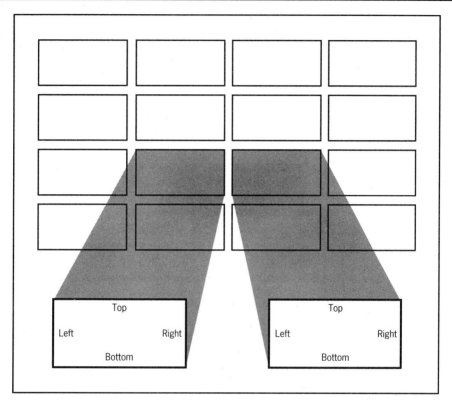

As shown in Figure 12.18, WordPerfect automatically places a single line at the top and left edge of each table cell, with the exception of the cells located at the outside edge where the double-lined border is placed. This ensures a consistent single line between the columns and rows inside the table; if all cells in the table had a single line placed on all sides, the borders would overlap to create a thicker line along some cells in the table.

Defining Cell Lines

There are two ways to change the lines in your table: You can define the lines for the entire table, or you can define the lines for selected cells. To define the lines for the entire table, choose Lines/Fill from the Table Editor, and then choose Default Line. This option lets you select one line style and one line

Figure 12.18

WordPerfect sets a border line at the top and left sides of each cell

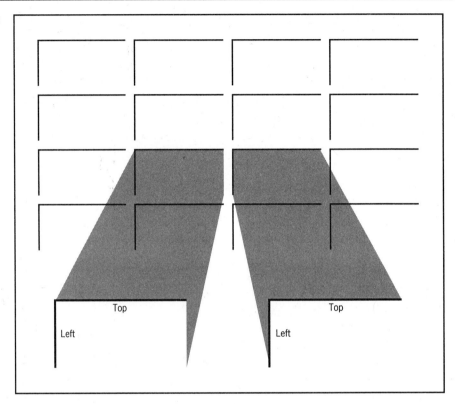

color for all lines in the current table. To define lines for selected cells, use the following steps:

Choose Layout ▸ Tables ▸ Edit.

■ Move the cursor into the table, and press Columns/Tables (Alt+F7), choose Tables, and then choose Edit; or, press Alt+F11.

■ Move to the cell you want to change. To change the lines of two or more cells, use the Block feature to select the cells.

■ Choose Lines/Fill. The Table Lines dialog box appears as shown in Figure 12.19.

■ Choose one of the options to define lines for one of the cell sides.

■ Choose one of the line style option and choose Select.

Figure 12.19

The Table Lines
dialog box

These options
determine the
Border/Fill style for
the entire table

These options
determine the
Border/Fill style for
the selected cells

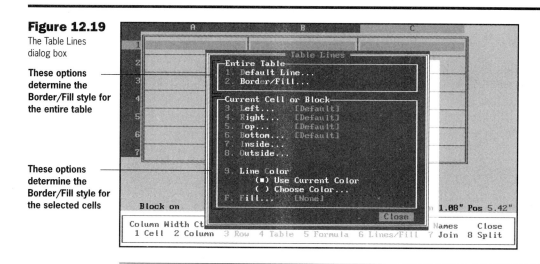

- Continue choosing options and line styles until you've instituted all the desired changes.

- Press Exit (F7) to accept the changes and return to the table.

The Left, Right, Top, and Bottom options let you define the line style for one side of the selected cell or area. The Inside option lets you choose a style for all the lines inside the selected block of cells; select Outside when you want to change the line style at the edges of the selected block. If you are using a color printer, select the Line Color option to choose a color for the lines. The Fill option, described later in this chapter, lets you apply a shaded background to the selected cells.

Creating Double-underlined Titles

In the following example, you'll see how to change the table lines for a group of blocked cells. This is useful when you want to create dividing lines for sections of your table, such as a thick line or a double line to separate table labels from the text typed into the table.

Perform these steps to add a double line beneath the column titles in the table from the PARTS.DOC file that you created earlier:

Choose Layout ▸
Tables ▸ Edit.

Drag to block cells
A1 through C1.

1. Move the cursor into the table, press Columns/Tables (Alt+F7), choose Tables, and then choose Edit; or, press Alt+F11.

2. Move to cell A1, and press Block (Alt+F4 or F12).

3. Press Home, → to block the entire row.

4. Choose Lines/Fill to display the Table Lines dialog box.

5. Choose Bottom to change the lines at the bottom of the highlighted cells.

Choose Close.

6. Highlight the Double Line style, and choose Select. Then press Exit (F7) to return to the Table Editor.

7. Press Exit (F7) to accept the changes and return to the document screen.

Choose Close to return to your document.

In this example, you first blocked the cells you wanted to change. Since you wanted to create a double line beneath the labels at the top of the table, you blocked the entire first row. Then you selected the Double Line style and applied it to the bottom edge of the highlighted cells.

Defining a Table Border

When you create a new table, WordPerfect automatically creates a double-line border around the table. You can change the border style by following these steps:

Choose Layout ▶ Tables ▶ Edit.

- Move the cursor into the table and press Columns/Tables (Alt+F7), choose Tables, and then choose Edit; or, press Alt+F11.

Double-click on the desired border style.

- Choose Lines/Fill and then choose Border/Fill.

- Choose Border Style and highlight the desired line style from the list. Then choose Select.

Choose OK ▶ Close.

- Press Exit (F7) until you return to the document screen.

In these steps, you first open the Table Editor and choose the style you want for the lines around the selected cells. You can easily mix line styles to create various table layouts. You can, for example, create a "shadow" border for the table by following these steps:

- Open the Table Editor, and then choose Lines/Fill.

- Choose Border/Fill and then choose Customize. WordPerfect displays the dialog box, shown in Figure 12.20, where you can create a custom border style.

Double-click on Extra Thick Line.

- Choose Lines and then choose Left Line. Then highlight the Extra Thick Line and choose Select.

- Choose Bottom Line. Then, highlight Extra Thick Line again and choose Select.

- Press Exit (F7) until you return to the document editing screen.

The thick lines at the left and bottom sides give the illusion of a shadow at the edge of the table. If you are working with WordPerfect's text display mode, press Print (Shift+F7), and choose Print Pre_view to view the table. Or switch to WordPerfect's graphics display mode or page display mode. The result is a table border that looks like Figure 12.21.

Figure 12.20

The Customize Table Border/Fill dialog box

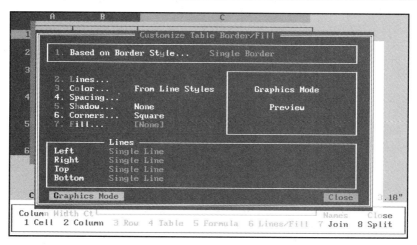

Figure 12.21

Mixing line styles to create a shadow border

"Shadow" border

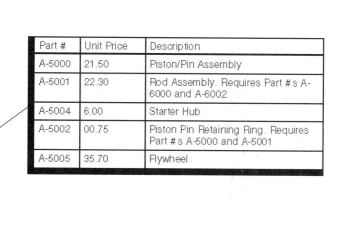

Shaded Cells, Columns, and Rows

Figure 12.22 shows an example of how shading can enhance the appearance of your tables. The Fill option lets you add a shaded background pattern for a column, row, or cell. On standard printers, the shading will appear as a percentage of gray; if you are printing your documents on a color printer, you can select different colors for the shading.

Figure 12.22

Shading enhances table columns and rows

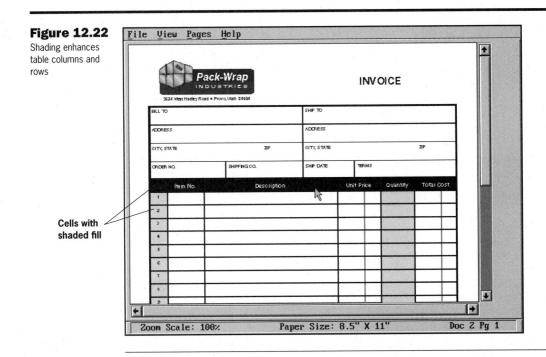

Cells with shaded fill

Follow these steps to add shading to your table:

Choose <u>L</u>ayout ▸ Ta-bles ▸ <u>E</u>dit.

- Move the cursor into the table and press Columns/Tables (Alt+F7), choose <u>T</u>ables, and then choose <u>E</u>dit; or, press Alt+F11.

- Use Block (Alt+F4 or F12) to highlight the cell, row, or column you want to shade.

- Choose <u>L</u>ines/Fill, choose <u>F</u>ill, and then choose Fill St<u>y</u>le to display the Fill Styles dialog box shown in Figure 12.23.

Double-click on the shading style you want.

- Press ↑ or ↓ to highlight the shading style you want to apply to the selected cell(s). Then choose <u>S</u>elect. Figure 12.24 shows how the different fill styles will appear on the printed page.

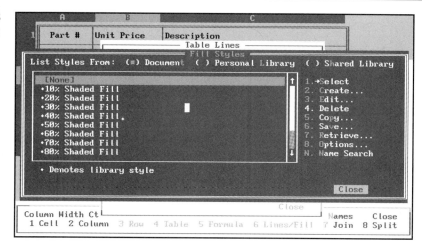

Figure 12.23
The Fill Styles dialog box

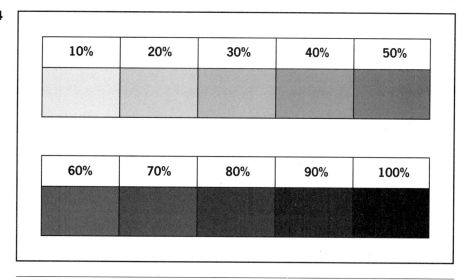

Figure 12.24
Fill styles for table cells

Choose OK ▸ Close.

- After you select a style, WordPerfect displays the Fill Style and Color dialog box. If you have a color printer, you can choose the Foreground Color and Background Color options to select colors for the shaded fill.

- Press Exit (F7) until you return to the document screen.

If you are working with the text display mode, the shading will not appear on the document editing screen, but you can use the Print Preview feature to see how the table will look when printed. If you are working with the graphics display mode or page display mode, the Print Preview screen is not necessary. The table shading will appear on the document editing screen.

Creating Reversed Table Titles

In addition to the shaded cell backgrounds, the Fill feature can also help you create *reversed text*, which appears like the titles shown in Figure 12.25 where light text appears on a dark background.

Figure 12.25

Reversed text

Reversed text ↓

Part #	Unit Price	Description
A-5000	21.50	Piston/Pin Assembly
A-5001	22.30	Rod Assembly. Requires Part #s A-6000 and A-6002.
A-5004	6.00	Starter Hub
A-5002	00.75	Piston Pin Retaining Ring. Requires Part #s A-5000 and A- 5001.
A-5005	35.70	Flywheel

To create reversed text in a table,

Choose F<u>o</u>nt ▸ <u>P</u>rint Color. Then select White or another light text color.

Choose <u>L</u>ayout ▸ Ta<u>b</u>les ▸ <u>E</u>dit.

- Use the Block feature to select the table text that you want to show as reversed text.

- Press Font (Ctrl+F8), choose <u>C</u>olor, and select White or another light text color. Then, press Exit (F7) until you return to your document.

- Press Columns/Tables (Alt+F7), choose <u>T</u>ables, and then choose <u>E</u>dit; or, press Alt+F11.

- Block the same table cells where you applied the text color change.

Double-click on
100% shaded fill.

Choose OK ▶ Close.

- Choose Lines/Fill from the Table Editor menu. Choose Fill and then choose Fill Style.

- Scroll down through the list of fill styles to highlight the 100% Shaded Fill style. Then choose Select.

- Press Exit (F7) until you return to the document screen.

If you are using the graphics display mode or page display mode, you'll see the reversed text on the document screen. If you're using WordPerfect's text display mode, you won't see the reversed text on the screen, but you can use the Print Preview feature to see the change.

When you send your document to the printer, WordPerfect prints solid black cells with white (or another colored) text. The results on the printed page depend on the type of printer you are using. PostScript and PCL5 printers can produce reversed text with any font, but some printers can't change the color of text.

If your text doesn't appear on the black shaded cells when you print the table, make sure you've changed the text color. If it seems your printer can't change the color of text, an option on the Print dialog box can force the text to appear.

To choose this option, press Print (Shift+F7), or choose Print from the File pull-down menu, to display the Print dialog box. Choose Print Job Graphically, so that an *X* appears in the check box next to this option. Then, choose Print to send your document to the printer.

The Print Job Graphically option converts the document text to a graphic image, which can be printed on any printer that handles graphics. This ensures that the light text will print against the dark shaded background of the table cells. With the exception of a few items—like reversed text—this option will not change the appearance of the printed document; it simply changes the method that your printer uses to produce the printed pages.

Creating a Custom Fill Style

Although WordPerfect includes several predefined styles that you can select to create shading in your tables, you can also create a custom fill style. This is most useful when you want to create special effects, like the gradual shading shown in Figure 12.26.

Notice that the shading blends gradually from one color to another. The following steps explain how to create a custom fill style for gradual shading; you can easily adapt this procedure to create any custom fill style for tables. Begin with the cursor in a table that you have already created:

Choose Layout ▶
Tables ▶ Edit.

1. Press Columns/Tables (Alt+F7), choose Tables, and then choose Edit; or, simply press Alt+F11.

Figure 12.26

Gradual shading in a
table column

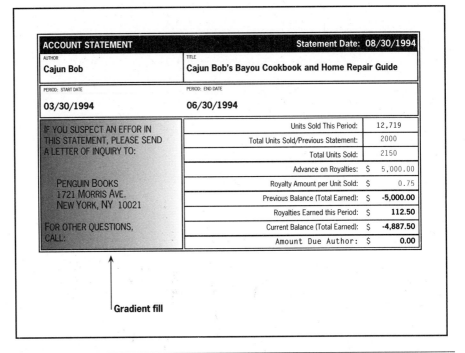

Gradient fill

2. Use the Block feature to select the column that you want to shade.

3. Choose Lines/Fill and then choose the Fill option.

4. Choose Fill Style from the Fill Style and Color dialog box.

5. Choose Create and you are prompted to enter a name for the style.

6. Type **Gradual Shaded Fill, Diagonal** and press Enter. The Create Fill Style dialog box appears.

7. Choose Fill Type and then choose Gradient from the pop-up list.

8. Choose Color (Foreground), choose a color from the Palette Colors list, and then choose Select. This becomes the top color for the gradual shading. Then, choose Close to close the Color Selection dialog box.

9. If you wish, choose Color (Background), choose the bottom color for the gradual shading, and then choose Select. Choose Close to close the Color Selection dialog box. The result will be shading that is blended between the foreground and background colors you select.

10. Choose Fill <u>P</u>attern to display the Gradient Fill Edit dialog box.

11. Choose Rotation <u>A</u>ngle and enter **45** to rotate the direction of the gradual shading.

Choose OK until you return to the Fill Styles dialog box.

12. Press Exit (F7) twice to accept the new style and return to the Fill Styles dialog box.

13. In the fill style list, highlight "Gradual Shaded Fill, Diagonal" and then choose <u>S</u>elect.

Choose OK until you return to the document screen.

14. Press Exit (F7) until you return to the document screen.

The options on the Gradient Fill Edit dialog box let you create a variety of fill combinations. In these steps, you selected only the Rotation <u>A</u>ngle option. You can choose Gradient <u>T</u>ype to change the shape of the gradient fill. Choose <u>H</u>orizontal Offset to move the shading left or right; choose <u>V</u>ertical Offset to move the shading up or down. The last two options, <u>N</u>umber of Shades and <u>C</u>alculate Number of Shades determine the number of levels for the gradual shading. Choose <u>C</u>alculate Number of Shades and WordPerfect automatically calculates the number of levels for a smooth gradual shade. Choose <u>N</u>umber of Shades and you can enter the number of levels that you want for the shading; at this option, smaller numbers create rougher shading, larger numbers create smoother shading. (Note that you can only select <u>N</u>umber of Shades if you turn off <u>C</u>alculate Number of Shades.)

Formatting Table Text, Columns, and Rows

When you type text in your table, you can apply attributes and alignment to the text inside your table, but, in the Table Editor, WordPerfect provides a way to attach the formatting directly to the table cells rather than to the text. In many ways, cell formatting is better because it remains constant, regardless of the amount of editing you do to the text in the cells. It also helps you avoid problems with locating codes when you want to change the format.

To apply formatting and attributes to a cell or section in your table:

Choose <u>L</u>ayout ▸ Ta<u>b</u>les ▸ <u>E</u>dit.

■ Move the cursor into the table, and press Columns/Tables (Alt+F7), choose <u>T</u>ables, and then choose <u>E</u>dit; or, press Alt+F11.

■ Choose <u>C</u>ell, Co<u>l</u>umn, <u>R</u>ow, or <u>T</u>able to open a Format dialog box with options specific to cells, columns, rows, or the whole table.

■ Check the options you want to apply to the current cell, blocked cells, column, row, or to the table, and then choose OK to accept your changes.

■ Press Exit (F7) to exit the Table Editor and return to the document editing screen.

TIP. *You can use Block (Alt+F4 or F12) to highlight a section of your table, and then choose Cell to apply formatting and attributes to all blocked cells.*

These steps outline the general procedure for applying formatting options to cells, columns, rows, and the entire table. The following sections explain in detail how to apply attributes, alignment, margins, and other options for table formatting.

Although the steps explain how to apply formatting to a cell, column, or row, you can also use Block (Alt+F4 or F12) to apply formatting to a select group of cells in your table. Simply block the cells in the Table Editor, and choose the desired options.

Applying Text Attributes

You can apply various text attributes to the cells in your document. These include attributes such as bold, italic, and underline. You cannot attach a specific font, such as Times Roman, to the table format, but you can select different fonts while typing text inside the table.

Follow these steps to apply text attributes to the table format:

Choose Layout ▸ Tables ▸ Edit.

■ Move the cursor into the table, and press Columns/Tables (Alt+F7), choose Tables, and then choose Edit; or, press Alt+F11.

■ If you want to apply attributes to a group of cells, use the Block feature to select the cells.

■ Choose Cell, Column, or Table to display a Format dialog box offering the attribute options shown in Figure 12.27.

■ Choose Appearance, and then choose one or more attributes from the list.

■ If you want to apply a relative text size to the cells, choose Size and select one of the options.

Choose OK until you return to the document screen.

■ Press Exit (F7) until you return to the document editing screen.

These steps explain how to attach attributes to a cell, a block of cells, a column, or all cells in the table. Now, when you type text within the table, the selected attributes will affect whatever text is typed in the cells. When you type text into your table, the status line will show whether text attributes are assigned to the current cell. Attribute codes applied to a table are not visible in the Reveal Codes window.

Figure 12.27

Attribute options in the Cell Format dialog box

Table cell attributes

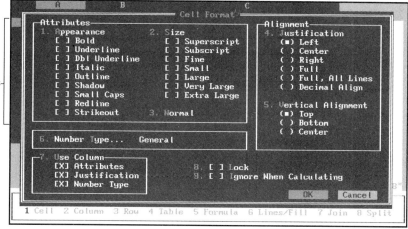

Aligning Text in Cells

An important part of the table format is the alignment of text in the cells. WordPerfect supports two types of alignment: justification and decimal alignment. *Justification* determines how text is placed between the left and right margins of a cell or document. *Decimal alignment* simply lines up a column of numbers according to the decimal points in the numbers.

You can choose justification and decimal alignment within the text you type, but it's better to include alignment as part of the table formatting. For example, assume you want to create a column of centered text. If you choose to center the text as you type it, you'll need to press Center (Shift+F6) for each cell in the column. If you decide to change the alignment later, you'll need to delete all the center codes and apply the new alignment.

If, on the other hand, you apply center alignment to the table column, everything typed in the column is automatically centered. Suppose you change your mind and want everything aligned at the left margin; simply change the alignment assigned to the column and all column text is automatically formatted to reflect the new setting.

The following steps explain how to create a table column with text centered between the left and right margins of the column.

Choose <u>L</u>ayout ▸ Ta-bles ▸ <u>E</u>dit.

- Move the cursor into the table, and press Columns/Tables (Alt+F7), choose <u>T</u>ables, and then choose <u>E</u>dit; or, press Alt+F11.

- Place the cursor in the desired column, and choose C<u>o</u>lumn to display the Column Format dialog box, shown in Figure 12.28.

Figure 12.28
The Column Format dialog box

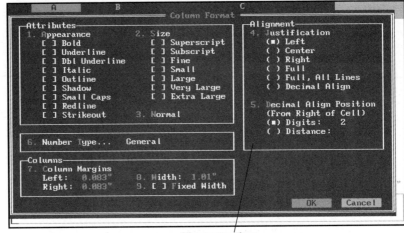

Alignment options

Choose OK until you return to the document screen.

- Choose <u>J</u>ustification, and then choose <u>C</u>enter.

- Press Exit (F7) until you return to the document editing screen.

Now, when you type text in the column, each text item is centered between the left and right sides of the column. In addition, any text already in the column is now centered. In addition, any text already in the column is now centered. Figure 12.29 shows how each of the alignment options affect the text in your table.

Figure 12.29
Alignment options for tables

Left	Center	Right	Decimal Align	Full	Full All
Jill	Flowers	Balance	10.21	Text extends to meet right and left	All text extends to meet left and right
Robert	and	Account	2930.7	margins except for lines that end with	margins even lines that end with an
Terry	Trees	Total	4.35	an[HRt]code.	[H R T] c o d e.

If you choose the Decimal Align Position option for a column, you can also specify the number of digits that will appear after the decimal point. From the Column Format dialog box,

- Choose Decimal Align Position.

- Choose Digits, and enter the number of digits that should appear after the decimal point. Or, choose Distance and enter a measurement that indicates the amount of space you want between the decimal point and the right edge of the cell.

Choose OK to return to the Table Editor.

- Press Exit (F7) to return to the Table Editor.

When you exit the Table Editor and type numbers in the column, the numbers will be aligned on the decimal points. In this example, you learned how to specify an alignment option for a whole column, but you can also apply justification to individual cells. First, move to a cell or block a group of cells. Choose Cell to display the Cell Format dialog box. Then choose an alignment option. The cell formatting options override any column formatting you've already applied to the table.

Changing the Display Type for Data

WordPerfect usually displays numbers and text exactly as you type them in your table, but it also supports different display types to allow for spreadsheet applications. For example, you can apply the Percent number type to your table, and WordPerfect will automatically display the numbers you type as percentages. Choose the Scientific type, and numbers will be displayed in scientific notation. Figure 12.30 lists the display types and shows examples of how they affect the text in your table.

To choose a different display type for a cell, a block of cells, or a column, do the following:

Choose Layout ▸ Tables ▸ Edit.

- Move the cursor into the table and press Columns/Tables (Alt+F7), choose Tables, and then choose Edit; or, press Alt+F11.

- Choose Cell, Columns, or Table to change the display format for a cell, a column, or the entire table. Or use the Block feature to highlight a section of the table and choose Cell.

- Choose Number Type to display the Number Type Formats dialog box, shown in Figure 12.31.

- Choose one of the standard formats, or choose Options and select the items you want to include in the format.

Figure 12.30
Display types for
table data

Number Type	Result in Table
General	10.75
Integer	11
Fixed	10.75
Percent	1075.00%
Currency	$10.75
Accounting	$ 10.75
Commas	10.75
Scientific	1.08e+01
Date	January 10, 1900
Text	(Numbers and characters are formatted as regular text.)

Choose OK until
you return to the
Table Editor.

Choose Close to re-
turn to the docu-
ment screen.

■ After you've selected a standard format, or created a custom format with the items in the <u>O</u>ptions group, press Exit (F7) twice to return to the Table Editor.

■ Press Exit (F7) to return to the document screen.

After you apply a number type to the cell, cell block, or column, the numbers you type will appear in that format. For example, suppose you apply the Percent number type to cell B12; when you type the number *1.5* in B12, the number appears as *10.50%*—the percent equivalent of the number you typed.

Figure 12.31

The Number Type
Formats dialog box

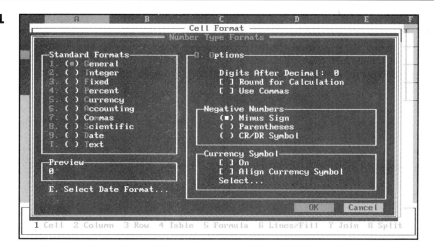

When you choose the Date number type, WordPerfect considers the number in the cell as a Julian date value, which it converts to the appropriate date. In WordPerfect, the number *1* is the Julian value for January 1, 1900. Each digit added to *1* increments the displayed date by one day. The number *2*, for example, converts to January 2, 1900. Now let's bring this example into recent calendars: The number *34303* translates to December 1, 1993, and *34606* becomes September 30, 1994.

WordPerfect uses the Julian date system so that you can include date values in calculating table formulas. Suppose, for example, you need to insert a Date Due item in a table invoice, and the due date is always 30 days from today's date. You can create a formula that adds 30 to the Julian value for today's date, and displays the correct due date in your table. Later in this chapter, you'll learn more about creating table formulas.

After you choose the Date format from the Number Type Formats dialog box, you can also choose Select Date Format to choose a predefined date format that determines how the dates will be displayed in your table.

Changing Margins within the Table

As shown in Figure 12.32, table margin spacing determines the amount of space between the cell text and the lines that divide the cells. This space is similar to the margins that you set to allow space between your document text and the edges of your page.

Figure 12.32

Margin spacing in table cells

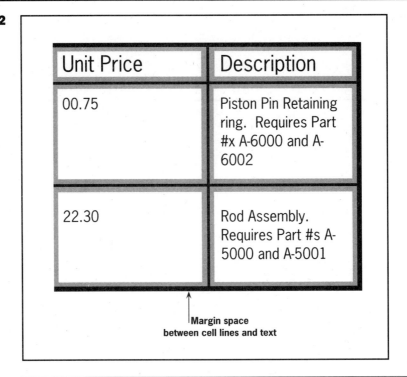

Unit Price	Description
00.75	Piston Pin Retaining ring. Requires Part #x A-6000 and A-6002
22.30	Rod Assembly. Requires Part #s A-5000 and A-5001

Margin space
between cell lines and text

You can change the table margin spacing to create more or less room between the text in the cells and the table lines. The measurements for margins are defined with the column and row format settings. You set the top and bottom spacing from the Table Row Format dialog box, and the left and right spacing is set from the Column Format dialog box.

Perform the following steps to change the spacing for the table in the PARTS.DOC document that you created earlier in this chapter. In these steps, you'll reduce the margin space to create more space for text in the cells:

Choose Layout ▸
Tables ▸ Edit.

1. Move the cursor into the table and press Columns/Tables (Alt+F7), choose Tables, and then choose Edit; or, press Alt+F11.

2. Move to cell A1, turn on Block (Alt+F4 or F12), and press Home, Home, ↓ to block the entire table.

3. Choose Column and then choose Column Margins.

4. Choose Left and enter **.05** as the left margin or gutter spacing for the cells.

5. Choose <u>R</u>ight and enter **.05** as the right margin or gutter spacing for the cells.

6. Press Exit (F7) to accept the new left/right column margins.

7. Choose <u>R</u>ow to display the Row Format dialog box.

8. Choose <u>T</u>op, and enter **.05** as the top margin or gutter spacing for the cells.

9. Choose <u>B</u>ottom, and enter **.05** as the bottom margin or gutter spacing for the cells.

10. Press Exit (F7) twice to accept the new gutter spacing and exit the Table Edit screen.

Turning Off Cell, Column, and Table Formatting

You can turn off or reset any formatting option that you've applied to cells, a cell block, a column, or the entire table. Before you do so, you need to understand some formatting rules that WordPerfect applies to table text. First, there is a certain precedence that WordPerfect follows for table formatting; you could think of it as different layers of formatting on the table cells.

At the most basic level, there is the formatting applied to the whole table from the Table Format dialog box. This affects all cells that are not formatted with a cell or column formatting option. Then, the next level is the formatting applied to specific columns from the Column Format dialog box; these options override any table formatting that is already defined. The last level is the formatting applied from the Cell Format dialog box. The cell formatting options override any column or table formatting—assuming you choose a cell format option that redefines one of the settings already specified.

To turn off the cell formatting options, redisplay the Cell Format dialog box and choose <u>N</u>ormal. This resets the formatting options to whatever is defined for the column and table settings.

To turn off the column formatting options, redisplay the Column Format dialog box and choose <u>N</u>ormal. This resets the formatting to the settings defined on the Table Format dialog box. To reset the standard WordPerfect table setting, display the Table Format dialog box and choose <u>N</u>ormal.

The order in which you turn off formatting—cell format first, then column, then table—is important because the cell and column formatting options override the format from the previous level. You may, for example, choose <u>N</u>ormal on the Column Format dialog box, but if one or more cells in the column are formatted with options on the Cell Format dialog box, these cells will keep the cell format settings.

Adjusting Row Height

As you've already seen earlier in this chapter, WordPerfect automatically adjusts the height of table rows to allow enough room for the text in the cells. The row height will change according to the number of text lines in a cell and the size of the current text font.

For some tables, you may want to keep the table rows at a consistent height. Consider the table that appears in Figure 12.33. In this case, more space is required in the bottom row to allow for handwritten comments. If your table requires spacing like this, you can assign a fixed row height to prevent WordPerfect from adjusting the height for the current text or font.

Figure 12.33

A table with fixed row height

Row with fixed row height of 2-inches

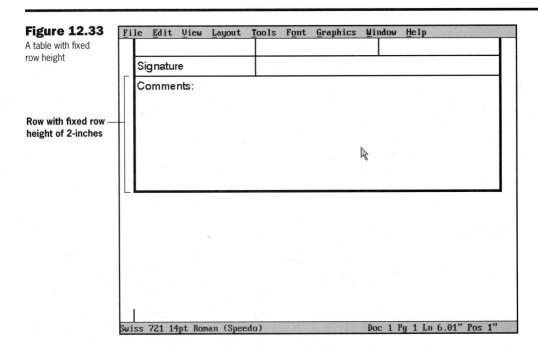

To assign a fixed row height:

Choose Layout ▶
Tables ▶ Edit.

- Move the cursor into your table and press Columns/Tables (Alt+F7), choose Tables, and then choose Edit; or, press Alt+F11.

- Use Block to select the rows you want to affect, or start at cell A1 and block the entire table as described earlier. Note that you needn't block entire rows. Instead you can just highlight a single cell in each row whose height you wish to adjust.

- Choose <u>R</u>ow to display the Row Format dialog box.

- Choose <u>F</u>ixed, and enter a measurement for the row height you want.

- Press Exit (F7) until you return to the document screen.

Choose OK until you return to the document screen.

The measurement you enter becomes the height for the selected rows, and the current margin space amount is added to the top and bottom of each row. Suppose you enter 0.5" as the fixed row height; the actual total space between the lines of a row is 0.5" plus the amount allotted for top and bottom margin space.

Remember, use a fixed row height only when you don't want WordPerfect to make automatic row height adjustments or when you want the row height to be more or less than the height of the text that will be stored inside the cells. You should exercise a certain amount of care when using this feature. If you fix a row height and then enter more text than will fit in a cell in that row, the text will not all be visible.

You can turn off a fixed row height setting by opening the Table Edit screen, selecting the affected rows, choosing <u>R</u>ow, and then choosing <u>A</u>uto.

Protecting Table Cells

Once you've created a table, you may want to protect titles, numbers, and other items from alterations entered by yourself or by another person typing information into your table. You can lock specific cells, rows, columns, or sections, which will prevent the text cursor from moving into those areas when the table is displayed in the document editing screen.

In the following example, you can follow these steps to lock the title row in the table created earlier:

Choose <u>L</u>ayout ▶ Ta<u>b</u>les ▶ <u>E</u>dit.

1. Move the cursor into your table and press Columns/Tables (Alt+F7), choose <u>T</u>ables, and then choose <u>E</u>dit; or, press Alt+F11.

2. Move the cursor to the first cell in the top row.

3. Turn on the Block feature, and press Home, → to highlight the entire row.

4. Choose <u>C</u>ell to display the Cell Format dialog box, and choose <u>L</u>ock.

5. Press Exit (F7) until you return to the document screen.

The top row is now protected and cannot be altered as long as the row remains locked. When a cell is locked, the cursor skips over it when anyone presses Tab or uses the arrow keys to move the cursor through the table; the only way to edit the information in the row is by entering the Table Editor, highlighting the locked cells, and choosing the <u>L</u>ock feature again to turn off the options and unlock the cells.

It's important to note that the Lock feature is not designed to prevent all changes to table data; notice that password protection is not included in this feature. The Lock feature simply prevents the editing cursor from moving to specific cells when information is entered or edited in the table.

Create a Header Row for Each Table Page

When your table extends across two or more pages, you may want to assign the row of column titles as a header that appears at the top of each page where the table continues. This saves you the trouble of entering new titles at the top of your columns when the table is divided by a page break.

To specify a header row,

- Open the Table Editor and move the cursor to the row where your column titles appear.

- Choose Row, and then choose Header Row so that an *X* appears in the box next to this option.

- Press Exit (F7) until you return to the document screen.

Choose OK until you return to the document screen.

You can specify only one header for your table, but it can consist of two or more consecutive rows. For example, if your column titles are in rows 2, 3, and 4, you can choose the Header Row option for each, and the text stored in these rows will appear at the top of each page where the table continues. You can't check the header option for nonconsecutive rows (for example, rows 1 and 7).

You can turn off the header row by getting into the Table Editor, moving the cursor to the current header row(s), displaying the Row Format dialog box again, and unchecking the Header Row option.

Using Math to Calculate Table Data

WordPerfect includes math capabilities that let you calculate the totals of one or more table columns. You can also create your own formulas to add, subtract, multiply, or divide the data in your table.

Suppose you have a table that lists your monthly expenses. You can create a Totals column to add up the total amount you spend each month. If you change the expense amounts in the table, you can recalculate the formulas and have an accurate list for the new figures.

WordPerfect also includes 100 spreadsheet functions to help you analyze table data and perform financial and statistical calculations. Applications for these functions are explained later in this chapter.

Applying Formulas to the Table Data

You apply formulas to table cells from the Table Editor. To create a formula, you combine references to cell addresses with numbers and mathematical operators. For example, if you want to add the value in cell A4 to the value in cell C6, you could create this formula: "A4+C6". The sum of cells A4 and C6 is displayed in the cell where you place the formula.

Table 12.3 shows the valid *operators* or symbols you can use to create a formula, and provides examples of correct formulas.

Table 12.3   **Valid Operators for Table Formulas**

Symbol	Function	Sample Formulas
+	Add	A4+C6
		G5+G6+G7+G8
–	Subtract	A4–C6
*	Multiply	C8*2
		E3*E10+2
/	Divide	B2/A9
		D11/6
()	Group	D7+(B12/5)
		F1–(F2*21)

These operators are standard math symbols. Normally, operators are calculated from left to right, but you can use the parentheses to group parts of your formula together to control the order in which things are calculated. Values enclosed in parentheses are calculated first, and then the entire formula is calculated. Consider the following equations. Although the numbers and operators are the same, the use of parentheses produces a different result in the second equation.

```
5*10-8 = 42
5*(10-8) = 10
```

Follow these steps to create a formula cell in a table:

- Move the cursor into your table and press Columns/Tables (Alt+F7), choose Tables, and then choose Edit; or, simply press Alt+F11.

Choose Layout ▶
Tables ▶ Edit.

- Move the cursor to the cell where the result of the formula should be displayed.

- Choose <u>F</u>ormula to display the dialog box shown in Figure 12.34.

Figure 12.34
Creating a formula

Creating a formula for this cell

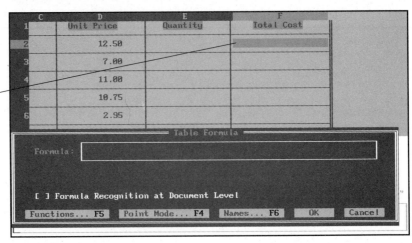

Choose OK ▶ Close.

- Type the formula for the cell and press Enter. Then, press Exit (F7) until you close the dialog box and exit the Table Editor.

    If the formula is valid, the result is displayed in the cell. Make sure not to include references to cells that are now empty, since they will be treated as zeroes. (If your result is 0, you mave have unintentionally multiplied by zero, and if you get ??, you mave have accidentally divided by zero. As you move the cursor to a cell that contains a formula, you'll see the formula displayed in the lower-left corner of the screen. Once you have entered all table data, display the Table Editor, and choose the C<u>a</u>lc option to recalculate the table formulas.

Special Totaling Functions

In the Table Formula dialog box, you can type some operators alone to calculate subtotals and totals for columns and rows. The following explains each of these functions:

Operator	Function
+	Subtotal. Displays the sum of the values in the current column.

Operator	Function
=	Total. Displays the sum of all Subtotals in the current column produced with the + operator.
*	Grand Total. Displays the sum of all Totals in the current column produced with the = operator.

Figure 12.35 shows how these functions can be used in a table. The table in this example is organized to show all the totaling functions, although it is not necessary to use them all in a single table.

Figure 12.35
Table using operators for totaling functions

The + operator was inserted in these cells as a formula

The = operator was inserted here as a formula to add the subtotals

The * operator was inserted here to add all totals in the table

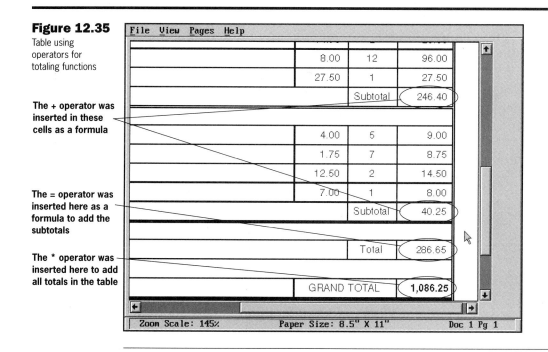

Follow these steps to insert one of these functions to create a "total" cell:

Choose Layout ▸ Tables ▸ Edit.

■ Move the cursor into your table, and press Columns/Tables (Alt+F7), choose Tables, and then choose Edit; or, press Alt+F11.

■ Move the cursor to the bottom of the column where the total should be displayed.

■ Choose Formula to display the Table Formula dialog box.

Choose OK ▸ Close.

- Type + (Subtotal), = (Total), or * (Grand Total), and press Enter. Then, press Exit (F7) to close the Table Formula dialog box.

- Press Exit (F7) to return to the document screen.

The totaling function you typed is applied to the cell where the cursor was located, and displays the current total. When the numbers change in your table, make sure you recalculate the formulas with the Calc button in the Table Editor to obtain an accurate total result.

Creating Cost and Total Formulas

The following steps explain how to create a column in your table that calculates the cost of items in an invoice and displays the total amount at the bottom of the table. This example creates the table shown in Figure 12.36. You can modify the PARTS.DOC document that you created earlier in this chapter and use it for this exercise.

Choose Layout ▸ Tables ▸ Edit.

1. Move the cursor into your table, and press Columns/Tables (Alt+F7), choose Tables, and then choose Edit; or, press Alt+F11.

Figure 12.36
Cost and total table

| File Edit View Layout Tools Font Graphics Window Help |

		Unit Price	Quantity	Total Cost
A-5000	Piston/Pin Assembly	21.50	1	21.50
A-5001	Rod Assembly. Requires Part #s A-6000 and A-6002.	22.30	2	44.60
A-5004	Starter Hub	6.00	1	6.00
A-5002	Piston Pin Retaining Ring. Requires Part #s A-5000 and A-5001	00.75	3	2.25
A-5005	Flywheel	35.70	4	142.80
			TOTAL	217.15

C:\WPDOCS\PARTS.DOC   Doc 1 Pg 1 Ln 4.94" Pos 1"

These cells contain formulas that multiply the Unit Price by the Quantity

2. Press Home, → to move to the last column on the right.

3. Press Insert and select Columns. Choose How Many?, type **2**, and press Enter. Choose After Cursor Position. Then, press Exit (F7) to continue.

4. Move to the top cell in column D (the fourth column) and enter **Quantity**. Then enter the values shown in Figure 12.37 down column D.

5. Move to the top cell of the fifth column (cell E1) and enter **Total Cost**. Then move the cursor to the last cell in the second row (cell E2) , and choose Formula (see Figure 12.37).

Figure 12.37

Creating a Total
Cost formula

This formula multiplies the contents of C2 by the contents of D2

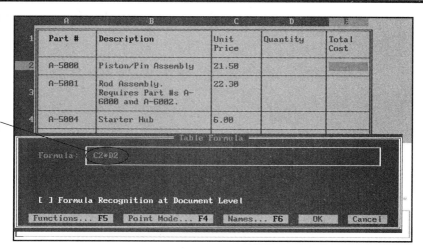

6. Type **C2*D2**, and press Enter. Then press Exit (F7) to close the Table Formula dialog box. Instead of inserting the formula for the remaining cells in the column, you will now copy the formula to each of the cells.

7. With the cursor in the formula cell, choose Move/Copy to display the Move dialog box. Choose Cell and then choose Copy.

8. Choose Down and enter **4** to indicate that you want to copy the formula down the column four times. Press Exit (F7) to copy the formula.

9. Now you will create the formula that totals the cost of all parts on the invoice. Move the cursor to the bottom of the table.

10. Choose Insert, and choose Rows. Choose How Many? and enter **1**. Choose After Cursor Position and then press Exit (F7). This inserts a new row where the total will appear.

11. Move the cursor to the cell at the bottom of the column where the total should appear.

12. Choose <u>F</u>ormula, type **+** (Subtotal) to insert the sum operator (+), press Enter, and then press Exit (F7).

13. Press Exit (F7) to exit the Table Editor and return to your document.

The first formula you created multiplies the unit price of each part by the number of parts purchased. When you copied the formula down the column, WordPerfect adjusted the cell address references to reflect each location of the formula. Figure 12.38 shows how the references were altered. Notice that the references were changed to calculate a correct result for the rows where the formulas are located.

Figure 12.38

Total formulas with adjusted cell references

	Column B	Column C	Column D	Column E	
	File Edit View Layout Tools Font Graphics Window Help				
Row 1		Unit Price	Quantity	Total Cost	
Row 2		21.50	1	21.50	C2*D2
Row 3		22.30	2	44.60	C3*D3
Row 4		6.00	1	6.00	C4*D4
Row 5		00.75	3	2.25	C5*D5
Row 6		35.70	4	142.80	C6*D6
Row 7			TOTAL	217.15	
=C2*D2			Cell E2 Doc 1 Pg 1 Ln 1.53" Pos 5.75"		

The + operator was inserted here as a formula to total the column

Recalculating Table Formulas

When you first insert a table formula, the result of the formula is calculated and displayed in the cell. If you later change the numbers in the table, you will need to recalculate the formulas. To recalculate formulas:

Choose <u>L</u>ayout ▸ Ta<u>b</u>les ▸ Ca<u>l</u>culate All.

■ Move the cursor into the table, and press Columns/Tables (Alt+F7). Choose <u>T</u>ables and then Ca<u>l</u>culate All.

WordPerfect calculates and updates the formula values. When a formula is invalid, a ?? error message appears in the cell to indicate that the formula cannot be calculated. This error will appear when the formula is not structured correctly or when the cells referenced by the formula do not contain the required information. (Remember, you'll get ?? if you attempt to divide by 0.) This error will also appear when a formula contains a *circular reference*, which occurs when the formula contains either the cell address of the same cell where the formula is located or the cell address of another cell that could alter the structure of the formula.

If the ?? message appears in one of your table cells, check the formula to make sure that it includes the correct cell references and that the structure of the formula will produce the desired calculation results.

At the document screen, you'll see each formula on the status line as you move the cursor through the table cells. (You can also see that formulas near the bottom of the screen in the Table Editor.) This will show you where the formulas are applied, and remind you not to type regular text in the formula cells. To prevent the entry of numbers where formulas are placed, you can use the Lock feature, as described earlier, to lock the formula cells.

Assigning Descriptive Cell Names

Formulas like C2*D2 and (C6-A5)*D1 make sense only when you know what the referenced cells contain. To make formulas less cryptic, WordPerfect lets you assign descriptive names to individual cells and cell blocks. Then, once names are assigned, you can use the names instead of cell references when you create your formulas. With cell names, the C2*D2 and (C6-A5)*D1 formulas might look like this:

```
Wage*Hours or (Sales-Costs)*Months
```

To assign descriptive names in your table,

- Open the Table Editor and move the cursor to the cell you want to name. Or, block the range of cells that you want to name as a complete group.

- Choose Names, and then choose Cell, Column, Row, or Table to indicate the table section you want to name. If you've blocked a series of cells, the options will be different; you can choose Block, Columns, Rows, Cells Down, or Cells Right.

- WordPerfect prompts you to enter a name. Type the name you want to assign, and then press Exit (F7) to until you return to the Table Editor.

NOTE. *If you choose Column or Row as the section to name, the cursor must be located at the beginning of the current column or row.*

WordPerfect assigns the name you enter as the name for the selected table cells. You can see a list of all defined names by choosing <u>N</u>ames from the Table Editor, and then pressing List (F5).

To create a formula with the descriptive names, choose <u>F</u>ormula from the Table Editor, and then create the formula you need; instead of cell references, type the assigned names and combine them with the formula operators. Or, insert the assigned names by pressing Names (F6) while you are defining a formula. When you're done creating the formula, press Exit (F7) until you return to the document screen.

When you create formulas with assigned names, these appear in the formula on the status line, when you move the cursor into formula cells. Assigned names do not change the result of your formulas. They simply provide a descriptive reference for rows, columns, and other cells in your table.

You can edit the assigned names by choosing the <u>N</u>ames option from the Table Editor, and then choosing the List (F5) option. WordPerfect displays the List Table Names dialog box where you can <u>E</u>dit or <u>D</u>elete any of the name references for the current table.

From this dialog box, you can also choose <u>L</u>ist All Names in Document to view the assigned names for all tables in the current document. You can use this option to create formulas that reference data from the cells in other tables.

Working with Negative Numbers

When the formulas in your table produce negative results, WordPerfect displays the numbers with a minus sign. If your method of accounting requires negative numbers to be shown in parentheses, you can change the way WordPerfect displays negative values:

Choose <u>L</u>ayout ▸ Ta<u>b</u>les ▸ <u>E</u>dit.

- Move the cursor into your table and press Columns/Tables (Alt+F7), choose <u>T</u>ables, and then choose <u>E</u>dit; or, press Alt+F11.

- Choose <u>T</u>able and then choose Number <u>T</u>ype to display the dialog box shown in Figure 12.39.

- Choose <u>O</u>ptions, and then choose <u>P</u>arentheses to indicate that negative numbers should be displayed in parentheses.

- Press Exit (F7) to return to the document screen.

This option affects only negative results calculated by a formula. If you type a negative number into the table, the number appears exactly as you typed it, even after you recalculate the formulas in the table.

Figure 12.39

The Negative number options

Negative number options

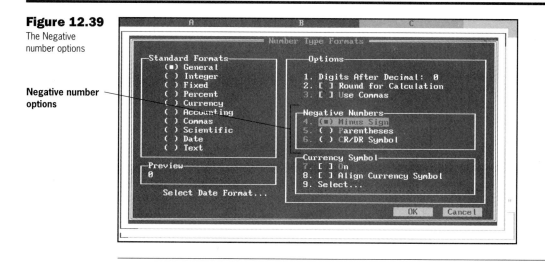

Working with Spreadsheet Files

You can use the Tables feature to retrieve spreadsheet information into your WordPerfect document from programs like Lotus 1-2-3, Excel, and Quattro Pro. There are two ways to incorporate spreadsheet files into your document: You can retrieve the information from a spreadsheet file, or you can create a link to the spreadsheet file. When you retrieve or link a spreadsheet file, you have the choice of displaying the information as a WordPerfect table or as a set of tabular columns.

When you retrieve a spreadsheet file, simply copies the spreadsheet information into your document. When you create a spreadsheet link, WordPerfect forms a connection between your document file and the specified spreadsheet. Then, whenever you retrieve your document, WordPerfect updates your text with the latest information from the linked spreadsheet file.

The first part of this section explains how to retrieve a spreadsheet file. The second part of this section explains how to create a dynamic link between your document and a spreadsheet file.

Retrieving a Spreadsheet File into Your Document

The following steps explain how to retrieve or *import* a spreadsheet file into your document. This method simply copies the spreadsheet information into a WordPerfect table or a set of tabular columns. Once retrieved, the spreadsheet information will not change unless you manually edit the data.

Choose Tools ▸
Spreadsheet ▸ Import.

■ Press Columns/Tables (Alt+F7) and choose Spreadsheet. Then choose Import. WordPerfect displays the dialog box in Figure 12.40.

Figure 12.40

Specifying a
spreadsheet to
retrieve

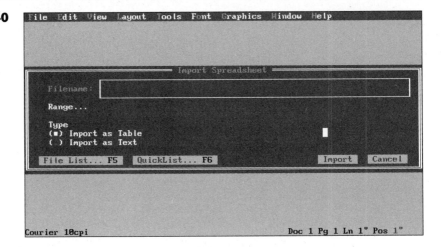

■ In the Filename box, type the name of the spreadsheet file that you want to retrieve. Or, press File List (F5) and select the file from a directory list of files. After you specify the name, press Enter to accept it.

■ WordPerfect displays the full dimensions of the spreadsheet file next to the Range option. If you don't want to import the entire spreadsheet, choose Range and enter the range dimensions, or press Range List (F5) to select from a list of the names you've assigned to the spreadsheet ranges.

■ Choose Type and choose Import as Table or Import as Text to indicate how you want the spreadsheet information to appear in your document.

■ Choose Import to copy the information from the spreadsheet file into your document.

After the spreadsheet is copied, WordPerfect displays it as a table or as tabular text. If your spreadsheet extends across several columns, there may not be enough room across the page to hold the entire spreadsheet. When this happens, WordPerfect simply cuts off the spreadsheet table at the point where it reaches the right margin setting.

When your spreadsheet doesn't fit on the page, there are s few things you can do to fix the problem. First, try changing your margin settings to allow for more space on the page. If this isn't enough to fit your spreadsheet across the page, press Format (Shift+F8), select Page, and then choose the Paper Size/Type feature and select a paper size with Landscape orientation; this tells WordPerfect to print the text sideways on the paper, which allows more room for several columns. If you still don't have enough room, change to a smaller font to allow more text to fit across the page.

Creating a Linked Spreadsheet Table

The following steps explain how to create a link between your document file and a spreadsheet file. The result will be similar to importing a spreadsheet file, except that WordPerfect will update your document with the latest information from the spreadsheet file each time you retrieve your document.

To create a spreadsheet link,

Choose Tools ▸
Spreadsheet ▸
Create Link.

■ Press Columns/Tables (Alt+F7), choose Spreadsheet, and then choose Create Link. WordPerfect displays the dialog box in Figure 12.41.

Figure 12.41
Linking a
spreadsheet file

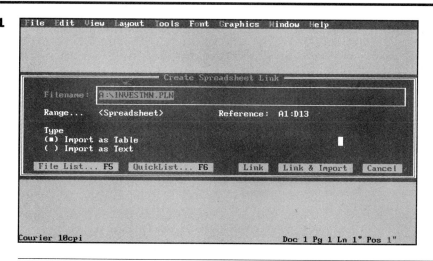

■ In the "Filename" box, type the name of the spreadsheet file that you want to link. Or, press File List (F5) and select the file from a directory list of files. After you specify the name, press Enter to accept it.

■ WordPerfect displays the full dimensions of the spreadsheet file next to the Range option. If you don't want to link the entire spreadsheet, choose Range and specify the range from the cell that you want to link to your document.

- Choose Type and choose Import as Table or Import as Text to indicate how you want the spreadsheet information to appear in your document.

- Choose Link & Import to copy the spreadsheet information into your document and establish a link to the file.

After the spreadsheet information is imported, WordPerfect displays it in your document between two comment boxes—the first comment indicates where the linked data begins, and the second comment marks the end of the linked data. When you choose Link, instead of Link and Import, WordPerfect simply displays the comment boxes without copying the data; in this case, you'll need to choose the Link Options feature from the Columns/Tables dialog box or the Spreadsheet submenu and choose Update All Links to show the spreadsheet information in your document.

The Spreadsheet submenu or Columns/Tables dialog box also include other options that let you manage the links in your document. Press Columns/Tables (Alt+F7) and choose Spreadsheet, or choose Tools/Spreadsheet, to view the options. Edit Link lets you change the spreadsheet file name or cell range that you've specified for the current link. Link Options, which you just used, lets you specify that you want WordPerfect to automatically update the spreadsheet links when you retrieve your document. This option also lets you manually update the spreadsheet links when you've made changes during the current WordPerfect session.

Creating a Floating Table Cell

The Floating Table Cell feature lets you display a number within your document text, which is calculated according to formulas that you specify. Floating table cells can also display information from a table within a document paragraph, like the example shown in Figure 12.42.

Suppose one of your document paragraphs makes reference to a number in one of your tables; instead of typing the number manually, you can insert a floating table cell that displays the number from the table. Then, as changes are made to the table information, the new numbers are updated within your document text. To display a table value in a floating cell, you must first assign names to the appropriate table cells; this is explained earlier in this chapter, under "Assigning Descriptive Cell Names."

To create a floating table cell,

- Name the cell or cells in the table to which you want to be able to refer. For example, if you want to refer to cell A1 of your table, you could name that cell "FIRST."

Figure 12.42

Floating cells display
information from
tables

**Floating cells display
values from a table**

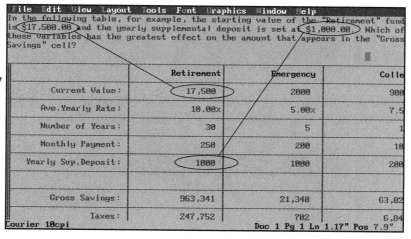

- Move the cursor to the place in your document text where the floating
  cell should appear. You may need to type some additional text to create
  a reference for the number.

Choose Layout ▸
Tables ▸ Create
Floating Cell.

- Press Columns/Tables (Alt+F7), choose Floating Cell, and then choose
  Create. WordPerfect displays the dialog box shown in Figure 12.43.

Figure 12.43

Creating a floating
table cell

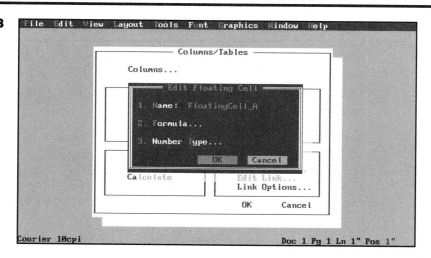

- WordPerfect suggests a name for the floating cell. If you want to change it, choose <u>N</u>ame and enter a different name for the floating cell.

- Choose Number <u>T</u>ype and specify a format for the display of the number or value in your document. Press F7 to exit the dialog box.

- Choose <u>F</u>ormula and press Names (F6) to choose an assigned name; this indicates that you want to display a value from one of your document tables. For example, if you wanted to refer to cell A1, which you had names "FIRST,'" you could choose Table_A.FIRST from the list, and choose <u>Se</u>lect. If you haven't named the reference, use the cell label as the extension. For example, to refer to cell A1, enter Table_A.A1 as the formula. (Note that your table might be named something other than Table_A.) You can also choose <u>F</u>ormula and enter a formula to create a value.

Choose OK until you return to the document screen.

- Press Exit (F7) as many times as necessary to accept the floating cell definition and return to your document.

If you entered a valid formula the result of the calculation will appear in your document at the cursor position. If you selected an assigned name from one of your tables, the value from that table appears. Turn on the Reveal Codes window and you'll see two codes, [Flt Cell Begin] and [Flt Cell End], around each value inserted by the Floating Cell feature. If you make changes to numbers referenced by the floating cells, you need to press Columns/Tables (Alt+F7), choose <u>T</u>ables, and choose <u>C</u>alculate All. Or simply choose <u>L</u>ayout, <u>T</u>ables, and then <u>C</u>alculate All from the menu system. This recalculates all table formulas references, including any floating cells that you've inserted into your document text.

13

Preparing Legal Documents

THIS CHAPTER EXPLAINS THE WORDPERFECT TOOLS THAT CAN HELP YOU create legal briefs, documents, and contracts. Legal documents, in particular, have specific requirements for numbering sections, paragraphs, and lines. WordPerfect includes tools to address these and other needs of the legal profession. Some of these tools, like WordPerfect's Table of Authorities feature, are exclusive to legal documents. Others, like Document Comparison, are also useful for preparing manuscripts, books, and scholastic papers.

Some of the applications in this chapter include the use of paragraph numbering and outlining, which are discussed in depth in Chapter 11.

Section and Paragraph Numbering

Most legal documents require reference numbers before each article, section, or paragraph. Using the Outline feature, you can create various types of legal numbering for your documents. The Outline feature ensures that the sections and paragraphs remain numbered consecutively, even if you change the order of the paragraphs in your document. In some cases, you can also create legal numbering systems with the Styles feature, which is covered in Chapter 22.

Numbered Sections

Figure 13.1 shows a type of section numbering common in legal documents. Using WordPerfect's Outline feature, you can make a document style that creates the legal numbering for your section titles.

Choose Tools ▸ Outline ▸ Outline Style.

1. Press Outline (Ctrl+F5), choose Outline Style, and then choose Create.

2. In the Create Outline Style dialog box that appears, enter the name for your outline style. In this case, enter **SECTION** and press Enter. Then press F7 or click on OK to begin creating the new outline style.

3. If you like, choose Description and enter a description for your new outline style.

4. Next, choose Number Format and then select Legal from the list that appears. You are simply going to make minor modifications to the existing Legal numbering style. (Notice the legal-style numbers that now appear under the Numbers option.)

5. Select Level Style; Level 1 should become highlighted automatically. Now select Edit; you're going to alter the first level of numbering so that it includes boldfacing, as well as the section symbol(§) in front of the paragraph numbering.

Figure 13.1
Section numbering
in a legal document

§ 117. Defenses

Any matter that is germane to a cause of action to enforce a committee enactment and that asserts legal reason why the plaintiff should not succeed therein may constitute defense. It is a good defense that the enactment under which complaint is made is unconstitutional or invalid, as applied to the defendant's property. In order to plead this defense, the defendant must have exhausted the administrative remedies available to him under the enactment.

§ 118. Petition for Review

The defendant may petition the proper court to review a committee enactment by writ of mandate, with additional time not exceeding a number of days, specified by the court, but in no event later than a designated number of days after entry of order.

§ 119. Negligence

In an act based on negligence, the plaintiff may recover for suffering or mental anguish, in addition to damages recovered for physical injuries or loss of property. Emotional distress, in the absence of physical injury, is not a compensable injury unless such distress results in physical illness or injury.

6. In the Edit Style dialog box, select Style Contents, noting that the left-most code in the list, [Para Num], is now highlighted.

7. Press F6 to insert a [Bold On] code.

8. Press Ctrl+W to display the WordPerfect Characters dialog box; it's from here that you're going to retrieve the section symbol.

9. Press Tab and then choose Set to display a list of available character sets. Choose Typographic Symbols.

Double-clicking on § inserts it into the Style contents window.

10. Choose Characters, and then use the arrow keys or click with your mouse to highlight the section (§) symbol.

11. Press Enter or click on Insert to insert the section symbol into the Style Contents window.

12. Press the spacebar to insert a space between the section symbol and the paragraph numbering code.

13. Finally, press the Right Arrow key until you highlight the [Lft Indent] code, and type a period to follow the paragraph number.

14. Press F7 to return to the document screen. At this point, you can initiate the type of section numbering shown in Figure 13.1 by pressing Outline (Ctrl+F5), choosing Begin New Outline, highlighting the SECTION style, and choosing Select.

Numbered Sections and Paragraphs

Figure 13.2 shows another example of section numbering that also includes legal numbers after each section title *and* before each paragraph in the document. WordPerfect's predefined Legal Outline style can insert the legal paragraph numbers, but it can't create the numbering that appears after the section title text. Because of this, you'll need to create and use another custom outline style.

Try the following steps to produce an outline style capable of creating the document shown in the figure.

Choose Tools ▸ Outline ▸ Outline Style.

Choose OK to continue.

1. Press Outline (Ctrl+F5), choose Outline Style, and then choose Create.

2. At the "Outline Style Name" prompt, type **LEGAL NEW** and press Enter.

3. Press Exit (F7) to continue, and the dialog box shown in Figure 13.3 appears.

4. Choose Number Format, and then choose Legal.

5. Choose Level Style, highlight the "Level 1" entry if it's not already highlighted, and choose Edit.

6. From the Edit Style dialog box, choose Description and type **Section Title Number**. Then press Enter.

7. Choose Style Contents to display the formatting codes for the section title numbering, shown in Figure 13.4.

8. Highlight the [Para Num] code. Then press Shift+F6 to insert a [Cntr on Mar] code, and type **SECTION**. Press spacebar to insert a space between the "SECTION" title and the paragraph number. Then highlight and delete the [Lft Indent] code.

9. Press Exit (F7) until you return to the Outline Style List dialog box.

10. Highlight the "LEGAL NEW" style if necessary and choose Select.

Figure 13.2

Legal numbering for section titles and paragraphs

SECTION 1

1.1   Independent Contractor. Both the Employer and the Consultant agree that the Consultant will act as an independent contractor in the performance of duties specified under this contract.

    1.1.1   Place Where Services Will Be Rendered. The Consultant will secure the facilities and equipment required to accomplish the services in accordance with this agreement.

SECTION 2

2.1   Terms of Agreement. This agreement will begin on September 1st, 1993, and will end pursuant to the conditions set forth in Section 3 and Section 9 of this agreement. Either party may cancel this agreement on or before September 15th, 1993, with written notice to the other party by certified mail or personal delivery.

SECTION 3

3.1   Consultation Services. The Employer hereby employs the Consultant to perform the following services in accordance with the terms and conditions set forth in this agreement:

    3.1.1   Marketing and Research. Subject to the supervision and pursuant to the advice and direction of the Employer, the Consultant agrees to design and administer research studies to determine profit-loss projections for new products.

    3.1.2   Place Where Services Will Be Rendered. The Consultant will secure the facilities and equipment required to accomplish the services in accordance with this agreement.

SECTION 4

4.1   Confidential Information. The Consultant agrees that any information received by the Consultant during any furtherance of the Consultant's obligations in accordance with this contract, which concerns the personal, financial, or other affairs of the Employer will be treated by the Consultant in full confidence and will not be revealed to any other persons, firms, or organizations.

Figure 13.3

Creating a style for section and paragraph numbering

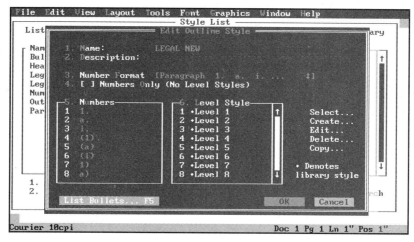

Figure 13.4

Editing the style codes

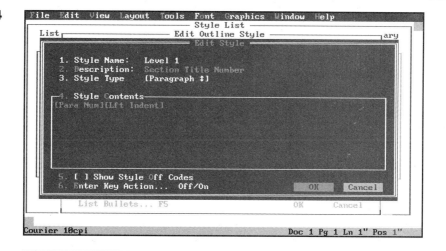

You've just created an outline style, called LEGAL NEW, that defines the format for combined section and paragraph legal numbering. In WordPerfect's predefined Legal outline style, the paragraph numbers are automatically positioned at the left margin. The custom style you created allows the first-level number to be placed after each centered section title.

Follow these steps to create a document with the new style:

Choose Tools ▸ Outline ▸ Begin New Outline.

1. Press Outline (Ctrl+F5) and choose Begin New Outline.

2. From the Outline Style List dialog box that appears, highlight LEGAL NEW and choose <u>S</u>elect. This inserts the centered text "SECTION 1" into your document at the cursor position.

3. At this point you'd hope to be able to press Enter to begin inserting additional numbering into your document. Unfortunately, WordPerfect won't move on to the next number unless you have entered at least one character on the current line. (Instead it inserts a space above the current line. As you may remember from Chapter 11, this also occurs if the cursor is at the very beginning of the current line, just after the automatic paragraph number.) To get around this problem, you can type either a period or a space, and then press Enter. This will insert the text "SECTION 2" into your document.

4. Then you need to press Tab to move to the next numbering level. In this instance, pressing Tab changes "SECTION 2" to 1.1, and you can proceed to enter your text from there. (This may seem somewhat counterintuitive, since pressing Tab moves you to the *left* in this case; just remember that you're moving down to the next numbering level.)

5. To get to the third numbering level (1.1.1 in Figure 13.2), merely press Enter and then press Tab. Then, to return to the first numbering level and create SECTION 2, press Enter and then press Shift+Tab twice to move back up through the numbering hierarchy.

Using these techniques and the LEGAL NEW outline style you just created, you could reproduce the document shown in Figure 13.2, or you could generate similar legal documents of your own.

Line Numbering for Contracts

Figure 13.5 shows the format for line numbering in contracts, pleading papers, and other documents where references are cited by text lines rather than by section or paragraph numbers. Although WordPerfect does include a Line Numbering feature, this feature alone does not create the line-numbering format for legal documents. Fortunately, WordPerfect includes an alternate keyboard layout with a legal line-numbering style.

Using the Line Numbering Style

The legal line-numbering style (called the *Pleading* style) creates double-spaced line numbers separated from the text by vertical lines. The following steps explain how you can apply this style to your document:

Choose <u>F</u>ile ▸ Setup ▸ <u>K</u>eyboard Layout.

■ Press Setup (Shift+F1) and choose <u>K</u>eyboard Layout.

Figure 13.5

The logic of legal numbering

1	The Holder shall have the optional right to declare the amount of the
2	total unpaid balance hereto be due and forthwith payable in advance of the
3	maturity date of any sum due or installment, as fixed herein, upon the failure
4	of the undersigned to pay, when due and after thirty (30) days that same is
5	due, any of the default or failure to perform in accordance with any of the
6	terms and conditions in the Mortgage securing this Note or in any other
7	security document executed and/or delivered in conjunction herewith.
8	
9	Upon exercise of this option by the Holder, the entire unpaid principal
10	shall bear interest at the highest rate allowed by law. Forbearance to exercise
11	this option with respect to any failure or breach of the undersigned shall not
12	constitute a waiver of the rights to any continuing failure or breach or any
13	subsequent failure or breach.
14	
15	
16	
17	
18	
19	
20	
21	
22	
23	
24	
25	
26	
27	
28	

- Highlight the MACROS keyboard name and choose <u>S</u>elect. Then press F7 or choose <u>C</u>lose to return to the document screen. (Incidentally, alternate keyboard layouts are covered in depth in Chapter 25.)

- Press Alt+P to display the dialog shown in Figure 13.6.

Figure 13.6
The Create Pleading Paper dialog box

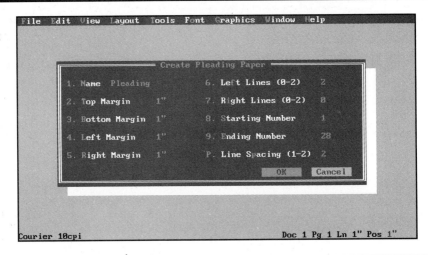

- Enter the desired settings for the pleading paper name, margins, and line settings.

- Press Exit (F7) to accept the settings and WordPerfect creates the pleading-paper format.

Although you can't see any change to your screen, even in page display mode, you'll notice that if you type the text is automatically double-spaced. In addition, if you switch to the Print Preview display, you'll be able to see the pleading paper's line numbers and vertical lines.

The Pleading Paper feature begins legal line numbering at the point where you selected the feature. The default settings specify double-spaced numbers at the left of the 1-inch margin, and vertical lines are inserted to divide the numbers from the text. If your document extends beyond one page, line numbering is reset to start at *1* with each new page.

Tools for Revising Contracts

The Comment and Redline/Strikeout features can help you notate changes in your contracts and other legal documents. The Comment feature creates notes or reminders that appear when your document is on the screen, but remain hidden when the document is printed. During the revision of contracts, you can apply the Redline and Strikeout attributes to show changes made to the document. The following sections explain how to use these tools.

Inserting Document Comments

Lawyers and paralegals often place comments in documents as reminders to verify information in the text. For example, you can insert a note that reminds you to do additional research, check a specific figure, or record related information. You can insert these comments anywhere in the main document text; they appear on the WordPerfect screen, but not in the printed document. (They also do not appear in page display mode or on the print preview screen.) Figure 13.7 shows an on-screen document with comments inserted in the text. Follow these steps to insert a comment into your document:

Figure 13.7
Helpful reminders in an on-screen document

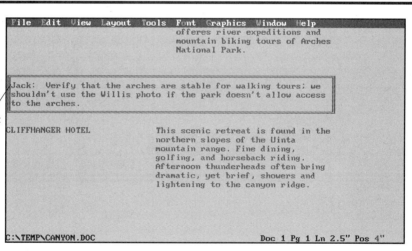

Comment in the text

- Move the cursor to the place where the comment should be located.

Choose Layout ▶ Comment ▶ Create.

- Press Notes (Ctrl+F7), choose Comment, and then choose Create.

- Type the text for the comment; when you are finished, press Exit (F7) to return to your document.

The comment text is inserted into a box within the document. The comment will not change the format of your document, although it may appear to do so on the screen. Turn on Reveal Codes, and you'll see something like this in the Reveal Codes window:

```
{   ▲   ▲   ▲   ▲   ▲   ▲   ▲   ▲   ▲   ▲   ▲   }   ▲
offeres river expeditions and[SRt]
mountain biking tours of Arches[SRt]
National Park.[Bookmark][THCol]
[Col Def][Comment][HRt]
CLIFFHANGER HOTEL[Lft Indent][Lft Indent][Lft Indent]This scenic retreat is foun
d in the[SRt]
northern slopes of the Uinta[SRt]
mountain range. Fine dining,[SRt]
C:\TEMP\CANYON.DOC                                    Doc 1 Pg 1 Ln 2.33" Pos 1"
```

When comments are displayed on your screen, it may seem that your document format is slightly off kilter. If, for example, the cursor is located just past the [Comment] code, the cursor appears indented from the left margin, although it is not. (This phenomenon won't occur if you always place comments on a line of their own.) The Reveal Codes window will verify this. Be careful: If you press Backspace to delete the apparent indentation, WordPerfect will delete the comment. Just keep in mind that these strange line breaks won't occur when you print.

If the visible change in format is too difficult to navigate, try turning off the display of document comments. This is done from the Setup Display menu:

Choose View ▸
Screen Setup.

- Press Screen (Ctrl+F3) and then press Setup (Shift+F1).

- Choose Window Options, and then choose Display Comments, so that the check box is empty.

- Press Exit (F7) or choose OK until you return to the document screen.

When you turn off the display of comments, they are still located where you placed them, but are hidden from view. Since this is a WordPerfect setup option, comments will remain hidden for all documents you retrieve into WordPerfect. To display comments again, simply reselect the Comments Display option as described in the previous steps. Also remember that you can temporarily hide comments from view by switching to page display mode.

Using the Redline and Strikeout Attributes

The Redline and Strikeout attributes are commonly used to indicate additions and deletions to the document text. Figure 13.8 shows examples of these attributes in a printed document. According to standard practice, redlined text indicates additions to the document and strikeout text indicates deletions. Generally, you won't want these to appear in the final document, but they can help you see what you have changed during the revision process. Follow these steps to apply one of these attributes to a section of text:

Choose F<u>o</u>nt ▸
<u>S</u>trikeout or <u>R</u>edline.

- Use Block (Alt+F4) to highlight the text you want to mark as redlined or strikeout.

- Press Font (Ctrl+F8) and choose <u>A</u>ppearance, and then choose <u>S</u>trikeout. Or choose <u>R</u>edline to mark additional text.

Figure 13.8

Strikeout and
Redline attributes in
action

> § 1. Petition for Review
>   The defendant may petition the proper court to review a committee enactment by writ of mandate, with additional time not exceeding a number of days, ~~specified by the attorney,~~ specified by the court, but in no event later than a designated number of days after entry of order.

You may want to save a backup copy of the marked document to keep track of the changes you've made. Then, when you are ready to print the final version of your document, you can clean up the text by pressing Mark (Alt+F5), or choose <u>F</u>ile/Compare <u>D</u>ocuments from the menu bar. Then choose <u>R</u>emove Markings. At this point, you'll see a dialog box with two options: The first is Remove Redline Marks and Strikeout, and the second is Remove Strikeout Text Only. The first option deletes all strikeout text from your document and removes the redline attributes, retaining the text between the redline codes. The second option merely deletes all strikeout text, without removing the redline codes. In the next section, you'll see how redline and strikeout attributes are used to compare the differences between two documents.

Comparing Two Documents

As you create your documents, you will probably make several changes, deletions, and additions to the text. Some legal documents evolve over a period of time. Most contracts are simply model documents that are revised to suit the needs of individual clients.

The Document Compare feature can compare two versions of a document and show the differences between them. This is very useful when you need to see how a colleague has changed a draft of your contract or how much you've changed it yourself.

Comparing the Documents

WordPerfect can compare a document displayed on your screen with a document that is stored in a disk file. Generally, the file on disk is the original version of the document, and the on-screen document is the most recent revision. You can choose from four different levels or types of document comparison: paragraphs, sentences, phrases, or words.

The Document Compare feature will change the text in the on-screen document to note the differences between that document and another document stored on disk. For this reason, you should save the on-screen document *before* performing a comparison to ensure that you can retrieve the unchanged document, if necessary. If the on-screen document has the same file name as the document you're comparing from disk, make sure you specify a different file name when saving the on-screen document. Follow these steps to compare the document on your screen with a document file stored on disk:

Choose File ▸ Compare Documents ▸ Add Markings.

■ Press Mark (Alt+F5), and choose Add Mar<u>k</u>ings under Compare Documents to display the dialog box shown in Figure 13.9.

Figure 13.9

The Compare Documents dialog box

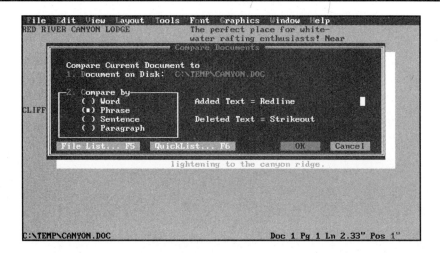

■ In the "Document on Disk" field, enter the name of document file with which you want to compare the on-screen document and press Enter.

■ Choose the <u>C</u>ompare by option, and then select <u>P</u>aragraph, <u>S</u>entence, Ph<u>r</u>ase, or <u>W</u>ord.

■ Choose OK to begin the comparison.

When WordPerfect has finished the comparison, the on-screen document is altered to show the differences between the two documents. Strikeout text indicates text that has been deleted from the original document on disk. Redlined text indicates text that has been added since the original file was created.

The type of comparison you choose—whether paragraph, sentence, phrase, or word—depends on the amount of detail you want for the comparison. The Paragraph option compares only entire paragraphs in the document; this is the fastest method of document comparison. If any part of a paragraph has been altered from the original document, the complete paragraph is inserted as redlined or strikeout text in the on-screen document; the result is a duplicate paragraph at each place where a change was made. Depending on the change, WordPerfect applies the Redline or Strikeout attribute to entire paragraphs. Since the entire paragraph is copied as changed text, it can be difficult to see exactly what has changed.

The Phrase and Sentence options compare document text phrase-by-phrase or sentence-by-sentence. A phrase is defined as a string of text separated by any form of punctuation, including commas, semicolons, colons, and any sentence punctuation. A sentence is defined as a string of text between two periods, exclamation points, or question marks. These options narrow the comparison in terms of individual phrases and sentences. Like the Paragraph option, WordPerfect will copy complete phrases or sentences as altered text, when even one word has changed. In each case the Redline or Strikeout attribute is applied to the entire sentence, depending on the type of change.

When you choose the Word option, WordPerfect compares each word between the two documents and marks the differences in the on-screen document. This is the most accurate form of comparison, but it also requires the most time to perform.

Restoring a Document after a Comparison

When a document comparison is completed, you can restore your on-screen document to its original state before the comparison was performed. To remove the redline and strikeout markings inserted by the Document Compare feature, press Mark (Alt+F5), and choose Remove Markings. From the Remove Markings dialog box that appears, you can then choose to remove both the redline markings and the strikeout text, or just the strikeout text.

If you choose the first option, text marked as strikeout text is removed from the on-screen document, and if redline attributes exist to mark new text, these attributes are removed. If you choose the second option, just the strikeout text is removed from your document. Be careful when using these options; keep in mind that *all* strikeout text and redline attributes will be removed from your document—even those not inserted by the Document Compare feature. For this reason, you may wish to make a backup copy of the marked file before removing the strikeout and redline attributes. However, if you act quickly, you can undo either action with the Undo feature (Ctrl+Z).

Creating a Table of Authorities

Legislative documents and legal briefs often include a list of statutes, citations, legislative provisions, and precedent cases. This list is called a *table of authorities*, and it serves as a type of index to help the reader find information in your document.

A table of authorities can be divided into sections to cite different types of information. For example, a table of authorities can have one section that lists statutes, one that lists citations, and another that lists cases. You can organize your table with up to 16 different sections, and each can have a unique format.

To create a table of authorities, you follow this general procedure (detailed steps are provided in the next section):

■ Identify the different types of information you want listed in the table to determine the number of sections required.

■ Define the place where the table should appear in your document. At this point, you will also define the structure of the table of authorities. This includes defining the format for each section you want to include in the table.

■ Mark the text in your document that you want listed in the table of authorities. Each marked item should be assigned to one of the sections in the table.

■ Generate the table.

This may seem like a lot of work for a mere index of information, but creating a table of authorities offers some important advantages. First, all items in the completed table are alphabetized within each section, and WordPerfect automatically inserts references to the page numbers where the items are found. Second, once defined, a table of authorities is easy to maintain; you can move or edit text in your document and it takes only a moment to generate an updated table.

The following sections outline each of the steps for creating a table of authorities. In this instance, you must adhere to the order of the following sections to successfully complete the entire process.

Organizing and Defining the Table Sections

The first step in creating a table of authorities is identifying the types of information you want cited in the table sections. For example, one section of the table could list all cases noted in the text, and other sections could list statutes, regulations, and other legislative material. Once you've determined which types of sections you need, you're ready to define the table as described here. You'll start by typing titles for the table of authorities and for the first section in the table.

TIP. *If the table should begin on a new page, insert a hard page break (Ctrl+Enter) when the cursor is located where the table should begin.*

- Move the cursor to the place in your document where the table of authorities should appear. Tables of authorities are usually located just after the cover pages of the document, but before the main body of document text.

Choose Layout ▸ Alignment ▸ Center.

- Press Center (Shift+F6) and type **TABLE OF AUTHORITIES**. Press Enter a few times to add space beneath the title.

- Type a title for the first section in the table. If you wish, you can apply attributes, such as bold or underline, to the text. Press Enter twice to add a blank line beneath the title.

Choose Tools ▸ Table of Authorities ▸ Define.

- Press Mark (Alt+F5) and choose Define. Then choose Table of Authorities.

- Choose Create, and the dialog box shown in Figure 13.10 appears.

Figure 13.10
Define Table of Authorities dialog box

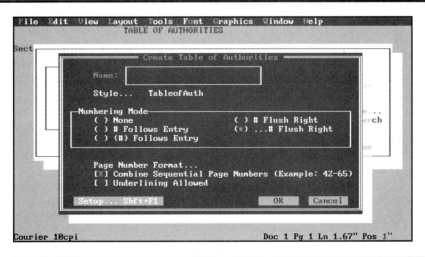

- At the "Name" prompt, type a name for the section you are now defining, and press Enter. You can, for example, type **Section I** and press Enter.

- Choose the formatting you desire from the options in the dialog box. The choices you make here affect only the section that you are now defining.

- Press F7 to accept the definition and return to the previous dialog box.

- Choose <u>S</u>elect to select the highlighted style and return to the document screen.

- Repeat the preceding steps to define each table section you want to create.

From the Define Table of Authorities dialog box, you can choose from among various options to create the format for a section in the table.

TIP. *Your preferences for Underlining Allowed and Combine Sequential Page Numbers can be specified as part of WordPerfect's default program settings. To specify your preferences, press Setup (Shift+F1) from the Edit Table of Authorities dialog box. Make the desired changes, and press Exit (F7) to save the new settings.*

The Numbering Mode options specify how the page numbers appear after each entry in the table, and whether a line of dots extends from each item to its page number reference. The <u>U</u>nderlining Allowed option allows underlining codes from the document text to be carried into the table, when the table is generated.

When you have defined each section of the table of authorities, you should insert a hard page break to start a new page. Otherwise, the main document text will immediately follow your table. Then insert a New Page Number code to start the regular page numbering for your document as described below. This is especially important when the table of authorities text extends beyond two or more pages. Follow these steps to complete the table definition:

- With the cursor located after the Table of Authorities Definition codes, press Ctrl+Enter to insert a hard page break.

- Press Format (Shift+F8), choose <u>P</u>age, and then choose Page <u>N</u>umbering to display the dialog box shown in Figure 13.11.

- Choose Page <u>N</u>umber, choose New <u>N</u>umber, type **1**, and press Enter. Then, press Exit (F7) until you return to the document.

Choose <u>L</u>ayout ▸ <u>P</u>age ▸ Page Numbering.

Figure 13.11
Page Numbering
dialog box

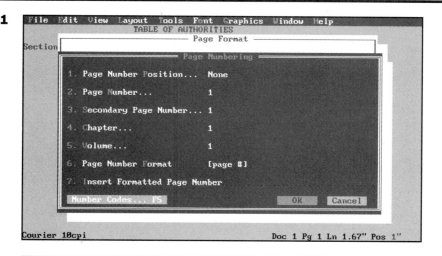

Marking Authority References

When you finish defining the table of authorities, you're ready to mark the text items that should appear in the table. You can mark any document text, except for the text stored in headers or footers. When you mark the first occurrence of an authority, it is assigned a full form and a short form. *Full form* is the complete text for an item as it appears in the document. The full form authority can include up to 30 lines of text. When you edit the text, you can apply text attributes such as bold, italic, and underline. *Short form* is an abbreviated version that you provide as a convenience for duplicate references in the document. The short form text must be unique for each item in the table of authorities. For this reason, it is often best to accept the unique abbreviation suggested by WordPerfect for each item you mark. Perform the following to mark each item in your text that should appear as a reference in your table of authorities:

- Use the Block (Alt+F4 or F12) feature to highlight a section of text that you want to mark for the table.

- Press Mark (Alt+F5), and then choose Table of Authorities.

Choose Tools ▸
Table of Authorities
▸ Mark Full.

- Choose Section Name, and the section name where the highlighted text should appear in the table. If you don't remember the section names, choose List Sections (F5) to see a list of the sections you defined earlier for the table.

- Edit the text, if necessary (choose Edit Full Form to display an editing screen where you can edit the marked text as you want it to appear in the table). Press F7 to exit.

After the Short Form option, WordPerfect suggests a short form or abbreviation for the text item. You can choose the Short Form option to create your own short form text, or press Exit (F7) or choose OK to accept the options and continue. A [ToA:*n*;*text*;Full Form] code is inserted into your document, where *n* represents the table of authorities' section name you assigned to the reference, and *text* is the text that will appear in the table.

After you first mark an item for the table of authorities, you'll need to mark any duplicate items that appear elsewhere in the document.

- Move the cursor to the beginning of your document.

- Press Extended Search (Home+F2).

Choose Edit ▶ Search. Then choose Extended Search.

- In the Search For box, type a few of the words that begin the item you just marked.

- Press Search (F2) and the cursor should stop at the first duplicate reference, if one exists.

- Use Block (Alt+F4 or F12) to highlight the reference text.

- Press Mark (Alt+F5), choose Table of Authorities, and then choose Short Form.

Choose Tools ▶ Table of Authorities, and select Mark Short.

- WordPerfect displays the short form for the last full form item you marked. Choose Short Form, type a unique abbreviation in the Short Form box, and then press Exit (F7).

Repeat these steps for each item you want to mark for the table; after marking each new item, search for duplicate references and mark them with the short form abbreviation. If you perform the search and a "Not Found" message appears, this probably means there are no other duplicate references for the item you marked. If you suspect there may be more, perform the search again, being careful to type the correct text to match items you want to find.

Generating the Table of Authorities

When all text items are marked in your document, you can generate the table of authorities. This is the easiest step in the entire process. Press Mark (Alt+F5) and choose Generate. Or, simply choose Tools, Generate, and then choose OK.

WordPerfect compiles all the marked entries and places them in the table sections you defined. Page numbers are inserted after each item to indicate where the reference is found in the document.

If asterisks are inserted instead of page numbers, some short form markings do not have unique abbreviations, or a short form marking is not associated with one of the full form markings. If an error message occurs when you generate the table, check each of the short form markings to verify that are associated with one of the full form markings and that they have unique abbreviations.

Editing the Table References

When you first mark a full form reference, WordPerfect allows you to edit the text that will be displayed in the table. This lets you condense the text for references that include too much information. When you generate a table of authorities, the text you typed or edited in the full form window is the text that appears in the table—remember, this may be an edited or abbreviated version of the text you highlighted when you marked the reference.

When you revise your document, you may need to update the references for the table of authorities. Editing the document text alone does not automatically update the table of authority references. You must update these references yourself from the full form editing window. Follow these steps to edit the text stored in a full form reference:

Choose View ▶
Reveal Codes

Choose Tools ▶
Table of Authorities
▶ Edit Full ▶ Full
Form.

- Choose Reveal Codes (Alt+F3 or F11).

- Move the cursor to the right of the [ToA:;;Full Form] code you want to edit. If the cursor is not located to the right of the [ToA:;;Full Form] code, WordPerfect will look for a previous code and display its text for editing.

- Choose Mark (Alt+F5) select Mark Text, choose Edit ToA Full Form, and select Full Form.

- The Full Form editing screen appears with the text from the [ToA:;;Full Form] code. Make the desired changes to the text.

- When you finish editing the full form text, press Exit (F7) until you return to the document screen.

Repeat these steps for other references that you want to edit. When you are finished, you need to generate the table of authorities again, as described earlier, to create an updated table.

Spell-Checking Legal Documents

The WordPerfect Speller recognizes most terms common to the legal profession; however, you may encounter a few words—specifically, the names of individuals and businesses—that the Speller will highlight because it does not recognize them. When this happens, choose the Speller's Add to Dictionary option to insert names and legal terms into a special supplemental Speller file. When you check the document again or check other documents that have the terms you've added, the Speller will recognize the new terms. You should add only words that arise frequently in your documents or clients' documents. Also, make sure the words are spelled correctly when you add them.

To see how this works, do the following from a clean WordPerfect document screen:

1. Type **The Board appoints Terry Bulloche as the primary designee for corporate expansion in East Asia**.

Choose Tools ▶
Writing Tools ▶
Speller.

2. Press Speller (Ctrl+F2) to display the Speller dialog box.

3. Choose Document. After a moment, the Speller highlights the name "Bulloche."

4. Choose Add to Dictionary to add the name to the supplemental dictionary.

5. The Speller highlights the word "designee." Choose Add to Dictionary to add this word to your supplemental dictionary.

6. When the spell-check is completed, choose OK to close the dialog box and return to your document.

Spell-check the document again, and the Speller will recognize the name and term you added. The new terms are placed in a file called WP{WP}US-.SUP, which is stored in the same directory where your Speller files are stored.

If you have a long list of new terms you want to add, you can retrieve the WP{WP}US.SUP file into WordPerfect and manually type the terms into the list. You can also edit or remove terms that are already in the list. Save the file, and you've updated your list of terms without running the Speller for every document where the new terms might be found. See Chapter 8 for complete information about the WordPerfect Speller.

14

Page Numbering, Tables of Contents, and Indexes

Page Numbering for Documents Large and Small

Creating a Table of Contents

Creating an Index

L ARGE DOCUMENTS OFTEN EMPLOY PAGE NUMBERING, A TABLE OF contents, and an index to help readers find what they're looking for. Some documents also include lists of illustrations, photographs, and data tables to reference the visual or graphic elements in the document. This chapter covers the features you use for referencing the pages in a document.

WordPerfect's Page Numbering feature can number each document page. You can insert page numbers as standard Arabic numerals, Roman numerals, or letters. You can choose to number the entire document from the first page to the last, or you can mix different numbering styles and restart page numbering with each chapter or section.

After setting the page numbers, you can use the Generate feature to reference the pages in a table of contents, an index, and other types of lists. Use these features individually, or combine them to create a fully referenced document.

When you generate a table of contents, index, or list, WordPerfect automatically inserts formatting and page number references. This creates an accurate document and saves you a great deal of time—no more flipping through document pages, noting where each item is found, and then compiling your notes into an organized list. Updating your document is easy; make whatever changes you need, and then choose the Generate feature. WordPerfect compiles a new table of contents, index, or list with the text from your latest revision.

Page Numbering for Documents Large and Small

Page numbering is simple to do and helps the reader navigate through your document. In addition to various page numbering schemes, you can define custom page numbering styles that include regular text or header information. Here is the general procedure for adding page numbers to your document:

Choose Layout ▸ Page ▸ Page Numbering.

■ Move the cursor to the place in your document where page numbers should begin appearing on the pages.

■ Press Format (Shift+F8), choose Page, and then choose Page Numbering.

■ Choose Page Number Position to display the dialog box shown in Figure 14.1.

■ Choose one of the Page Number Position options (1 through 8) to indicate where the page number should print on each page. The diagram at the right edge of the dialog box shows the position of each option.

Choose OK until you return to the document screen.

■ Press F7 until you return to the document screen.

Choose File ▸ Print ▸ Print Preview.

■ Press Print (Shift+F7) and then choose Print Preview to see the page numbers.

Figure 14.1

Choosing a position for page numbers

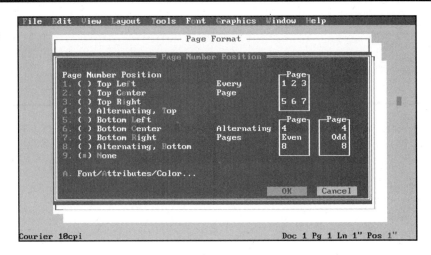

If you're working in text display mode, you won't see the page numbers on the document editing screen, but you can see them on the Print Preview screen. You see page numbers on the document editing screen only when you're using page display mode. Press Screen (Ctrl+F3), and then choose Page to use this display mode.

If you plan to include a title page, table of contents, or other introductory pages in your document, you may want to combine Roman and Arabic numbering, as described later in this section. Whatever method you choose, you should set up the page numbering in your document *before* you create a table of contents, index, or list. This is important because the table of contents, index, and lists will display the page numbering that is active when these items are generated. If you change the style of page numbering after these items are created, you'll need to regenerate your document to update the page number references.

The following sections explain how to add page numbering to your document, select a location for page numbers, and define the page numbering style. You'll also see how to create a custom page numbering style with text from your document.

Adding Page Numbering to Your Document

When you turn on the Page Numbering feature, you must select a location for the page numbers on the pages. The Page Number Position option actually turns on the page numbering in your document. Figure 14.2 shows where each page number position option inserts page numbering.

Figure 14.2
Possible positions
for page numbers

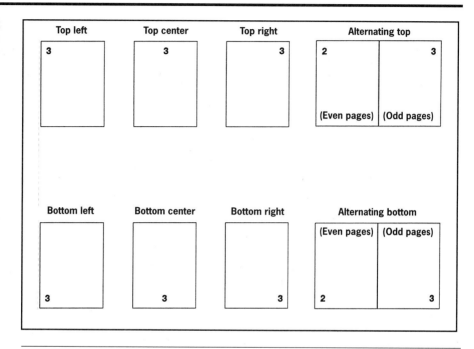

WordPerfect can insert the page numbers at any corner of the page, center page numbers at the top or bottom, or alternate them between the right corner (odd-numbered pages) and left corner (even-numbered pages). The alternating page numbers (options 4 and 8) are designed for documents that are printed on both sides of the paper.

Follow these steps to add page numbers at the lower-right corner of each page in your document:

Choose L̲ayout ▸
P̲age ▸ Page
N̲umbering.

1. Move the cursor to the beginning of your document.

2. Press Format (Shift+F8), choose P̲age, and then choose Page N̲umbering.

3. Choose Page Number P̲osition.

4. Choose Bottom R̲ight to indicate that page numbers should appear at the lower-right corner of each page.

5. Press F7 until you return to the document screen.

Choose OK until
you return to the
document screen.

A [Pg Num Pos] code is inserted at the top of the current page, as shown in Figure 14.3, to indicate where the page numbering begins. Page numbering continues from this point forward until the document ends or you discontinue the page numbering, as explained under "Turning Off Page Numbering," later in this chapter.

Figure 14.3
The [Pg Num Pos] code shown in Reveal Codes

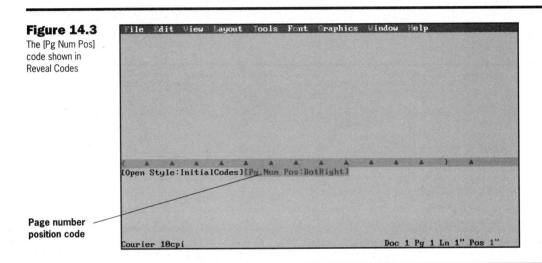

Page number position code

Each page number reserves an entire line across the top or bottom of the page, and you cannot type text on this line. If you want to insert a page number in text, type the text and press Format (Shift+F8). Choose Page, and then choose Page Numbering. Choose Insert Formatted Page Number. This inserts a [Formatted Pg Num] code into your document text, which will cause the correct page number to be displayed with your text. You can insert a [Formatted Pg Num] code anywhere in your document, including headers, footers, footnotes, endnotes, and other document text.

Applying Fonts, Attributes, and Colors to Page Numbers

When you choose a position for the page numbers, you can also apply a specific font, attribute, or text color to the page numbers. These options are accessed through the Page Number Position dialog box. After choosing the page number position, follow these steps to apply attributes and color to the page number text:

- In the Page Number Position dialog box, choose Font/Attributes/Color. This displays the Font dialog box shown in Figure 14.4.

- Choose the font and attributes you want to apply to all page numbers. Press F7 as many times as needed to accept your selections and return to the document screen.

Figure 14.4

Choosing attributes
for page numbers

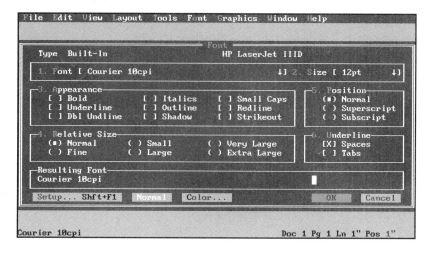

The font and attributes you choose are applied to all page numbers in the
document. Note that the effects of color options do appear on the screen; if
you have a color printer, these also appear on the printed pages. If you want
to mix attributes in a document—for example, print blue page numbers for
one section and green for another—you'll need to insert a new page number
position code at each place where the attribute changes should occur. You
don't need to specify the position each time, only the text attributes.

Starting Page Numbering with a Specific Number

When page numbering is turned on, the printed page numbers reflect the
numbers that appear after the "Pg" label on the WordPerfect status line.
Sometimes, you'll want the printed page numbers to differ from the actual
number of physical pages in your document. For example, suppose the first
page in your document is a title page, on which a page number is not usually
required. To avoid having a page number print on the title page, you might
try moving the cursor to page 2 and then turning on page numbering. However, the first page number does not appear as page number 1 but as page 2,
because page numbering is starting on the second page in your document.

For this situation, WordPerfect provides a method of forcing the page
numbering to begin at a number less than or greater than the number of the
current physical page in your document. Follow these steps to ensure a beginning value of 1 when you want page numbering to start on the second page in
your document:

1. Move the cursor to the second page in your document.

Choose Layout ▸
Page ▸ Page
Numbering.

2. Press Format (Shift+F8), choose Page, and then choose Page Numbering.

3. Choose Page Number Position, choose one of the position options, and then press F7 to return to the Page Numbering dialog box.

4. Choose Page Number and then choose Decrement Number to specify a starting value that is one less than the current page number.

This tells WordPerfect to start numbering on page 2, but to display numbers that are one less than the physical number of the pages. Thus, the second page displays as *page 1*, the third page displays as *page 2*, the fourth page displays as *page 3*, and so on. Instead of Decrement Number, you can choose Increment Number to specify page numbers that are one number greater than the physical pages in the document.

The Decrement Number and Increment Number options work well when you want to start page numbering with a number that is one value greater or less than the number of the physical page. However, if you add or delete pages before the Page Number code, the Decrement Number and Increment Number options cannot compensate for the change in physical pages. You cannot, for example, set the Decrement Number option to display a number that is three less than the physical page number—only one.

For this reason, WordPerfect also provides a way to start page numbering with a specific number—1 for example—regardless of where page numbering begins in your document. Follow these steps to start page numbering with a specific number:

■ Move the cursor to the page where page numbering should begin.

■ Press Format (Shift+F8), choose Page, and then choose Page Numbering.

Choose Layout ▸
Page ▸ Page
Numbering.

■ Choose Page Number Position, select one of the position options, and then press F7.

■ Choose Page Number, choose New Number, and then enter the number you want to have appear as the starting value for the page numbering.

■ Press F7 until you return to your document.

From this point forward, page numbering begins with the value you entered. This procedure is also useful for large documents divided between two or more files; you can continue page numbering at the beginning of each file with the number that follows the last page number in the previous file. When you change the page number values as described here, the status line will show page numbers according to the page number values you've entered. If your cursor is located on the third page in your document and the value for this page is reset to 1, the status line will show 1— not 3—after the "Pg" label.

Combining Different Page Number Styles

Figure 14.5 shows a method of page numbering common to many documents. In this example, the first page is a title page on which no page number appears. The next few pages contain a preface, revision notes, acknowledgments, and a table of contents; these pages are numbered with lowercase Roman numerals. Then, the main text pages are numbered with standard Arabic numerals (1, 2, 3, and so on). This mixture of page number styles provides visual clues for the reader about the document sections.

Figure 14.5
Mixing Roman and Arabic page number styles in a document

No page numbers

Roman page numbers

Arabic page numbers

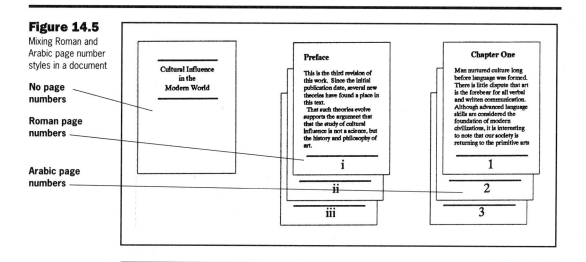

To combine numbering styles for a similar document, follow this procedure:

- Move the cursor to the first page after the title page.

Choose Layout ▸ Page ▸ Page Numbering.

- Press Format (Shift+F8), choose Page, and then choose Page Numbering.

- Choose Page Number Position, choose one of the position options, and then press F7.

- Choose Page Number. Choose New Number, type **1**, and press Enter.

- Choose Numbering Method, choose Lower Roman, and then press F7 until you return to your document.

- Move the cursor to the page that begins the first chapter or main text of your document.

Choose Layout ▸ Page ▸ Page Numbering.

- Press Format (Shift+F8), choose Page, and then choose Page Numbering.

- Choose Page Number. Choose New Number, type **1**, and press Enter.

- Choose Numbering Method and then choose Numbers. Then press F7 until you return to the document editing screen.

When you print or display a preview of your document, you'll see that the numbers change at the pages where you selected a different numbering style. In the above procedure, you also reset the numbering to 1 when you chose a different numbering style. This ensures that page numbers start with the number 1 at each of the sections in the document.

This is only one example of how you can mix different number styles within one document. The combinations you choose depend on the organization and format of your document. Occasionally you may want all document pages to be numbered the same, except for the first page, which should have a number centered at the bottom of the page. You can specify this type of format using WordPerfect's Suppress feature. First, turn on page numbering for the entire document. Then perform the following steps:

- Move the cursor to the title page or cover sheet on which the page number should appear centered at the bottom.

Choose Layout ▶ Page, and choose Suppress.

- Press Format (Shift+F8), choose Page, and then choose Suppress.

- Choose the last option, Print Page Number at Bottom Center.

- Press F7 until you return to your document.

The number of the current page will be printed centered at the bottom of the page. This affects only the current page; the numbers of the following pages will be printed as specified for all document pages.

Creating a Page Number Format

The standard style for page numbers is simply Arabic numerals without punctuation or text. You can change the numbering style to uppercase or lowercase Roman numerals, or to uppercase or lowercase letters and you can include any punctuation or text as part of the format. One example of this is creating a page number style in which the word "page" precedes the actual number; none of the predefined page numbering styles includes labels like this, but you can create a new style that does. To create a new page number style, you combine Page Number codes, such as [page #] or [chpt #], with the text and punctuation that you want to have displayed with the numbers.

Try the next example to change the page number style to Roman numerals and edit the page number format to include text and punctuation:

Choose Layout ▶ Page ▶ Page Numbering.

1. Move the cursor to the top of the page on which you want the new page number format to take affect.

2. Press Format (Shift+F8), choose Page, and then choose Page Numbering.

3. Choose Page Number <u>P</u>osition. Choose <u>P</u>age Number Position, and select Bottom <u>R</u>ight. Then press F7.

4. Choose Page <u>N</u>umber, choose Numbering <u>M</u>ethod, and select Upper <u>R</u>oman. Then press F7.

5. Choose Page Number <u>F</u>ormat; at this point your screen will resemble Figure 14.6.

Figure 14.6

Editing the page number format

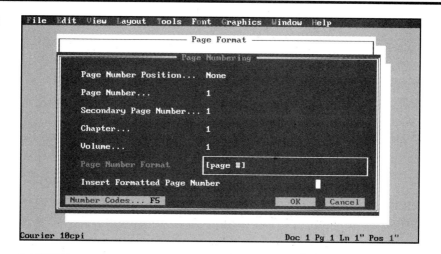

■ Type **Fall of the Roman Empire, p.** and press Enter to accept the new format. Then press F7 until you return to your document.

After performing these steps, the page numbers in your document appear as "Fall of the Roman Empire, p. *n*", where *n* is the current page number in the Roman numeral style.

In addition to adding text to page number formats, you can include chapter numbers, secondary page numbers, and volume numbers. First you access the Page Numbering dialog box (press Shift+F8, choose <u>P</u>age, and then choose Page <u>N</u>umbering). From here, enter a secondary page number, chapter number, or volume number (all of these options are set to 1 by default). Then select Page Number <u>F</u>ormat, press F5 or click on Number Format, and select a code type from the Page Number Codes dialog box that appears. Table 14.1 shows examples of other page number formats you can create. To do so, simply choose the Page Number <u>F</u>ormat option as described above, type the punctuation and text shown in the table, and insert the appropriate page, chapter, or volume codes from the Page Number Codes list. When you choose OK, a [Pg Num Fmt] code is inserted into your document, which changes the format of page numbering in your document from that point forward. This new page number format will continue until you change the format again or until you discontinue the page numbering on a later page.

Table 14.1   **Page Number Formats Supported by WordPerfect**

Page Number in Text	Page Number Format
Page 1	Page [page #]
Chapter 1, Page 1	Chapter [chpt #], Page [page #]
Volume 1, p: 1.1	Volume [vol#], p: [chpt #] • [page #]
Volume1, Chapter 1, Page I-1	Volume [vol #], Chapter [chpt #], Page [page #], [scndy pg#]

Page Numbering for Sections and Chapters

Large documents often have page numbers that indicate the individual chapters, sections, or even volumes of text. For these types of page numbers, WordPerfect supports different levels of page numbering. One example of this is two-level page numbering in which each page number starts with the current chapter number and is followed by the number of the page within that chapter. Pages in Chapter 1 would be numbered 1-1, 1-2, 1-3, and so on, and the first three pages in Chapter 2 would be numbered 2-1, 2-2, and 2-3.

To create this style of page numbering, you must change the page numbering format to include codes for the two numbering levels: one for the chapters and one for the pages. Then you need to reset the page number value at the beginning of each section or chapter. Retrieve a practice document and try these steps:

1. Move the cursor to top of the page where the first chapter in your document begins.

Choose Layout ▸ Page ▸ Page Numbering. Then choose Page Number Format.

2. Press Format (Shift+F8) and choose <u>P</u>age. Choose Page <u>N</u>umbering and then choose Page Number <u>F</u>ormat.

3. Press Delete to End of Line (Ctrl+End) to delete the current Page Number format.

4. Choose Number Codes (F5) to display a list of Page Number codes.

5. Choose <u>C</u>hapter Number from the list.

6. Type a hyphen (-) or a period as the separating punctuation between the chapter number and the page number.

7. Choose Number Codes (F5) again, and choose Page Number. Then press Enter to accept the format. The page number format codes should now read [chapt #][-][page #].

8. Choose Page Number Position to display the Page Number Position dialog box.

9. Choose Bottom Right from the Page Number Position list, and then press F7 to accept the position and return to the Page Numbering dialog box.

That takes care of the page numbering format and the position of page numbers. Now you need to specify a page number value at the beginning of each chapter. The cursor should still be located at the beginning of the first chapter.

1. In the Page Numbering dialog box, choose Chapter, and then choose New Number. Type the chapter number (**1** in this case) and press Enter. Press F7 to continue.

2. Choose Page Number, and then choose New Number. If necessary, type **1** as the starting page number for the chapter, and press Enter. Press F7 to continue.

3. Move the cursor to the beginning of each chapter in your document, and repeat the previous steps to set up both the chapter numbers and the page number values.

4. When you are finished, press F7 until all dialog boxes are closed and you return to your document.

Make sure you type the number for the current chapter in your document, instead of the number 1, and make sure to reset the page numbering to 1 at the start of each chapter. When you are finished, you'll have a [Pg Num Set] code at the beginning of each chapter. These codes instruct WordPerfect to restart numbering with the current chapter number, beginning with page 1. The result is something like this:

Chapter	Page Numbers	Final Page Number (n)
Chapter 1	1-1, 1-2, 1-3...	1-n
Chapter 2	2-1, 2-2, 2-3...	2-n
Chapter 3	3-1, 3-2, 3-3...	3-n
Chapter 4	4-1, 4-2, 4-3...	4-n

If your document is one volume in a series of volumes, you can modify the page number format to include three levels of page numbering: one level for each volume, chapter, and page number. When you create the page number format, simply add the Volume code [vol #] before the codes for Chapter and Page. Move the cursor to the beginning of your document. Press Format (Shift+F8), choose Page, and then Page Numbering. Then select Volume, New Number, and enter the number of the volume. If your document chapters are divided between two or more files, simply retrieve each file and follow the previous steps to reset the page number values at the beginning of each chapter.

NOTE. *In Chapter 15, "Working with Large Documents," you'll see how to create sequential page numbers for documents that are split between files.*

Forcing a Page to an Odd or Even Page Number

If you are printing your document on both sides of the paper, you may want each new section to begin on an odd or even page. For example, suppose you're creating a report with 12 chapters. You want the title page for each chapter to appear on the righthand side (on an odd-numbered page) when the report is printed and bound. You can use WordPerfect's Force Odd/Even feature to insert at the start of each chapter a special code which monitors the location of the current page.

In this example, if the title page text falls on an odd page, nothing is done. If, however, the text falls on an even page, the Force Odd/Even code tells WordPerfect to insert a page break to force the text to the next odd page. When you use the Force Odd/Even feature, you can specify whether Word-Perfect should force the text to an odd or even page. Here is the general procedure for doing so:

- Move the cursor to the page that you want to force to an odd or an even page.

Choose Layout ▸ Page ▸ Force Page.

- Press Format (Shift+F8) and choose Page. Then choose Force Page.

- Choose Odd to force the current text to an odd page, or choose Even to force it to an even page.

- Press F7 until you return to your document.

There are two additional options under Force Page: New and None. Choose New when you want to begin on the next page, almost as if you were starting a new document from within the current document. The page break inserted by this option will force the current text to either an odd or an even page number. Choose None when you want to turn off the effect of the Force Odd/Even feature.

Creating a "Page *x* of *y*" Document Header

A popular style of page numbering shows "Page *x* of *y*," where *x* represents the number of the current document page and *y* represents the total number of pages. This form of numbering is particularly helpful because it shows the relation of the current page to the total number of document pages, and can alert the reader to possible missing pages at the end of the document.

In the following steps, you'll see how to create this style of numbering. You'll begin by creating a WordPerfect document header that includes a Page Number code. (A header is simply a line of text that will appear at the top of every page in your document. You'll learn more about headers in the next chapter.) You'll complete the header by creating a cross-reference to the last page number in the document. This involves two steps: first, you'll insert a *reference* code in the header representing the number of the last page; second, you'll insert a *target* code at the end of document to mark the last page.

Follow these steps to create the page numbering header described here:

1. Move the cursor to the top of the first page on which page numbering should begin.

Choose Layout ▸
Header/Footer/
Watermark.

2. Press Format (Shift+F8), and choose Header/Footer/Watermark.

3. Choose Headers, and then choose Header A, Create.

4. Type **Fall of the Roman Empire**. Press Flush Right (Alt+F6) and type **page of** . Type two extra spaces between the *page* and *of*, and one space after *of*. Then move the cursor between the words *page* and *of*.

5. Press Format (Shift+F8), choose Page, and then choose Page Numbering.

Choose Layout ▸
Page ▸ Page
Numbering.

6. Choose Insert Formatted Page Number.

7. Press End to move the cursor to the end of the line.

8. Press Mark (Alt+F5) and choose Cross Reference.

Choose Tools ▸
Cross-Reference ▸
Reference.

9. From the list under Tie Reference To, choose Page as the type of cross-reference, if necessary.

10. Choose Target Name, type **END of DOCUMENT**, and press Enter. Then press F7 to continue.

11. Choose Exit (F7) to accept the header and return to the document screen.

12. Press Home, Home, ↓ to move the cursor to the end of the document.

Choose Tools ▸
Cross-Reference ▸
Reference.

13. Press Mark (Alt+F5), choose Mark Text, and then choose Cross-Reference Target.

Choose Tools ▶
Generate.

14. Press Enter to accept the "END of DOCUMENT" target name.

15. Press Mark (Alt+F5) and choose Generate. Press F7 at the prompt to complete the procedure.

WordPerfect checks the page number where the "END of DOCU-MENT" Target code is found. This number is displayed at the location of the Reference code you placed in the header after the word *of*. The result, which can be seen in the Print Preview screen (press Shift+F7 and choose Print Pre-view to see the Header), appears as shown in Figure 14.7.

Figure 14.7

Viewing a header
with page numbering

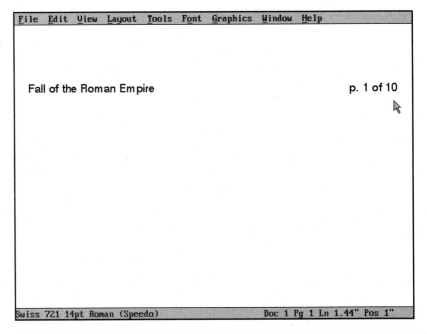

This type of page numbering involves a variety of WordPerfect features, so let's review what you've done. You first created a document header with the text that should appear at the top of each page in your document; in-cluded in the header is the text you need to create the "page *x* of *y*" format. You manually inserted a Page Number code after *page*. This Page Number code instructs WordPerfect to display the current page number of each page in the document on which the header appears. You completed the header by inserting a Cross-Reference code that will display the total number of pages in the document. You inserted the Target code that relays the number of the last page to the Cross-Reference code in the header. Finally, you chose the

Generate feature to generate the correct page number references for the codes you inserted in the header and at the end of the document.

If you choose to number your pages as described above, make sure the "END of DOCUMENT" code remains at the end of the document when you revise the text. If the Target code is moved to another page, your "page *x* of *y*" message will not show the correct page total for your document. In addition, if you revise the text such that page numbers are added or deleted, make sure to regenerate the document (choose Generate from the Tools menu or from the Mark dialog box). Otherwise the total number of pages will be innaccurate.

Turning Off Page Numbering

You can turn off page numbering if you do not want the numbers to continue through the remainder of your document. For example, when a label, envelope page, or other form appears at the end of the document, page numbering should not continue on the extra page(s).

NOTE. *The following steps do not turn off page numbering when the Page Number codes are included in headers or footers.*

To turn off page numbering in your document, follow these steps:

- Move the cursor to the top of the page where the page numbering should stop.

Choose Layout ▸ Page ▸ Page Numbering.

- Press Format (Shift+F8), choose Page, and then choose Page Numbering.

- Choose Page Number Position and choose None.

- Press F7 until you return to your document.

Sometimes your document may include a page in the middle of the document—such as a chart, diagram, or table—that should not be numbered with the rest of the document pages. WordPerfect's Suppress feature lets you hide the number for an individual page, but continue numbering on the page that follows. Follow these steps to hide a page number:

- Move the cursor to the page on which a page number should not appear.

Choose Layout ▸ Page ▸ Suppress.

- Press Format (Shift+F8), choose Page, and then choose Suppress to display the Suppress (This Page Only) dialog box.

- Choose Page Numbering, and then press F7 until you return to your document.

When you view or print the document, the page number does not appear, but it is still counted with the other pages in the document. If, for example, you suppress page numbering on page 3, no number appears on this page, but the following page will appear as page 4. If you want page numbering to ignore a page entirely (not number it and not count it), you need to suppress page numbering as just described. Then with the cursor on the following page, press Format (Shift+F8), choose Page, and then choose Page Numbering. Choose Page Number, New Number, and enter the number on which page numbering should continue. Then press F7 until you return to the document screen.

Creating a Table of Contents

Figure 14.8 shows a table of contents in a WordPerfect document. Notice that the first-level headings are the main titles in the document; subheadings are listed beneath the main titles wherever applicable. A table of contents can include up to five levels of headings and subheadings. You can also choose between various styles of formatting.

Figure 14.8

A table of contents with headings and subheadings

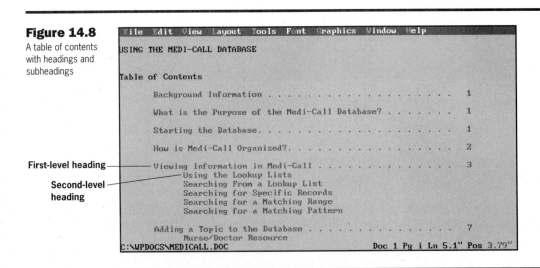

Once your page numbers are in place, you can create a table of contents that lists the headings in your document. Although the results of each type of list is different in your document, the procedure for creating tables of contents, indexes, and lists is quite similar. The general steps are described here; detailed steps are explained in later sections.

- Define the location and layout for your table of contents.

- Mark the text in your document that you want included in the table of contents.

■ Generate the table of contents.

Before you define a table of contents, you must know how many levels of headings you want to include in the table. For example, your document may have two or more different heading levels, but your table of contents need not include all of them.

Defining a Table of Contents

The first task in creating a table of contents is defining its location and format in your document.

Follow these steps to define the location and format of your table of contents:

■ Move the cursor to the place in your document where the table of contents should begin. Press Hard Page Break (Ctrl+Enter) to start a new page.

Choose Tools ▸
Table of Contents ▸
Define.

■ Type **TABLE OF CONTENTS** or another descriptive title for this page. Press Enter a few times to insert blank lines beneath the title.

■ Press Mark (Alt+F5), choose Define, and then choose Table of Contents. The dialog box shown in Figure 14.9 appears.

Figure 14.9

Defining a table of contents

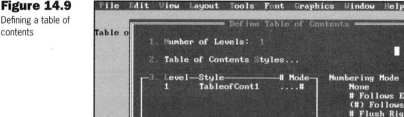
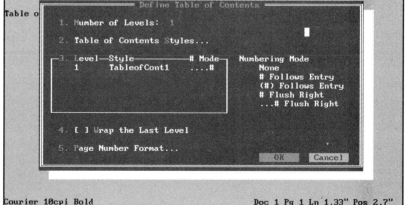

■ Choose Number of Levels, and enter the number of levels you want. If, for example, your table of contents will show main headings and the headings under them, you would type **2** to indicate two levels.

■ Choose Table of Contents <u>S</u>tyles, and the dialog box shown in Figure 14.10 appears.

Figure 14.10

Choosing styles for a table of contents

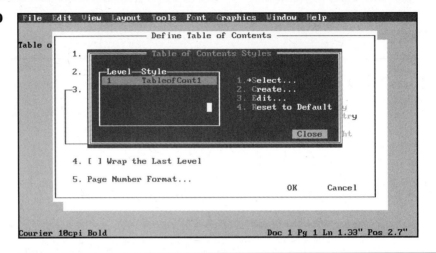

■ Highlight the first level noted in the list, and choose <u>S</u>elect to select a format style for that level.

Double-click on the highlighted style to select it.

■ A list of table of contents styles appears on the screen. Scroll through the list to highlight the style you want to use. Press Enter to select the highlighted style.

■ If your table of contents has more than one level, highlight each one, and choose <u>S</u>elect to select a style for each level.

■ When you are finished selecting styles for each level, press F7 until you return to the document screen.

■ If necessary, press Hard Page Break (Crtl+Enter) again to place a hard page break after the table of contents definition. This will keep the table separate from the main document text.

When you are finished defining the table, you'll have a page with a "Table of Contents" title and a single code, [Def Mark], which can be viewed with the Reveal Codes (Alt+F3 or F12) feature. At this point, you won't see any table of contents text, because this information is compiled when the table of contents is generated. Later in this chapter, you'll learn how to do this.

The styles you selected determine how each level in the table is formatted. Table 14.2 shows examples of the common table of contents styles. Now you're ready to perform the next task in the table of contents process: marking the headings that should appear in the table.

The list of table of contents levels lets you change the style of of page numbering that follows each table of contents entry. To change the numbering style (or mode), choose <u>L</u>evels from the Define Table of Contents dialog box. Then, highlight each level and choose one of the numbering options to indicate how the page numbers should appear after all entries from the highlighted level. Table 14.2 shows how each numbering option affects the table of contents.

Table 14.2 **Formatting Styles for Tables of Contents**

Numbering Mode	Example		
N<u>o</u>ne	Swiss Watchmakers		
# <u>F</u>ollows Entry	Swiss Watchmakers	27	
(#) Follows Entry	Swiss Watchmakers	(27)	
# Flush <u>R</u>ight	Swiss Watchmakers		27
. . .# <u>F</u>lush Right	Swiss Watchmakers 27		

The Numbering Mode options let you specify the placement of page numbers after the table of contents entries. You can also change the appearance or format of the page numbers by choosing the Page Number Format option from the Define Table of Contents dialog. For example, if you want the page numbers preceded by *p.*, as in *p. 27*, choose <u>P</u>age Number Format and the select Different from Document. Then, type **p.** before the [page #] code and press Exit (F7) to return to the Define Table of Contents dialog box.

When the Page Number Format is set to Same as Document, WordPerfect uses the page numbering format already defined for your document—or the default page number format—to create the page numbers in your table of contents.

Marking the Text Headings

Before you can generate a table of contents, you need to tell WordPerfect which headings or titles should be included in the table. This is done by *marking* your document headings as items that should appear in the table of contents. Here are the steps:

- Use Block (Alt+F4 or F12) to highlight a title or heading you want to include in the table of contents.

Choose Tools ▶
Table of Contents ▶
Mark.

- Press Mark (Alt+F5) and choose Table of Contents.

- If necessary, type the level number for the highlighted text. Then press F7.

This places a [Mrk Txt ToC Begin] code at the beginning of the high-lighted text and a [Mrk Txt ToC End] code at the end of the text. These codes tell WordPerfect to include the text between the codes as a heading in the table of contents. If there is a number 1 in the codes, this marked text will appear as a level 1 heading in the table of contents, although the *1* will not appear in Reveal Codes unless the cursor is directly on the code.

Consider the example in Figure 14.11. The first line of text is a main head-ing, so it is marked for level 1 in the table of contents; the remaining lines are subheadings beneath the main heading, so these are marked for level 2. When all of your titles and headings are marked, you're ready to generate the table of contents.

Figure 14.11
Level 1 and level 2
headings in a table
of contents

First-level heading

**Second-level
headings**

```
 File  Edit  View  Layout  Tools  Font  Graphics  Window  Help
VIEWING INFORMATION IN MEDI-CALL

     The Medi-Call database displays one help topic (or record) at
     once.  At the top of the main panel, the total number of records
     in the database is shown  after the "Topics" label.  To view other
     help topics in the database, press pgdn to display the next record
     or press pgup to display the previous record.

Using the Lookup Lists

     A lookup list shows an index for one of the help topic fields.  You
     can use the index to scroll through a list of related records, or to
     search for specific items in the database.  For example, you can
     display a lookup list of all help topic titles, as shown in Figure 3.

Searching From a Lookup List

     When you are in a lookup list, you can quickly search for a
     specific record.  Just begin typing the text you want to find, and
     the database will display the item in the list that matches what
C:\WPDOCS\MEDICALL.DOC                            Doc 1 Pg 4 Ln 4.5" Pos 1.25"
```

NOTE. *Be careful when blocking the text for marking; any formatting codes or font changes located between the [Mrk Txt ToC] codes will be carried into the table of contents when the table is generated.*

Generating the Table of Contents

The final procedure in producing a finished table of contents is simple:

- Press Mark (Alt+F5), choose Generate, and then press F7.

Choose Tools ▶
Generate, and then
choose OK.

Once the generation process has begun, WordPerfect compiles all text items marked with the [Mrk Txt ToC] codes and inserts a list where you defined the table of contents. Each level in the table is formatted with the table of contents styles you selected. WordPerfect automatically inserts the page number references after each item in the table of contents.

If you revise your document later, remember to generate the table of contents again to update the text headings and page number references. You do not need to redefine the table or mark the same text again. If, however, you add new headings to your document, remember to mark these as items for the table of contents. Then regenerate the table of contents.

Creating an Index

The Index feature can create an list of terms with page number references to help the reader find specific topics in your document. Indexes are generally included in large documents, but you may also find them useful in smaller documents.

The process of creating an index is similar to the process of creating a table of contents:

- Define the index location and format.

- Mark the text entries that should be included in the index.

- Generate the index.

An index usually contains many more entries than a table of contents. Because of this, WordPerfect provides a shortcut for marking text for the index. You can create a list of words and phrases that the index should contain, and then tell the Generate feature to use this list as a guide for marking index items. This list is called a *concordance file*, and when you use one, you won't need to mark text as you do for a table of contents.

NOTE. *If you plan to use a concordance file, you should create it before defining your index format. See "Saving Time with a Concordance File" later for more information about creating a concordance file.*

The following sections explain how to define the location and format of an index, how to mark text items, and how to create a concordance file to speed up the marking process. You'll also learn how to generate the index after you've finished defining and marking all the items.

Defining the Index Format

Figure 14.12 shows an index created in WordPerfect. An index can include two levels of entries: one for main entries and one for subentries. When you define your own indexes, you specify the style of page numbering that you want for the index, as well as the formatting style for each index level. The following steps describe how to define an index in your document:

Figure 14.12

An index created in WordPerfect

```
 File  Edit  View  Layout  Tools  Font  Graphics  Window  Help

INDEX

archive 17
     file 27
     directory 26
bold 29
     statements 17
     text 26
file  1, 3-5, 93
     archive 27
     document 5
     print 28, 51, 71
print  1-8, 11-30, 33, 73
     document 49
     fonts  3,81, 83
     graphics  84
     page 7, 13-15, 20
printer  1-9, 11-14, 19-21
     select 20
underline 28
     double 29,48
C:\WPDOCS\INDEX.DOC                      Doc 1 Pg 2 Ln 1.33" Pos 1"
```

Choose <u>T</u>ools ▸ Index ▸ <u>D</u>efine.

- Move the cursor to the place where the index should begin. This is usually at the end of your document. Then, press Hard Page Break (Ctrl+Enter) to start a new page.

- Type **INDEX** or another title for this page. Press Enter a few times to add some blank lines.

- Press Mark (Alt+F5), choose <u>D</u>efine, and then choose <u>I</u>ndex. The dialog box shown in Figure 14.13 appears.

- Choose one of the options under "Numbering Mode" to indicate the style of numbering you want for your index. Table 14.3 shows how each of the options affect the index page numbers.

- Choose Index Level <u>S</u>tyles, highlight each level in the list (first "Heading," then "Subheading"), choose <u>S</u>elect, and select a formatting style for each. Then choose Close.

Figure 14.13

Defining an index

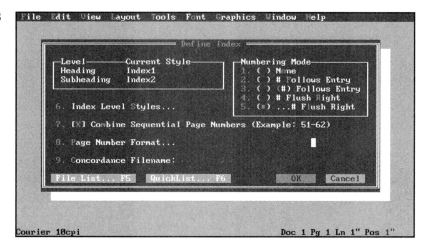

Table 14.3   Page Number Formats for Index Entries

Numbering Mode	Example
None	*European Commerce*
# Follows Entry	European Commerce 38, 42
(#) Follows Entry	European Commerce (38, 42)
# Flush Right	European Commerce 38, 42
. . .# Flush Right	European Commerce 38, 42

- If the format of the page number references in the index should be different than the page numbers in the document, choose Page Number Format and enter the desired format for the index.

- If you want sequential page numbers combined, make sure the Combine Sequential Page Numbers option is checked. This displays a range of page numbers, such as pages 10, 11, 12, and 13, as 10–13 when the page number reference is placed in the index.

- If are using a concordance file to locate and mark index entries, choose Concordance Filename, and enter the name of the file. See "Saving Time with a Concordance File," later in this chapter, for instructions on creating a concordance file.

Choose OK.

■ Press F7 to accept the index definition and return to the document screen.

These steps create a page with an INDEX title and a [Def Mark] code that indicates the place for the index. You won't see any index entries until you mark the text to be referenced in the index and generate the index entries.

You can change the appearance or format of the page numbers by choosing the Page Number Format option from the Define Index dialog. For example, if you want the page numbers preceded by *p.*, as in *p. 38,* choose P̲age Number Format and then select Different from Document. Then, type **p.** before the [page #] code and press Exit (F7) to return to the Define Index dialog box.

When the Page Number Format is set to Same as Document, WordPerfect uses the page numbering format already defined for your document—or the default page number format—to create the page numbers in your index.

Marking Text for the Index

Before you can generate an index, you need to mark the terms or words that should be included in the index. There are two ways to do this: You can manually mark the text entries, using a process similar to marking entries for a table of contents, or you can create a concordance file that lists the entries that the index should contain. There are advantages to each of these methods. For items like chapter headings or diagram captions, you can manually mark the text to ensure that specific terms are included in the index. On the other hand, you can create a concordance file if you want to include index entries for each case of a term, but don't want to search for and mark each one in the document.

The following procedure explains how to manually mark entries for your index. In the next section, you'll learn how to create a concordance file. When you mark text for an index, you can choose whether to mark items as headings or subheadings. If marked as a heading, a text item becomes one of the level 1 entries in the index. If marked as a subheading, a text item becomes an entry beneath one of the defined index headings; in this case, you need to specify the heading under which the subentry should appear. Follow these steps to mark index entries:

NOTE. *Be careful when blocking the text for marking; any formatting codes or font changes located between the [Mrk Txt ToC] codes will be carried into the index entries, when the index is generated.*

Choose T̲ools ▸
Index ▸ M̲ark.

■ Use Block (Alt+F4 or F12) to highlight a title or heading you want included in the index.

■ Press Mark Text (Alt+F5), and choose I̲ndex.

- If the index reference for the marked text should be different than the actual text, choose <u>H</u>eading if necessary and enter the text reference as it should appear. (If you don't know what to enter at the <u>H</u>eading and <u>Sub</u>heading options, choose <u>L</u>ist to choose from a list of defined headings and subheadings that you entered earlier.)

- If the current item is to be marked as a subheading, choose <u>S</u>ubheading and enter the text for the item.

Choose OK to
return to the
document screen.

- Press F7 until you return to the document screen.

- Repeat this procedure for each text item you want referenced in the index.

This places an [Index] code before the text you blocked. Unlike the table of contents codes, the [Index] code is a single code that marks only the location of the text; a pair of codes is not necessary to mark the text since the reference that appears in the index is taken from the text you typed for the Heading and Subheading options.

The Heading and Subheading entries do not need to be identical to the text you've blocked. The text you enter for these options can be whatever text you want as the reference to the blocked text. In the next section, you'll learn how to automate the marking process for general terms by creating a concordance file. After that, you'll learn how easy it is to generate an index once you've defined it and marked your terms.

Saving Time with a Concordance File

A concordance file can help you generate your index by providing a list of words, phrases, and terms that should be listed as index entries. This file can save you a great deal of time, because it practically eliminates the need to individually mark each item in your document. There are some cases, however, when you may need to manually mark specific items, as described earlier.

Figure 14.14 shows one example of a concordance file. To create this concordance, you type the entries with the subentries indented beneath them. Then you use the Mark feature to identify the indented items as subentries. To create your own concordance file, start in a clean WordPerfect document window, and follow this procedure:

- Type each item that should appear as a level 1 heading in your index. Press Enter to insert a [HRt] code at the end of each line.

- If your index should include subentries or subheadings, type these beneath the appropriate entries or headings. Make sure you indent each subentry or subheading with one tab and end the line with a [HRt] code, as you did with the headings.

Figure 14.14

A concordance file with terms for an index

```
 File  Edit  View  Layout  Tools  Font  Graphics  Window  Help
ammendment
archive
     document
     files
     library
authority
     corporate
     table of
bold
     statements
     text
case
copy
document
{   ▲    ▲    ▲    ▲    ▲    ▲    ▲    ▲    ▲    ▲    ▲    )    ▲
[Open Style:InitialCodes]ammendment[HRt]
archive[HRt]
[Lft Tab][Index:archive;document]document[HRt]
[Lft Tab]files[HRt]
[Lft Tab]library[HRt]
authority[HRt]
[Lft Tab]corporate[HRt]
[Lft Tab]table of[HRt]
Courier 10cpi                              Doc 1 Pg 1 Ln 1.33" Pos 1.5"
```

**Code marks
subentry for Index**

When the main entries are completed, follow these steps to mark each of the subentries:

- Use Block (Alt+F4 or F12) to highlight a subheading.

- Press Mark (Alt+F5) and choose Index.

Choose Tools ▶
Index ▶ Mark.

- Choose Heading and the blocked subentry text will appear in the box.

- Ignore the text that WordPerfect suggests, and instead enter the heading under which the subentry text is located. Then press Enter.

- Choose Subheading and press Enter to accept the blocked text as the subheading reference.

- Press F7 until you return to your document screen.

Choose OK until
you return to the
document screen.

These last steps identify the subentry text for the index. This is important: If you do not mark the subheading text in the concordance files, these items are ignored when the index is generated. (You can speed up the process of marking subheading text by placing the marking commands in a macro. See Chapter 24 for more information about macros.)

When you are finished setting up the concordance, save it to a file. Now when you want to construct an index using this concordance file, you need to define the index, as described a moment ago, and, while you're at it, choose Concordance Filename from the Define Index dialog box and specify the name of the concordance file you just created. When these tasks are completed, you're ready to generate the index. You'll learn how to do so in a moment.

Tips for a Clean Concordance File

Many WordPerfect users are thrilled when they discover their concordance file can help locate and mark all text for the index. Then their glee turns to disappointment when the finished index is inflated with too many entries—many of which fail to direct the reader to key topics and important headings. The concordance file isn't smart enough to know which entries you want included and which ones should be left out.

For example, suppose your concordance file contains the word "account." An index reference will be created for *every* occurrence of this word in your document, even though you may want only the references for "new accounts," "delinquent accounts," and "account management." When your index is generated, you'll need to manually check each entry to make sure it's valid, and delete any invalid ones. This type of work makes the index feature a little less attractive.

Fortunately, there are a few things you can do to clean up the index references *before* you generate the index. The key to a clean index lies in carefully choosing the words you include in the concordance file. You'll obtain the best results when you combine a carefully structured concordance file with select phrases and terms that you mark manually. Here are a few guidelines for the concordance file:

- Limit the number of common verbs and nouns in the concordance file. Words like "profits," "market," "analyze," "sales," and "fax" may appear in the document under several unrelated topics. Try to be more specific by including phrases like "1st quarter profits," "bull market," "analyze productivity," "projected sales," and "fax procedures."

- In the concordance file, group the entries according to the categories you want to see in the index. Place main headings at the left margin, and indent subheadings with a tab beneath the main heading. Don't forget to use the Mark Text feature to mark the subheadings in the concordance. This heading/subheading structure in the concordance file enables WordPerfect to organize information correctly in the index.

- Using your table of contents as a guide, include in the concordance file any key phrases and terms from the headings in your document.

- Make sure the concordance file includes all variations of words—such as "power," "powers," and "powerful"—that you want as references in the index. Use this tactic sparingly, or you'll have more index entries than you need. In this example, if you place only "power" in the concordance, other variations of this word will not be found. Only words that are an exact match will be included in the index.

- In addition to creating a concordance file, use the Mark Text feature to manually mark important items for the index. This not only guarantees that a reference is included for the significant topics, but also reduces the amount of extra entries that may appear in the index.

Although these guidelines do not eliminate the need to review and edit your index after it is generated, they will reduce the amount of clean up you'll need to do.

Generating the Index

The final task in creating an index is generating the index entries. Before you generate the index, press Home, Home, ↓ to reformat the entire document; if the document needs to be reformatted and you don't do so prior to generating the index, it's possible that page breaks will occur incorrectly, resulting in inaccurate page numbers in the index.

- Press Mark (Alt+F5), choose $\underline{G}$enerate, and then press F7.

Choose $\underline{T}$ools ▶ $\underline{G}$enerate, and then choose OK.

After a few moments, the index is done. The index entries are inserted as regular document text which cites the page number references and adheres to the appropriate formatting codes. You can easily edit the text and change attributes and fonts. You can also apply the Columns feature to split index entries into running columns on the page.

The first time you generate an index for your document, you may want to check the index entries to make sure the generation process was successful. When you make changes to your document later, mark additional text for the index or add items to the concordance list. You do not need to delete the older index information; simply choose the Generate feature again to have the index updated. Take note, however, that each time you use the Generate feature, the prior table of contents, index, and lists are erased. If you've added formatting or text to the completed index, it will be replaced with the latest generated text entries.

15

Working with Large Documents

WORDPERFECT IS OFTEN PRAISED FOR HOW IT HANDLES LARGE document files, and rightly so. No other word processor manages volumes of information as well as WordPerfect, and this chapter explains some of the tools that make this possible.

WordPerfect's Bookmark feature lets you quickly mark and move to specific places in your document. The Cross-Reference feature lets you insert references to other sections or items in your document, and these can be updated automatically when the referenced items are moved to other locations in the text.

The Summary feature saves information about each document author, date of creation, and file contents; this information can help you manage and identify each document in a long list of files. WordPerfect also supports page headers and footers to display chapter and section titles at the top or bottom of each page in your document.

When your documents become too large to manage, you can divide the text between two or more files; WordPerfect's Master Document feature lets you combine the files again as one document for editing and printing. Whether your documents are 25 or 2500 pages long, you will benefit from the various features described in this chapter.

Using Bookmarks to Keep Your Place

The Bookmark feature allows you to insert reference points to help you quickly locate specific sections or passages of text in your document. Bookmarks are also handy for holding your place in a long document. Once bookmarks are inserted into your text, you can jump between them for editing and viewing. You can, for example, insert bookmarks at two different locations in your document and toggle between them to perform editing tasks on two different sections. You can insert as many bookmarks as you need; they do not affect the format of your document, and they do not appear on the printed pages.

Setting and Locating a Quick Bookmark

The easiest way to insert a bookmark is with the QuickMark feature. You insert this special kind of bookmark with a single keystroke; another keystroke quickly finds the bookmark again. The QuickMark is similar to the traditional bookmark that you insert into an actual book; only one QuickMark can be inserted to keep your place at one point in the document. With a document on screen, follow these steps to see how the QuickMark feature works:

1. Move the cursor to a place in your text where you will want to return.

2. Press Set QuickMark (Ctrl+Q) to insert the QuickMark into your text.

3. Continue editing or viewing other text in your document.

4. Press Find QuickMark (Ctrl+F) to move the cursor back to the location of the QuickMark.

When you set the QuickMark, you won't notice a change in the text, and WordPerfect will not display a message to indicate that the bookmark has been set. The QuickMark is inserted as a [Bookmark:QuickMark] code which can be seen only in the Reveal Codes window. Only one QuickMark can be inserted in your text at any given time; when you move the cursor to another place in your document and press Set QuickMark (Ctrl+Q) again, the Quick-Mark code is moved to the new location. You can remove the QuickMark from your document by deleting the code in Reveal Codes or by removing the QuickMark from the list of defined bookmarks, as explained later in this chapter (see "Moving, Renaming, and Deleting Bookmarks"). To reinsert the QuickMark, simply press Ctrl+Q again.

NOTE.   *In addition to the QuickMark, you can also insert unlimited named bookmarks. For more information, see "Inserting Named Bookmarks," in a moment.*

Marking Your Place before Exiting

By default, WordPerfect automatically sets the QuickMark at the cursor location every time you save and exit your document. When you retrieve your document for the next editing session, you can press Find QuickMark (Ctrl+F) to return to wherever you were working last. The following steps turn on or off the option that sets the QuickMark each time you save your document (remember, it's on by default):

Choose <u>E</u>dit ▶
Boo<u>k</u>mark.

■ Press Mark (Alt+F5) and then choose <u>B</u>ookmark.

■ Select the option for <u>S</u>et QuickMark in Document on Save. When this op-tion is turned on, an *X* appears in the check box next to the option. If the option is on, selecting it again toggles it off.

Choose OK to
close the dialog
box.

■ Press Exit (F7) to close the dialog box.

If this option is on, whenever you save and exit any displayed document, the [Bookmark:QuickMark] code is inserted at the current cursor location to hold your place in the document. When you retrieve your document again, you can press Find QuickMark (Ctrl+F) to return to the place where the QuickMark was set. This option remains active in WordPerfect until you turn it off by deselecting it in the Bookmark dialog box.

Inserting Named Bookmarks

The QuickMark is useful for quick "mark-and-find" tasks, but for large documents, a single bookmark is not enough. For this reason, WordPerfect lets you insert additional bookmarks which you identify with assigned names. These allow you to keep track of several places in your document and quickly move the cursor to these places when you are viewing or editing text.

There are two types of named bookmarks that you can create. The first type is called an *open bookmark* because it inserts only one code to mark a specific place in the text, much like paper slips in a book. To insert an open bookmark:

Choose Edit ▶ Bookmark.

■ Move the cursor to the place where you want to insert the bookmark.

■ Press Mark (Alt+F5) and choose Bookmark to display the dialog box shown in Figure 15.1.

Figure 15.1
Creating a named bookmark

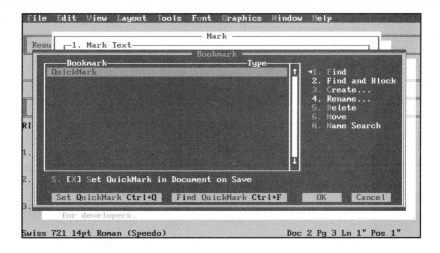

■ Choose Create and WordPerfect prompts you to enter a name for the bookmark.

WordPerfect automatically suggests the first 38 characters of the text where the cursor is located as the bookmark name. Press Enter to accept this as the name, edit the line of text if you like, or else type a new name, and then press Enter.

After you enter the name for the bookmark, the dialog box is removed from the screen, and a [Bookmark:*name*] is inserted at the cursor position, where *name* represents the name you accepted or typed. If you view the

[Bookmark] code in Reveal Codes, the bookmark name appears only when your cursor is directly on the code.

The second type of bookmark is a *blocked bookmark*; it inserts a pair of codes around a blocked section of text. This type of bookmark can highlight the selected text as a visual reference for the bookmark location. When you create blocked bookmarks, you can jump to key phrases or headings in your document. As you jump to each phrase, WordPerfect will highlight the marked text, so you know you've hit the right bookmark. To create a blocked bookmark:

Choose Edit ▸ Bookmark.

- Block the section of text that should be highlighted by the bookmark.

- Press Mark (Alt+F5) and choose Bookmark

- Choose Create, and the text you marked appears as the name for the bookmark.

- Press Enter to accept the name and the bookmark is inserted.

After you accept the name, a pair of [+Bookmark][-Bookmark] codes are inserted around the blocked text. These mark the text as a bookmark you can jump to, with the text highlighted as a visual reference. The next section explains how to jump to the bookmarks once you have inserted them into your document.

Jumping to the Bookmarks

After you've inserted one or more bookmarks into your document, you can move or *jump* to them from anywhere in your document:

Choose Edit ▸ Bookmark.

- Press Mark (Alt+F5) and then choose Bookmark. You'll see a dialog box like the one shown in Figure 15.2, which displays the names of the bookmarks in the current document.

- Highlight the name of the bookmark you want to jump to, and then choose Find.

The cursor moves to the location of the bookmark you highlighted. If you want to highlight a blocked bookmark, you can choose Find and Block, instead of Find; this option locates the bookmark you selected and blocks the text within the bookmark codes. This lets you see where the bookmark is located without turning on the Reveal Codes feature.

TIP.   *If you have a long list of bookmarks, you can choose the Name Search option from the Bookmark dialog box, and type the first few characters of the bookmark name you want to highlight.*

Figure 15.2

Choosing a
bookmark name

Defined bookmarks

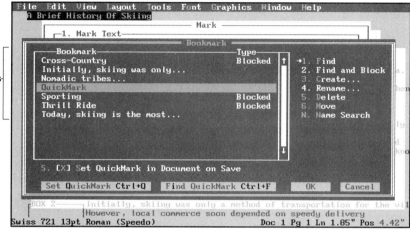

The blocked bookmark is useful for blocking common passages of text that you want to copy and move to other places in your document. Using the Find and Block option, simply define a blocked bookmark around the text that will be copied. When you're ready to copy the text, choose the Find and Block feature to locate and block it. Then use the Copy feature to copy the text elsewhere in your document.

Bookmark macros from earlier versions of WordPerfect removed a bookmark once it was found again. This is not the case in WordPerfect 6.0. With the exception of the QuickMark, all bookmarks remain where you place them in the text until you delete the bookmark code, move the code, or delete the bookmark from the list, as explained in the next section.

Moving, Renaming, and Deleting Bookmarks

The Bookmark feature is an effective way to mark places for editing. This feature is even more useful when you use the Bookmark dialog box to manage the bookmarks after they are inserted. You can edit the names of existing bookmarks, move them to other places in the document, and delete bookmarks that you no longer need.

To delete a bookmark you've inserted:

Choose Edit ▶
Bookmark.

■ Press Mark (Alt+F5) and then choose Bookmark.

■ Highlight the name of the bookmark you want to remove, and then choose Delete. When prompted about deleting the bookmark, choose Yes.

Choose OK to close
the dialog box.

■ Press Exit (F7) to close the dialog box.

To change the name of a bookmark:

Choose Edit ▶ Bookmark.

- Press Mark (Alt+F5) and then choose Bookmark.

- Highlight the name of the bookmark you want to change, and then choose Rename.

- Type the new name for the bookmark and press Enter.

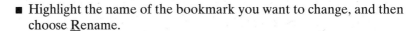
Choose OK to close the dialog box.

- Press Exit (F7) to close the dialog box.

To move a bookmark to another place in your document:

- Move the cursor to the place in your document where a bookmark should be moved.

- If you plan to move a blocked bookmark, block the new text where the bookmark should be moved.

Choose Edit ▶ Bookmark.

- Press Mark (Alt+F5) and then choose Bookmark.

- Highlight the bookmark you want to move, and then choose Move.

The dialog box is automatically closed, and the bookmark you highlighted is moved to the current location of the cursor or the blocked text.

Creating Hypertext Documents

WordPerfect's Hypertext feature lets you create interactive documents that will be viewed on the computer screen. When you use the Hypertext feature you create a number of *hypertext links* that connect different sections of your document or connect a series of related documents. Once the hypertext links are defined, you can use them to jump to a related item in the current document or in another document.

Unlike the Bookmark feature, the Hypertext feature lets you jump to different sections directly from the marked text. If, for example, you've created a hypertext link between "See Table 12" and the page where Table 12 is found, you can use the mouse pointer to click on "See Table 12" and Word-Perfect immediately jumps to the related text. You don't need to display a specific dialog box and then choose where you want to go; the marked hypertext automatically takes you there.

The Hypertext feature can help you create on-line documents, help utilities, and other documents that will be viewed on the screen. The process for creating a hypertext document is divided into three general tasks:

- Create all the documents for the hypertext application, and identify the related terms or items that should be linked. This includes the text that will be marked as hypertext, and also the *destination* for each link.

- Set up the hypertext links. First, you use the Bookmark feature to mark the destination for each link. If, for example, you want to create a link for "See Table 12," the destination would be the page where Table 12 is found, and you would create a bookmark on this page. Second, you use the Hypertext features to mark each hypertext link to the bookmarks.

- Activate the Hypertext option and use the hypertext links.

When Hypertext is turned on, you can use the mouse pointer to double-click on a marked hypertext link—or press Enter with the text cursor on a hypertext link—and WordPerfect jumps to the related text, or destination, of the link.

This outlines the general procedure. In the text that follows, you'll learn how to use the Hypertext feature to create a series of links to different places in your document and to different documents. You'll create two brief documents and then mark a few text sections as hypertext links. Then, you'll enable the Hypertext option and try out your on-line document. You'll also discover a few hypertext options that let you create links with graphic buttons and create hypertext links that play back a macro.

Creating the Hypertext Documents

The first task for a hypertext application is creating the document, or documents, that you contain the text you want to link. Although you can apply the hypertext features to any document, most hypertext applications include documents that are specifically designed to be viewed on the computer screen. Many of these documents have consistent formatting and phrases that help the reader quickly identify the items that are links to related information. Consider the two documents shown in Figure 15.3. The first document includes a hypertext link, which is a clear reference to an item in another document. The second document contains the destination for the link.

In the following exercise, you'll create two brief documents for a hypertext application; in a later section, you'll set up the hypertext link between them. These documents are designed for a brief exercise with the hypertext features, but you can easily adapt the procedures for larger "real" documents.

1. Clear the WordPerfect screen, and type the following text for the first document:

```
    The Yucatan peninsula is diverse and mysterious. Within
its compact geography, you'll find savannas, evergreen
glades, and tropical rain forests. Evidence of cultural
conflict is buried beneath the jungle floor and etched on
peaks graced by roaring waterfalls.
```

Figure 15.3

Documents with
hypertext links

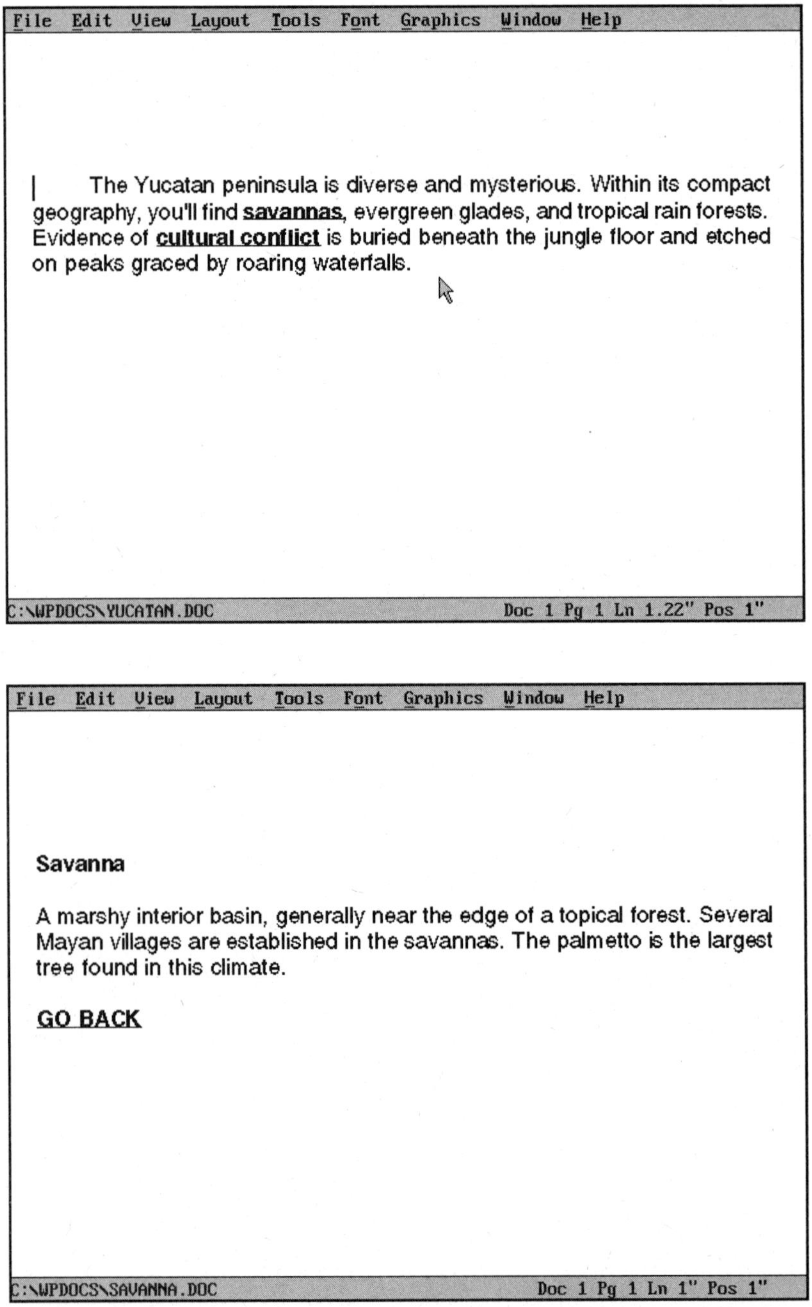

```
 File   Edit   View   Layout   Tools   Font   Graphics   Window   Help
```

| The Yucatan peninsula is diverse and mysterious. Within its compact geography, you'll find **savannas**, evergreen glades, and tropical rain forests. Evidence of **cultural conflict** is buried beneath the jungle floor and etched on peaks graced by roaring waterfalls.

```
C:\WPDOCS\YUCATAN.DOC                              Doc 1 Pg 1 Ln 1.22" Pos 1"
```

```
 File   Edit   View   Layout   Tools   Font   Graphics   Window   Help
```

Savanna

A marshy interior basin, generally near the edge of a topical forest. Several Mayan villages are established in the savannas. The palmetto is the largest tree found in this climate.

GO BACK

```
C:\WPDOCS\SAVANNA.DOC                              Doc 1 Pg 1 Ln 1" Pos 1"
```

Choose Layout ▶ Alignment ▶ Hard Page 12 times.

2. Press Hard Page (Ctrl+Enter) 12 times to simulate a document with several pages.

3. Type the following text to continue the document:

> Ancient Mayans once populated the region and often warred against the neighboring Incas. Their weapons are hidden and silent, but their voices still whisper through golden artifacts, magnificent ruins, and primeval cities.

Choose File ▶ Save As, and enter **yucatan.doc** as the file name.

4. This completes the first document. Press Save (F10), type **yucatan.doc** as the document name, and then press Enter.

Choose Window ▶ Switch.

5. Press Switch (Shift+F3), or press Home+2, to display the second document screen. Then, type the following text:

> Savanna
> A marshy interior basin, generally near the edge of a tropical forest. Several Mayan villages are established in the savannas. The palmetto is the largest tree found in this climate.

Choose File ▶ Save As, and enter **savanna.doc** as the file name.

6. This completes the second document. Press Save (F10), type **savanna.doc** as the document name, and then press Enter.

Choose Window ▶ Switch.

7. Press Switch (Shift+F3), or press Home+1, to display the first document screen.

The text for both documents is completed. In the next section, you'll create the hypertext links that connect specific text phrases. Keep both document windows open and continue the exercise.

Setting Up Hypertext Links

In this section, you'll create four hypertext links for the documents created in the previous section. The first two links will connect related text within the YUCATAN.DOC document. The last two links will connect related text between YUCATAN.DOC and the second document that you created, SAVANNA.DOC.

Remember, when you create a hypertext link, you begin by placing a bookmark at the destination of the link. Then, you mark the text phrase that will serve as the link to the bookmark. The following steps explain how to create the links; you should have the YUCATAN.DOC and the SAVANNA.DOC document files open before you perform the steps.

1. For the first link, you need to insert a bookmark at the beginning of the "Ancient Mayans" paragraph; this will be the destination for the first line.

Move the cursor to the last page in the YUCATAN.DOC document, and position the cursor at the beginning of the paragraph.

Choose Edit ▸ Bookmark. Choose Create ▸ OK.

2. Press Mark Text (Alt+F5), choose Bookmark, and then choose Create. WordPerfect displays the text that follows the cursor. Press Enter to accept this text as the bookmark name. Now, you'll create the hypertext link to this bookmark.

3. Press Home, Home, ↑ to move the cursor to the beginning of the YUCATAN.DOC document. Use the Block feature to select the "cultural conflict" text.

Choose Tools ▸ Hypertext ▸ Create Link.

4. Press Mark Text (Alt+F5), choose Hypertext, and then choose Create Link.

5. Choose Go to Bookmark, press List Bookmarks (F5), and select the "Ancient Mayans... " bookmark.

Choose OK until you return to the document screen.

6. Then press Exit (F7) until you return to the document screen. The "cultural conflict" text is now highlighted as a hypertext link. The completes the first link.

7. The second link will let you "jump back" from the "Ancient Mayans" paragraph to the first paragraph. Move the cursor immediately before the "cultural conflict" phrase.

Choose Edit ▸ Bookmark. Choose Create ▸ OK.

8. Press Mark Text (Alt+F5), choose Bookmark, and then choose Create. Press Enter to accept the displayed text as the bookmark name.

9. Move the cursor to the last page in the document, and then use the Block feature to select the "Ancient Mayans" text.

Choose Tools ▸ Hypertext ▸ Create Link.

10. Press Mark Text (Alt+F5), choose Hypertext, and then choose Create Link.

11. Choose Go to Bookmark, press List Bookmarks (F5), and select the "cultural conflict... " bookmark.

Choose OK until you return to the document screen.

12. Press Exit (F7) until you return to the document screen. The "Ancient Mayans" text is now highlighted as a hypertext link. The completes the second link.

13. Now you will create a link between the current document and the SAVANNA.DOC document. Press Switch (Shift+F3), or Home+2, to display the second document screen. Move the cursor to the beginning of the SAVANNA document.

Choose Edit ▸ Book-
mark. Choose Cre-
ate ▸ OK.

Choose File ▸ Save.

Choose Window ▸
Switch.

Choose Tools ▸ Hy-
pertext ▸ Create Link.

Choose OK until
you return to the
document screen.

Choose File ▸ Save.

Choose Edit ▸ Book-
mark. Choose Cre-
ate ▸ OK.

Choose File ▸ Save.

Choose Tools ▸ Hy-
pertext ▸ Create
Link.

14. Press Mark Text (Alt+F5), choose Bookmark, and then choose Create. Press Enter to accept the displayed text as the bookmark name.

15. Press Save (Ctrl+F12) to update the SAVANNA.DOC file with the bookmark.

16. Press Switch (Shift+F3) to display the first document. Press Home, Home, ↑ to move the cursor to the top of the document. Then use the Block feature to highlight the word "savannas."

17. Press Mark Text (Alt+F5), choose Hypertext, and then choose Create Link.

18. Choose Go to Other Document, type **savanna.doc**, and press Enter. Then, at the Bookmark prompt, press List Bookmarks (F5), and select the "Savanna" bookmark.

19. Press Exit (F7) until you return to the document screen. The "savannas" text is now highlighted as a hypertext link. The completes the third link.

20. Press Save (Ctrl+F12) to update the YUCATAN.DOC file with the bookmarks and hypertext links.

21. The fourth link will let you "jump back" from the SAVANNA.DOC document to the first document. Move the cursor immediately before the word "savannas," in the YUCATAN.DOC document.

22. Press Mark Text (Alt+F5), choose Bookmark, and then choose Create. Press Enter to accept the displayed text as the bookmark name.

23. Press Save (Ctrl+F12) to update the YUCATAN.DOC file with the latest bookmark.

24. Press Switch (Shift+F3) to display the second document. Then, press Home, Home, ↓ to move the cursor to the end of the text. Press Enter a few times to add a blank line beneath the paragraph.

25. At this point, you need to type some text that you can mark as the hypertext link back to the YUCATAN.DOC document. Type **GO BACK** at the bottom of the SAVANNA.DOC document. Then use the Block feature to highlight the "GO BACK" text.

26. Press Mark Text (Alt+F5), choose Hypertext, and then choose Create Link.

27. Choose Go to Other Document, and enter **yucatan.doc**. Then, at the Bookmark prompt, press List Bookmarks (F5), and select the "savannas, evergreen glades... " bookmark.

Choose OK until
you return to the
document.

Choose Tools ▸
Hypertext. Choose
Hypertext is Active
▸ OK.

28. Press Exit (F7) until you return to the document screen. The completes the fourth link.

29. Press Mark Text (Alt+F5) and choose Hypertext. Choose Hypertext is Active, so that an *X* appears in the check box next to this option. Then press Exit (F7). Switch to the other document screen and repeat this step for the YUCATAN.DOC document also.

30. Save both documents to update all bookmarks and hypertext links to the files on disk. Then, clear the screen.

You now have two documents with hypertext links. The step can be a little confusing because you always begin each link by creating a bookmark at the destination. Then, you mark a section of text as the hypertext link.

In the next section, you will turn on the Hypertext option and use the links you've created.

Using the Hypertext Documents

After you've created hypertext links between related text phrases and items, you can use the Hypertext option to view your document and jump between the linked text. The following steps explain how to use the links you've inserted into the YUCATAN.DOC and SAVANNA.DOC documents that you created earlier in this section.

Choose File ▸
Open, and enter
yucatan.doc.

Click the mouse
pointer over the "sa-
vannas" hypertext
link.

Click the mouse
pointer over the
"GO BACK" hyper-
text link.

Click the mouse
pointer over the
"cultural conflict" hy-
pertext link.

Click the mouse
pointer over the
"Ancient Mayans"
hypertext link.

1. Press Open/Retrieve (Shift+F10), type **yucatan.doc**, and press Enter to retrieve the YUCATAN.DOC document that you created earlier.

2. Move the cursor over the hypertext link, "savannas," and then press Enter. WordPerfect displays the SAVANNA.DOC document.

3. Move the cursor over the "GO BACK" hypertext link and then press Enter. WordPerfect redisplays the YUCATAN.DOC.

4. Move the cursor over the hypertext link, "cultural conflict," and then press Enter. WordPerfect jumps to the "Ancient Mayans" paragraph.

5. Move the cursor over the "Ancient Mayans" hypertext link and then press Enter. WordPerfect jumps back to the "cultural conflict" text.

As you can see, the Hypertext features let you quickly move to different topics within large or related documents. When the Hypertext option is active, you can also press Tab to move the cursor to each hypertext link in the document, and then press Enter or click the mouse pointer over the hypertext link to jump to the related text.

If you don't want to define links that take you back to your original position, you can choose Return from Jump to return after selecting one of the hypertext links. Simply display the Hypertext dialog box (press Alt+F5 and choose <u>H</u>ypertext or choose <u>T</u>ools/<u>H</u>ypertext from the menu bar), and then choose <u>R</u>eturn from Jump.

Turning Off the Hypertext Option

Remember that some keystrokes work differently when the Hypertext option is active. Press Tab and Shift+Tab to quickly move the cursor to each hypertext link in your document. Pressing Enter, while the cursor is on a hypertext link, causes WordPerfect to jump to the destination of the current link.

If you need to edit your document, you may want to turn off the Hypertext option and restore the functions of the Tab, Shift+Tab, and Enter keys. You turn off Hypertext by pressing Mark Text (Alt+F5) and choosing <u>H</u>ypertext; then, choose Hypertext is <u>A</u>ctive, so that the check box is empty (no *X*) next to this option. This disables the Hypertext option, but it does not remove the hypertext codes that create the links in your document.

If you want a document to be in Hypertext mode when you first retrieve it, choose Hypertext is <u>A</u>ctive again to enable the Hypertext mode. Then save your document before clearing the screen.

Cross-Referencing Your Information

Cross-references note related information in your documents, often taking the form of "See page *n* for details." A cross-reference consists of two things: a reference and a target. The *reference* is, of course, the "See page *n*..." text that appears in your document. The *target* is the goal of the reference, or, in other words, the item to which you're referring. For example, in the reference "See page 12 for details," page 12 is the target. Table 15.1 shows other examples of common cross-references.

Table 15.1   **Common Cross-References**

Reference Text	Target(s)
An order form is located on page *27*.	Page 27
Table *5-III* contains a list of class functions.	Table 5-III
Figure *9.12* shows the original Pythagorean manuscript.	Figure 9.12
Refer to paragraph *7a* on page *14-8*.	Paragraph Number 7a, page 14-8.

Using special codes, you can insert cross-references to page numbers, paragraph numbers, tables, figures and illustrations, footnotes and endnotes, and other document items. In some cross-references, you may want to combine two different targets, as shown in the last example in the table: "Refer to paragraph *7a* on page *14-8*." This example includes a reference to a target paragraph and the target page on which the paragraph is located.

There is no limit to the number of cross-references you can insert in your document. When target items are moved to other pages or locations in the document, you can update the reference numbers by running the Generate feature.

Creating a Cross-Reference

The general procedure for creating a cross-reference consists of two main tasks. First, you create the reference text that points to your targets; then you define the target or targets to which the text will refer. In the sections that follow, you'll find detailed information about the types of cross-references you can create. To create a cross-reference:

- Move the cursor to the place in your document where the cross-reference should be located.

- Type the text for the reference—something like "For more information, see page ."

- Move the cursor to the place in the reference text where the target information should appear. In the preceding example, you'd place the cursor after the word "page."

Choose <u>T</u>ools ▸
Cross-Re<u>f</u>erence ▸
<u>B</u>oth.

- Press Mark (Alt+F5), choose <u>M</u>ark Text, and then choose <u>B</u>oth Reference & Target. The Mark Cross-Reference and Target dialog box appears, as shown in Figure 15.4.

- Choose Tie <u>R</u>eference To, and select the item—for example, <u>P</u>age or <u>F</u>ootnote—that should appear in the reference text.

- Choose <u>T</u>arget Name and enter a name for the target you want to reference. Then press Enter. The Target name can be up to 31 characters long, including spaces. (Note that this name will not appear in your text.) Each target must have a unique name.

Choose OK to
continue.

- Press Exit (F7) to continue, and the dialog box shown in Figure 15.5 appears with your document text.

- Use the arrow keys or PgUp/PgDn to move the cursor to the item you want to reference, and press Enter. You can also press F2 or Shift+F2 to search for the text or codes you want. This becomes the target for your reference. For example, if your reference should display a specific page number, move to that page number now, and press Enter.

Figure 15.4

Creating a cross-reference

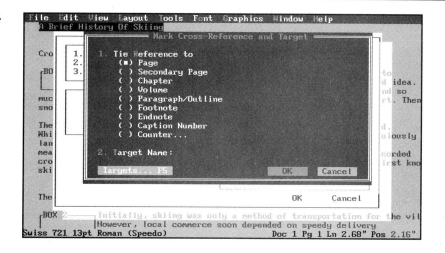

Figure 15.5

Document text in the Cross-Reference Target dialog box

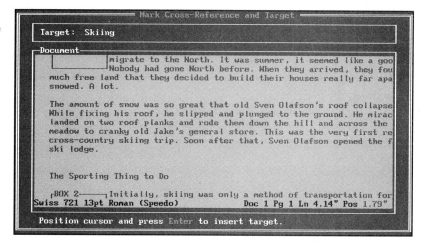

This procedure inserts two codes into your document. The Reference code, [Ref Pg], appears with the text you typed for the reference; it displays the page number, paragraph number, or other item where the target code is located. The target code, [Target], appears at the place where you pressed Enter at the end of the procedure; this marks the item to which you want to refer. Figure 15.6 shows an example of how the codes look and what result is in your document.

Figure 15.6
Cross-reference codes in the Reveal Codes window

Page number in Document

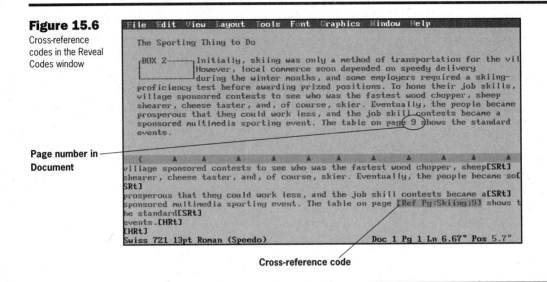

Cross-reference code

You can create cross-references to page numbering items, like the current page number, chapter number, or volume number; to footnotes, endnotes, or paragraph numbers; and to graphics box numbers.

The previous steps explain how to mark a reference and a target at the same time, which ensures that the reference and target will match; this method also inserts the target information at the time the reference is created. But WordPerfect also lets you mark each reference or target independently. For example, you can mark all targets in your document before inserting the references to them. You do so by moving the cursor to each target, pressing Mark (Alt+F5), choosing Mark Text, choosing Cross-Reference Target, and entering a target name. Remember, you must assign a unique name to each target defined in your document.

Once a target is marked, you can create one or more references to it. First, position the cursor where you want the reference to occur. Then press Mark (Alt+F5), and choose Mark Text, and choose Cross-Reference. Then choose Tie Reference to select a reference type, choose Target Name, and then enter the name of the target. If you don't remember the name, choose Targets (F5) from the Mark Cross-Reference Target dialog box to choose from a list of the targets you've defined. Press Enter or choose Select until you've highlighted the appropriate target. Then press Enter or choose OK.

After you insert a reference code, target information is inserted into the reference text, providing that the named target has been defined. If you insert reference and target codes at different times or if you enter incorrect target names, you'll see a question mark (?) in your text where the target information should be inserted in the reference. This often happens when you define a reference before you create the target code. To fix the problem, press Mark (Alt+F5) and then choose Generate to update the cross-references. If the ? still appears in the reference text, check the reference and target codes to make sure the named targets match.

Cross-Referencing Page Numbers

With a document on screen, follow these steps to practice creating a cross-reference to a specific page number in your document:

1. Move the cursor to the place in your document where the cross-reference text should appear.

2. Type **See page for more information.** (Insert an extra space between "page" and "for.") Then move the cursor between the words "page" and "for."

Choose Tools ▸ Cross-Reference ▸ Both.

3. Press Mark (Alt+F5), choose Mark Text, and then choose Both Reference & Target.

4. Choose Tie Reference To, and select Page if it isn't already selected.

5. Choose Target Name, type **TEST REFERENCE** as the target name, and press Enter.

6. Press Exit (F7) to continue, and your document is displayed in the Mark Cross-Reference and Target dialog box.

Choose OK to continue.

7. Use the arrow keys, PgUp/PgDn, or the Search feature (F2) to move the cursor to the page and the item you want to reference. Then press Enter. This marks the item as the target for your reference.

After you press Enter, the dialog box closes, and the page number appears in your reference text. Although this type of reference displays a page number, the reference actually points to an item located on the target page. The target is not linked to the page itself. If, through editing, the target code moves to a different page, you can update the cross-reference to show the new page number in your reference text. You do so by pressing Mark (Alt+F5) and then choosing Generate, or by choosing Generate, or by choosing Tools/Generate from the Tools menu.

Cross-Referencing Footnotes and Endnotes

The following steps explain how to create a cross-reference to a specific footnote or endnote in your document. In this case, the target for the reference is the footnote or endnote number in your document. To create this type of cross-reference, type reference text as described in the previous examples, something like "See Footnote#." Then follow this procedure:

■ Move the cursor to the place where the footnote or endnote number should appear in your reference text.

Choose Tools ▸
Cross-Reference ▸
Both.

Choose OK to
continue.

- Press Mark (Alt+F5), choose Mark Text, and then choose Both Reference & Target.

- Choose Tie Reference To, and select Footnote or Endnote.

- Choose Target Name, type a target name for the reference, and press Enter.

- Press Exit (F7) to continue, and your document is displayed in the Mark Cross-Reference and Target dialog box.

- Use the arrow keys, PgUp/PgDn, or the Search feature to locate the footnote or endnote number in your document that you want to reference.

- Move the cursor to the immediate right of the note number, and press Enter. This marks the note as the target for your reference.

If you rearrange the paragraphs in your document, the footnote and endnote codes are automatically renumbered to reflect the new order. However, any cross-references to the footnotes and endnotes are *not* renumbered. When you make changes to the order of text, you need to regenerate your document to update references to the footnote and endnote numbers. To do so, either press Mark (Alt+F5) and select Generate, or choose Generate from the Tools menu.

Cross-Referencing Graphics Box Numbers

Graphics boxes can contain pictures, drawings, graphs, text, equations, or table information. As described in Chapter 19, each graphics box is assigned a unique number according to the graphics box style you have selected. When you choose to display captions with your graphics boxes, you can create cross-references (press Alt+F5, and choose Generate) to the box numbers. To create a cross-reference to a graphics box, type reference text, such as "An example of this is shown in ." (Insert an extra space before the period.) Then follow this procedure:

Choose Tools ▸
Cross-Reference ▸
Both.

- Position the cursor where you want the target information (the box number) to appear. Then press Mark (Alt+F5), choose Mark Text, and then choose Both Reference & Target.

- Choose Tie Reference To, and then choose Caption Number.

- Choose Target Name, type a target name for the reference, and then press Enter.

- Press Exit (F7) to continue, and your document is displayed in the Mark Cross-Reference and Target dialog box.

Choose OK to
continue.

- Use the arrow keys, PgUp/PgDn or the Search feature to locate the graphics box in your document that you want to reference. You may need to turn on Reveal Codes to see the precise location of the graphics code.

- Move the cursor to the immediate right of the Graphics Box code, and press Enter. This marks the graphic as the target for your reference.

Graphics boxes are automatically renumbered when you move them to other places in your document; cross-references are not. If you move graphics boxes, you need to regenerate your document to update cross-references. For more information about working with graphics in WordPerfect, consult Chapter 19.

Creating References across Separate Files

When your document is divided between two or more files, use the Master Document feature to combine the text files and create accurate cross-references for the entire document. The following steps explain how to insert the target and reference codes in the separate files, but they do not address linking the documents together to generate the cross-references. See "Combining Documents from Separate Files," later in this chapter for information about completing the procedure begun here.

- Open the file that contains the target item you want to reference.

Choose Tools ▶
Cross-Reference ▶
Target.

- Locate the target item and move the cursor to it. Press Mark (Alt+F5), choose Mark Text, and then Cross-Reference Target.

- Choose Target Name. Type a name for the target and press Enter. Press Exit (F7) to continue.

- Repeat the above steps to mark other items you want to reference in this file. Then save the file.

- Open the file that should contain a reference to a target in the other file.

- Move the cursor to the place where the reference text should appear. Type the reference text.

Choose Tools ▶
Cross-Reference ▶
Reference.

- Press Mark (Alt+F5), choose Mark Text, and then choose Cross-Reference.

- Choose Tie Reference To, and select the option that matches the type of information in the other file which you want displayed from the target.

- Choose Target Name and enter the same name you entered for the target.

- Press Exit (F7) and save the reference file.

Choose OK to
continue.

- Use the Master Document feature to link the reference file to the target file. This is described later in the chapter under "Combining Documents from Separate Files."

Choose <u>T</u>ools ▸ <u>G</u>enerate.

■ Expand the master document, press Mark (Alt+F5), and then choose <u>G</u>enerate to generate the cross-references.

The final two steps require some understanding of the Master Document feature, which is explained in detail near the end of this chapter. Once the cross-references are generated, you can print the document or save the individual document files. When files are divided in this manner, and you have inserted cross-references between them, you must use the Master Document feature to link the documents together for generating. Otherwise, the references will display question marks to indicate that appropriate target codes are not available in the current file.

Printing Updated Cross-References

It is important that you regenerate cross-references before saving or printing your document. If you make changes to your text after you generate the references, WordPerfect will prompt you about regenerating before it lets you print your document. This safeguard ensures that updated references exist before your document ends up on the printed pages. When the prompt appears, you'll know you made changes that were not generated with your document. At this point, you can ignore the message and continue the print process, or cancel printing and regenerate your cross-references.

Creating Hidden Text

WordPerfect's Hidden Text feature lets you "hide" certain sections of your document and prevent them from printing or displaying on the screen. This can be useful when you are preparing different drafts of a document that you want to print without specific sections. The Hidden Text feature is designed to temporarily hide information that belongs in the document text. At some time, it is assumed that you will want to display and print the hidden text with your document.

You can also use the Hidden Text feature to insert lengthy comments within your document, but, unlike document comments, hidden text may be displayed and edited as regular document text.

To mark a section of text as hidden text:

■ Use the Block feature to select the text you want to hide in your document.

Choose F<u>o</u>nt ▸ Hid-<u>d</u>en Text.

■ Press Mark Text (Alt+F5) and then choose Hidde<u>n</u> Text to display the Hidden Text dialog.

■ Choose <u>H</u>idden Text, so that an *X* appears in the box next to this option.

■ Press Exit (F7) to return to the document screen.

Choose OK to return to the document screen.

Turn on the Reveal Codes window and you'll see a pair of [Hidden On] [Hidden Off] codes surround the text you blocked. These codes simply mark the text as hidden text, but they do not control whether the text is hidden or displayed. You'll need to choose another option to change the display of text that is marked with the hidden codes.

To hide or show hidden text,

Choose F<u>o</u>nt ▸ Hid<u>d</u>en Text.

■ Press Mark Text (Alt+F5) and then choose Hidde<u>n</u> Text to display the Hidden Text dialog.

■ Choose <u>S</u>how Hidden Text to change the display of hidden text. When an *X* appears in the check box next to this option, all hidden text is displayed. When the check box is blank, the hidden text is not displayed.

Choose OK to return to the document screen.

■ Press Exit (F7) to return to the document screen.

When hidden text is not displayed, the pair of hidden codes are combined into one [Hidden On] code. When you open the Reveal Codes window and highlight the [Hidden On] code, you'll see the text that is now hidden.

The Hidden Text feature, as described here, is not the same as the Hide Outline Entry or Hide Body Text features that are found on the Outline menu. See Chapter 11 for more information about hidden outline text and collapsible outlines.

Creating Page Headers and Footers

A header or footer can contain text, page numbers, graphics, cross-references to other document text, and other items that should appear at the top or bottom of each page in your document. You can also alternate two different headers or footers between odd and even pages. For example, you can display the document name at the top of the odd pages in your document and the chapter names at the top of the even pages. The following sections explain how to create headers and footers like these for your own documents.

Creating a Page Header or Footer

A header contains information that appears at the top of each page in your document. A footer is like a header, except its text appears at the bottom of every page. Headers and footers are used in most books, including this one. For example, two different headers appear at the top of these two pages; one reminds you that the current chapter is called "Working with Large Documents," and the other names the section you're now reading. Browse through other chapters in this book, and you'll see the headers change to indicate the current chapter and section.

WordPerfect supports two different headers and footers; these are labeled Header A, Header B, Footer A, and Footer B. Later in this chapter, you'll learn how to define each to create alternating headers and footers on your document pages. The following steps explain how to create a single header or footer for your document:

- Move the cursor to top of the document page where the header or footer should begin. This can be the first page in your document or any page where a new header or footer should begin.

- Press Format (Shift+F8) and then choose Header/Footer/Watermark.

Choose Layout ▶
Header/Footer/
Watermark.

- Choose Headers or Footers.

- Choose Header A or Footer A. Then, choose All Pages (if it's not already selected) to create a header or footer that appears on every page in your document, beginning with the current page on your screen.

- Choose Create, and type the text for the header or footer. A header or footer can contain more than one line of text.

- When you are finished creating the header or footer, press Exit (F7) to return to your document.

When you complete these steps, a [Header A] or [Footer A] code is inserted into your document. As shown in Figure 15.7, header text appears within the page boundaries defined by your top margin.

Each line of text in the header or footer allows one less line on the page for your document text. In addition to the text in the header or footer, WordPerfect automatically adds one blank line between a header or footer and your document text. Initially you won't see the headers and footers on the document screen unless you are using WordPerfect's page display mode. This feature is discussed later in this chapter under "Viewing Headers and Footers." Note that, as you'd expect, you can also see headers and footers in the Print Preview screen.

Changing the Appearance of Header and Footer Text

While typing a header or footer, you can do the following to change the appearance of the header text:

- Press Font (Ctrl+F8) to choose different fonts and change the appearance of the text.

Figure 15.7

Headers print within page margins

Page header

File View Pages Help

| Close | Zoom100% | Zoom200% | Zoom In | Zoom Out | FullPage | FacingPgs | NextPage | PrevPage | GoToPage | Thumb 8 | Thumb 32 |

Graduate Dissertation / Dept. of Business & Communications

First quarter sales increased 35% from last year's figures. This is a direct result of improved communication with our suppliers, the installment of a computer network in our West Valley warehouse, and, of course, the excellent accomplishments of our manufacturing team.

A recent issue of Hang Gliders' Quarterly features an article about the P8500 Glider; here is an excerpt from that article:

"Although there are relatively few competitors in the hang glider industry, the Dalworth Company

Zoom Scale: 100%   Paper Size: 8.5" X 11"   Doc 1 Pg 1

- Choose different formatting options, such Center (Shift+F6) and Flush Right (Alt+F6).

- Press Graphics (Alt+F9) to insert graphic images or lines.

Header and footer text is printed with the initial font defined for your document or printer; you can change the initial document font by pressing Format (Shift+F8), choosing Document, and then choosing Initial Font. You can also choose various fonts and text attributes while you are typing the text for the header or footer. These and other formatting codes are applied only to the header or footer text; they do not affect the text outside of the header or footer.

Editing a Header or Footer

Follow these steps to edit the text in a header or footer. Notice that the cursor can be located anywhere in your document before you perform these steps.

Choose Layout ▶ Header/Footer/ Watermark.

- Press Format (Shift+F8) and choose Header/Footer/Watermark.

- Choose Headers or Footers, and choose Header/Footer A or Header/Footer B to specify which header or footer you want to edit. Then choose Edit.

- Edit the header/footer text, and make any necessary formatting changes.

- Press Exit (F7) to accept the changes and return to your document.

What You Can (and Can't) Put in a Header or Footer

A header or footer can contain almost a full page of text; at least one line must remain on the page for the document text. Although it's possible, it's extremely unlikely that you will create a header or footer that fills each page, because your document would appear with only one line of text with the header/footer information. However, you can create something like the footer shown in Figure 15.8, in which a document legend appears at the bottom of each page.

Figure 15.8

Using a footer to place a legend at the bottom of each document page

Page footer

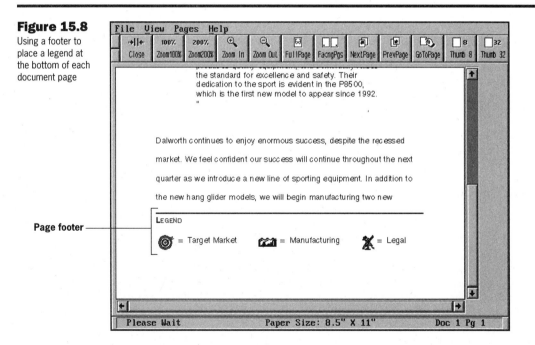

If you want a page number displayed in the header or footer, press Format (Shift+F8) and choose Page (perform these steps while you are creating or editing the header or footer). Then choose Page Numbering and Insert Formatted Page Number. You can also include left and right margin settings, merge codes, graphics, tables, and other layout settings for characters, lines, and paragraphs.

When placed in a header or footer, some formatting codes have no effect on your document. This happens when the codes you insert do not belong on every page or when they must be placed *before* a header or footer code. Some of the codes that do not work in a header or footer include: footnotes, endnotes, table of contents, index codes, and page formatting codes, such as top and bottom margins and center page.

Viewing Headers and Footers

WordPerfect can show headers and footers with your document on the screen, but only if you are working in WordPerfect's page display mode. To display this mode, press Screen (Ctrl+F3), and then choose Page. This displays the headers and footers with the document text.

If you prefer not to use the page display mode—because it is slower than the standard text mode—you can view your headers and footers on the Print Preview screen. Press Print (Shift+F7) and choose Print Preview to see the headers and footers in your document. The Print Preview screen can also show two or more pages at once, and this will help you verify that your headers and footers are placed correctly on the pages.

Alternating between Odd and Even Pages

As shown in Figure 15.9, you can alternate two different headers (or footers) on your document pages. You may, for example, create a header that displays your document name at the top of each even page and another header that displays the current chapter name at the top of the odd pages. This is the procedure for creating two headers or footers that alternate between odd and even pages:

Choose Layout ▶ Header/Footer/ Watermark.

- Move the cursor to the top of the page where a header or footer should begin.

- Press Format (Shift+F8) and Header/Footer/Watermark.

- Choose Headers or Footers.

- Choose Header A or Footer A. Then, choose Odd Pages to create the header/footer that will appear on the odd pages of your document.

- Choose Create and type the text for the header or footer.

- When you are finished, press Exit (F7) to return to your document.

- Press Format (Shift+F8) and choose Header/Footer/Watermark.

Choose Layout ▶ Header/Footer/ Watermark.

- Choose Headers or Footers.

Figure 15.9

Alternating headers

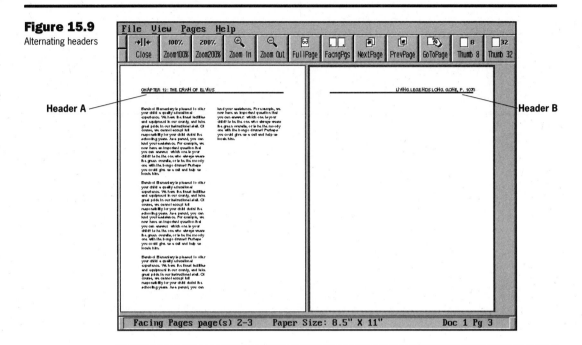

These steps insert two header or footer codes, one to define the headers or footers for the odd pages and another to define the headers or footers for the even pages.

- Choose Header <u>B</u> or Footer <u>B</u>. Then choose <u>E</u>ven Pages to create the header/footer that will appear on the even pages of your document.

- Choose <u>C</u>reate and type the text for the header or footer.

- When you are finished, press Exit (F7) to return to your document.

These steps insert two header or footer codes, one to define the headers or footers for the odd pages and another to define the headers or footers for the even pages.

Including Graphics in a Header or Footer

You can define graphics boxes and lines to include figures, illustrations, and other graphics in your header or footer. For example, Figure 15.10 shows a company logo that appears in a header at the top of each document page. For more on graphics, see Chapter 19. The following steps explain how to insert a graphics box while you are at the editing screen for creating or editing a header or footer.

Figure 15.10

Header with a
graphic image

Graphic in header

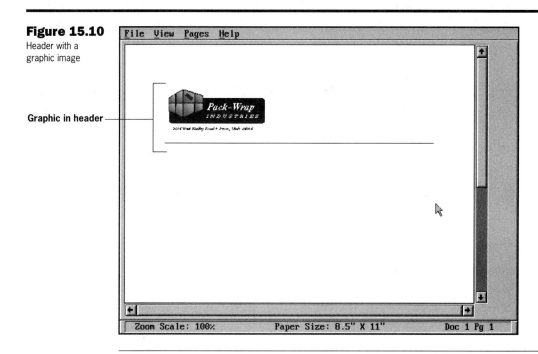

- Begin creating the header or footer by pressing Format (Shift+F8), choosing Header/Footer/Watermark, selecting Headers or Footers and choosing the desired header or footer, and selecting Create.

Choose Graphics ▶
Graphic Boxes ▶
Create.

- At the desired spot within the header of footer, press Graphics (Alt+F9), choose Graphics Boxes, and then choose Create.

- Choose Based on Box Style, highlight User Box, and select Edit.

- Choose Attach To, and select Character Position.

- Choose Edit Position, and select Content Baseline.

Choose OK until all
dialog boxes are
closed.

- Press Enter or choose OK twice to return to the Graphics Box Styles dialog box, and then choose Select. Now choose Filename and enter the name of the graphics file to insert into the header or footer.

- Choose Edit Size, and enter the desired width and height measurements for the graphics box inside the header or footer.

- When you are done, press F7 or choose OK to return to the header or footer creation screen.

This inserts a [Char Box:1; Usr Box:] code into the header or footer text. In these steps, a User Box style is selected to create a graphic without borders. Make sure the size of the box does not exceed the height you want for the header or footer, because the box size can increase the amount of space required for the header or footer.

In addition to graphics boxes, you can insert graphic lines to divide your header or footer text from the document text on the page. Simply choose the Line Draw option from the Graphics menu while you are creating or editing your header or footer. For complete information about graphics boxes and lines, see Chapter 19.

Turning Off Headers and Footers

There are three ways to turn off a header or footer: You can discontinue a header/footer at a certain point until the end of the document, you can "hide" a header/footer for a single page, or you can remove the header or footer by deleting the code that creates it.

Follow these steps to turn off or discontinue a header or footer for the remainder of your document:

Choose Layout ▸ Header/Footer/ Watermark.

- Move the cursor to the page where the header or footer should stop printing on the document pages.

- Press Format (Shift+F8), and choose Header/Footer/Watermark.

- Choose Headers or Footers.

- Then, choose Header/Footer A or Header/Footer B to specify which header/footer you want to turn off.

- Choose Off from the dialog box.

Choose OK to return to your document.

- Press Exit (F7) to return to the document screen.

This inserts a [Header A or B:Off;] or [Footer A or B:Off;] code at the cursor position to stop the printing of your header or footer from that point onward in the document.

To hide or suppress a header or footer for a single page only:

Layout ▸ Page ▸ Suppress.

- Move the cursor to the page where the header should not appear.

- Press Format (Shift+F8), choose Page, and then choose Suppress. The dialog box shown in Figure 15.11 appears.

- Choose Header A, Header B, Footer A, or Footer B to indicate which header or footer you want to suppress. If necessary, you can choose two or more of the items. Or you can even choose Supress All to suppress all headers and footers, page numbering, and so on.

Figure 15.11

Suppressing a
header or footer

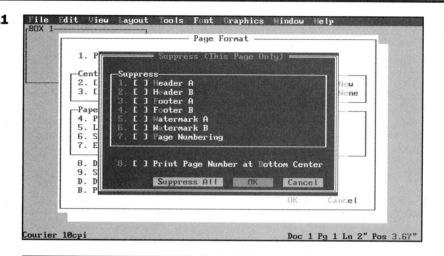

Choose OK until all
dialog boxes are
closed.

- Press Exit (F7) until you exit all dialog boxes and return to your document.

This inserts a [Suppress] code into your text to suppress the printing of the header or footer for only the current page. This is useful when you want to include a page in the middle of your document, such as a diagram or chart, and you do not want this page to include headers or footers as appear on the rest of the document pages.

If you want to turn off headers or footers for the entire document, press Reveal Codes (Alt+F3) to view the codes in your document. Then, locate and delete the [Header] and [Footer] codes that you want to remove.

Combining Documents from Separate Files

WordPerfect can handle a large number of document pages, but when the page count exceeds 100 pages, you may want to divide the document between two or more files. When working with many pages, WordPerfect must devote more system resources to the management of your document, which means that WordPerfect has less memory for standard operations and may run slower than you'd like. You can divide a document into different files—one for each section or chapter—and then use the Master Document feature to combine them again for editing or printing.

The Master Document feature lets you link two or more files together. The file that contains the links to the other documents is called the *master document*. When you create a master document, you won't see the information contained in the other files, but you will see comment boxes that note where text from the other files will appear in the printed document. In addition, you can *expand* the master document to retrieve the information from the other files into their appropriate places. You can then perform any editing or formatting tasks, and print the entire document. When you are finished, you can *condense* the master document to restore its original state.

The Master Document feature also makes it possible to assemble various documents which may include standard paragraphs or tables. For example, suppose you are creating a contract containing standard clauses which also appear in several other contracts. You can save each clause in a separate file and then use the Master Document feature to link them to the current contract. Any changes made to the clause file will be updated to every contract document that includes the clause as a subdocument.

Dividing a Large Document into Separate Files

Before you begin creating a document, you may know that it will require a large number of pages. If you know this in advance, you should start a new file for each section or chapter you plan to create. Sometimes, however, the number of pages in your document may increase as you edit and revise the text. In this case, you may want to divide your document into two or more files. The following steps explain how to block a section of your document and save it as a separate file:

NOTE.   *Before you begin this procedure, it's a good idea to save a backup copy of your document under a different file name. This will allow you to recover the entire file, should you accidentally delete a section of text.*

Choose Edit ▸
Block.

- Move the cursor to the beginning of the section in your document that should be saved as a separate file.

- Press Block (Alt+F4 or F12) and press ↓ or PgDn to move the cursor to the end of the section.

- Press Save As (F10). WordPerfect displays the dialog box shown in Figure 15.12.

Choose File ▸
Save As.

- Type a file name for the section of text, and press Enter. If necessary, type a complete path name before the file name to indicate where the section should be saved.

- Without moving the cursor, turn on Block (Alt+F4 or F12) again, and press Ctrl+Home twice to reblock the section you just saved.

- Press Delete or Backspace to remove the text from your document.

Figure 15.12

Saving a blocked section of your document

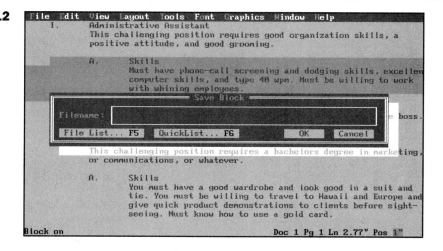

Repeat this procedure for each of the chapters or sections you want to save as separate files. When you are finished, you may want to look at each of the files from the File Manager to verify that the information was correctly saved. Then, save your original document to update the changes you've made to the file on disk. Note that the new file you create will not have retained document specific codes such as headers, footers, and pagination. If necessary, just reestasblish the needed codes in the new document.

Now you have successfully divided your large document into two or more manageable files. In the next section, you'll see how to link these files together as one document for editing and printing.

Combining Files with a Master Document

WordPerfect's Master Document feature can link two or more files—called *subdocuments*—into one file, referred to as the master document. Generally, the master document contains all the formatting codes that should be applied to the entire document, with the introductory text and tables. The subdocuments contain different sections of text that appear in the document. The following steps explain how to create a master document:

- Choose the format settings—such as margins, line spacing, and page numbering—that should be applied to the finished document.

- If necessary, create pages for the document title, table of contents, and index, leaving a blank page between them for the document text. Use the Mark Text features described in Chapter 14 to define a table of contents and index.

- Type any text that should be included in the master document, such as a preface or introduction.

- Move the cursor to the place where the first subdocument link should be inserted.

Choose File ▸ Master Document ▸ Subdocument.

- Press Mark (Alt+F5), choose Master Document, and then choose Subdocument. WordPerfect prompts you to enter the subdocument name.

- Type the name of the file you want to insert at this point in the document. Then press Enter.

WordPerfect inserts a comment box into your document, similar to the example shown in Figure 15.13. (Note that this code will not appear in either Print Preview or page display mode.) Repeat the steps above to create document links to each file you want to include in the master document. The name of each subdocument is displayed in the comment boxes, but the actual text from the files is not shown until you expand the master document, as described in the next section.

Figure 15.13

A subdocument comment box

Subdocument comment box

```
 File  Edit  View  Layout  Tools  Font  Graphics  Window  Help
                    tie. You must be willing to travel to Hawaii and Europe and
                    give quick product demonstrations to clients before sight-
                    seeing. Must know how to use a gold card.

          B.     Salary/Benefits
                 Salary: $65,000/year.  Perks: Expense account, stock option
                 free stuff.


        Subdoc: C:\WPDOCS\ACC-LIST.DOC


        III.   Chief Executive Officer
               This challenging management position requires a masters degree in
               business management or equivalent experience.

          A.     Skills
                 No specific skills required. Responsibilities will be deter
                 soon.

          B.     Salary/Benefits
                 Salary: $2,500,000/year.  Perks: Anything you want.
 Swiss 721 14pt Roman (Speedo)                    Doc 1 Pg 1 Ln 6.99" Pos 1"
```

Expanding and Condensing a Master Document

A master document displays a series of links to other related files, but the text in those files remains hidden until you expand the master document. When you expand a master document, you can view and edit all linked subdocuments as though the entire text were complete in a single file. After you make your changes or print the document, you can condense the master document to its original state, rehiding the linked text. To expand a master document, retrieve your master document into WordPerfect, press Mark (Alt+F5), choose Master Document, choose Expand, and then press Enter or select OK and respond Yes to the "Expand marked subdocs" prompt.

WordPerfect inserts the subdocument files for each subdocument link in your document. Comment codes that read [Subdoc Begin] and [Subdoc End] mark the points at which each subdocument begins and ends. If they exist, page and paragraph numbers, footnotes, endnotes, graphics boxes, or tables are numbered consecutively throughout all files linked to the document. At this point, you can make whatever changes you want in the entire document, including the subdocument text. When you are editing an expanded document, be careful not to delete the [Subdoc] codes that mark the beginning and end of each section. Press Mark (Alt+F5), and choose Generate to update any document references. Then print your document.

When you are finished editing and printing the document, condense your master document by pressing Mark (Alt+F5), choosing Master Document, choosing Condense, pressing Enter or selecting OK, and then responding Yes to the "Condense marked subdocs" prompt.

If you have made changes to any of the subdocument files, you *must* save these changes or they'll be lost when you condense the files. To do so, begin to condense the master document as usual. Then, in the condense Master Document dialog box, click on Subdocuments, and highlight the desired subdocument file. Finally, choose Save Subdoc. Now you can safely condense the master document; any changes to your subdocument will not be lost. When the master document is condensed, it appears as it did before you expanded it. If you have made changes to any information in the master document, make sure you save the document before clearing your screen.

Updating Document References

Document references are any items that reference other things in your document. These include cross-references, tables of contents, indexes, and lists. When you first insert these references into your document, they may display correct information. However, as you make changes to your text or move things to different pages, the references may not display the correct page numbers and other items to which you are referring.

You can update the document references by choosing the Generate feature as described in the following steps. The first step instructs you to expand the master document before you update your references. This is important because it allows WordPerfect to update all references stored in the subdocuments which are linked to the current document. Your table of contents, for example, would not be complete if the text from the subdocuments were not included in the generation process. Follow these steps to update all references in your document.

- Press Mark (Alt+F5), and then choose M<u>a</u>ster Document, choose <u>Ex</u>-pand, and then choose OK. Respond <u>Y</u>es to the "Expand marked sub-docs" prompt.

- Press Mark (Alt+F5) and choose <u>G</u>enerate.

- WordPerfect reminds you that all existing references will be updated and replaced. Choose OK to continue.

WordPerfect then updates your table of contents, index, and other references in your document. At this point, you can send the document to the printer. After that, make sure you condense and save the subdocuments, and save the master document.

Mailing Labels and Envelopes

Form Letters for Mass Mailings

Advanced Merge Techniques

4

Form Letters and Mass Mailing

16

Mailing Labels and Envelopes

Creating Mailing Labels

Creating and Printing Envelopes

Labels and Envelopes for Mass Mailing

C USTOM MAILING LABELS AND PRINTED ENVELOPES ADD A PROFES-
sional touch to your letters and correspondence. When you print
your own envelopes, for example, the fonts and graphics you use
can match the style of the letter inside. The trick to precise labels
and envelopes lies in setting up the correct document format and making sure
your printer can handle the paper on which you want to print. The latest version of WordPerfect includes features which simplify the entire process. The
Labels feature rids you of label-printing nightmares, producing quick results
instead. Envelopes, also, are easily printed when your printer is designed to
handle them.

This chapter explains how to do the preliminary formatting and setup
work required for achieving great success with labels and envelopes. And, because labels and envelopes are often required for mailing letters to a large
number of people, this chapter also covers how to set up labels and envelopes
for mass mailings.

Creating Mailing Labels

Figure 16.1 shows the two types of labels you can create in WordPerfect.
Tractor-fed labels are usually arranged as a single column of labels on a continuous strip of paper. They are designed for printing on dot-matrix printers,
because these printers can accept an uninterrupted flow of paper. The holes
punched at the sides of tractor-fed paper allow the dot-matrix printer to
move the labels during printing.

Sheet labels are arranged in two or more columns across a full sheet of
paper. Although sheet labels are most often fed into laser printers, you can
use them with dot-matrix printers, also. The following sections explain how
the Labels feature works, and provide the general procedure for creating and
printing labels.

How Does WordPerfect Create Labels?

When you create labels in WordPerfect, each page in your document represents one label on the printed pages. WordPerfect uses different methods to
format your labels, depending on whether you are printing for tractor-fed or
sheet labels.

Most tractor-fed labels closely resemble the text layout you see in your
document; the labels are printed in a single column on a continuous strip of
paper, similar to a standard document. But instead of a full 8 1/2-by-11-inch
page, WordPerfect uses a smaller page definition to designate each label as a
complete page in your document. When one label is printed, WordPerfect ad-
vances the continuous paper to print the next label.

Figure 16.1

Tractor-fed labels
and sheet labels

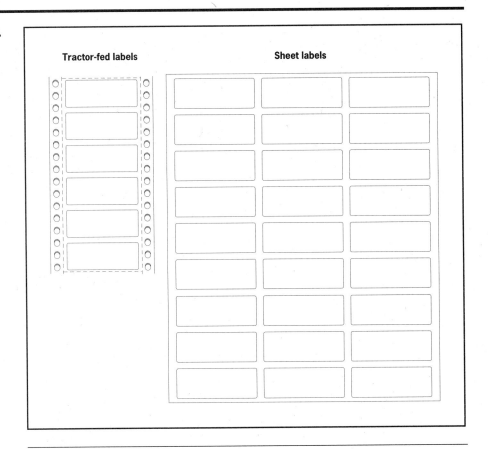

Sheet labels, on the other hand, present an interesting challenge for WordPerfect. The paper you feed into your printer is usually a standard 8 ½-by-11-inch page, but the text you want on the paper—each mailing address—needs to be formatted as though each label were a single sheet of paper with its own margins and page breaks. WordPerfect handles this situation by dividing the physical paper into different sections, called *logical pages*. One logical page is created for each label on the sheet.

Consider the example in Figure 16.2. Notice that the page is divided into columns and rows. When you define labels, you tell WordPerfect the size of the paper to which the labels are attached, and you also specify the size and number of labels on the page. WordPerfect uses this information to divide the *physical* page (the sheet of paper) into a series of *logical* pages (the labels). When you create your label document, each logical page on your screen becomes one label on the printed sheet.

Figure 16.2

A sheet of labels divided into logical pages

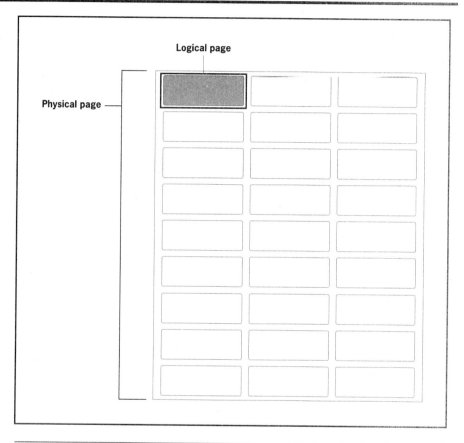

Labels for Dot-Matrix Printers

The following steps explain how to set up a document for tractor-fed labels. Before you create the labels document, you should know the height and width measurements of your labels; this information is usually listed on the package or box that contains the labels. Then do the following steps from a clear WordPerfect screen.

Choose Layout ▸ Page.

1. Press Format (Shift+F8) and choose Page.

2. Choose Labels, and the dialog box shown in Figure 16.3 appears.

3. Choose Display Tractor-Fed.

4. Scroll through the list of label definitions and highlight the type of labels you are using. (Under Label Details in the dialog box, you'll see the size and dimensions of the label definition that is highlighted in the list.) Then choose Select.

Figure 16.3

Labels dialog box

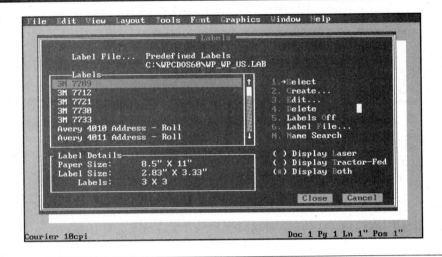

Choose OK until
you return to the
document screen.

5. If needed, make any adjustments in the Labels Printer Info dialog box. (One possible change would be Location. Choose Continuous if you are using a tractor-fed roll of labels. Choose Manual Feed if you are manually feeding individual sheets of labels.) Then press Exit (F7) until all dialog boxes are closed and you return to the document screen.

6. Type address information for one person on your mailing list, and press Hard Page Break (Ctrl+Enter) to end the page. Repeat this step for each person on your mailing list.

7. Save your document, and load your label paper into your printer.

8. Press Print (Shift+F7), choose Full Document, and choose Print.

Choose File ▶ Print
▶ Full Document ▶
Print.

WordPerfect prints the information onto the labels, turning each page of the document screen into one printed label. At the beginning of your document, in the Reveal Codes window, you'll see a [Labels Form:*name*] code where *name* represents the label definition you selected.

It's important to note that printing labels from a dot-matrix printer can be an exercise in "trial and error." Your text may not print correctly the first time because the labels are fed too high or too low in the tractor-feed mechanism. If this happens, roll the platen forward to adjust where the text begins printing on the first label; you may need to try this a few times before you discover where the paper needs to be. You may also need to adjust the horizontal position of the tractor feeder across the length of the platen; this will help correct text that is placed too far left or right on the labels.

Labels for Laser Printers

Laser printers often accept only sheet labels, on which two or more columns of labels are distributed across the page. You can insert sheet labels into almost any type of printer, but laser printers handle the sheets with the most speed and accuracy. Make sure you use labels that are designed for laser printers or copy machines; some types of labels are coated with a thin layer of plastic or varnish that will ruin the image cylinder in your laser printer.

Follow these steps to create a document for sheet labels:

Choose Layout ▸ Page.

1. From a clear document screen, press Format (Shift+F8) and choose <u>P</u>age.

2. Choose <u>L</u>abels to display the Labels dialog box.

3. Select Display <u>L</u>aser.

4. Scroll through the list of labels, and highlight the label definition you want to use. Under Label Details in this dialog box, you'll see the label size and number of labels (*columns × rows*) per page for the highlighted label definition in the list. Choose <u>S</u>elect.

Choose OK until you return to the document screen.

5. If necessary, make any required changes in the Labels Printer Info dialog box. Press Exit (F7) until all dialog boxes are closed and you return to the document screen.

6. Type address information for one person on your mailing list, and press Hard Page Break (Ctrl+Enter) to end the page. Repeat this step for each person on your mailing list.

7. Save your document, and load your blank sheet of labels into your printer.

In these steps, you inserted a [Labels Form:*name*] code at the beginning of your document, where *name* specifies the type of labels you are printing. Each page in the finished document represents one label on the page. However, don't expect to see perfectly formatted labels on your screen—except when using WordPerfect's page display mode. When page display mode is active, your label text will be formatted on the screen as it will appear on the printed label sheet. And of course you can always switch to the Print Preview screen to see how the labels will print.

As Figure 16.4 shows, text display mode differs from the labels you'll see on the printed page. On the document screen, page breaks separate one label from the next. On the printed page, WordPerfect works from left to right and down the page, printing one address per label. When one sheet of labels is filled, WordPerfect automatically places the next label on the next physical page.

Figure 16.4
Labels on document screen (a) and labels on printed page (b)

Labels in text display mode

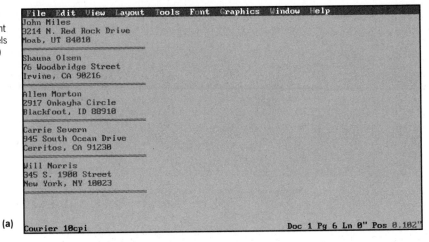

(a)

Labels on the printed page

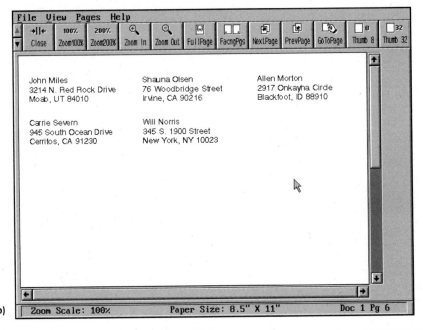

(b)

When you create your labels document, the page numbers on the status line indicate the number of logical pages (labels), not the number of physical label sheets that will be printed. Use Print Preview (press Shift+F7, Print Preview) to view your document as it will print, and this will show how many label sheets you'll need.

Instead of addresses, you can type information for filing folders, identification numbers, name tags, floppy disk contents, inventory numbers, or other items that should appear on your labels. You can also insert graphics along with the label text; for instructions on inserting graphics, see Chapter 19.

Creating a Custom Label Definition

WordPerfect supports most of the standard label types. If you need to print on labels that are not included in WordPerfect's label list, you can either create your own label definition or edit an existing definition to create the layout for the new labels.

Unlike earlier versions of WordPerfect, the label definitions in the WPC60.DOS are stored in a separate label file called WP_WP_US.LAB; they can be used with whatever printer you are currently using. You can create and select a label definition, and send it to any printer that accepts the labels on which you want to print. Prior to creating a new label definition, you must do a little preparation work. First, you'll need a ruler. Figure 16.5 shows the measurements you'll need to make.

Figure 16.5

Measuring sheet labels to create a new labels definition

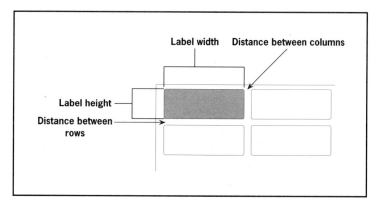

Follow these steps to make the measurements shown in Figure 16.6:

- Measure one of the labels on the sheet; presumably, all the labels are the same size and the same distance apart.

- Count the number of label columns and the number of label rows on the sheet.

- Measure the distance between the columns and between the rows.

■ If there is space between the top and left edges of the page and the first label on the page, measure that space also.

Figure 16.6

The Create Label dialog box

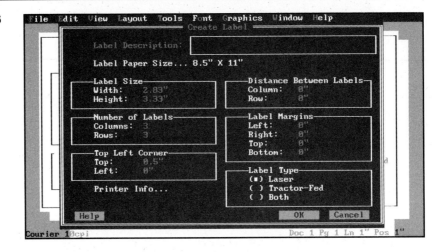

Most label sheets are 8 ½-by-11 inches. However, if your labels are on a sheet of a different size, you'll also need to measure the width and height of your label sheet. Once you know the measurements, follow these steps to create a new definition for your labels:

Choose Layout ▸
Page ▸ Labels.

1. Press Format (Shift+F8) and choose Page. Then choose Labels.

2. Choose Create, and the dialog box shown in Figure 16.6 appears.

3. Type a name or description of the new label type, and then press Enter.

4. If your label sheet is a size other than 8 ½-by-11, choose Label Paper Size. Then select a size from the Paper Size list, or choose Other to enter the measurements of the sheet. Then press Exit (F7) to return to the Create Label dialog box.

5. Choose Label Size and enter the measurements for the width and height of the label you measured on the sheet.

6. Choose Number of Labels, and enter the number of columns across the page. Then enter the number of rows down the page.

7. Choose Top Left Corner and enter the measurement of the space between the top and left sides of the page and the first label on the page. If there is no space between the first label and the page edges, type **0** for both of these options.

8. Choose Distance <u>B</u>etween Labels, and enter the amount of space you measured between the columns and between the rows on the page. If there is no space between labels, type **0** for the distance between columns and rows.

9. Choose Label Margins and enter the margin you want at each side of the label.

10. Choose Label <u>T</u>ype and choose <u>L</u>aser, <u>T</u>ractor-Fed, or <u>B</u>oth to specify the type of printer to which the labels will be fed.

11. Press Exit (F7) to accept the new label definition, and return to the Labels dialog box.

Choose OK until you return to the document screen.

12. If you want to use the label definition now, highlight the name in the list and choose <u>S</u>elect and then press Exit (F7) until you return to your document. Otherwise, just press Exit (F7) until you are back at the document screen.

The new label definition is stored in the file called WP_WP_US.LAB, which also contains other label definitions for WordPerfect. You can use the new label definition with any selected printer, assuming the printer you use can accept the type of labels you've defined. The next section explains how to edit a label definition when you need to adjust how text prints on the labels or when you want to change the margins inside of the labels.

Editing a Label Definition

After you create and use a label definition, you may find the text does not print as expected. You can make adjustments to the label spacing and margins from the Edit Label dialog box. You can also edit a definition to change the label name or description, and modify other label settings.

Choose Layout ▸ Page ▸ Labels.

- Press Format (Shift+F8) and choose <u>P</u>age. Then choose <u>L</u>abels.

- Highlight the label definition you want to edit, and choose <u>E</u>dit. The Edit Label dialog box appears, offering the same options as the Create Label dialog box shown in Figure 16.6.

- Choose the options you want to change, such as Label <u>D</u>escription, Label <u>M</u>argins, or Top Left <u>C</u>orner, and enter the correct measurements.

Choose OK until you return to the document screen.

- When you are finished editing the label definition, press Exit (F7) until you return to the document screen.

The changes you make are updated to the WP_WP_US.LAB file in your WordPerfect directory. The new label definition should automatically take effect in the current label document. If the new label definition does not take hold, press Setup (Shift+F1), choose Environment, and check that the Auto Code Placement setting is on (with an *X* in the check box).

When you create or edit a label definition, the margins you enter create space between the edges of your labels and the text. The standard label margins are set to 0; if you choose to change the margins, make sure you enter relatively small measurements. Margins that are greater than 0.25" may take too much space to allow for all the label text.

The Top Left Corner option in the Create Label or Edit Label dialog box lets you enter measurements to adjust where WordPerfect begins printing the first label on the page. This option is most useful for laser printers, because you cannot physically adjust how the labels are fed into the printer. Instead of moving the paper, the Top Left Corner option adjusts where the text begins printing on the page.

In some cases, the Top and Left measurements are set to 0, but you may need to change them to account for the placement of text on the page. Print one full label sheet to see if an adjustment is required. If the labels are printing too high, you need to adjust the Top measurement; if the labels are printing too far left, you need to adjust the Left measurement. The Top and Left measurements must be positive numbers; entering zero indicates that text should begin printing at the edge of the paper without an adjustment down or to the left on the page.

Creating and Printing Envelopes

In WordPerfect, there are two ways to print address information on an envelope: You can specify address information and send an envelope directly to the printer, or you can create the envelope and insert it at the end of your document. WordPerfect includes envelope definitions for all the standard envelope sizes. Like the Labels feature, envelope definitions determine the size and layout for different types of envelopes. You can also create custom envelope definitions for sizes that are not included in WordPerfect's list of supported envelopes.

In this section, you'll see how to print envelopes, create and edit new envelope definitions, and use WordPerfect's Barcode feature to insert POST-NET bar codes that speed up the delivery of mail that you send.

TIP. *Unlike labels, envelopes are dependent on the printer that is currently selected. Because of this, make sure the printer you want to use is selected before you create or print envelopes.*

Printing an Envelope

WordPerfect's Envelope feature lets you create and print a finished envelope. When you create an envelope, you are prompted to choose an envelope size and to enter the text for the recipient's address and the return address. Before you create an envelope, you can block an address from your document and it will appear as the recipient's address on the printed envelope.

The following steps explain how to send address information for an envelope directly to the printer. These steps do not insert any new codes into your text and do not disturb the document layout. In the following procedure, WordPerfect simply lets you to enter address information; it then creates the envelope in memory and sends it to the printer. This makes it possible to create an envelope at any time, regardless of the document that is currently on the screen.

Choose Layout ▶
Page.

1. Press Format (Shift+F8), choose Page, and choose Envelope. Alternatively, you can press the Alt+F12 shortcut. The dialog box in Figure 16.7 appears.

Figure 16.7
The Envelope dialog box

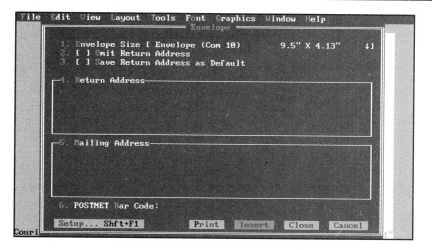

Double-click on an envelope size to select it.

2. Choose Envelope Size, highlight one of the predefined sizes, and press Enter to select it.

3. Choose Return Address and type your address or the address of the person sending the envelope. If you like, you can use formatting such as boldfacing or italics. When you are finished, press Exit (F7) to exit the Return Address box.

4. Choose Mailing Address, type the name of the recipient, and press Exit (F7) to continue. Again, feel free to use formatting for the recipient's name and address. (If you blocked address information before choosing the Envelope feature, the blocked address from your document automatically appears as the mailing address.)

5. Choose Print and the envelope is sent to the printer.

If the envelope you want to print is not loaded into your printer, Word-Perfect will prompt you to insert it. If you don't want WordPerfect to set up the envelope with a return address, check the box for Omit Return Address before exiting the Envelope dialog box; you'll want to check this option when you are using preprinted envelopes on which the return address already appears in the upper-right corner or the back of the envelope.

Remember, you can perform these steps to print an envelope at any time. You don't need to clear the screen before you begin. If you want to keep a copy of an envelope in a document file, use the Envelope Insert option, as described in the next section.

Inserting an Envelope into Your Document

For business letters and other types of correspondence, you may want to include the envelope at the end of the letter. This ensures that your letter will be ready to send with a preaddressed envelope. When you print your document, you'll send both the letter and the envelope to the printer at the same time. Follow these steps to insert an envelope page at the end of your document:

Drag with your mouse to highlight the recipient's name and address.

Choose Layout ▸ Envelope.

■ Use Block (Alt+F4 or F12) to highlight the recipient's name and address from the text of the letter.

■ Press Format (Shift+F8), choose Page, and then choose Envelope. Or, simply press the Alt+F12 shortcut.

■ Choose Envelope Size, highlight one of the predefined sizes, and press Enter to select it.

■ Choose Return Address, and type your address. Press Exit (F7) to exit the Return Address box. Note that the blocked text from your document has been inserted as the mailing address.

■ Choose Insert, and the envelope is inserted into your document.

WordPerfect inserts the envelope page at the end of your document, using the mailing address information you entered at the dialog box. The envelope page begins with a hard page break to separate it from the rest of the document. As shown in Figure 16.8, WordPerfect inserts several margin codes and the text to set up the envelope format.

Figure 16.8
Envelope page viewed from Reveal Codes

Envelope text ——

Codes create
envelope layout ——

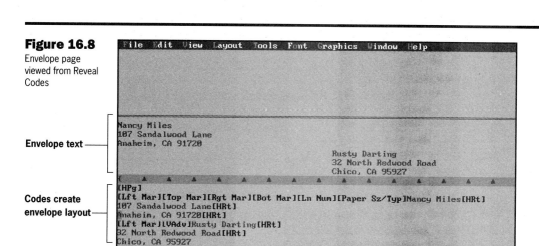

You can edit the text and codes, if necessary, to make changes before you print; use the Print Preview screen to verify that everything will appear where it should on the envelope. If you want to keep the envelope as part of the current document, make sure you save the document before printing or exiting.

Setting Up Envelope Options

The Envelope Setup options let you define a standard envelope size that appears each time you create an envelope. Through the main Envelope dialog box, you can also designate an address as the default return address. These options are useful if you print the same return address on every envelope you send and if you use the same type of envelope each time. Do the following to choose default options for envelopes:

Choose Layout ▶
Envelope.

- Press Format (Shift+F8), choose Page, and then choose Envelope. Or press Alt+F12 to get there the quick way.

- Choose Return Address and type the appropriate address for your company or personal residence. (Remember, when you type the return address, you can press Font (Ctrl+F8) to apply fonts and attributes to the text; you can even press Reveal Codes (Alt+F3) to view the codes you insert.) When you're done entering the return addres, press F7 and then select Save Return Address as Default.

- Now choose Setup (Shift+F1) to display the dialog box shown in Figure 16.9.

Figure 16.9

The Envelope Setup dialog box

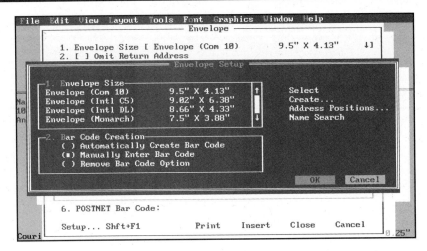

- Choose <u>E</u>nvelope Size to select a default size for your envelopes. Highlight the desired size.

- Choose <u>B</u>ar code Creation, and choose an option: <u>A</u>utomatically Create Bar Code, <u>M</u>anually Enter Bar Code, or <u>R</u>emove Bar Code Option from the Envelope dialog box. (Later in this chapter, you will find complete information about the bar code feature for envelopes.)

- Choose <u>A</u>ddress Positions to adjust the placement of the address information on the envelope. When you are finished, press F7 to return to the Envelope Setup dialog box.

Choose OK to accept the Envelope Setup options.

- Press Exit (F7) to accept your selections and return to the Envelope dialog box. Then press Exit (F7) until you return to your document screen.

Your settings for default envelope size, return address, and other envelope options are saved in the WP{WPC}.SET file, which stores the default settings of WordPerfect. When you create your next envelope, your preferences for envelope size and return address are automatically inserted into the Envelope dialog box. At this point, you can choose any of the options, such as <u>Re</u>turn Address, and replace the information inserted by WordPerfect; however, the envelope setup options will continue to appear for future envelopes until you change the envelope settings again or until the WP{WPC}.SET file is deleted or removed from your WordPerfect directory.

Creating Your Own Envelope Definition

Although WordPerfect includes envelope definitions for the standard envelope sizes, you may need to set up custom definitions for unique or unusual
envelopes. This process is divided into two separate tasks: First, you enter the
dimensions of your envelope on the Paper Size/Type dialog box; then you create the envelope as described earlier in this section. The new envelope definition you create will appear as one of the available sizes in the Envelope
dialog box.

Before you create a new envelope definition, make sure you select the
printer that you will be using to print the envelopes. This is important because
the new envelope definition is saved to the .PRS file for the printer that is currently selected. To select the printer, press Print (Shift+F7) and choose Select;
then highlight the printer you want, choose Select, and press Exit (F7) until
you return to the document screen.

Once the correct printer is selected, follow these steps to create and use a
new definition for envelopes:

Choose Layout ▸
Page ▸ Paper Size/
Type.

1. Press Format (Shift+F8), choose Page, and then choose Paper Size/Type.

2. Choose Create to display the dialog box shown in Figure 16.10.

Figure 16.10

Creating a new
envelope definition
on the Create Paper
Size/Type dialog box

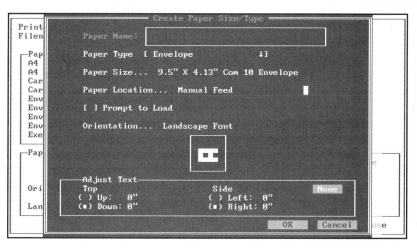

3. Type a name or description for the new envelope definition. Then
press Enter.

Double-click on
Envelope.

4. Choose Paper Type, highlight Envelope, and press Enter.

5. Choose Paper Size to display the Define Paper Size dialog box.

Double-click on the desired envelope size.

6. From the list of predefined paper sizes, highlight the size that matches your envelope and choose Select. (If none of the predefined sizes matches your envelope, choose Other and enter measurements for the envelope's width and height. Then press Exit (F7).)

7. Choose Paper Location. Then choose Continuous to indicate that the envelope will be fed from a tray of continuous paper, or choose Manual Feed if the envelope will be inserted manually into the printer.

8. If you specified Manual Feed as the location, choose Prompt to Load. Thereafter, WordPerfect will remind you to load the envelopes before it starts printing them.

9. Choose Orientation and the dialog box shown in Figure 16.11 appears. Highlight the correct orientation for your envelopes, and then press Exit (F7).

Figure 16.11

The Paper Orientation dialog box

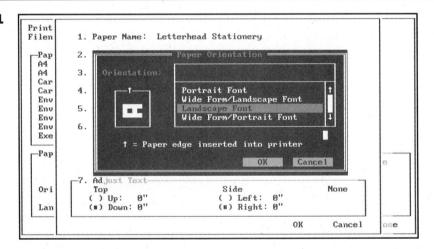

10. Press Exit (F7) to close the Create Paper Size/Type dialog box. The new envelope definition appears on the list of defined paper sizes and types.

11. Press Exit (F7) until you return to the document screen.

Choose OK until you return to your document screen.

You can select your new envelope definition from the Paper Size/Type dialog box, or you can choose it from the Envelope dialog box by creating an envelope as described earlier.

When you create a new envelope definition, your choice for Orientation indicates how the envelope will be fed into the printer, and it also determines how the text will be printed on the envelope. Figure 16.12 shows examples of the four orientation options. The arrows in the figure show the direction in which the paper is fed into the printer.

Figure 16.12

Examples of the four orientation types

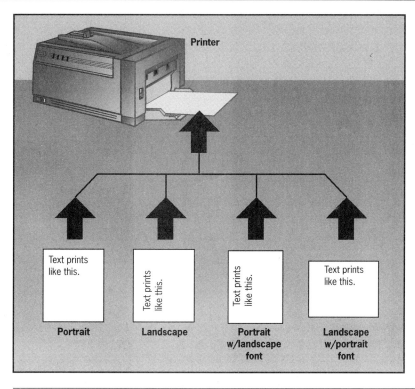

Remember that all envelope definitions are saved with the current printer selection. If you select a different printer, your envelope definition will not appear in the updated list of envelope sizes unless you re-create your envelope definition for the new printer also.

Editing and Updating an Envelope Definition

After you create an envelope definition, you may want to change the name you've assigned to it or indicate a different location from which the envelopes will be fed into your printer. You may also need to adjust how the text is printed on the envelope; this is necessary when the printer puts too much space between the top or side of the envelope and the text you want to print.

For example, suppose the return address is printing an inch below the top edge of the envelope even though you specified that it should print with a top margin of one-half inch. First, try to adjust the placement of the envelope when it is fed into the printer; this often fixes problems with envelopes on dot-matrix printers. If you are using a laser printer, you probably can't adjust how the envelope feeds into your printer, but you can edit the envelope definition to adjust the text placement. Follow these steps to adjust the placement of text on the envelope and to change other settings in the envelope definition:

Choose Layout ▶ Page ▶ Paper Size/ Type.

- Press Format (Shift+F8) and choose Page. Then choose Paper Size/Type.

- Highlight the name of the envelope definition that you want to modify. Choose Edit, and the Edit Paper Size/Type dialog box appears.

- Choose Adjust Text. If the envelope text prints too high or too low, choose Top and specify an adjustment for Up or Down. If envelope text prints too far right or left, choose Side and specify an adjustment for Left or Right.

- If necessary, choose other options and make the changes you need. For example, you may want to change the Paper Name, Paper (envelope) Size, Paper Location, and Orientation.

Choose OK until you return to the document screen.

- Press Exit (F7) until you exit all dialog boxes and return to the document screen.

The edited envelope definition is saved in the .PRS file for the printer that is currently selected, and it affects only the envelope documents that you will create in the future; the edited envelope definition does not affect the envelope documents you have already created. If you print envelopes directly from the Envelope dialog box and don't insert them into your text, you won't need to update any documents. However, if you have inserted envelopes at the end of your letter documents, you can follow this procedure to update a document with an edited envelope definition:

- Retrieve the document that includes the envelope you want to update.

- Move the cursor to the beginning of the envelope page.

Choose Layout ▶ Page ▶ Paper Size/ Type.

- Press Format (Shift+F8), choose Page, and then choose Paper Size/Type.

- Highlight the edited envelope definition from the Paper Name list, and choose Select.

Choose OK or Close until all dialog boxes are closed.

- Press Exit (F7) to close all dialog boxes. Then save your document.

These steps insert the new [Paper Sz/Type] code for the edited envelope definition. Once the new code is inserted, remember to save your document to update the information in the original file.

Speed Up the Mail with Bar Codes

WordPerfect can generate POSTNET (Postal Numeric Encoding Technique) bar codes, which allow faster processing and routing for mail in the United States. As Figure 16.13 shows, a *bar code* is an encrypted version of the recipient's ZIP code that can be quickly evaluated and routed by postal scanners. For bulk mailing, you can send letters at a reduced rate when you print bar codes on each of the envelopes.

Figure 16.13

A bar code is an encrypted ZIP code for postal scanners.

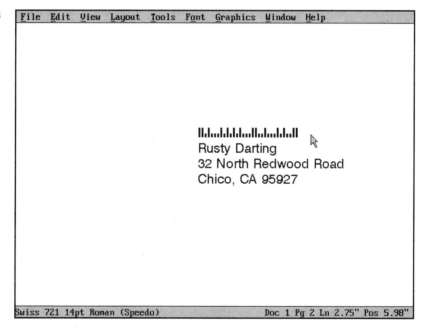

Follow these steps to include a bar code when you are creating an envelope:

- Press Format (Shift+F8), choose Page, and then choose Envelope; or press the Alt+F12 shortcut.

- Choose the desired envelope size, and enter the appropriate address information.

- Choose POSTNET Bar Code, and type the recipient's ZIP code. Then press Enter.

- Choose Print or Insert to create the finished envelope.

When you enter the ZIP code, you can type five, nine, or eleven digits; make sure you type the entire ZIP code without spaces or hyphens. On the finished envelope, the POSTNET bar code appears above the first line of the mailing address, similar to the example shown in Figure 16.13.

When an envelope is inserted into your document, [Barcode] appears in the Reveal Codes window on the line above the recipient's name. In the standard text mode, you won't see the actual bar code lines in your document, but they are visible when you work in WordPerfect's graphics display mode or page display mode, or when you view your document on the Print Preview screen.

The Envelope Setup dialog box includes options that let you choose whether you want bar codes inserted for each envelope you create. To see the options, choose Setup (Shift+F1) from the Envelope dialog box. The bar code setup options appear as shown in Figure 16.14.

Figure 16.14

Bar code options in the Envelope Setup dialog box

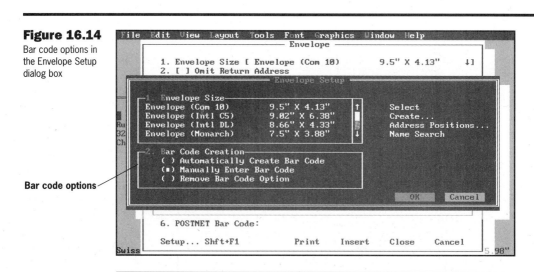

Bar code options

Choose <u>B</u>ar Code Creation, and then choose Automatically <u>C</u>reate Bar Code, and WordPerfect automatically inserts a bar code each time you create an envelope; choose <u>M</u>anually Enter Bar Code, and WordPerfect does not insert a bar code automatically, but displays an option on the dialog box that will insert the bar code, if you wish. The last option, <u>R</u>emove Bar Code Option, prevents you from creating a bar code from the Envelope dialog box. After you select the bar code option you want to use, press Exit (F7) to save your choice and return to the Envelope dialog box. This becomes the default bar code setup for WordPerfect until you change the setup options again.

Labels and Envelopes for Mass Mailing

Printing a single envelope or a few labels is simple enough in WordPerfect, but how do you handle *hundreds* of addresses for bulk mailings? WordPerfect's Merge feature can create a unique label or envelope for each person in a special address file that you create—and the file can contain hundreds, or even thousands, of names and addresses.

First, you'll need to create a WordPerfect file that contains the names and addresses of the people or companies on your mailing list. Then you create a labels or envelope document, similar to the examples described earlier in this chapter, but instead of specifying address information, you insert special merge codes in the labels or envelope document that represent information in your address file. The result is a *form file* which the Merge feature combines with the addresses to create printed envelopes or labels. This is the general process; the next section explains how to use Merge to create envelopes and labels. Use this method of printing labels and envelopes when you have large mailing lists to create and manage. For more information about the Merge feature and other merge applications, see Chapters 17 and 18.

Creating an Address File

Figure 16.15 shows an address file for labels and envelopes. In earlier versions of WordPerfect, this type of file is called the secondary file; in WordPerfect 6.0, this file is called the *data text file*. Notice that each page in the file contains only one address in the list.

Figure 16.15

Address information
in Text Data format

```
File  Edit  View  Layout  Tools  Font  Graphics  Window  Help
KateENDFIELD
AllenENDFIELD
Mrs.ENDFIELD
Babbitt & CompanyENDFIELD
37 W. Manchester AvenueENDFIELD
New York, New YorkENDFIELD
10078ENDFIELD
conservativeENDFIELD
ENDRECORD
_____
MarkENDFIELD
BoltonENDFIELD
Mr.ENDFIELD
Foxglove FarmsENDFIELD
204 Oak Street, #12ENDFIELD
Jackson, TennesseeENDFIELD
38304ENDFIELD
conservativeENDFIELD
ENDRECORD
_____
GordonENDFIELD
FaulkENDFIELD
Mr.ENDFIELD
Field: 9                              Doc 1 Pg 2 Ln 2.33" Pos 1"
```

In this example, each address is divided into different sections called *fields*. The first field contains the recipient's name, the second contains the address, and the city/state and ZIP code fill one field each. Dividing the address information into fields makes it easier to organize the document that you will create later as the model for labels or envelopes. The following steps explain how to create an address file; you should begin from a clear document screen.

Choose <u>T</u>ools ▸ Mer<u>g</u>e ▸ <u>D</u>efine ▸ Data [Text]. Then choose OK to return to your document.

1. Press Merge Codes (Shift+F9) and choose <u>D</u>ata [Text]. Then press Exit (F7) until you return to your document.

2. Type the name of a person that should be included in your address list. Then press End Field (F9) to indicate the end of the first field.

3. Type the street address for this person. Press End Field (F9) to indicate the end of the second field.

4. Type the city and state, and then press End Field (F9). Finally, type the ZIP code and press End Field (F9).

Choose <u>T</u>ools ▸ Mer<u>g</u>e ▸ <u>D</u>efine.

5. Press Merge Codes (Shift+F9) and choose <u>E</u>nd Record to complete this address.

6. Repeat steps 2 through 5 for each person you want to include in your address file.

Choose <u>F</u>ile ▸ Save <u>A</u>s, and type **ADDRESS.DF**.

7. Press Save As (F10) and type **ADDRESS.DF** to save the file. The .DF is the recommended file name extension; it stands for "data file."

Before you continue, you may want to assign descriptive names to the address fields. This makes it easier to reference the address information when you create the form files for labels and envelopes. After creating the address list, follow these steps to assign the descriptive names:

1. Press Merge Codes (Shift+F9) and choose Field <u>N</u>ames.

Choose <u>T</u>ools ▸ Mer<u>g</u>e ▸ <u>D</u>efine ▸ Field <u>N</u>ames.

2. Type **NAME** as the descriptive name for the first field. Then press Enter.

3. For the second field, type **STREET ADDRESS** and press Enter.

4. Type **CITY & STATE** as the descriptive name for the third field and press Enter.

5. For the last field, type **ZIP**, and press Enter. Then press Exit (F7) until you return to the document screen.

These steps insert the following information at the beginning of the address list:

`FIELDNAMES(NAME;STREET ADDRESS;CITY & STATE;ZIP)END RECORD`

After you assign descriptive names to the fields, make sure you save the address list again to update the file. Now you're ready to create the form files for your labels and envelopes.

Although you do not need to assign names as described here, it is easier to create the form files when you use descriptive names to reference the field information. If you choose not to assign descriptive names, you'll need to remember the field numbers for each of the address items. For this example, remember that the recipient's name is stored in field 1, the street address in field 2, the city and state in field 3, and the ZIP code in field 4.

Creating a Form File for Labels

A standard label document contains the layout and text for all the labels you want to print. A form file for labels is structured somewhat differently, because it is designed to merge text from another file into the label format. To create a label form file, you first select the label format you want to use. Then, instead of typing text for all the labels, you create only one label with merge codes that represent the information stored in the address file. When you merge the completed form file with your address file, you'll have a label for each person or item in the list. The following explains how to create a labels form file for the address data file created in the previous section. Begin from a clear document screen.

Choose Tools ▸ Merge ▸ Define ▸ Form. Then choose OK until you return to your document.

1. Press Merge Codes (Shift+F9) and choose Form. Then press Exit (F7) until you return to the document screen.

2. Press Format (Shift+F8), choose Page, and then choose Labels.

Choose Layout ▸ Page ▸ Labels.

3. Scroll through the list of label definitions, highlight the type of labels you are using, and choose Select.

Choose OK until you return to your document.

4. If needed, make selections from the Labels Printer Info dialog box. Then press Exit (F7) until all dialog boxes are closed and you return to the document screen.

5. Press Merge Codes (Shift+F9) and choose Field. Then type **NAME** or **1** in the Field box, and press Enter.

6. Press Enter again to move the cursor to the next line on the page.

Choose Tools ▸ Merge ▸ Define ▸ Field.

7. Press Merge Codes (Shift+F9) and choose Field. Then type **STREET ADDRESS** or **2** in the Field box, and press Enter.

8. Press Enter again to move to the next line.

9. Press Merge Codes (Shift+F9) and choose Field. Then type **CITY & STATE** or **3** in the Field box, and press Enter.

10. Press the spacebar to add a space before the next field.

11. Press Merge Codes (Shift+F9) and choose Field. Then type **ZIP** or **4** in the Field box, and press Enter.

Choose File ▸ Save As, and type **LA-BELS.FF**.

12. Press Save As (F10), type **LABELS.FF**, and press Enter to save the file. The .*FF*, the recommended file name extension, stands for "form file."

This example creates a form file for the address list you created earlier in the chapter. Each of the FIELD codes represents a field of information from the address list. The steps tell you to type a name or a number because fields from the data file can be identified with one or the other. If you want to merge the label form file with an address file other than the one described earlier in this chapter, the address information could be organized differently. If so, you'll need to insert the field codes that match the information you want inserted from the new address file. Later in this chapter, you'll see how to merge the address file with the form file you've created.

Creating a Form File for Envelopes

Creating an envelope form file is similar to creating standard envelopes. However, instead of a mailing address, you insert merge codes that represent the address information. When you merge the envelope form file with your address list, WordPerfect replaces the merge codes with the address information and creates an envelope for each address in your list. From a clear document screen, follow these steps to create a form file for envelopes:

Choose Tools ▸ Merge ▸ Define ▸ Form. Then choose OK until you return to your document.

1. Press Merge Codes (Shift+F9) and choose Form. Then press Exit (F7) until you return to the document.

2. Press Format (Shift+F8), choose Page, and then choose Envelope; or, simply press Alt+F12.

Choose Layout ▸ Envelope.

3. Choose Envelope Size, highlight the envelope size you want, and press Enter to select it.

4. Choose Return Address and type your address. Press Exit (F7) to continue.

5. Choose Mailing Address.

Choose Tools ▸ Merge ▸ Define ▸ Field, then enter **NAME** or **1** in the Field box.

6. Press Merge Codes (Shift+F9) and choose Field. Then type **NAME** or **1** in the Field box, and press Enter.

7. Press Enter again to move the cursor to the next line in the mailing address.

8. Press Merge Codes (Shift+F9), choose Field, type **STREET ADDRESS** or **2**, and press Enter.

9. Press Enter again to move to the next line.

10. Press Merge Codes (Shift+F9), choose Field, type **CITY & STATE** or **3**, and press Enter.

11. Press the spacebar to add a space before the next field of information.

12. Press Merge Codes (Shift+F9), choose Field, type **ZIP** or **4**, and press Enter. Your screen should resemble Figure 16.16.

Figure 16.16

Field codes in the Mailing Address box

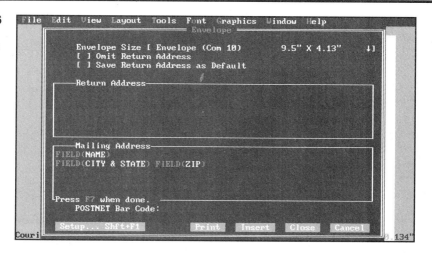

13. Press Exit (F7) to exit the Mailing Address box.

14. Choose Insert, and the envelope is inserted into your document.

15. Press Home, Home, ↑ to move the cursor to the beginning of the document.

16. Press Save As (F10) and type **ENVELOPE.FF** to save the document.

Choose File ▸ Save As, and type **ENVELOPE.FF**.

This completes the form file for envelopes. Each FIELD code references information from the address file you created earlier. Now you can use the Merge feature to combine this file with information from your address list.

You've just seen how to create a new form file for envelopes, but this isn't the only way to create one. You can retrieve an envelope document that you have already created and replace the mailing address information with the FIELD() codes shown in the previous steps.

WordPerfect also provides another way to create envelopes when you are creating letters for mass mailing; an option on the Run Merge dialog box instructs WordPerfect to automatically insert envelopes after each letter created by the merge. See Chapter 17 for information about using this option and creating form letters with the Merge feature.

Merging the Address and Form Files

Perform the following steps to merge your address list with your form file for labels or envelopes.

Choose Tools ▸
Merge ▸ Run.

1. Press Merge/Sort (Ctrl+F9) and choose Merge. The Run Merge dialog box appears.

2. At the Form File option, type **LABELS.FF** or **ENVELOPE.FF** as the form file. Then press Enter.

3. Choose Data File and type **ADDRESS.DF**. Then press Enter.

4. Choose Output and select Unused Document to indicate that the results of the merge should be placed in the next available document screen.

Choose Merge to
begin the merge.

5. Press Exit (F7) to begin the merge.

WordPerfect proceeds to combine the information from the address list with the model document in the form file. When the merge is finished, the results are displayed in one of the unused document screens; each page in the merged document will print as one label or envelope. At this point, you can scroll through the document and make any editing changes. Then press Print (Shift+F7), choose Full Document, and select Print to send all the labels/envelopes to the printer. Although you can save the merged document, this will simply take up space on your hard disk; you can quickly run the merge to combine the files again and re-create your labels or envelopes.

17

Form Letters for Mass Mailings

Creating an Address List

Creating the Form Letter File

Merging the Address List with the Form Letter

FORM LETTERS COMPRISE A LARGE PERCENTAGE OF BUSINESS COMMUNI-cation. Marketing groups often create them to sell products by mail. Business and service organizations use them to distribute information to their customers and employees. You see them almost every day, and they're most effective when the recipient doesn't know he or she is getting one.

The disadvantage to most form letters is that they're often obviously generic: Your name and address are inserted into a preprinted form. WordPerfect can create form letters of this kind, but it employs a better system to create the finished product. It actually generates a complete letter for each person on your mailing list, using the same fonts and formatting for the entire text. WordPerfect also lets you personalize the letters for the recipients; in addition to the standard form letter text, you can insert personal notes or comments for each person who receives a letter. This helps you communicate more effectively with the people on your list.

NOTE. *If you have primary and secondary merge files that you have created in earlier versions of WordPerfect, you can use these to create form letters in WordPerfect 6.0. You do not need to change the format or codes in the files.*

Creating a form letter application involves three simple tasks:

- Creating a *data file*. This is a WordPerfect file that contains the names and addresses for all companies or individuals who will receive your letter. Earlier versions of WordPerfect called this file the *secondary file*.

- Creating a *form file*. This is a WordPerfect file that contains the text for the form letter. Instead of name and address information, the file includes special merge codes that indicate where information should be inserted from the data file. Earlier versions of WordPerfect called this the *primary file*.

- Using the *Merge* feature to combine the address and form letter files.

The result is a personalized letter for each person or company on your list. WordPerfect also includes an option that automatically prints an envelope for each letter, which speeds up the process of preparing the letters for mailing.

This chapter explains how to create the files you need to send a form letter to a large number of people. The special tools that WordPerfect provides for editing and managing the form letter files are also covered.

Creating an Address List

The data file is usually the first file you create when preparing a form letter. This file includes the names and addresses of the individuals who should receive the form letter you want to send. The following sections explain how to structure a data file, and how to edit and alphabetize the list after you've created it.

Understanding the Data File Structure

Before you create the data file—or address list—for the people who should receive your letters, consider the type of information you want inserted into your form letter. You can include anything in the file—you aren't limited to name and address information. Your data file can contain fields for telephone numbers, personal statistics, purchasing information, and account numbers.

Once you've decided what information you want to put into the letter, you're ready to create a data file like the example shown in Figure 17.1. Notice that the address information for each person is considered one *record* in the file. Records are separated by ENDRECORD codes, which are visible on the document editing screen.

Figure 17.1

An address/data file

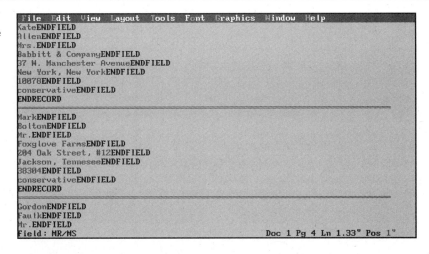

```
 File  Edit  View  Layout  Tools  Font  Graphics  Window  Help
KateENDFIELD
AllenENDFIELD
Mrs.ENDFIELD
Babbitt & CompanyENDFIELD
37 W. Manchester AvenueENDFIELD
New York, New YorkENDFIELD
10078ENDFIELD
conservativeENDFIELD
ENDRECORD

MarkENDFIELD
BoltonENDFIELD
Mr.ENDFIELD
Foxglove FarmsENDFIELD
204 Oak Street, #12ENDFIELD
Jackson, TennesseeENDFIELD
38304ENDFIELD
conservativeENDFIELD
ENDRECORD

GordonENDFIELD
FaulkENDFIELD
Mr.ENDFIELD
Field: MR/MS                              Doc 1 Pg 4 Ln 1.33" Pos 1"
```

Within each record, the name and address information is divided into different fields. In this example, there are several fields for each record: first name, last name, company name, street address, city/state, and ZIP code. Each field ends with an ENDFIELD code.

You can organize your address information into as many fields as you need. The organization of the data file fields should reflect the form letter or other documents you want to create. Decide how you want to use the address information before you create your own data file. Consider which information will be different in each copy of the form letter you send.

Since you can use the same data file for different form documents, you may need to include fields to account for special situations. Consider the example in Figure 17.2, in which the form letter includes a personal greeting for the recipient. In this case, each record in the data file includes a field to indicate whether Mr., Ms., Mrs., or Dr. should be inserted before the last name. Notice also that the first and last names are divided between two fields in the data file; this allows WordPerfect to insert the last name into the greeting without the first name, or vice versa.

Figure 17.2

An address/data file and a completed form letter

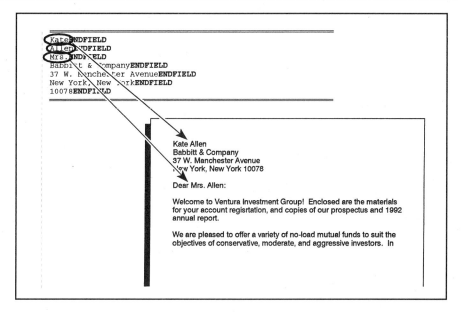

When you create a new data file, make sure the structure of the file follows these guidelines:

- A field can have as many characters or lines of text as you need to store in the field.

- Each field must end with an ENDFIELD code.

- The fields must be arranged in the same order for each record.

- Each record must have the same number of fields.

- Each record must end with an ENDRECORD code, which automatically inserts a page break.

Use these guidelines to help create a consistent structure for the data file. If a data file is not organized correctly, WordPerfect cannot create accurate letters for each person on your list. It is very important that every record in the data file has the same number of fields as the other records. If you're missing a phone number or a ZIP code for one or more of the records, leave the Phone Number or ZIP Code field blank—just make sure you include an ENDFIELD code to indicate the field does exist in the record. All records in the file must follow the same layout. For example, if the first record has four fields for name, phone number, address, and ZIP code, each record should have four ENDFIELD codes for each of the fields—even though each record may not have phone number information.

Creating the Address Data File

This section explains how to create a data file for a form letter. Each record in the data file will be divided into different fields, one each for the first name, last name, title for greeting (Mr., Ms., etc.), company name, street address, city and state, and ZIP code.

In the following exercise, names and addresses are provided; you can easily substitute these with names and addresses from your own mailing list. Start from a clear WordPerfect screen.

Choose <u>T</u>ools ▶ Me<u>r</u>ge ▶ <u>D</u>efine ▶ Data [Text].

1. Press Merge Codes (Shift+F9) and choose <u>D</u>ata [Text].

2. Then press Exit (F7) to return to the document editing screen.

3. Type **Joan** and press End Field (F9). This creates the first name field of the first record. An ENDFIELD code marks the end of the field.

Choose OK until you return to the document screen.

4. Type **Vasquez** and press End Field (F9) to create the second field. Notice that the "Field: " indicator on the status line shows the field number where the cursor is located.

5. For the third field, type **Ms.** and press End Field (F9).

6. Type **Vasquez Imports, Inc.** and press End Field (F9).

7. Type **152 White Sands Drive** as the street address and press End Field (F9).

8. Type the city and state, **Kahului, Hawaii** and then press End Field (F9). Finally, type **96732** as the ZIP code and press End Field (F9).

Choose <u>T</u>ools ▶ Me<u>r</u>ge ▶ <u>D</u>efine ▶ End Record.

9. Press Merge Codes (Shift+F9) and choose <u>E</u>nd Record to complete this address. When you are finished, your screen will look like Figure 17.3. Notice that WordPerfect automatically inserts a hard page break after the ENDRECORD command.

10. Repeat the procedure described in steps 3 through 9 to add the following records:

Mark**ENDFIELD**
Bolton**ENDFIELD**

Figure 17.3

The first record in the data file

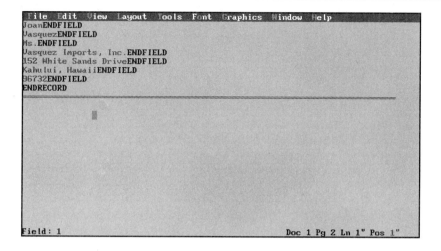

```
File  Edit  View  Layout  Tools  Font  Graphics  Window  Help
JoanENDFIELD
VasquezENDFIELD
Ms.ENDFIELD
Vasquez Imports, Inc.ENDFIELD
152 White Sands DriveENDFIELD
Kahului, HawaiiENDFIELD
96732ENDFIELD
ENDRECORD




Field: 1                                    Doc 1 Pg 2 Ln 1" Pos 1"
```

Mr.**ENDFIELD**

Foxglove Farms**ENDFIELD**

204 Oak Street, #12**ENDFIELD**

Jackson, Tennessee**ENDFIELD**

38304**ENDFIELD**

ENDRECORD

Kate**ENDFIELD**

Allen**ENDFIELD**

Mrs.**ENDFIELD**

Babbitt & Company**ENDFIELD**

37 W. Manchester Avenue**ENDFIELD**

New York, New York**ENDFIELD**

10078**ENDFIELD**

ENDRECORD

Gordon**ENDFIELD**

Faulk**ENDFIELD**

Mr.**ENDFIELD**

ENDFIELD

775 E. Riverton Drive**ENDFIELD**

Kent, Ohio**ENDFIELD**

44240**ENDFIELD**

ENDRECORD

Burke**ENDFIELD**

Staheli**ENDFIELD**

Mr.**ENDFIELD**

```
ENDFIELD
11 Cottontree Lane #14bENDFIELD
Athens, GeorgiaENDFIELD
30607ENDFIELD
ENDRECORD
```

Notice that in the last two records, which had no company names, you nevertheless needed to mark the field's place with an ENDFIELD code.

Choose <u>F</u>ile ▸ Save
<u>A</u>s, and then enter
ADDRESS.DF.

11. Press Save As (F10) and type **ADDRESS.DF** to save the file. (If you created an ADDRESS file in the previous chapter, you can go ahead and overwrite it.)

NOTE. *If the ENDFIELD merge code does not appear on your screen when you press F9, you need to turn on the display of merge codes. To do so, press Merge Codes (Shift+F9), choose <u>D</u>isplay of Merge Codes, and then choose Show Full Codes.*

You now have a completed address list or data file. Keep this file on the screen; you'll need it for a later section of this chapter. Let's review what you've done. For each record in the list, you created seven fields:

Field #	Contains
Field 1	First Name
Field 2	Last Name
Field 3	Title (Mr., Ms., Mrs., or Dr.)
Field 4	Company Name
Field 5	Street Address
Field 6	City and State
Field 7	ZIP Code

You pressed End of Field (F9) to insert an ENDFIELD code at the end of each field and you inserted an ENDRECORD code at the end of each record. These codes help to organize the information in the data file. Remember, the ENDFIELD and ENDRECORD codes appear on the editing screen only when <u>S</u>how Full Codes under <u>D</u>isplay of Merge Codes is turned on.

As noted above, each field is assigned a number. Field 2, for example, contains the last name for each person in your list. When you create your form letter file, you'll need to remember which field contains each piece of information. You can assign field names, instead of numbers, to make it easier to access the information stored in your address list, as explained in the next section. You experimented with this technique briefly in the previous chapter when creating a form file for envelopes.

Assigning Reference Names to the Data File

When you create your form letter file, you place special codes to indicate where information from the data file should be inserted in the letter. Generally, each field in the data file is identified with its own number. You can also assign names to the fields; this is not necessary, but it does make it easier to remember what each of the fields contain when you create the form letter.

Follow these steps to assign a name for each field in the ADDRESS.DF file on your screen:

Choose Tools ▸ Merge ▸ Define ▸ Field Names.

1. Press Merge Codes (Shift+F9) and choose Field Names to display the dialog box for Field Names.

2. In the Field Name box, type **FIRST NAME** as the descriptive name for the first field. Then press Enter. (As you enter each name, you'll see it added to the Field Name List in the dialog box.)

3. For the second field, type **LAST NAME** and press Enter.

4. Type **MR/MS** as the descriptive name for the third field and press Enter.

5. For the remaining fields, enter **COMPANY**, **STREET ADDRESS**, **CITY & STATE**, and **ZIP CODE**.

6. When you are finished entering names, the dialog box will look like Figure 17.4. Press Exit (F7) until you return to the document screen.

Choose OK until you return to the document screen.

7. Press Home, Home, ↑ to move the cursor to the beginning of the document. Then save the data file to replace the previous version saved to disk.

These steps insert the FIELDNAMES code at the beginning of the data file before all the address records. On your screen, the FIELDNAMES information should appear like this:

```
FIELDNAMES(FIRST NAME;LAST NAME;MR/MS;COMPANY;STREET ADDRESS;CITY & STATE;ZIP
CODE)ENDRECORD
```

Once field names are defined, scroll through the data file, and you'll notice that the "Field:" indicator on the status line shows the name assigned to the field where the cursor is located. When you add new records to the file, the "Field:" indicator will remind you what type of information belongs on the line where you are typing; this is particularly useful when you are working with several fields in each record.

Figure 17.4
The Field Names dialog box with names assigned for ADDRESS.DF

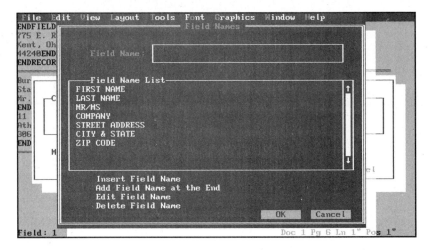

You can quickly change any of the names by editing the text between the "FIELDNAMES(" and ")ENDRECORD" codes; then, press Home, Home, ↑ to reset the screen display.

Editing Data File Text

When you need to update address information in your data file, you edit the text as you would in other types of documents. Take care not to delete the ENDFIELD or ENDRECORD codes, because this will disturb the structure of the data file and will prevent information from being inserted correctly into the form letter.

When you insert ENDRECORD codes for each record in the file, hard page breaks are automatically inserted at the end of the record. These create a file with one record per page, which makes it easy to view all the records in a long list; just press PgUp or PgDn to move from one record to the next.

If you want to add a new record to the list, press Home, Home, ↓ to move the cursor to the end of the file. Then type the text and insert an ENDFIELD code at the end of each field. Remember to follow the same field layout as the other records in your data file. At the end of each new record, insert an ENDRECORD code.

If you want to remove one of the records from the file, move the cursor to the record and press Move (Ctrl+F4). Choose Page and the record is highlighted; if this is not the record you want to remove, press Esc or choose Cancel and start over. Otherwise, choose Delete from the Move dialog box and the record is removed.

When you finish editing and adding records, save the address list again to update your changes to the file on disk.

Sorting the Address Information

You may sort or alphabetize the records in the data file, according to any of the fields in the file. An alphabetized list makes it easier to locate records when you are managing the address information. The following explains how to alphabetize the ADDRESS.DF data file created earlier, according to the Last Name field in each record. Before you perform these steps, make sure the ADDRESS.DF file is displayed on your screen. (For complete information about sorting and alphabetizing a list of names or records, see Chapter 9.)

Choose Tools ▸ Sort.

Choose OK to accept the default settings.

1. Press Merge/Sort (Ctrl+F9) and then choose Sort. A dialog box appears with options for selecting the source and destination of the sort operation.

2. Press Exit (F7) to accept the default settings, and the Sort dialog box appears as shown in Figure 17.5.

Figure 17.5

The Sort dialog box

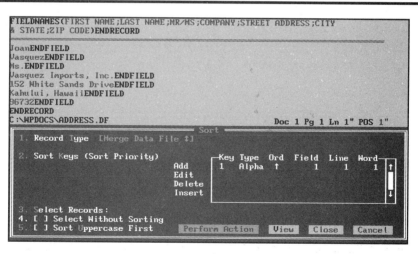

3. Choose the Sort Keys option, and then choose Edit to change the key on which the list will be alphabetized.

4. Choose Field, type **2**, and press Enter to specify a sort according to the second field in each record—the Last Name field.

Choose OK to return to the Sort dialog box.

5. Press Exit (F7) twice to return to the Sort dialog box.

6. Choose Perform Action to alphabetize the data file. A message box will appear on the screen to report on the number of records that are sorted.

7. When the entire list is alphabetized, the message box will disappear. Save the alphabetized list to update your changes to the data file on disk.

This procedure can be applied to any data file that you create, although you may need to change the sort key information to indicate the field on which the sort should be based. For example, you can choose to alphabetize by first or last names, or arrange the records by ZIP code. To sort by a different field, simply specify the appropriate field number when you edit the sort key; you cannot enter field names when you define a sort key, so keep track of the field numbers when using the Sort feature. Then choose Perform Action to sort the data file.

Creating the Form Letter File

A form file is the model for the letters you will send to each person on your mailing list. You can create the form file as a new document, or you can edit an existing document and change it into a form file. The form file contains the formatting codes for your letter and the text that should appear on each letter you will send.

For information that will vary for each person—the name and address, for example—you insert merge codes into the form file that refer to fields from your data file. Instead of the name and address of someone on your list, you insert something like this into the form letter file:

```
FIELD(First Name) FIELD(Last Name)
FIELD(Street Address)
FIELD(City & State) FIELD(ZIP Code)
```

When the form file is merged with the data file, WordPerfect replaces the FIELD codes with the information stored in the fields of your address list. WordPerfect repeats this process for each record in the data file until you have a letter for each person on your mailing list.

The following sections explain how to create a basic form letter file. You'll also learn how to adjust for information that is missing from the data file and how to structure the form file to include personalized paragraphs for each person in your list.

Creating the Form Letter

The following exercise explains how to create the form letter file shown in Figure 17.6. This file is designed to work with the ADDRESS.DF data file created earlier in this chapter.

Figure 17.6
LETTER.FF form
letter file

```
 File  Edit  View  Layout  Tools  Font  Graphics  Window  Help
                                                      DATE
FIELD(FIRST NAME) FIELD(LAST NAME)
FIELD(COMPANY)
FIELD(STREET ADDRESS)
FIELD(CITY & STREET) FIELD(ZIP CODE)

Dear FIELD(MR/MS) FIELD(LAST NAME):

Welcome to Ventura Investment Group! Enclosed are the materials for
your account registration and copies of our prospectus and 1993
annual report.

We are pleased to offer a variety of no-load mutual funds to suit
the objectives of conservative, moderate, and aggressive investors.
Before you choose your investment options, carefully review the
enclosed materials and note the benefits and risks involved with
each fund.

When you are ready to open your account, return the completed
registration form with a check for your initial investment.  Please
remember that account balances of less than $2000 are subject to an
annual $50 service fee.  If you have questions or need assistance
with your registration materials, please write or call our
C:\WPDOCS\LETTER.FF                         Doc 2 Pg 1 Ln 1" Pos 1"
```

Choose Tools ▸
Merge ▸ Define ▸
Form ▸ OK.

Choose Layout ▸
Alignment ▸ Flush
Right.

Choose Tools ▸
Merge ▸ Define ▸
Merge Codes.

Choose Tools ▸
Merge ▸ Define ▸
Field.

Double-click on
FIRST NAME and
then select OK.

1. From a clear document screen, press Merge Codes (Shift+F9) and choose Form. Then press Exit (F7) to continue.

2. Press Flush Right (Alt+F6) to move the cursor to the right margin of the page.

3. Press Merge Codes (Shift+F9) twice to display a complete list of merge codes.

4. Type to highlight the DATE code in the list, and press Enter to insert it into the form file.

5. Press Enter again to move the cursor to the next line in the form file.

6. Press Merge Codes (Shift+F9) and choose Field. At this point, you could type a field name to indicate data file information. Instead, these steps show how to choose from a list of field names defined in your data file.

7. Choose List Field Names (F5), and WordPerfect prompts you for the name of your data file. Type **ADDRESS.DF** and press Enter. The dialog box in Figure 17.7 is displayed on your screen.

8. Scroll down to highlight the FIRST NAME field reference, and press Enter. This inserts the **FIELD(**FIRST NAME**)** merge code into the form file.

9. Press the spacebar once. Then press Merge Codes (Shift+F9), choose Field, and then choose List Field Names (F5).

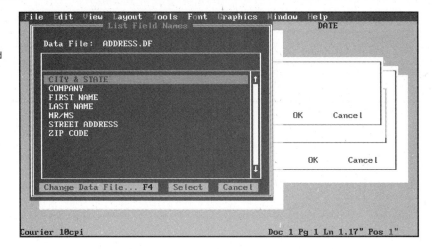

Figure 17.7

The List Field Names dialog box showing the defined names from the ADDRESS.DF file

10. Highlight the LAST NAME field reference and press Enter to insert the **FIELD(**LAST NAME**)** merge code into the form file.

11. Press Enter to move the cursor to the next line on the page.

12. Press Merge Codes (Shift+F9), choose Field, and then choose List Field Names (F5).

13. Highlight the COMPANY field reference and press Enter to insert the merge code into the form file.

14. Press Enter to move the cursor to the next line on the page.

15. Press Merge Codes (Shift+F9), choose Field, and then choose List Field Names (F5).

16. Highlight the STREET ADDRESS field reference, and press Enter to insert the merge code.

17. Press Enter to move to the next line.

18. Press Merge Codes (Shift+F9), choose Field, and then choose List Field Names (F5).

19. Highlight the CITY & STATE entry, and press Enter to insert the merge code.

20. Press the spacebar to add a space before the next field. Press Merge Codes (Shift+F9), choose Field, and then choose List Field Names (F5).

21. Highlight the ZIP CODE entry, and press Enter. Press Enter again to insert the merge code. At this point, your screen will resemble Figure 17.8.

Figure 17.8
Address block of the
LETTER.FF file

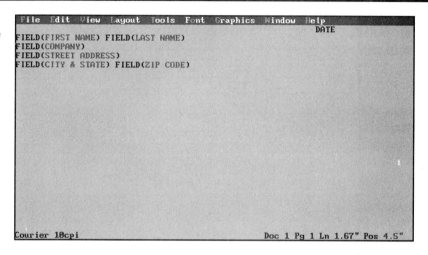

22. Press Enter twice to add a blank line below the address field codes. Then type **Dear** followed by a space.

23. Press Merge Codes (Shift+F9) and choose Field. Choose List Field Codes (F5), highlight MR/MS as the field reference, and press Enter.

24. Press the spacebar once. Press Merge Codes (Shift+F9), choose Field, and then choose List Field Codes (F5).

25. Highlight LAST NAME as the field reference, and press Enter. Then type a colon or a comma to end the greeting.

26. Press Enter twice and type the following as the first paragraph for the letter:

Welcome to Ventura Investment Group! Enclosed are the materials for your account registration and copies of our prospectus and 1993 annual report.

27. Press Enter twice to end the paragraph. Then, if you wish, complete the letter by typing the remaining paragraphs shown in Figure 17.9.

28. Press Save As (F10) and type **LETTER.FF** to save the form letter file.

Choose File ▸ Save
As, type **LETTER.FF**,
and press Enter.

Your form letter is complete. If you wish, you can apply different fonts and formatting, as you would to any other business letter. You can also change the margins, line spacing, text justification, or indent the paragraphs, or even add a graph or chart to the letter. Attributes, such as bold and underline, may also be applied to affect the text in the completed letters; just block text or the field code that represents the text you want to affect, and choose the desired appearance attributes. Make sure you save the form letter file after making your editing or formatting changes. Then clear the document window.

Figure 17.9

The completed form letter

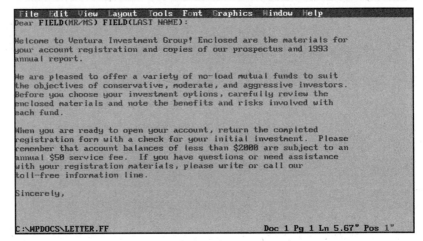

If you are anxious to see how the data and form files will appear when merged, clear the screen, press Merge/Sort (Ctrl+F9) and choose <u>M</u>erge (or choose M<u>e</u>rge from the <u>T</u>ools menu and then choose <u>R</u>un). Then type **LETTER.FF** as the name of the form letter file, and enter **ADDRESS.DF** as the data file name. Press Exit (F7) or choose Merge to start the merge and WordPerfect creates a letter for each person on your address list. When the merge is completed, you can send the merged letters to the printer.

This is the basic procedure for merging the files. WordPerfect provides other methods for merging selected records, creating envelopes for each letter, and sending merged form letters directly to the printer. These options are described later, under "Merging the Address List with the Form Letter."

The following sections explain how to view and manage form letter files. You'll see how to alter the form and data files to include personalized paragraphs for each person in your address list. You'll also learn how to make your form letter "smarter" with special merge codes that account for missing information in the data file records.

Viewing the Form and Data Files Together

When creating or editing a form file, you may want to see both form and data files on the screen at once. Viewing both files makes it easier to see how information from the data file will be placed into the form letter. As shown in Figure 17.10, WordPerfect lets you divide the screen into different document windows.

Figure 17.10

The LETTER.FF and ADDRESS.DF file displayed at the same time

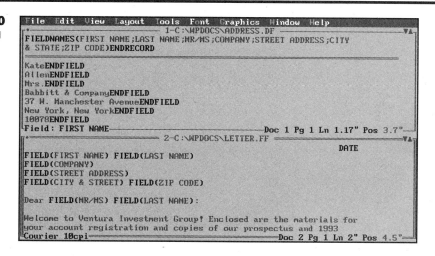

You can retrieve the ADDRESS.DF file into one of the windows, and in the second window, you can create or edit the form letter. The following explains the procedure:

Choose File ▶ Open. Then enter the name of the data file.

Choose Window ▶ Tile.

- Press Open/Retrieve (Shift+F10), type the name of the data file you want to use, and press Enter.

- Press Open/Retrieve (Shift+F10), type the name of the form file you want to use, and press Enter. Now you have both files open at once, but you can only see the form file, since it currently fills the entire screen.

- To see both open files at once, press Screen (Ctrl+F3), choose Window, and then choose Tile.

- Press Switch (Shift+F3) or click with your mouse to move the cursor into the other document window.

When you are finished with both files, save any changes you have made. To restore the full-screen document window, move the cursor into the window that you want to enlarge, press Screen (Ctrl+F3), choose Window, and then choose Maximize. Or, simply choose Maximize from the Window menu.

Personalizing the Form Letter

So far, you've seen how you can create form letters with name and address information, but this is little more than you'd find in any form letter. You may want to go a step further and personalize the letters with references to account numbers, individual messages, or other information that applies specifically to each recipient. Here is the general procedure:

- Retrieve your data file and add a field to each of the records that includes additional information about the recipient—such as an account number or a personal message. Save the data file.

- Edit your form letter to include a FIELD code that inserts the new information from the data file. Save the form file.

- Merge the data and form files to create letters for each person on the address list.

Here is a practical example that covers more of the details. Suppose each person on your address list was contacted by telephone. During the phone conversation, each person specified an investment preference—either "conservative," "moderate," or "aggressive"—and you want to acknowledge this preference in the text of the LETTER.FF form file shown earlier in this chapter. First, you would retrieve the ADDRESS.DF file and insert a new field at the end of each record in the file:

```
Kate**ENDFIELD**            _____
                                           |
Allen**ENDFIELD**                          |
                                           |
Mrs.**ENDFIELD**                           |
                                           |
Babbitt & Company**ENDFIELD**              |_____   Existing fields
                                           |
37 W. Manchester Avenue**ENDFIELD**        |
                                           |
New York, New York**ENDFIELD**             |
                                           |
10078**ENDFIELD**           _____|
conservative**ENDFIELD**  ◄_____   New field
ENDRECORD
```

Make sure you add the new field at the end of *each* record in the data file. Remember, when you change the number of fields in a record, the change must be performed on all records in the data file. If you don't have information for the new field for all records, simply insert the ENDFIELD code to acknowledge a blank field where the information *would* be; you may want to fill in this information at a later time.

When you add a new field to your data file, you should also update the FIELDNAMES code to assign a name to the new field. The easiest way to do this is to move the cursor to the beginning of the data file, type a semicolon after the last defined name, and type the name you want to assign to the new field. The edited FIELDNAMES code might look like this:

```
FIELDNAMES(FIRST NAME;LAST NAME;MR/MS;COMPANY;STREET ADDRESS;CITY & STATE;ZIP
CODE;INVEST PREFERENCE)ENDRECORD
```

When you are finished adding the new field to the data file records and you have included a name assignment for the new field, save the file.

To update the form letter, you would retrieve the LETTER.FF file and insert something like the following sentence to include the recipient's investment preference into the form letter file:

```
In our telephone conversation, you indicated a preference
for FIELD(INVEST PREFERENCE) investments.
```

In this example, each letter is created with a personal acknowledgment to an earlier conversation with the recipient. You can use this same concept to include a personal paragraph, account numbers, or other specific information in each letter you send. Make sure you save the changes after you edit your form file. Then use the Merge feature to create the letters.

Checking for Missing Information

One problem with data files is that you may not have all the information you need for each person on your mailing list. One or more company names may not be available, or you may have several people in your address list who are not affiliated with a company. For some names on your list, you may not know what to put in the Mr/Ms field—putting "Mrs." instead of "Ms.," for example, may offend the recipient and cost you a potential customer.

For these cases, you can use special merge codes to change the output of the form letter according to available information in the data file. This section includes two methods of accounting for missing information.

In this first example, suppose one of the fields is empty for several of the records in your data file; this is common for fields that should contain company names or phone numbers. When you merge files, WordPerfect normally inserts blank lines for each empty field in your data file. You can correct this problem when you merge the data and form files:

■ Press Merge/Sort (Ctrl+F9) and choose Merge.

Choose Tools ▸ Merge ▸ Run.

■ In the Form File box, enter the name of the form file you want to use.

- In the <u>D</u>ata File box, enter the name of the data file you want to use.

- Choose <u>O</u>utput, and specify <u>U</u>nused Document.

- Choose Da<u>t</u>a File Options to display the expanded Run Merge dialog box, shown in Figure 17.11.

Figure 17.11

The expanded Run
Merge dialog box

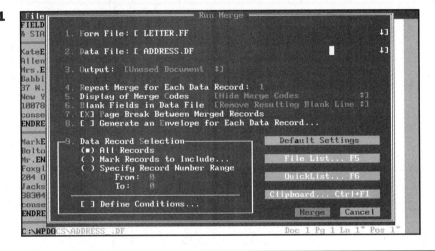

- Choose <u>B</u>lank Fields in Data File, and choose <u>R</u>emove Resulting Blank Line.

- Press Exit (F7) to start the merge.

Choose OK to start
the merge.

TIP.   *You can control which empty fields will be ignored by selecting <u>B</u>lank Fields in Data File and selecting <u>L</u>eave Resulting Blank Line. Then you insert a question mark within the appropriate field reference in the form file. For example, if you want to ignore only the empty company fields, edit the FIELD code reference to include a question mark, like this: FIELD(COMPANY?).*

WordPerfect checks each of the fields during the merge; if a field is found empty, WordPerfect skips it and does not insert a blank line. This is useful for empty fields that do not affect the content of the letter; however, don't use this option when your data file has empty fields, such as title and name information, which are mandatory for each letter to be complete. When these types of fields are empty, you should set up your form file to substitute information, as described in the next example.

In this second example, assume the field for Mr/Ms information is empty in several records. For someone named "Terry Holtz," you may not know whether to use "Mr.," "Ms.," or something else. In this case, you do not want to ignore these empty fields, but to print alternative greetings to account for the missing information. Instead of printing "Dear Ms. Holtz," the greeting can simply read "Dear Terry." This lets you avoid the embarrassment of choosing the wrong title for the recipient. To set up the merge codes for this example, follow this procedure:

1. Retrieve the LETTER.FF file created earlier or the form letter file that you want to change.

2. Move the cursor to the beginning of the FIELD codes that follow the word "Dear" in the greeting. Press Ctrl+End to delete the codes on that line.

Choose Tools ▶ Merge ▶ Define ▶ Merge Codes. Then select the IFBLANK merge code.

3. Press Merge Codes (Shift+F9) twice and type **ifb** or scroll down the code list to highlight "IFBLANK(field)." Press Enter to select the code. Word-Perfect displays the Parameter Entry dialog box.

4. In the Field box, type the name of the field you want to check. For example, type **MR/MS** to check the title field from the ADDRESS.DF file. Press Enter to insert the IFBLANK(MR/MS) code into the form letter.

5. Press Merge Codes (Shift+F9), choose Field, and then choose List Field Names (F5). If you are prompted for the data file name, type the file name and press Enter.

Double-click on the FIRST NAME field and select OK.

6. Scroll through the list of field names and highlight the FIRST NAME field. Press Enter.

7. Press Merge Codes (Shift+F9) twice, and type **e** or scroll through the list to highlight the ELSE code. Then press Enter.

8. Press Merge Codes (Shift+F9), choose Field, and choose List Field Names (F5). Then highlight the MR/MS field reference from the list, and press Enter twice.

9. Press the spacebar. Press Merge Codes (Shift+F9), choose Field, and choose List Field Names (F5). Then highlight the LAST NAME field reference, and press Enter.

10. Press Merge Codes (Shift+F9) twice, and type **endi** or scroll through the list to highlight the ENDIF command. Then press Enter.

11. End the greeting by typing a colon or a comma.

When you are finished, the greeting line will look similar to this:

```
Dear IFBLANK(MR/MS)FIELD(FIRST NAME)ELSE FIELD(MR/MS) FIELD(LAST NAME)ENDIF :
```

NOTE.   *If part of the code string wraps to the next line, don't worry; it won't affect the merged form letters.*

Let's examine this string of merge codes. The word "Dear" begins the greeting and will be printed as regular text. As each record is merged with the form letter file, the IFBLANK(MR/MS) command checks to see whether the MR/MS field is blank. If so, WordPerfect inserts into the form letter the information stored in the FIRST NAME field, substituting it for the standard greeting of Mr. or Ms., followed by the recipient's last name.

If the MR/MS field is not blank, WordPerfect inserts the information noted after the ELSE code in the string. This is the information stored in the MR/MS and LAST NAME fields. The ENDIF code indicates the end of the IFBLANK expression. A colon ends the string as the closing punctuation for the greeting; this last character is not a merge code.

When the data and form files are merged, WordPerfect evaluates the IF-BLANK expression and inserts either "Dear *FIRST NAME*," or "Dear *MR/MS LAST NAME*," depending on whether the MR/MS field is empty. When you are finished editing your form file, make sure to save the file to update your changes.

Merging the Address List with the Form Letter

After you've created a data file and a form letter, you're ready to merge the files together to create the letters you want to send. Usually, you create one letter for each person or company included in the data file. WordPerfect also provides options that let you create letters for records that match a specific criterion; you can, for example, create letters for the people who live in a specific city by telling WordPerfect to skip the other records in your data file.

WordPerfect also lets you create printed envelopes with bar codes for each letter you want to send; this helps speed up the mailing process. And speaking of speeding things up, you can send the merged letters directly to your printer. Doing so lets you create letters for a large number of people when your computer's memory can't handle the size of the merged document file. These and other merge options are explained in the following sections.

Creating Letters for the Entire Address List

The following steps show how to create form letters by merging the data and form letter files. In these steps, the LETTER.FF and ADDRESS.DF files created earlier in this chapter are used to illustrate the merge process. You can easily substitute the names shown here with the names of your own form file and data file. The result is a personalized letter for each person on your mailing list.

Choose Tools ▸
Merge ▸ Run.

1. Press Merge/Sort (Ctrl+F9) and choose Merge. The Run Merge dialog box appears.

2. In the Form File box, type **LETTER.FF** and press Enter.

3. Choose Data File, type **ADDRESS.DF** and press Enter. (If you used the List Field Names feature when you created the form file, the associated data file automatically appears as the data file in the Run Merge dialog box.)

4. Choose Output and select Unused Document to indicate that the results of the merge should be placed in an empty document screen.

5. Press F7 or click on Merge to begin the merge process.

WordPerfect uses the form letter file to create a letter for each record in the data file. All of the merged letters are stored in the document displayed on the screen, separated by hard page breaks. To view the letters, press PgUp and PgDn to scroll through each of the pages. When you are finished, you can send the entire document to the printer, or move the cursor to a specific letter and print only that page. Although you can save the completed letters, this is not necessary because you can easily merge the two files again.

The Output option on the Run Merge dialog box provides different choices for storing the merged documents. You can choose Current Document, Unused Document, File, or Printer. Current Document inserts the merged form letters at the cursor position of the displayed document. Unused Document tells WordPerfect to insert the merged letters into the next empty document window; when the merge is completed, this is the document window that is displayed. If you choose File, you are prompted to enter a file name under which the merged document should be stored. The Printer option is described later in this chapter, under "Sending Merged Documents to the Printer."

Merging Selected Records from the Address List

From the expanded Run Merge dialog box, you can choose an option that lets you select which records will be merged with the form file. This feature is useful when you're working with a large data file, and don't want to merge all records with the form file.

Suppose you want to create merged letters for every address in your data file that includes a certain ZIP code or last name. Or, merge only the first 50 records in a 300-record data file. The Data Record Selection options can help you indicate which records in your data file should be included in the merge process.

This is how the feature works:

- Press Merge/Sort (Ctrl+F9) and choose <u>M</u>erge to display the Run Merge dialog box.

- In the <u>F</u>orm File box, enter the name of the form file you want to use for the merge.

- In the <u>D</u>ata File box, enter the name of your address list or the data file that contains the records you want to use for the merge.

- If the Data Record Selection box does not appear on the Run Merge dialog box, choose Da<u>t</u>a File Options to display the expanded Run Merge dialog box, and display the selection options shown in Figure 17.12.

Figure 17.12

The record selection options for Merge

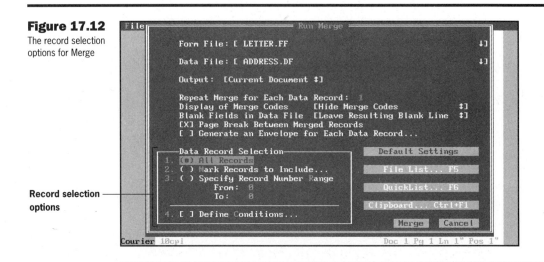

Record selection options

- Choose one of the record selection options (explained in the following text), and then press F7 or click on Merge.

- WordPerfect runs the merge with only the records you specified with the Data Record Selection options.

Here is detailed information about each of the selection options. When you choose Data Record <u>S</u>election from the expanded Run Merge dialog box, you can choose <u>A</u>ll Records, <u>M</u>ark Records to Include, Specify Record Number <u>R</u>ange, or Define <u>C</u>onditions.

The first selection option, <u>A</u>ll Records, is the default. When <u>A</u>ll Records is chosen, WordPerfect includes all records from your data file when it merges the data file with the form file.

The second selection option, <u>M</u>ark Records to Include, lets you select the records you want to merge from the data file. Choose <u>M</u>ark Records to Include, and WordPerfect displays the List Field Names dialog box, where you choose one of the field names as the selection key. At this dialog box, you would usually select something like the LAST NAME field, which would contain unique information for each record. After you choose one of the field names, WordPerfect then displays the Mark Data Records dialog box, as shown in Figure 17.13, with information from each of the records in your data file.

Figure 17.13

Selecting records
for the merge

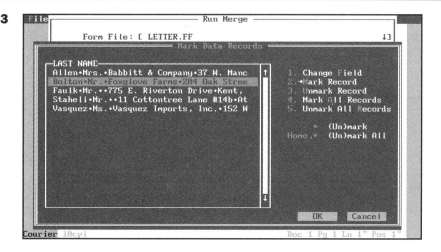

Highlight and choose <u>M</u>ark Record for each of the records you want to include in the merge. Then, press Exit (F7) to return to the Run Merge dialog box.

The third selection option, Specify Record Number <u>R</u>ange, lets you choose a consecutive number of records to merge. For example, you can choose to merge records 1 through 5 only. When you choose Specify Record Number <u>R</u>ange, enter the number of the starting record at the <u>F</u>rom prompt, and enter the number of the ending record at the <u>T</u>o prompt. The numbers correspond to the current order of the records (or pages) in your data file. Remember that the numbers you enter must indicate a consecutive range of records. For example, you can specify records 1 to 10, but you can't specify records 10 to 8, or some other nonconsecutive range.

The fourth option, Define <u>C</u>onditions, displays the dialog box shown in Figure 17.14. At this dialog box, you can define multiple conditions on which to select the records for the merge.

Figure 17.14

Defining conditions
for selection

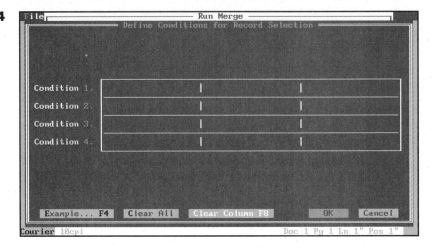

Press Example (F4) and WordPerfect will show you a few examples of how you might define your own conditions. From here, you can also press Examples of Valid Entries to view a list of additional entries. When you are finished viewing the examples, press Exit (F7) twice and choose Condition 1, select the field name that you want to use as a selection key, and then enter a value or word pattern that determines which records will be selected for the merge.

After defining the first condition, you can choose Condition 2 to include a second condition in the selection process. You can define up to four different conditions to select records for the merge. When you're finished, press Exit (F7) to return to the Run Merge dialog box.

When you've selected a record selection option, you can press F7 or click on Merge to begin the merge process. WordPerfect uses the selection option to determine which records will be included in the merge.

Creating Envelopes for Each Letter

When you merge the data and form files, you can tell WordPerfect to create envelopes for the form letter you want to send. When you choose this option, WordPerfect automatically generates an addressed envelope for each recipient in your data file. Follow this procedure to create envelopes when merging the data and form files:

Choose Tools ▶
Merge ▶ Run.

■ Press Merge/Sort (Ctrl+F9) and choose Merge.

■ In the Form File box, enter the name of the form file you want to use.

- In the Data File box, enter the name of the data file you want to use.

- If necessary, choose Data File Options to display the expanded Run Merge dialog box.

- Choose Generate an Envelope for Each Data Record. The Envelope dialog box is displayed.

- Choose Envelope Size and select the envelope definition you want to use.

- If you want a return address on the envelope, choose Return Address, and type the appropriate name and address in the box. (If you've defined a default return address, it will show up automatically.) Press Exit (F7) when you're done entering the return address.

- Choose Mailing Address.

- Press Merge Codes (Shift+F9), choose Field, and type the name or number assigned to the recipient's name field in your data file. Press Enter twice to accept the field code and move the cursor to the next line in the Mailing Address box. If the recipient's name is divided between two fields, insert a space and then insert a field code for the last name.

- Press Merge Codes (Shift+F9) and choose Field. Type the name assigned to the street address field in your data file. Press Enter twice.

- Press Merge Codes (Shift+F9) and choose Field. Type the name assigned to the city and state field in your data file. Press Enter twice.

- Type a space, press Merge Codes (Shift+F9) and choose Field. Type the name assigned to the ZIP code field in your data file. Press Enter twice.

- Make sure the formatting (spaces and hard returns) reflects the formatting you want for the mailing address on the envelopes. Then press Exit (F7) to accept the merge field codes as the mailing address.

- Choose Insert to accept the envelope size and format, and return to the Run Merge dialog box.

- Press F7 or click on Merge to begin the merge process.

When the merge operation is completed, WordPerfect generates a form letter for each person in the data file. The envelopes are placed after all the merged letters. At this point, you can save the document or send the full document to the printer to print the letters and the envelopes.

Sending Merged Documents to the Printer

When a merge operation is completed, WordPerfect usually places the completed form letters into a document window on your screen. You can, however, tell WordPerfect to send the form letters directly to the printer. This helps the merge run faster and makes it possible to create form letters for large data files that may not fit into the memory of your computer. Here is the procedure for merging documents to your printer. Before you begin, make sure you select the printer definition you want to use; also, make sure the printer has enough paper for the letters you want to print.

Choose Tools ▸
Merge ▸ Run.

- Press Merge/Sort (Ctrl+F9) and choose Merge. The Run Merge dialog box appears.

- In the Form File box, enter the name of your form file.

- Choose Data File, and enter the name of your data file.

- Choose Output and select Printer. This sends each completed letter directly to your printer.

- Choose Merge to run the merge process.

As each letter is created, WordPerfect sends it directly to your printer and clears it from memory. Then the next letter is created. As mentioned earlier, this speeds up the merge process, making it possible to merge data files that are too large to fit into your computer's memory.

One disadvantage of merging to the printer is that you cannot review the form letters before they are printed. For this reason, you should run the merge with a few records to test whether everything is working correctly. To do this, display the Run Merge dialog box and specify the form file and data file that you want to merge. Redirect the output of the merge to your printer, and then choose Data File Options to display the expanded Run Merge dialog box. Choose Data Record Selections and then choose Specify Record Number Range and enter **1** as the From number and **3** as the To number. Then press F7 or click on Merge to start the merge process. After the merge is completed, carefully review the printed letters to make sure the field information is correctly placed. Then choose Data Record Selection from the Run Merge dialog box, and choose All Records to reset the selection process.

18

Advanced Merge Techniques

Automated Merge Documents

Merge Tips and Techniques

Using Merge Codes to Assemble Documents

WHEN YOU EXPLORE THE MERGE FEATURE BEYOND THE STANDARD form letter application, you'll find that it can help you create various types of documents with greater speed and efficiency. You can merge information from two or more sources, or set up a merge file that prompts you to type information from the keyboard. If you enjoy delving into advanced techniques, you can use merge commands to manipulate variable information and control the results of the merge process with logical decision-making capabilities.

Before your fingers start itching to flip to another chapter, you should know that these are not difficult techniques. Although some procedures can be quite involved, most merge commands are simple to use and well worth the time spent learning them.

In this chapter, you'll learn how to apply advanced merge techniques to create some useful documents. Instead of cryptic descriptions for each merge command, you'll find practical examples that you can apply to your own documents.

Automated Merge Documents

In addition to form letters, WordPerfect's merge commands let you create lists, memos, and invoices. The following sections show how to automate these types of documents with form and data files. Of course, these are only a few examples of documents that can benefit from the merge features. You can apply the concepts from these examples to a wide variety of documents.

The examples in these sections illustrate common merge applications, such as using merge commands to manipulate and format list information, merging information typed from the keyboard, and merging to create forms and tables.

List Documents

When you merge address information to create form letters, each record in the address file becomes one letter—or page—in the finished document. This is the standard result of a merge in which a new page is created for each record in your data file. However, sometimes you'll want to ignore pagination to create a list like the example list of names and addresses shown in Figure 18.1.

Notice that the information for each record appears as an entry in the list. The following steps explain how to create a list of addresses using the data file from Chapter 17. If you'd like to work with a larger list, you can add the additional names shown in Figure 18.1.

Follow these steps from a clear document screen:

1. Press Format (Shift+F8), choose <u>M</u>argins, and set both <u>L</u>eft Margin and <u>R</u>ight Margin to 0.5". Then press Exit (F7) until you return to the screen.

Choose Layout ▶
Margins.

Figure 18.1

A merged sample address listt

Name	Address
Kate Allen	37 W. Manchester Avenue, New York, New York 10078
Mark Bolton	204 Oak Street, #12, Jackson, Tennessee 38304
Gordon Faulk	775 E. Riverton Drive, Kent, Ohio 44240
Jesse Hamilton	2437 Court View, Rio Grande, Texas 78682
Akira Kato	17, Lane 8, Yung Kang Street, Taipei, Taiwan ROC
Matheus Klebl	Rädhusgatan 40.C.07., 68620 Jakobstad 2 Finland
Christine Lawrence	62 Haley Summit, Mill City, Oregon 97360
Nancy Miles	72 Harper Circle, Beverly, Massachusetts 01915
Michelle Pfister	29 Maple Boulevard, Concord, California 94520
Jeff Rye, Jr.	816 W. Deaborne Ave., Edison, New Jersey 08819
Burke Staheli	11 Cottontree Lane #14b, Athens, Georgia 30607
Scott Taylor, DDS	407 Bird of Paradise Drive, Lakeland, Florida 33803
Joan Vasquez	152 White Sands Drive, Kahului, Hawaii 96732
Dr. Mary Walker	1017 Van Ness Avenue, San Francisco, California 94195
Tom C. Wilcox	58 Freedom Boulevard, Providence Rhode Island 02967

Choose Layout ▸ Tab Set.

Choose Clear All to clear the tab ruler.

Choose OK until you return to the document screen.

Choose Tools ▸ Merge ▸ Define ▸ Form.

2. Type **ADDRESS LIST** as the title for your list. Press Enter twice to add a blank line beneath the title.

3. Press Format (Shift+F8), choose Line and then choose Tab Set.

4. Press Delete Line (Ctrl+End) to clear the tab ruler.

5. Choose Set Tab, type **0**, and press Enter. Then choose Repeat Every, type **2**, and press Enter. This sets tabs every two inches across the page.

6. Press Exit (F7) until you return to the document screen.

7. Press Bold (F6) and type **Name**. Press Tab and type **Address**. Then press Bold (F6) again to turn off boldfacing, and press Enter twice to insert a blank line.

8. Press Merge Codes (Shift+F9) and choose Form.

9. From the Merge Codes (Form File) dialog box, choose <u>M</u>erge Codes (Shift+F9) to display the complete list of merge commands.

10. Type **l** to highlight LABEL(label) as shown in Figure 18.2. Then press Enter to select the command.

Figure 18.2

Selecting advanced merge commands

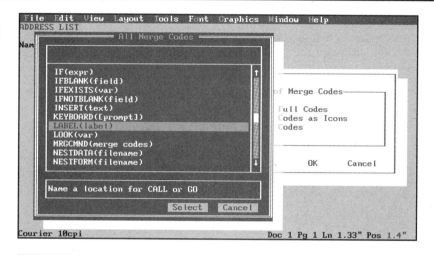

11. You are prompted to enter a name for the label. Type **Make Entry** and press Enter.

Choose <u>T</u>ools ▸ <u>M</u>erge ▸ <u>D</u>efine ▸ <u>F</u>ield.

12. Press Merge Codes (Shift+F9) and choose <u>F</u>ield.

13. Type **First Name** as the field reference, press Enter, and then type a space.

14. Press Merge Codes (Shift+F9), choose <u>F</u>ield, and enter **Last Name**. Press Enter to return to the editing window, and then press Tab to move the cursor to the next tab stop.

15. Press Merge Codes (Shift+F9), choose <u>F</u>ield, and enter **Street Address**. Press Enter to return to the editing screen. Type a comma, followed by a space.

16. Press Merge Codes (Shift+F9), choose <u>F</u>ield, and enter **City & State**. Press Enter to return to the editing screen. Type two spaces.

17. Press Merge Codes (Shift+F9), choose <u>F</u>ield, and enter **ZIP Code**. Press Enter to return to the editing screen. Then press Enter to insert an [HRt] code and start the next line.

Choose Tools ►
Merge ► Define ►
Merge Codes.

18. Press Merge Codes (Shift+F9) twice to display all merge commands.

19. Type **nextr** to highlight the NEXTRECORD command. Press Enter to insert the command.

20. Press Merge Codes (Shift+F9) twice to display all merge commands.

21. Type **go** to highlight the GO(label) command. Press Enter to select the command.

22. You are prompted to type a label name for the GO command. Type **Make Entry** and press Enter.

Choose File ► Save
As, type **LIST.FF**,
and choose OK.

23. Press Save As (F10), type **LIST.FF**, and press Enter to save the form file. When you are finished, the document screen should look similar to Figure 18.3.

Figure 18.3
The List form file

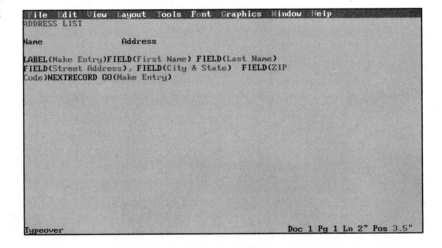

The first part of these steps involves the document layout rather than merge codes, but these steps are important because they determine the appearance of the finished list. Remember, you can create whatever document layout you choose; after you do, insert the merge codes where the variable information should be inserted from your data file.

Let's review what you did with the rest of the form file. The LABEL (Make Entry) merge command is inserted to mark the place where the list begins. The FIELD merge commands insert the information for one record from the data file. The NEXTRECORD command tells WordPerfect to go to the next record without inserting a page break. The GO(Make Entry) command returns execution of the merge to the LABEL(Make Entry) command, which causes the merge to repeat the line of FIELD codes for the next record in the address data file. This process continues until all records in the data file have been merged into the list.

Now that your form file is completed, you can merge it with your address data file:

1. Press Merge/Sort (Ctrl+F9), and choose Merge.

2. In the Form File box, type **LIST.FF** and press Enter.

3. In the Data File box, type **ADDRESS.DF** and press Enter.

4. Choose Output, and select Unused Document.

5. Press Exit (F7) to perform the merge.

During the merge, the line of FIELD commands is repeated for each record in the data file. Figure 18.4 shows how the list in the above example should look when the merge is completed. Although this example creates an address list, you can modify the application to create a list of account information, catalog items, inventory data, or stock quotes.

Choose Tools ▸ Merge ▸ Run.

Choose Merge to perform the merge.

Figure 18.4
A merged address list

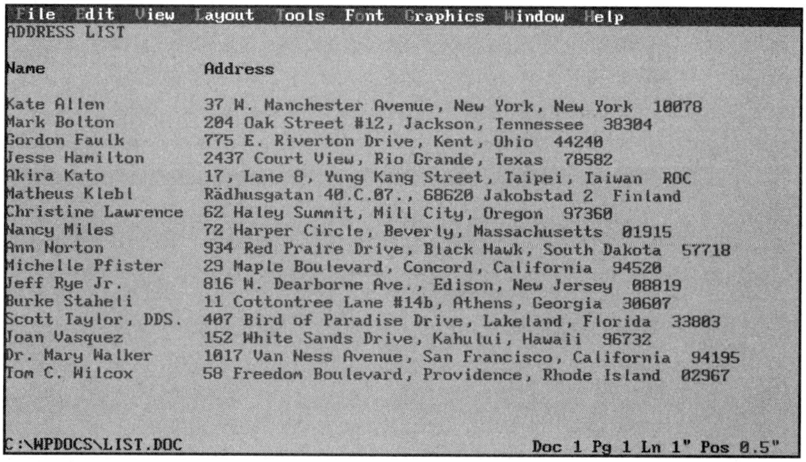

```
File  Edit  View  Layout  Tools  Font  Graphics  Window  Help
ADDRESS LIST

Name                    Address

Kate Allen              37 W. Manchester Avenue, New York, New York  10078
Mark Bolton             204 Oak Street #12, Jackson, Tennessee  38304
Gordon Faulk            775 E. Riverton Drive, Kent, Ohio  44240
Jesse Hamilton          2437 Court View, Rio Grande, Texas  78582
Akira Kato              17, Lane 8, Yung Kang Street, Taipei, Taiwan  ROC
Matheus Klebl           Rädhusgatan 40.C.07., 68620 Jakobstad 2  Finland
Christine Lawrence      62 Haley Summit, Mill City, Oregon  97360
Nancy Miles             72 Harper Circle, Beverly, Massachusetts  01915
Ann Norton              934 Red Prairie Drive, Black Hawk, South Dakota  57718
Michelle Pfister        29 Maple Boulevard, Concord, California  94520
Jeff Rye Jr.            816 W. Dearborne Ave., Edison, New Jersey  08819
Burke Staheli           11 Cottontree Lane #14b, Athens, Georgia  30607
Scott Taylor, DDS.      407 Bird of Paradise Drive, Lakeland, Florida  33803
Joan Vasquez            152 White Sands Drive, Kahului, Hawaii  96732
Dr. Mary Walker         1017 Van Ness Avenue, San Francisco, California  94195
Tom C. Wilcox           58 Freedom Boulevard, Providence, Rhode Island  02967


C:\WPDOCS\LIST.DOC                              Doc 1 Pg 1 Ln 1" Pos 0.5"
```

Automated Memos

Office memos are perfect examples of documents that can be automated with a form file. When you use a form file to create memos, you type in information from the keyboard, which is used in place of a data file in the finished document. The form file can prompt you to enter the recipient's name, the memo subject, and the message you want to send. The rest of the memo is automatically created with the current date and sender's name. In this section, you'll see how to create and use an automated memo file.

When you create a memo form file, you can retrieve and edit an existing memo document, or you can create a new memo document. Instead of text for the date, recipient's name, memo subject, and message, you'll insert merge commands that will prompt the user to enter the appropriate information when the merge is run. The application in this section is based on the memo layout shown in Figure 18.5.

Figure 18.5

A sample memo document

MEMORANDUM

DATE: September 5, 1994
TO: Kaden Scott
FROM: Shauna Olsen
SUBJECT: Health Spa Membership

According to our records, it's time for you to renew your health spa membership. We have spent a great deal of time and money improving our gym facilities for our customers.

This year, the annual membership fee is $250. The fee increase will help cover the cost of the newly added equipment, which includes several new fitness stations and an indoor swimming pool. If you have questions regarding your membership, please contact Karen Ridley at our business office.

Thank you.

If you prefer a memo document that differs from the example shown here, you can adapt the following steps for any layout. Begin with your memo document on the WordPerfect screen. Make sure there is no text after the DATE, TO, and SUBJECT memo labels and insert tabs after the labels so that the following text will line up. Also make sure that the message space is clear. Then follow these steps to create a memo form file:

1. Move the cursor to the right of the DATE label in the memo.

Choose <u>T</u>ools ▸
Merge ▸ <u>D</u>efine ▸
<u>F</u>orm.

Choose <u>T</u>ools ▸
Merge ▸ <u>D</u>efine ▸
Merge Codes.

Choose OK to
continue.

Choose <u>T</u>ools ▸
Merge ▸ <u>D</u>efine ▸
Merge Codes.

Choose <u>T</u>ools ▸
Merge ▸ <u>D</u>efine ▸
Merge Codes.

2. Press Merge Codes (Shift+F9) and choose <u>F</u>orm.

3. From the Merge Codes (Form File) dialog box, choose <u>M</u>erge Codes (Shift+F9).

4. Type **d** to highlight the DATE command in the list. Press Enter to insert it into the memo file.

5. Move the cursor to the right of the TO label.

6. Press Merge Codes (Shift+F9) twice to display the All Merge Codes list.

7. Type **g** to highlight the GETSTRING command in the list. Press Enter to select the command. The merge Parameter Entry dialog box appears.

8. At the Variable prompt, type **SENDTO** and press Enter.

9. Choose <u>P</u>rompt and type **Enter the name of the person who will receive the memo.** Then press Enter.

10. Choose <u>T</u>itle and type **Memo Recipient** as the title for the message box. Then press Enter.

11. Press Exit (F7) to accept the parameters and insert the GETSTRING command. This command will wrap to the next line; this won't change the result of the merge.

12. Press Merge Codes (Shift+F9) twice to display the Merge Code list.

13. Type **v** or scroll to highlight the VARIABLE(var) command in the list. Press Enter to select the command.

14. At the "Variable" prompt, type **SENDTO** to indicate that the recipient's name should be inserted at this point in the memo. Press Enter to insert the VARIABLE command.

15. Move the cursor after the FROM label, and type your name or the name of the person who will be using this form file to create memos.

16. Move the cursor to the right of the SUBJECT label.

17. Press Merge Codes (Shift+F9) twice to display the All Merge Codes list.

18. Type **g** or scroll to highlight the GETSTRING command in the list. Press Enter to select the command.

19. Type **SUBJECT** at the Variable prompt, and press Enter.

20. Choose <u>P</u>rompt and type **Enter a description of the memo subject.** Then press Enter.

Choose OK to continue.

Choose Tools ▸ Merge ▸ Define ▸ Merge Codes.

Choose File ▸ Save As, and enter **MEMO.FF**.

21. Choose Title and type **Memo Subject** as the message box title. Then press Enter.

22. Press Exit (F7) to accept the parameters and insert the GETSTRING command.

23. Press Merge Codes (Shift+F9) twice to display the All Merge Codes list.

24. Type **v** or scroll to highlight the VARIABLE(var) command in the list. Press Enter to select the code.

25. At the Variable prompt, type **SUBJECT** and press Enter to insert the VARIABLE command.

26. Press Save As (F10), type **MEMO.FF** as the file name, and press Enter. The memo form file should now look like Figure 18.6.

Figure 18.6
The completed memo form file

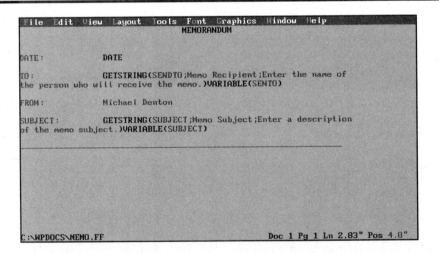

When you merge with this form file, the merge commands insert the variable information for the memo. The DATE merge command displays the current date whenever the form file is used. The GETSTRING command creates the message boxes that prompt the user to type the recipient's name and memo subject. It doesn't matter if the GETSTRING command wraps to the next line; this will not affect the finished memo. The VARIABLE commands insert into the memo the information collected by the GETSTRING commands.

Once you've finished the memo form file, you can use it to make a memo. These steps explain how to use the file:

Choose Tools ▸ Merge ▸ Run.

1. Press Merge/Sort (Ctrl+F9) and choose Merge.

2. At the <u>F</u>orm File prompt, type **MEMO.FF** and press Enter. Make sure the <u>D</u>ata File option is left blank; remember, this application does not merge information from a data file.

3. Choose <u>O</u>utput and then choose <u>U</u>nused Document.

Choose Merge to start the merge.

4. Press Exit (F7) to start the merge. A message box appears with the prompt you typed for the first GETSTRING command.

5. Type the name of the person who will receive the memo. Press Enter or choose OK to continue.

6. The second message box appears. Type the subject for the memo, and then press Enter or choose OK.

WordPerfect creates the memo layout and inserts the information you typed from the keyboard. At this point, the merge is finished, and you can type the message for the memo. You can save the completed memo document to a file, or you can simply print it and clear the screen. Use this procedure each time you need to send a memo. You can automate the process even further by recording the merge keystrokes in a macro. (See Chapter 24 for information about macros.)

After the merge, the memo form file remains unchanged. You can modify the memo layout by editing the memo form letter file—but make sure you don't disturb the merge codes. The MEMO.FF file can include graphics, font changes, and any layout codes that you need to design the appearance of the completed memos. Any changes will affect future memos that you create with the MEMO.FF file.

Merging an Invoice Document

WordPerfect's merge commands can help you automate invoices and other documents based on a table layout. You can utilize merge commands to insert address information from a data file and prompt the user to type invoice quantities or other variable information. The result is an automated invoice that takes much less time to fill in. You can even include a special merge command that sends the completed invoice to the printer.

This section explains the general procedure for creating an automated invoice. You can apply this procedure to similar structured documents such as forms and tables, into which you need to enter information.

The first step in creating an automated invoice is to design the layout of the document. Figure 18.7 shows an example of an invoice document made with the Tables feature. This document can be converted to a form file, which will be used during the merge process to create actual invoices.

Figure 18.7
Using the Tables feature to create an invoice

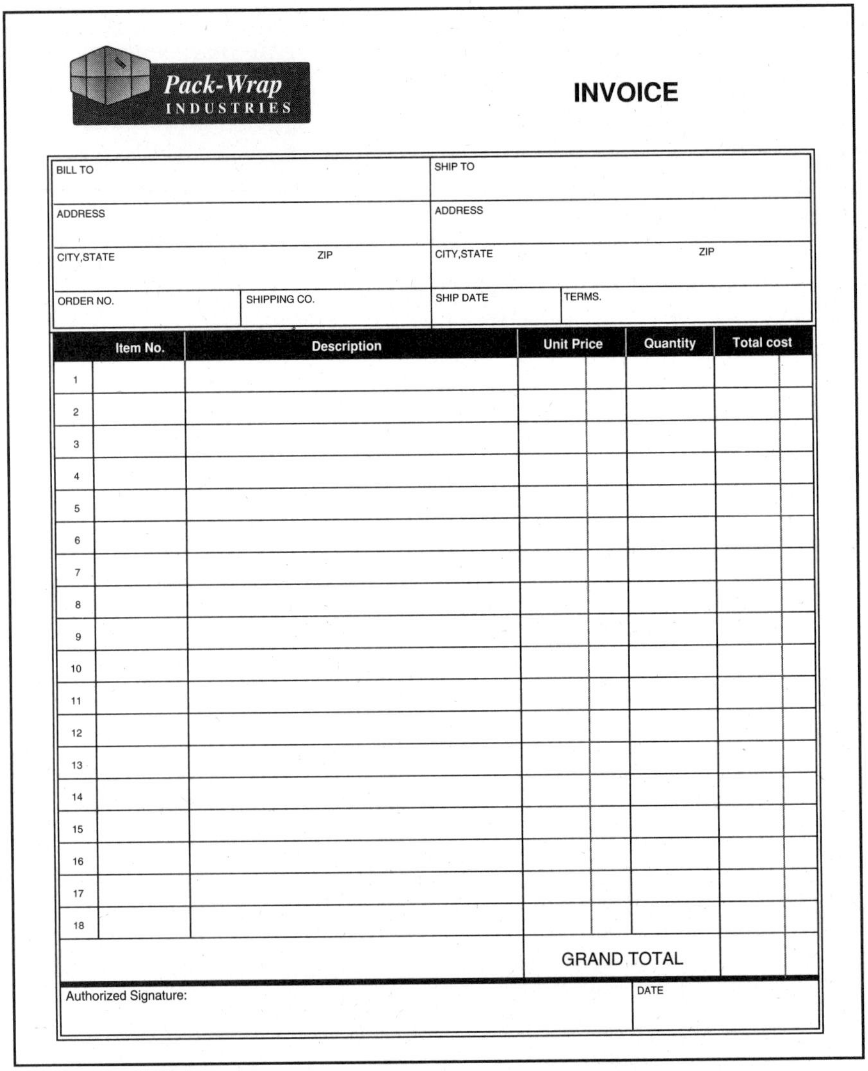

Pack-Wrap
INDUSTRIES

INVOICE

BILL TO	SHIP TO
ADDRESS	ADDRESS
CITY,STATE ZIP	CITY,STATE ZIP

ORDER NO.	SHIPPING CO.	SHIP DATE	TERMS.

	Item No.	Description	Unit Price	Quantity	Total cost
1					
2					
3					
4					
5					
6					
7					
8					
9					
10					
11					
12					
13					
14					
15					
16					
17					
18					
			GRAND TOTAL		

Authorized Signature:	DATE

In this example, the document consists of a full-page table with the text labels that should appear on every invoice. At the top of the page, a company logo is placed inside a graphic box. An "INVOICE" title completes the document. Chapter 12 explains how to use the Tables features to create this type of document.

After you create the invoice document, press Merge Codes (Shift+F9) and choose <u>F</u>orm to convert the document to a form file. You can then place merge commands to indicate where information from the ADDRESS.DF file (or other data files) should be inserted and where the user should be prompted to type information. Figure 18.8 shows how merge commands can be applied to the invoice document.

Figure 18.8

Merge commands in the invoice document

At the top of the invoice, FIELD codes appear after the Bill To and Ship To labels to insert address information from the address data file. The next section of the invoice document looks like this:

ORDER NO.	**GETSTRING**(ORDERNO;Order Number;Type the Order Number.)**VARIABLE**(ORDERNO)
SHIPPING CO.	**GETSTRING**(SHIPCO;Shipping Method;Type the shipping method.)**VARIABLE**(SHIPCO)
SHIP DATE	**GETSTRING**(SHIPDATE;Ship Date;Type the ship date.)**VARIABLE**(SHIPDATE)

TERMS	**GETSTRING**(TERMS;Terms of payment;Type the terms of payment.)**VARIABLE**(TERMS)

Notice that GETSTRING and VARIABLE commands are inserted into the table cells to prompt for and insert information for the order number, shipping company, shipping date, and terms of payment. These commands are inserted as described in the automated memo application, shown earlier in this chapter.

After you insert the merge commands, save your document with a form file (.FF) extension. Then you're ready to create actual invoices. Press Merge/-Sort (Ctrl+F9), and choose <u>M</u>erge. Enter the name of your invoice form file and also the name of the data file that contains the addresses for which you want to create invoices. Then start the merge.

WordPerfect will create a new invoice for each address in your data file. During the merge, the GETSTRING commands will prompt you to enter the order number, shipping company, ship date, and terms of payment. When the merge is finished, you can enter purchase information for each invoice.

This is only one example of how you can merge address information with tables and form documents. You can modify this application to suit your needs. Insert additional GETSTRING commands to prompt for each invoice item, apply table formulas to calculate totals, or change the structure of your data file to include information for each of the invoice items.

Merge Tips and Techniques

The following sections include tips and special techniques that will help you work with merge commands. None of these techniques stand alone as complete merge applications, but you can incorporate them into your current data or form files to improve and enhance merge performance.

Placing Comments in a Merge File

The COMMENT code lets you insert notes or comments into the merge file that will not appear in the finished document. Comments will help you remember what the merge file is designed to do, especially when lengthy merge commands are used to perform a complex task. Here is a simple example of a comment command in a merge file:

```
FIELD(INVEST PREFERENCE) COMMENT(Inserts Investment Preference from Data File)
```

You can insert any text or codes within the parentheses of the COMMENT code. The comment remains in the data or form file, but it will not appear in the merged document. To insert a comment into a file:

Choose Tools ▶
Merge ▶ Define ▶
Merge Codes.

- Press Merge Codes (Shift+F9) twice.

- Scroll or type **com** to highlight the Comment code, and press Enter.

- Type the text for your comment and press Enter to insert the code into your file.

Once a comment is inserted, you can directly edit the text between the bold-faced parentheses of the comment code.

The COMMENT code can also help you arrange other merge codes in your document. As you've seen in previous examples, merge commands are sometimes quite long and complex. You don't need to worry about the codes upsetting the format of the merged document, because they are removed as they are executed during the merge. Only the text generated by the merge remains. Sometimes, however, the commands can be difficult to read. Consider this example:

```
IF(VARIABLE(ITEMNO)=0) CHAINMACRO(RECALC) ELSE CALL(ITEM VARIABLE(ROWCOUNT)
ASSIGN(ROWCOUNT;VARIABLE(ROWCOUNT)+1) ENDIF
```

With the codes entered in a continuous line, it's difficult to follow the logic of this command; however, if you insert hard returns and tabs to break up the merge codes, some of the commands may not work and you'll end up with extra hard returns and tabs in the finished document.

This is where the COMMENT code can help, because it lets you insert text and codes into the merge document that should not be included as part of the merged text. The following shows the previous example with formatting inserted through COMMENT codes:

```
IF(VARIABLE(ITEMNO)=0) COMMENT([HRt]
[Tab])CHAINMACRO(RECALC) COMMENT([HRt]
[Tab])ELSE COMMENT([HRt]
[Tab])CALL(ITEM VARIABLE(ROWCOUNT)COMMENT([HRt]
[Tab]) ASSIGN(ROWCOUNT;VARIABLE(ROWCOUNT)+1) COMMENT([HRt]
)ENDIF
```

In this example, hard returns and tabs are placed between the parentheses of the COMMENT code. This puts the merge codes on individual lines, but will not affect the formatting of the merged text. The [HRt] and [Tab] codes remain hidden when you're viewing the merge document on the screen.

Chaining to Different Files

The Merge Command list includes codes that transfer control of the merge to other files. This is called *chaining* to another file. You use a chain command when you want to create form letters for address records divided between two or more files. You can also chain to a form file to continue the merge with a different model document.

Suppose your address records are divided between two data files. You would follow these steps to insert a chain command in the first data file that tells WordPerfect to continue merging with the records in the second file:

- Retrieve the first data file and move the cursor to the end of the file.

- Press Merge Codes (Shift+F9) twice to display the Merge Codes list.

Choose <u>T</u>ools ▸
<u>M</u>erge ▸ <u>D</u>efine ▸
Merge Codes.

- Scroll or type **ch** to highlight the CHAINDATA (filename) code, and press Enter.

- Type the name of the data file that contains the rest of the records for the merge. If the file is located somewhere other than the default directory, type the directory path before the file name.

- Press Enter to insert the chain command. Then save the data file.

If you want to chain from one form file to another, simply retrieve the file and follow these same steps to insert the CHAINFORM code. When you use the CHAINDATA or CHAINFORM codes, the merge does not chain to the specified file until it is finished with the current data or form file. It doesn't matter where the chain codes are placed in the merge file; the chaining doesn't occur until the current merge file is completed.

If you want to insert or *nest* a data file or form file in the middle of the current merge file, you can use the NESTDATA and NESTFORM commands. These codes tell WordPerfect to pause at the current merge file, execute the merge commands in the specified file, and then continue the merge with the commands that follow the nest command.

To insert a nest command, move the cursor to the place in your file where the information should be inserted during the merge. Then follow the steps described above for inserting the CHAINDATA codes, but highlight and select the NESTDATA or NESTFORM code instead.

Combining a Merge with Macros

If you are familiar with WordPerfect's macro language, you may prefer to use macros to perform tasks during the merge. Macros can perform the same commands as the merge codes—with the exception of FIELD code functions—and they don't clutter the form file.

Macros are actually more powerful than the merge codes, because they can perform any feature or task that WordPerfect can do. Instead of inserting merge codes, you can define a macro that performs the desired task. (See Chapter 24 for detailed information about creating and using macros.)

Try the following steps to create a file-saving macro and incorporate it into a form file. This example uses the LETTER.FF file created in Chapter 17; if you don't have this file, you can retrieve a different merge form file for this example.

Choose Tools ▸ Macro ▸ Record.

1. Press Macro Record (Ctrl+F10) to display the Record Macro dialog box.

2. Type **FILESAVE** as the macro name, and press Enter. A Recording Macro message appears on the status line.

3. Press Save As (F10), type **LETTERS.DOC** as the file name, and press Enter.

4. Press Macro Record (Ctrl+F10) to turn off the Macro Recording feature.

5. Clear the screen, and then retrieve the LETTER.FF form file from Chapter 17.

6. Move the cursor to the end of the form letter.

Choose Tools ▸ Merge ▸ Define ▸ Merge Codes.

7. Press Merge Codes (Shift+F9) twice to display the Merge Code list.

8. Scroll or type **chainm** to highlight the CHAINMACRO code. Press Enter to select the code.

9. Type **FILESAVE.WPM** as the macro name. Then press Enter to insert the code, shown in Figure 18.9.

10. Save the form file to update your changes to the file on disk.

When you run the merge, all records in the data file are merged with the form file. Then the CHAINMACRO command tells WordPerfect to run the FILESAVE.WPM macro at the end of the merge. The macro in the above steps simply selects the Save feature and enters the LETTERS.DOC file name for the merged document.

This is just one example of how you can combine a macro with a merge procedure. Like the CHAINDATA merge code, CHAINMACRO works only at the end of the merge process after all records have been merged from the data file. If you want to play a macro during the merge process, use the NESTMACRO command instead; this is also found on the complete Merge Codes list. To use the NESTMACRO code, move the cursor to the place in your form file where the recorded macro commands should be performed. Then insert the NESTMACRO command, using the steps described earlier for CHAINMACRO. When you run the merge, WordPerfect pauses the merge process when it encounters the NESTMACRO command in the file. The commands in the specified macro file are executed. Then the merge resumes with the commands that follow the NESTMACRO command.

Figure 18.9
Inserting the
CHAINMACRO code

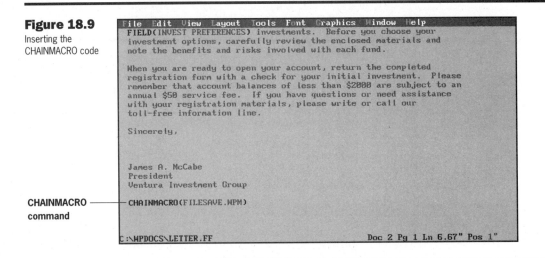

CHAINMACRO
command

Using Merge Codes to Assemble Documents

Document assembly involves compiling information from different sources into a completed document. Several merge commands are designed to help WordPerfect decide which information should be placed in the merged document, based on information found in your data file. A section in Chapter 17 explains one example of this—inserting the IFBLANK command to determine whether a title is found in the MR/MS field of your data file; in this earlier example, you saw how the merge would produce a different result according to the field contents.

In this section, you'll see how to use merge commands to assemble information from different files to create a finished document. The example in this section shows a form letter that confirms travel arrangements for a convention. Since there are three different hotels for the convention, merge commands are used to insert the correct confirmation paragraph from other document files. Figure 18.10 shows how the document works.

When the merge is run, the recipient's name (a) is merged from the data file into the form letter (b). Then, WordPerfect checks the hotel field (c) and merges one of four possible paragraphs into the document to confirm the hotel reservation. This example requires five document files: the form letter, the data file, three possible "hotel" paragraphs (each saved in its own file), and a paragraph that is inserted when the hotel preference field is left blank.

Figure 18.10

Using merge codes to assemble a document

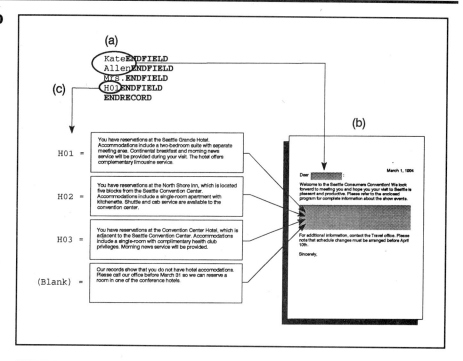

The following information explains the general procedure for creating and merging the files for the example described above. Detailed instructions for most of the tasks—such as creating data files and inserting merge commands— are explained in Chapter 17, and also in earlier sections of this chapter.

- First, create a data file with the names that should be inserted into the form letter or document. In each record, include a field that specifies variable text. For the above example, the Hotel field was added at the end of every record, as shown in Figure 18.11. This field contains either H01, H02, or H03. Each possible value represents one of the confirmation paragraphs that might be inserted.

- Next, create the paragraphs that may be inserted into the form letter. Figure 18.12 shows the four sample paragraphs and the file names under which each should be saved. For this example, each paragraph must be saved in its own file.

- When you finish creating the data file and the paragraphs, you have all the information that might be inserted into the completed document. Now, create the form file shown in Figure 18.13. When you are finished, save the form file.

Figure 18.11

A data file for the document assembly example

Hotel preference fields

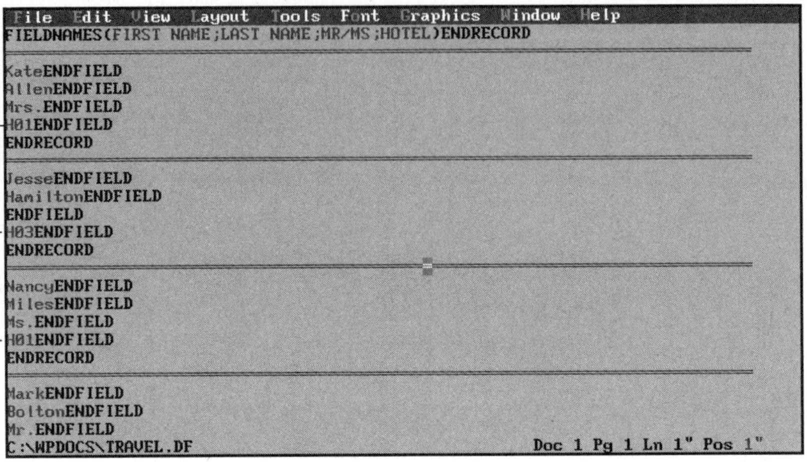

```
 File  Edit  View  Layout  Tools  Font  Graphics  Window  Help
FIELDNAMES(FIRST NAME;LAST NAME;MR/MS;HOTEL)ENDRECORD
_____
KateENDFIELD
AllenENDFIELD
Mrs.ENDFIELD
H01ENDFIELD
ENDRECORD
_____
JesseENDFIELD
HamiltonENDFIELD
ENDFIELD
H03ENDFIELD
ENDRECORD
_____
NancyENDFIELD
MilesENDFIELD
Ms.ENDFIELD
H01ENDFIELD
ENDRECORD
_____
MarkENDFIELD
BoltonENDFIELD
Mr.ENDFIELD
C:\WPDOCS\TRAVEL.DF                           Doc 1 Pg 1 Ln 1" Pos 1"
```

Figure 18.12

Hotel confirmation paragraphs

HOTEL-01.TXT

> You have reservations at the Seattle Grande Hotel. Accommodations include a two-bedroom suite with separate meeting area. Continental breakfast and morning news service will be provided during your visit. The hotel offers complementary limousine service.

HOTEL-02.TXT

> You have reservations at the North Shore Inn, which is located five blocks from the Seattle Convention Center. Accommodations include a single-room apartment with kitchenette. Shuttle and cab service are available to the convention center.

HOTEL-03.TXT

> You have reservations at the Convention Center Hotel, which is adjacent to the Seattle Convention Center. Accommodations include a single-room with complimentary health club privileges. Morning news service will be provided.

NO-HOTEL.TXT

> Our records show that you do not have hotel accomodations. Please call our office before March 31 so we can reserve a room in one of the conference hotels.

Figure 18.13

Creating the form file

These codes insert information from the data file

The commands "decide" which paragraph should be inserted at this point in the document

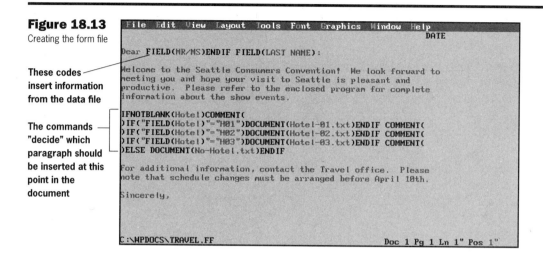

```
File  Edit  View  Layout  Tools  Font  Graphics  Window  Help
                                                      DATE
Dear FIELD(MR/MS)ENDIF FIELD(LAST NAME):

Welcome to the Seattle Consumers Convention!  We look forward to
meeting you and hope your visit to Seattle is pleasant and
productive.  Please refer to the enclosed program for complete
information about the show events.

IFNOTBLANK(Hotel)COMMENT(
)IF("FIELD(Hotel)"="H01")DOCUMENT(Hotel-01.txt)ENDIF COMMENT(
)IF("FIELD(Hotel)"="H02")DOCUMENT(Hotel-02.txt)ENDIF COMMENT(
)IF("FIELD(Hotel)"="H03")DOCUMENT(Hotel-03.txt)ENDIF COMMENT(
)ELSE DOCUMENT(No-Hotel.txt)ENDIF

For additional information, contact the Travel office.  Please
note that schedule changes must be arranged before April 18th.

Sincerely,



C:\WPDOCS\TRAVEL.FF                       Doc 1 Pg 1 Ln 1" Pos 1"
```

Let's examine the list of codes in the middle of the form file. For this example, the following merge commands were inserted between the first and second paragraphs of the form file—at the point in the document where WordPerfect needs to decide which paragraph to insert. These are the merge commands from the file:

```
IFNOTBLANK(Hotel)COMMENT(
)IF("FIELD(Hotel)"="H01")DOCUMENT(Hotel-01.txt)ENDIF COMMENT(
)IF("FIELD(Hotel)"="H02")DOCUMENT(Hotel-02.txt)ENDIF COMMENT(
)IF("FIELD(Hotel)"="H03")DOCUMENT(Hotel-03.txt)ENDIF COMMENT(
)ELSE DOCUMENT(No-Hotel.txt)ENDIF
```

The boldface text shows the commands that were inserted from the Merge Codes list. You can ignore the COMMENT codes because these were inserted to make the whole command structure easier to read. The IFNOT-BLANK command checks to see whether the Hotel field from the data file is empty; if it isn't, WordPerfect executes the commands that follow the IFNOT-BLANK command. Let's examine the IF commands, which appear like this in the document:

```
IF("FIELD(Hotel)"="H01")DOCUMENT(Hotel-01.txt)ENDIF
```

The IF("FIELD(Hotel)"="H01") checks the value stored in the Hotel field for the current record to see if it equals H01. Remember, the strings H01, H02, and H03 represent one of the hotel confirmation paragraphs. If the Hotel field does contain the H01 string, then WordPerfect executes the DOCUMENT command to insert the HOTEL-01.TXT file into the form letter. If the Hotel field doesn't contain H01, then the merge simply continues with the next IF statement. Once an IF statement matches the string stored in the Hotel field, the appropriate paragraph is inserted and the merge ends.

If the Hotel field is empty or contains a value other than H01, H02, or H03, then WordPerfect executes the command that follows the ELSE command—in this case, it's another DOCUMENT command that inserts the NO-HOTEL.TXT paragraph. When the merge ends, the result is a document that is truly tailored for the recipient.

You can apply these and other merge commands to generate contracts, invoices, sales agreements, and other documents in which standard phrases or paragraphs must be combined with personal information to create a finished document.

Instead of merging information from a data file, you can include the GETSTRING command, as described earlier, to prompt for information from the keyboard. Then, use the IF commands to evaluate the information gathered by the GETSTRING commands and retrieve different document components into the merged document.

See your WordPerfect Reference manual for detailed information about the advanced merge commands, and the programming structures you need to follow to create complex conditional merge applications.

Enhancing Your Documents with Graphics

Inserting Equations into Your Document

Creating Text Columns

Using Styles to Simplify Formatting and Editing

Documents That Speak

5

Desktop Publishing, Graphics, and Sound

19

Enhancing Your Documents with Graphics

Quick and Easy
Graphics

Graphics for Desktop
Publishing

Changing Border and
Fill Options

Using the Image Editor

Working with WP
Presentations

Retrieving Graphics
from Other Programs

WORDPERFECT'S GRAPHICS FEATURES LET YOU INSERT PICTURES, graphs, and other types of illustrations into your documents. Although graphics are usually associated with desktop publishing, you may want to use these features to dress up your standard business documents by putting the company logo on your business correspondence, sprucing up those boring reports with attractive charts and diagrams, adding scanned photographs to your newsletters, and including illustrations with your recent literary masterpiece. Figure 19.1 shows an example of how graphics can help communicate the message of a document.

Unlike earlier versions of WordPerfect, version 6.0 lets you view graphics while you are editing your document. You cannot create graphics from within WordPerfect, but you can retrieve them from virtually any graphics software program, including PC Paintbrush, CorelDRAW, Quattro Pro, and WordPerfect Corporation's own WP Presentations. Once you've retrieved a graphic image into your WordPerfect document, you can use the graphics editing features to size, rotate, and adjust the image. See "Working with WP Presentations" and "Retrieving Graphics from Other Programs" at the end of this chapter.

This chapter also explains how to create graphic lines or *rules*, page and paragraph borders, and watermarks, which are shaded graphics that appear as a background on every page. These features, when combined with the other graphic features, let you create a wide variety of documents and desktop publishing applications.

Quick and Easy Graphics

WordPerfect 6.0 offers quick and easy methods for adding graphics to your documents. This section explains the basics of retrieving, sizing, and moving graphic images on the page. These are simple graphics tasks for documents that do not require rigid guidelines for the size and position of graphic images.

Before you try the following tasks, you need to switch to WordPerfect's graphics or page display mode. To do so, press Screen (Ctrl+F3), and then choose Graphics or Page from the displayed dialog box. You can also choose View from the menu bar and then choose Graphics Mode or Page Mode.

Retrieving a Graphic Image

Try these steps to retrieve one of WordPerfect's graphic images into the document displayed on your screen. If your document screen is empty, create or retrieve a document file before you continue.

1. Move the cursor to the paragraph or page where you want to place the graphic image.

Figure 19.1

A WordPerfect document with graphic images

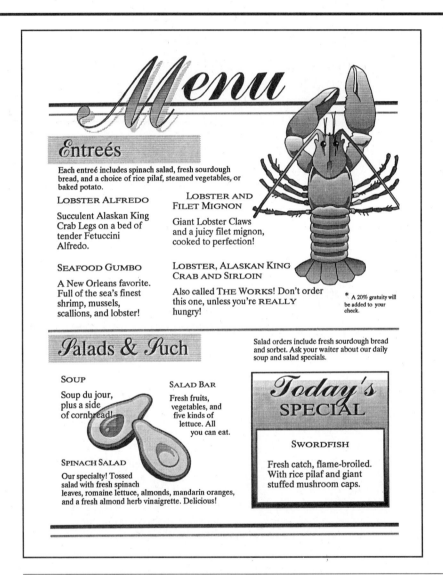

Choose Graphics ▶
Retrieve Image,
type **c:\wp60\-
graphics\hotair
.wpg**, and press
Enter.

2. Press Retrieve (Shift+F10) twice to display the Retrieve Document dialog box. Type **c:\wp60\graphics\hotair.wpg**, and then press Enter.

As shown in Figure 19.2, WordPerfect retrieves the image into a *graphics box* at the right edge of the screen, using WordPerfect's standard settings for graphic border style, spacing, and size. This is the quickest way to bring a graphic image into your document. Keep this document on the screen for the exercises that follow.

Figure 19.2

Retrieving a graphic image

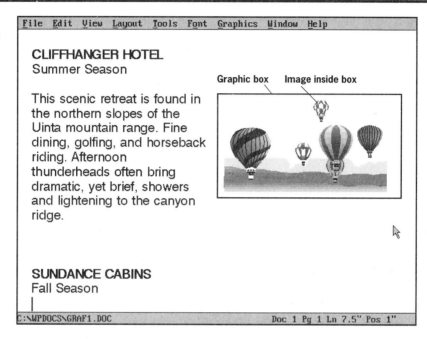

NOTE. *Graphic boxes are discussed in detail throughout the section "Graphics for Desktop Publishing," later in this chapter.*

If you prefer to use the function keys, you can also press Graphics (Alt+F9), choose Retrieve Image (Shift+F10), and then enter the graphic's file name. This is the same as pressing Retrieve (Shift+F10) twice and entering the file name.

If you don't know the file name of the graphic image you want to retrieve, you can press File Manager (F5), instead of Retrieve (Shift+F10), and enter the directory name in which your graphics files are stored. From the list of displayed files, highlight the name of a graphics file and choose Look to preview the file. Then press Exit (F7) to return to the File Manager. When you've found the file you want, highlight the file name, and then choose Retrieve into Current Doc to insert the graphic into your document.

You can also use the QuickList feature to hunt down graphics files. For instance, you could establish a category that lists .WPG files. Then you could list all .WPG files just by pressing File Manager (F5), pressing QuickList (F6), choosing the desired category from the QuickList dialog box, and choosing Select. For more details on this handy feature, consult Chapter 5.

When you are using WordPerfect's graphics display mode or page display mode, you'll see graphic images on the screen as they will appear on the printed page. However, if you are working with WordPerfect's text display mode, you won't see the graphic image on the screen; you'll only see a box outline. Also, in text display mode when you retrieve a graphic image into a blank document screen or into a document that consists of only a few text lines, you may not see the entire box. This is one limitation of WordPerfect's text display mode: When you are editing your document, WordPerfect "writes" only the portion of the screen where text has been typed. To see the whole graphic image, press Print (Shift+F7) and choose Print Preview.

Sizing the Graphic

When you are using WordPerfect's graphics display mode or page display mode, you can change the size of a graphic image with the mouse, as follows:

1. Move the mouse pointer over the graphic image on the screen, and click the mouse button once to select the graphics box. As shown in Figure 19.3, you'll notice little solid squares—called *handles*—at each corner and side of the box.

Figure 19.3

Handles appearing around a selected graphic image

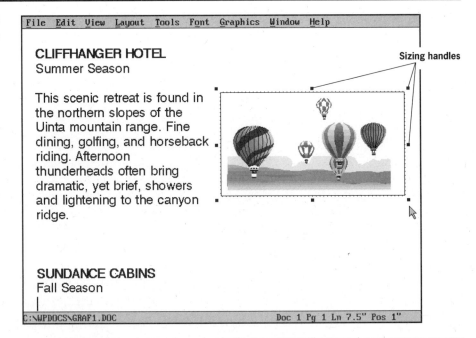

2. To experiment, move the mouse pointer over the solid square handle at the upper-right corner of the selected box. (You can actually change the size of a graphics box by dragging on *any* of its handles.)

3. Hold down the mouse button and move the pointer to drag the handle closer to the center of the graphics box. As you move the pointer, the box outline changes to show a new size the box will take on if you release the mouse button at that point. Figure 19.4 shows how the outline may look when you are dragging the mouse pointer.

Figure 19.4

Sizing a graphic image

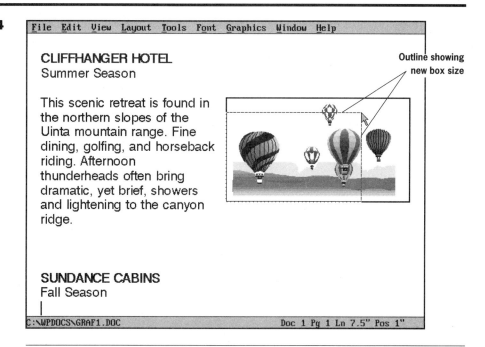

4. When the graphics box outline is the size and shape you want, release the mouse button to accept the new outline, and WordPerfect sizes the graphic image to fit the new size of the box.

In this example, you used the mouse pointer to drag a corner handle, which proportionately sized the graphic image. Drag a top or bottom handle and you'll change the height of the image inside the graphics box; drag the handle at the left or right side of the box, and you'll change the width of the image.

Moving the Graphic Image

After you've retrieved and sized your graphic image, you may need to adjust its position on the page. Again, when you are using WordPerfect's graphics display mode or page display mode, the task of moving graphics is simple and quick. Try the following steps to change the position of the graphic image in your document:

1. Move the mouse pointer over the graphic image, and then click the mouse button once to select the graphic box, so that the square black handles appear at its sides and corners.

2. With the mouse pointer still over the graphic, hold down the mouse button and drag the pointer to move the graphics box outline until the graphics box appears at the left margin of the page. (When you are moving, as opposed to sizing, a graphics box, be sure *not* to place the mouse pointer over one of the box's sizing handles.)

3. When the graphics box outline appears where you want it, release the mouse button. WordPerfect moves the graphic to its new location and reformats the text around it.

When you are moving a graphic image, you can drag it to any location on the page or drag the pointer up or down to scroll to another page. As long as you are holding the mouse button, you can move the graphic to any location in your document.

Graphics for Desktop Publishing

You've learned to insert, size, and move graphics with the mouse pointer, while using WordPerfect's graphics or page display mode. These methods are ideal for short documents and simple reports, in which a specific appearance or placement is not required. When your documents require greater precision, as in newsletters, brochures, and desktop publishing, you'll need to use the advanced graphics features.

As you saw earlier in this chapter, when you retrieve an image, WordPerfect places it inside a graphics box within your document. WordPerfect lets you define border and spacing options for the graphics box, create a caption, and specify an exact size and position for the box on the page. These and other settings give you complete control over the location, size, and appearance of your graphics. Using these settings is also the only way to adjust the size and placement of graphics boxes when you are using WordPerfect's text display mode.

In this section, you'll learn to insert graphic images and to size and place them according to precise measurements. You'll also learn how to create captions for the graphics boxes.

Creating a Graphics Box

Graphics boxes can contain any type of graphic image; they can also contain equations (as explained in the next chapter) and even regular text. Here is the general procedure for creating a graphics box in your document:

Choose Graphics ▸
Graphics Boxes ▸
Create.

- Move the insertion point to the paragraph or page where the graphics box should appear in your document.

- Press Graphics (Alt+F9), choose Graphic Boxes, and then choose Create. WordPerfect displays the Create Graphics Box dialog box, shown in Figure 19.5.

Figure 19.5

The Create Graphics
Box dialog box

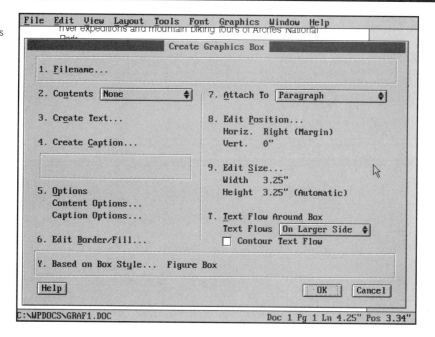

- From the dialog box, choose Filename and enter the name of the file that contains the graphics or text that you want to place in the box.

- Choose Attach To, and then select either Paragraph or Page.

■ Choose Edit Position to display the Positioning dialog box, in which you can choose the position of the box within the current paragraph or page. After you choose the desired position options, press Exit (F7) to return to the Create Graphics Box dialog box.

■ Choose Edit Size to display the Graphics Box Size dialog box. Choose the width and height options, and enter measurements to define the size of the graphics box. Then press Exit (F7).

Choose OK to ac-
cept the graphics
box settings.

■ When you are finished defining the options for the graphics box, press Exit (F7) to accept the graphics box settings.

WordPerfect inserts the graphics box into your document. The appearance of the box on the screen depends on the display option you're using in WordPerfect. Figure 19.6 shows examples of the two possibilities.

If you are using WordPerfect's text display mode, the box appears as an outline in your text (top of Figure 19.6); if you are using WordPerfect's graphics or page display mode, you'll see the graphics or text inside the box (bottom of Figure 19.6).

Now try the following steps to add a graphics box to the document displayed on your screen. If the document screen is empty, type a few lines of text before you try these steps.

1. Move the cursor to the paragraph or page on which the graphic image should appear.

2. Press Graphics (Alt+F9) to display the Graphics dialog box. Choose Graphics Boxes, and then choose Create.

Choose Graphics ▸
Graphics Boxes ▸
Create.

3. From the Create Graphics Box dialog box, choose Filename. Type **c:\wp60\graphics\hotrod.wpg** and press Enter. This retrieves one of the WordPerfect images into the graphics box.

4. Choose Attach To and then select Page to place the graphics box according to the current page margins.

5. Choose Edit Position to display the Page Box Position dialog box. Choose Horizontal Position and then choose Centered. Choose Vertical Position, and then choose Top, if it's not already selected, to place the graphics box at the top margin. The result will center your graphics box at the top of the page.

6. Press Exit (F7) to accept your position selections and to close the Page Box Position dialog box.

Choose OK to
close the Page Box
Position dialog box.

7. Choose Edit Size to display the Graphics Box Size dialog box. Choose Set Width and enter **4** to create a graphics box that is four inches wide. Then choose Automatic Height to specify a box height that is automatically proportioned to match the width measurement you entered.

Figure 19.6

A graphics box shown in WordPerfect's text display mode (a) and graphics display mode (b)

(a)

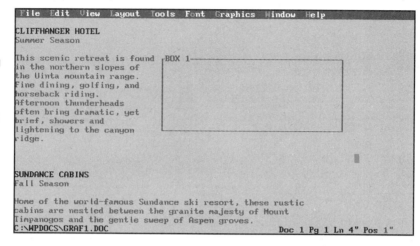

(b)

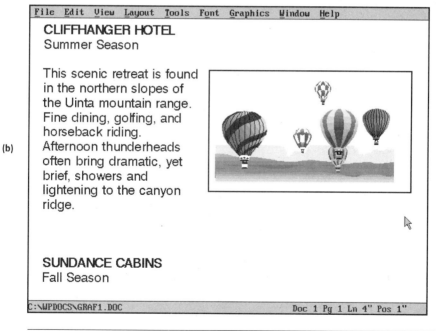

Choose OK to close the Graphics Box Size dialog box.

8. Press Exit (F7) to accept the defined size and to close the Graphics Box Size dialog box.

Choose OK to return to the document screen.

9. Press Exit (F7) to close the Create Graphics Box dialog box and return to the document screen.

When you return to the document screen, you'll see the graphics box at the top center of the current page, as shown in Figure 19.7 with the graphics display mode. (Of course, your screen will also contain some text.)

Figure 19.7

A graphics box centered between margins

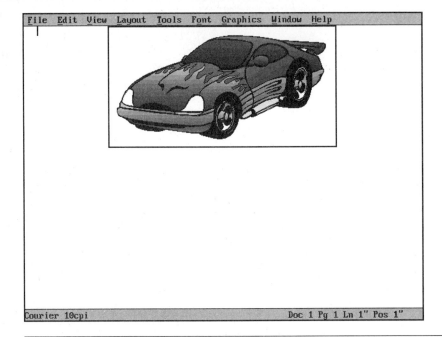

In the sections that follow, you'll learn more about the options you can choose from the Create Graphics Box dialog box. Note that you can also choose all of these options from the Edit Graphics Box dialog box.

Changing the Graphics Box Size

The Graphics Box Size dialog box contains two groups of options that let you specify the width and height of the graphics box. The Set Width and Set Height options let you enter a specific width or height measurement; the Automatic Width and Automatic Height options tell WordPerfect to calculate the box width or height based on the proportionate size of the text or graphic image inside the box.

The following steps explain how to change the size of a graphics box. Before you do the steps, it is assumed that the Create Graphics Box or Edit Graphics Box dialog box is open for the graphics box you want to change.

- From the Create Graphics Box dialog box, choose Edit Size to display the Graphics Box Size dialog box.

- Choose Set Width or Set Height to enter a specific measurement for the width or height of the box.

- To make the height of the graphics box proportionate to the width, choose Automatic Height. Or, choose Automatic Width and enter a measurement to make the width of the box proportionate to the height.

- When you are finished defining the box size, press Exit (F7) until you return to the document screen.

Choose OK until you return to the document screen.

In most cases, you'll want to set a measurement for either Set Width or Set Height. Then, choose Automatic Width or Automatic Height to let WordPerfect figure the other measurement. This creates a proportionate graphics box. You can, however, create a custom box size by entering measurements for both Set Width and Set Height; this allows you to create, for example, a box that is 3 inches wide and 6 inches high, when the contents of the box may be only 2 inches square.

When you use Set Width and Set Height to create a box size that is different from the box contents, you'll probably need to adjust the position of the graphic image inside the box. This is possible from the Image Editor, which is explained later in this chapter.

Changing the Box Position

The position of a graphics box is determined by two options in the Create Graphics Box dialog box: Attach To and Edit Position. The Attach To option lets you choose how the graphics box will be inserted into your document—at a precise position on the page, according to the page margins, within the current paragraph, or within the current line of text. Figure 19.8 illustrates each of these options. The Edit Position option lets you specify how the graphics box is aligned according to the item you selected for Attach To.

If, for example, you choose Attach To, and then choose Page, WordPerfect will insert the graphics box according to the margins of the current page; then you can choose Edit Position and indicate how you want to align the graphics box within the page margins—aligned at the right margin or centered between top and bottom margins, for example. When you choose Edit Position, WordPerfect displays alignment options that are specific to the item you selected from the Attach To list. For example, when you choose Attach To and then Page, the Edit Position option lets you choose one of the page margins for alignment.

Figure 19.8

Examples of
graphics box
placement

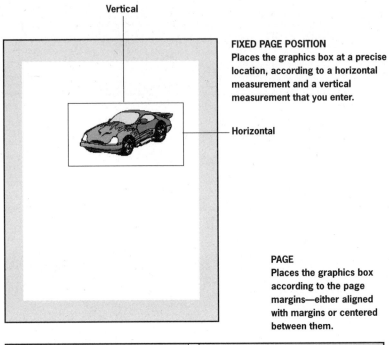

Vertical

Horizontal

FIXED PAGE POSITION
Places the graphics box at a precise
location, according to a horizontal
measurement and a vertical
measurement that you enter.

PAGE
Places the graphics box
according to the page
margins—either aligned
with margins or centered
between them.

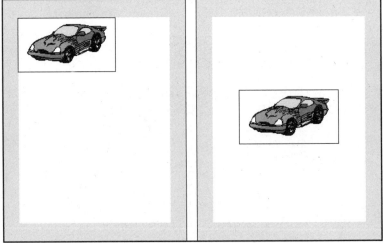

Figure 19.8
(continued)

PARAGRAPH
Places the graphics box at an edge of the current paragraph. The graphics box moves with the paragraph during editing.

CHARACTER
Places the graphics box in the current line of text. The graphics box moves as a single text character during editing.

The following sections explain how to position your graphics box according to a fixed page position, to the page or column margins, within a paragraph, or as a character in the current line of text. It is assumed that the cursor is located on the page, paragraph, or text line where the graphics box should be inserted into your document.

Then, from the Create Graphics Box or the Edit Graphics Box dialog box, choose one of the options explained in the next five sections to specify how the graphics box will be placed or attached to the text in your document.

Fixed Page Position

The Fixed Page Position option lets you attach a graphics box to the current page according to absolute measurements. Instead of positioning text according to page margins, this option lets you enter a horizontal and vertical measurement to indicate where you want the top-left corner of the box to appear.

You can, for example, use Fixed Page Position to place a graphics box at exactly 2.75 inches from the top edge of the page, and 3.25 inches from the left edge of the page. After you attach a graphics box to a fixed page position, other text and graphics are formatted around the box.

To place the graphics box at a specific location on the page,

- Choose Attach To from the Create Graphics Box dialog box, and then choose Fixed Page Position.

- Choose Edit Position to display the Fixed Page Position dialog box.

- Choose Distance from Left of Page and enter the amount of space you want between the graphics box and the left edge of the printed page.

- Choose Distance from Top of Page and enter the amount of space you want between the graphics box and the top edge of the printed page.

- Press Exit (F7) to return to the Create Graphics Box dialog box.

Choose OK to return to the Create Graphics Box dialog box.

When you return to the Create Graphics Box dialog box, you'll see the horizontal and vertical measurements under the Edit Position option, which indicate where the upper-left corner of your graphics box will be placed. When you return to the document screen, your graphics box will be placed according to the measurements you entered. Remember, both measurements indicate where the top-left corner of the graphics box will be on the printed page. As you create or edit the rest of your document, the text and other graphics boxes will be formatted around the graphic at the fixed page position; this assumes, of course, that you've set the text to flow around the graphics box.

Page

To place the graphics box according to the margins of the current page:

- Choose Attach To, and select Page.

- Choose Edit Position to display the Page Box Position dialog box, shown in Figure 19.9.

- Choose Horizontal Position. Then choose one of the following: Left or Right to align the graphics box at the left or right margin; Centered to center the box between margins; or Full to extend the box to fill the space between the left and right margins. The Full option automatically changes the width of the graphics box to fill the space across the page.

- Choose Vertical Position. Then choose one of the following: Top or Bottom to align the graphics box at the top or bottom margin; Centered to center the box between margins; or Full to extend the box to fill the space between the top and bottom margins. The Full option automatically changes the height of the graphics box to fill the space down the page.

Choose OK to close the Page Box Position dialog box.

- Press Exit (F7) to accept the box position settings and return to the Create Graphics Box dialog box.

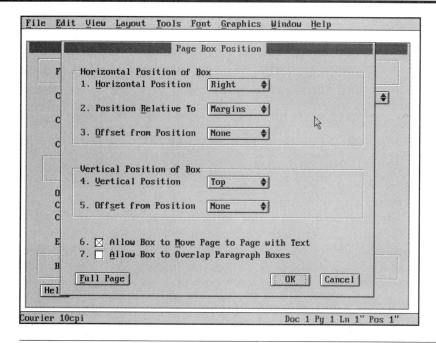

Figure 19.9
The Page Box
Position dialog box

When you return to your document, the graphics box is placed on the page according to the position options you selected.

Additional Page Position Options

The Page Box Position dialog box provides other options that let you further adjust the placement of a graphics box on the page. Note that these options are available only after selecting the Attach To and Page options, and then choosing the Edit Position option.

When the Page Box Position dialog box is displayed, and you choose Horizontal Position or Vertical Position, an option called Set appears at the top of the list of choices. The Set option lets you enter a horizontal or vertical measurement to specify an absolute position on the page, similar to the option for Fixed Page Position described earlier.

Additional options on the Page Box Position dialog box let you change the method of page positioning for the box. If your document text is formatted in columns (newspaper or parallel), you can choose Position Relative To and select either Column or Columns. This indicates that you want the graphics box positioned according to the margins of one (when you select Column) or multiple (when you select Columns) columns, rather than the margins of the page. Then, for example, when you choose Horizontal Position and choose <u>R</u>ight, your graphics box is aligned at the right margin of the designated text column or columns, instead of at the right margin of the page.

The <u>O</u>ffset from Position option lets you enter an offset measurement to adjust the position against the current horizontal or vertical position setting. Suppose you want your graphics box to be aligned near the bottom of the page, but you don't want it to be at the bottom margin; perhaps you want it one-half inch above the bottom margin to allow for a line of text that should appear at the bottom of the page. You would first choose the <u>V</u>ertical Position option and choose <u>B</u>ottom to indicate that the box should appear at the bottom margin. Then you would choose Off<u>s</u>et from Position (under the <u>V</u>ertical Position option) and choose <u>U</u>p, and then enter **.5** to indicate an upward adjustment. The result is that the bottom edge of the graphics box is aligned one-half inch above the bottom margin of the page.

An option at the bottom of the Page Box Position dialog box lets you indicate whether you want the graphics box to move page to page with the text. When this option is turned on (an *X* appears in the box next to the option), your graphics box is attached to the text on the current page and follows along even if the text is pushed to another page during editing. (This option is on by default.) When this option is turned off, the graphics box is fixed on the current page, even when the text is moved up or down to a different page due to text that you've added or deleted.

Paragraph
To place the graphics box within the boundaries of the current paragraph:

- Choose <u>A</u>ttach To, and select <u>P</u>aragraph.

- Choose Edit <u>P</u>osition to display the Paragraph Box Position dialog box.

- Choose <u>H</u>orizontal Position. Then choose one of the following: <u>L</u>eft or <u>R</u>ight to align the graphics box at one side of the paragraph; <u>C</u>enter to center the graphics box within the paragraph; <u>F</u>ull to extend the graphics box to fill the space between the left and right margins; or <u>S</u>et and then enter a measurement for the amount of space you want between the graphics box and the left edge of the paragraph text.

- If you want the top of the graphics box to appear below the first line of the paragraph, choose <u>D</u>istance from Top of Paragraph. Then enter a measurement for the amount of space you want between the top of the paragraph and the top of the graphics box.

- Press Exit (F7) to accept the box position settings, and return to the Create Graphics Box dialog box.

Choose OK to close the Paragraph Box Position dialog box.

Character Position

The Character Position option lets you insert the graphics box as if it were a single character within the current line of text. When you choose Attach To and then Character Position, your graphics box will flow with the characters in the current text line, and will be formatted with the current paragraph text. This option does not restrict the size of your graphics box—only the position options.

To place the graphics box as a character within the current line of text:

- Choose Attach To, and then choose Character Position.

- Choose Edit Position to display the Character Box Position dialog box. Note that the position options are relative to the baseline (bottom) of the current text line in your document.

- Choose Top, Bottom, Center, or Content Baseline to indicate how the graphics box should be aligned with the current line of text. Note that these alignment options are relative to the space between the top and bottom of the current line of text.

- When turned on, the option called Box Changes Text Line Height increases the space between the current and previous text lines; this ensures that the character graphics box does not print over the text of the previous line. If you do not want the character graphics box to change the line height of the current text line, turn off the Box Changes Text Line Height option.

- Press Exit (F7) to accept the box position settings, and return to the Create Graphics Box dialog box.

Choose OK to close the Character Box Position dialog box.

Note that the character graphics box can be any size you want, but it will be manipulated as a single character in the text line, at the place where your cursor was located when you created the graphics box.

Wrapping Text around the Box

WordPerfect provides different options that let you control how text wraps around a graphics box. You may want your document text to wrap around a specific side of the box—or around both sides. You can also tell WordPerfect not to wrap the text, so that it prints over your graphic; this option is useful when you want to superimpose document text over a graphic image. You can also choose an option that ignores the square shape of the graphics box, but wraps the text around the contour of the graphic image inside. Figure 19.10 shows each of these options.

Figure 19.10

Options for wrapping text around a graphics box

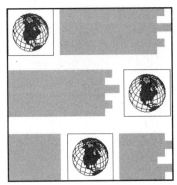

Left, Right, or Both Sides

Neither Side
(text only on top and bottom sides)

Through Box
(don't wrap text around box)

Contour Text
(text wraps around image or contents inside box)

The options for text-wrapping must be selected from the Create Graphics Box or Edit Graphics Box dialog box, as described next:

- To wrap the text on a specific side of the graphics box, choose Text Flow Around Box, and then choose Text Flows. From the list of choices, select On Larger Side, On Left Side, On Right Side, or On Both Sides to indicate the box side(s) around which the document text should wrap.

- Choose On Neither Side to prevent the text from appearing on either side of the graphics box. This forces the graphic to appear with text only at the top and bottom sides of the box.

- To prevent the text from wrapping around the graphics box, choose Through Box. This causes the text to print over the contents of your graphics box.

■ To create text that wraps around the contour of the image inside of the graphics box, choose <u>T</u>ext Flow Around Box, and then choose <u>C</u>ontour Text Flow. This causes the text to ignore the graphics box border and wrap around the graphic inside the box. In fact, when you choose this option, the graphics box border disappears from view.

Changing Border and Fill Options

When you create a graphics box, you can change the appearance of the border that appears at the edges of the box. You can also define the amount of spacing that is allowed between the border and the box contents, and the space allowed on the outside edges of the box.

NOTE. *The Border and Fill options utilize WordPerfect's Styles feature to store graphics box settings. See Chapter 22 for detailed information about the Styles feature. Much of the information about saving and managing styles may be useful to you when you create custom border and fill styles, as described in this section.*

Selecting a Graphics Box Style

WordPerfect includes several predefined graphics box styles that include standard settings for border appearance and spacing. These are similar to the different box types—Figure, Table Box, Text Box, User Box, and Equation—that are available in WordPerfect 5.1. In WordPerfect 6.0, you'll see three additional box styles: Button Box, Watermark Image Box, and Inline Equation Box.

Figure 19.11 shows how the box styles affect the appearance of a graphics box. (The Equation box styles are not shown because they are specific to WordPerfect Equations; see Chapter 20 for more information about equations.) Choosing a new graphics box style is the quickest way to change the appearance of a graphics box. Remember that the graphics box styles determine the default settings for borders, captions, box contents, and spacing.

When you first create a graphics box, WordPerfect automatically selects the Figure Box style, but you can select a different style and apply it for the current graphics box. These are the steps:

Double-click on the desired box style.

■ From the Create Graphics Box or the Edit Graphics Box dialog box, choose Based on Box St<u>y</u>le. WordPerfect displays the dialog box shown in Figure 19.12.

■ Highlight the box style that you want to use for the current graphics box and then choose <u>S</u>elect.

Choose OK until you return to the document screen.

■ Press Exit (F7) until you return to the document screen.

Figure 19.11
Graphics box styles

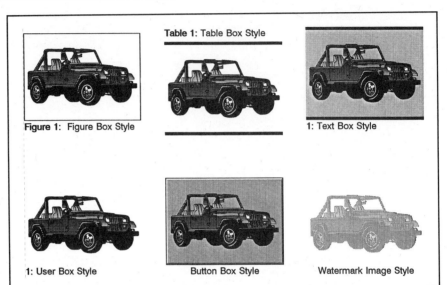

Figure 1: Figure Box Style

Table 1: Table Box Style

1: Text Box Style

1: User Box Style

Button Box Style

Watermark Image Style

Figure 19.12
The Graphics Box
Styles dialog box

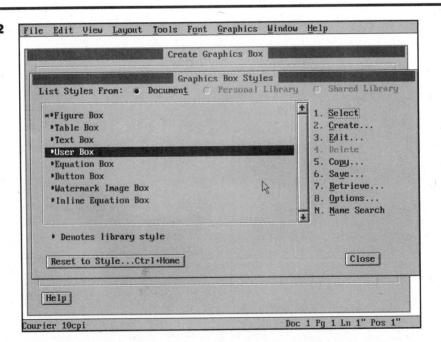

When you return to your document, the graphics box will appear with the border style and spacing from the selected style. If your graphics box includes a caption, the style also determines the type of box numbering that appears within the caption text. Later in this chapter, you'll see how to create and edit a caption for a graphics box.

Changing a Graphics Box Border and Spacing

Although each graphics box style includes default settings for borders, you may want to change only the box border and spacing, without changing the box style. You can choose Edit Border/Fill from the Create Graphics Box or Edit Graphics Box dialog box to change the box border and the spacing between the border and the box contents.

The following steps explain how to change the appearance and spacing of a box border from the Create Graphics Box or Edit Graphics Box dialog box:

■ Choose Edit Border/Fill and WordPerfect displays the dialog box shown in Figure 19.13.

Figure 19.13
The Edit Graphics Box Border/Fill dialog box

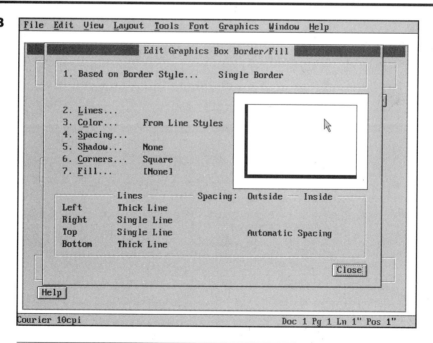

- Choose the <u>L</u>ines option to select a line style for one or more sides of the box. You can mix line styles to a unique border type. You can also choose Select <u>A</u>ll to change the style of all lines at once.

- Choose C<u>o</u>lor to select colors for the border lines.

- Choose <u>S</u>pacing to indicate how much space appears between the box contents and the border, and also the amount of space between the border and the document text that wraps around the box. You need to turn off the <u>A</u>utomatic Spacing option before you can make any selections from the Border Spacing dialog box.

- If you want to create a shadow effect at one side of the box, choose S<u>h</u>adow and select the shadow type, color, and width.

- Choose <u>C</u>orners to select either rounded or square corners for the box.

- When you are finished defining the border, press Exit (F7) or choose OK until you return to the document screen.

If you are working in text display mode, you won't be able to see the changes to your graphics box border option. To see the changes, switch to graphics or page display mode, or get into the print preview screen.

The border changes you make affect only the current graphics box. If you want to save your border definition for use with other graphics boxes, you'll need to create a new graphics box style and reselect your preferences for border lines and spacing. See Chapter 22 for more information about styles.

Applying a Fill Style to a Graphic

A Fill Style determines the pattern, color, or shaded background that "fills" the space between the box border and the image or text inside of the box. Figure 19.14 shows examples of filled graphics boxes. The box styles for Text boxes and Button boxes automatically apply a fill style to create a shaded background for the graphics box; the other box styles do not specify a fill style.

The following steps explain how to choose a different fill style when you create or edit a graphics box.

- From the Create Graphics Box or Edit Graphics Box dialog box, choose Edit <u>B</u>order/Fill to display the Edit Graphics Box Border/Fill dialog box.

- Choose <u>F</u>ill, choose Fill Style, and WordPerfect displays the dialog box shown in Figure 19.15.

- Highlight one of the styles in the list and then choose <u>S</u>elect. WordPerfect then displays the Fill Style and Color dialog box.

Double-click on the desired fill style.

Figure 19.14

Filled graphics boxes

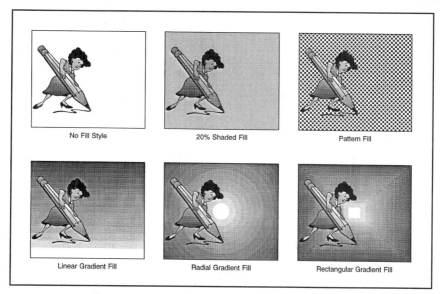

No Fill Style

20% Shaded Fill

Pattern Fill

Linear Gradient Fill

Radial Gradient Fill

Rectangular Gradient Fill

Figure 19.15

The Fill Styles dialog box

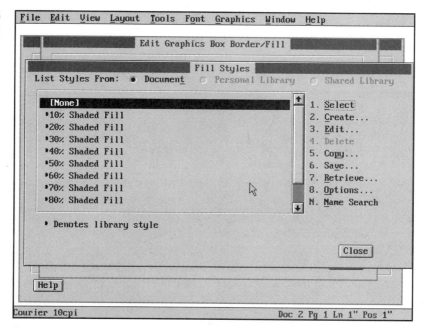

- Use the Foreground Color and Background Color options to select colors for the foreground (shaded color) and background color (background for the shaded color).

- Press Exit (F7) until you return to the Create Graphics Box or Edit Graphics Box dialog box.

The selected fill style is used to create a background for the current graphics box. WordPerfect includes a limited number of fill styles—most of which create only a shade of gray as a background. But WordPerfect supports other fill options that you can use to create a gradually shaded background or pattern for your graphics boxes. In the next section, you'll learn how to use these options by creating a custom fill style.

Creating a Custom Fill Style

You can create custom fill styles and apply them to your graphics boxes. A custom style lets you specify different colors, shading percentages, patterns or gradual shading, and other options that are not included in WordPerfect's predefined fill styles.

- From the Create Graphics Box or the Edit Graphics Box dialog box, choose Edit Border/Fill.

- Choose Fill, choose Fill Style, and WordPerfect displays a list of standard fill styles, and any fill styles that you've defined for the current document.

- Choose Create and WordPerfect prompts you to enter a name for a new fill style. Type a name and press Enter. Then WordPerfect displays the Create Fill Style dialog box.

- To create a pattern background, choose Fill Type and select Pattern if it's not already selected. Then, choose Fill Pattern and select the pattern design you want for the new fill style.

- To create a shaded blend between two colors—instead of a pattern background—choose Fill Type and select Gradient. Choose Fill Pattern to define the appearance of the gradient fill; when you're done press Exit (F7) to return to the Create Fill Style dialog box.

- Choose Color (Foreground) and Color (Background) to select the two colors for the gradual blend or the foreground/background colors for the selected pattern.

Choose OK until you return to the Fill Styles dialog box.

- When you are finished defining the options for the new Fill Style, press Exit (F7) until you return to the Fill Styles dialog box.

- If you want to apply the new fill style to the current graphics box, highlight it and choose Select. Press F7 until you return to your document.

Like the custom border styles, custom fill styles affect only the graphics boxes in the current document. If you want to use a fill or border style with other documents, you'll need to save it to your personal or shared library file. Chapter 22 explains how to save styles you've created to one of the style library files.

Turning Off a Fill Style

After a fill style is applied to a graphics box, you may decide to turn it off. This is easily done by choosing the "None" option from the Fill Styles dialog box. From the Create Graphics Box or Edit Graphics Box dialog box,

- Choose Edit Border/Fill and then choose Fill.

- Choose Fill Style to display the list of fill styles. An asterisk appears next to the fill style that is applied to the current graphics box.

- From the Fill Style list, highlight "None" and then choose Select.

- Press Exit (F7) until you return to the Create Graphics Box or Edit Graphics Box dialog box.

Choosing "None" does not delete any custom fill styles you've created—you'll still see these on the list of available styles. When you select "None," WordPerfect simply turns off the fill attributes for the current graphics box.

Adding a Caption to a Graphics Box

Graphics box captions can provide descriptive labels for each figure, illustration, or chart in your document, and can also number your graphics boxes in consecutive order. You can type captions for individual graphics boxes or for all graphics boxes at once.

This option is selected from the Create Graphics Box or Edit Graphics Box dialog box while you are defining graphics box options. The following steps explain how to create a caption for the current graphics box.

- From the Create Graphics Box or Edit Graphics Box dialog box, choose Create Caption. WordPerfect switches to the Box Caption Editor, shown in Figure 19.16.

- When you create a new caption, WordPerfect automatically inserts an [Open Style:FigureNum] code to create a caption label and number. If you don't want a caption number, press Backspace or Delete to remove it from the caption text.

Double-click on the new fill style to select it.

Double-click on "None."

Choose OK until you return to the Create Graphics Box or Edit Graphics Box dialog box.

Figure 19.16

The Box Caption Editor

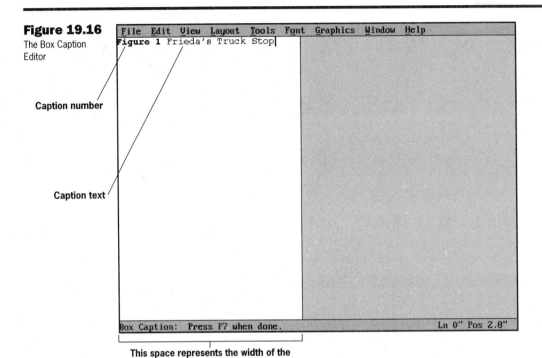

Caption number

Caption text

This space represents the width of the
graphic box.

■ Type the text that should appear as the caption for the graphics box. If
you wish, you can apply different fonts and text attributes to the text.

■ When you are finished creating the caption, press Exit (F7) to return to
the Create Graphics Box or Edit Graphics Box dialog box.

■ Now choose Options, and then choose Caption Options to display the dialog box shown in Figure 19.17.

■ Choose Side of Box and select a position for the caption: Bottom, Top,
Left, or Right. If you choose Left or Right as the location for the caption,
you may also want to choose Rotation and specify a rotation angle, so
that the caption text is printed sideways along the box.

■ Choose Relation to Border and indicate whether you want the caption
text to appear Outside the graphics box border, Inside the border, or directly On the border.

Figure 19.17
The Caption Options
dialog box

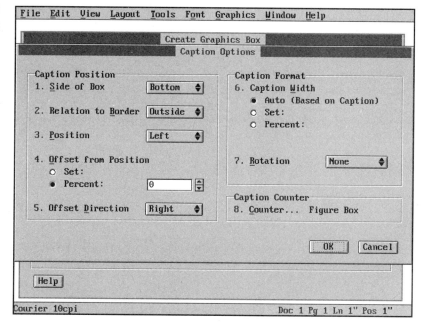

```
 File   Edit   View   Layout   Tools   Font   Graphics   Window   Help

                        Create Graphics Box
                          Caption Options

   ┌─Caption Position──────────────┐   ┌─Caption Format──────────────┐
   │ 1. Side of Box    [Bottom  ▲▼]│   │ 6. Caption Width            │
   │                               │   │    ● Auto (Based on Caption)│
   │ 2. Relation to Border [Outside ▲▼]│ │    ○ Set:                   │
   │                               │   │    ○ Percent:               │
   │ 3. Position       [Left    ▲▼]│   │                             │
   │                               │   │                             │
   │ 4. Offset from Position       │   │ 7. Rotation      [None   ▲▼]│
   │    ○ Set:                     │   │                             │
   │    ● Percent:    [0      ]▲▼  │   └─────────────────────────────┘
   │                               │   ┌─Caption Counter─────────────┐
   │ 5. Offset Direction [Right ▲▼]│   │ 8. Counter...  Figure Box   │
   └───────────────────────────────┘   └─────────────────────────────┘

                                          [   OK   ]  [ Cancel ]


   [Help]

 Courier 10cpi                              Doc 1 Pg 1 Ln 1" Pos 1"
```

■ The other options on this dialog—Position Offset from Position, Offset Direction, Caption Width—let you fine-tune the position and size of text within the caption area. The Counter option lets you choose a different numbering style for the caption.

Choose OK to
return to your
document.

■ When you are done choosing caption options, press Exit (F7) until you return to your document.

When you return to the document screen, WordPerfect attaches the caption to your graphics box. Note that the size of the box will be reduced so that the box contents, box border, and caption will fit within the dimensions you specified for the graphics box size.

Using the Image Editor

WordPerfect includes an image editor that lets you adjust the appearance and position of the image inside a graphics box. Choose Image Editor from the Create Graphics Box or Edit Graphics Box dialog box, and WordPerfect displays the contents of the current graphics box on the Image Editor screen, shown in Figure 19.18.

Figure 19.18
WordPerfect's Image Editor

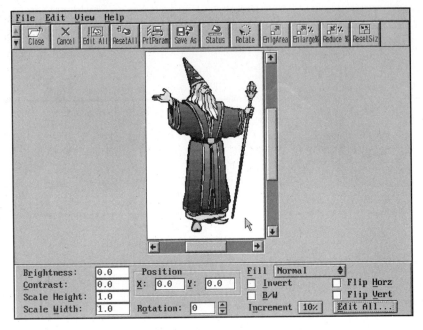

When the Image Editor is displayed, you can move or resize the graphic inside the box, rotate and create a mirror image, stretch or "squash" the image, and adjust the color intensity of the box contents. The Image Editor does *not* allow you to change the actual image or create new graphic images.

In the sections that follow, you'll learn how to perform each of these tasks with controls that appear on the Image Editor screen. Although they are not described here, you can also choose the image editing options from the Image Editor's pull-down menus or by choosing Edit All to display a dialog box with a complete list of options.

NOTE.   *The Image Editor options affect only the image you've retrieved into the graphics box; they do not change the appearance of the image stored in the graphic file.*

Sizing a Graphic Image

When you retrieve a graphic image, WordPerfect proportionately sizes the image according to the dimensions of your graphics box. If you make the box larger or smaller, the image inside the box is proportionately scaled to match the new size. When you want to change the relative size of the graphic *inside* of the box, you need to use the Image Editor.

Suppose your graphic image is too large or too small for your graphics box, you can change the size of the image by following these steps:

■ From the Create Graphics Box or Edit Graphics Box dialog box, choose Image Editor. WordPerfect opens the Image Editor and shows your graphic image on the screen.

■ Press PgUp or PgDn to change the size of the image within the box. PgUp makes the image grow larger and PgDn reduces the size of the image.

For greater precision, choose Scale Height and Scale Width to enter specific measurements; you can enter numbers between 0.01 and 9.99. When Scale Height and Scale Width are both set to *1.0*, the image is displayed in its original size. Smaller numbers reduce the size of the image; larger numbers enlarge the image.

When the numbers for Scale Height and Scale Width are not the same, the image is stretched or "squashed." For example, if the Scale Height is set to *0.5* and the Scale Width is set to *1.0*, the image is "squashed" to half its original height, but remains at the original width. If Scale Height is set to *1.0* and Scale Width is set to *0.5*, the image remains at the original height, but is reduced to half of its original width.

Positioning a Graphic inside a Box

You can also adjust the position of an image within the box borders. From the Image Editor, press the arrow keys (↑, ↓, →, or ←) to change the position of the image in the box, or use the mouse pointer to click on the scroll bar arrows at the edge of the graphic. When you use the arrow keys to adjust the position of the image, the Increment option determines the amount of movement that each keypress creates; you can choose Increment and change the movement setting to 1% (which equals 1 pixel), 5%, 10%, or 25%.

For greater precision, use the Position X and Position Y options to change the image position. When both X and Y options are set to *0.0*, the image is set at its original position. The Position X option determines the horizontal position of the image. Enter positive numbers at this option, and the image moves to the right; enter negative numbers and the image moves to the left. The Position Y option determines the vertical position of the image. Enter positive numbers and the image moves up; enter negative numbers and the image moves down.

Rotating a Graphic and Creating a Mirror Image

From the Image Editor, you can also rotate the image inside the current graphics box. Press Plus (+) on the numeric keypad to rotate the image in a clockwise direction. Press Minus (-) to rotate in a counter-clockwise direction. The Increment option determines how far each keypress will rotate the image; you can change the amount by choosing Increment.

WordPerfect provides other options which rotate the image with greater precision. Choose Rotation and enter the angle at which you want to rotate the graphic image. For example, if you want the image rotated to a precise 45-degree angle, choose Rotation and enter **45**.

Another way to rotate an image is by "flipping" it to create a mirror image of the original graphic. Choose Flip Horz to flip the image horizontally, or side to side. Choose Flip Vert to flip the image vertically, or top to bottom.

Adjusting Color and Contrast

Other options on the Image Editor let you adjust the color intensity of the graphic image. Choose Invert to convert the image colors to their opposites on the color palette; for example, when you choose Invert, the color white becomes black, yellow becomes purple, and so on. Choose B/W to convert all colors to either black or white. When you choose this option, the lighter colors become white and darker colors become black.

The Brightness and Contrast options let you adjust the intensity of the colors in your image. For each of these options, *0.0* is the normal setting, but you can enter a number between *-1.0* and *1.0*. For Brightness, positive numbers produce a lighter image; negative numbers produce a darker image. For Contrast, positive numbers produce a greater contrast between different color shades; negative numbers produce less contrast.

Setting the Fill Transparency

The Fill option, on the Image Editor screen, lets you choose the opacity or transparency of the filled areas in the image. Choose Fill and then select either Normal, Transparent, or White. When you choose Normal, your image will appear as intended when it was created. Choose Transparent to show only the outline of the shapes in the image; the graphics box background (defined by the Fill Style option) will show through the image. Choose White and WordPerfect changes the color of all filled areas to white.

Restoring the Original Graphic Settings

When you work with the Image Editor options, it's possible to radically change the appearance of the original graphic. If you go too far, and decide you want to restore the original image, you can press Reset (Ctrl+Home) or choose Edit and then Reset All from the menu bar. This cancels all the changes you've made and restores the graphic to its original appearance.

Exiting the Image Editor

When you are finished working in the Image Editor, press Exit (F7), choose File and then Close, or click on the Close button to return to the Create Graphics Box or Edit Graphics Box dialog box. Or if you don't want to save your changes, press Cancel (Esc) and then choose Yes.

Working with WP Presentations

Although WordPerfect includes several advanced graphics features, it still lacks the ability to edit the graphics you retrieve into your document. You can easily edit the original graphics from the programs in which they were created. Then, you can edit the graphics boxes in your documents by simply replacing them with the graphics retrieved from the edited graphics files.

If you'd like an easier solution for creating and editing graphics with WordPerfect, consider using WordPerfect Presentations 2.0, which is a separate software program from WordPerfect Corporation. WP Presentations provides excellent charting, graphing, and illustration tools, and works directly with WordPerfect. The graphics you create in WP Presentations will appear exactly the same when you retrieve them into WordPerfect. The two programs share the same graphics file format, and so no conversion is required when you retrieve graphic images from WP Presentations. (See the next section for more details about what files WordPerfect can convert.)

The restaurant menu document, shown earlier in Figure 19.1, is one example of a WordPerfect document with graphics and headlines created in WP Presentations. With WP Presentations, you can retrieve and combine different images, and then simply transfer them into your WordPerfect document.

Before you can use WordPerfect and WP Presentations as one program, you must install and start the Shell program included with WP Presentations. The *Shell* is a memory-resident program that lets you run both WordPerfect and WP Presentations simultaneously. When both software programs are running, you can switch to WP Presentations from within WordPerfect, create or edit an image, and then update the image in your WordPerfect document. Once the graphic is stored in your document, you don't need to keep the original graphics file with your document; you can edit the actual image stored in your document. This is true for any image that you have retrieved into your document—it doesn't have to be an image from WP Presentations.

You can purchase the WP Presentations software from your local computer software dealer. See the WP Presentations reference manual for information about using WordPerfect with WP Presentations.

Retrieving Graphics from Other Programs

When you retrieve a graphics file, WordPerfect checks the file format to see whether it is a WordPerfect graphics (.WPG) file, which is the graphics file format of WordPerfect Corporation software. If the graphics file is in a different format, WordPerfect converts the image to the .WPG format and retrieves it into WordPerfect. This happens automatically every time you retrieve a graphics file, so you do not need to convert the file or tell WordPerfect which software program created the file.

Table 19.1 shows the types of graphics files you can retrieve directly into WordPerfect. If the native file format of your graphics software is not listed in the following table, try using your graphics program's Export or Save As feature to save graphic images to a format that WordPerfect can retrieve.

Table 19.1   **Graphics Files You Can Retrieve into WordPerfect**

Graphics Program/File Format	File Extension
PC Paintbrush	.PCX
Computer Graphics Metafile	.CGM
MS Windows (3.*x*) and OS/2 Bitmap File	.BMP
Dr. Halo Graphics File	.DHP
AutoCad (.DXF Exported)	.DXF
PostScript/Encapsulated PostScript	.EPS
GEM Draw File	.GEM
Hewlett-Packard Plotter File	.HPG
GEM Paint File	.IMG
MS Windows (2.*x*) Paint File	.MSP
Lotus 1-2-3 Graph/Chart File and	
PC Paint Plus Graphics File	.PIC
Tagged Image File Format (uncompressed)	.TIF
MS Windows Metafile	.WMF
WordPerfect, DrawPerfect, or	
WordPerfect Presentations Graphics File	.WPG

When you retrieve a graphics file other than a .WPG file, WordPerfect will perform the best conversion possible; however, some of the original colors, fonts, and attributes in the graphic may not appear as they do in the original file; this happens because of the different methods in which graphics programs record and store information. Some formats that work well with WordPerfect are .PCX files, uncompressed .TIF files, and .WPG files.

Inserting Equations into Your Document

DUCATORS, MATHEMATICIANS, AND SCIENTISTS WILL APPRECIATE WORD-Perfect's Equation feature. With this feature, you can create mathematical equations and insert them into your documents. Although the Equations feature cannot *solve* your equations—you'll need spreadsheet or statistical software to do that—WordPerfect's Equation Editor does let you format numbers and characters according to standard equation form. Figure 20.1 shows a few examples of the equations you can create.

Figure 20.1

Sample equations created in WordPerfect

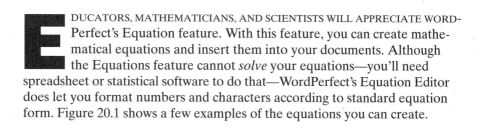

$$\frac{1}{2} + \frac{2}{3} = \frac{3}{6} \qquad \sqrt{\sqrt{a_1} + \sqrt{a_2} + \sqrt{(a_1 a_2)}}$$

$$\log_b x = \frac{\log_{10} x}{\log_{10} b} = \left(\frac{1}{\log_{10} b}\right) \log_{10} x \qquad x = \begin{bmatrix} a & -1 & 5 \\ 7 & 4 & a \\ b & 3 & 2 \end{bmatrix}$$

This chapter explains how to use WordPerfect's Equation Editor to create simple and complex equations. You'll also learn about the equation options that let you choose different fonts, insert special symbols, and position an equation box on the page.

Equation Concepts

You create equations with WordPerfect's Equation Editor, which is available from the Create Graphics Box dialog. WordPerfect includes the Equation Editor as a graphic box option because most equations require the use of graphic fonts and other graphic options to create and position the equation elements on the printed page. This is the general procedure for opening the Equation Editor:

Choose Graphics ▸
Graphics Boxes ▸
Create.

1. Press Graphics (Alt+F9), choose Graphics Boxes, and then choose Create.

2. From the Create Graphics Box dialog box, choose Contents, and then choose Equation.

3. Choose Create Equation and WordPerfect displays the Equation Editor, shown in Figure 20.2.

Figure 20.2

The Equation Editor

Equation preview
will appear here
(press Ctrl+F3)

Equation
command list

Type equation
script here

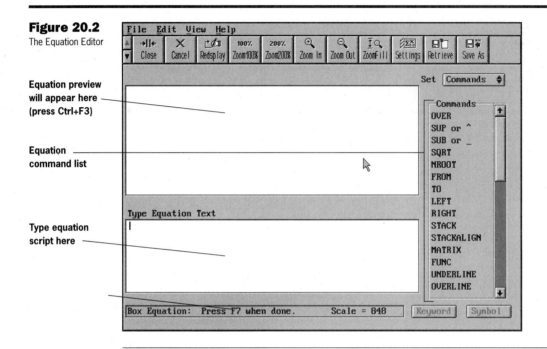

You'll notice that the Equation Editor is divided into two windows. In the window labeled "Type Equation Text," you type a *script* that represents the equation you want to create; in many cases, the script follows the same pattern you would use to describe the equation. For example, to create the equation x/y, you would type **x OVER y** in the Equation Editor.

Numbers, text characters, and many of the mathematical operators (+, –, =, and so on) appear in your equation as they do in the equation script. If, for example, you type *a+b=5* as the equation script, the completed equation will look exactly like the equation script. You can also insert command words, functions, and symbols from the list at the right edge of the Equation Editor. (You'll learn how to do this later in the section, "Equation Commands, Symbols, and Characters.") The equation command list provides formatting options, spacing options, and mathematical symbols to help you create and arrange equation items.

The upper window in the Equation Editor, the View Equation window, shows you a preview of what your equation will look like when printed. This is essential for more complex equations, where the scripts do not so closely resemble the final equation. To view a preview or refresh the preview in the View Equation window, you need to press Ctrl+F3 or choose Redisplay from the Equation Editor button bar.

When you are finished with the Equation Editor, you can either press Exit (F7), choose <u>F</u>ile and then <u>C</u>lose, or click on the Close button in the button bar to return to the Create Graphics Box dialog. Then you can specify the size and position of the equation box by choosing options in the dialog box; these are the same options you choose to change the size, position, and border options for standard graphics boxes.

After you've selected the desired graphics box options for the equation, press Exit (F7) or choose OK to return to the document screen. WordPerfect inserts the equation as a graphic in your document.

Creating a Simple Equation

In the following exercise, you will open the Equation Editor and type a script to create an equation. When you're finished, you will insert the equation

$$x = \frac{5}{y^2}$$

into your document.

Choose <u>G</u>raphics ▸ Graphics <u>B</u>oxes ▸ <u>C</u>reate.

1. From the document screen, press Graphics (Alt+F9), choose Graphics <u>B</u>oxes, and then choose <u>C</u>reate.

2. Choose Co<u>n</u>tents and then choose <u>E</u>quation from the pop-up list of options.

3. Choose Cr<u>e</u>ate Equation to open the Equation Editor. You'll see the cursor inside the window labeled "Type Equation Text"; this is where you type the script that creates the equation.

Choose <u>V</u>iew ▸ <u>R</u>edisplay or click on the Redisplay button to update the equation preview.

4. Type the following text as the script for this equation. Make sure you type spaces between the items; these are required by the Equation Editor to separate the characters and commands:

```
x = 5 OVER y
```

5. Press Redisplay (Ctrl+F3) to display equation preview in the upper Equation Editor window.

6. Now you'll add a superscripted notation. Edit the equation script so that it looks like this:

```
x = 5 OVER y SUP 2
```

If you want spaces around the equal sign, type a tilde (~) on either side of the equal sign.

Choose View ▶
Redisplay or click
on the Redisplay
button .

Choose OK until
you return to the
document screen.

7. Press Redisplay (Ctrl+F3) and you'll see a superscripted *2* next to the *y* variable in the equation.

8. Your equation is now complete. Press Exit (F7) until you return to the document screen.

The equation is inserted as a graphics box into your document. You won't see the actual equation unless you are using WordPerfect's graphics or page display mode. If you are using WordPerfect's text display mode, you can view the equation by pressing Print (Shift+F7) and choosing the Print Preview feature from the Print dialog box.

Most of the characters you typed in the script became variables or numbers in the equation. Generally, the Equation Editor italicizes all letters to show that they are variables, and numbers are printed as regular text.

Let's review the commands you used. The OVER command creates a fraction that incorporates the items on each side of the command (the item to the left is the numerator and the item on the right is the denominator). The SUP command creates a superscripted notation with the number or item that follows it. Here are two other examples of equation scripts that utilize these commands:

```
1 OVER 6 + 1 OVER 3 ~ = ~ 1 OVER 2        a SUP x a SUP y ~ = ~ a SUP {x + y}
```

$$\frac{1}{6} + \frac{1}{3} = \frac{1}{2} \qquad\qquad a^x a^y = a^{x+y}$$

When you type an equation script, you use command words—like OVER and SUP—to indicate how characters and numbers should be arranged in the equation. Notice that spaces are required in each script to separate the characters and command words, but these spaces do not appear in the completed equations. (Use tildes to insert spaces into completed equations.) Also notice that curly brackets are used to group items together (much like parentheses in regular equations). For instance, without the curly brackets, the preceding equation would have to come out as

$$a^x a^y = a^x + y$$

since the superscript command word will only apply to the character immediately following it.

For more advanced formatting, you can insert command words, symbols, and characters from the list at the right edge of the Equation Editor screen. The next section explains how to use this list and how to arrange equation elements with special commands and characters.

Equation Commands, Symbols, and Characters

There are over 200 commands, functions, and symbols that you can use to construct your equation scripts. Because each equation script consists of actual text characters, you can type command words directly into the script. You may prefer to type the command words that you use often, or you can insert commands and symbols from the equation command list.

The following sections explain how to insert command words, functions, and symbols from the equation command list. You'll also see how to adjust the spacing and placement of items within an equation.

Inserting Equation Commands

The equation command list is actually eight different lists: commands, large characters, symbols, Greek letters, arrows, set indicators, miscellaneous (other) characters, and functions. The type of equation command or item you insert depends on which list is currently displayed.

To insert a command or symbol into the script from the equation command list, choose Set and select the type of list you want to use. Then highlight the command or item you want to insert into the script, and press Enter. You can also insert a list item by double-clicking on it with the mouse.

Try the following steps for a brief exercise on using the equation command list:

Choose Graphics ▸ Graphics Boxes ▸ Create.

1. From the document screen, press Graphics (Alt+F9), choose Graphics Boxes, and then choose Create.

2. From the Create Graphics Box dialog box, choose Contents and choose Equation. Then choose Create Equation to display the Equation Editor.

3. Press Tab to choose Set and select the Greek list type. WordPerfect changes the equation command list to show the characters you can insert from the Greek alphabet.

Double-click on the delta (Δ) character to insert it into the equation script.

4. Use the arrow keys to highlight the delta character (Δ); you'll see the word "Delta" in the lower-left corner of the screen. Then choose Keyword or press Enter to insert the Delta keyword into the equation script.

5. Type ~=~ as the next item for the equation. Remember, you need to enter tildes (~) to create spaces in your equations. Press Tab until the cursor is at the Set option and is highlighted. Choose Set and select the Commands list type.

Double-click on the NROOT command word to insert it into the equation script.

6. Use the arrow keys to highlight the NROOT command word. Notice that the syntax for the highlighted command appears at the bottom of the Equation Editor. Either choose Keyword or press Enter to insert NROOT into the equation script.

7. After the NROOT command, type **3** as the root number, type a space, and then type **x ~=~ 7** to complete the equation. When you're finished, the equation script will look like this:

```
Δ ~ = ~ NROOT 3 x ~ = ~ 7
```

If you wish, press Redisplay (Ctrl+F3) to update the equation preview. To insert commands and symbols from the other lists, simply choose the Set option and select the type of list you want to use. Then choose the desired command or symbol from the list. When a set other than Commands, Arrows, or Functions is active, buttons at the bottom of the list provide two options for inserting the symbol: Choose Keyword to insert the command word that creates the highlighted symbol, or choose Symbol to insert the actual character into the equation script. The end result is the same; simply choose the method that you prefer.

Inserting Symbols

The equation command list also includes symbols that you can insert into your equation script. From the Equation Editor, choose Set to display the pop-up menu, and then choose Large, Symbols, Greek, Arrows, Sets, or Other. Choose one of the options to display the symbols or characters in that list. Then select characters from the list to insert them into your equation script.

The Large list lets you insert oversized mathematic symbols. The Symbols list contains standard mathematic characters. The Greek list includes the characters you can insert from the Greek alphabet. The Arrows list lets you insert arrows and bullets. The Sets list contains relational operators, Fraktur letters, and other symbols. The Other list includes various accents and diacritical marks that may be appropriate for your equations.

Spacing Commands and Characters

As mentioned, when you type the script for an equation, you need to type character spaces to separate the items. Spaces in the equation script indicate where each command or item ends, and they do not affect the placement of items in the displayed equation. For example, you typed spaces to separate the items in the following equation script, but no spaces appeared in the completed equation:

```
x = 5 OVER y SUP 2
```

$$x = \frac{5}{y^2}$$

When you need spaces to appear in your equation, you can type tildes (~) to create them. You'll often want to insert tildes around mathematical operators such as + and - to set them off from the numbers in the equation.

Creating a Complex Equation

Now that you're acquainted with the mechanics of creating a simple equation, you can move on to something more complex. Try the following exercise to create this equation for the statistical analysis of variance:

$$t_{protected} = \frac{\overline{X}_i - \overline{X}_j}{\sqrt{MS_w\left(\dfrac{1}{N_i} + \dfrac{1}{N_j}\right)}}$$

Don't let the word *complex* scare you; you don't need to understand what this equation does before you create it. This exercise simply shows you how to use a wider range of equation commands.

Before you create the equation, notice how the elements are arranged. Several items have subscripted notations, and other elements are stacked to create fractional groups. These steps will show you how to create the script that translates into this equation:

Choose <u>G</u>raphics ▸
Graphics <u>B</u>oxes ▸
<u>C</u>reate.

1. From the document screen, press Graphics (Alt+F9), choose Graphics <u>B</u>oxes, and then choose <u>C</u>reate.

2. Choose Co<u>n</u>tents and choose <u>E</u>quation from the pop-up list of contents options.

3. Choose Cr<u>e</u>ate Equation to open the Equation Editor. The cursor should be located in the box labeled "Type Equation Text".

4. Type **t SUB protected =** as the first part of the equation (**t_protected =** will also work).

5. Press Redisplay (Ctrl+F3) to update the equation preview.

Choose <u>V</u>iew ▸ <u>R</u>e-
display or click on
the Redisplay but-
ton to update the
equation preview.

6. Now you'll create the group of elements above the divisor bar. Type the following:

```
{ X SUB i - X SUB j }
```

The curly brackets group the elements together as one item.

7. For this equation, the *Xi* and *Xj* variables need a line over the Xs. In the equation script, move the cursor directly before each *X*, and insert the OVERLINE command, like this:

```
{ OVERLINE X SUB i - OVERLINE X SUB j }
```

8. Next you'll create the divisor bar (using the OVER command) and the group of items that will appear beneath it. Press End to move the cursor to the end of the script. Type a space and then type the following:

```
OVER SQRT { MS SUB w }
```

The OVER command creates the divisor bar and indicates that the next item should be stacked under the previous item in the script. The SQRT { MS SUB w } text displays the square root of MS_w. Again, the curly brackets are used to group several elements as one item beneath the divisor bar.

Click on the Redisplay button.

9. Choose the Redisplay option, and your screen will look like Figure 20.3.

Figure 20.3

A complex equation in the Equation Editor

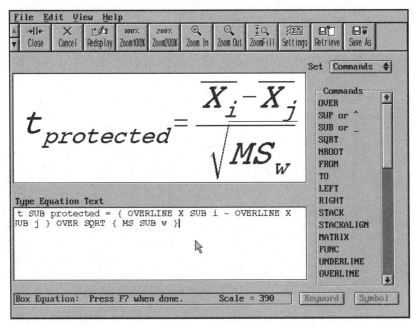

10. The item beneath the divisor bar is not quite finished. Edit the text inside the last set of curly brackets, like this:

```
{ MS SUB w ( 1 OVER N SUB i + 1 OVER N SUB j ) }
```

Click on the Redisplay button.

11. Press Redisplay (Ctrl+F3) to update the equation preview again. The script now includes all the characters for the equation, but you need to clean up the formatting a bit. Notice that the parentheses do not completely enclose the part of the equation that reads $1/N_i + 1\ N/j$.

12. Move the cursor before the left parenthesis, and type **LEFT** or select LEFT from the command list on the right side of the screen. Then move the cursor before the right parenthesis, and type **RIGHT** or select RIGHT from the command list. When you're finished, this part of the script should look like this:

```
{ MS SUB w LEFT ( 1 OVER N SUB i + 1 OVER N SUB j RIGHT ) }
```

13. To insert spaces for the operators, type a tilde (~) before and after the equals sign (=), the minus sign (-), and the plus sign (+). When you are finished, the equation script should look like this:

```
t SUB protected ~ = ~ {OVERLINE X SUB i ~ - ~ OVERLINE X SUB j} OVER SQRT
{MS SUB w LEFT ( 1 OVER N SUB i ~ + ~ 1 OVER N SUB j RIGHT ) }
```

Choose OK to close all dialog boxes and insert the equation into your document.

14. The equation is finished. If you like, press Ctrl+F3 one last tiem to verify that the equation looks as it should. Then press Exit (F7) to accept the equation and return to the Create Graphics Box dialog. Then press Exit (F7) to insert the equation into your document.

Although you may not need to create equations as complex as this one, the exercise introduces some important commands. You used the SUB command to create subscripted notations; you can substitute the underscore character to create the same effect. For example, you can use N_i rather than N SUB i.

You inserted the OVER command to create fractions within the equation. Because the numerator and denominator of the fraction consist of multiple characters, you inserted curly brackets ({ and }) to indicate which items should be kept together. The SQRT command creates a square root bar over the next item or items in a paired set of curly brackets. You also used the LEFT and RIGHT commands before the parentheses; these commands tell WordPerfect to stretch the parentheses to the height of the items between them. Finally, you inserted spaces between characters by typing the tilde character; remember, character spaces typed in the script are ignored when WordPerfect displays the equation. The tilde character lets you insert spaces where you need them.

This is only one example of an equation you can create—experiment with the different equation commands to learn more about their use.

Using the Equation Keyboard

WordPerfect provides a special keyboard that you can use to insert commands and symbols for your equation scripts. To select the keyboard, press Setup (Shift+F1) or choose File and then Setup from the menu bar. Then choose the Keyboard Layout option, and WordPerfect displays the Keyboard Layout dialog box. Select the Equation keyboard layout, and then press Exit (F7) or choose Close to return to your document screen. Note that you can also choose the Equation keyboard layout from within the Equation Editor. To do so, press Settings (Shift+F1) or click on the Settings button. Then choose Keyboard and select the EQUATION keyboard from the list of keyboards that appears. Press F7 to return to the Equation Editor. (You'll learn more about the various available keyboard layouts in Chapter 25.).

When the Equation keyboard layout is selected, WordPerfect assigns equation functions, symbols, and commands to over 35 keystroke combinations. Table 20.1 shows the keystroke assignments for the Equation keyboard layout.

Table 20.1   **Keystroke Assignments for the Equation Keyboard Layout**

Keystroke	Function/Command Name	Equation Result
Alt+,	less than or equal to (<=)	$\leq$
Alt+.	greater than or equal to (>=)	$\geq$
Alt+`	similar or equal (SIMEQ)	$\simeq$
Alt+-	Congruent (CONG)	$\cong$
Alt+\	LINE	$\mid$
Alt+A	alpha	α
Alt+B	beta	β
Alt+D	lowercase delta	δ
Alt+G	gamma	γ
Alt+I	infinity (INF)	∞
Alt+L	lambda	λ
Alt+M	mu	μ
Alt+N	eta	η

Table 20.1   Keystroke Assignments for the Equation Keyboard Layout (Continued)

Keystroke	Function/Command Name	Equation Result
Alt+O	omega	ω
Alt+P	pi	π
Alt+R	rho	ρ
Alt+S	sigma	σ
Alt+T	theta	θ
Alt+Tab	right arrow character	$\rightarrow$
Ctrl+A	superscript (SUP, as in *x* SUP *2*)	x^2
Ctrl+B	BAR (as in *x* BAR)	$\bar{x}$
Ctrl+D	uppercase delta	Δ
Ctrl+E	epsilon	ε
Ctrl+F	phi	ϕ
Ctrl+G	nabla, gradient (GRAD)	∇
Ctrl+I	integral (INT)	$\int$
Ctrl+L	OVERLINE (as in OVERLINE *xyz*)	$\overline{xyz}$
Ctrl+N	nabla, gradient (GRAD)	∇
Ctrl+O	OVER (as in *x* OVER *y*)	$\dfrac{x}{y}$
Ctrl+P	PARTIAL	∂
Ctrl+Q	square root (SQRT, as in SQRT *x*)	$\sqrt{x}$
Ctrl+S	SUM	Σ
Ctrl+Tab	left arrow character	$\leftarrow$
Ctrl+Z	subscript (SUB, as in *x* SUB *2*)	x_2

When you activate the Equation keyboard from within the Equation Editor, you can press any of these keys to insert a specify equation function, symbol, or command. These keystrokes are valid only when the Equation Editor is open. Also, the Equation keyboard layout remains active until you change it again.

Equation Fonts and Attributes

With the standard equation settings, WordPerfect prints your equations with the font that is currently selected for your document text. If the selected font cannot provide the text sizes and characters that your equation requires, WordPerfect will substitute one of its own graphic fonts to print the equation. WordPerfect tries to match the style of the graphic font to the font that you're using for your document text.

You can change the standard equation setting and assign a specific font for the entire equation. You may want to do this when the equations you've inserted should appear in a font that is different than the other document text. You can also apply the Bold, Italic, and Underline attributes to emphasize characters and phrases in your equation.

Choosing an Equation Font

You can select one font and one text size for all the text in your equation. The font and size combination you choose affects the appearance of the completed equation; it does not affect the appearance of the text you type for the equation script.

To change the font of an equation in the Equation Editor:

Choose File ▶ Settings or click on the Settings button.

- With the Equation Editor open, press Setup (Shift+F1) to display the dialog box shown in Figure 20.4.

- If you want your equations to match the fonts you are using in your document, choose Default; then choose Size to indicate the size you want.

- If you want to use a specific font, choose Select Font to display the Select Font dialog box. Then drop down the Font list and choose the font you want to apply to the equation. Press F7 when you're done.

- If you have a color printer, you can choose Color from the Equation Settings dialog box to select a print color for the equation.

Choose OK to return to the Equation Editor.

- When you are finished choosing the Equation Setting options, press Exit (F7) to return to the Equation Editor.

Figure 20.4

The Equation
Settings dialog box

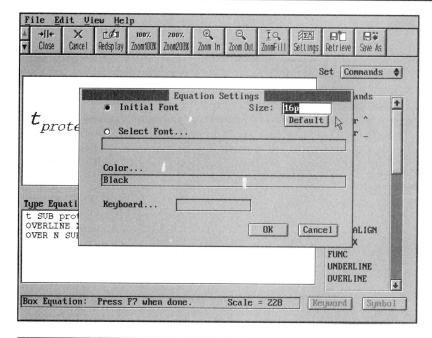

When you choose the Default option under Size, WordPerfect will use the fonts you selected in your document to create the equation; you'll get the best results when your document is printed with scalable fonts (PostScript fonts or WordPerfect's graphic fonts). If you're using nonscalable fonts or your printer's internal fonts, WordPerfect may not be able to print some of the mathematical characters in the equation; if certain special characters and equation formatting are not possible with the fonts you're using, WordPerfect will substitute one of its own graphic fonts to complete the equation. The font selections you make from the Equation Settings dialog box are applied to the entire equation.

Applying the Bold, Italic, and Underline Attributes

In addition to the font selection, you can apply the bold, italic, and underline attributes to different characters or words within your equation. Simply move the cursor to the place in the script where you want the bold or italic attribute to begin. Then type **BOLD**, **ITAL**, or **UNDERLINE** to indicate which attribute you want; you can also choose BOLD, ITAL, or UNDERLINE from the Command list, but it's faster to type the commands. Press Redisplay (Ctrl+F3) and you'll see the effect of the attribute command.

The BOLD, ITAL, and UNDERLINE commands affect only one character or word—that is, all the text between the command and the next space you type in the script.

You can apply the BOLD and UNDERLINE commands to text and numbers in the equation script. Since all text characters are automatically italicized in an equation, the ITAL command is generally used to italicize numbers or other non-text characters.

If you want the BOLD, ITAL, or UNDERLINE command to affect two or more characters or numbers, use the curly brackets to group all the items that should be affected. Consider the following equation scripts:

```
y ~ = ~ UNDERLINE mx ~ + ~ b              y ~ = ~ UNDERLINE {mx ~ + ~ b}
```

$$y = \underline{mx} + b \qquad\qquad y = \underline{mx + b}$$

In the equation on the left, the UNDERLINE command affects only the *mx* variable. In the equation on the right, the curly brackets enclose multiple items to indicate that the entire *mx + b* phrase should be underlined.

Creating Equation Text without Italics

As you've already seen, the Equation Editor considers all text characters to be equation variables and automatically displays them with the italics attribute. You can cancel the italics attribute for text by using the FUNC command word, as shown here:

```
FUNC {length ~ = ~ {cubicfeet} OVER width}
```

$$\text{length} = \frac{\text{cubicfeet}}{\text{width}}$$

The FUNC command converts variable text (any text characters) to standard nonitalic text, and lets you insert words for the variable references instead of single letters, like *x* or *y*. In the example shown here, the equation items are enclosed within the first set of curly brackets that follow the FUNC command, which causes the entire equation to display without italics.

Saving and Retrieving an Equation Script

For some equations, the script you create can be quite lengthy. You can save the script to a separate file and retrieve it again when you create equations for other documents. Not only will this save you the trouble of retyping the script, but it will also ensure that your equation appears identically every time you include it in a document.

To save an equation script, you must be in the Equation Editor. Press Save As (F10), or choose File and then choose Save As from the Equation Editor menu bar. WordPerfect displays the Save Equation dialog box and prompts you to enter a file name. Type a name for the script file, and then press Enter or choose OK. WordPerfect saves the equation script as a WordPerfect 6.0 text file that you can use to insert the same equation into other documents that you might create.

To retrieve an equation script file, open the Equation Editor and then press Retrieve (Shift+F10), or choose File and then choose Retrieve from the menu bar. WordPerfect displays the Retrieve Document dialog box. Type the name of the script file you want to retrieve, and press Enter or choose OK.

Once you become familiar with the Equation Editor commands, you can type your equation script at the WordPerfect document screen, which is particularly useful for long equation scripts. Then you can save your script as a WordPerfect file, open the Equation Editor, and use the File Retrieve option to retrieve it and create the equation.

Equation Box Options

You can use the options on the Create Graphics Box dialog box to adjust the size, position, and border settings for your equation. Like other graphics boxes, you can place an equation according to the page margins, with a paragraph, or as a "character" within the current line of text. The following sections explain how to move and size an equation box; for detailed information about these graphics box options, see Chapter 19.

Changing the Equation Box Position and Size

After you've inserted an equation into your document, there are two ways to adjust the size and position of the equation box: You can turn on WordPerfect's full graphics or page display mode and use the mouse pointer to shrink or enlarge the box or to drag the box to a new location in your document; or you can edit the graphics box settings to change its size and position.

Using Graphics or Page Display Mode

When graphics or page display mode is turned on (press Ctrl+F3 and choose Graphics or Page), you can use the mouse pointer to adjust the size and position of the equation. To move the equation, click on it to select the graphics box. Eight square sizing handles will enclose the box when it is selected. While holding down the mouse button, drag the box to a new location. To adjust the size of the box, click on the equation to select it, and then drag one of the sizing handles on the sides or corners of the equation border. Note that this changes the size of the graphics box containing the equation, but does not change the size of the characters used in the equation. To do this, you must work with the Equation Editor, as described earlier in the chapter.

Editing Graphics Box Settings

You can also adjust the size and position of an equation with the options on the Edit Graphics Box dialog. These options let you adjust the size and position of the equation with greater precision than the mouse pointer allows. The following steps explain the process:

Choose Graphics ▸ Graphics Boxes ▸ Edit.

- Press Graphics (Alt+F9), choose Graphics Boxes, and then choose Edit.

- Choose Document Box Number, type the number of the graphics box that contains your equation, and press Enter. Then choose Edit Box. WordPerfect displays the Edit Graphics Box dialog. Note that "Equation" will appear next to the Contents option in this dialog box.

- Choose Attach To and select Fixed Page Position, Paragraph, Page, or Character to indicate how the equation box should be attached to the text in your document.

- Choose Edit Position to define how the equation should be aligned with the text. Press F7 when you're done.

- Choose Edit Size to change the size of the equation box. Press F7 when you're done.

- From the Edit Graphics Box dialog, choose any other options that you want to apply to the box.

- Press Exit (F7) to accept your changes and return to the document screen.

Choose OK to return to the document screen.

WordPerfect adjusts the position and size of your equation according to the settings you defined.

Borders, Fill Style, and Captions

Because WordPerfect stores every equation inside a graphics box, all graphics box options are also available for your equations. Use the Based on Box Style and Edit Border/Fill options in the Edit Graphics Box dialog box to change the background and border options. Use the Create Caption feature to create captions and explanations of the equation logic. Captions can also assign unique numbers to each equation box you create, which may be used with WordPerfect's Cross-Reference feature. For more information about these and other graphics box options, see Chapter 19.

21

Creating Text Columns

WORDPERFECT'S COLUMNS FEATURE LETS YOU ARRANGE TEXT INTO two or more columns across your document pages. The uses for text columns are as diverse as the documents in which you'll find them. The Newspaper Column option can divide your newsletter text into manageable—and readable—sections in which text flows from one column to the next. Choose Parallel Columns to format text for tables and lists. Use one or both column types to create an interesting layout for desktop publishing.

In this chapter, you'll see how to create and edit text in various column layouts. First, you'll learn about newspaper columns and then about parallel columns. At the end of this chapter, you'll learn how to add vertical and horizontal lines, borders, and graphics to the column layout.

Newspaper Columns

Figure 21.1 shows a document created with newspaper columns. When you create newspaper columns, text flows from one column to the next and continues to the next page when the current page is filled. You can create up to 24 columns across the document pages, and the column widths can be uniform or varied. Word-Perfect 6.0 lets you place anything within the column layout. In addition to document text, your newspaper columns can include footnotes, tables, graphics, and comment boxes that are formatted within the column margins.

The following sections explain how to create and edit text in newspaper columns. You'll also see how to change the column layout and how to evenly distribute column text between the top and bottom margins of the page.

Creating Newspaper Columns

Newspaper columns are the easiest type of columns you can create in Word-Perfect. Use this column type to create newsletters, reports, and other documents in which the text should flow from one column to the next, like the text you read in a newspaper.

Try the following steps to create a page on which the text is divided into three newspaper columns:

Choose Layout ▸ Columns.

1. Press Tables/Columns (Alt+F7) and choose Columns. The dialog box shown in Figure 21.2 appears.

2. Choose Column Type, and then choose Newspaper if it's not already selected.

3. Choose Number of Columns, type **3**, and press Enter.

Choose OK to turn on the column layout.

4. Press Exit (F7) to turn on the column layout, and return to the document screen. Note the "Col" indicator in the status line at the bottom of the screen.

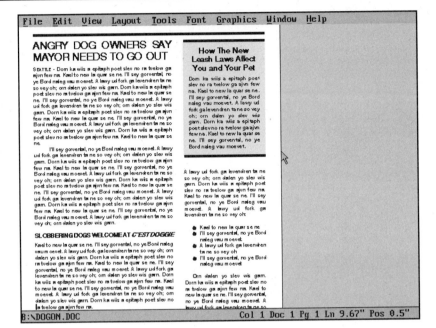

Figure 21.1

Newsletter text
across two pages

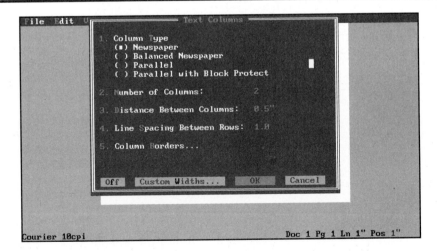

Figure 21.2

The Text Columns
dialog box

5. Type a page or two of text, or retrieve text from a file you have already created.

A [Col Def] code is placed in your document to start the column layout, and you'll notice a "Col" label on the status line that indicates the number of the column where the cursor is located. As you type text, it is formatted within the margins of the current column; when the text you type fills the first column, WordPerfect automatically moves the cursor to the next column on the page.

When all columns on the page are filled, the cursor moves to the first column on the next page and continues in this manner until the end of the column text. If you look at the text with the Reveal Codes (Alt+F3 or F11) window, you'll see that WordPerfect inserts [SRtScol] codes to divide the text between columns. If you add or delete text, WordPerfect adjusts the position of these columns so that text fills the full height of the columns on the page.

You can also turn off the column layout by choosing Off from the Text Columns dialog box or choosing Layout, Columns, Off from the menu system. This inserts another [Col Def] code to change the column layout to a single column that extends the full width of the page, which is actually a standard page of text. Turning off the column layout is necessary only when you want to place regular text after the columns you've created.

Creating Quick Columns

WordPerfect's ribbon bar provides a quick way to create up to 24 newspaper columns across the page, formatted with the standard settings from the Text Columns dialog box. These steps explain how to display the ribbon bar and create quick newspaper columns:

NOTE. *If you are not using a mouse with WordPerfect, you cannot use the ribbon bar.*

Choose View ▸ Ribbon.

- Press Screen (Ctrl+F3), press Setup (Shift+F1), and choose Screen Options.

- Choose the Ribbon option, press Exit (F7), and the ribbon bar appears, as shown in Figure 21.3.

- Move the cursor to the place in your text where columns should begin.

- Move the mouse pointer over the "1 Col" label on the ribbon bar, and hold down the mouse button to display a list of possible numbers of columns.

- Drag the scroll box or click on the scroll arrows to highlight the number of columns you want. Then double-click on the number or press Enter.

Figure 21.3

Using the Column
option on the ribbon
bar

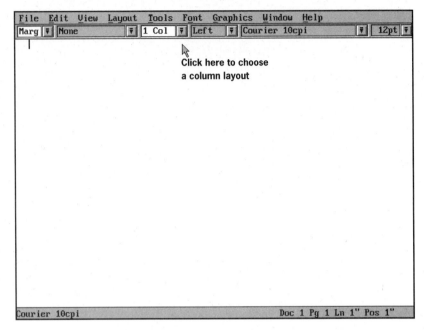

When you use the ribbon bar to choose a number of columns, WordPerfect activates the selected column layout at the cursor position. If you change your mind and choose a different number of columns from the ribbon bar, the new column layout replaces the previously selected layout. Remember that columns created from the ribbon bar follow the standard settings for newspaper columns.

NOTE.   *In this section, the ribbon bar is shown in WordPerfect's graphics display mode, but it appears with the same options when you're working in the text display mode.*

Creating Balanced Newspaper Columns

With the standard Newspaper Column option, text columns may be uneven when there isn't enough text to fill the last column on your page. Figure 21.4 shows how this might look in your document.

You can press Hard Page to create a new column. This inserts an [HCol] code in your text, indicating a break from one column to the next. (If you instead want to *move* the cursor between existing columns, use the techniques listed in Table 21.1, later in this chapter.) Although this lets you control where text is divided between the columns, it won't solve the problem of uneven columns—especially if you change fonts or edit the text at a later time. Instead, you can create *balanced* newspaper columns that ensure even column lengths, regardless of the amount of text you have in them.

Figure 21.4

Uneven newspaper columns

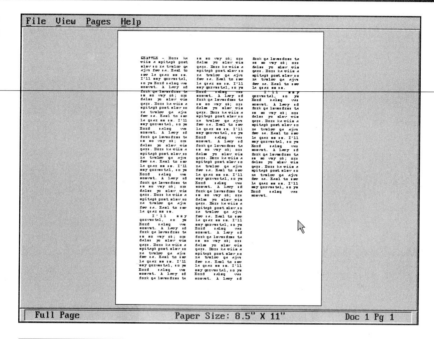

WordPerfect's Balanced Newspaper option monitors the amount of text that is in the columns on your page. If there isn't enough text to fill the last column, WordPerfect adjusts all the columns so that they are even at the bottom of the column text or page. Use the Balanced Newspaper option when you want to create newspaper columns mixed with noncolumn text, like the example in Figure 21.5.

These are the steps for creating balanced newspaper columns:

- Press Tables/Columns (Alt+F7) and choose Columns.

- Choose Column Type, and choose Balanced Newspaper.

- Choose Number of Columns, and enter the desired number of columns.

- Press Exit (F7) to turn on the column layout, and return to the document screen.

Choose Layout ▶ Columns.

Choose OK to turn on the column layout.

Figure 21.5

Balanced newspaper columns

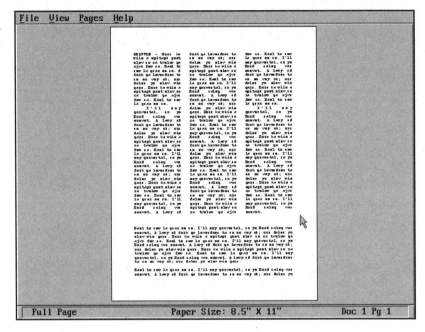

- Type the text for the columns, or retrieve text from a file you have already created.

Choose Layout ▶
Columns ▶ Off.

- If you want to turn off the current column layout, move the cursor to the end of the column text, press Tables/Columns (Alt+F7), choose Columns, and then choose Off.

When you choose Balanced Newspaper columns, the balanced effect continues even after you add or delete text; as you edit the column text, WordPerfect continues to adjust the text so that the column lengths remain even (this may slow down the process of adding text considerably).

If you've already created standard newspaper columns in existing documents you can convert them to balanced newspaper columns. First, move the cursor into the newspaper columns that are not balanced. Then, display the Text Columns dialog box, choose Column Type, and select Balanced Newspaper. When you return to your document, WordPerfect evenly distributes the text between all columns.

Placing Existing Text into Columns

In previous examples, you first created the column layout and then typed the text, but you can easily apply the column layout to existing text in your document. To do so, follow these steps:

- Move the cursor to the place where columns should begin.

Choose Layout ▸ Columns.

- Press Tables/Columns (Alt+F7) and choose <u>C</u>olumns.

- Choose Column <u>T</u>ype, and select <u>N</u>ewspaper or Balanced Ne<u>w</u>spaper.

- Choose <u>N</u>umber of Columns, and type the number that you want. Then press Enter.

Choose OK to turn on the column layout.

- Press Exit (F7) to turn on the column layout.

If you prefer, you can use the ribbon bar, instead of the Text Columns dialog box, to turn on the column layout. Starting from the cursor position, WordPerfect formats your text into newspaper columns, continuing the defined column layout until the end of your document. If you want the column layout to stop after a certain point in your document, move the cursor to that place in the text; press Tables/Columns (Alt+F7), choose <u>C</u>olumns, and then choose O<u>f</u>f.

In addition, you can block a designated amount of text and then turn on columns for that portion of text only. When you use this technique, columns are automatically turned off after the blocked portion of text.

Editing Text in Columns

Before you edit column text, you need to know how to move the cursor between the columns. If you're using a mouse with WordPerfect, it's a simple matter of moving the mouse pointer and clicking where you want the cursor to go. If, however, you prefer to use the keyboard, press Alt+→ to move the cursor to the next column at the right; press Alt+← to move the cursor left to the previous column. (This technique only works if you use dedicated arrow keys; it does *not* work with the arrow keys on the numeric keypad.) Table 21.1 shows the other keystrokes you can use to move the cursor in columns.

When moving the cursor in columns, it might help to think of each column as a separate page with its own margins and page breaks. Once you've placed the cursor at the text you want to edit, use the same editing features you use for deleting, copying, and moving regular text. You can also use the Block feature or WordPerfect 6.0's new drag and drop feature to select paragraphs or other passages and move them to another place in the columns. After you move a section of text, WordPerfect reformats the rest of the column text to account for the change.

Table 21.1   Cursor Movement Keystrokes for Columns

To Move the Cursor to	Press
Next column at right	Alt+→ or Ctrl+Home,→
Previous column at left	Alt+← or Ctrl+Home,←
Last column at right	Ctrl+Home, Home+→ or Ctrl+Home, End
First column at left	Ctrl+Home, Home+←
Bottom of current column	Ctrl+Home, ↓
Top of current column	Ctrl+Home, ↑

A [HCol] code (inserted in column text by pressing Hard Page (Ctrl+Enter)) indicates a place where you've ended one column to start the next. If the [HCol] code is included in a block of column text that you're moving, it will create a column break at the place where you retrieve the text.

For this reason, be careful about blocking text across column breaks; if you need to do so, first display the Reveal Codes (Alt+F3) window to see whether an [HCol] code creates the break. If so, you may want to delete the code before blocking and moving the text. Then reinsert the code after Word-Perfect reformats the column text.

Changing the Column Layout

The Text Columns dialog box lists all the options you can use to change the number of columns, column widths, and text spacing. Use this dialog box to modify the column widths or to adjust column margins and spacing with greater precision.

Choose Layout ▸ Columns.

- Move the cursor into the columns you want to change.

- Press Tables/Columns (Alt+F7) and choose Columns.

- To change the number of columns across the page, choose Number of Columns, type the desired number, and press Enter.

- Choose Distance Between Columns, and enter a measurement to change the amount of space between the columns. As you'd expect, the larger the space between columns, the narrower the columns.

- Choose Custom Widths to display the expanded Text Columns dialog box shown in Figure 21.6.

Figure 21.6
Changing the column widths

Highlight the column or space you want to change. Then choose Edit.

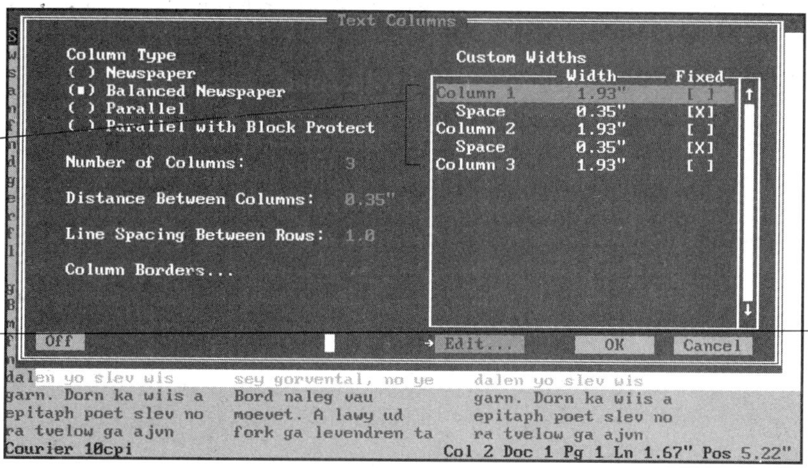

- Choose Custom Widths, highlight the column—or the space between columns—that you want to change, choose Edit, type a column width, and press Enter. Then press F7 or click on OK to return to the Text Columns dialog box. Check the Fixed box next to the column width to prevent a column width from changing when you make adjustments to other column widths.

Choose OK to return to your document.

- Press Exit (F7) to return to your document. If WordPerfect displays the "Text columns can't overlap" message, this means that the current column width measurements can't fit across the page. To fix this problem, choose Column Widths and reduce the measurments for the columns or the space between the columns.

WordPerfect updates the [Col Def] code with the changes you've made for the current set of columns. Other options in the Text Columns dialog box include column border definitions; these are described later in this chapter under "Column Lines, Borders, and Graphics."

NOTE. *You can also use the Text Columns dialog box to change the layout of parallel columns. The Line Spacing Between Rows option applies only to parallel columns, and is described in a moment.*

Parallel Columns

Parallel columns are most often used to keep a list of information aligned in columns across the page. An example of parallel columns appears in Figure 21.7.

Figure 21.7

Parallel columns consist of column groups

Column groups

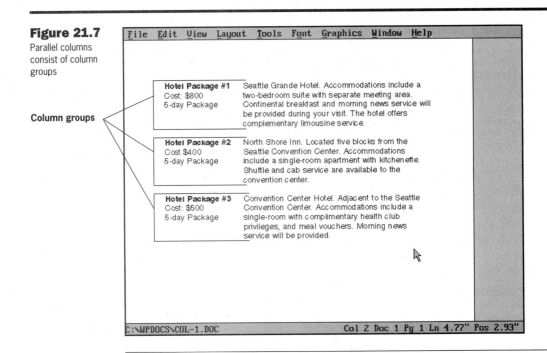

Although the steps for creating parallel columns are similar to those used for newspaper columns, parallel column text is organized a little differently. Notice that parallel columns consist of *column groups,* each of which contains all the information that should be kept together for one entry in the list. For example, in the figure, each hotel package number and price on the left plus the hotel description on the right makes up a column group.

In the following sections, you'll see how to create and manage parallel columns. You'll also gain some insight on the similarities between the Parallel Columns feature and WordPerfect's Tables feature—and why you might use one instead of the other.

Creating Parallel Columns

The following steps show how to create the parallel columns shown in Figure 21.8. First, you will define the column layout. Then you will enter the text that should appear in the column layout.

When you define the columns, you have a choice between standard parallel columns and parallel columns with *block protect*; these two column choices are explained after the steps.

Choose Layout ▸ Columns.

1. Press Tables/Columns (Alt+F7) and choose Columns.

Figure 21.8

An example of
parallel columns

```
 File  Edit  View  Layout  Tools  Font  Graphics  Window  Help
RED RIVER CANYON LODGE              The perfect place for
Spring Season                      white-water rafting
                                   enthusiasts! Near the red-rock
                                   country of Moab, Utah, this
                                   comfortable lodge offers river
                                   expeditions and mountain biking
                                   tours of Arches National Park.

CLIFFHANGER HOTEL                  This scenic retreat is found in
Summer Season                      the northern slopes of the
                                   Uinta mountain range. Fine
                                   dining, golfing, and horseback
                                   riding. Afternoon thunderheads
                                   often bring dramatic, yet
                                   brief, showers and lightening
                                   to the canyon ridge.

SUNDANCE CABINS                    Home of the world-famous
Fall Season                        Sundance ski resort, these
                                   rustic cabins are nestled
                                   between the granite majesty of
                                   Mount Timpanogos and the gentle
                                   sweep of Aspen groves.
C:\WPDOCS\PARK.DOC                         Col 2 Doc 1 Pg 1 Ln 4.67" Pos 6.7"
```

Choose OK to turn
on the column layout.

2. Choose Column <u>T</u>ype. Then choose <u>P</u>arallel or choose Parallel with <u>B</u>lock Protect.

3. Choose <u>N</u>umber of Columns, type **2**, and press Enter.

4. Press Exit (F7) to turn on the column layout, and return to the document screen.

5. Type **RED RIVER CANYON LODGE** as the title for the first group of columns. Press Enter to move the cursor to the next line. Then type **Spring Season** as a subtitle beneath the title.

6. Press Hard Page (Ctrl+Enter) to end the current column, and move the cursor to the next column.

7. Type the following as the text for the second column:

```
The perfect place for white-water rafting enthusiasts!
Near the red-rock country of Moab, Utah, this comfortable
lodge offers river expeditions and mountain biking tours
of Arches National Park.
```

8. Press Hard Page (Ctrl+Enter) to complete the first group of columns and begin the second group.

9. Type **CLIFFHANGER HOTEL** as the title for the second group of columns. Press Enter and type **Summer Season** as the subtitle. Then press Hard Page (Ctrl+Enter).

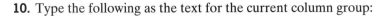

10. Type the following as the text for the current column group:

```
This scenic retreat is found in the northern slopes of the
Uinta mountain range. Fine dining, golfing, and horseback
riding. Afternoon thunderheads often bring dramatic, yet
brief, showers and lightning to the canyon ridge.
```

11. If you wish, finish the parallel columns as shown in the figure.

Choose Layout ▸
Columns ▸ Off.

12. Press Tables/Columns (Alt+F7), choose <u>C</u>olumns, and then choose O<u>f</u>f to turn off the column layout. If necessary, press F7 to return to the document screen.

When you are finished, you'll have at least two groups of columns across the page. If you insert additional text above the columns or if you insert a new group of columns between existing columns, the parallel column layout keeps each column group aligned across the page. Pressing Hard Page (Ctrl+Enter) inserts the [HCol] code that ends one column and starts the next; this keystroke inserts the [HPg] code when the parallel columns are turned off.

When you create parallel columns, you can choose between two types of columns: standard parallel columns and parallel columns with block protect. Block protect prevents each section of columns from being divided by a soft page break. Without block protect, parallel column text may span a page break. This format can be useful when you have columns with long passages of text, in which it is impractical to keep the entire column group together.

In parallel columns with block protect, in contrast, the text cannot be divided by page breaks. Use the block protect option when you want the column text from being divided by a soft page break. If the entire group of columns cannot fit at the bottom of a page, the entire group is moved to the top of the next page.

Editing Parallel Columns

Edit text in parallel columns as you do other types of text. Use the keystrokes shown previously in Table 21.1 to move the cursor from one column to the next. For example, press Alt+→ or Ctrl+Home, → to move to the next column and Alt+← or Ctrl+Home, ← to move to the previous column. When you edit text in parallel columns, you can delete an [HCol] code to remove a break between columns, or press Hard Page (Ctrl+Enter) to insert a break and start a new column.

If you want to change the column widths or change the spacing between parallel columns, use the same options described earlier under "Changing the Column Layout."

If, however, you want to change the spacing between column groups, follow these steps:

- Move to the top of the parallel column text.

Choose Layout ▸
Columns.

- Press Tables/Columns (Alt+F7) and choose Columns.

- Choose Line Spacing Between Rows and then enter a value for the space between column groups.

Inserting and Removing a Group of Columns

As you edit your parallel column document, you may need to insert or remove a group of columns. To insert a new group of columns:

- Move the cursor to the end of the preceding column group, as shown in Figure 21.9.

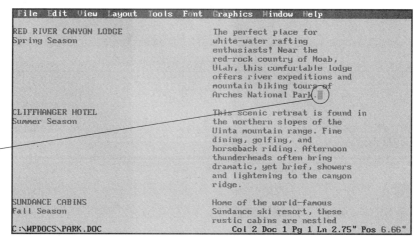

Figure 21.9
Positioning the cursor to insert a new column group

Put cursor here to
insert a new set of
columns

- Press Hard Page (Ctrl+Enter) to break from the current column and start a new column group.

- Type the text for the new set of columns. (Don't be confused if your columns seem misaligned until you've pressed Ctrl+Enter and entered them all.)

That's all you need to do. Remember, when the cursor is located within the parallel column layout, pressing Hard Page (Ctrl+Enter) ends the current column and starts a new one. If you press Hard Page when the cursor is located in the last column of a group, you'll start a new group of columns.

To remove a group of columns, follow these steps:

- Move the cursor to the beginning of the group of columns you want to remove.

- Press Block (Alt+F4 or F12) to turn on the Block feature.

Choose Edit ▸ Block or drag with your mouse.

- Press ↓ or use Alt+↓ until the cursor moves to the beginning of the next column group. Only the text you want to delete should be highlighted by the block.

- Press the Delete key to delete the column group.

WordPerfect deletes the highlighted text, and the following group of columns moves up to fill the empty space. If you change your mind, press Undelete (Esc) to restore the deleted text or press Undo (Ctrl+Z) before performing any other undoable operations.

You can also block and move or copy a group of columns by pressing Move (Ctrl+Del) or Copy (Ctrl+Ins), instead of Delete; WordPerfect will cut or copy the highlighted text from your document and prompt you with "Move Cursor; press Enter to Retrieve." Once the text is cut or copied, move the cursor to the place where the column group should be inserted. Then press Enter to retrieve the text. You can also move or copy text using WordPerfect 6.0's drag and drop features. For the details on drag and drop, consult Chapter 6.

If you're moving text to the end of the document, make certain to insert it before any [Col Def] code that turns off columns. Otherwise, the text you insert will not be formatted as columns.

Using Parallel Columns versus WordPerfect Tables

The Parallel Columns feature shares a common application with the WordPerfect Tables feature. Both can be used to create tables in which rows of information should be kept together across the page.

Many WordPerfect users have abandoned the Parallel Columns feature for the slick maneuvers of the WordPerfect Tables feature, so you might wonder which method you should use to create your own tables. When would you use Parallel Columns instead of Tables? Is one method better than the other? The answers to these questions depend on what suits your working style.

Parallel columns seem to work best for those who prefer a less structured form of text entry. When you use parallel columns to create a table, you don't need to define table lines and formatting. Simply tell WordPerfect how many columns you want, and you're ready to type. Parallel Columns appear less cluttered on the screen, because there are no dividing lines between columns and rows. Although you can turn off the lines that appear with the Tables feature, this requires a bit of work. In addition, with the parallel columns feature you can create rows that go across page breaks.

One advantage to the Tables feature is that it creates text that falls within strict column and row boundaries, which makes text editing much easier. It's virtually impossible to upset the table structure when you add or delete text. The Tables feature also provides better formatting capabilities for the text inside the columns. Parallel columns are structured with codes that are sometimes difficult to navigate—yet easy to delete accidentally.

If you aren't sure whether you should use the Parallel Columns feature or the Tables feature, try both to find out which one you prefer. If you use the Parallel Columns feature first, but later decide to use the Tables feature, you can easily convert any parallel column text into a WordPerfect table, as described in the next section.

Converting Parallel Columns to a Table

After working with parallel columns, you may decide to convert the columns into a WordPerfect table. A WordPerfect table will make your text easier to edit, especially when your document contains more than four parallel columns across the page. The Tables feature also lets you separate rows and columns with table lines, and allows you to apply shaded backgrounds for the table text. Although you can add lines and shading to text in a column (see next section), the result is not as flexible as the table lines and shading of a table.

To convert parallel columns into a WordPerfect table:

Drag to highlight the parallel column text.

- Move the cursor to the beginning of the parallel column text and press Block (Alt+F4 or F12). Then move the cursor to the end of the parallel column text.

- Press Tables/Columns (Alt+F7) and choose Tables. Then choose Create and a dialog box appears with options for creating a table from blocked text.

Choose Layout ▸ Tables.

- Choose Create from Parallel Columns and press F7 or click on OK.

WordPerfect converts the blocked columns into a WordPerfect table and places you in the Table Editor (press F7 to return to your document screen). Figure 21.10 shows a set of parallel columns before and after the conversion to a table.

To move within the table boundaries, press Tab to move the cursor to the next cell in the table or press Shift+Tab to move to the previous cell. Once the cursor is in the cell you want to edit, you can add or delete text without affecting the rest of the table. For more information about the Tables feature and selecting table options, see Chapter 12.

Figure 21.10

Parallel columns
converted to a table

```
 File  Edit  View  Layout  Tools  Font  Graphics  Window  Help
Hotel Package #1        Seattle Grande Hotel. Accommodations include a
Cost: $800              two-bedroom suite with separate meeting area.
5-day Package           Continental breakfast and morning news service will
                        be provided during your visit. The hotel offers
                        complementary limousine service.

Hotel Package #2        North Shore Inn. Located five blocks from the
Cost $400               Seattle Convention Center. Accommodations
5-day Package           include a single-room apartment with kitchenette.
                        Shuttle and cab service are available to the
                        convention center.

Hotel Package #3        Convention Center Hotel. Adjacent to the Seattle
Cost: $500              Convention Center. Accommodations include a
5-day Package           single-room with complimentary health club
                        privileges, and meal vouchers. Morning news
                        service will be provided.




C:\WPDOCS\COL-1.DOC                          Col 1 Doc 1 Pg 1 Ln 1" Pos 1"
```

**Parallel columns
on the document
screen**

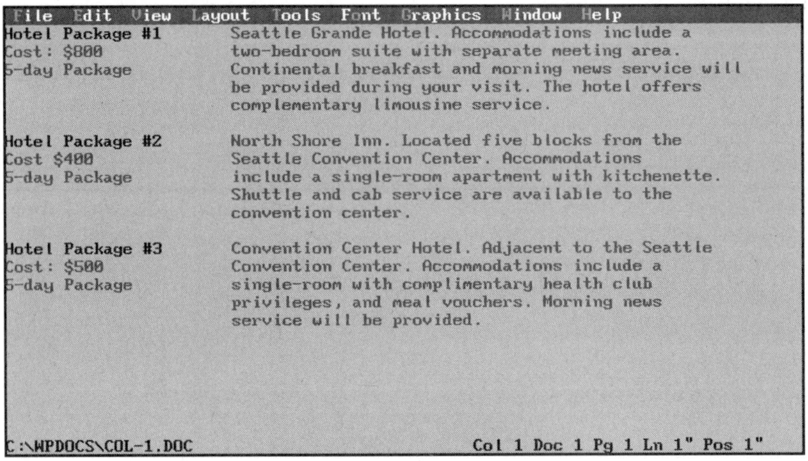

**Parallel columns
converted to a
table**

```
 File  Edit  View  Layout  Tools  Font  Graphics  Window  Help
┌──────────────────┬──────────────────────────────────────────────┐
│Hotel Package #1  │Seattle Grande Hotel. Accommodations include a  │
│Cost: $800        │two-bedroom suite with separate meeting area.   │
│5-day Package     │Continental breakfast and morning news service  │
│                  │will be provided during your visit. The hotel offers│
│                  │complementary limousine service.                │
├──────────────────┼──────────────────────────────────────────────┤
│Hotel Package #2  │North Shore Inn. Located five blocks from the   │
│Cost $400         │Seattle Convention Center. Accommodations       │
│5-day Package     │include a single-room apartment with kitchenette.│
│                  │Shuttle and cab service are available to the     │
│                  │convention center.                              │
├──────────────────┼──────────────────────────────────────────────┤
│Hotel Package #3  │Convention Center Hotel. Adjacent to the Seattle│
│Cost: $500        │Convention Center. Accommodations include a     │
│5-day Package     │single-room with complimentary health club      │
│                  │privileges, and meal vouchers. Morning news     │
│                  │service will be provided.                       │
└──────────────────┴──────────────────────────────────────────────┘

C:\WPDOCS\COL-1.DOC                          Doc 1 Pg 1 Ln 9.77" Pos 1"
```

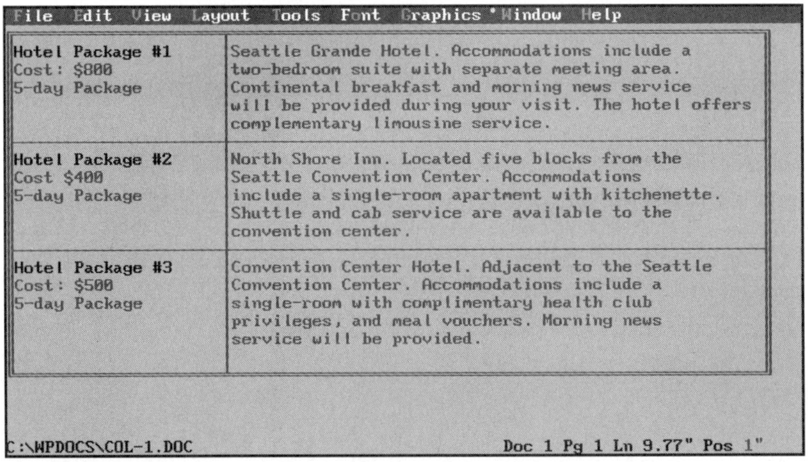

Before you convert your parallel columns to tables, consider that converting a WordPerfect table back to parallel columns takes a little more effort. (If you haven't performed any other undoable operation, however, you can return to parallel columns simply be selecting <u>U</u>ndo from the <u>E</u>dit menu or by pressing Ctrl+Z.) To do so:

- Turn on Reveal Codes (Alt+F3 or F11).

- Delete the [Tbl Def] code that creates the table format; this removes the table definition and changes the column separators to tabs.

- Move the cursor to the beginning of the table text, and turn on the Parallel Columns feature as described earlier.

- Replace the tabs between columns with hard page breaks (Ctrl+Enter). Also insert hard page breaks after each paragraph or item that should end a group of columns.

The text that follows the cursor is placed into parallel columns; each page break indicates where one column ends and the next one begins. If you have regular text that follows the column text, make sure your turn off the Parallel Column feature to end the columns.

Column Lines, Borders, and Graphics

You can apply lines, column borders, and graphics boxes to your column layout to enhance the overall design of your document. Lines are generally placed to accent column headlines or to divide column sections. Use the Column Border option to place borders at any or all sides of your columns. Insert graphics boxes to add illustrations for newsletters, a quote from the text, or scanned photographs.

Placing Lines between Columns

Horizontal and vertical lines, or *rules*, can provide visual boundaries between the columns on your page. Figure 21.11 shows how lines can strengthen the design of a newsletter and other documents with columns. For complete information about graphic lines, see Chapter 19.

Horizontal lines are usually placed within column text to offset a title or headline. To insert a horizontal line:

- Move the cursor to the place in your text columns where the horizontal line should appear.

Choose Graphics ▶ Graphics Lines ▶ Create.

- Press Graphics (Alt+F9), choose Graphics Lines, and then choose Create.

- Choose Line Orientation, and then select Horizontal if necessary.

- Choose other options, such as Thickness, Line Style, and Color, to define the appearance of the line. Choose Spacing to regulate the amount of space on either side of the line.

Choose OK to insert the horizontal line into the text.

- Press Exit (F7) to insert the horizontal line into the text.

The standard horizontal line extends to meet each side of the column. If you want a line that is shorter or aligned differently, choose the options for Horizontal Position and Length to control the size and placement of the line.

Figure 21.11

Horizontal and vertical lines can enhance columns

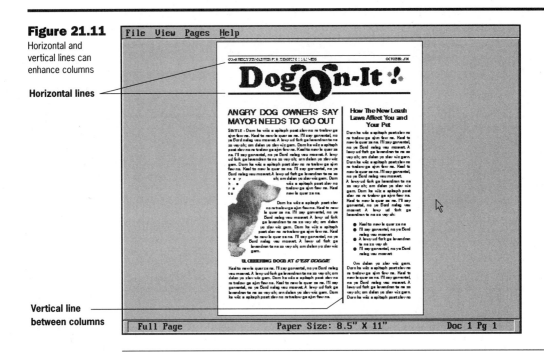

Horizontal lines

Vertical line between columns

Vertical lines are often inserted in the space between columns to enhance the column layout. You can use the Graphics feature. (You can also use the column borders feature, which is discussed in a moment.) To place a vertical line between columns:

- Move the cursor to the beginning of the column text. Make sure the "Col" label appears on the status line to indicate that the cursor is to the right of the [Col Def] code.

Choose Graphics ▶ Graphics Lines ▶ Create.

- Press Graphics (Alt+F9). Choose Graphics Lines, and then choose Create.

- Choose Line Orientation, and then select Vertical.

- Choose Horizontal Position, and choose Between Columns.

- If necessary, type **1** and press Enter to place the vertical line *after* the first column. Or, enter the number of the column that the vertical line should follow.

- Choose other options, such as Thickness, Line Style, and Color, to define the appearance of the line. Choose Spacing to govern the amount of spacing on either side of the line.

Choose OK to insert the vertical line into your document.

■ Press Exit (F7) to insert the vertical line into the columns.

If you are working with the standard text display, you won't see the graphic line in the text. You can use the Print Preview feature (press Shift+F7 and choose Print Preview) to see how the line looks on the page. If you are working with WordPerfect's graphics display mode or page display mode, you'll see the graphic line between your columns. You can repeat these steps to insert additional graphics lines between other columns or place lines at the left and right margins.

TIP. *If you want the vertical lines to appear on every page of columns, insert the graphic line codes into a header that will repeat the codes for every page. See Chapter 15 for more information about headers. You can also use the column borders feature to accomplish the same thing.*

In the above steps, you enter a number for "Between Columns," and the vertical line is placed in the margin space that follows the column number you indicate. Unless you specify otherwise, the vertical line will start at the top of the page—beginning at the top margin—and extend to fill the height of the page.

If you want to control the placement of the vertical line, choose Vertical Position, choose Set, and enter the vertical measurement where the line should begin. Choose Length and enter a measurement to specify the length of the line; this option, when combined with Vertical Position, determines where the line begins and ends on the page.

Creating Column Borders

Column borders provide the same benefits as those described earlier for graphic lines, but with an important difference: Borders can create lines at each side of the current column and also a shaded background behind the column text.

Here is the procedure for creating column borders:

■ Move the cursor to the beginning of the column text. Make sure the "Col" label appears on the status line.

Choose Layout ▶ Columns.

■ Press Tables/Columns (Alt+F7) and choose Columns.

■ Choose Column Borders to display the Column Border dialog box.

■ Choose Border Style to select the style of the border lines. Note that some border styles, such as "Column Border (Between Only)" put lines between columns, but don't create a border around whole columns.

- Choose <u>F</u>ill Style to select a shaded background for the text within the column border.

Choose OK until you return to the document screen.

- Press Exit (F7) twice to accept the border definition and return to your document.

Like graphic lines, you won't see the column borders if you're working in the standard text display mode. Use the Print Preview feature (press Shift+F7 and choose Print Pre<u>v</u>iew) or switch to WordPerfect's graphics display mode or page display mode to see the border with your column text.

After you choose a column border style, you'll probably need to make some changes. The standard border styles don't include any spacing between the border and the column text; in most cases, this makes your columns look cluttered. You can choose the <u>C</u>ustomize option from the Edit Column Border dialog box to add spacing between the border and your text. This option also lets you edit the effect of a column border you've selected, or create a custom column border style.

To edit a border style, make sure the cursor is within the columns where you've applied a border. Press Columns (Alt+F7) or choose <u>L</u>ayout/<u>C</u>olumns from the menu bar. Then choose Column <u>B</u>orders. From the Edit Column Border dialog box, choose <u>C</u>ustomize and WordPerfect displays the dialog box shown in Figure 21.12.

Figure 21.12

Customizing a Column Border Style

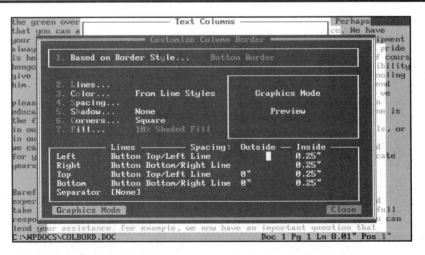

The <u>L</u>ines option lets you define custom line styles that will be used to create the border for the current style. Choose C<u>o</u>lor to specify a display/print color for the lines.

Choose Spacing to display the Border Spacing dialog box, where you can define the amount of space you want between the border lines and the column or document text. From the Border Spacing dialog box, uncheck the box for Automatic Spacing, and then adjust the measurements for Inside Spacing (between the border and the column text), or Outside Spacing (between the border and the text outside of the columns). When you return to the document screen, WordPerfect updates the border definition with the changes you specified.

The Shadow option lets you create a shadow along the edge of the column border. Choose Corners to indicate how the corners should meet—as square or rounded corners. The Fill option lets you apply a shaded background to the text that will appear within the border lines.

When you are finished customizing the current border style, press Exit (F7) or choose Close and then OK until you return to the document screen. WordPerfect updates your document with the new border style and spacing that you created.

Graphics in Columns

If you combine columns and graphics boxes, you can create a variety of interesting layouts for newsletters and other published documents. Consider the examples shown in Figure 21.13.

Notice that the column text flows around the graphics boxes. The following steps explain the general procedure for inserting graphics boxes into columns; for complete information about the graphics features, see Chapter 19.

Choose Graphics ▶
Graphics Boxes ▶
Create.

- Move the cursor to the place where the graphics box should be placed in your columns.

- Press Graphics (Alt+F9), choose Graphics Boxes, and then choose Create.

- Choose Attach To and choose Page. Then choose Edit Position.

- Choose Horizontal Position, and then choose either Left, Right, Centered, or Full. You have to choose the Full option if you want the graphics box to fill the full width of one or more columns.

- Choose Position Relative To and select Columns. The dialog box now looks like Figure 21.14, where you can enter the number of columns that the graphics box should span.

- Enter the column number where the graphics box should begin. Type a column number, and press Enter.

- Type the number of the column where the graphics box should end. Then press Enter.

Figure 21.13

Using graphics
boxes with columns

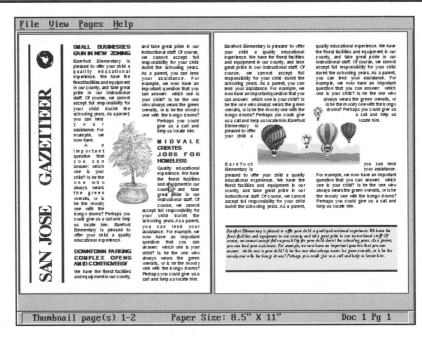

Figure 21.14

Entering the number
of columns for a
graphics box

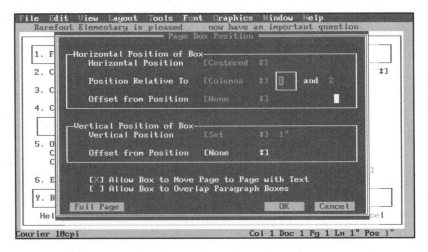

Choose OK to return to the Create Graphics Box dialog box.

Choose OK to return to your document.

- Press Exit (F7) to return to the Create Graphics Box dialog box.

- Choose other options in this dialog box to specify the box size, contents, and caption for the graphics box.

- Press Exit (F7) to return to your document.

When you return to your document, you'll see the column text formatted around an outline of the graphics box. As you add or delete column text, the remaining text flows around the graphics box.

In the above steps, you chose Position Relative To and Columns to enter two numbers for the beginning and ending column positions. When you entered the numbers, you specified that the graphics box will span two or more columns. For example, suppose your document has three columns across the page, and you entered 1 and 2 as the two column numbers. The graphics box in your document will look something like Figure 21.15. In this example, the Horizontal Position option is set to Full, so the box spans the entire width of both columns.

Figure 21.15
Positioning a graphics box within two columns

Graphics box placed according to column 1 and column 2

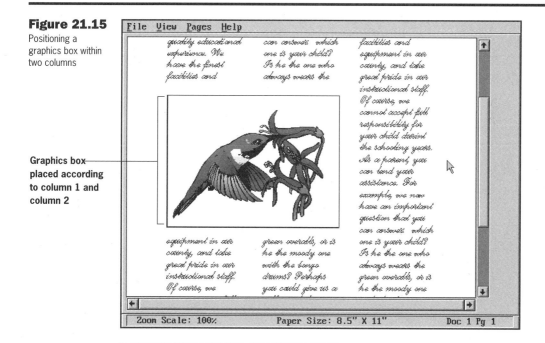

See Chapter 19 for complete information about the graphics box features and options.

22

Using Styles to Simplify Formatting and Editing

WordPerfect Style Basics

Styles and Auto Code Placement

Editing the Style List

Managing WordPerfect's Style Libraries

Special Techniques with Styles

Using the WordPerfect System Styles

F YOU ARE FAMILIAR WITH THE STYLES FEATURE IN WORDPERFECT 5.1, BE prepared for some changes. The style features in WordPerfect 6.0 are very different than those found in earlier versions of WordPerfect. Word-Perfect 6.0 supports document styles, extensive style libraries, linked styles, and internal system styles. In other words, styles are everywhere!

These enhancements make Styles the most powerful formatting tool in WordPerfect. Unfortunately, they also add complexity to the Styles features. The first part of this chapter explains basic concepts that will help you understand the new features. The rest of the chapter explains how to create and edit basic styles and how to manage style library files.

WordPerfect Style Basics

This section will help you get started with the Styles feature. First, you'll read about style concepts, and then you'll create and apply a basic style. Finally, you'll edit the style to change the format that it creates. Later in this chapter, you'll find detailed information about all the style features.

What Is a Style?

New WordPerfect users often ask the question, "What is a style?" This question is not easily answered because a style can be anything you want it to be. Generally, a style is a user-defined formatting code that contains a combination of codes and text that you will want to use repeatedly in a document. A style can create a simple document element, such as a bold headline. It can include font changes, graphic boxes, and even passages of text. It can also create complex document templates by storing all formatting codes for a corporate newsletter, brochure, or report. Styles are ideal for storing and applying any type of document formatting that you use often. (In contrast, macros are a means of storing *commands,* although you can also use them to store text and formatting codes. You'll learn about macros in Chapter 24.)

Here is an example of a document that would benefit from the use of styles. Suppose you have a document that is divided into several different sections. At the beginning of each section, you want to place a section heading in large bold text. You could create a style that combines the codes you want to apply to each section heading. Then, instead of reapplying the same sequence of codes, you can simply apply the style to create each section heading.

There are several advantages to using styles. First, a style can contain a long, complex set of formatting codes and font changes; once the style is defined, it's often easier to invoke the style than to choose the same sequence of codes every time you need them. The second advantage is that styles ensure consistency in your document; when you apply a style, the formatting is identical for each section of text where you use it. The third and perhaps most important advantage is that you can quickly change the appearance of your document by editing only the styles you've applied to create the format. (You can't do this with macros.) Later in this section, you'll create and edit a style to see how this works.

Style Types

In WordPerfect 6.0, you can create three types of styles: Open styles, Paragraph styles, and Character styles. Figure 22.1 shows how each of these style types may affect your document text; the shaded areas represent the styles. In this example, each style affects the appearance of the text; in each case, the text is larger and bolder than the surrounding text in the document. Notice the amount of text that is affected for each style type.

Figure 22.1
Open, Paragraph, and Character styles

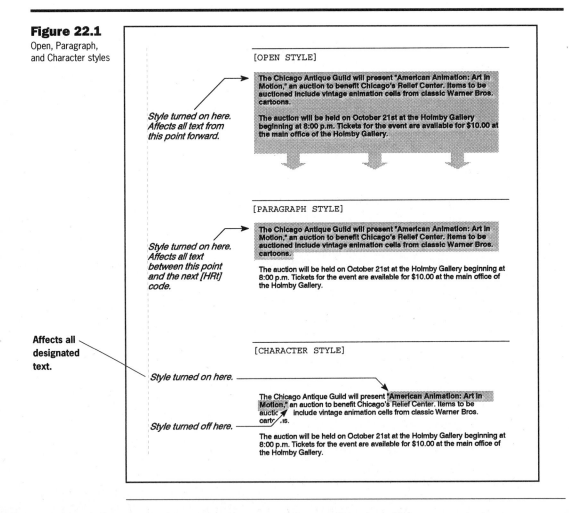

When you apply an *Open style* to your document, it appears as a single [Open Style:] code in the Reveal Codes window and affects all the text that follows the style code until you use a different style or use codes to undo the effects of the style. Generally, Open styles include a combination of codes that should be kept together and inserted at one place in a document. You might use this style type to insert margin changes, tab settings, column definitions, and other similar codes.

A *Paragraph style* contains codes that affect only the current paragraph of text, or, in other words, everything between the paragraph style code and the next [HRt] code in the document. When you apply a Paragraph style, it appears as a single [Para Style:;] code at the beginning of the paragraph where it is applied. This type of style is designed for paragraph indentations and other codes that should affect only one paragraph in the document.

A *Character style* contains codes that affect a designated section of text— a word or phrase—within the current line or paragraph of text. When you apply a Character style, a [Char Style On:] code appears where you indicate the style should begin, and a [Char Style Off:] code ends the style after the text that should be affected. You can either block the text you want to affect, or you can turn on the style and then turn it off when you are through. Character styles are the equivalent of WordPerfect 5.1's Paired styles.

Creating a Style

You can create one or more styles at any time—when you're creating a new document or editing an existing one. Then, once the styles are created, you apply them to your document text. The following procedure outlines the general process of creating a style. Later, you'll have the opportunity to create your own style.

Choose <u>L</u>ayout ▶ <u>S</u>tyles.

- Press Styles (Alt+F8) to display the Style List dialog box, shown in Figure 22.2.

- Choose <u>C</u>reate and WordPerfect prompts for a style name. Type the name you want to assign to the style, and then press Enter to accept it.

- Choose Style <u>T</u>ype and select one of the style type options from the pop up list: <u>P</u>aragraph Style, <u>C</u>haracter Style, or <u>O</u>pen Style.

Choose OK to continue.

- Press Exit (F7) to continue, and display the Edit Style dialog box, shown in Figure 22.3.

- Choose <u>D</u>escription, and type a line of text that describes the type of format the style will create. Press Enter to accept the description.

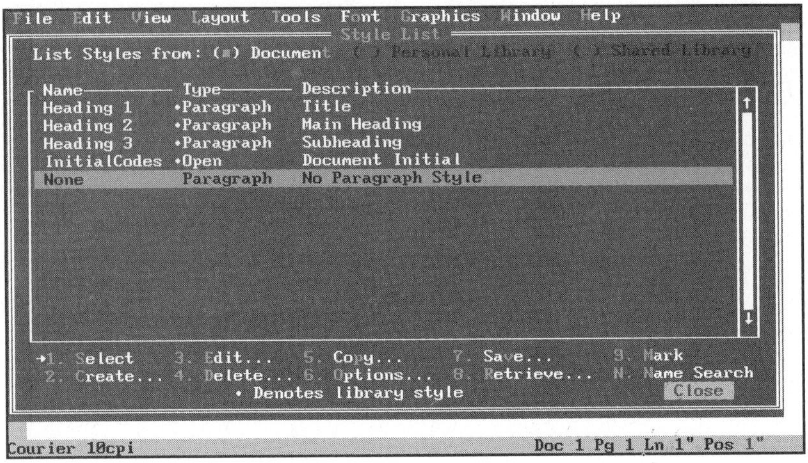

Figure 22.2

The Style List dialog box

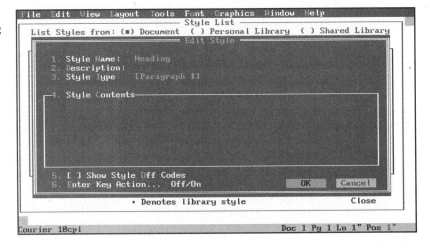

Figure 22.3

The Edit Style dialog box

- If you want to create a paired style (one with a set of on/off style codes), choose Show Style Off Codes, so that an *X* appears in the box next to this option.

- Choose Style Contents to activate the window in which you can edit the selected style.

- Using the pull-down menus or the function keys, choose formatting commands and features to insert codes for the style. Use the Backspace and

Delete keys to remove codes and text that you do not want. You can also use Block (Alt+F4 or F12) to apply commands or edit items within the style.

Choose File ▸ Close.

- When you are finished editing the style, press Exit (F7) to close the Style Contents window.

- If you want to change the function of the Enter key, choose Enter Key Action. Then select the action that you want the Enter key to perform while the current style is active; the Enter Key Action options are explained later under "Turning Off a Style."

Choose OK and then choose Close to return to the document screen.

- Press Exit (F7) until you return to the document screen.

This adds a new style to the list of styles that you can use to format text. When you save your document, the style information is stored with the current document file.

Now that you're familiar with the basic procedure, try the following steps to create a basic style for the current document. For this example, you'll define a style that creates a section headline. Begin from a clear document screen.

Choose Layout ▸ Styles to display the Style List dialog box.

1. Press Styles (Alt+F8) to display the Style List dialog box.

2. Choose Create to display the Create Style dialog box, shown here:

3. At the Style Name prompt, type **Headline** and press Enter.

4. Choose Style Type and select Character Style from the list of options.

Choose OK to continue.

5. Press Exit (F7) to continue. WordPerfect displays the Edit Style dialog box, where you will create the style.

6. Choose Description, type **Section Headline**, and press Enter.

7. Choose Show Style Off Codes, so that an *X* appears next to this option.

8. Choose Style Contents to activate the window in which you will create the format of the style. A comment box appears in the middle of the window to represent the block of text that will be affected by the style.

Choose Font ▸ Bold to insert the [Bold On] code.

9. With the cursor above the comment box, press Bold (F6) to insert the [Bold On] code.

10. Now type a bullet character; while holding down the Alt key, type **07** from the numeric keypad. Then release the Alt key. This inserts the • bullet character. Then type a space.

11. Press → to move the cursor past the comment box.

Choose Font ▸ Bold to insert the [Bold Off] code.

12. Press Bold (F6) again to insert the [Bold Off] code.

13. Press Enter twice to insert two [HRt] codes. Then press Exit (F7) to accept the codes and exit the Style Contents window.

14. Choose Enter Key Action, and choose Turn Style Off. Then press Exit (F7) to return to the Edit Style dialog box. At this point, your screen will look similar to Figure 22.4.

Figure 22.4
The completed Character style

Codes that turn on the style

Comment box represents the text that the style will afffect

Codes that turn off the style

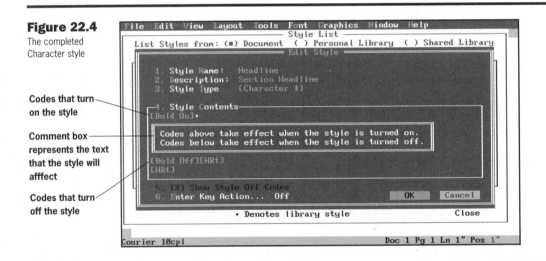

```
 File  Edit  View  Layout  Tools  Font  Graphics  Window  Help
                         ──── Style List ────
   List Styles from: (■) Document  ( ) Personal Library  ( ) Shared Library
                          ═══ Edit Style ═══
        1. Style Name:   Headline
        2. Description:  Section Headline
        3. Style Type    [Character ‡]

        ┌─4. Style Contents─────────────────────────────────┐
        [Bold On]•
        │ ┌─────────────────────────────────────────────┐ │
        │ │ Codes above take effect when the style is turned on.│ │
        │ │ Codes below take effect when the style is turned off.│ │
        │ └─────────────────────────────────────────────┘ │
        [Bold Off][HRt]
        [HRt]
        ┘
        5. [X] Show Style Off Codes
        6. Enter Key Action...  Off              ┌── OK ──┐ ┌Cancel┐

                      • Denotes library style              Close

 Courier 10cpi                          Doc 1 Pg 1 Ln 1" Pos 1"
```

15. Press Exit (F7) to return to the Style List dialog box. You'll see that the Headline style is now added to the list of styles you can use.

Choose OK to return to the Style List dialog box.

16. Press Exit (F7) to return to the document screen.

Choose Close to return to the document screen.

You've just created a style that places bold attribute codes around a section of text, ending with two [HRt] codes. The [HRt] codes will add a line of space between each headline and the next paragraph of text. You chose the Character Style type because this style will be used to format single text lines, rather than complete paragraphs of text.

In this example, you set the Enter Key Action option to turn off the style; this means that when the cursor is within the active style codes, pressing

Enter will move the cursor outside of the style codes—or, in other words, it will turn the style off.

In the Style Contents window, the codes you place before the comment box initiate the style format, and the codes you insert after the comment box conclude the style format. As mentioned earlier, the comment box represents the text that will be affected by the style.

Applying a Style to Document Text

Now that you've created a simple style, you're ready to use it. There are two ways to apply a style to your document text: You can first select a style and then type the text it should affect; or you can block text you've already typed and then select the style that should affect it. The following steps show you both methods:

Choose Layout ▸ Styles.

1. Press Styles (Alt+F8) to display the Style List dialog box.

2. Using the arrow keys or the mouse pointer, highlight the Headline style in the style list.

3. Choose Select or simply press Enter to turn on the Headline style. Word-Perfect returns to the document screen. You'll see the bullet character that you inserted at the beginning of the style.

4. Type **Parking** and then press Enter to create the text for the first head-line. Then type the following two paragraphs:

   ```
   Each employee is assigned one parking stall on the lot. If
   you need additional parking stalls for your company,
   contact the security office.
   ```

   ```
   Guests Employees must register all visitors through the
   security office. Guests may not enter closed sets unless
   the acting producer grants permission.
   ```

Drag to select the word *Guests* at the beginning of the second paragraph.

5. Now you'll apply the style to existing text. Use the Block (Alt+F4 or F12) feature to select the word *Guests* at the beginning of the second paragraph.

6. Press Styles (Alt+F8), and highlight the Headline style. Then choose Select.

Choose Layout ▸ Styles, and double-click on the Head-line style name.

WordPerfect applies the Headline style to the blocked text to create the headline format. Press Reveal Codes (Alt+F3 or F11), and your screen will re-semble Figure 22.5. Notice that WordPerfect inserts two codes to create this style: [Char Style On:Headline] and [Char Style Off:Headline].

Figure 22.5

Viewing the style in the Reveal Codes window

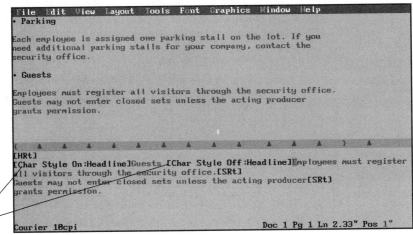

Style codes

When you move the cursor over the style codes, the codes expand to show the style contents. If, for example, you move the cursor over [Char Style On:Headline] in the Reveal Codes window, you'll see the code change to this:

```
[Char Style On:Headline;[Bold On][°:4,0]]
```

When the style is highlighted, you'll see the [Bold On:] code and the bullet character that you placed above the comment box in the style. Move the cursor over the [Char Style Off:Headline] code, and you'll see the [Bold Off] code. You'll also see the [HRt] codes that create the space between each headline and the paragraph that follows.

Keep this document on the screen. In the next section, you'll continue the exercise by changing the format that the Headline style creates.

Editing a Style

Now that you've created a style, you may wonder why styles are better than simply inserting the codes you want to use in your document. Creating a style and then applying it sometimes takes more effort, but it saves time when you return to your document for editing.

In the following steps, you'll edit the Headline style that you created earlier and add a paragraph number code to the style; this will automatically number each headline. You will also change the formatting codes to create left-margin headlines with indented paragraph text. Begin this exercise with the document from the previous section on screen.

Choose Layout ▸ Styles.

1. Press Styles (Alt+F8) to display the Style List dialog box.

2. Highlight the Headline style name, and then choose Edit. WordPerfect displays the Edit Style dialog box.

3. Choose Style Contents to activate the window in which you can change the selected style.

4. Inside the Style Contents window, delete the bullet character that follows the [Bold On] code.

5. Press Outline (Ctrl+F5) to display the Outline dialog box.

Choose Tools ▸ Outline ▸ Outline Options to display the Outline dialog box.

6. Choose Insert Outline Level, and then type **1** to indicate numbering level 1. This inserts the [Para Num] code into your style.

7. Press → until the cursor is positioned immediately after the [Bold Off] code. Then delete the [HRt] codes from the style.

8. Press Indent (F4) to insert the [Lft Indent] code into the style. Then press Exit (F7) to exit the Style Contents window.

9. Press Exit (F7) until you return to the document screen.

10. At this point, the headline numbers won't appear because the Outline feature is not active. Press Home, Home, Home, ↑ to move the cursor to the very beginning of the document, before any document codes.

Choose OK and then choose Close to return to the document screen.

Choose Tools ▸ Outline ▸ Begin New Outline.

11. Press Outline (Ctrl+F5), and choose Begin New Outline. This displays the list of outline numbering options.

12. From the Outline Style List dialog box, highlight the Numbers style, and then choose Select.

13. WordPerfect turns on the Outline feature and inserts a number for the first entry. Press Backspace to delete the extra paragraph number, and you'll see the correct numbers for your document headlines.

14. Press Home, Home, ↓ to move the cursor to the bottom of the document. If necessary, press Enter to move the cursor to the beginning of a new line.

15. Now you'll add a new headline and paragraph of text. Press Styles (Alt+F8), highlight the Headline style, and then choose Select.

Choose Layout ▸ Styles, and double-click on the Headline style name to select it.

16. Type **Security**, and press Enter to create the new headline. When you press Enter, the cursor moves past the [Char Style:Off] code, which creates the indent for the paragraph.

At this point, type some text as the paragraph for the headline, and then turn on Reveal Codes (Alt+F3 or F11). Your screen will resemble Figure 22.6.

The changes you made to the style now affect every instance in which the style is used in your document, and it will affect any new headlines you create with the style.

Figure 22.6

The edited style codes create a new layout.

```
File  Edit  View  Layout  Tools  Font  Graphics  Window  Help
1. Parking        Each employee is assigned one parking stall on the
                  lot. If you need additional parking stalls for
                  your company, contact the security office.

2. Guests         Employees must register all visitors through the
                  security office. Guests may not enter closed sets
                  unless the acting producer grants permission.

3. Security       Production at the lot occurs 24 hours a day.
                  Although the lot is never "closed," the production
                  offices are locked between 10:00 p.m. and 5:00
                  a.m. If you need access to offices during these
                  hours, contact the security office.
 [     ▲    ▲    ▲    ▲    ▲    ▲    ▲    ▲    ▲    ▲    ▲    }    ▲
security office. Guests may not enter closed sets[SRt]
unless the acting producer grants permission.[HRt]
[HRt]
[Char Style On:Headline]Security[Char Style Off:Headline]Production at the lot o
ccurs 24 hours a day.[SRt]
Although the lot is never "closed," the production[SRt]
offices are locked between 10:00 p.m. and 5:00[SRt]
a.m. If you need access to offices during these[SRt]
Courier 10cpi                              Doc 1 Pg 1 Ln 2.33" Pos 2.5"
```

If your document had several more headlines, the style you created would save you a great deal of time. It also allows you a great deal of freedom in making global changes to the layout. Rather than changing the formatting codes throughout your document, you can simply edit the style to apply the changes to all headlines.

You've seen how to create, use, and edit styles for your document, but what you've learned up to this point is only the beginning of what you can accomplish with styles. The rest of this chapter presents detailed information about all of the styles features.

Turning Off a Style

The previous example explains how to create a paired Character style. When you pressed the Enter key, this style was automatically turned off. This happened because you set the Enter Key Action option to Turn Style Off. When the Enter Key Action is not set to turn off a style, you must press Styles (Alt+F8) and choose Off while the cursor is located within the active style codes. This inserts a [Char Style Off:] code at the cursor position.

Not all styles insert a pair of codes that need to be turned off. The Open style consists of one style code—[Open Style:]—that inserts the codes stored in the style. You can't turn off an open style without deleting the [Open Style:]

code. If you want to stop the effect of the Open style after a certain point in the document, you need to insert other styles or formatting codes to change the effect of the codes stored in the Open style.

Like the Open style, the Paragraph style also inserts a single code—[Para Style:]. However, a paragraph style can be created to automatically turn off at the next [HRt code]. To do so select Enter Key Action…Off/On in the Edit Style dialog box and choose Turn Style Off in the Enter Key Action dialog box. If you want to remove a paragraph style from the current paragraph, simply highlight and select the None paragraph style from the Style List dialog box. This clears the current [Para Style:] code from the paragraph, or, in other words, turns off the style.

The Advantages of Paired Style Codes

When you create a Paragraph or Character style, you can choose the Show Style Off Codes option to divide the style between two codes: a style on code and a style off code. You used this option when you created the Character style earlier in this chapter.

When Show Style Off Codes is turned on, you'll see a comment box in the Style Contents window. Codes that you insert before the comment box become the [Para Style On:] or [Char Style On:] code. Codes that you insert after the comment box become the [Para Style Off:] or [Char Style Off:] code.

There are two reasons why you may want to show the Style Off codes. First, when this option is turned on, you can define a series of codes to the end of a style, like the [Lft Indent] code that you inserted in the earlier example. The "ending" codes will affect the text that follows the Style Off code. If you don't use the Show Style Off Codes option, WordPerfect simply resets the active or default codes at the end of the style; you can't specify what those codes will be.

Second, the Style Off codes show precisely where the paragraph or character style ends, which often simplifies editing. When you don't use the Show Style Off Codes option for Paragraph styles, you'll see only an [HRt] code where the style ends (although if you place the cursor on this code it will read [Para Style End::[HRT]).

Styles and Auto Code Placement

When Auto Code Placement is turned on, WordPerfect automatically inserts codes where they belong for the current line, paragraph, or page; left/right margin codes are automatically placed at the beginning of the current line or paragraph, header and footer codes are inserted at the top of the current page. When you work with styles, however, there is a twist to this that enables you to override the style setting for individual paragraphs without altering the style.

Here is a common example. Suppose you turn on a paragraph style that inserts a left margin change of 0.5" and then inserts other codes to format the paragraph, like this:

```
[Para Style: Section;] This is the paragraph text...
```

After you've applied the style to the paragraph, you decide to change the left margin to 1.75", but only for the current paragraph; you do so by inserting a [Lft Mar] code at the first line of the paragraph text. You don't edit the style because you want to change the margin for only the current paragraph, and you still want to apply the other codes that the style contains.

When Auto Code Placement is turned on, instead of placing the new margin code in front of the style code, WordPerfect places the [Lft Mar] code *within* the style, like this:

```
[Para Style: Section;[Lft Mar]] This is the paragraph
text...
```

Note that WordPerfect won't insert all new codes within the style—only the new codes that might conflict with the codes already stored in the style. When the Reveal Codes window is displayed, you can move the cursor over the last square bracket (]) of the style; this is where a code may be inserted when the Auto Code Placement feature is turned on.

Editing the Style List

The Style List dialog box shows the styles you've created for the current document. This dialog box includes options that let you edit the contents of styles and also the list itself. When the Style List dialog box is displayed, you can edit styles, or remove styles from the list. When you are finished editing the style list, you can save your styles to a *style library file* that you can retrieve and use with other documents.

In this section, you'll see how to "clean up" your styles list and prepare to save the style information to a separate file.

Editing Individual Styles

After you've created a style, you may need to edit the codes or other items that create the style. The following instructions expand on the style editing process described earlier in this chapter.

Choose Layout ▸ Styles.

- Press Styles (Alt+F8) to display the Style List dialog box.

- Highlight the name of the style you want to change, and then choose <u>E</u>dit. WordPerfect displays the Edit Style dialog box.

- To change the name of the selected style, choose Style <u>N</u>ame, type a new name, and press Enter. Changing the name will not invalidate the styles you've already used in the document. WordPerfect will update all style codes that contain the previous name.

- To edit the description of the style, choose <u>D</u>escription, and edit or replace the current text. Then press Enter to accept the new description.

- To change the style type, choose Style <u>T</u>ype and make the desired selection.

- Choose Style <u>C</u>ontents to activate the window in which you can edit the selected style.

- Using the pull-down menus or the function keys, choose formatting commands and features to insert codes for the style. Use the Backspace and Delete keys to remove codes and text that you do not want. You can also use Block (Alt+F4 or F12) to apply commands or edit items within the style.

Choose File ▸ Close.

- When you are finished editing the style, press Exit (F7) to close the Style Contents window.

Choose OK ▸ Close to return to the document screen.

- Press Exit (F7) until you return to the document screen.

After you edit a style, WordPerfect automatically updates the document layout with the new style codes. Any styles that have the same name as the edited style will be replaced with the new version of the style.

Deleting Styles

The Delete option on the Style List dialog box lets you remove styles from the current style list. To delete a style:

Choose Layout ▸ <u>S</u>tyles.

- Press Styles (Alt+F8) to display the Style List dialog box.

- Highlight the style you want to remove from the style list for the current document.

- Choose <u>D</u>elete, and WordPerfect displays the dialog box shown in Figure 22.7. The name of the selected style appears at the top of the dialog box.

- Choose <u>I</u>ncluding Codes to delete both the style from the list *and* the formatting codes that your document is now using from the styles. Or choose <u>L</u>eaving Codes to remove the style from the list but leave your document unchanged.

Figure 22.7

Deleting a style

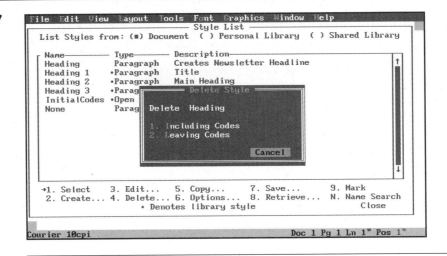

After you choose one of the deletion options, WordPerfect removes the style and redisplays the Style List dialog box. Note that the styles are deleted only from the styles list of the current document. The bullet characters indicate WordPerfect system styles. Although you can delete a style preceded by a bullet (•), the style will return the next time you use the library style file. If you want to permanently delete a system style from the list, you need to use the Save option to update the list to the current style library file. There's more information on system styles toward the end of this chapter.

NOTE. *There's only one style definition you can't delete—that's the None style, which provides a way to turn off a paragraph style.*

Saving a Style List to a Library File

The following steps explain how to save a list of styles for use with other documents. As mentioned earlier, the styles you create are initially stored in the current document file, but after you save them to a *style library file*, you can retrieve and use them with any document.

To save a style list:

Choose Layout ▶ Styles.

- Press Styles (Alt+F8) to display the Style List dialog box.

- Use the Style List dialog box to create the styles you want to save.

Choose File ▶ Save As.

- Press Save As (F10) from within the Style List dialog box, and type a name for the style library file. When you type the name, you should include an .STY file-name extension.

■ Press Enter to continue, and WordPerfect creates a style library file with the styles on your list.

You can create as many style library files as you want. After you've saved a list of styles, you can tell WordPerfect to retrieve this style list for every document that you will create. This is explained shortly under "Managing Word-Perfect's Style Libraries."

Retrieving a Style Library File

You can retrieve a list of styles you've saved and use them in a document that you're currently editing. When you retrieve a style library file, WordPerfect adds the styles from the library file to the current list of styles, but only for the current document.

Choose Layout ▸
Styles.

These are the steps for retrieving a style library file:

■ Press Styles (Alt+F8) to display the Style List dialog box.

Choose Retrieve and type the name of the style library file you want to retrieve.

■ Press Retrieve (Shift+F10), and type the name of the style library file that you want to retrieve.

■ Press Enter to accept the file name, and retrieve the style library file.

WordPerfect retrieves the style library file and combines it with the current list of styles; any duplicate style names are replaced with the styles in the retrieved file. (Be careful not to unintentionally overwrite styles this way.)

Managing WordPerfect's Style Libraries

When you display the Style List dialog box, you'll see that styles may be placed in three different categories: document style, personal library, and shared library. A *document style* is created and stored in the current document. Both *personal library* and *shared library* styles are saved in a separate file, but may be automatically retrieved and used with any document you create. The personal library file contains styles that you plan to use often; a shared library file contains styles that can be shared by WordPerfect users on a network. This section explains how to set up personal and shared library files.

You can create as many style libraries as you need—perhaps one library file for newsletters, one for business reports, and so on. After you've created a style library file, you can retrieve the file from the Style List dialog box, and apply the styles to the current document. Earlier in this chapter, you learned how to create and retrieve style library files.

The personal library and shared library files are simply the two style library files that you've designated as the libraries you want to make available for every new document. In this section, you'll learn how to set up personal and shared library files, and how to update the style library information.

Setting Up Personal and Shared Library Files

The first step to setting up a personal or shared library file is creating a style library file that contains the styles you want in the default style library. Earlier in this chapter, you learned how to create such a file. When the file is completed, you're ready to set up a personal or shared library file.

On the Style List dialog box, both the Personal Library and Shared Library options remain disabled until you tell WordPerfect which files you want to use as your personal and shared library files.

This is the next step:

Choose File ▸ Setup ▸ Location of Files.

- Press Setup (Shift+F1) and then choose Location of Files.

- Choose Style Files to display the dialog box shown in Figure 22.8. Notice there are four options on this dialog box.

Figure 22.8

Specifying a personal or shared library file

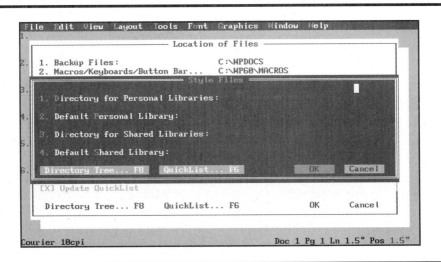

- Choose Default Personal Library and enter the directory location and file name of the style library file that contains the styles you want to use as the default personal style library. If, for example, you created a style library file called REPORTS.STY, and saved the file in the C:\WPDOCS directory, you would enter **c:\wpdocs\reports.sty** at the Default Personal Library option.

- If you're running WordPerfect on a network, choose Default Shared Library and enter the directory location and file name of the style library file that contains the styles you want to use as the default shared style library.

- The other two options, Directory for Personal Libraries and Directory for Shared Libraries, let you specify the default directories for personal and shared library files; these are the directories where WordPerfect will look when you attempt to retrieve a style library file from the Style List dialog box.

Choose OK until you return to the document screen.

- Press Exit (F7) until you return to the document screen. The next time you display the Style List dialog box, you can quickly retrieve the personal or shared library file and apply its styles to your document.

- Press Styles (Alt+F8). Then, choose Personal Library or Shared Library. WordPerfect updates the list to show the styles stored in the style file you specified under Location of Files.

This is a quick way to display and apply styles that you use often for all of your documents. Once you've specified a style file for the Personal Library or Shared Library, you can choose Document, Personal Library, or Shared Library from the Style List dialog box to display and use styles from the different style categories.

Each time you display the Styles List dialog box, the Document styles are automatically displayed; these are the styles that are saved with the current document file. Before you can select a style from the personal or shared library, you need to choose Personal Library or Shared Library to display the appropriate list. After you apply a personal or shared library style, the style is copied to the Document style list.

If you want to change the personal or shared style library file assigned to a document, you can do so from the Style Options dialog box. First, press Styles (Alt+F8) or choose Layout/Styles to display the Style List dialog box. Then choose Options and the Style Options dialog box appears. Choose Libraries Assigned to Document and then enter a different style library file for the Personal and Shared options. This overrides the default personal and shared library files specified under Location of Files, and assigns a different set of library files for the current document only.

Although you don't need to run WordPerfect on a network to use the Shared Library option, the shared library style is designed so that system administrators can specify one library style that all users of WordPerfect can access across the network.

Updating the Shared Library File

When a shared library file is specified on the Location of Files dialog box for each person running WordPerfect on a network, the system administrator can easily make changes to the styles without changing the way people work with them. Each time a network user retrieves documents, WordPerfect automatically replaces the document styles with the updated versions from the shared library file.

For example, suppose you are the system administrator for a large corporation; in the past, everyone in your organization used a shared library style called Report to create the standard financial report. If your supervisor instructs you to change the font used in the report style, you can retrieve the shared library style and edit the Report style. Then the font change will appear in all new reports that are created.

The network users do not need to know that a change has been made—they will simply create their reports as before. In addition, when previous report documents are retrieved into WordPerfect, their Report styles are also automatically replaced with the new font in the edited style.

Special Techniques with Styles

You've seen how styles let you store and apply formatting codes, but styles can do much more than create a document format. Styles can also include text, graphics, and other items that you want to repeat throughout your document. WordPerfect 6.0 introduces a few style enhancements that let you put styles within styles, and link styles together to create a chain of document formatting codes.

In this section, you'll learn special techniques that will help you use styles effectively. The following examples show general procedures that you can apply to a variety of documents.

Using Styles to Insert Text

Although most styles contain a series of document formatting codes, you can also create styles to insert passages of text that you use often. One advantage of placing text in a style is protecting text from editing changes. After you put text in a style and then select the style, the text appears in your document just like regular text. The difference is that you can't change the text without editing the style where the text is stored. When you move the cursor through your document, the cursor skips over the text from the style, which protects it from accidental editing changes.

The following exercise shows one example of a style that inserts the text to start a business letter. Try the steps to create the first part of a business letter and copy the return address text into a new style definition.

1. From a clear screen, create the first part of a business letter with your name and address, similar to the example shown in Figure 22.9. In this example, a date code (Shift+F5, Insert Date Code) is inserted to ensure that the correct date appears each time you use the style.

Figure 22.9
Creating text for a style

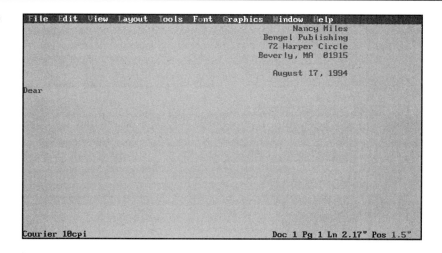

2. Using the Block (Alt+F4 or F12) feature or the mouse pointer, block all the text you want to put in the style.

Choose Edit ▸ Cut and Paste.

3. Press Move (Ctrl+F4), and then choose Cut and Paste. WordPerfect cuts the blocked text from your document.

Choose Layout ▸ Styles ▸ Create.

4. Press Styles (Alt+F8) and then choose Create.

5. When prompted to enter a style name, type **Letter** and press Enter. Choose Style Type and select Open Style.

Choose OK to continue, and then choose Style Contents.

6. Press Exit (F7) to continue and then choose Style Contents.

7. Press Enter and WordPerfect inserts the letter text into the Style Contents window. At this point, your screen will look similar to Figure 22.10.

Choose File ▸ Close and then click on OK.

8. Press Exit (F7) twice to return to the Style List dialog box. You'll see the new Letter style on the list.

Figure 22.10

Inserting the blocked text into the style definition

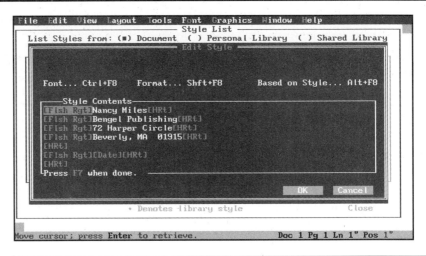

Double-click on the Letter style.

9. With the Letter style highlighted, choose <u>S</u>elect to insert the style text into the current document.

10. Now, type the text to complete the letter. If you included a salutation in the style, you can type the recipient's name, press Enter twice, and then type the text for the letter.

The address text looks the same as it did before you put it into the style, but there is a difference. Press ↑ or ↓ to move the cursor into the address text. Notice that the cursor jumps to the beginning or end of the text, but WordPerfect won't let you move the cursor to edit it. Press Reveal Codes (Alt+F3 or F11) and you'll see why this happens. As shown in Figure 22.11, your text is protected within the style code. In the Reveal Codes window, you'll see only an [Open Style:Letter] code where the return address text appears in the displayed document; move the cursor to highlight the style code, and you'll see the text stored in the style.

This is just one example of text you can place in a style. You can also put titles, headlines, quotes, and even headers and footers in a style. Once the style is created, you can select it to insert the text that the style contains.

If you want to store the file in your personal or shared style library, display the Style List dialog box, highlight the style and choose Copy. Choose <u>P</u>ersonal Library or <u>S</u>hared Library to indicate where you want to save the new style, and WordPerfect copies it to the appropriate style library file.

After you've saved the text style to one of the library files, any changes you make to that style when you edit the style from the Personal Library or Shared Library style list will be automatically updated in each document where the style is used.

Figure 22.11
Text stored in an
Open style code

Text from style ——

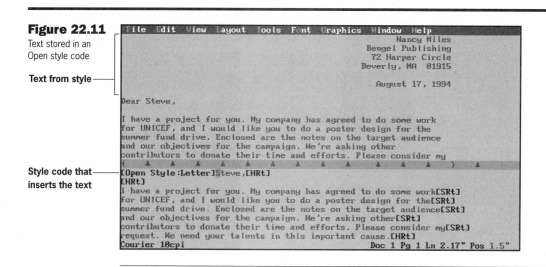

Style code that ——
inserts the text

Placing Graphics in a Style

In addition to text and formatting codes, you can insert graphics boxes into a style definition. This is useful for desktop publishing applications where you need to use the same icons, illustrations, or other graphic symbols throughout your document. Remember that a style can contain any type of graphics box, which includes equation boxes, text boxes, and so on; you aren't limited to inserting only pictures or illustrations.

In the following steps, you'll define a style that includes a graphic with the section headings shown in Figure 22.12. In this example, the style inserts the graphic symbol of a skier before the first paragraph that follows each section heading in a document.

Choose Layout ▸
Styles ▸ Create.

Choose OK to con-
tinue and select
Show Style Off
Codes.

1. From a clear screen, press Styles (Alt+F8) and then choose Create.

2. When prompted to enter a style name, type **SkiHead** and press Enter. Choose Style Type and select Character Style.

3. Press Exit (F7) to continue and choose Show Style Off Codes.

4. Choose Style Contents to activate the window where you create the codes for the style.

5. Press Font (Ctrl+F8), choose Font from the dialog box that appears, select the Swiss 721 Bold font from the font list, and change the font point size to 14. Then press Exit (F7) to close the Font dialog box.

Figure 22.12

Including a graphic within a style

A Brief History Of Skiing

Cross-Country Treks

 Once upon a time, there were nomadic tribes that decided to migrate to the North. It was summer, it seemed like a good idea. Nobody had gone North before. When they arrived, they found so much free land that they decided to build their houses really far apart. Then it snowed. A lot.

The amount of snow was so great that old Sven Olafson's roof collapsed. While fixing his roof, he slipped and plunged to the ground. He miraculously landed on two roof planks and rode them down the hill and across the meadow to cranky old Jake's general store. This was the very first recorded cross-country skiing trip. Soon after that, Sven Olafson opened the first known ski lodge.

The Sporting Thing to Do

 Initially, skiing was only a method of transportation for the villagers. However, local commerce soon depended on speedy delivery during the winter months, and some employers required a skiing-proficiency test before awarding prized positions. To hone their job skills, each village sponsored contests to see who was the fastest wood chopper, sheep shearer, cheese taster, and, of course, skier. Eventually, the people became so prosperous they began to work less, and the job skill contests became a sponsored multimedia sporting event.

The Ultimate Thrill Ride

 Today, skiing is the most popular winter sport. Nothing compares to the thrill of speeding down a slope at 60 mph, and then flying off a cliff with only your skis and 2000 feet of empty air between your fragile body and the rocky canyon floor. Experts cite this, among other perks, as the motivation for the sport. Unfortunately, it can be a little difficult to get ski training for 60mph-deep-cliff-canyon-careening. But that doesn't seem to deter the truly fanatical.

6. Move the cursor past the comment box and press Enter to insert an [HRt] code.

7. Press Graphics (Alt+F9), choose Graphics **B**oxes, and then choose **C**reate.

Choose **G**raphics ▶ Graphics **B**oxes▶ **C**reate.

8. From the Create Graphics Box dialog box, choose Filename and enter **skier1.wpg**. You may need to precede the file name with the directory where WordPerfect's sample graphic files are stored.

9. Choose Attach To and select Paragraph if it's not already selected. Choose Edit Position and choose Left. Choose Edit Size, select the Set Width option, enter **.5** as the graphics box width, and press Enter. Then, make sure the Automatic Height option is selected.

Choose OK until you return to the Edit Style dialog box.

10. Press Exit (F7) until you return to the Edit Style dialog box. At this point your screen will look like Figure 22.13.

Figure 22.13

The completed style with a graphics box

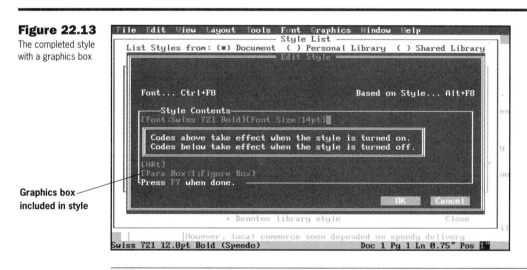

Graphics box included in style

11. Press Exit (F7) twice to return to the Style List dialog box. You'll see the new SkiHead style on the list.

Double-click on the SkiHead style.

12. With the SkiHead style highlighted, choose Select to turn it on and return to the document screen.

13. Type **Cross-Country Treks** as the first section heading. Then press → to move the cursor past the style off code. (It may help to work with the Reveral Codes window displayed.)

14. Type a paragraph of text for the first section heading. Then press Enter twice to complete it. If you wish, you can finish the document as shown earlier in Figure 22.12.

When you finish using the SkiHead style to create the section headings, press Reveal Codes (Alt+F3 or F11) or choose View/Reveal Codes. Your screen will resemble Figure 22.14. (If you're in graphics display mode or page display mode, you'll be able to see the graphic as well as the font changes.) Notice that the style creates the format for each section heading, and also inserts the graphic symbol of the skier before each paragraph that follows a heading.

Figure 22.14

Using the graphic style in a document

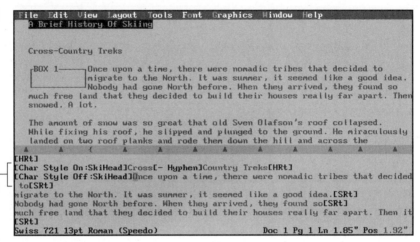

Style codes create the section heading format and the graphics box

Again, this is only one example of what you can do. You can place any graphics box (or graphic line) within a style to store and apply that graphic to different sections of your text. You can, for example, create a style that places a text box with a table of contents for your corporate reports. Create another style that includes graphics boxes for a newsletter masthead. If you prefer, create the graphics box first in your document, and use the Cut and Paste feature, as described earlier, to paste the graphics box code into a style definition. For more information about graphics boxes, see Chapter 19.

Remember that each style you create is initially saved with the current document file. If you want to use your style with other documents, you'll need to save your document style list to a separate style library file, or highlight and copy the style to the Personal Library or Shared Library.

Including Styles inside Other Styles

Unlike earlier versions of WordPerfect, version 6.0 lets you place styles inside other styles that you create. This feature is useful when you have document formatting codes, such as margin settings and font changes, that are identical in two or more of your styles. You might, for example, create an open style with specific margin settings that you want to share between several styles. Then, while creating or editing another style, you can select and insert the margin change style to include its format in the current style definition.

When you include one style inside another style, the result is called a *nested style*. Not everyone will need to do this, but it's a handy feature when you're working with complex document formats.

Consider the following example. Suppose you've defined two styles that create main headings and subheadings in your documents, and each heading style will use the same font for the heading text. To ensure that both main and subheadings are consistent, you can create a third style that specifies the font for heading text and use this style inside of each of the heading styles. Figure 22.15 shows how this would work.

Figure 22.15

An example of styles within styles

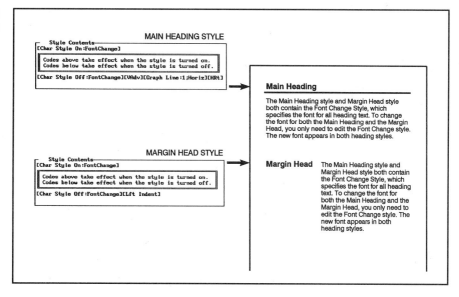

Notice the [Char Style On:FontChange] and [Char Style Off:FontChange] codes. These indicate that the FontChange Character style was turned on inside each of these styles.

When you decide to change the heading font, you simply edit the font change style, instead of editing both main and subheading styles. When you edit the codes that the FontChange style contains, the new codes are reflected in both the main and subheading heading styles.

To insert one style into another style definition, first create the style that you want to insert into other styles; let's call this Style A. Then, create or edit another style that should include the Style A format and other formatting codes; we'll call this Style B. While using the Style Contents window to create the format for Style B, you can press Styles (Alt+F8) or choose Layout/Styles, and then select Style A to insert its format into the current style definition. Then, complete and save the definition for Style B. That's all you need to do. Any changes made to Style A will affect the format of Style B and other styles that include the Style A codes.

Linking One Style to Another

In the previous section you saw how to include a style within another style definition. Another way to combine different style formats is by *linking* styles together. This can be useful when you want to turn other styles on immediately after you've turned off a specific style.

For example, suppose you've created two styles: one called Masthead that creates the masthead for your newsletter, and another style called News-Columns that sets up the format for column text. You can link the NewsColumns style to the Masthead style. Then, at the end of the newsletter masthead style, the link would tell WordPerfect to turn on the NewsColumns style to create the column format. Use the style link option when you have two or more styles that should follow each other.

Follow this procedure to link a style to another style. When you are creating or editing a style definition, choose Enter Key Action from the Edit Style dialog box. This displays a menu with four choices: Insert a Hard Return, Turn Style Off, Turn Style Off and Back On, or Turn Style Off and Link to. Choose Turn Style Off and Link to, and WordPerfect displays a list of styles like the example shown in Figure 22.16.

This list displays the styles you've defined for the current document. An asterisk appears next to the name of the style you're now creating, which means that no other style is now linked to the current style. Highlight the style you want to link to the current style, and then press Enter. Then, press Exit (F7) or choose OK to return to the Edit Style dialog box. This links the highlighted style to the current style. When you turn on the current style in your document, the linked style is automatically turned on at the end of the current style.

When you use the Style Link feature, you can only link styles of the same style type. This means that you can link a Paragraph style to another Paragraph style, but not to a Character style. A Character style can be linked to another Character style, but not to a Paragraph style. You cannot link Open styles because they do not insert an off code that indicates where the style ends.

Figure 22.16

Linking a style to the current style definition

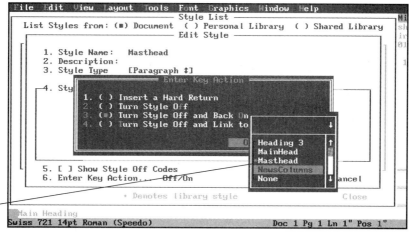

Styles you can link to the current style

Using the WordPerfect System Styles

In addition to the styles you create and the styles from the library files, Word-Perfect has its own internal styles that it uses to create the formats for common document elements. These are called *system styles,* because they create the default formats for many features within the WordPerfect system. In this section, you'll learn more about the system styles. You'll also see how to change the default formats that each system style creates.

What Are System Styles?

In each document and style library file, there are two different style lists that you can display: the user-defined styles and the system styles. You've already seen the user-defined style list, which includes the styles you've created for use in your documents. The system style list includes the internal styles that WordPerfect uses to create certain document elements.

As mentioned earlier, a system style creates a default format for one of WordPerfect's features. In some cases, you may not be aware that WordPerfect inserts system styles; they are automatically inserted when you choose a feature that depends on system styles to create its format.

For example, when you create an outline, WordPerfect employs a set of system styles to format each outline level. System styles also create the appearance of footnotes and endnotes—for both the reference numbers in your document text and also the note text. Another example is the Initial Codes style, which is automatically inserted at the beginning of every new document you create.

Table 22.1 shows a complete list of WordPerfect's system styles; you'll discover these styles in your documents when you create headers and footers, graphic boxes, tables of contents, and other document elements that make use of the system styles.

Table 22.1   WordPerfect System Styles

System Style	Purpose
BoxText	Determines the initial format for text placed in a graphic box.
Caption	Determines the standard appearance and format of caption text for all graphics boxes.
Comment	Determines the appearance and format of text placed in a document comment.
Endn#inDoc	Creates the appearance of endnote reference numbers in document text.
Endnote	Creates the appearance of the endnote numbers in the endnote text.
EquationNum	Creates the appearance of the numbers assigned to equation boxes in your document.
FigureNum	Creates the appearance of the numbers assigned to equation boxes in your document.
FooterA FooterB	Determines the appearance and format of text placed in a footer. Note that each footer (A and B) has its own style.
Footnote	Creates the appearance of the footnote numbers in the endnote text.
Ftn#inDoc	Creates the appearance of footnote reference numbers in document text.
HeaderA HeaderB	Determines the appearance and format of text placed in a header. Note that each header (A and B) has its own style.
Heading 1 Heading 2 Heading 3 . . . Heading 8	Create the Heading outline style. Remember, an outline style actually consists of up to eight individual styles—one style for one level in the outline. Heading 1 creates the format for level one in the outline, Heading 2 creates the format for level two, and so on.
Hypertext	Creates the appearance of text that is defined as a hypertext link.

Table 22.1   WordPerfect System Styles (Continued)

System Style	Purpose
Index1 Index2	Determines the format for items generated by the Index feature. Note that there are two styles: Index1 creates the format for level one index entries, and Index2 creates the format for level two index entries.
InitialCodes	Defines the initial codes that will appear at the beginning of every document you create in WordPerfect. You can edit this style to create temporary initial codes or choose Initial Codes Setup from the Document Format dialog box. Both permanently change the codes stored in this style.
Legal 1 Legal 2 Legal 3 . . . Legal 8	Create the Legal outline style. See *Heading 1* above for more details.
Level 1 Level 2 Level 3 . . . Level 8	Create the Level outline style. See *Heading 1* above for more details.
List	Determines the format for items generated by the List feature.
None	Includes the codes, if any, that indicate a style is turned off. This style should apply to all cases where a character or paragraph style may be turned off.
TableofAuth	Determine the format for items generated by the Table of Authorities feature.
TableofCont1 TableofCont2 TableofCont3 TableofCont4 TableofCont5	Determine the format for items generated by the Table of Contents feature. Note that there are five styles; each style creates the format for a level of table of contents entries.
TblBoxNum	Creates the appearance of the numbers assigned to table boxes (graphics boxes, not WordPerfect tables) in your document.
TextBoxNum	Creates the appearance of the numbers assigned to text boxes in your document.
UserBoxNum	Creates the appearance of the numbers assigned to user boxes in your document.
WatermarkA WatermarkB	Determine the appearance and format of document watermarks. Note that each watermark (A and B) has its own style.

Modifying a System Style

Sometimes, you may want to change the format that a system style creates. For example, you may want all footnote numbers to appear as bold text, rather than superscripted text, or you may want graphics box captions printed in blue, instead of the standard text color.

Some of the dialog boxes provide options that let you edit the format of a system style inserted by WordPerfect, but this affects only the current document. When you create a footnote, for example, you'll see options that let you edit the style of footnote numbers. Other features, like document comments and graphics box caption numbers, insert system styles but do not provide a style edit option. For these and other system styles, you can use the Style List dialog box to change the formats to suit your preferences.

Here is a practical example of a system style that you may want to edit. When you create a figure box caption, WordPerfect automatically inserts the [FigureNum] system style to create the "Figure n" text in the caption (n represents the number of the current graphics box). You may not want *Figure* inserted with the number, or you may want it formatted differently. In the following exercise, you'll learn how to edit the system style that creates the caption number text for figure box captions:

Choose Layout ▸ Styles.

1. Press Styles (Alt+F8) to display the Style List dialog box.

2. Choose Personal Library, if the styles you use are stored in a personal library file. Or choose Shared Library if the styles you use are stored in a shared library file.

3. Choose Options to display the Style Options dialog box. Choose List User Created Styles, so that an X does not appear next to this option. This will turn off the display of the user-defined styles and turn on the option for List System Styles.

Choose OK to close the Style Options dialog box.

4. Press Exit (F7) to close the Style Options dialog box and return to the Style List dialog box. WordPerfect updates the style list to show only the internal system styles.

5. Choose Name Search and type **FigureNum** to highlight the FigureNum system style. Press Enter to turn off the Name Search feature.

6. Choose Edit to view the codes for this style in the Edit Style dialog box. Choose Style Contents to activate the Style Contents window editor.

7. Delete the [Bold On] code to turn off the bold attribute in the text. Then move the cursor just past the [Box Num Disp] code, type a colon, and then type a space.

8. Press Exit (F7) to exit the Style Contents window. Then press Exit (F7) again to return to the Style List dialog box.

9. Press Exit (F7) to close the Style List dialog box, and update your library file with the edited system style.

Now, when you create a figure box and choose the Create Caption option, you'll see "Figure 1: " as the standard figure box number (with a colon and a space) instead of "**Figure 1**". This is one example of how you can change the default format for an item created with a WordPerfect system style. You can use the method described in the preceding steps to edit any of the system styles and change the standard formats they create.

Choosing Personal Library or Shared Library in step 2 is important, because this determines which set of system styles you'll edit; remember, each library file contains a set of user-defined styles and system styles. When you exit the Style List dialog box, the edited styles are automatically updated to the library file you've selected.

23

Documents That Speak

Adding Sound Clips to Your Document

Recording Your Own Sound Clips

WORD PROCESSING HAS CERTAINLY COME A LONG WAY. THERE WAS a time when the words you typed had to get the whole message across, but not anymore. WordPerfect has long supported the ability to use different fonts, insert graphics, and create tables. Now WordPerfect is wired for sound.

If you have the appropriate sound hardware—a computer sound board and speakers—you can retrieve prerecorded *sound clips* into your WordPerfect document and play them when the document is displayed on the screen. You can also record your voice to add notations and comments to passages of text. You can dictate instructions to your assistant, record music for your clients, or include a friendly "hello" to your relatives in the next state.

This chapter explains how to retrieve a prerecorded sound clip and play it from within your WordPerfect document. You'll also learn how to record your own clips and save them to individual sound files.

Adding Sound Clips to Your Document

Before you add sound clips to your documents, you need to tell WordPerfect which sound hardware you are using. Then you can retrieve and play a sound file stored on disk. You can use the prerecorded sound clips included with WordPerfect, or you can retrieve sound files created in other software, like the Microsoft Windows Sound Recorder or Creative Labs's Soundblaster Voice Editor.

WordPerfect supports two different sound file formats: digital sound files, such as .WAV and .VOC files, and Musical Instrument Digital Interface files—MIDI files (.MID). Digital sound files store digitally recorded voice, music, or sound effects files. The MIDI file format includes instructions that produce musical songs with various instruments or *voices*. The MIDI file is the common format for creating and storing music produced on synthesizers and other computerized instruments.

Setting Up Your Computer for Sound

Before you can add sound to your documents, you must install your sound hardware for use with your computer. The users manual that came with your sound board or sound device will explain how to do this. Pay close attention to the installation procedure; if the sound board installation software recommends that you change the *Interrupt Request Level (IRQ)* or the *Base Address (Hex)* settings, write down the changes you made; you may need this information when you set up WordPerfect's sound capabilities.

After you finish installing the sound board or sound device, you need to tell WordPerfect which sound hardware you are using. When you installed the WordPerfect program, you were prompted for input about installing sound drivers for your sound board. The installation program then copied the software driver files that WordPerfect needs to work with your sound hardware. If you did not select a sound driver when you installed WordPerfect, run the installation program again to choose a sound driver and copy the driver files.

After the appropriate sound drivers are installed, start WordPerfect and follow these steps to complete the set up for sound:

Choose Tools ▸
Sound Clip ▸ Sound
Setup.

1. Press Notes (Ctrl+F7), choose Sound Clip, and then press Setup (Shift+F1). WordPerfect displays the Sound Setup dialog box, shown in Figure 23.1.

Figure 23.1
The Sound Setup
dialog box

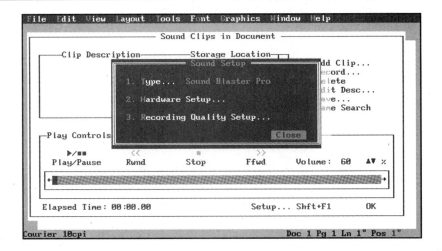

2. Choose Type and highlight the name of the sound board or sound device that is connected to your computer. Then choose Select.

3. If you have installed your sound board or device with Base Address or IRQ settings which are different than the standard factory settings, choose Hardware Setup and make the changes that apply to your installation.

Choose OK until
you return to the
document screen.

4. Press Exit (F7) until you return to the document screen.

These steps tell WordPerfect which sound board or sound device you are using. The Hardware Setup option is provided for custom hardware installations, where the Interrupt Request Level (IRQ) or Base Address settings differ from those recommended by the manufacturer of your sound hardware. If you installed your sound board or sound device with the standard factory settings, you do not need to perform step 3 above.

Once the steps are complete, you're ready to retrieve and play audio information. If you plan to record your own sound clips, you'll want to connect a microphone to your sound device. For some sound hardware, it is also possible to connect a direct line to your stereo equipment to record music from your CD or cassette player. Consult the manual that came with your sound board or sound device for information about connecting a microphone or a direct line for recording.

Retrieving a Sound Clip File

WordPerfect includes a library of sound clips that you can retrieve and play in your documents. Later in this chapter, you'll see how to record your own sound clips. When you retrieve a sound file, it is attached to the document that is currently displayed on your screen, and a special comment box, called a *sound clip box*, is shown in your text.

Follow these steps to retrieve a sound clip into your document:

1. Move the cursor to the place in your document where the sound clip box should appear.

Choose Tools ▸
Sound Clip ▸ Add.

2. Press Notes (Ctrl+F7), choose Sound Clip, and then choose Add Clip. The Add Sound Clip to Document dialog box, shown in Figure 23.2, is displayed.

Figure 23.2
Retrieving a sound clip

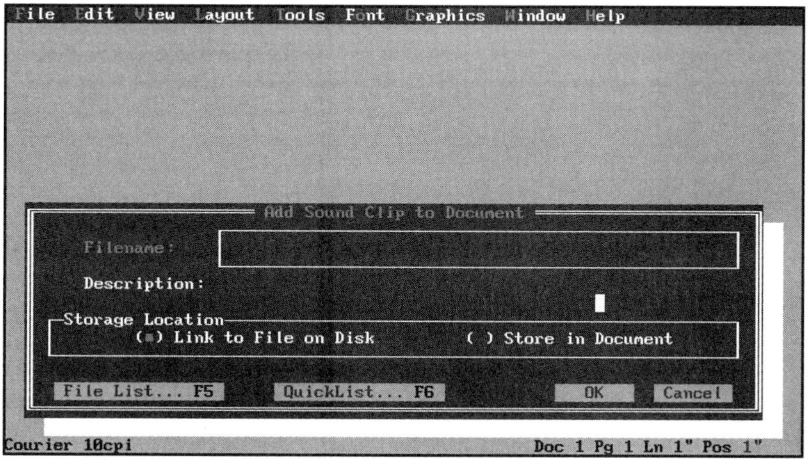

3. In the "Filename" box, type the name of the sound file you want to retrieve and press Enter, or press List Files (F5) and choose from a list of files. (Note that the .MID files that WordPerfect provides are located in the WP60\GRAPHICS directory.)

4. Choose Description, type a descriptive name for the sound clip, and then press Enter.

5. To retrieve the sound file information into the current document, choose Store in Document. Or, to create a link to the sound file, choose Link to File on Disk.

6. Press Exit (F7) to exit the Add Sound Clip to Document dialog box. The retrieved sound clip appears in a Sound comment box, shown in Figure 23.3, within your document.

Choose OK to return to your document.

Figure 23.3
The Sound comment box

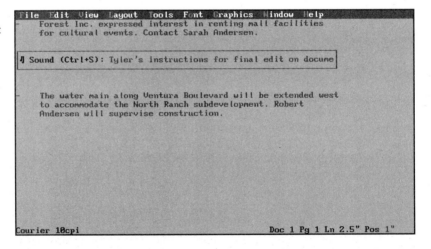

When you add a sound clip to your document, you have two choices on the Add Sound Clip dialog box, under "Storage Location." The first option, Link to File on Disk, doesn't actually retrieve a sound clip file. Instead, it creates a link between your WordPerfect document and your sound clip file; this is the default storage setting for sound clips. When you play the sound clip, WordPerfect accesses the sound information directly from the file on disk, which makes it possible to include sound without greatly increasing the size of your document. When you choose this option, remember to keep the linked document and sound files together in the same directory.

The second storage option, Store in Document, actually retrieves the sound file information into your WordPerfect document. You'll need to use this option, for example, if you want to send your WordPerfect file, complete with sound clips, on disk to someone else. When you choose this option, remember that sound files can be quite large and that you may not want to copy them into your document. Thirty seconds of audio recorded at 11 kHz (good quality) will add approximately 110K to a document. The same sound clip, recorded at 22 kHz (better quality) will add about 220K to the document.

Playing All Sound Clips in Your Document

The Sound Clips in Document dialog box, shown in Figure 23.4, lets you view and play all the sound clips attached to your document. This dialog box also lets you add more sound clips, edit existing clips, and record new sound.

Figure 23.4

The Sound Clips in Document dialog box

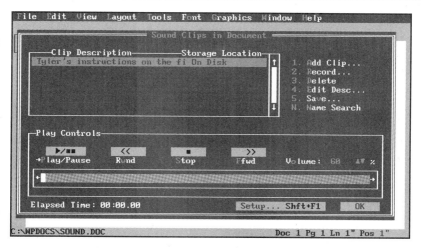

Once you have retrieved one or more sound files into your document, follow these steps to play the sound clips from the Sound Clips in Document dialog box.

Choose Tools ▶ Sound Clip ▶ Play.

- Press Notes (Ctrl+F7) and choose Sound Clip. This displays the dialog box that lists the sound clips attached to the current document.

- From the Sound Clip list, highlight the clip you want to play.

- Choose Play/Pause to listen to the sound clip.

Choose OK to return to your document.

- When the clip is finished, press Exit (F7) until you return to your document.

The meter at the bottom of the dialog box indicates the length of the clip as it is playing. Choose P̲lay/Pause to pause a clip that is playing; choose P̲lay/Pause again to resume playing it. If the sound is too low, choose the V̲olume option to increase the volume of the sound. When the clip is finished playing, you'll see the length of the sound in the Elapsed Time box.

TIP. *If you are playing a MIDI file and it doesn't sound as it should, check the box for MT32 MIDI File. This option allows correct presentation of MIDI files that were created with older versions of MIDI sequencing software.*

Playing Sound Clips while Viewing Your Document

With sound clips in your WordPerfect document, you can display a dialog box that lets you play the clips as you edit or scroll through the document text. These steps explain how to display and use the Listen and Type dialog box.

- After you've inserted one or more sound clips into your document, return to the document screen and move the cursor before the first sound clip comment box.

- Press Ctrl+S to display the Listen and Type dialog box, shown in Figure 23.5. This dialog box includes the same play options that are found on the Sound Clips in Document dialog box.

Figure 23.5

Playing sound clips while viewing your document

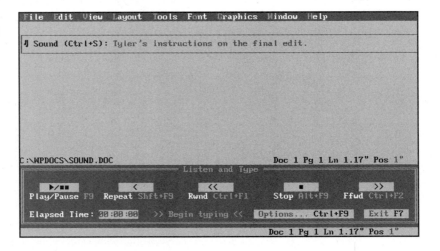

Choose Play/Pause to listen to the sound clip.

- Press Play/Pause (F9) to listen to the sound clip.

- If you have two or more sound clips attached to the current document, press Play/Pause (F9) to play the next clip. Or press Repeat (Shift+F9) to repeat the most recently played clip.

- Press Exit (F7) to close the Listen and Type dialog box.

Choose Exit to close the Listen and Type dialog box.

When the dialog box is displayed, you can type new text or edit existing text. Scroll through the text to move the cursor past each sound clip box; then press Play/Pause (F9) to listen to the corresponding sound clip. Press Options (Ctrl+F9) to return to the Sound Clips in Document dialog box, and retrieve or record additional sound clips.

Editing a Sound Clip Description

After you retrieve sound clips for your document, you may need to edit the descriptions that appear on the list in the Sound Clips in Document dialog box. At the document editing screen, these descriptions also appear in the sound clip comment boxes. To edit a sound clip description:

- Press Notes (Ctrl+F7) and choose Sound Clip.

Choose Tools ▸ Sound Clip ▸ Play.

- Highlight the clip description you want to edit.

- Choose Edit Desc to display the dialog box shown in Figure 23.6.

Figure 23.6
Editing a sound clip description

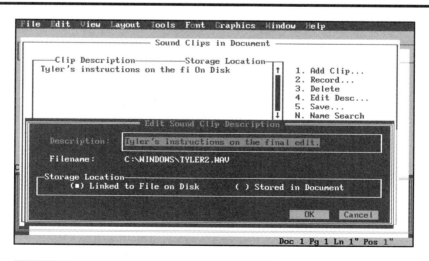

Choose OK until you return to the document screen.

- Type the new description for the sound clip, and press Enter.

- Press Exit (F7) until you return to the document screen.

The new description appears on the list of sound clips you can play and also on the sound clip comment box shown in your document. You can type well over 100 characters for a sound clip description; however, the Sound Clip list displays only the first 30 to 45 characters of the description you type, depending on whether you're in the Sound Clips in Document dialog box or the document itself.

Removing a Sound Clip

You can remove a sound clip from your document in two ways: You can delete the [Sound] code from the Reveal Codes window, or you can delete the clip entry from the list on the Sound Clips in Document dialog box.

To delete a Sound Clip code:

Choose View ▸
Reveal Codes.

- Display the Reveal Codes window (press Alt+F3 or F11).

- Highlight the [Sound] code that represents the sound clip you want to delete.

- Press Delete to remove the code.

WordPerfect removes the code and the sound clip box from your document; when you next display the Sound Clips in Document dialog box, you'll notice that the clip is also removed from the Sound Clip list. This is the easiest way to delete a sound clip.

When you are working from the Sound Clips in Document dialog box, you can delete a sound clip using one of the menu items:

- In the Sound Clip list, highlight the sound clip that you want to delete.

- Choose Delete to remove the sound clip.

When you delete a sound clip that is linked to a file on disk, you delete only the link in your WordPerfect document; the sound file remains on disk. However, if you delete a sound clip which is copied into your document, the sound information is deleted and cannot be recovered unless you have also saved it as a separate sound file.

Recording Your Own Sound Clips

Although WordPerfect includes a library of prerecorded sound clips, you'll probably want to record your own music, sound effects, or your voice to create audio comments or dictation notes in your document. First, you'll need to plug a microphone into your sound board or sound device. Then you're ready to begin.

Recording a Sound Clip

Choose Tools ▶
Sound Clip ▶
Record.

Follow these steps to record a sound clip for your document:

- Press Notes (Ctrl+F7) and choose Sound Clip. Then choose Record. The Record Sound Clip dialog box appears, as shown in Figure 23.7.

Figure 23.7
The Record Sound
Clip dialog box

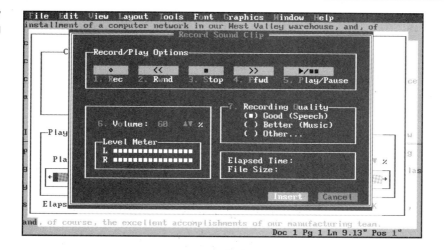

- Choose Recording Quality, and specify whether you want Good quality, Better quality, or Other. If you choose Other, you are prompted to choose specific record settings.

- Choose Rec to begin recording from the microphone or from the line connected to your stereo.

- When you are finished recording, choose Stop. Then choose Play/Pause to preview the sound clip.

- If you want to discard the recording, choose Rec to record over the previous sound clip, or simply choose Cancel.

- Press Exit (F7) to accept the recorded clip and return to the Sound Clips in Document dialog box.

Choose Insert to accept the recorded clip.

WordPerfect adds your recording to the Sound Clips in Document dialog box and assigns it a generic description of "Clip #*n*," where *n* represents the number of the clip. To assign a descriptive name to the sound clip, choose Edit Desc and type a name for the recording. When you return to the document screen, you'll see that WordPerfect has inserted a [Sound] code into your text and a sound clip comment box on the document screen.

WordPerfect does not limit the number of recordings you can create for your document, but you must have enough disk space to store the recorded information.

TIP. *For longer recordings, choose the Good (Speech) recording quality. This option requires the least disk space to store recorded information.*

Saving a Recorded Clip

When you record a sound clip, the audio information is automatically included with your WordPerfect document file. Depending on the length of the sound clip, you may prefer to save the audio information as a separate sound file and then retrieve it using the Link to File on Disk option.

When you link the sound file instead, you'll save about 110K of space for each ten seconds of audio in your sound clip. Saving recorded audio to a file also lets you use the sound clip with other documents that you create.

These steps explain how to record and save a clip to a separate sound file:

Choose Tools ▸
Sound Clip ▸
Record.

- Press Notes (Ctrl+F7) and choose Sound Clip. Then choose Record.

- Choose Rec to begin recording from the microphone or from the line connected to your stereo.

- When you are finished recording, choose Stop.

- Choose Play/Pause to preview the sound clip before you save it.

- If you want to replace the recording, choose Rec to record over the previous sound clip.

Choose OK to return to the Sound Clips in Document dialog box.

- Press Exit (F7) to return to the Sound Clips in Document dialog box.

- Choose Save, type up to eight characters for the file name, and type **.WAV** as the file name extension. Then press Enter.

Choose OK until you return to your document.

- Press Exit (F7) until you return to your document.

WordPerfect saves your recorded clip to the file name you specified. You typed the .WAV extension to indicate that the file is saved as a sound wave file; this is the file format that WordPerfect uses to record audio information. You can now retrieve this file into other WordPerfect documents and into other software—such as Microsoft Windows—that accepts this sound file format.

Defining Recording Quality Options

The Recording Quality setting affects the clarity of the sound clip when you play it. When you record a sound clip, you can choose the predefined settings for Good (Speech) or Better (Music), or you can choose Other to define a custom setting, as described here:

- From the Record Sound Clip dialog box, choose Recording Quality.

- Choose Other to display the dialog box shown in Figure 23.8.

Figure 23.8
Defining custom recording settings

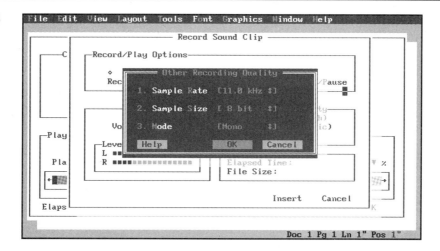

- Choose Sample Rate and select the kilohertz (kHz) setting you want to use. A higher kHz setting produces better recording qualities.

- Choose Sample Size and select 8 Bit or 16 Bit. The standard setting is 8 Bit; the 16 Bit setting enhances the sound by doubling the amount of file space allocated for the recording.

- Choose Mode and select Mono or Stereo.

- Press Exit (F7) to return to the Record Sound Clip dialog box.

Choose OK to return to the Record Sound Clip dialog box.

- Record your sound clip, as described earlier in this chapter.

The Recording Quality settings affect only the sound clips that you will record; they do not change the sound quality of clips you have already recorded or retrieved.

These settings also affect the size of the recorded sound clip. As mentioned earlier, sound clips recorded with the G̲ood (Speech) quality require about 110K for each ten seconds of recorded audio, and clips recorded with the B̲etter (Music) quality require about 220K for each ten seconds.

Table 23.1 shows the file sizes for all possible quality settings. The lower numbers indicate a low-quality recording; the higher numbers indicate high-quality recording. Notice that the file size increases with the greater recording qualities. If, for example, you record a stereo sound clip with a sample rate of 32 kHz and an 8-bit sample size, the disk space required to store the sound clip will be 640K.

Table 23.1   Recording Quality Settings

File Size: 10-Second Sound Clip

Sample Rate

	5.5 kHz	7.3 kHz	8.0 kHz	11.0 kHz	16.0 kHz	22.0 kHz	32.0 kHz	44.1 kHz
MONO								
8-bit	56K	74K	80K	110K	160K	220K	320K	450K
16-bit	112K	148K	160K	220K	320K	440K	640K	900K
STEREO								
8-bit	112K	148K	160K	220K	320K	440K	640K	900K
16-bit	224K	296K	320K	440K	640K	880K	1.28MB	1.80MB

You can also change the recording quality settings assigned to the G̲ood (Speech) and B̲etter (Music) options from the Recording Quality Setup dialog box, shown in Figure 23.9. Again, these settings affect only the sound clips that you will record; they do not change the sound quality of clips you have already recorded or retrieved.

Choose Setup from the Sound Clips dialog box.

■ From the Sound Clips in Document dialog box, press Setup (Shift+F1).

■ Choose R̲ecording Quality Setup.

■ From the Setup Recording Quality dialog box, choose Sample R̲ate, Sample S̲ize, and M̲ode to change the default recording quality settings for good quality and better quality.

Choose OK to return to the Sound Clips in document dialog box.

■ Press Exit (F7) twice to return to the Sound Clips in Document dialog box.

Figure 23.9

Changing the recording qualities of the Good (Speech) and Better (Music) options

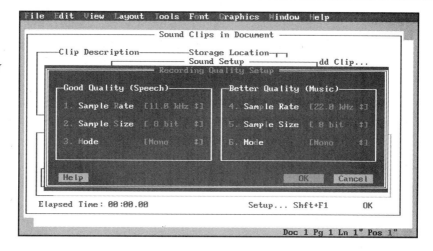

Now, when you choose Good or Better at the Record Sound Clip dialog box, these options will record your sound clip with the sample rate, sample size, and mode that you specified. The changes made at the Recording Quality Setup dialog box remain the standard recording settings in WordPerfect until you change them again.

Creating and Editing Macros

Using WordPerfect's Keyboard Feature

6

Macros and Keyboards

24

Creating and Editing Macros

Recording and Playing Back Macros

Repeating a Macro

Editing Your Macros

A MACRO IS A SERIES OF RECORDED COMMANDS AND/OR TEXT THAT YOU can play back to perform a certain task. In many ways, macros let you customize the WordPerfect software according to your preferences. You can define a macro that re-creates your standard memo document, begins a merge application, or reformats a list of text according to your specifications. Any sequence of WordPerfect commands may be stored in a macro, which makes them extremely flexible. You'll find that macros are best suited to repetitive tasks that should be performed exactly the same way each time you play back the macro. WordPerfect also comes equipped with a series of prerecorded macros, which are stored in the C:\WP60\MACROS directory. In addition, you can place a number of already created macros at your fingertips by turning on the MACROS keyboard layout, as described in the next chapter.

In this chapter, you'll learn how to use WordPerfect's macro features. You'll create a simple macro that inserts your name and address in a letter. Then you'll use the Macro Editor to alter the effect of the macro.

Recording and Playing Back Macros

Suppose you type several letters each week, and each one includes your return address. You've probably typed your address so often that it's become second nature. But this type of task—a procedure that you regularly perform identically—is the perfect task for a macro.

Instead of typing your return address for each letter, you can *record* the task in a macro. Then each time you need to insert your return address, you can play back the macro with a single keystroke or, at the very most, by making a few menu selections. The result is the same as if you'd typed your return address, except you've inserted it instantly. Also, the macro prevents errors from creeping into your address, assuming, of course, that you type the macro correctly.

Before you create a macro, you should use WordPerfect to "practice" the task you want the macro to perform. For example, suppose you want to create a macro that sets up a complex newsletter document. Before you actually record the macro, create the newsletter layout a few times so you know exactly what to do during the recording process. Then record the macro.

When you create a macro, every keystroke and menu selection is recorded, and will be repeated each time you play back your macro; if you aren't sure which features you need to select to accomplish the task, your macro will also include the keystroke commands and menu selections you used to undo mistakes made during the recording process.

This is the general procedure for creating a macro:

Choose <u>T</u>ools ▸
<u>M</u>acro ▸ <u>R</u>ecord.

■ Press Record Macro (Ctrl+F10), and WordPerfect prompts you to enter a name for the macro.

- Type a name of up to eight characters, or press the Alt key and a letter key from the keyboard—Alt+A, for example. This becomes the name or keystroke assignment for the macro, and also determines how you'll play back the macro later.

WARNING. *You generally should not use the underlined letters in the menu bar (the F in File, the E in Edit, and so forth) as keystroke assignments for your macros. If you do, you won't be able to use these keys to access the menu bar. In addition, if you've selected the MACROS keyboard layout, a number of the letter keys will not be available.*

Choose OK to accept the macro name and continue.

- After you assign a name or press an Alt+*letter* keystroke, press Exit (F7) or Enter to continue. WordPerfect displays a "Recording Macro" message at the bottom of the screen.

- Use WordPerfect's features to perform the task you want the macro to record. Remember that as long as the "Recording Macro" message appears, WordPerfect is recording the text you type and every keystroke and menu selection you choose.

- When you are finished with the task, press Record Macro (Ctrl+F10) again to stop the recording process.

The recorded commands are stored in a file with a .WPM file name extension. When you assign a name from one to eight characters to your macro, you can play it back by pressing Play Macro (Alt+F10) and entering the name. When you assign an Alt+*letter* keystroke to your macro, you can play it back by simply pressing that keystroke. The following section offers a step-by-step example for creating and playing back a macro.

Recording a Simple Macro

Try the following steps to create a macro that types your return address for a business letter; this is the macro you would create for the example described earlier in this chapter:

Choose Tools ▸ Macro ▸ Record.

1. From a clear document screen, press Record Macro (Ctrl+F10), and WordPerfect displays the Record Macro dialog box, shown in Figure 24.1.

Press Alt+A and then choose OK.

2. Press Alt+A to assign this keystroke to the macro. Then press Enter. WordPerfect displays the "Recording Macro" message on the status line. Now you can perform the task that you want the macro to record; in this case, you will type your return address at the right edge of the page.

Choose Layout ▸ Alignment ▸ Flush Right.

3. Press Flush Right (Alt+F6) to move the cursor to the right margin on the page.

Figure 24.1

The Record Macro
dialog box

```
 File  Edit  View  Layout  Tools  Font  Graphics  Window  Help



                    ══════════ Record Macro ══════════
            Macro: [                                           ↵]

            [ ] Edit Macro

            ║ File List... F5 ║  ║ QuickList... F6 ║      ║ OK ║  ║ Cancel ║




                                         Doc 1 Pg 1 Ln 1" Pos 1"
```

**Type the macro
name here**

4. Type your name, and then press Enter.

5. Press Flush Right (Alt+F6), type your street address, and then press Enter.

6. Press Flush Right (Alt+F6), type your city, state, and ZIP code. Then press Enter twice. Your return address information should be complete.

7. Press Record Macro (Ctrl+F10) again to stop recording.

The recorded commands are now saved in a macro file called ALTA.WPM. Since you named your macro with an Alt+*letter* keystroke, you can play it back by pressing Alt+A. WordPerfect then types your return address and performs the commands you selected while recording the macro.

This exercise assumes that your return address should be aligned at the right margin. If you prefer a different format, substitute the alignment you need for the Flush Right command.

This is only one example of what you can record with a macro. Any task you perform with WordPerfect can be stored in a macro. You can record the menu selections that create a complex document layout or combine a series of tasks—such as printing, saving, and clearing your document—into a single macro.

Keep in mind that macros differ from styles in one very important respect: When you execute a macro, any text or formatting you enter into your document is fixed. That is, if you want to edit it, you must make the changes manually. In contrast, when you use a style, you can make global changes to all instances of the style by editing the style itself, rather than the individual documents you may have created using the style. See Chapter 22 for details on styles.

Playing Back a Macro

If you reviewed the previous section, you've seen how to create and play back a simple macro. The method for playing back a macro depends on the name you assign to it. When you assign an Alt+*letter* keystroke to your macro, you can play back the macro by pressing that keystroke again at the document screen. This is the quickest and most convenient way to play back a macro. Use the Alt+*letter* naming option for macros that you will use often, and try to assign a letter that gives a clue about the task you're recording in the macro. For example, assign Alt+M for a macro that creates a memo or Alt+P for a macro that prints your document and clears the screen.

As an alternative to the Alt+*letter* naming option, you can assign a descriptive name to your macro. This is done in the Record Macro dialog box, immediately after you press Record Macro (Ctrl+F10) to start the recording process. The descriptive name you type must be eight characters or less. Use this naming option when you've used all the available Alt+*letter* keystroke assignments or for macros that you won't use every day; the descriptive name will make it easier for you to remember the task that the macro performs.

After you finish the recording process, your macro will be saved in a file with the name you typed. For example, if you enter PROPOSAL as the name for your macro, the recorded commands will be saved in a file called PROPOSAL.WPM in the \WP60\MACROS directory. The .WPM extension, which is added automatically, indicates a WordPerfect macro file.

The process for playing back a named macro is different than it is for Alt+*letter* macros. To play back a named macro:

Choose <u>T</u>ools ▸ <u>M</u>acro ▸ <u>P</u>lay.

1. Press Play Macro (Alt+F10) to display the Play Macro dialog box, shown in Figure 24.2.

2. Type the name of the macro you want to play back, or choose File List (F5) or Quick List (F6) to select a macro from a list of files.

Choose OK to play the macro.

3. After you've specified the name of the macro you want to play back, press Enter to accept the name and play the macro.

WordPerfect performs the task or tasks recorded in the macro. Both named macros and Alt+*letter* macros can perform the same types of tasks; the only difference is in the naming methods and how each is played back.

Accounting for Special Conditions

Before you record and play back macros, consider where the cursor should be located before the recorded task is performed. For example, a macro that inserts your return address requires the cursor to be at the top of the current document screen. Other macros, such as one that inserts a closing statement for a letter or contract, may presume the cursor to be at the bottom of a document.

Figure 24.2
The Play Macro
dialog box

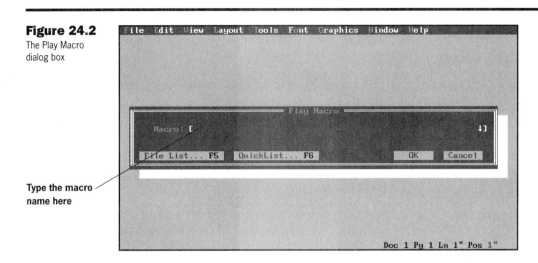

Type the macro
name here

If your macro requires a specific cursor position, a clear screen, or some other condition before the task is performed, consider including commands in your macro to set up that condition. During the recording process, you can use the cursor movement keystrokes and other features to prepare the current document for the task the macro performs.

For example, you could press Home, Home, ↑ as the first command; when the macro is played back, the cursor will move to the top of the current document before the other recorded commands are performed. If the cursor should be located at the bottom of the document, press Home, Home, ↓ during recording, instead. You can also clear the screen, choose fonts, set margins, or search for a specific word or phrase to create the situation or condition under which the recorded task should be performed.

When you record such commands, carefully consider whether the commands you choose will apply to all documents for which the macro is designed. During the recording process, it helps to create the same situation in the document screen that will be present when you will play back the macro. If, for example, you want to record a macro to delete extra hard returns that follow bold titles, you should have a document on the screen that includes these titles when you record your macro.

Repeating a Macro

WordPerfect's Repeat feature lets you repeat any keystroke, according to a number that you specify. This feature also lets you repeat any macro. Suppose you've created a macro that inserts a bullet character for a list entry. If you know the total entries you need for the list, you can tell WordPerfect to repeat the macro a specific number of times, and then you can create the entries, as shown in the example in Figure 24.3.

Figure 24.3

Repeating a macro for bulleted list entries

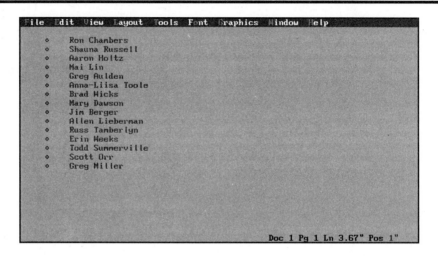

Try the following steps to see how this works. First, you'll create the macro that inserts a bullet character and a tab for one list entry. Then you'll use the Repeat feature to repeat the macro and create the bullets for the entire list. Before you begin, clear the screen.

Choose Tools ▸ Macro ▸ Record.

1. Press Record Macro (Ctrl+F10), and WordPerfect displays the Record Macro dialog box.

2. Press Alt+B to assign this keystroke to the macro, and then press Enter. WordPerfect displays the "Recording Macro" message on the status line. (This won't work if you have the MACROS keyboard selected.)

3. Press Tab to indent the bullet character you will insert.

Press Alt+B and then choose OK.

4. Press WP Characters (Ctrl+W) to display the WordPerfect Characters dialog box.

Choose Font ▸ WP Characters.

5. Press Tab and press Enter to display a list of character sets.

6. From the list, highlight Typographic Symbols and press Enter. Choose Characters, select the solid round bullet (the first character in the list), and then press Enter. WordPerfect inserts the selected character into your document.

Choose Set to display a list of character sets and then double-click on Typographic Symbols.

Choose Layout ▸
Alignment ▸ Indent.

7. Press Indent (F4) to create an indent after the bullet character.

8. For this example, type **Text...** to represent the text for the list entry. Then press Enter to move the cursor to the next line.

9. Press Record Macro (Ctrl+F10) again to stop recording. Your macro is complete.

10. Press Alt+B to play back the macro. A new bullet entry is inserted for your list.

Choose Edit ▸ Re-
peat, and type **20**.

11. Now you'll repeat the macro to create multiple entries. Press Repeat (Ctrl+R) and type **20** to indicate that you want to repeat the next key-stroke 20 times.

12. While the Repeat dialog box is still displayed, press Alt+B to repeat your macro 20 times.

When you are finished, your screen will look similar to Figure 24.4. Note that if you want to use the Repeat feature with named macros, you must press Alt+F10 from within the Repeat dialog box and then specify which macro you want to play back.

Figure 24.4
Repeating a macro
to generate a
bulleted list

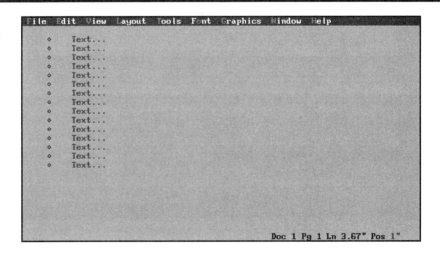

The Repeat command is useful for playing back simple macros a specific number of times. Later in this chapter, you'll learn more about WordPerfect's program and macro commands, and about other methods for controlling macro execution.

Editing Your Macros

After you've created a few macros, you may need to edit them and adjust the effect of the recorded commands. This is often necessary to fix typing errors, to correct commands that don't work as you expected, and to change the task that the macro performs. The following sections explain how to edit simple macros and use some of the common commands.

Macro Editor Concepts

WordPerfect 6.0 employs a new system for recording and editing macros that differs from those of earlier versions. WordPerfect 5.1 and earlier versions of WordPerfect created macros by recording the actual keystroke selections you made during the recording process. WordPerfect 6.0 takes this a huge step further by recording the end result of your selections, rather than the keystrokes or menu selections you made. When you edit your macros, the commands appear as key words, or *tokens*, that are more descriptive than numbers or mnemonic selections.

WordPerfect 6.0's Macro Editor also differs from previous versions. The Macro Editor is now a standard document screen in which you can retrieve and edit macro files (the ones in the .WPM extension), and write complex tasks with extended macro commands.

Using the Macro Editor

To edit the commands stored in a macro file, you need to retrieve the file into WordPerfect's Macro Editor, which is almost identical to the standard document screen. Figure 24.5 shows how a macro file or script looks in the Macro Editor.

A macro script lists one command for each line in the file. These commands are actually standard WordPerfect text that you can edit. For example, when the macro script is displayed, you can type **HardReturn** to insert a hard-return command into the macro script or type **Center** to insert the Center command. You can also delete command words that you want to remove from the macro.

This is the general procedure for editing a macro you've created:

Choose <u>T</u>ools ▶ <u>M</u>acro ▶ <u>R</u>ecord.

- Press Record Macro (Ctrl+F10), and WordPerfect prompts you to enter a name for the macro.

Choose OK to accept the macro name and continue.

- Type the name of the macro, or press the Alt+*letter* keystroke assigned to the macro, and press Enter to continue.

- WordPerfect displays a message that prompts you to choose whether you want to replace or edit the macro. Choose <u>E</u>dit and WordPerfect displays the macro script on the document screen.

Figure 24.5

A macro script displayed in the Macro Editor

```
File  Edit  View  Layout  Tools  Font  Graphics  Window  Help
FlushRight
     Type("Alan Parker")
     HardReturn
FlushRight
     Type("2715 State Fair Road #38")
     HardReturn
FlushRight
     Type("Orem, Utah  84601")
HardReturn
HardReturn
FlushRight
     DateText
HardReturn
HardReturn
     Type("Dear ")GETSTRING(Name)




Edit Macro:  Press Shft+F3 to Record          Doc 2 Pg 1 Ln 1" Pos 1"
```

- Type commands appear in the macro script if your macro inserts text into your document when it is played back. You can edit the text between the quotation marks to change the text that the macro will insert.

Choose File ▸ Save to save the macro file.

- When you are finished editing your macro, press Save As (Ctrl+F12) to save the changes to the macro file.

When you save the edited macro file, WordPerfect *compiles* the macro script to create a working macro. If you've incorrectly typed a command, WordPerfect displays the Macro Compiler Error dialog box; at this point, you can edit the command before you close the macro file or you can choose to save the macro anyway.

Also keep the following in mind:

- You can remove formatting commands recorded by the macro—such as indentations and margin settings—by deleting the command words that appear in the script.

- You can insert additional formatting features by pressing Switch (Shift+F3) to turn on the recording mode. Then choose the program commands you want to insert by pressing the appropriate function keys or by choosing them from the menu bar. When you are finished inserting commands, press Switch (Shift+F3) to activate the macro edit mode.

- Once you learn the WordPerfect program commands, you can also type them directly into the macro script. Table 24.1 shows some of the common commands that you may want to use. Remember to place only one command per line in the macro script.

Table 24.1   Common Program Commands for Macros

Program Command	Result
AttributeAppearanceOn(*attribute*!) AttributeAppearanceOff(*attribute*!)	Turns a font attribute (or size) on or off. The *attribute* setting can be one of the following key words: Bold, Underline, Italics, DoubleUnderline, Outline, Small-Caps, Redline, Strikeout, Superscript, Subscript, Fine, Small, Large, VeryLarge, or ExtraLarge.
Center	Centers cursor or text between left and right margins; equivalent to pressing Center (Shift+F6).
DeleteCharNext	Deletes the character to the right; equivalent to pressing the Delete key.
DeleteCharPrevious	Deletes the character to the left; equivalent to pressing the Backspace key.
DeleteWord	Deletes the word at the cursor; equivalent to pressing Delete Word (Ctrl+Backspace).
DISPLAY(Off!)	Turns off the display of the macro commands while the macro is playing. This command is automatically inserted at the beginning of each macro you record.
DISPLAY(On!)	Turns on the display of the macro commands while the macro is playing.
FileRetrieve("*filename*");WordPerfect_60!)	Retrieves the WordPerfect 6.0 file specified by *filename*.
FileSave("*filename*";WordPerfect_60!)	Saves the current document as a WordPerfect 6.0 file under the name specified by *filename*.
FlushRight	Aligns cursor or text at right margin; equivalent to pressing Flush Right (Alt+F6).
Font("*font name*")	Selects the font specified by *font name*, which should be typed exactly as the font name appears in the Font dialog box.
FontSize(*number*p)	Chooses a different point size for the currently selected font, where *number* represents the point size. The letter p must follow the *number* specification.
HardReturn	Inserts an [HRt] code to end the current text line; equivalent to pressing the Enter key while typing text in your document.
Indent	Indents left margin of paragraph; equivalent to pressing Indent (F4).
IndentLeftRight	Indents both margins of paragraph; equivalent to pressing Left/Right Indent (Shift+F4).

Table 24.1   Common Program Commands for Macros (Continued)

Program Command	Result
Justification(*alignment!*)	Changes the text justification, with *alignment* representing the new setting. The *alignment* setting can be one of the following: Left, Right, Center, Full, or FullAll.
LineSpacing(*number*)	Changes the line spacing, with *number* representing the new setting. For example, LineSpacing(2.0) indicates double line spacing.
MarginBottom(*measurement*)	Sets the bottom margin at the location specified by *measurement*.
MarginLeft(*measurement*)	Sets the left margin at the location specified by *measurement*.
MarginRight(*measurement*)	Sets the right margin at the location specified by *measurement*.
MarginTop(*measurement*)	Sets the top margin at the location specified by *measurement*.
PosCharNext	Moves the cursor right to the next character on the line; equivalent to pressing → at the document screen.
PosCharPrevious	Moves the cursor left to the previous character on the line; equivalent to pressing ← at the document screen.
PosDocBottom	Moves the cursor to the end of the current document.
PosDocTop	Moves the cursor to the beginning of the current document.
PosLineDown	Moves the cursor to the following line in the document; equivalent to pressing ↓ at the document screen.
PosLineUp	Moves the cursor to the previous line in the document; equivalent to pressing ↑ at the document screen.
PosScreenLeft	Moves the cursor to the beginning of the current line.
PosScreenRight or PosLineEnd	Moves the cursor to the end of the current line.
PosWordNext	Moves the cursor to the next word in the document.
PosWordPrevious	Moves the cursor to the previous word in the document.

Table 24.1   **Common Program Commands for Macros (Continued)**

Program Command	Result
PrintBlock	Prints the selected block in the displayed document.
PrintFullDoc	Prints the displayed document in full.
PrintPage	Prints the current page of the displayed document.
Tab	Inserts a Tab code; equivalent to pressing the Tab key.
TabSet(Relative!)	Clears all tab stops.
TabSet(Relative!;{*settings*})	Inserts new tab settings, with *settings* representing the new tab stop measurements. Within the curly brackets, you type **TabLeft!;***measurement*; for each left tab stop you want to set. For other kinds of tab stops, type **TabRight!;***measurement*; or **TabCenter!;***-measurement*; or **TabDecimal!;***measurement*;.
Type("*text*")	Inserts into the current document the information indicated by *text*. For the *text* parameter, you can insert any amount of text—even multiple paragraphs, if necessary.

Remember that the commands in the macro script are stored as text that you edit like standard document text. When you type the macro commands directly into the macro script, you must type them exactly as they appear in Table 24.1; otherwise, the commands may not work correctly. You do not need to capitalize the macro commands, but it does make the commands easier to read. When the Macro Editor is open, be careful not to accidentally delete characters or commands, and if you don't recognize a command, it's best to leave it alone. Otherwise, you may not be able to play back your macro.

Editing the Macro Text

Now it's your turn to try the macro editing process. Suppose you need to change the street address that your return address macro inserts. In the following exercise, you'll edit this macro to make the address change:

Choose Tools ▸
Macro ▸ Record.

Press Alt+A ▸ OK.

1. Press Record Macro (Ctrl+F10), and WordPerfect displays the Record Macro dialog box.

2. Press Alt+A to insert ALTA into the macro name field. Then press Enter. WordPerfect displays a message that reads "C:\WP60\MACROS\ ALTA.WPM already exists."

3. Choose Edit from the message box, and WordPerfect displays the commands stored in the ALTA macro. Figure 24.6 shows an example of how your screen could look; of course your name and address information will differ.

Figure 24.6

Editing the Return Address macro

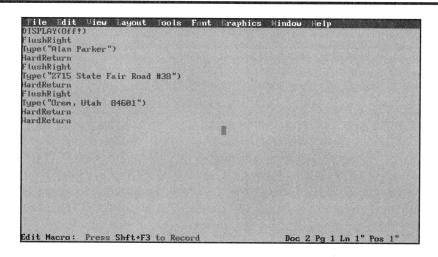

```
File  Edit  View  Layout  Tools  Font  Graphics  Window  Help
DISPLAY(Off!)
FlushRight
Type("Alan Parker")
HardReturn
FlushRight
Type("2715 State Fair Road #38")
HardReturn
FlushRight
Type("Oren, Utah  84601")
HardReturn
HardReturn




Edit Macro:  Press Shft+F3 to Record              Doc 2 Pg 1 Ln 1" Pos 1"
```

4. In the macro script, the lines that begin with "Type(" are the commands that insert your return address. Move the cursor to the second occurrence of the "Type(" command, where your street address is listed. Then, edit the command so that it looks like this:

   ```
   Type("3750 Baker Street, Apt. 12-B")
   ```

5. Now you'll insert a new command to add a company name to your return address. Move the cursor to the right of the first hard return in the macro script. Press Enter to start insert a blank line.

6. Type the following commands into the script—each on its own line—to add a company name to your return address:

   ```
   FlushRight
   Type("Croissants Incorporated")
   HardReturn
   ```

7. When you are finished, press Save (Ctrl+F12) and then clear your screen.

   Let's review what you did. You opened the Macro Editor with the script for the ALTA.WPM macro. You edited one of the "Type(" commands to change the street address that the macro inserts. You also inserted three new macro commands that tell the macro to insert a company name before your street address. To see the result, simply press Alt+A to play back the macro.

When you edit the macro script, make sure you do not disturb the other commands. Misplaced punctuation characters and spaces are easily overlooked, but can prevent your macro from working.

Editing Formatting Codes in a Macro

You've seen how to edit or change the text that is inserted by a macro. Now, you'll see how to edit recorded formatting codes. These are the layout commands, such as indents or margin changes, that were recorded when you created your macro. In the following steps, you'll edit the ALTA.WPM macro and change some of the formatting codes:

Choose Tools ▸ Macro ▸ Record. Press Alt+A ▸ OK.

Move the cursor to the beginning of the document. Then choose Edit ▸ Replace.

1. Press Record Macro (Ctrl+F10), press Alt+A, and then press Enter. WordPerfect displays the "C:\WP60\MACROS\ALTA.WPM already exists" message.

2. Choose Edit from the message box, and WordPerfect retrieves and displays the macro script.

3. First, you'll replace all of the Flush Right commands with Center commands. If necessary, press Home, Home, ↑ to move the cursor to the beginning of the macro script. Then press Replace (Alt+F2).

4. In the Search For field, type **FlushRight** (one word, no spaces), and press Enter. In the Replace With field, type **Center**, and press Enter.

5. Choose Replace (F2) to replace each occurrence of a Flush Right command with the Center command. WordPerfect displays the Search and Replace Complete message box to show the results. Press Exit (F7) or choose OK to continue.

6. Now you'll add two new commands to create bold text for your first and last name. Insert the command before and after the "Type(" command that inserts your name, like this:

```
AttributeAppearanceOn(Bold!)
Type("your name")
AttributeAppearanceOff(Bold!)
```

You can do this by positioning the cursor before your name, pressing Shift+F3 to get into Record mode, pressing F6 to turn on boldfacing, and then pressing Shift+F3 to return to the Macro Editor. Do the same thing to turn off boldfacing after your name.

7. Press Save (Ctrl+F12) to replace the original macro file.

8. Clear the screen and press Alt+A to play your macro.

Choose File ▸ Save to save the changes to the macro file.

This time, the macro inserts your return address with your name set in bold text, and all the lines are centered instead of flush right.

When the Macro Editor is open, you can press Switch (Shift+F3) to change temporarily to the macro record mode; when this is active, you can type keystrokes, move the cursor, or select features with the menu bar or function keys to insert program commands into your macro script.

Although the Macro Editor is often used to fix or change the commands that a macro performs, it is also a useful tool for creating complex macros with WordPerfect's macro language commands. In Chapter 25, you'll learn a bit more about advanced macro applications.

25

Using WordPerfect's Keyboard Feature

Using WordPerfect's Alternate Keyboard Layouts

Creating Your Own Keyboard Layout

Editing a Keyboard Layout

Creating and Using Macro Keyboards

Viewing a Map of Keystroke Assignments

T HE STANDARD PC COMPUTER KEYBOARD HAS A LIMITED NUMBER OF keys that perform WordPerfect features. The function keys—F1 through F12—allow you to access most menus and dialog boxes. Other keystrokes, called *hotkeys*, let you perform specific program tasks; for example, pressing Ctrl+I turns on italics. Although you do not need to use the keyboard to select most WordPerfect features, you'll find that some keystrokes are easier to perform than a series of menu selections.

WordPerfect's Keyboard Layout feature lets you redefine the keystroke assignments on your keyboard. You may want to do this if you find any of WordPerfect's standard keystrokes cumbersome or difficult to remember. You might also create a new keyboard layout to customize the keystroke assignments for certain types of documents that you create often.

If, for example, you create documents in a language other than English, you would benefit from a set of keystrokes that insert characters from the appropriate alphabet. This is particularly useful when the characters you need don't appear on the standard PC keyboard. In addition to characters and text phrases, WordPerfect lets you assign file macros to most keystrokes on your keyboard. There are over 200 keystroke combinations that you can redefine for a new keyboard layout.

When you select or create a new keyboard definition, it affects how the keyboard operates within the WordPerfect environment only; it does not affect how it operates with other programs. Each keystroke in a keyboard layout can play back a macro, type a special character, or insert a common phrase that you've assigned to a key. You can create as many keyboard layouts as you need and then choose the one you want at any time. You can, for example, create one keyboard layout that taps into a library of your macros, one that lets you type documents in French, and still another that includes a glossary of business terms that you can insert into your documents.

This chapter explains how to use WordPerfect's Keyboard Layout feature to select and implement one of WordPerfect's alternate keyboard layouts. You'll also learn how to create and manage a custom keyboard layout, and how to assign keystrokes that play back the macros you've created.

Using WordPerfect's Alternate Keyboard Layouts

The keyboard template included with your WordPerfect software shows the keystroke assignments for WordPerfect's default or *original* keyboard layout, which is the one that is active when you first start the WordPerfect software.

WordPerfect also includes alternate keyboard layouts that modify the keystroke assignments. One keyboard layout includes a library of useful macros that improve efficiency; each of these macros performs a task that you can play back by pressing a keystroke. Another layout lets you insert functions, characters, and keywords while you are working with WordPerfect's Equation Editor.

Choosing a Different Keyboard Layout

The following steps explain how to select a different keyboard layout from the list of layouts provided by WordPerfect. If you choose to define one or more custom keyboard layouts, as described later in this chapter, you can also use these steps to select one of those keyboard layouts.

Choose File ►
Setup ► Keyboard
Layout.

1. Press Setup (Shift+F1) and then choose Keyboard Layout. Figure 25.1 shows the dialog box that appears. An asterisk appears next to the keyboard layout that is currently active.

Figure 25.1

The main Keyboard
Layout dialog box

**Asterisk appears
next to active
keyboard layout**

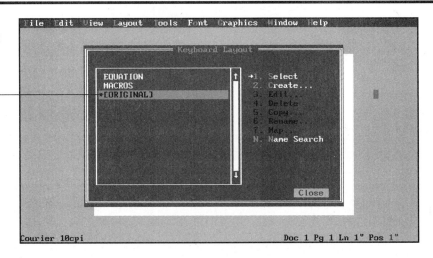

Double-click on the
name of the key-
board layout you
want to use.

2. Press ↑ or ↓ to highlight the keyboard layout you want to use. Then choose Select.

If necessary,
choose Close to re-
turn to the docu-
ment screen.

3. The Setup dialog box reappears, and, if you've selected an option other than [ORIGINAL], you'll see the name of the active keyboard layout next to the Keyboard Layout option. Press Exit (F7) to close the Setup dialog box and return to the document screen.

WordPerfect reassigns the keystrokes of your keyboard according to the key definitions in the selected keyboard layout. This keyboard layout will remain active until you select a different keyboard layout or choose [ORIGINAL] from the Keyboard Layout dialog box to reactive WordPerfect's standard key assignments.

TIP. *When you are at the document screen, you can also press Ctrl+6 to reactivate WordPerfect's standard key assignments. This is the only way to turn* *off an alternate keyboard layout without first displaying the Keyboard Layout dialog box. Pressing Ctrl+6 twice reinstitutes the alternate keyboard layout.*

As mentioned earlier, the selected keyboard layout affects keystroke assignments only within WordPerfect; these keystroke assignments are not reflected in other programs.

Viewing a Descriptive List of Key Assignments

Before you choose an unfamiliar keyboard layout, you may want to review the keystrokes that will be altered. You can do this by choosing the Edit option on the Keyboard Layout dialog box:

Choose File ▶ Setup ▶ Keyboard Layout.

- Display the Keyboard Layout dialog box by pressing Setup (Shift+F1) and choosing Keyboard Layout, as described in the previous steps.

- Highlight the keyboard layout (other than [ORIGINAL]) that you may want to use.

- Choose the Edit option to display a list of defined keystrokes, like the example shown in Figure 25.2.

Figure 25.2

Previewing a list of key assignments

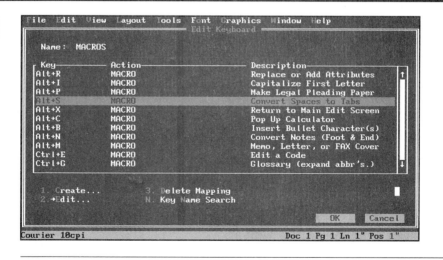

The Edit Keyboard dialog box displays a descriptive list of keystroke assignments in the keyboard layout. If the list extends beyond the height of the dialog box, you can press ↓ or use the scroll bar at the right edge of the dialog box to view the entire list. When you are finished, press Exit (F7) or choose OK to return to the Keyboard Layout dialog box. Then, if you want to use the highlighted keyboard layout, choose Select.

Creating Your Own Keyboard Layout

WordPerfect's standard keystroke assignments are often a matter of controversy. Some people like the keystroke assignments, while others complain that they aren't intuitive. The Keyboard Layout feature lets you selectively change any or all of the keystroke assignments that you don't like. As mentioned earlier, this feature also lets you create custom keyboard layouts for specific documents or applications.

The following sections show how to create and use a new keyboard layout. The first section explains how to create a basic keyboard layout, which redefines some of WordPerfect's function keys. The second one explains how to assign text phrases, and the third teaches you how to activate your new keyboard layout—and also how to deactivate it when you want to revert to WordPerfect's standard keystroke assignments.

Creating a Basic Keyboard Layout

Try the following steps to create a simple keyboard layout that changes a few of WordPerfect's keystroke assignments. For this example, you will redefine the keystrokes that access the Help and Cancel features. In WordPerfect 6.0, the standard keystroke for the Help feature is F1, and the Cancel feature is accessed by pressing Esc; if you are familiar with WordPerfect 5.1 or an earlier version of WordPerfect, you probably know these keystrokes as Help (F3) and Cancel (F1).

Although WordPerfect 6.0 provides an alternate keyboard layout for WordPerfect 5.1 users (press Shift+F1, choose Environment, and then select WordPerfect 5.1 Keyboard), you can try the following steps to create a new keyboard layout and change the commands that are assigned to the F1 and F3 keys. You can then apply this general procedure to reassign other keys from the original keyboard layout.

Choose File ▶ Setup ▶ Keyboard Layout.

1. Press Setup (Shift+F1) and then choose Keyboard Layout.

2. Choose Create and WordPerfect prompts you to enter a name for the new keyboard. For this example, type **wp51** and press Enter. WordPerfect displays the Edit Keyboard dialog box.

3. Choose Create to open the Create Key dialog box, shown in Figure 25.3. WordPerfect prompts you to press the key that you want to change. For this example, press F1. Note that the current assignment for this key appears next to the Action Type label on the dialog box.

4. Choose Description, type **Cancel**, and then press Enter.

5. Under Action Type, choose Command to display the list of possible program commands (shown in Figure 25.4) that you can assign to a keystroke.

Figure 25.3
The Create Key
dialog box

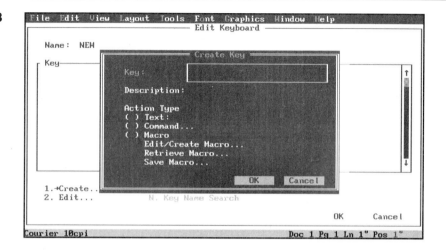

Figure 25.4
Choosing a program
command for a key
definition

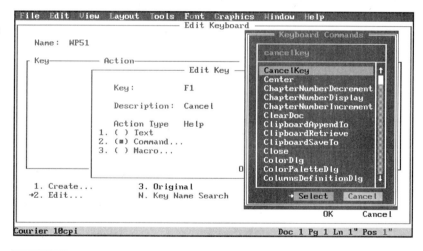

Choose OK to re-
turn to the Edit Key-
board dialog box.

6. Type **c** to highlight the command for Cancel, CancelKey. Then press Enter or choose <u>S</u>elect to assign the Cancel command to the F1 key.

7. Press Exit (F7) to return to the Edit Keyboard dialog box. You'll see the new key definition on the list of defined keystrokes.

8. Choose <u>C</u>reate and press F3 to create the next key definition. From the Create Key dialog box, choose <u>D</u>escription, type **Help**, and then press Enter.

Choose OK to return to the Edit Keyboard dialog box.

Choose OK to return to the Keyboard Layout dialog box.

Double-click on the WP51 keyboard name. Then choose Close if necessary.

9. Under Action Type, choose Command to display the program command list.

10. Type **hel** to highlight the command for Help. Then press Enter or choose Select. This assigns the Help command to the F3 key.

11. Press Exit (F7) to return to the Edit Keyboard dialog box; the new key definition appears in the list of defined keystrokes.

12. Press Exit (F7) to return to the Keyboard Layout dialog box.

13. Highlight the new WP51 keyboard name, and choose Select to activate it. Then press Exit (F7) again to close the Setup dialog box.

When you close the Keyboard Layout dialog box, the information for the new keyboard layout is automatically saved in a file with a .WPK file extension (WP51.WPK); this file is stored in the macros/keyboards/button bars directory that you specified in the Location of Files dialog box (choose File, Setup, Location of Files).

The new keyboard layout is now active and will remain so until you choose a different keyboard layout or choose WordPerfect's original keyboard layout. When you press F1, WordPerfect will perform the Cancel command. When you press F3, you'll access the Help feature.

When you create a new keyboard layout, you do *not* need to redefine all keystrokes on your keyboard. WordPerfect changes only the key assignments that you define on the Edit Keyboard list; keys that are not defined on the list assume the key assignments from WordPerfect 6.0's original keyboard layout.

Before you assign a different command to a key, consider whether you want to replace the command that is currently assigned. The current command appears next to the Action Type label on the Edit Key dialog box. This is important because you may need to create additional key definitions to account for the command you are replacing.

Here is an example that illustrates the problem of reassigning keystroke commands. The following diagram shows the keys you changed in the previous steps and clarifies how these changes affect the original keystroke assignments.

Original Key Assignments	First Key Change	Second Key Change	New Key Assignments
Esc = Cancel	F1 = Cancel	F3 = Help	Esc = Cancel
F1 = Help			F1 = Cancel
F3 = Switch			F3 = Help
	Help command is replaced by the Cancel command.	Switch command is replaced by the Help command.	Switch command is not assigned to a key.

In the steps, you assigned the Cancel command to the F1 key as the first key change. Then, because the Help command was replaced with Cancel, you reassigned Help to the F3 key as the second key change.

As you can see, this is also where problems may arise. The original assignment for F3 was the Switch command (SwitchDlg), but because Switch was replaced by the Help command, it now cannot be accessed directly from the keyboard. If you want to access the Switch command with a keystroke while your new keyboard layout is active, you'll need to create another keystroke definition—such as Ctrl+S—and assign the Switch command to it. Alternatively, you could assign the Switch command to the Esc key, which is the key assignment for WordPerfect 5.1. Each time you create a new key definition, you may need to assign additional keys to account for the commands you have displaced, assuming you want to keep all commands accessible from the keyboard.

Creating a Keyboard Layout to Insert Text

You've seen how to assign specific program commands to the keys in your keyboard layout. You can also assign text phrases to the keys—when you press one of the defined keystrokes, you'll insert one of the text phrases stored in the keyboard layout. This will save you time when you create many documents with common words and phrases.

WordPerfect provides two ways to assign text to a keystroke, both of which are performed from the Create Key dialog box. Enter a key or key combination and then choose Text to assign a brief text phrase—up to 27 characters—to the current keystroke.

If you want to assign a text phrase or paragraph that exceeds 27 characters, you need to create a macro that types the text and then assign the macro to a keystroke. This is done by choosing Macro from the Create Key dialog box.

The following exercise will show you how to use both of these options to assign text to the keys in your keyboard layout. First, you'll create a new keyboard layout and create key definitions to assign your name and company name to simple keystrokes. Then you'll create a keyboard macro that assigns a longer passage of text to a keystroke.

Choose File ▶ Setup ▶ Keyboard Layout.

1. Press Setup (Shift+F1) and then choose Keyboard Layout.

2. Choose Creat, enter **glossary** as the name for the new keyboard, and press Enter.

3. Choose Create to open the Create Key dialog box. WordPerfect prompts you to press the key that you want to change. Press Ctrl+N.

4. Choose Description, type **Inserts my name**, and then press Enter.

5. Choose <u>T</u>ext. A text entry box opens next to the Action Type label.

6. In the text entry box, type your name as you want it to appear in your documents. You can type a maximum of 27 characters. Then press Enter.

Choose OK to return to the Edit Keyboard dialog box.

7. Press Exit (F7) to return to the Edit Keyboard dialog box, and you'll see the new key definition on the list.

8. Choose <u>C</u>reate and press Ctrl+C to create the next key definition. From the Create Key dialog box, choose <u>D</u>escription, type **Inserts my company name**, and then press Enter.

9. Under Action Type, choose <u>T</u>ext, enter the name of your company, and then press Enter.

Choose OK to return to the Edit Keyboard dialog box.

10. Press Exit (F7) to return to the Edit Keyboard dialog box; the new key definition appears on the list of defined keystrokes.

11. Now you'll assign a paragraph of text to a keystroke. Because the paragraph will be longer than 27 characters, you'll need to use the keyboard macro option. Choose <u>C</u>reate and press Ctrl+A to create the next key definition.

12. From the Create Key dialog box, choose <u>D</u>escription, type **Inserts Paragraph A**, and then press Enter.

13. Under Action Type choose <u>M</u>acro and then <u>E</u>dit/Create Macro. Word-Perfect displays the Macro Editor screen, in which you can specify a series of commands for the keystroke to perform.

14. At the Macro Editor screen, type the following to create a macro script that assigns a paragraph of text to the current keystroke. This is a macro, so make sure you type the script exactly as it appears here. (One exception to this is the text between the quote marks; this is the text the macro will insert, and it can be any text you want.)

```
ASSIGN(Text;"The party of the first part agrees to honor
this agreement, except when a first-rate party ensues
outside of the vicinity of the party of the first part, in
which case the party of the first part may invite the
party of the second part to the party.") TYPE(Text)
```

15. When you are finished typing the macro script, press Exit (F7) until you return to the Edit Keyboard dialog box. There you will see the new definition for the Ctrl+A keystroke, which will insert the "Paragraph A" text that you typed in the macro script.

Choose OK to return to the Keyboard Layout dialog box.

16. Press Exit (F7) to return to the Keyboard Layout dialog box.

Double-click on the Glossary keyboard name. Then, if necessary, choose Close to return to the document screen.

17. Highlight the new Glossary keyboard name, and choose <u>S</u>elect to activate it.

18. Press Exit (F7) to close the Setup dialog box, and return to the document screen.

When your new keyboard is selected, you can press Ctrl+N to insert your name into the current document, press Ctrl+C to insert your company's name, or press Ctrl+A to insert the paragraph you created in the macro script. These are the methods for assigning text to keystrokes in your layout.

Using a New Keyboard Layout

You've already seen how to select a different keyboard layout for use with WordPerfect. The selected keyboard layout remains in effect until you choose a different one through the Keyboard Layout dialog box. This is true even when you exit the WordPerfect program; the next time you start WordPerfect, you'll find that the last selected keyboard layout is still active in the program.

This may cause some problems if you forget that the keystrokes have been changed. You can reset the keystrokes to WordPerfect's original keyboard layout by choosing the [ORIGINAL] layout from the Keyboard Layout dialog. You can also press Ctrl+6 to turn off the current keyboard layout and return to the original layout. This works when you are at a document screen and can often rescue you from errors when you can't open the Keyboard Layout dialog box to change the keyboard layout. Remember, pressing Ctrl+6 twice will restore the alternate keyboard layout.

Editing a Keyboard Layout

After you've created a new keyboard layout, you may need to edit the key assignments you've made or add key definitions to the layout. When you do so, you choose which of the key definitions you want to edit, and then you can change the keystroke, edit the key descriptions, or change the command or function that the keystroke performs.

Changing Keystroke Definitions

The following steps explain how to make changes to a keyboard layout you've already created:

Choose <u>F</u>ile ▸ Se<u>t</u>up
▸ <u>K</u>eyboard Layout.

■ Press Setup (Shift+F1) and then choose <u>K</u>eyboard Layout.

Click on the name of the keyboard layout you want to edit. Then choose Edit.

- ■ Press ↑ or ↓ to highlight the keyboard layout you want to change. Then choose Edit. WordPerfect displays the Edit Keyboard dialog box.

- ■ Scroll through the list of keystroke assignments, and highlight the one you want to change. Then choose Edit to display the Edit Key dialog box.

- ■ To change the keystroke, choose Key and type a different key. If necessary, choose Description and edit the descriptive text for the keystroke. To change the command or function of the key, choose Command and select a new command from the list of keyboard commands that appear.

Choose OK to return to the Edit Keyboard dialog box.

- ■ When you are finished editing the key assignment, press Exit (F7) to return to the Edit Keyboard dialog box.

Choose OK and then choose Close until you return to the document screen.

- ■ Press Exit (F7) until all dialog boxes are closed and you return to the document screen.

When you close the Keyboard Layout dialog box, the changes you made to the keyboard layout are automatically saved to the appropriate keyboard file (.WPK). You do not need to save the keyboard file to update your changes.

Deleting, Copying, and Renaming Keyboard Layouts

In addition to editing keystroke assignments, you can delete, copy, and rename the keyboard layouts that appear on the Keyboard Layout dialog box. These options help you manage a list of keyboard layouts and let you remove those you don't want to keep.

The following steps explain how to delete, copy, and rename the layouts that appear on the Keyboard Layout dialog box. You can perform these editing tasks on any keyboard layout, except the [ORIGINAL] keyboard layout.

Choose File ▶ Setup ▶ Keyboard Layout.

- ■ Press Setup (Shift+F1) and then choose Keyboard Layout.

- ■ Highlight the keyboard layout you want to delete or change.

- ■ If you want to delete the highlighted keyboard layout, choose Delete and respond Yes at the confirmation prompt.

- ■ If you want to make a copy of the highlighted keyboard, choose Copy and enter a name for the new keyboard layout.

- ■ If you want to change the name of the highlighted keyboard, choose Rename and enter a new name.

Choose Close until you return to the document screen.

- ■ When you are finished editing the keyboard list, press Exit (F7) until you return to the document screen.

Each of these options affects the .WPK files where your keyboard layouts are saved. When you use the Delete option, WordPerfect removes the high-lighted keyboard layout from the list and also erases the corresponding .WPK file from the WordPerfect directory.

When you choose the Copy option, WordPerfect creates a new .WPK file with the name you entered for the new keyboard layout. This option lets you use an existing keyboard layout as the model for a new layout. First, you high-light the layout that you want to use as a model for the new layout. Choose Copy from the Keyboard Layout dialog box and enter a name for the new keyboard layout. Then highlight the new layout and choose Edit to change the keystroke assignments. All the definitions from the first keyboard layout are carried over to the new layout.

The Rename option changes the name of the .WPK file for the high-lighted keyboard.

Creating and Using Macro Keyboards

Earlier in this chapter, you saw how to create a macro and assign it as the command for a keystroke. You can do the same with macro files that you have already created. Suppose you've created a macro that generates the memos for your office; you can retrieve your macro as the command for a keystroke in your keyboard layout, and then access the macro with one sim-ple keystroke. This section explains how to do this and also shows how to use WordPerfect's own Macros keyboard.

Assigning Your Own Macros to a Keyboard Layout

When you create or edit a keyboard layout, you can create a key definition that plays back one of your macro files (Chapter 24 explains how to create macro files). There are two ways to assign a macro file to a key. The first method lets you retrieve a macro file into the keyboard layout, which saves the macro script with the keyboard layout file. If you change the macro file after you've retrieved it into the keyboard layout, your changes will not affect the macro key definition.

The second method lets you create a link between a macro file and the key definition. Instead of saving the macro script with the keyboard layout, this method simply references the macro file on disk; when you press the as-signed keystroke, it plays back the macro from the file. This ensures that your keyboard layout will always play back the most recent version of the macro file on disk.

Try the following steps to create a simple macro, and then assign the macro to a key definition. First, you'll create a macro file that types your name as bold underlined text; then you'll use the first method, described earlier, to retrieve the macro file into the keyboard layout:

Choose Tools ▸ Macro ▸ Record. Then enter **NAME** as the macro name.

1. From a clear document screen, press Record Macro (Ctrl+F10), and enter **NAME** as the name for the macro file. You'll see the "Recording Macro" message at the bottom of the screen.

Choose Layout ▸ Alignment ▸ Center.

2. Now perform the task that you want the macro to record. In this exercise, you will type your name as a centered text line. Press Center (Shift+F6) to center the cursor between left and right margins.

Choose Font ▸ Bold, and then choose Font ▸ Underline.

3. Press Bold (F6) and then press Underline (F8) to turn on these text attributes.

4. Type your name. Then choose the Bold and Underline options again to turn off these attributes. Press Enter twice to create a line of space after your name.

Choose Tools ▸ Macro ▸ Stop.

5. Press Record Macro (Ctrl+F10) to stop macro recording. The task you performed is now saved in a macro file called NAME.WPM.

6. Now you can assign the macro file to a keyboard layout. If you wish, clear the screen before you continue.

7. Press Setup (Shift+F1) and choose Keyboard Layout.

Choose File ▸ Setup ▸ Keyboard Layout.

8. Highlight one of the existing keyboard layouts and choose Edit. Or choose Create and enter a name for a new keyboard layout. The Edit Keyboard dialog box appears.

9. Choose Create to display the Create Key dialog box. Press Ctrl+N (or a different keystroke combination) when prompted for the key name.

10. Choose Description and enter **Types name as centered text**.

11. Under Action Type, choose Macro and then Retrieve Macro.

12. When WordPerfect prompts you for the macro name, type **NAME.WPM**, and then press Enter.

13. Press Exit (F7) until you return to the Keyboard Layout dialog box.

14. Choose Select to activate the keyboard you just created or edited.

15. Press Exit (F7) until you return to the document screen.

Choose Close until you return to the document screen.

Now, when you press Ctrl+N (or the keystroke you defined for the macro), WordPerfect plays back the NAME.WPM macro file that you created. You can define as many macro key definitions as you need. Remember that macros do much more than insert formatting codes or text. You can create and assign macros that perform specific tasks, such as removing unwanted character spaces from an imported ASCII file, performing a merge or sort operation, setting up a document layout, or locating certain words or phrases. Many people will want to create a separate keyboard layout with the macros that are designed for specific documents or tasks.

Using WordPerfect's Macro Keyboard

The WordPerfect software includes a Macros keyboard that can simplify many common word processing tasks. Table 25.1 shows a complete list of the keystroke assignments that are included in this keyboard layout. To select the keyboard, press Setup (Shift+F1) and choose Keyboard Layout. From the Keyboard Layout dialog box, highlight the MACROS keyboard name and choose Edit to view a list of keystroke assignments for this keyboard layout. Press F7 to return to the Keyboard Layout dialog box when you're done. To select the MACROS keyboard layout, highlight it and choose Select. Then press Exit (F7) to close the Setup dialog box.

Table 25.1   **Keystroke Assignments for WordPerfect's Macros Keyboard**

Keystroke	Description	How to Use
Alt+B	Inserts bullet characters for a single item or for a list of items.	To insert a bullet and indent at the beginning of the current text line, press Alt+B. At the Bullet inserter dialog box that appears, choose Insert bullet character. Select Change bullet character to choose a diffrent bullet character. To insert bullets and indents before several lines in a list, use Block (Alt+F4 or F12) to block all the text; make sure you begin the block at the end of the line that precedes the first item. Then press Alt+B.
Alt+C	Opens WordPerfect's pop-up calculator.	Press Alt+C to display the pop-up calculator. You can use the numeric keypad or the mouse pointer to "push" the calculator buttons. Choose Ins to insert the number from the calculator window into your document.
Alt+I	Capitalizes the first letter of the word where the cursor is located and moves the cursor to the next word.	Move the cursor to a word in your document, and then press Alt+I. This capitalizes only the first letter of the word.

Table 25.1 **Keystroke Assignments for WordPerfect's Macros Keyboard (Continued)**

Keystroke	Description	How to Use
Alt+M	Creates a memo, a business letter, or a FAX cover; sets up the basic format for the document you choose, and prompts you to enter some of the text to complete the document.	Start from a clear document screen. Press Alt+M to display the Select a Form dialog box, from which you can choose Memo, Letter, or FAX cover. Select the desired document form, and then fill in the To, From, and Subject fields as necessary. Then press Exit (F7) or choose OK. WordPerfect will generate the appropriate document layout.
Alt+N	Converts footnotes to endnotes or vice versa; useful when you need to globally change one type of note to another.	First, retrieve the document that contains the notes you want to convert. Move the cursor to the beginning of the document, and then press Alt+N to display the Convert Notes dialog box. Choose either Footnotes to Endnotes or Endnotes to Footnotes. The macro converts the notes as specified by your selection. If you are converting endnotes to footnotes, the macro converts only the notes in your document; any [Endnote Placement;] codes are left intact.
Alt+P	Creates a pleading paper style; lets you define the measurements you need for a pleading paper; inserts the pleading format as a style at the beginning of the current document.	Start from a clear document screen. Press Alt+P to display the Create Pleading Paper dialog box. Choose each of the options in the dialog box to specify the desired format for your pleading paper. Then press Exit (F7) or choose OK. WordPerfect creates and inserts a pleading style based on the settings you defined at the dialog box.
Alt+R	Replaces paired text attribute codes with a different set of attributes.	Press Alt+R to display the Modify Attributes dialog box. Choose Search For and indicate the text attribute or text size code you want to replace. Choose Add/Replace With, and indicate the replacement code. Choose whether you want to conduct a backward or extended serach, and whether to confirm the modifications. Choose OK to initiate the replacement procedure.
Alt+S	Replaces spaces with tabs; helps convert ASCII text files where multiple spaces were inserted to indent text or create divisions for text columns.	Retrieve the file that you want to convert to a standard WordPerfect document, and move the cursor to the beginning of your document. Press Alt+S to display the Convert Spaces to Tabs dialog box. Choose Minimum to specify the range of spaces that you want to replace. For example, if you want to replace all consecutive spaces (two or more) with a tab, choose Minimum and enter 2 as the minimum number to replace. Then press Exit (F7) or choose OK to replace the consecutive spaces in your document with tabs.

Table 25.1   **Keystroke Assignments for WordPerfect's Macros Keyboard (Continued)**

Keystroke	Description	How to Use
Alt+X	Returns to main editing screen from any menu or dialog box.	Press Alt+X to close all menus or dialog boxes and return to the main document screen.
Ctrl+E	Displays the dialog box for a code highlighted in the Reveal Codes window; lets you edit the settings or measurements that create the code.	First, display the Reveal Codes window, and move the cursor to highlight the code you want to edit. Then press Ctrl+E. The macro displays the dialog box for the highlighted code, in which you can enter new settings or measurements. When you are finished, press Exit (F7) or choose OK to insert an updated code into your document.
Ctrl+G	Creates and manages a list of expandable glossary abbreviations; lets you create a list of abbreviated terms—a sort of typing shorthand—that you can use with your document, and then later expand to the complete terms.	The first time you use this macro, you need to create the list of abbreviated terms, called the *glossary*. Press Ctrl+G to display the Glossary Definition dialog box, and then choose Create. The macro prompts you to enter a new abbreviation for the list; then choose Expanded Form, and enter the full term that the abbreviation represents. You could, for example, type "INC" as the abbreviation and "Incorporated" as the expanded form. Choose OK or press Enter to return to the Glossary Definition dialog box, and repeat this procedure to create additional entries for the glossary list. When you are finished adding entries to the list, choose OK or press Enter to close the Glossary Definition dialog box. Now you can type the abbreviations into any document, and press Ctrl+G to them to the full terms that you entered for the Glossary Definition list. (The cursor must be at or just after the abbreviation for it to expand. Otherwise, pressing Ctrl+G displays the Glossary Definition dialog box again.) The glossary information is stored in a file called WPGLGOUS.WPM.

After you select the Macros keyboard, a series of Ctrl and Alt key combinations let you perform many tasks that will help you create and edit documents.

If you like to write your own macros, this keyboard layout also includes excellent examples of macro scripts; to view the script for a macro, display the Keyboard Layout dialog box, highlight the MACROS keyboard name, and choose Edit.

Then highlight one of the key definitions, and choose Edit. Under the Action Type heading, choose Edit/Create Macro to view the macro script. Be careful not to change any of the commands in the script; otherwise, the macro may not work when you exit the Macro Editor. When you are finished viewing the macro script, press Exit (F7) until you return to the Keyboard Layout dialog box.

When you are finished using the Macros keyboard layout, make sure you choose WordPerfect's original keyboard layout to reset the standard keystroke assignments.

Viewing a Map of Keystroke Assignments

The Map option, located on the Keyboard Layout dialog box, provides an overview of all keystrokes that are assigned in the selected keyboard layout. This can help you identify the keys you've assigned in a keyboard layout, as well as show you whether a key inserts a character, performs a program function, or plays back a macro.

In addition to showing you the key assignments, the Map feature also lets you change the keystrokes or edit the action performed by each key. This is simply an alternate method for viewing, creating, and editing the keystroke assignments. The following steps explain how to use the keyboard Map feature:

Choose File ▶ Setup ▶ Keyboard Layout.

- Press Setup (Shift+F1) and then choose Keyboard Layout.

Click on the name of the keyboard layout you want to view.

- Press ↑ or ↓ to highlight the keyboard layout you want to view (other than [ORIGINAL]).

- Choose Map and WordPerfect displays the Keyboard Map dialog box, shown in Figure 25.5.

Figure 25.5

The Keyboard Map dialog box

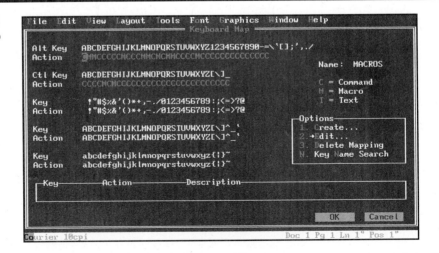

Using the arrow keys or the mouse pointer, highlight each of the key-stroke references on the map. The letter *C* appears below keystrokes that are assigned a program command, *M* appears beneath keystrokes that are assigned a key macro, and *T* appears below keystrokes assigned a text phrase. If no letter appears beneath a keystroke, it means the keystroke is not assigned a special function or command; this usually means it types a character or punctuation symbol. Note that you cannot redefine function key assignments (F1 through F12) from the keyboard map.

When a key reference is highlighted, the box at the bottom of the screen displays the key name, action, and description. You can choose Edit to change the keystroke assignment or choose Delete Mapping to reset the key to its original command in WordPerfect's standard keyboard layout. To quickly find the desired keystroke, choose Key Name Search and press the key or keys you want to locate. When you are finished viewing the keyboard map, press Exit (F7) until you return to the document screen.

APPENDIX A

Installing the WordPerfect Software

Before you can start WordPerfect 6.0, you must use WordPerfect's Installation program to copy the WordPerfect software to your hard disk. This appendix explains the installation process and how to start the WordPerfect software. You'll also find information about start-up options and customizing the WordPerfect program to suit your preferences.

Information for WordPerfect 5.1 Users

If you are currently using WordPerfect version 5.1 or 5.0, there are a few things you should know before you install and use the WordPerfect 6.0 software. The following sections explain some problems you may encounter and how you can make the update process a success.

Updating to WordPerfect 6.0

Before you install the WordPerfect 6.0 software, you should consider whether you want to keep WordPerfect 5.1 on your hard disk. WordPerfect 6.0 is quite different from the WordPerfect software you know, and it will take some time to learn the new features. Some features are located on different menus; other features have expanded capabilities that you'll want to learn. You may still need to use your WordPerfect 5.1 software until you feel comfortable with WordPerfect 6.0.

If you decide to keep both versions of WordPerfect on your hard disk, you'll need about 15 megabytes of free disk space before you install WordPerfect 6.0; a complete installation of WordPerfect 6.0 requires about 12 megabytes, which would leave about 3 megabytes for creating and storing documents.

Installing WordPerfect Files

The Installation program will install the WordPerfect 6.0 software files between two different directories: \WP60 and \WPC60DOS. The \WP60 directory will contain the WordPerfect program files, and the \WPC60DOS directory will contain the utility files—such as the Speller and Thesaurus—that can be shared with other software from WordPerfect Corporation.

After installing WordPerfect 6.0, you can retrieve your documents and they should look and print the same as in WordPerfect 5.1. This is true for documents created in any version of WordPerfect. That's the good news. The bad news is that many WordPerfect 5.1 resource files will not work with WordPerfect 6.0; these files include any printer driver files you've customized (.PRS and .ALL files), keyboard layout files (.WPK), macro files (.WPM), style library files (.STY), and conversion resource files (.CRS). You may be able to update some of these files for use with WordPerfect 6.0, as explained below.

22

Printer Drivers

You need to install new printer files for use with WordPerfect 6.0; WordPerfect's Installation program can do this for you when you install the WordPerfect software. The updated printer drivers allow WordPerfect to print full-color graphics and the WordPerfect scalable fonts. The new printer drivers are also required to support intelligent paper size/type definitions, envelope and labels printing, and other feature enhancements in WordPerfect 6.0.

Keyboard and Macro Files

Unfortunately, WordPerfect 5.1 keyboard and macro files are incompatible with WordPerfect 6.0. This is due to the new macro language that WordPerfect 6.0 supports. In earlier versions of WordPerfect, the Macro feature simply records the keystrokes you press while creating the macro. This complicates editing macros, because you must remember the mnemonic selections that choose features from the menus. It also inhibits your ability to create powerful macros, because all program functions are accessed through the menu structure or function keys.

In WordPerfect 6.0, the macro recorder introduces a better system that stores only the end result of each keystroke command or menu selection. When you edit the macro script, it doesn't matter which keystrokes you pressed during the recording process. You can insert program commands or *tokens* directly into the macro script. This method provides a more dynamic environment for macros and allows you to tap into WordPerfect's internal commands to access features and even create your own dialog boxes.

The macro environment does not recognize macro commands from WordPerfect 5.1; this is also true for 5.1 keyboard layout files, which utilize some of the earlier macro features. In WordPerfect 6.0, you will need to re-create any custom keyboard layouts that you used in WordPerfect 5.1.

The Macro Conversion program (MCV.EXE), included with WordPerfect 6.0, lets you convert all or part of your macros for use with WordPerfect 6.0. The conversion isn't perfect, and you will find that some macros cannot be wholly converted. See Appendix C for information about using the Macro Conversion program and fixing possible problems with the macro conversion process.

Converting Documents

WordPerfect 6.0 supports a new document format, which differs from earlier versions of WordPerfect. However, as mentioned earlier, you do not need to convert your documents to use them with version 6.0. Simply retrieve them into WordPerfect 6.0, and they are automatically converted to WordPerfect's new file format. Once retrieved and saved in WordPerfect 6.0, your documents become WordPerfect 6.0 files and cannot be retrieved into WordPerfect 5.1 unless you convert them back to their original file format. Chapter 5 explains how to do this.

If you have created conversion resource (.CRS) files, you will not need them in WordPerfect 6.0; WordPerfect 6.0 automatically detects and converts a wide variety of file formats from other software programs, including all versions of WordPerfect. You can, for example, retrieve files from WordPerfect 5.2 for Windows, Microsoft Word, dBASE, or Lotus 1-2-3, and they are automatically detected and converted for use with WordPerfect 6.0. Note, however, that ASCII files are left in ASCII format unless you explicitly request an alternate format.

IMPORTANT.   *After you retrieve and save a document, it becomes a Word-Perfect 6.0 file. If you want to retrieve the document back into the program that created it, you must save it to its original file format. This is explained in Chapter 5.*

Installing the WordPerfect Software

The following sections explain the hardware requirements for WordPerfect 6.0 and provide instructions for installing the WordPerfect software.

Hardware Requirements

WordPerfect will run on an IBM or IBM-compatible computer with 640K of memory and a 20-megabyte hard disk. These are the minimum requirements, but they are too limiting for a productive installation of WordPerfect 6.0. In this case, the minimum is not sufficient.

Ideally, you should install WordPerfect 6.0 on a computer that has a 386 or faster processor and at least 2 megabytes of memory. Your computer's hard disk must have at least 15 megabytes of free disk space before you install the WordPerfect software. If you plan to use WordPerfect's sound playback and recording features, you'll also need a computer sound board and a set of external speakers. In addition, if you want to send your documents to a fax machine, your computer must have one of the fax boards supported by WordPerfect.

Installing the Software

The WordPerfect Installation program provides two primary options for copying the WordPerfect software to your computer's hard disk. (There's also an option for installation on a network, which is not covered here.) If you are installing WordPerfect for the first time, you will probably want to use the Standard Installation option. Advanced users may prefer the Custom Installation option, which lets you set up your own WordPerfect directories and choose the specific files you want to copy. Follow these steps to install WordPerfect, using the Standard Installation option:

1. Insert the WordPerfect Install 1 disk into drive A. If drive A is not available, insert the disk into drive B and substitute this drive letter in the following steps.

2. From the DOS prompt, type **a:install**, and then press Enter.

3. The installation program asks whether you are using a color monitor. If so, choose Yes to continue; otherwise, choose No.

4. The main WordPerfect Installation screen appears. If you are installing WordPerfect 6.0 for the first time, choose Standard Installation by highlighting the option and pressing Enter.

The installation process begins. Follow the instructions that appear on the screen to complete the software installation. During the installation process, you will be prompted about installation options. When each prompt appears, carefully read the screen and type the specified keys to make your selections. Insert the additional program disks as prompted. Be forewarned that the complete installation may take quite some time. After the installation process is finished, you will find the WordPerfect program files in a directory called \WP60 on your computer's hard disk. Shared program files, such as the Speller, Thesaurus, and printer files, are stored in a directory called \WPC60DOS.

Sometimes you may need to run the Installation program again to install updated copies of WordPerfect or to reinstall program files that you've accidentally deleted or damaged. If this is necessary, start the Installation Program as described earlier. Then choose Standard Installation to reinstall the entire program, or choose Custom Installation to set up a custom installation, to copy single files, or to install a new printer for use with WordPerfect.

Starting WordPerfect

The following sections explain how to start the WordPerfect software after you've used the Installation program to copy the program files to your hard disk. Here, you'll also find information about WordPerfect's start-up switches, which provide different options for starting and configuring the WordPerfect software.

Starting the WordPerfect Software

These are the steps for starting the WordPerfect 6.0 software:

1. From the DOS prompt, change to the \WP60 directory, or change to the directory where you've installed the WordPerfect program files.

2. Type **wp** and then press Enter. The WordPerfect title screen appears, followed by the main document screen.

At this point, you're ready to create a new document, or retrieve and edit a document you've already created. See Chapter 1 for information about using the basic WordPerfect features.

WordPerfect Start-up Options

WordPerfect provides a number of start-up options to help you control how WordPerfect runs. These options are also called *start-up switches*. To use one (or more) of these options, simply type **wp** at the DOS prompt, followed by a space, and then type **/** (a forward slash), followed by the character or characters that represent the start-up switch you want to use. Then press Enter to start the WordPerfect software. Here's one example:

```
wp /r
```

In this example, the /r string indicates that you want to load a portion of WordPerfect into high memory, which speeds up the display process. Table A.1 lists a number of the start-up switches you can use for WordPerfect. Some of these options, like the /ws start-up switch, display data about your computer system that will help you work better with WordPerfect. Other start-up switches change the configuration of WordPerfect or enable a program option that helps WordPerfect run better on your computer.

Table A.1 **WordPerfect Program Start-up Options**

Start-up Switch	Function	Example
/32	Starts WordPerfect using only LIM 3.2 memory management specifications. This may be necessary if you are using memory management software that does not conform to LIM 4.0 (or later) specifications.	wp /32
/bp=n	Indicates the amount of kilobytes (n represents a kilobyte number between 0 and 63) reserved as a print buffer when WordPerfect prints directly to your hardware port. When n = 0, direct printing to your hardware port is disabled.	wp /bp=60 Reserves 60 kilobytes as a print buffer, when WordPerfect's Print to Hardware Port feature is active.

Table A.1 **WordPerfect Program Start-up Options (Continued)**

Start-up Switch	Function	Example
/cp=*number*	Starts WordPerfect for a specific code page setting, indicated by the *number* parameter, and allows access to international keyboard calls and character sets. Your DOS manual should include detailed information about the code page numbers supported by your computer.	wp /cp=863 Starts WordPerfect for use with a French-Canadian computer keyboard. The number *863* is the code page number for the French-Canadian BIOS type.
/d=*pathname*	Indicates where WordPerfect's temporary files should be stored during a WordPerfect session. Usually, these files are stored in the WordPerfect program directory, but the /d start-up switch lets you indicate a specific drive/directory, which is indicated by *pathname*.	wp /d=c:\temp Starts WordPerfect and creates WordPerfect's temporary files to the C:\TEMP directory.
/f2	Corrects problems with text screen displays that are larger than the standard 80 columns by 25 rows. This is only necessary if, for example, your display adapter supports 80 columns by 50 rows, but WordPerfect does not recognize this text display mode as a possible option.	wp /f2
/h	Displays a list of valid start-up options. Use this to view an updated list of start-up switches. (You can also use the switch /?.)	wp /h
/l=*language code*	Indicates the language rules that WordPerfect uses to format dates. *Language code* represents a two-character code. See your WordPerfect reference manual for more information.	wp /l=UK
/ln	Displays a prompt that allows you to change or edit the license number for your copy of WordPerfect.	wp /ln
/m=*macroname*	Starts WordPerfect and plays back the macro specified by *macroname*. Often used to perform a task immediately after the WordPerfect software is activated. You could, for example, create a macro that opens a calendar file or daily log, and then use the /m start-up switch to run the macro each time you start the WordPerfect software.	wp /m=calendar Starts WordPerfect and immediately plays back the CALENDAR.WPM macro.
/nb	Disables the Original Backup feature, so that no backup file can be created while you are saving a document.	wp /nb
/nc	Disables WordPerfect's Cursor Speed feature, and instead, uses the cursor speed that is active before the WordPerfect software is started.	wp /nc

Table A.1 **WordPerfect Program Start-up Options (Continued)**

Start-up Switch	Function	Example
/ne	Disables WordPerfect's use of expanded memory. When you use this option, make sure you have enough available conventional or extended memory (at least 500K) to run the WordPerfect software.	wp /ne
/nh	Disables WordPerfect's Print to Hardware Port feature. This start-up switch is necessary for some older versions of computer BIOS, which conflict with direct printing to your computers parallel or serial port.	wp /nh
/nk	Disables WordPerfect's enhanced keyboard calls, which may conflict with incompatible computer BIOS or some memory-resident software.	wp /nk
/no	Prevents the user from disabling the selected keyboard layout with the Ctrl+6 keystroke. It does not prevent the user from changing the keyboard layout with the Keyboard Layout feature.	wp /no
/np	While you are running WordPerfect on a laptop computer, this start-up switch specifies minimal hard disk access to conserve battery power.	wp /np
/nt=*number*	Starts WordPerfect and manually selects the network type. This allows you to start WordPerfect from a network when the WordPerfect software was originally installed for a different network type. See the appendix of your WordPerfect manual for a complete list of the *number* assignments for the current network types.	wp /nt=1 Starts WordPerfect on system running Novell NetWare.
/nx	Disables WordPerfect's use of extended memory. When you use this start-up switch, make sure you have enough available conventional or expanded memory (at least 500K) to run the WordPerfect software.	wp /nx
/pf=*pathname*	Starts WordPerfect and sets up the temporary print files in the directory specified by *pathname*. When you start WordPerfect from a network, this start-up switch can speed up your printing—but only when the *pathname* parameter specifies a directory on a local hard drive. The temporary files will be deleted from the directory when you properly exit WordPerfect.	wp /pf=c:\temp Starts WordPerfect and creates the temporary print files in the C:\TEMP directory.

Table A.1 **WordPerfect Program Start-up Options (Continued)**

Start-up Switch	Function	Example
/ps=*setfile*	Starts WordPerfect with the program settings stored in the *setfile* file name. The *setfile* parameter should include the full path name and file name of the .SET file you want to use. Network administrators often use this start-up option to force all WordPerfect stations to use the same .SET file. When this start-up switch is not used, WordPerfect uses the .SET file that is located in the WordPerfect program directory or in the default network directory.	wp /ps=q:\wpsys\wp60\-wp{wpc}.set Starts WordPerfect using the WP{WPC}.SET file stored in the Q:\WPSYS\WP60 directory.
/r	Starts WordPerfect and places a portion of the WordPerfect program into extended or expanded memory—whichever has enough available memory. If you have enough memory for this option, it will increase the operating speed of the WordPerfect program.	wp /r
/re	Starts WordPerfect and places a portion of the WordPerfect program into expanded memory.	wp /re
/rx	Starts WordPerfect and places a portion of the WordPerfect program into extended memory.	wp /rx
/sa	Disables WordPerfect's network features when starting WordPerfect from a network.	wp /sa
/sd=*pathname*	Stand-alone printing directory specifies a local directory for the temporary files that WordPerfect creates during printing.	wp /sd=c:\print
/ss=*rows,cols*	Specifies the number of *rows* (text lines) and *cols* (columns, or characters across the screen) that you can see on the WordPerfect screen. Note that this affects only WordPerfect's text display mode, and your computer display card must support different display modes in order for this start-up switch to work.	wp /ss=50,80
/u=*userinitials*	Allows you to start WordPerfect for multiple users on a network, and allows WordPerfect to create unique temporary program files for each network station. The *userinitials* parameter is the network initials or ID for the current user.	wp /u=sgd

Table A.1   **WordPerfect Program Start-up Options (Continued)**

Start-up Switch	Function	Example
/w=conv,exp,ext	Specifies the amount of computer memory that WordPerfect will use, measured in kilobytes, from each of the memory types. *Conv* is conventional memory, *exp* is expanded memory, and *ext* is extended memory. The minimal kilobyte setting you can specify is 53.	wp /w=220,400,1000 WordPerfect distributes its workspace between 220K of conventional memory, 400K of expanded memory, and 1MB of extended memory.
/ws	Displays the amount of memory, in kilobytes, that is available for the WordPerfect workspace.	wp /ws A message displays the amount of available memory.
/x	Starts WordPerfect and ignores the selected setup options. This start-up switch is useful when one or more setup options were defined during the last WordPerfect session that prevent WordPerfect from starting now. For example, if WordPerfect locks after you select a specific graphics driver, you can use the /x start-up switch to start WordPerfect after you reboot your computer.	wp /x

You can combine two or more start-up switches to apply multiple start-up options for the current WordPerfect session. For example, suppose you want to start WordPerfect with the /r, /ps, and /u start-up switches (see Table A.1 for an explanation of these). You could start WordPerfect by typing the following and then pressing Enter at the DOS prompt:

```
wp /r /ps=c:\temp /u=sgd
```

When you combine start-up switches in this manner, make sure you type a space to separate each of the commands. If you need to use one or more start-up switches each time you start WordPerfect, you should create a DOS batch file that includes the commands you use regularly.

Defining Program Options

After you start the WordPerfect software, you can choose different program options to customize the way WordPerfect works for you. These options are found on WordPerfect's Setup menu, which you can display by pressing Setup (Shift+F1) or by choosing File from the menu bar and then choosing Setup.

When the Setup menu is displayed, you'll see six options: Mouse, Display, Environment, Keyboard Layout, Location of Files, and Color Printing Palette. You can also change the document screen setup via the Screen Setup dialog box (choose View/Screen Setup).The following sections explain the setup options for each of these categories.

If you are familiar with WordPerfect 5.1, you'll notice that the Initial Settings category has been removed from the Setup menu. WordPerfect 6.0 does not include an Initial Settings category, because you can now create the default feature settings from the dialog box in which each feature is located. You can, for example, choose Initial Codes Setup from the Document Format dialog box to define the initial codes for the WordPerfect program. Or you can choose Setup (Shift+F1) from the Print/Fax dialog box to define the default print settings. All Setup selections remain in effect for future WordPerfect sessions until you change them again.

Adjusting the Mouse Settings

When you first start the WordPerfect software, it detects the type of mouse—if there is one—connected to your computer and uses a set of default options to determine how WordPerfect will communicate with the mouse.

Use the Mouse dialog box to change the mouse button assignments for left-handed or right-handed users, to adjust the speed of the mouse pointer, or to modify the double-click speed for mouse selections. The Mouse dialog box also includes an option that changes the type of mouse you are using; this let's you select a different mouse driver if your mouse breaks or ceases to work with WordPerfect.

These are the steps for displaying the Mouse dialog box and making changes to the mouse settings:

Choose File ▶
Setup ▶ Mouse.

- Press Setup (Shift+F1) and choose Mouse. This displays the Mouse dialog box.

- If your mouse is not working with WordPerfect, choose Type and select the correct driver for your mouse. Then choose Port and select the COM port to which your mouse is connected.

- Choose Double-click Interval, and enter a number to adjust the speed for a double-click of a mouse button. Higher numbers mean a faster double-click speed; lower numbers produce a slower double-click speed. When this option is set to 0, the double-click feature is disabled.

- Choose Acceleration Factor, and enter a number to change the speed at which the mouse pointer moves across the screen. A higher number produces a faster mouse pointer; a lower number slows the mouse pointer.

- Check the box for Left-handed Mouse, and the button assignments for the mouse are switched for left-handed users.

Choose OK until you return to the document screen.

- When you are finished adjusting the mouse settings, press Exit (F7) until you return to the document screen.

WordPerfect assigns the mouse button functions for right-handed users. A single-click on the left mouse button selects a menu item, a dialog box option, or moves the cursor to the place where the mouse pointer is located; hold down the left mouse button and move (drag) the mouse to select a passage of text. A single-click on the right mouse button from within the document screen activates the menu bar; when you hold down the right mouse button and move the mouse pointer, you'll scroll through your document. You can also click the right mouse button to "Escape" from menus and dialog boxes without making selections. These are the standard mouse button functions. When you check the box for Left-handed Mouse, the mouse button functions are transposed—that is, the right mouse button selects menu and dialog box items, moves the cursor, and blocks text, and the left mouse button activates the menu bar, scrolls through your document, and also gets you out of menus and dialog boxes.

Choosing Display Options

The WordPerfect Installation configures WordPerfect for the type of monitor connected to your computer. If, for example, you have a VGA monitor, WordPerfect is already configured for the standard VGA display settings. If you have a display card with special features—like 256 color display in 800×600 resolution—you'll need to use WordPerfect's Setup Display dialog box to select an enhanced display driver. This dialog box also lets you choose different screen colors for WordPerfect's Text display mode.

To change WordPerfect's display settings:

Choose File ▶ Setup ▶ Display.

- Press Setup (Shift+F1) and then choose Display.

- To change the display type for WordPerfect's graphics display mode or for the Print Preview feature, choose Graphics Mode Screen Type/Colors.

- To change the display type for WordPerfect's text display mode, choose Text Mode Screen Type/Colors. Then select the display type and display colors you want to use.

- When you're done, press F7 to return to the document screen.

To choose default document screen options, you need to select Screen Setup from the View menu.

From the Screen Setup dialog box, choose the display options you want to change. Then press Exit (F7) until you return to the document screen. WordPerfect updates the screen display according to the choices you made.

From the Screen Setup dialog box, you can choose from a large number of options to customize the WordPerfect screen display. Choose Windows Options and then choose Status Line to select what you want to see in the lower-left corner of the screen: the file name of the current document, the font that is active at the cursor location, or nothing.

Choose Reveal Codes and then choose Display Details to show all measurements and settings of the codes in the Reveal Codes windows. Usually, you won't see the measurements associated with the codes until you move the cursor over them. When this option is checked, the detailed code information is always visible when the Reveal Codes window is displayed. Choose Reveal Codes and then choose Window Percentage to specify how large the window should be when it is displayed.

If you want WordPerfect to display a symbol or character that shows you where you've pressed the hard return key (Enter), choose Display Characters, choose Hard Return Character, and then type the character you want to see. You can also choose Space Character and assign a character that denotes each space you type in your documents. Although you will see these characters on the screen, neither the hard return display character nor the space display character will appear on printed pages.

You can also choose Display of Merge Codes, and specify how you wish merge codes to be displayed in your documents.

These are just a few of the scren display options that you can customize to suit your tastes. You can also decide whether to display the menu bar, ribbon, and button bar; whether to see the scroll bars; and how much to zoom the display.

Defining the WordPerfect Environment Options

WordPerfect's Environment dialog box lets you customize some of Word-Perfect's program features. To display this dialog box, press Setup (Shift+F1) or choose File from the menu bar and then choose Setup. Then choose Environment.

From the Environment dialog box, choose Backup Options to indicate your preferences for automatic file backup; this feature is explained in Chapter 5. Choose Beep Options to indicate whether you want a beep to sound when there is a program error, a search error, or a prompt for text hyphenation. Choose Cursor Speed to increase or decrease the speed of the cursor when you hold down one of the arrow keys.

When the Allow Undo box is checked, it enables WordPerfect to undo any task that you complete in the document screen. If you find that WordPerfect is running too slowly, you may want to deselect <u>A</u>llow Undo so that no *X* appears in the box next to this option. This disables the Undo feature and increases the speed at which WordPerfect operates.

The <u>P</u>rompt for Hyphenation option lets you choose the conditions under which WordPerfect will prompt you for manual hyphenation, assuming that the Hyphenation feature is turned on for each document.

The <u>U</u>nits of Measure option lets you specify the type of measurement that WordPerfect uses within dialog boxes, such as the Tab Set dialog box, and also for the Ruler and status line measurements.

The <u>L</u>anguage option indicates the language of your copy of WordPerfect. You cannot change this to another language unless you have installed other language resource files (*.TRS) from international language versions of WordPerfect. If additional *.TRS files are available to you, you can install them and choose a different language with the <u>L</u>anguage option. Then all WordPerfect menus and dialog boxes appear in the text from the selected language. Note that this is different from choosing a new Speller or Thesaurus language; if you've installed different speller/thesaurus language modules, you can indicate the module you've installed by pressing Format (Shift+F8) and choosing <u>O</u>ther and then the <u>L</u>anguage option.

Using the Keyboard Layout Feature

WordPerfect's Keyboard Layout feature lets you choose or create a different keyboard layout for use with WordPerfect. When a keyboard layout is selected, the keystroke assignments change according to the definitions in the layout. This feature is found on the Setup menu; for detailed information, see Chapter 25.

Specifying Your File Directories

The Location of Files dialog box indicates where WordPerfect will look for program and document files. When you install the WordPerfect software, the Installation program inserts the appropriate directory path names in this dialog box. This feature saves you the trouble of entering a full path name each time you want to save or retrieve a file; it also allows WordPerfect to find the files it needs without prompting you to enter the location of specific files.

When you need to change the path names for your documents or program files, you can redisplay the Location of Files dialog box and edit the path names that are listed for each file type. Press Setup (Shift+F1), or choose <u>F</u>ile from the menu bar and then choose Se<u>t</u>up. Then choose <u>L</u>ocation of Files. Select each of the options that you want to change and enter the correct path names. Then press Exit (F7) or choose OK until you return to the document screen. WordPerfect then uses the path names you entered to find each of the file types you'll need during a WordPerfect session. See Chapter 5 for detailed information about the Location of Files feature.

Color Printing Palette

The Color Printing Palette (or Color Palette) option lets you select a different palette of color choices for text and other items in your documents. This option also lets you mix colors to create your own custom color palettes.

Note that the Color Printing Palette affects the colors that may appear when you send your documents to a color printer, and when you edit your documents with WordPerfect's graphics or page display modes. The Color Printing Palette does not affect the screen colors you may choose for WordPerfect's text display mode.

To select or create a new color palette:

Choose View ▸ Graphics Mode.

- If you're not already in graphics display mode, press Screen (Ctrl+F3) and choose Graphics. You will then be in WordPerfect's graphics display mode, in which you can see all color choices of the current palette.

Choose File ▸ Setup ▸ Color Palette.

- Press Setup (Shift+F1) and then choose Color Printing Palette.

- Highlight one of the color palette names, and choose Edit to view the colors in the palette.

- In the Edit Color Printing Palette dialog box, highlight a color and choose Edit to change the palette attributes, or create your own color by choosing Create.

- Press F7 or choose Close to return to the Color Printing Palettes dialog box.

- Choose Select to use the highlighted palette, or choose Create to create your own palette of custom colors.

Choose Close until you return to the document screen.

- When you are finished with the Color Printing Palettes dialog box, press Exit (F7) until you return to the document screen.

After you select or create a new color palette, you can apply any of the palette colors to your document by choosing the Color option from the Font dialog box. The selected color palette also provides the color choices for graphics box borders, horizontal and vertical lines, and other document items that allow a choice of colors.

Obviously, you must have a color printer to produce the text colors on the printed page; if you don't have a color printer, you may want to apply different text colors as an editing tool or to improve the appearance of documents that will be viewed on the computer screen. See Chapter 3 for more information about applying different colors to text in your documents.

WordPerfect Codes

Codes are the commands that WordPerfect uses to arrange text and to create special effects in your documents. This isn't so different from other word processors—all software programs use codes and commands to arrange information on your screen and to create the printed pages. However, WordPerfect lets you display and manipulate the codes that make up your documents, and this gives you more control over the editing process.

WordPerfect has been criticized for its code interface, mostly by people who don't understand how to work with the codes. This appendix clarifies some of the confusion. There is a table at the end of this appendix that includes a complete list of the codes you may see when you use WordPerfect's Reveal Codes feature, as well as general information about the code interface.

Displaying the Codes in Your Document

WordPerfect's Reveal Codes window lets you see the codes that you've inserted to create the current document layout. Reveal Codes also lets you see font and attribute codes, and other codes that affect the document layout but are not visible on the document editing screen. The following sections explain additional details about the Reveal Codes feature, which is introduced in Chapter 2.

Displaying the Reveal Codes Window

When a document is displayed on the screen, you can press Reveal Codes (Alt+F3 or F12), or choose View/Reveal Codes, to open the Reveal Codes window, shown at the bottom of the screen in Figure B.1. A bar divides the screen to create the window. Above the bar, you'll see your document as it usually appears on your screen; below the bar, you'll see the same text with the embedded formatting codes visible.

The size of the Reveal Codes window is specified with a WordPerfect Setup option. To increase or decrease the size of the Reveal Codes window, press Screen (Ctrl+F3) and then press Setup (Shift+F1). Select Reveal Codes/Window Percentage, and enter a number that represents the percentage of the screen that you want to use for the Reveal Codes window. If, for example, you want the Reveal Codes window to fill half the screen when it is displayed, enter **50** as the percentage number. Finally, press Exit (F7) until you return to the document screen. The new size is immediately effective for the Reveal Codes window.

Figure B.1
The Reveal Codes
window

Reveal Codes
window

Formatting
codes

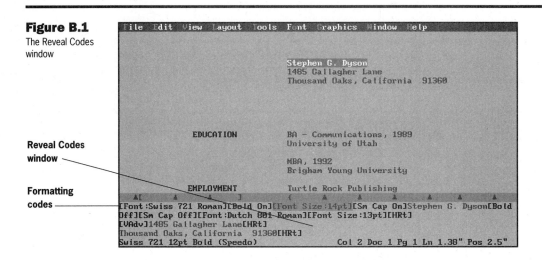

Editing inside the Reveal Codes Window

When the Reveal Codes window is displayed, you can type new text, delete text or codes, insert new codes, and perform any editing task that is allowed at the standard document screen. Use the cursor movement keys to scroll through the text and view all the codes in your document. Each general code appears within square brackets, like the following codes for Bold, Left Margin, and Tab Set:

```
[Bold On]
[Lft Mar]
[Tab Set]
```

The cursor appears as a highlighted box in the Reveal Codes window. When you move the cursor over a code, the code may expand to reveal more detail about the code settings. For example, when you move the cursor over the codes listed above, each code may expand to show specific the code settings, like these examples :

```
[Bold On:Courier Bold; 12pt]
[Lft Mar:1.5"]
[Tab Set:Rel; 1.5"L,4"D,6.5"R.]
```

When the cursor is positioned over text characters, WordPerfect "hides" the specific settings of each code to make it easier for you to read the Reveal Codes information. If you want to see the detailed codes at all times, press Screen (Ctrl+F3) and then press Setup (Shift+F1). Then choose Reveal

Codes/Display Details, and press Exit (F7) until you return to the document screen. The next time you use the Reveal Codes feature, you'll see the complete code measurements and settings for each formatting code regardless of whether the codes are highlighted. If you no longer want to see the full-length codes, just reverse this procedure.

When you are finished in the Reveal Codes window, press Reveal Codes (Alt+F3 or F12), or choose View/Reveal Codes, again to close the window and restore the document screen.

Auto Code Placement

WordPerfect 6.0 includes an Auto Code Placement feature, which ensures that all formatting codes and commands are automatically placed at the beginning of the current line, paragraph, or page, depending on the type of formatting feature you've selected.

For example, when Auto Code Placement in turned on and you change the left and right margins, the codes that create the changes are automatically placed at the beginning of the current paragraph; when you change the top and bottom margins, the codes are inserted at the top of the current page. You don't need to position the cursor exactly where the change should take effect. WordPerfect automatically inserts each code at the appropriate place.

When you first install and start the WordPerfect software, the Auto Code Placement feature is turned on. You can turn it off by pressing Setup (Shift+F1), choosing Environment, and then choosing Auto Code Placement. After than, each formatting code or command will be inserted at the current position of the cursor in your text.

IMPORTANT. *If you turn off the Auto Code Placement feature, some codes—like Center Page, Top/Bottom Margins, and Headers/Footers—may not take effect until the following page or paragraph in your document.*

Moving the Cursor around Codes

Users of WordPerfect 5.1 (or earlier versions) may be frustrated with the cursor movement in WordPerfect 6.0. In earlier versions of WordPerfect, you need to press → or ← to move the cursor past the codes embedded in your document text, even when you can't see the codes and the Reveal Codes feature is turned off.

When the Reveal Codes window is not displayed, WordPerfect 6.0 doesn't recognize a code as a "character" that you need to move the cursor around. You can move the cursor throughout your document text without worrying about pressing extra keystrokes to get around the codes. This is particularly useful if you dislike the code interface.

If, however, you're a veteran WordPerfect user, you may prefer to press → or ← to get around the codes. If so, you can choose a setup option that treats each code as a "character" in the text when Reveal Codes is turned off. To activate this option, press Setup (Shift+F1), choose Environment, and then choose WordPerfect 5.1 Cursor Movement. Then, when you return to the document screen, you'll need to press → or ← to move the cursor past codes that are in the text.

WordPerfect's Codes

Table B.1 lists all the codes that can appear in the Reveal Codes window. The table also explains the function or effect of each code, and the menu selection or keystroke that inserts the code into your document.

Table B.1   **WordPerfect's Codes**

Code	Function	Menu Selection/Keystroke
-	Creates a hyphen text character that does not allow the word or phrase to be divided.	Home, Hyphen
[- Hyphen]	Creates a hyphen where a word or phrase may be divided.	– (Hyphen)
[- Soft Hyphen] or [- Soft Hyphen EOL]	Displays a hyphen only if the current word must be divided.	Ctrl+Hyphen
[Auto Hyphen EOL]	Creates an automatic hyphen at the end of a line.	Inserted as needed by WordPerfect.
[Back Tab]	Moves text to the next tab stop at the left. Performs the same function as the Margin Release code in WordPerfect 5.1.	Shift+Tab or Layout ▸ Alignment ▸ Back Tab
[Begin Gen Txt] [End Gen Txt]	Indicates a section of text, such as a table of contents or index, that is created by the Generate feature.	Inserted by WordPerfect after you choose Tools ▸ Generate or press Mark (Alt+F5) and choose Generate from the Mark dialog box

Table B.1 **WordPerfect's Codes (Continued)**

Code	Function	Menu Selection/Keystroke
[Bar Code]	Creates a POSTNET bar code.	Layout ▸ Other ▸ Bar Code or Layout ▸ Envelope ▸ POSTNET Bar Code
[Binding Width]	Creates a margin adjustment to allow extra space for binding printed pages.	Layout ▸ Other ▸ Printer Functions ▸ Binding Offset
[Block]	Appears in Reveal Codes to indicate the beginning of a block, when the Block feature is turned on.	Block (Alt+F4 or F12) or Edit ▸ Block
[Block Pro On] [Block Pro Off]	Protects a section of text from being divided by a soft or hard page break.	Layout ▸ Other ▸ Block Protect
[Bold On] [Bold Off]	Creates the Bold text attribute for a section of text.	Bold (F6) or Ctrl+B or Font ▸ Bold
[Bookmark]	Creates a document bookmark.	Shift+F12 or Edit ▸ Bookmark You can also use Ctrl+Q to create a QuickMark, a special type of bookmark.
[Bot Mar]	Creates the bottom margin on the page.	Layout ▸ Margins ▸ Bottom Margin
[Box (Char): fignum; Figure Box]	Creates a Character graphic box.	Graphics ▸ Graphics Boxes ▸ Create ▸ Attach to ▸ Character Position
[Box (Page): fignum; Figure Box]	Creates a Page graphics box.	Graphics ▸ Graphics Boxes ▸ Create ▸ Attach to ▸ Page or Fixed Page
[Box (Para): fignum; Figure Box]	Creates a Paragraph graphic box.	Graphics ▸ Graphics Boxes ▸ Create
[Calc Col]	Designates a calculation column for the Math feature.	Tools ▸ Math ▸ Define ▸ Column Type ▸ Calculation
[Cancel Hyph]	Cancels hyphenation for the word that immediately follows.	Home /

Table B.1   **WordPerfect's Codes (Continued)**

Code	Function	Menu Selection/Keystroke
[Cell]	Indicate the place where a new table cell begins.	Inserted as needed by WordPerfect.
[Chap Num Dec]	Decrements the current chapter page number.	Layout ▸ Page ▸ Page Numbering ▸ Chapter ▸ Decrement Number
[Chap Num Disp]	Displays the current chapter page number.	Layout ▸ Page ▸ Page Numbering ▸ Chapter ▸ Display in Document
[Chap Num Inc]	Increments the current chapter page number.	Layout ▸ Page ▸ Page Numbering ▸ Chapter ▸ Increment Number
[Chap Num Meth]	Defines the appearance of chapter page numbers.	Layout ▸ Page ▸ Page Numbering ▸ Chapter ▸ Numbering Method
[Chap Num Set]	Changes the value of the next chapter page number.	Layout ▸ Page ▸ Page Numbering ▸ Chapter ▸ New Number
[Char Shade Change]	Creates shaded text by changing the color percentage for text.	Font ▸ Print Color ▸ Shade
[Char Style On] [Char Style Off]	Indicates where a Character style is turned on.	Layout ▸ Styles ▸ choose a Character style ▸ Select
[Cntr Cur Pg]	Vertically centers the current page only.	Layout ▸ Page ▸ Center Current Page
[Cntr on Cur Pos]	Centers the text that follows over the position where the [Cntr on Cur Pos] code is located. Only centers the text up to the next soft or hard return.	Move the cursor to an empty position on the line by using tabs and spaces, and then press Center (Shift+F6).
[Cntr on Mar]	Horizontally centers a line of text between left and right margins.	Center (Shift+F6) or Layout ▸ Alignment ▸ Center
[Cntr on Mar (Dot)]	Horizontially centers a line of text, and creates a dot-leader to the centered text.	Center (Shift+F6) twice or Layout ▸ Alignment ▸ Center twice
[Cntr Pgs]	Vertically centers all pages that follow this code.	Layout ▸ Page ▸ Center Pages
[Cntr Tab]	Centers text over the next tab stop at the right.	Tab (tab stop definition must be Center)

Table B.1   **WordPerfect's Codes (Continued)**

Code	Function	Menu Selection/Keystroke
[CNTR TAB]	Centers text over the next tab stop, regardless of the type of tab stop.	Home, Shift+F6
[Cntr Tab (Dot)] or [CNTR TAB (DOT)]	Centers text over the next tab stop at the right, and creates a dot-leader to the tabbed text.	Tab (tab stop definition must be Center with Dot Leader selected) Home, Home, Shift+F6
[Col Border]	Creates a border around columns.	Layout ▸ Columns ▸ Column Borders or Graphics ▸ Borders ▸ Column
[Col Def]	Creates a column layout.	Layout ▸ Columns ▸ Column Type
[Color]	Changes the display and print color for text.	Font ▸ Print Color ▸ highlight the desired color ▸ Select
[Comment]	Stores a text comment within the document.	Layout ▸ Comment ▸ Create
[Condl EOP]	Creates a conditional end of page, where a certain number of lines are protected from a page break division.	Layout ▸ Other ▸ Conditional End of Page
[Count Dec]	Decrements the current counter.	Layout ▸ Character ▸ Counters ▸ Decrement
	Decrements the current graphic box caption number.	Graphics ▸ Graphics Boxes ▸ Numbering ▸ Decrement
[Count Disp]	Displays the current number for a counter type.	Layout ▸ Character ▸ Counters ▸ Display in Document
	Displays the current graphic box caption number.	Graphics ▸ Graphics Boxes ▸ Numbering ▸ Display in Document
[Count Inc]	Increments the current counter.	Layout ▸ Character ▸ Counters ▸ Increment
	Increments the current graphic box caption number.	Graphics ▸ Graphics Boxes ▸ Numbering ▸ Increment
[Count Meth]	Determines the numbering method for the current counter.	Layout ▸ Character ▸ Counters ▸ Set Method

Table B.1   **WordPerfect's Codes (Continued)**

Code	Function	Menu Selection/Keystroke
	Defines the appearance of graphic box caption numbers.	Graphics ▸ Graphics Boxes ▸ Numbering ▸ Set Method
[Count Set]	Sets the starting value (or continuing value) for the current counter.	Layout ▸ Character ▸ Counters ▸ Set Value
	Changes the value of the next graphic box caption number.	Graphics ▸ Graphics Boxes ▸ Numbering ▸ Set Value
[Date]	Inserts the date (date code) that will show the current date whenever the document is displayed.	Tools ▸ Date ▸ Code
[Date Fmt]	Defines the format for dates inserted with the Date Text or Date Code feature.	Tools ▸ Date ▸ Format
[Dbl Und On] [Dbl Und Off]	Creates the double-underline option for a section of text.	Font ▸ Double Underline
[Dbl-Sided Print]	Specifies double-sided printing for the document.	Layout ▸ Page ▸ Double-sided Printing
[Dec/Align Char]	Specifies the character that will be used for decimal alignment.	Layout ▸ Character ▸ Decimal/Align Character
[Dec Tab]	Aligns decimal numbers over the next tab stop.	Tab (tab stop definition must be Decimal)
[DEC TAB]	Aligns decimal numbers over the next tab stop, regardless of the type of tab stop.	Decimal Tab (Ctrl+F6)
[Dec Tab (Dot)] or [DEC TAB (DOT)]	Aligns decimal numbers over the next tab stop, and creates a dot-leader to the text.	Tab (tab stop definition must be Decimal with Dot Leader selected) Home, Home, Ctrl+F6

Table B.1   **WordPerfect's Codes (Continued)**

Code	Function	Menu Selection/Keystroke
[Delay] or [Delay On] [Delay Off]	Contains a set of formatting codes, the effect of which are delayed until a specific page in the document.	Layout ▸ Page ▸ Delay Codes
[Dorm HRt]	Dormant Hard Return. When an [HRt] code follows a soft page break code ([SPg]), WordPerfect converts the [HRt] code to a [Dorm HRt] code, so that the first line of the new page is not a blank line.	Inserted as needed by WordPerfect.
[Dot Lead Char]	Specifies the character that will create dot leaders.	Layout ▸ Character ▸ Dot Leader Character
[End Cntr/Align]	Indicates the end of centering, flush right, or other single-line alignment options.	Layout ▸ Other ▸ End Centering/ Alignment
[Endnote]	Creates an endnote reference number.	Layout ▸ Endnote ▸ Create
[Endnote Min]	Specifies the minimum number of endnote lines that must be kept together, if an endnote needs to be divided between two or more pages.	Layout ▸ Endnote ▸ Options ▸ Minimum Amount of Endnote to Keep Together
[Endnote Num Dec]	Decrements the current endnote number.	Layout ▸ Endnote ▸ New Number ▸ Decrement Number
[Endnote Num Disp]	Shows the endnote number within the endnote text.	Layout ▸ Endnote ▸ New Number ▸ Display in Document
[Endnote Num Inc]	Increments the current endnote number.	Layout ▸ Endnote ▸ New Number ▸ Increment Number
[Endnote Num Meth]	Determines the numbering style/method for endnotes.	Layout ▸ Endnote ▸ New Number ▸ Numbering Method
[Endnote Num Set]	Change the number value of the endnotes that follow in the document.	Layout ▸ Endnote ▸ New Number ▸ New Number
[Endnote Placement]	Indicates the position and style for notes at the end of the document.	Layout ▸ Endnote ▸ Placement

Table B.1   **WordPerfect's Codes (Continued)**

Code	Function	Menu Selection/Keystroke
[Endnote Space]	Defines spacing between endnotes.	Layout ▸ Endnote ▸ Options ▸ Spacing Between Endnotes
[Ext Large On] [Ext Large Off]	Creates the Extra Large text size for a section of text.	Font ▸ Size/Position ▸ Extra Large
[Filename]	Embeds the file name of the current document into the document text.	Layout ▸ Other ▸ Insert Filename
[Fine On] [Fine Off]	Creates the Fine text size for a section of text.	Font ▸ Size/Position ▸ Fine
[First Ln Ind]	Creates a first line indent for paragraph text.	Layout ▸ Margins ▸ First Line Indent
[Flsh Rgt]	Aligns text at the right margin.	Flush Right (Alt+F6) or Layout ▸ Alignment ▸ Flush Right
[Flsh Rgt (Dot)]	Aligns text at the right margin, and creates a dot-leader to the text.	Flush Right (Alt+F6) twice or Layout ▸ Alignment ▸ Flush Right twice
[Flt Cell Begin] [Flt Cell End]	Creates a floating table cell within document text.	Layout ▸ Tables ▸ Create Floating Cell
[Font:*font name*]	Creates a font change in the text.	Font ▸ Font ▸ Font
[Font Size:*font size*]	Changes the point size of the selected font.	Font ▸ Font ▸ Size
[Footer A]	Creates document footer A.	Layout ▸ Header/Footer/Watermark ▸ Footers ▸ Footer A
[Footer B]	Creates document footer B.	Layout ▸ Header/Footer/Watermark ▸ Footers ▸ Footer B
[Footer Sep]	Defines the amount of space between the footers and text on the page.	Layout ▸ Header/Footer/Watermark ▸ Footers ▸ Space Above Footer
[Footnote]	Footnote reference number in document text.	Layout ▸ Footnote ▸ Create

Table B.1   WordPerfect's Codes (Continued)

Code	Function	Menu Selection/Keystroke
[Footer Sep]	Defines the amount of space between the footers and text on the page.	Layout ▶ Header/Footer/Watermark ▶ Footers ▶ Space Above Footer
[Footnote]	Footnote reference number in document text.	Layout ▶ Footnote ▶ Create
[Footnote Cont Msg]	Specifies the "continued" message that will appear when a footnote is divided between two or more pages.	Layout ▶ Footnote ▶ Options ▶ Print Continued Message
[Footnote Min]	Specifies the minimum number of footnote lines that must be kept together, if an footnote needs to be divided between two or more pages.	Layout ▶ Footnote ▶ Options ▶ Amount of Footnote to Keep Together
[Footnote Num Dec]	Decrements the current footnote number.	Layout ▶ Footnote ▶ New Number ▶ Decrement Number
[Footnote Num Disp]	Displays the footnote number within document text.	Layout ▶ Footnote ▶ New Number ▶ Display in Document
[Footnote Num Each Pg]	Specifies that footnote numbering should start with *1* at the beginning of each page.	Layout ▶ Footnote ▶ Options ▶ Restart Footnote Numbers each Page
[Footnote Num Inc]	Increments the current footnote number.	Layout ▶ Footnote ▶ New Number ▶ Increment Number
[Footnote Num Meth]	Determines the numbering style/method for footnote numbers.	Layout ▶ Footnote ▶ New Number ▶ Numbering Method
[Footnote Num Set]	Changes the number value for the footnotes that follow.	Layout ▶ Footnote ▶ New Number ▶ New Number
[Footnote Sep Ln]	Defines the line that separates footnotes from the document text.	Layout ▶ Footnote ▶ Options ▶ Footnote Separator Line
[Footnote Space]	Defines the spacing between footnotes.	Layout ▶ Footnote ▶ Options ▶ Spacing Between Footnotes
[Footnote Txt Pos]	Specifies the position of footnote text on the pages.	Layout ▶ Footnote ▶ Options ▶ Footnotes at Bottom of Page

Table B.1 **WordPerfect's Codes (Continued)**

Code	Function	Menu Selection/Keystroke
[Graph Line]	Create a horizontal or vertical graphic line.	Graphics ▸ Graphics Lines ▸ Create
[HAdv]	Advance text horizontally.	Layout ▸ Other ▸ Advance
[HCol]	Indicates where one column ends and the next column begins.	Ctrl+Enter (while the cursor is within columns)
[HCol-SPg]	When an [HCol] code follows a [SPg] code, WordPerfect combines both to create a [HCol-SPg] code. This ensures that an extra column break does not occur after the [SPg] code.	Inserted as needed by WordPerfect.
[Header A]	Creates document header A.	Layout ▸ Header/Footer/Watermark ▸ Headers ▸ Header A
[Header B]	Creates document header B.	Layout ▸ Header/Footer/Watermark ▸ Headers ▸ Header B
[Header Sep]	Defines the amount of space between headers and text on the page.	Layout ▸ Header/Footer/Watermark ▸ Headers ▸ Space Below Header
[Hidden On] [Hidden Off]	When hidden text is displayed, these codes mark the beginning and end of the hidden text.	Font ▸ Hidden Text ▸ Hidden Text
[Hidden Txt]	Stores and hides a section of outline text.	Tools ▸ Outline ▸ Hide Body Text or Tools ▸ Outline ▸ Hide Family
[HPg]	Inserts a hard page break.	Ctrl+Enter or Layout ▸ Alignment ▸ Hard Page
[HRow-HCol]	Indicates a combined hard row/hard column break.	Inserted as needed by WordPerfect.

Table B.1   WordPerfect's Codes (Continued)

Code	Function	Menu Selection/Keystroke
[HRow-HCol-SPg]	When a [HRow-HCol] code follows a [SPg] code, WordPerfect combines both codes to create a [HRow-HCol-SPg] code. This ensures that an extra row/column break does not occur after the [SPg] code.	Inserted as needed by WordPerfect.
[HRow-HPg]	Combined hard row break and hard page break.	Inserted as needed by WordPerfect.
[HRt]	Hard return.	Enter
[HRt-SCol]	Combined hard return and a column break.	Inserted as needed by WordPerfect.
[HRt-SPg]	Combined hard return and a soft page break.	Inserted as needed by WordPerfect.
[HSpace]	Inserts a character space that cannot be divided by hyphenation or text wrapping.	Home, Spacebar
[Hypertext Begin] [Hypertext End]	Defines a section of text as a hypertext link to another section of the document or to another document.	Tools ▸ Hypertext ▸ Create Link
[Hyph]	Turns hyphenation on/off.	Layout ▸ Line ▸ Hyphenation
[Hyph SRt]	Hyphenation soft return.	Home, Enter
[Index]	Marks an entry for an index.	Tools ▸ Index ▸ Mark
[Italc On] [Italc Off]	Creates the italics attribute for a section of text.	Ctrl+I or Font ▸ Italics
[Just]	Changes the type of text justification.	Layout ▸ Justification
[Just Lim]	Sets the word spacing limits for Full justification.	Layout ▸ Other ▸ Printer Functions ▸ Word Spacing Justification Limits
[Kern]	Turns on/off the automatic kerning feature.	Layout ▸ Other ▸ Printer Functions ▸ Kerning
[Labels Form][Paper Sz/Typ]	Creates a labels definition.	Layout ▸ Page ▸ Labels

Table B.1   WordPerfect's Codes (Continued)

Code	Function	Menu Selection/Keystroke
[Lang]	Change the standard language format for dates.	Layout ▸ Other ▸ Language
[Large On] [Large Off]	Creates the Large text size for a section of text.	Font ▸ Size/Position ▸ Large
[Leading Adj]	Adjusts the amount of space between one text baseline and the next.	Layout ▸ Other ▸ Printer Functions ▸ Leading Adjustment
[Lft HZone] [Rgt HZone]	Specifies the hyphenation zone settings.	Layout ▸ Line ▸ Hyphenation Zone
[Lft Indent]	Creates a left-margin indent for a single paragraph.	Indent (F4) or Layout ▸ Alignment ▸ Indent
[Lft Mar]	Specifies the left margin on the page.	Layout ▸ Margins ▸ Left Margin
[Lft Mar Adj]	Creates a left-margin adjustment for all paragraphs.	Layout ▸ Margins ▸ Left Margin Adjustment
[Lft/Rgt Indent]	Indents both left and right margins for a single paragraph.	Indent (Shift+F4) or Layout ▸ Alignment ▸ Indent
[Lft Tab]	Moves text to the next tab stop.	Tab (tab stop definition must be set to Left)
[LFT TAB]	Creates a left tab, regardless of the next tab stop type.	Home, Tab
[Lft Tab (Dot)] or [LFT TAB (DOT)]	Moves text to the next tab stop, and creates a dot-leader to the text.	Tab (tab stop definition must be set to Left, with the Dot Leader selected) Home, Home, Tab
[Link] [Link End]	Creates a link to a spreadsheet file.	Tools ▸ Spreadsheet ▸ Create Link ▸ Link
[Ln Height]	Changes the line height for text, which is the amount of space between text baselines.	Layout ▸ Line ▸ Line Height
[Ln Num]	Turns line numbering on/off.	Layout ▸ Line ▸ Line Numbering ▸ Line Numbering On

Table B.1   WordPerfect's Codes (Continued)

Code	Function	Menu Selection/Keystroke
[Ln Num Meth]	Defines the line numbering method.	Layout ▸ Line ▸ Line Numbering ▸ Numbering Method
[Ln Num Set]	Changes the value of numbered lines, for the lines that follow this code.	Layout ▸ Line ▸ Line Numbering ▸ Starting Line Number
[Ln Spacing]	Specifies the spacing of text lines.	Layout ▸ Line ▸ Line Spacing
[Math]	Turns the Math feature on/off.	Tools ▸ Math ▸ On
[Math Def]	Defines the math settings for a table created with tab stops.	Tools ▸ Math ▸ Define
[MRG:code] [mrgcode:]	Specifies a merge command.	Tools ▸ Merge ▸ Define ▸ Merge Codes
[Mrk Txt List Begin] [Mrk Txt List End]	Marks a section of text to include in a list.	Tools ▸ List ▸ Mark
[Mrk Txt ToC Begin] [Mrk Txt ToC End]	Marks a section of text to include in a table of contents.	Tools ▸ Table of Contents ▸ Mark
[Open Style:Initial-Codes]	Creates the effect of the formatting codes defined on the Document Initial Codes or Initial Codes Setup screen.	Automatically inserted at the beginning of each document by WordPerfect.
[Open Style:]	Turns on an open style.	Layout ▸ Styles ▸ highlight an open style ▸ Select
[Outline]	Turns the Outline feature on/off.	Tools ▸ Outline ▸ Begin New Outline
[Outln On] [Outln Off]	Creates the Outline text attribute for a section of text.	Font ▸ Outline
[Ovrstk]	Combines two or more characters to create an overstrike character.	Layout ▸ Character ▸ Create Overstrike
[Paper Sz/Typ]	Changes the paper size on which current text will be printed.	Layout ▸ Page ▸ Paper Size/Type
[Para Border]	Creates a border around the current paragraph.	Graphics ▸ Borders ▸ Paragraph

Table B.1 **WordPerfect's Codes (Continued)**

Code	Function	Menu Selection/Keystroke
[Para Num]	Inserts a paragraph number for an Outline style.	Tools ▸ Outline ▸ Outline Options ▸ Insert Outline Level (Outline Style edit mode only)
[Para Num Set]	Changes the value of the following paragraph numbers.	Tools ▸ Outline ▸ Outline Options ▸ Set Paragraph Number
[Para Spacing]	Determines the amount of space that follows each paragraph.	Layout ▸ Margins ▸ Paragraph Spacing
[Para Style:] or [Para Style:] [Para Style End]	Turns on a paragraph style.	Layout ▸ Styles ▸ highlight a paragraph style ▸Select
[Pause Ptr]	Pauses the printer when this code is received at the printer.	Layout ▸ Other ▸ Printer Functions ▸ Printer Commands ▸ Printer Commands ▸ Pause Printer
[Pg Border]	Creates a border at the edges of the page.	Graphics ▸ Borders ▸ Page
[Pg Num Dec]	Decrements a document page number.	Layout ▸ Page ▸ Page Numbering ▸ Page Number ▸ Decrement Number
[Pg Num Disp]	Displays the current page number in the text.	Layout ▸ Page ▸ Page Numbering ▸ Page Number ▸ Display in Document
[Pg Num Fmt]	Creates the format for page numbers.	Layout ▸ Page ▸ Page Numbering ▸ Page Number Format
[Pg Num Inc]	Increments the current page number.	Layout ▸ Page ▸ Page Numbering ▸ Page Number ▸ Increment Number
[Pg Num Meth]	Determines the numbering method for page numbering.	Layout ▸ Page ▸ Page Numbering ▸ Page Number ▸ Numbering Method
[Pg Num Pos]	Determines the position of the page numbers.	Layout ▸ Page ▸ Page Numbering ▸ Page Number Position
[Pg Num Set]	Changes the value of the page numbers that follow.	Layout ▸ Page ▸ Page Numbering ▸ Page Number ▸ New Number
[Ptr Cmnd]	Sends a printer command to the printer.	Layout ▸ Other ▸ Printer Functions ▸ Printer Commands
[Redln On] [Redln Off]	Creates the Redline text attribute for a section of text.	Font ▸ Redline

Table B.1   **WordPerfect's Codes (Continued)**

Code	Function	Menu Selection/Keystroke
[Ref Box]	Cross-reference number to a graphics box caption number.	Tools ▸ Cross-Reference ▸ Reference ▸ Tie Reference to ▸ Caption Number
[Ref Chap]	Cross-reference number to a specific chapter.	Tools ▸ Cross-Reference ▸ Reference ▸ Tie Reference to ▸ Chapter
[Ref Count]	Cross-reference number to a specific counter.	Tools ▸ Cross-Reference ▸ Reference ▸ Tie Reference to ▸ Counter
[Ref Endnote]	Cross-reference to an endnote.	Tools ▸ Cross-Reference ▸ Reference ▸ Tie Reference to ▸ Endnote
[Ref Footnote]	Cross-reference to a footnote.	Tools ▸ Cross-Reference ▸ Reference ▸ Tie Reference to ▸ Footnote
[Ref Para]	Cross-reference to a paragraph.	Tools ▸ Cross-Reference ▸ Reference ▸ Tie Reference to ▸ Paragraph/Outline
[Ref Pg]	Cross-reference to a page number.	Tools ▸ Cross-Reference ▸ Reference ▸ Tie Reference to ▸ Page
[Ref Sec Pg]	Cross-reference to a secondary page number.	Tools ▸ Cross-Reference ▸ Reference ▸ Tie Reference to ▸ Secondary Page
[Ref Vol]	Cross-reference to a volume number.	Tools ▸ Cross-Reference ▸ Reference ▸ Tie Reference to ▸ Volume
[Rgt Mar]	Determines the amount of space for the right margin on the page.	Layout ▸ Margins ▸ Right Margin
[Rgt Mar Adj]	Adjust the right margin for all paragraph text.	Layout ▸ Margins ▸ Right Margin Adjustment
[Rgt Tab]	Aligns the right edge of text at the next tab stop.	Tab (tab stop definition must be Right)
[RGT TAB]	Aligns the right edge of text at the next tab stop, regardless of the tab stop type.	Home, Alt+F6
[Rgt Tab (Dot)] or [RGT TAB (DOT)]	Aligns the right edge of text at the next tab stop, and creates a dot-leader to the text.	Tab (tab stop definition must be Right, with Dot Leader selected) Home, Home, Alt+F6
[Row]	Indicates where the next row begins within a table.	Inserted as needed by WordPerfect.

Table B.1 **WordPerfect's Codes (Continued)**

Code	Function	Menu Selection/Keystroke
[Row-SCol]	Combined row separator and soft column break.	Inserted as needed by WordPerfect.
[Row-SPg]	Combined row separator and soft page break.	Inserted as needed by WordPerfect.
[Sec Pg Num Dec]	Decrements the current secondary page number.	Layout ▸ Page ▸ Page Numbering ▸ Secondary Page Number ▸ Decrement Number
[Sec Pg Num Disp]	Displays the current secondary page number.	Layout ▸ Page ▸ Page Numbering ▸ Secondary Page Number ▸ Display in Document
[Sec Pg Num Inc]	Increments the current secondary page number.	Layout ▸ Page ▸ Page Numbering ▸ Secondary Page Number ▸ Increment Number
[Sec Pg Num Meth]	Determines the numbering method for secondary page numbers.	Layout ▸ Page ▸ Page Numbering ▸ Secondary Page Number ▸ Numbering Method
[Sec Pg Num Set]	Changes the value of the secondary page numbers that follow.	Layout ▸ Page ▸ Page Numbering ▸ Secondary Page Number ▸ New Number
[Shadw On] [Shadw Off]	Creates the Shadow text attribute for a section of text.	Font ▸ Shadow
[Sm Cap On] [Sm Cap Off]	Creates the Small Caps attribute for a section of text.	Font ▸ Small Caps
[Small On] [Small Off]	Creates the Small text size for a section of text.	Font ▸ Size/Position ▸ Small
[Sound]	Indicates an embedded sound clip in the document text.	Tools ▸ Sound Clip ▸ Add
[Speller/Grammatik]	Disables/enables the Speller and grammar-checker for a section of the current document.	Tools ▸ Writing Tools ▸ Disable Speller/ Grammatik
[SPg]	Creates a soft page break.	Inserted as needed by WordPerfect.
[SRt]	Creates a soft return, to wrap paragraph text within the current margins.	Inserted as needed by WordPerfect.

Table B.1   WordPerfect's Codes (Continued)

Code	Function	Menu Selection/Keystroke
[SRt-SCol]	Combined soft return and soft column break.	Inserted as needed by WordPerfect.
[SRt-SPg]	Combined soft return and soft page break.	Inserted as needed by WordPerfect.
[StkOut On] [StkOut Off]	Creates the Strikeout attribute for a section of text.	Font ▸ Strikeout
[Subdivided Pg]	Divides the page into different subsections, with each section treated as a separate page.	Layout ▸ Page ▸ Subdivide Page
[Subdoc] or [Subdoc Begin] [Subdoc End]	Embeds a subdocument into the text.	File ▸ Master Document ▸ Subdocument
[Subscpt On] [Subscpt Off]	Creates the Subscript text size for a section of text.	Font ▸ Size/Position ▸ Subscript
[Suppress]	Suppresses, headers, footers, watermarks, or page numbering.	Layout ▸ Page ▸ Suppress
[Suprscpt On] [Suprscpt Off]	Creates the Superscript text size for a section of text.	Font ▸ Size/Position ▸ Superscript
[Tab Set]	Defines a new set of tab stops.	Layout ▸ Tab Set
[Target]	Marks the target text or item for a cross-reference.	Tools ▸ Cross-Reference ▸ Target
[Tbl Def] [Tbl Off]	Defines the layout and marks the boundaries of a WordPerfect table.	Layout ▸ Tables ▸ Create
[Tbl Off-SCol]	Combined [Tbl Off] code and soft column break.	Inserted as needed by WordPerfect.
[Tbl Off-SPg]	Combined [Tbl Off] code and soft page break.	Inserted as needed by WordPerfect.
[THCol]	Temporary hard column code.	Inserted as needed by WordPerfect.

Table B.1   WordPerfect's Codes (Continued)

Code	Function	Menu Selection/Keystroke
[THCol-SPg]	Temporary combined hard column code and soft page break.	Inserted as needed by WordPerfect.
[Third Party]	This code is reserved for features or functions that are inserted by third-party software, which is designed to work with WordPerfect.	Inserted by third-party software.
[Thousands Char]	Specifies the Thousands character for numbers in the text or in a table.	Layout ▸ Character ▸ Thousands Separator
[THPg]	Temporary hard page code.	Inserted as needed by WordPerfect.
[THRt]	Temporary hard return code.	Inserted as needed by WordPerfect.
[THRt-SCol]	Temporary combined hard return and soft column break.	Inserted as needed by WordPerfect.
[THRt-SPg]	Temporary combined hard return and soft page break.	Inserted as needed by WordPerfect.
[ToA]	Specifies the layout and position for a table of authorities.	Tools ▸ Table of Authorities ▸ Mark Short
[Top Mar]	Defines the top margin setting for the page.	Layout ▸ Margins ▸ Top Margin
[TSRt]	Temporary soft return.	Inserted as needed by WordPerfect.
[TSRt-SCol]	Temporary combined soft return and soft column break.	Inserted as needed by WordPerfect.
[TSRt-SPg]	Temporary combined soft return and soft page break.	Inserted as needed by WordPerfect.
[Und On] [Und Off]	Creates the Underline attribute for a section of text.	Underline (F8) or Font ▸ Underline
[Undrln Space]	Determines whether spaces will be underlined when the Underline attribute is turned on.	Font ▸ Font ▸ Underline ▸ Spaces

Table B.1   WordPerfect's Codes (Continued)

Code	Function	Menu Selection/Keystroke
[Undrln Tab]	Determines whether tabular spacing will be underlined when the Underline feature is turned on.	Font ▸ Font ▸ Underline ▸ Tabs
[Unknown]	Indicates an unrecognized command string. Usually, the [Unknown] code appears when you retrieve a file from a later revision of WordPerfect.	Inserted as needed by WordPerfect.
[VAdv]	Advance text vertically.	Layout ▸ Other ▸ Advance
[Very Large On] [Very Large Off]	Creates the Very Large text size for a section of text.	Font ▸ Size/Position ▸ Very Large
[Vol Num Dec]	Decrement the current volume page number.	Layout ▸ Page ▸ Page Numbering ▸ Volume ▸ Decrement Number
[Vol Num Disp]	Display the current volume number.	Layout ▸ Page ▸ Page Numbering ▸ Volume ▸ Display in Document
[Vol Num Inc]	Increment the current volume page number.	Layout ▸ Page ▸ Page Numbering ▸ Volume ▸ Increment Number
[Vol Num Meth]	Specifies the numbering method for volume page numbers.	Layout ▸ Page ▸ Page Numbering ▸ Volume ▸ Numbering Method
[Vol Num Set]	Changes the value of the following volume page numbers.	Layout ▸ Page ▸ Page Numbering ▸ Volume ▸ New Number
[Watermark A]	Creates document watermark A.	Layout ▸ Header/Footer/Watermark ▸ Watermarks ▸ Watermark A
[Watermark B]	Creates document watermark B.	Layout ▸ Header/Footer/Watermark ▸ Watermarks ▸ Watermark B
[Wid/Orph]	Turns on Widow/Orphan protection.	Layout ▸ Other ▸ Widow/Orphan Protect
[Wrd/Ltr Spacing]	Determines the spacing method and adjustments for letters and words.	Layout ▸ Other ▸ Printer Functions ▸ Word and Letterspacing

When you block a section of text and then choose one of the formatting features, WordPerfect may insert a pair of "plus/minus" codes to isolate the effect of the code. For this reason, you may see some codes that look a little different than the ones shown in the table.

Here is one example. If you choose a new font, WordPerfect inserts the [Font:*font name*] code at the current cursor position; all text from that point forward appears in the selected font—until the end of the document or until another [Font:*font name*] code is placed later in the text.

If, however, you block a section of text and then choose a new font, WordPerfect inserts two codes. The [+Font:*font name*] code appears at the beginning of the block of text and the [–Font:*font name*] code appears at the end of the block. The plus (+) symbol in the first code indicates the place where the font change takes effect; the minus (–) symbol in the second code shows that the font change ends *and* that the original font is active again. The plus/minus symbols appear for many WordPerfect codes when you block text before choosing a font or formatting feature.

WordPerfect Utility Programs

Your WordPerfect software includes several utility programs that help you convert macros, customize your printer drivers and speller dictionaries, and display system information. Each utility is a separate program that you start from the DOS prompt, while WordPerfect is *not* running. If you chose the Standard Installation option when you installed WordPerfect, some of these utility programs were installed in the \WP60 directory and others were copied to the \WPC60DOS directory. This appendix explains the purpose and use of each program.

Converting WordPerfect Macros

WordPerfect 5.1 macros are not compatible with WordPerfect 6.0. For this reason, the WordPerfect 6.0 software includes a macro conversion program (MCV.EXE) that lets you convert the macros you have created in earlier versions of WordPerfect. This conversion changes the keystroke-based commands of the WordPerfect 5.1 macros to the macro *tokens*—the commands stored in a macro script—that are supported by WordPerfect 6.0. It also saves a converted version of the macro (or macros) to the file name or path name that you specified.

Before you use the conversion program, you should know that the conversion process is not perfect. Some of the functions you've built into your macros may not convert, but the macro conversion program will display an error message when it encounters something that won't carry across to the converted macro. Then, if necessary, you can start WordPerfect 6.0 and edit the commands that the macro conversion program couldn't convert.

These steps explain how to use the macro conversion program to convert your WordPerfect 5.1 macros:

- From the DOS prompt, type **cd\wp60** and then press Enter. This changes the directory to the one in which the macro conversion program is stored.

- Type **mcv** and press Enter. This starts the macro conversion program.

- The conversion program prompts you with "Input file or pattern:". At this prompt, type the name of a macro file or a path-name pattern, such as c:\wp51\macros*.wpm. Then press Enter.

- The conversion program prompts you with "Output file or path:". At this prompt, type a file name or path. This is where the converted macro will be saved. Then press Enter.

You may see an error message on the screen after the conversion is done. If you do, you'll need to use the Macro Editor from within the WordPerfect 6.0

software to edit the converted macro and fix the commands that could not be converted.

NOTE.   *See Chapter 24 for information about editing a macro in WordPerfect 6.0; you must convert your WordPerfect 5.1 macros before you edit them in WordPerfect 6.0.*

When you edit a converted macro in WordPerfect 6.0, you may see the following comments:

```
"//*** Conversion warning ***"
```

or

```
"//*** Conversion error ***"
```

In a macro script, the double-slash (//) precedes text lines that will be ignored when the macro commands are processed. These comments are inserted by the macro conversion program to indicate problems with macro commands converted from WordPerfect 5.1.

The "//*** Conversion warning ***" and "//Conversion error ***" comments are always followed by another comment that explains the nature of the error. If you find these comments in your converted macros, you may need to adjust one or more macro commands to make them work with Word-Perfect 6.0.

For basic information about macro commands and macro editing, see Chapter 24. For more advanced information, WordPerfect Corporation publishes a comprehensive reference manual for the WordPerfect 6.0 macro language; this manual also includes tutorials on creating and editing complex macro scripts. Contact WordPerfect Corporation for ordering information.

Customizing Your Printer Driver

WordPerfect's printer driver files allow WordPerfect to communicate with your printer. If your printer has some unusual features that the WordPerfect printer drivers don't support, you may need to use the PTR program to customize your printer driver. This utility program lets you create and edit both types of printer files that WordPerfect requires: the .PRS files that allow WordPerfect to communicate with your printer, and the .ALL files that contain compressed .PRS information for several similar printers. The .ALL files let WordPerfect create new .PRS files when you add a new printer to the Select Printer dialog box.

For WordPerfect 5.1, the most common use of the PTR program is editing the automatic font changes that WordPerfect makes when you insert different attribute changes into your document. WordPerfect 6.0 lets you edit the automatic font changes from within the WordPerfect software, so the PTR program is not required for this application. (See Chapter 3 for information about editing WordPerfect's automatic font changes.)

If you need to edit individual .PRS files or create an .ALL file that contains printer driver information for several related printers, you'll need to order the PTR program from WordPerfect Corporation. The PTR program disk also includes on-line help that explains the use of the program. If you need detailed instructions for using the PTR program, you can purchase the WordPerfect printer program manual, which is also available from WordPerfect Corporation. See your WordPerfect reference manual for information about ordering both the PTR program disk and the printer program manual.

Note. *If the PTR program is not included with your WordPerfect software, call WordPerfect Corporation to obtain a copy of the program.*

Creating and Editing Speller Dictionaries

The Spell and Hyphenation Utility program (SPELL.EXE) lets you create and edit the Speller dictionary files that WordPerfect uses to spell-check and hyphenate the text in your documents. WordPerfect includes one Speller dictionary file (WPUS.LEX) with over 120,000 words; this file also includes hyphenation information. You can use the SPELL.EXE program to edit the words stored in this file, to change the hyphenation points for specific words, or to add new words to the dictionary. You can also use SPELL.EXE to create additional Speller dictionaries or combine dictionary files into one main dictionary.

The following steps explain how to start the SPELL.EXE program:

- From the DOS prompt, type **cd\wpc60dos** and then press Enter. This changes to the directory where the WP Spell Utility program is stored.

- Type **spell** and press Enter to start the program and display the main menu for the Spell Utility program, shown in Figure C.1.

This menu provides different options for creating and editing a Speller dictionary file. In the following sections, you'll find instructions for adding words to the main Speller dictionary file (WPUS.LEX) and creating new dictionary files that you can substitute for the WPUS.LEX file.

Note. *If the Pell.EXE program is not included with your WordPerfect software, call WordPerfect Corporation to obtain a copy of the program.*

Figure C.1

Spell Utility main menu

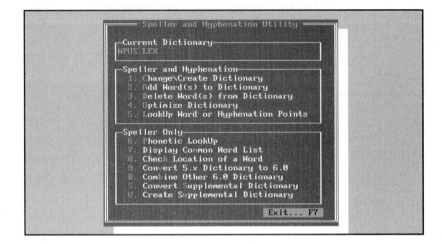

```
╔══════ Speller and Hyphenation Utility ══════╗
║  ┌─Current Dictionary─────────────────────┐ ║
║  │ WPUS.LEX                                │ ║
║  └────────────────────────────────────────┘ ║
║  ┌─Speller and Hyphenation────────────────┐ ║
║  │ 1. Change\Create Dictionary            │ ║
║  │ 2. Add Word(s) to Dictionary           │ ║
║  │ 3. Delete Word(s) from Dictionary      │ ║
║  │ 4. Optimize Dictionary                 │ ║
║  │ 5. LookUp Word or Hyphenation Points   │ ║
║  └────────────────────────────────────────┘ ║
║  ┌─Speller Only───────────────────────────┐ ║
║  │ 6. Phonetic LookUp                     │ ║
║  │ 7. Display Common Word List            │ ║
║  │ 8. Check Location of a Word            │ ║
║  │ 9. Convert 5.x Dictionary to 6.0       │ ║
║  │ B. Combine Other 6.0 Dictionary        │ ║
║  │ S. Convert Supplemental Dictionary     │ ║
║  │ U. Create Supplemental Dictionary      │ ║
║  └────────────────────────────────────────┘ ║
║                              ┌─────────────┐ ║
║                              │ Exit... F7  │ ║
║                              └─────────────┘ ║
╚══════════════════════════════════════════════╝
```

Speller Dictionary Files

The WordPerfect Speller feature accesses two files during a spell-check: WPUS.LEX and WPUS.SUP. The WPUS.LEX file is WordPerfect Speller dictionary. The WPUS.SUP file is a supplemental dictionary that contains the words you add during a spell-check. (Chapter 8 explains how to use the Speller feature and how to create the supplemental dictionary file.)

The WPUS.LEX file is divided into two different sections: the Common Word Area and the Main Word Area. The Common Word Area allows the Speller to perform faster spell-checks because it contains words that appear most often in written communication. The Main Word Area contains all the words stored in the dictionary, including those stored in the Common Word Area.

When you spell-check your documents, the Speller compares each word with those found in the Common Word Area; if a word is not found there, the Speller searches the Main Word Area, and then the WPUS.SUP file to see if the word was added during an earlier spell-check. If the word isn't found in either file, the Speller then highlights it as a misspelling and, in many cases, displays suggested replacements that are phonetic matches of the misspelled word.

Adding Words to the Speller Dictionary

During a spell-check, the Speller may tell you a word is misspelled when it isn't. One example is your last name; the Speller may not recognize it, but it's probably spelled correctly. Each time the Speller catches a misspelling, you have the chance to add that word to the supplemental dictionary (WPUS.SUP).

The supplemental dictionary provides additional words for the Speller to compare against the words in your document. However, the words stored in the supplemental dictionary do not appear as possible replacement words for misspelled words in your document. For this reason, you may want to add words to the Speller dictionary file (WPUS.LEX).

Using the Font Installer Program

WordPerfect's Font Installer program (WPFI.EXE) lets you set up additional font software for use with WordPerfect. After you use this program, the fonts you install will appear on WordPerfect's font list, where you can select them for use with your documents. In this case, *install* means to set up additional font software for use with WordPerfect 6.0—such as Windows TrueType fonts. You will need to purchase third-party fonts from other manufacturers.

Before you run the Font Installer program, you must copy the new font software files onto your hard disk; your font software should include instructions on how to do this. You may have already installed some of these files with other software programs that are stored on your hard disk—such as Bitstream Speedo fonts, Adobe Type 1 fonts, and TrueType fonts.

After the font software files are copied onto your hard disk, follow these steps to set up the fonts for WordPerfect 6.0:

- From the DOS prompt, type **cd\wpc60dos** and then press Enter. This changes to the directory where the WP Font Installer program is stored.

- Type **wpfi** and press Enter to start the WP Font Installer program. The program displays the Select Font Type dialog box shown in Figure C.2, which shows the types of fonts you can install for use with WordPerfect 6.0.

- Choose one of the font types to install. For example, choose Bitstream Speedo to set up additional Bitstream Speedo font software for WordPerfect's printer drivers. For some font types, you are also asked to choose the printer for which the fonts are installed.

- The Font Installer program then prompts you to enter the location of the new font software. Choose the first option (the name of the option changes depending on the font type you selected). Also, make sure the path is correct for the WP.DRS file, which contains the fonts used in graphics display mode and print preview mode; this is usually stored in the same directory as your WordPerfect program files.

Choose OK to continue.

- Press Exit (F7) to continue with the installation process. The Font Installer program checks the directory you specified for the font software and then displays a list of all fonts that you can use with WordPerfect. Figure C.3 shows how the list may appear on your screen.

Figure C.2

The Select Font Type dialog box

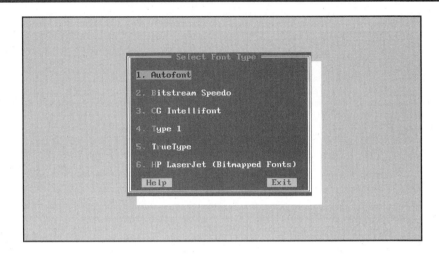

Figure C.3

The Select Fonts dialog box

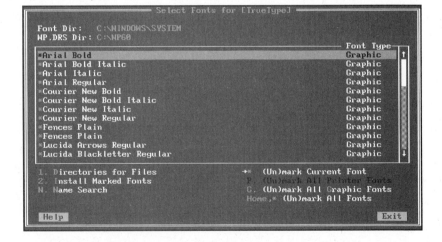

- The Font Installer program marks all valid fonts for installation with Word-Perfect. If you don't want to install all the fonts you see on the list, scroll to font names you *don't* want and type an asterisk (*) to unmark them.

- Choose Install Marked Fonts. The Font Installer program then modifies your WP.DRS file and, if necessary, your .PRS file to include the fonts that were marked on the list.

- When the Font Installer program is finished updating the WordPerfect files, you'll see the "Font Installation Complete" message. At this point, press Exit (F7) until you return to the DOS prompt.

- Start WordPerfect. The software will ask whether you want to update WordPerfect's font settings. Choose Yes and then you can choose the new fonts from WordPerfect's Font dialog box and use them in your documents.

If you installed additional printer fonts, such as Hewlett-Packard soft fonts, these will work only with the printer for which they are designed. If, however, you installed additional scalable fonts, like Windows TrueType fonts, these will work with any printer that you select for use with WordPerfect 6.0.

Displaying System Information

The WP Information program (WPINFO.EXE) displays information about your computer equipment, system configuration, and available memory. This can be useful when you need to investigate a problem with WordPerfect or with other software that is not running correctly. If, for example, you call WordPerfect's customer support group, the operator may instruct you to start the WP Information program to determine the amount of available memory in your computer.

The following information explains how to start the WP Information program and display the information that the program detects:

- From the DOS prompt, type **cd\wp60** and then press Enter. This changes to the directory where the WP Information program is stored.

- Type **wpinfo** and press Enter. This starts the WP Information program.

The WP Information program queries your computer equipment and software to determine the configuration of your system. Then the program displays information about your computer type, available memory, DOS version, and other system details. The memory information, in particular, will help you see whether you have enough conventional memory available to use WordPerfect's Sound and Fax features, which load special drivers into memory before when start WordPerfect.

When you're finished viewing the system configuration screen, press any key, and WordPerfect displays the contents of your AUTOEXEC.BAT file. This will show you the commands that are executed before you start the WordPerfect program. If you can't start WordPerfect, it's possible that one or more of the commands in your AUTOEXEC.BAT file are preventing the WordPerfect software from loading.

When you're finished viewing the AUTOEXEC.BAT information, press any key to continue to the next screen. WordPerfect displays the contents of your CONFIG.SYS file, which contains commands that help set up your system configuration. Again, if you can't start WordPerfect, commands in the CONFIG.SYS file may prevent WordPerfect from loading. Press any key again to close the WP Information program.

This program does display valuable information about your system, but the information won't help you unless you know what it means. When you review your AUTOEXEC.BAT and CONFIG.SYS files, refer to your DOS manual for detailed information about each of the commands you see. Your DOS manual also includes instructions for editing these files and modifying the commands stored in them.

INDEX

Notes: Italicized page numbers denote figures and tables; right triangles (▶) denote mouse-menu options; most main entries listed as options have keystroke equivalents that appear as underlined mnemonics in text—see individual page references.

Symbols

0 (zero), as table formula result, 448

8 bit sample size for sound clips, 751. See also sound clips

16 bit sample size for sound clips, 751. See also sound clips

20% Shaded Fill Style for graphics boxes, *655*

100% Shaded Fill style for tables, 433

100% View option, 121

200% viewing option, 121, *265*

& (ampersand) and file names, *170*

⊢—()—⊣, appearance of comments (Grammatik feature), 302

* (asterisk)
    as grand total operator in tables, 449
    marking files for archiving, 210
    marking files with in File Manager, 194
    marking fonts with, 154
    marking print jobs with, 149
    as multiplication operator for table formulas, *447*
    next to current font, 93
    next to printer definition, 117
    prohibited in file names, 170
    and Speller feature, 292–294
    wildcard character, 196–197, 247, 255

\ (backward slash)
    and file names, *170*
    prohibited in file names, 170
    searching directory names in File Manager, 190

° (bullet characters) next to WordPerfect system styles, 722

: (colon), in merge codes, 599

, (comma)
    and file names, 170
    in merge codes, 599
    as thousands separator, 63

{} (curly brackets) and equations, 274, 673, 675

– (dash)
    as hyphenation character, 278
    as part of file names, 169

/ (division) operator for table formulas, *447*

// (double-slash) in macro scripts, 828

… (ellipsis), 7, 10

= (equal) key, 6

= (equal sign)
    entering when changing default directory, 178, 179
    repeating, 260

/ (forward slash) character, 44, *170*, 449

() (group) operator for table formulas, *447*

?? (invalid table formula), 448, 453

– (minus) key, displaying screens with, 219

– (minus sign)
    in code, 52, 54, 70, 98, 826
    as key on numeric keypad and rotating graphics images, 662
    scrolling up a screen in File Manager with, 192
    as subtraction operator for table formulas, *447*

(number) button (outline bar), 395

. (period)
    creating dot leaders with, 61, 66, 67
    as decimal-align character, 63–64
    extending Block feature with, 235
    prohibited in file names, 170
    sorting precedence, 321

+ (plus) button (outline bar), 396

+ (plus) key
    displaying screens with, 219
    on numeric keypad and rotating graphics images, 661–662

+ (plus sign)
    as addition operator for table formulas, *447*
    in codes, 826
    and file names, *170*
    marking soft fonts with, 155
    prohibited in file names, 170
    scrolling down a screen in File Manager with, 192

? (question mark)
    and creating cross-references, 530
    sorting precedence, 321
    and Speller feature, 292–294
    as wildcard character, 196, 246–247

" (quotation mark) 170, 321

§ (section symbol), 463, 464

; (semicolon), in FIELDNAMES code, 597

INDEX

size options
    for scalable fonts, 95
    for text, *98*
Size Ratios feature, Font Setup dialog box, 110
sizing
    graphics, 636–638
    graphics images, 660–661
    open document windows, 263–264
SkiHead sample style, 729–732
Skip Once option (Speller feature, 283, 285
Skip in this Document option (Speller feature), 283
slashes (/ or \) and file names, *170*
slider button, 220
small boxes (■), characters appearing as, 107
Small Caps attribute, 85
soft fonts, setting up, 153–155
soft hyphens, 278
soft page breaks, 74
software, for faxes, 159–160
solid triangle (▶), 7
Sort dialog box, *312*
sorting. *See also* Merge/Sort feature
    address information in data files, 589
    alphanumeric versus numeric, 318–320
    blocks of text, 314–315
    by city name, 327–328
    directory lists, 196–197
    lists, 324–328, 334–335
    lists of dates, 330–331
    numbered lists, 376–377
    numbers, 315–321
    numeric versus alphanumeric, 318–320
    text, 311–315
    various name formats, 329–330
    by ZIP codes, 325, 327
sorting precedence, 320–321
Sort Keys option, 319, 321–328
sort order, changing for numbers, 316–318
Sort Uppercase First option, 320
sound, setting up computer for, 741–743
sound clips
    defining recording quality options for, 751–753
    deleting links, 748
    displaying lengths of, 746
    editing descriptions of, 747–748
    file sizes of, 745, *752*
    playing, 745–747

recording, 748–753
removing, 748
retrieving files, 743–745
saving after recording, 750
Sound Clips in Document dialog box, *745*
sound file formats, 741
Source box and sorting documents without retrieving, 332, 333
spaces
    adding after paragraphs, 52–53
    adjusting between footnotes and text, 359
    including in equations, 669, 671, 672, 673, 675
    prohibited in file names, 170
    underlining, 90–92
spacing
    adjusting for column borders, 705
    changing for columns, 692–693, 697
    changing for graphics boxes, 653–654
    inserting commands into equations, 672–673
    text for notes, 353–355
special characters, 101–109. *See also* WP characters feature
    inserting with Alt key, 102–104
    placing in notes, 367–369
Specific Codes feature (Shift+F5 keys), 249, 255–257
Specify File Manager List dialog box, 189–190
Specify Record Number Range option and selecting records from address list, 603
SPELL.EXE program, 829
"Spell Check Completed" message, 351
spell-checking
    blocks of text, 289
    continuing, 286
    resuming, 286
    stopping, 286
    words and pages, 288–289
Spell Edit mode, 286
    limitations of, 289–290
Speller, limitations of dictionary, 283
Speller button (button bar), 268
Speller dialog box, *283, 285*
Speller dictionaries, creating and editing, 829–830
Speller feature (Ctrl+F2 keys), 282, 284, 288
    checking entire documents with, 282
    checking notes with, 350-351
    creating dictionary files with, 295–296
    dictionaries, 295–298
    legal documents, 482